Gary L. Harmon

Susanna M. Harmon

SCHOLAR'S MARKET:

*AN INTERNATIONAL DIRECTORY
OF
PERIODICALS PUBLISHING LITERARY SCHOLARSHIP*

Introductory Essay: William White

Afterword: Richard Centing

Publications Committee
The Ohio State University Libraries
A Division of Educational Services
Columbus, Ohio
1974

Standard Book Number: 0-88215-033-2
Library of Congress Card Number: 73-620216
Printed in the United States of America
Copyright © 1974
Gary L. Harmon and Susanna M. Harmon
All Rights Reserved

TABLE OF CONTENTS

Acknowledgments v
What's An Introduction For?
        William White vi
A Coming of Age for Literary Scholarship
        Gary L. Harmon viii
Information Key for All Entries xxi
  I. Single and Multiple Author Periodicals..................... 1
       ● American.. 3
       ● European... 43
 II. Age and/or Nationality 105
       ● Comprehensive in Scope 107
       ● American.. 127
       ● American and English (sometimes including Continental) . 157
       ● English and British Commonwealth 185
       ● Continental (sometimes including English) 213
               Classical 215
               Medieval and Renaissance 225
       ● European: Post-Renaissance through Contemporary 243
       ● Baltic and Slavic......................................275
       ● Asian..297
       ● African, Caribbean, Latin American, and Near Eastern 311
III. Genres 327
       ● Poetry...329
       ● Theatre..345
       ● Prose: Fiction and Non-fiction 359
IV. American Ethnic Minorities 369
 V. Folklore 389
VI. Film...407
VII. Specialized Topics and Interdisciplinary Studies 441
       ● Interdisciplinary: Literature and Psychology, Religion,
         Politics, Philosophy, Science, or the Arts 443
       ● Popular Culture......................................461
       ● Theory of Literature 493
       ● Children's Literature, Satire, and Women's Studies 503
VIII. Teaching About Literature 509
 IX. Literary Reviews (Generous representation of graphics, poetry,
       fiction, and/or plays; essays on literature; and essays
       on non-literary subjects in some) 545

X. General Reviews (Essays from various fields included with some literary appraisals; poems or short stories on occasion) . .595
XI. Bibliographical and Library Resources 621
Tracing Literary Periodicals: An Afterword
  Richard R. Centing 651
Appendix A: Publishing Conventions for Manuscript Submissions. . . . 655
Appendix B: Reprint Companies Most Often Cited and Microfilm and Microfiche Companies 657
Author Index 659
Title Index 669

ACKNOWLEDGMENTS

To those who responded so generously with full information and, with few exceptions, copies of their periodicals for us to inspect, we owe special thanks. Without the help of editors, we could not have made this contribution to the profession, except with partial and second or third-hand information.

Various assistants have helped with some of the processing of letters, addresses, file cards, typing, and even library searching. Mary Jane Brown, G. Randall Colville, Gencie Rucker, and Ella Smith deserve our gratefulness for their efforts in these tedious matters. And Mrs. Alice Lantz and Mrs. Doris Gates, both secretaries, have given of their skills to coordinating some of the materials involved in the book's early creation.

Several scholars have supplied various-sized dollops of information, advice, and, always, encouragement. Richard Centing, Reference Librarian at The Ohio State University and Editor of both *Under the Sign of Pisces: Anais Nin and her Circle* and *The Widening Circle;* Warren French, Professor of English at Purdue University, Indianapolis; William White, Director of American Studies at Wayne State University; and Larry Tjarks, Texas Tech University—all these individuals share in our gratitude for their contributions.

Finally, we have been pleased with the research assistance of Ms. Nancy Rose Pollock whose skills and tenacity saw us through the head crunching rigors in the last phases of manuscript creation.

G.L.H.
S.M.H.

WHAT'S AN INTRODUCTION FOR?

At the risk of irreverence or flippancy unseemly for a periodical guide, I will begin with an excursion into autobiography. As a constant scribbler, I don't have to look for things to write articles about; they come looking for me. Several years ago, noting that a bunch of boys were whooping it up in a bunch of magazines about their favorite authors, I wondered how many periodicals there were devoted to the antics and work of an individual author. And, as has happened on hundreds of occasions, my wondering got into print. I wrote a piece with a list for *The American Book Collector* called "One Man's Meat," a title I swiped from E. B. White (no relation).

It's amazing (meaning, it amazes me) how a short article I gave no more thought to than dozens of others should have attracted as much attention as this one. I got all kinds of letters about it; people from all over told me of other such magazines (the addenda business is a thriving one); I wrote several folo stories (as they call them in newspapering); and one little magazine to which I am devoted, called *Literary Sketches* and produced in Williamsburg, Virginia, used an entire issue a year or two ago to listing, with full details, the largest number of such one-author journals and clubs I know of (with the exception of this book).

Beginning with one-author publications and then following their curiosity, the Harmons have come up—that's a niggling little phrase for months of back-breaking work—with this directory, a comprehensive, useful, up-to-date and accurate guide to periodicals that publish articles in English about literature. The result is a satisfying book of information that every scholar who wants to publish an article about literature—of virtually any sort—should have. Just to consult the book's various sections is an education in the diversity of resources for publishing or for research purposes.

I'm sure I'm not the only one who's been asked again and again by some young, and some not so young, writer of a piece on literature or on an author, "Where should I send it?" It's a natural question, and there is no easy answer. After all my years of scribbling, I even ask myself the same question.

Well, here's part of the answer: Send it to one of the 850 periodicals listed here. The information accompanying each entry will help you decide which one, though you still have only part of the answer to your query on where to send your contribution.

I'd suggest consulting this directory even before writing your final draft. Then I'd further suggest getting a copy of the periodical you'd like to send your piece to, and follow its style in your article—you'd be surprised how much that'll please the editor, for he won't have to go through your copy (if he accepts your piece) and edit it for consistency with the journal's editorial practices (that's short for capitalization, abbreviations, footnotes, punctuation, and other such bother).

What do you do if and when your opus comes back—rejected? Well, as you can see, there's more than one place to send it. I've always felt that if a writer of an article feels he's done a full job, researched thoroughly, written as well as he could, has been absolutely accurate (especially on quotations), and that his contribution is really a contribution and not just another "item" in his bibliography so he can get promoted to associate professor, then a rejection is not a death-blow. It just means that an editor (or a reader or maybe two) doesn't have room for the article, or maybe he doesn't like it. He may even tell you how to fix it up so he can publish it. Nevertheless, if you get it back, there's one thing to do: Send it off again, perhaps after you read it over to make sure it's as good as you thought it was when you first entrusted it to the U.S. Postal Service. Don't "file" it. Send it to another journal. (I once sent an A. E. Housman note to six periodicals before it was accepted, by *PMLA!*)

Of course there are many guides and directories, but there isn't one that's quite like this one. If it isn't absolutely complete, that's because journals are born and die all the time, and no matter how hard someone tries, some little journals seem to be well-kept secrets and don't get listed in places like this. With some good help from working scholars, maybe the next edition will be even more complete than this one.

And this is a book meant for use, not ostentation, to paraphrase what someone else said, years ago, in a wholly different connection. So use it, with care, periodical-style.

August, 1973

William White
Director, American Studies Program
Wayne State University
Editor, WALT WHITMAN REVIEW

A COMING OF AGE FOR LITERARY SCHOLARSHIP

Not long ago, Henry Miller was quoted in a press release, saying that within one hundred years people would not be reading books any more. His inference was most likely that people would be absorbing ideas and information in some other fashion than through books. For those who write articles about books, plays, poems, and authors, such an idea surely stuns the imagination—probably enough for literary scholars to reject Miller's contention soundly. There is much to recommend such doubt. After all, the birth pattern for periodicals publishing literary scholarship in the English language suggests that the times are better than ever for those who want to publish their scholarly observations about the literature of the world.

The pattern is a pronounced one, as the following tabulation reveals. Of the 821 periodicals indicated here (27 dates of the total 848 in the book were unknown), the first-issue dates produce a rapidly accelerating pattern:

34	16	18	31	43	71	141	306*	161
pre-1900	1900-09	1910-19	1920-29	1930-39	1940-49	1950-59	1960-69	1970+

Since the 1930's, it appears that, for these periodicals, the number founded, and still surviving, doubles every ten years.** It would seem that such periodicals have more than kept pace with the increasing number of libraries and scholars who use and support them. It is also obvious that the late 1960's and the early 1970's has been a period marked by strenuous activity in all phases of literary scholarship: Interpretation, theory, interdisciplinary speculations, comparative studies, bibliography, biography, history, and so on.

Some Reasons Why—And Is This Phenomenon Good?

Speculation about why this burst of periodicals has occurred amounts to a commentary on the current health of literary scholarship as a profession.

- Ph.D. programs which develop producing literary scholars have no doubt played an important part in causing a scholarly explosion.

- Postal rates have continued to favor inexpensive circulation of academic journals in the United States.

- New printing technology has become more available to scholars than before. (See *Future Shock*, pp. 278-280.)

- Increasing salaries of professors in the sixties may well have spurred the founding of journals that reflect individual interests and swelled the number of journals subscribed to by scholars.

---

* One hundred six were begun in the 1960-64 period, and 200 were founded in the 1965-69 period.

** This statement requires some modification, of course. A few periodicals no longer publishing are listed in this book because they are valuable to some scholars and because they are available through microfilm or microfiche editions. And a few not listed began and subsided in the same time span.

- Increasing competition for promotions, tenure, and even positions on faculties have created a "need" for scholarly expression.

- Established, older journals often have not been able to absorb the pressure from those who wish to publish.

- Literary scholars have become increasingly aware of interdisciplinary inquiry and some largely unexplored studies, such as Black culture, women's studies, or American studies.

- Various groups of scholars have slowly redefined the field itself—to include myth, film, popular culture, or oral literature.

Which among these is most important is hard to say. Together, they are a formidable set of pressures on literary scholars to publish. At the root of the phenomenon, however, is the technology, coupled with increased wealth and pressure to publish, which has brought about the rich confection of literary scholarship published in these journals.

English professors also seem to be extending their inquiries to other media, to other disciplines. But the recent vulnerability of our economy and the future shock pace of change in academia could stunt the growth of publication outlets for literary scholars. A recent item in the *PMLA* "Professional Notes and Comments" section, questioned whether "the civilizing benefits" of more publications "are reaching out to touch individuals and society effectively" and whether the printed product is "worth the energy expended, if a nation in crisis requires intellectual energy on other fronts." If such thinking becomes widespread, combined with unforeseen postal and printing cost increases—like the ones that felled *LIFE* magazine and others—then academic journals, which cannot depend on advertising revenue or mergers to bail them out, could be adversely affected.

Literary study is strongest when a pluralism of ideas and approaches can surface in the professional publications. Periodicals are for the literary scholar what the stage is for the actor. It is in writing that we practice—and develop—what we are to teach. Periodicals that disseminate a wide variety of views and approaches to thinking about literature and culture are always needed to enrich our thinking—or to avert standardization of thought and practice. If economic conditions should turn on academia, some of the leading journals and many of the struggling small ones that are not supported by affiliation with national or regional organizations could die. The late sixties and early seventies might then be regarded as a golden age for literary periodicals; if the growth pattern does not change, this period may be simply a silver age, laying a basis for the golden age that is to come.

What Sorts of Periodicals Are Included Here?

Those who use this book—the researching and the publishing scholars, librarians, and collectors—will see that the organization of this book is a kind of profile of the habits of literary scholars. They are grouped in such a way that scholars with particular interests—e.g., English literature, film, folklore, or bibliography—can find the needed publications together or through cross references.

Only those periodicals printed totally or partially in the English language are included. For this reason, such fine works as the Welsh Y GENHINEN, the Australian QUARBER MERKUR, the Swiss STENDHAL CLUB QUARTERLY, the French CAHIERS DU CINEMA, and the Italian CINEMA NUOVO, or the United States BULLETIN BAUDELAIRIEN (French text), the NUEVA NARRATIVA HISPANAMERICANA (Spanish test), and HISPAMERICA (Spanish text) are omitted. Even journals that print only occasionally a few pages in English are often omitted, as in the case of KIR OU KIRK (LETTER & LITERATURE): AN ARMENIAN PERIODICAL or HISPANOFILA.

Periodicals concerning literature were eliminated if they consisted of creative writing only, with no scholarly articles of any kind. Thus, POETRY NORTHWEST and the PARIS REVIEW, for example, and many campus literary magazines are not represented here. Fanzine type periodicals that do not attempt serious scholarly inquiry into literature were eliminated. It was striking to see hundreds of detective and science fiction fanzines circulating. Only the most significant of s-f journals were included, such as EXTRAPOLATION, a serious publication on science fiction, and THE ARMCHAIR DETECTIVE, which is useful as a bibliographical tool.

Otherwise, our effort was to be inclusive. We defined both periodicals and literature broadly. The periodicals in this book therefore include bulletins, newsletters, monthlies, quarterlies, triannuals, biannuals, and annuals. Some scholars have not regarded an annual as "periodical." Our definition, however, includes all journals of any size with a continuing title (which eliminates serials) and a common focus that are published periodically, and annuals that appear once a year, every year, meet these criteria. For this reason, the LESSING YEARBOOK, ANÁLES GALDOSIANOS, SHAKESPEARE RESEARCH AND OPPORTUNITIES, PIRANDELLO STUDIES, CONTEMPORARY LITERARY SCENE, MILTON STUDIES, and the NATHANIEL HAWTHORNE JOURNAL are examples of an increasing breed of annuals. Our interpretation of "literary scholarship" led us to include periodicals publishing studies in criticism, biography, bibliography, scholarship in publishing about literature and history. Moreover, journals combining the study of literature with other studies, such as the INTERNATIONAL JOURNAL OF SYMBOLOGY, COLLEGE LITERATURE, LITERATURE AND PSYCHOLOGY, NEO-HELLENIKA, were included. And finally, because so many members of the English profession have come to regard periodicals about film, folklore, popular culture, teaching about literature, and ethnic minorities as important sources for research and publishing, individual sections are provided for each.

The result is the eleven groups of periodicals, with their appropriate subgroups, named below, together with 1) the number of periodicals and cross references in each section, 2) the circulation ranges, and 3) the main characteristics of periodicals in the section.

I. SINGLE AND MULTIPLE AUTHOR PERIODICALS
   Total No.: 153;   Cross Refs.: 20

   AMERICAN
      Total No.: 60   Cross Refs.: 7
      Circulation Range: 50-6,000
      Periodicals focusing on individual American authors, mostly men, except for Flannery O'Connor, Emily Dickinson, and Willa Cather. Some groups also receive attention, such as the Transcendentalists.

EUROPEAN
Total No.: 93   Cross Refs.: 13
Circulation Range: 100-2,600
Periodicals focusing on single writers and groups of writers, such as the Wordsworth Circle. One Russian, Dostoevsky, is included here, rather than in a specially created category.

II. AGE AND/OR NATIONALITY
Total No.: 353   Cross Refs.: 78

COMPREHENSIVE IN SCOPE
Total No.: 33   Cross Refs.: 7
Circulation Range: 200-34,000 (though the NEW YORK REVIEW OF BOOKS circulates 100,000)
A few periodicals around the world print articles on any literature in the world as a particular effort. These are often comparative literature journals.

AMERICAN
Total No.: 54   Cross Refs.: 16
Circulation Range: 250-30,000
These periodicals focus on American literature and often inlcude interdisciplinary journals of American studies and history.

AMERICAN AND ENGLISH
Total No.: 45   Cross Refs.: 6
Circulation Range: 65-3,000
These periodicals reflect the long-standing dual interest of scholars on both sides of the Atlantic for work on the literatures of the U.S. and of Britain, occasionally including articles about Continental writing as well.

ENGLISH, AND THE BRITISH COMMONWEALTH
Total No.: 47   Cross Refs.: 9
Circulation Range: 250-3,900 (th ough BOOKS IN CANADA circulates 41,000)
Often among the oldest periodicals, the ones in this group are usually published in Europe and thus reflect the Anglophile focus.

CONTINENTAL (SOMETIMES INCL. ENGLISH)
Total No.: 37   Cross Refs.: 6
Circulation Range: 275-5,400
This section is subdivided into two groups: 1) Classical and 2) Medieval and Renaissance.

EUROPEAN: POST-RENAISSANCE THROUGH CONTEMPORARY
Total No.: 51   Cross Refs.: 10
Circulation Range: 300-13,400
Britain and the Continent are included here.

BALTIC AND SLAVIC
Total No.: 31   Cross Refs.: 2
Circulation Range: 400-30,000
This cluster of periodicals is part of a larger group of hundreds that is more historical and social-science oriented. Many indicate that they will publish articles about or involving literature; a good procedure is to inquire before submitting an article.

ASIAN
Total No.: 21   Cross Refs.: 4
Circulation Range: 200-3,200
These periodicals focus mainly on Indian, Japanese, and Chinese subjects, reflecting, in part, a curricular trend toward including the East as an important subject for non-Eastern students to choose.

AFRICAN, CARIBBEAN, LATIN AMERICAN, AND NEAR EASTERN
Total No.: 34   Cross Refs.: 18
Circulation Range 300-2,400
Mexico, Israel, and the Portuguese speaking world are among those included in this category.

III. GENRES
Total No.: 57   Cross Refs.: 8

POETRY
Total No.: 24   Cross Refs.: 3
Circulation Range: 300-9,000
The number in this section should surprise many who think that only poetry gets published and that poetry interpretation is slight.

THEATRE
Total No.: 21   Cross Refs.: 4
Circulation Range: 400-15,000
Periodicals of history, interpretation, bibliography, and theatre craft are in this group.

PROSE: FICTION AND NON-FICTION
Total No.: 12   Cross Refs.: 1
Circulation Range: 400-5,000
Though the number of journals concentrating on fiction or prose alone is few, the majority are of high quality and have originated in the last five years.

IV. AMERICAN ETHNIC MINORITIES
Total No.: 31   Cross Refs.: 5
Circulation Range: 350-20,000
Almost all of these journals have originated in the last ten years. Black, Chicano, and Indian periodicals are the focus.

V. FOLKLORE
Total No.: 27   Cross Refs.: 2
Circulation Range: 280-30,000
These periodicals are among the older developments in the profession, and many concentrate on state or regional folklore.

VI. FILM
Total No.: 55   Cross Refs.: 4
Circulation Range: 200-124,000
So many literature professors have come to write about film that it is perhaps the profession's newest development, along with current investigations of popular culture.

VII. SPECIALIZED TOPICS AND INTERDISCIPLINARY STUDIES
Total No.: 93   Cross Refs.: 10

INTERDISCIPLINARY (Literature and psychology, religion, history, politics, philosophy, and the like)
Total No.: 25   Cross Refs.: 1
Circulation Range: 100-6,500
This group often reflects the rather natural connection of literature with the central interests of so many other disciplines.

POPULAR CULTURE
Total No.: 47   Cross Refs.: 1
Circulation Range: 150-6,000
This fast-growing publication group contains both scholarly gems and fringe journals for literary scholarship (such as THE MYSTERY READER'S NEWSLETTER); the group will probably continue to grow for some time as the study of popular culture develops in the university curriculum.

THEORY OF LITERATURE
Total No.: 14   Cross Refs.: 6
Circulation Range: 350-2,550
Only seven journals appear to be devoted totally to literary theory.

CHILDREN'S LITERATURE, SATIRE, AND WOMEN'S STUDIES
Total No.: 7   Cross Refs.: 2
Circulation Range: 200-2,000 (except for HORN BOOK MAGAZINE which circulates 27,000)
This fringe group of periodicals reflects slowly emerging special interests of publishing scholars.

VIII. TEACHING ABOUT LITERATURE
Total No.: 56 Cross Refs.: 7
Circulation Range: 300-54,900
Many of these are official publications of state and regional English teaching organizations. While many more exist, the ones here include only those that have printed essays on literature teaching. Workaday problems of the English profession often dominate the space, however, and this has probably drained away some of the prestige they should have in the profession. With the renewed attention to teaching now taking place in the profession, these journals could reflect that attention by increasing space devoted to helping the young interpret and enjoy literary study.

IX. LITERARY REVIEWS
Total No.: 78 Cross Refs.: 2
Circulation Range: 300-6,000
This group represents the mix of an occasional scholarly article in the same issue with poetry, short stories, plays, photographs, drawings, and the like.

X. GENERAL REVIEWS
Total No.: 45 Cross Refs.: 8
Circulation Range: 300-325,000
Here are a number of popular magazines, such as the ATLANTIC MONTHLY, the AMERICAN SCHOLAR, or HARPER'S MAGAZINE. Such periodicals publish numerous articles on general subjects, with a few involving literature; occasional poetry or short stories are included, too.

XI. BIBLIOGRAPHICAL AND LITERARY RESOURCES
Total No.: 55 Cross Refs.: 11
Circulation Range: 200-35,000
This group forms the backbone of literary scholarship, for libraries, collectors, and scholars. Publishing information, bibliographies, and reviews are the main fare.

It is obvious that the profession is full of vitality, for scholars are inventing and investing in literary scholarship. It has not become a standardized profession, served and controlled by only a few monolithic journals; each area is served with a pluralism of interests and approaches. From a scholar's point of view, this is desirable, but a Susan Sontag might not be so generous, preferring to stand against interpretation—or, against too much interpretation. Scholars need to practice their craft of writing and interpreting. Because of the tendency for uneducated imaginations and unexamined lives to proliferate, the vitality of interpretive scholarship revealed in these journals can serve as a kind of corrective. Intelligent interpretation could not pose a clear and present danger to Miss Sontag's interest in preserving the sheer enjoyment of literature.

The Newer Periodicals

While some journals will have escaped inclusion in this book, the following table indicates the overall pattern of developments among the total of 219 periodicals founded from 1969 through 1973.

Section	No. of New Periodicals	Percent of Section or Subsection	Totals By Section	Sectional Percentage of Grand Total
I. SINGLE AND MULTIPLE AUTHOR FOCUS		*T=39.7	52	23.7
American	26	49.0		
European	26	32.5		
II. AGE AND/OR NATIONALITY		T=20.7	57	26.0
Comprehensive in Scope	5	19.2		
American	14	36.8		
American and English	6	15.4		
English and British Commonwealth	7	18.4		
Continental: Classical through Renaissance	5	16.7		
European: Post-Renaissance through Contemporary	4	9.8		
Baltic and Slavic	7	24.1		
Asian	4	23.5		
African, Caribbean, etc.	5	31.3		
III. GENRES		T=36.7	18	8.2
Poetry	7	33.3		
Theatre	3	17.6		
Prose: Fiction and Non-Fiction	8	72.7		
IV. AMERICAN ETHNIC MINORITIES	12	T=46.2	12	5.5
V. FOLKLORE	3	T=12.0	3	1.4
VI. FILM	10	T=19.6	10	4.6
VII. SPECIALIZED TOPICS AND INTERDISCIPLINARY STUDIES		T=45.8	38	17.4
Interdisciplinary	9	37.5		
Popular Culture	22	47.8		
Theory of Literature	4	50.0		
Children's Literature, etc.	3	60.0		
VIII. TEACHING ABOUT LITERATURE	10	T=20.4	10	4.6
IX. LITERARY REVIEWS	9	T=11.8	9	4.1
X. GENERAL REVIEWS	5	T=13.5	5	2.3
XI. BIBLIOGRAPHICAL AND LIBRARY RESOURCES	5	T=11.4	5	2.3
TOTALS	219		219	100%

*"T" (for "total") indicates that the percentage given is for the entire section.

Many implications arise from these patterns, but it is perhaps most interesting to see the extraordinary range and energy of the emerging periodicals. It is useful to notice the strength in numbers of the new single and multiple author focused publications, the newness of the section on fiction-focused periodicals, and the number and variety of periodicals about popular culture. Some of these latest entries into the literary scholar's market are unusually promising, and they deserve mention. The following discussion of these new publications moves through the book section by section.

One fifth of all the new periodicals represented in this book focus on single authors or small groups of writers, and half of these are about American writers. In short, they form ten percent of all growth among periodicals. Twenty years ago, a Faulkner newsletter subsided and reemerged as CRITIQUE. A new Faulkner publication, however, is the slim, mimeographed FAULKNER CONCORDANCE NEWSLETTER (1973), and since 1969, the FITZGERALD-HEMINGWAY ANNUAL (formerly the FITZGERALD NEWSLETTER—1958) has exemplified some sort of splendor in 360 pages of hardbound articles published by NCR/Microcard Editions.

A useful and professionally produced journal, PAIDEUMA: A JOURNAL DEVOTED TO EZRA POUND SCHOLARSHIP (1972) is a substantial journal, the first to succeed THE POUND NEWSLETTER, a valuable resource that ceased after ten issues in 1956. THE DREISER NEWSLETTER (1970) is growing in quality and size. For Whitman scholars, CALUMUS: AN INTERNATIONAL WHITMAN QUARTERLY (1970) is a welcome advent from a Japanese publisher and editor. Also, POE STUDIES (1972) graduated from the POE NEWSLETTER (1968), and the SINCLAIR LEWIS NEWSLETTER (1969) and the WALLACE STEVENS NEWSLETTER (1969) are examples of periodicals that are useful to scholars and improving all the time.

Single and multiple author focused publications are almost always about men, never about members of ethnic minorities as of this writing, and in eight instances about women. THE FLANNERY O'CONNOR BULLETIN (1972), a 90-page annual, is a fine one. Others are the WILLA CATHER PIONEER MEMORIAL AND EDUCATIONAL FOUNDATION NEWSLETTER (1957); EMILY DICKINSON BULLETIN (1968); UNDER THE SIGN OF PISCES: ANAÏS NIN AND HER CIRCLE (1970); BRONTË SOCIETY TRANSACTIONS (1895); the MARY WOLLSTONECRAFT NEWSLETTER (1972); VIRGINIA WOOLF QUARTERLY (1972); and the new VIRGINIA WOOLF MISCELLANY (1973). Women poets are represented in four Browning periodicals and the HIGGINSON JOURNAL OF POETRY (1971).

Among the Europeans, the BRECHT HEUTE/BRECHT TODAY (1971) annual publication of 200-240 pages is a successful attempt to combine contributions of Germanists, drama scholars, and persons in the practical theater, while the mimeographed COMMUNICATIONS: THE BRECHT NEWSLETTER (1971) reports on scholarly activities about the work of Bertolt Brecht. Both the DICKENS STUDIES ANNUAL (1970) and the DICKENS STUDIES NEWSLETTER (1970) print articles and information on Charles Dickens. Browning enthusiasts have BROWNING SOCIETY NOTES (1971), and Graves scholars have the multilithed FOCUS ON ROBERT GRAVES (1972). Slavic scholars use the INTERNATIONAL DOSTOEVSKY SOCIETY BULLETIN (1972). Finally, THE THOMAS HARDY YEARBOOK (1970) and the SPENSER NEWSLETTER (1970) keep Hardy and Spenser followers informed about current research with occasional articles about the authors' lives or works.

Another fifth of the 219 new periodicals concern national literatures, with a fourth of that total represented by United States-centered publications and the rest spread rather evenly among the sub-groups. Two remarkable examples of periodicals that are comprehensive in scope are REVIEW OF NATIONAL LITERATURES (1970), a handsome 200-page biannual review publishing critics from around the world, and RACKHAM LITERARY STUDIES (1971), another biannual, currently published by graduate students at The University of Michigan.

In the American group, the Canadians express their interest in the interplay between Canada and the United States with THE CANADIAN REVIEW OF AMERICAN STUDIES (1970), and a few Midwesterners have gotten together to launch several publications, among them the annual MIDAMERICA (1973) and THE GREAT LAKES REVIEW: A JOURNAL OF THE MIDWEST (1973), both focusing on Midwest culture. Three other publications show unusual promise: CONTEMPORARY LITERARY SCENE (1974) and LOST GENERATION JOURNAL (1973) are strong newcomers. And a periodical that has achieved almost instant prestige is Maurice Beebe's JOURNAL OF MODERN LITERATURE (1970), which includes strong features of the editor's earlier stint with MODERN FICTION STUDIES (1955) and adds some new ones.

For periodicals that concentrate on both American and British Commonwealth subjects, ENLIGHTENMENT ESSAYS (1970), THE ERASMUS REVIEW (1971), and two periodicals called ESSAYS IN LITERATURE, the one originating from Denver (1973), the other from Illinois (1974) are evidence of solid scholarly energy. One exemplary new journal is the quarterly IRISH UNIVERSITY REVIEW (1970), and one with an inexpensive format and high circulation (41,000) is the monthly BOOKS IN CANADA (1972) about all books published in Canada.

European studies, represented by a small group of periodicals, have added the impressive NEO-HELLENIKA: ANNUAL PUBLICATION OF THE CENTER FOR HELLENIC STUDIES (1970), the quarterly ENGLISH LITERARY RENAISSANCE (1971), and VIATOR: MEDIEVAL AND RENAISSANCE STUDIES (1970). Among other journals in the section is one that exhibits a new plateau of development among Hispanic studies, the JOURNAL OF SPANISH STUDIES: TWENTIETH CENTURY (1973).

While genre-focused periodicals comprise less than ten percent of the total listed new periodicals, journals publishing poetry criticism increased by a third, theatre journals by twenty percent, and periodicals publishing criticism on fiction about seventy percent. One explanation for such an increase is that other journals are not absorbing articles quite rapidly enough to satisfy the founders of these new journals. News about the older STUDIES IN SHORT FICTION (1963) receiving over 400 manuscripts per year helps explain the creation of FICTION INTERNATIONAL (1973), THE INTERNATIONAL FICTION REVIEW (1974), STUDIES IN AMERICAN FICTION (1973) and STUDIES IN THE NOVEL (1969)—all substantial periodicals with growing circulations. The highflyer among scholarly poetry periodicals is the tabloid-style THE AMERICAN POETRY REVIEW (1972), circulation 50,000, though PARNASSUS: POETRY IN REVIEW (1972) is a most impressive journal that deserves to grow from its 1973 circulation of 750.

About half of the periodicals on ethnic minorities have developed in the last five years though they comprise only one out of twenty in the total of new periodicals. AMISTAD: WRITINGS ON BLACK HISTORY AND CULTURE

(1970) apparently ceased after only two annual publications, though it was one of the very best of this group. The biannual AZTLAN: CHICANO JOURNAL OF THE SOCIAL SCIENCES AND THE ARTS (1970) is perhaps the most substantial of periodicals dealing with a minority other than Black culture. Those researching Black drama should see BLACK THEATRE, but only back issues are available now since its demise. THE BLACK SCHOLAR: JOURNAL OF BLACK STUDIES AND RESEARCH (1970), BLACK REVIEW (1971), BLACK BOOKS BULLETIN (1971), and BLACK ACADEMY REVIEW: QUARTERLY OF THE BLACK WORLD (1970) show promise, but the mortality rate in this segment of new periodicals is probably going to be high for a while. If financial health and demonstrated sustained interest in the Black studies endures, these journals have a strong chance for long-range survival and significance, much as the elder PHYLON (1940) has proven over the years.

While growth through publication outlets has not been a feature of scholarly folklore periodicals—the most notable addition being the FOLKLORE ANNUAL OF THE UNIVERSITY FOLKLORE ASSOCIATION (1969)—the number of scholarly film periodicals has increased by a third. The most admirable of these are the LITERATURE/FILM QUARTERLY (1973), the JOURNAL OF POPULAR FILM (1972), and THE FILM JOURNAL (1971), all quality publications with growing substantial circulations.

High circulation is not a feature of new interdisciplinary journals, but HARTFORD STUDIES IN LITERATURE: A JOURNAL OF INTERDISCIPLINARY CRITICISM (1969), DADA/SURREALISM (1971), INTERNATIONAL JOURNAL OF SYMBOLOGY (1969), and JOURNAL OF LITERARY SEMANTICS (1972) indicate the imagination used in new directions for literary study.

Periodicals about popular culture and about theory of literature have added to their number by more than fifty percent, with such journals as SCIENCE FICTION STUDIES (1973) to extend the subject covered very well by the 1959-founded EXTRAPOLATION: A JOURNAL OF SCIENCE FICTION AND FANTASY. THE MYSTERY AND DETECTION ANNUAL (1972) and MYTHLORE (1969) are among the more interesting, though none of the new publications seems to rival the now older (1967) JOURNAL OF POPULAR CULTURE. New periodicals on theory that deserve special mention are NEW LITERARY HISTORY: A JOURNAL OF THEORY AND INTERPRETATION (1969) and DIACRITICS: A REVIEW OF CONTEMPORARY CRITICISM (1971). And an unusually fine creation is the serious CHILDREN'S LITERATURE (1972), treating an important subject for almost the first time in an individual publication.

Three new periodicals among a group that might escape notice from traditional literary scholars should be mentioned: CONNECTIONS (1974) (formerly CONNECTIONS: THE RADICAL AMERICAN STUDIES JOURNAL— 1971), COLLEGE LITERATURE (1974), and POPULAR CULTURE METHODS (1972), all exhibiting the vitality of periodicals trying to cause teachers and scholars to reorient their work and ideas. As for literary reviews and general reviews, neither group has multiplied substantially among seeming myriads of national and local reviews; among the new ones, perhaps ANTAEUS (1970) and ANTHELION (1971) are showing the hardiest efforts to survive in a competitive group.

The important area of bibliography and library journals manifests little recent growth, but that growth has been quite significant. The new periodicals include both the MLA ABSTRACTS and the MLA INTERNATIONAL BIBLIOGRAPHY, which had been only parts of PMLA previously. RESOURCES FOR AMERICAN LITERARY STUDY (1971) is a strong bibliographical tool; in the long run, it may become a sort of cornerstone for literary scholarship on American subjects, and all the new sources of articles will cause the authors of chapters in the annual AMERICAN LITERARY SCHOLARSHIP (1963) much more research work. PROOF: THE YEARBOOK OF AMERICAN BIBLIOGRAPHICAL AND TEXTUAL STUDIES (1971) as well as SCHOLARLY PUBLISHING: A JOURNAL FOR AUTHORS AND PUBLISHERS (1969) are significant new additions to this section which deserve to be used . . . and to survive.

The Future?

What is the future for periodical publishing? To answer this may be to describe the future of scholars and of the culture. Henry Miller *could* be correct. We might not be reading books a hundred years from now. But because of our basic professional need to communicate scholarly thoughts to others—assuming that scholarship continues!—doubling the number of new literary periodicals every ten years may indeed continue. Periodicals, as now, may increasingly become annuals or biannuals. They may continue the pattern of joining literature study with other disciplines and of the interest in visual media, in popular culture, in single authors. They may even become more experimental, more reflective of practicing what we are busy teaching.

But: If some quirk in the energy or resource supply should develop—such as paper shortages, post office price increases, or a shift to visual/audio communication—then what must happen to continue the free flow of ideas? Perhaps we will be sending microfilms back and forth in the mails. Or, each of us might well have his or her own microfiche machine to use on the bedroom wall for journal reading before sleep. We may need a device that automatically disconnects our machine when we have dozed off, saturated for a day in the process of absorbing the wave upon wave of new schools of criticism, new interpretations of important works, newly unearthed information on our literary heritage, or a more complete bibliographical list than the last. Supra-agency publishers, representing a legion of cooperating periodical editors, could make available computerized abstracts of all articles written on a subject, and scholars could dial copies of complete articles long-distance on the ubiquitous office computers to have them read aloud while page after page is flashed on the screen before our thinking chair. Authors and editors could even be reimbursed by readers each time they dialed an author's work.

No paper. No subscriptions. No books or periodicals as we know them. But the profession will be at work, and, individually, we will continue to search for some idea, some observation, some information that *matters* to someone else who turns his or her machine on to sift through that new angle, flashed on the video wall by the computer teletyper, and to fumble for a fresher understanding than the one from the week before. Perhaps literary scholarship will always be coming of age.

Gary L. Harmon
University of North Florida

January, 1974

INFORMATION KEY FOR ALL ENTRIES

All entries—save those who did not reply or those who replied partially—provide the following information in this pattern:

- Title of periodical
- Editor's name(s) and address
- Subscription address
- Publishing schedule
- Circulation number
- Cost options
- Description of contents
- Are unsolicited mss. welcome?
- Specifically welcomed contributions
- Usual ms. length desired
- Style requirements
- Copyright holder of published material
- Time for editor's decision on accepting ms.
- Time for acceptance to publication
- Payment
- Are rejected mss. returned?
- Date of first issue, usual publication length, and other general information
- Back issue information: Cost, availability, where to inquire, reprint or microfilm availability

ABOUT THE INDEXES

If you know the title of the periodical for which you want information, one quick way to locate it is to consult the Title Index. If you wish to submit an article—or search for one—that focuses on an author, consult the Author Index; you may be surprised to find that there is a periodical that focuses on your author and that there are so many such author-focused periodicals.

I
SINGLE
AND
MULTIPLE
AUTHOR
PERIODICALS

AMERICAN

[Alger, Horatio]

NEWSBOY

EDITORIAL ADDRESS: SUBSCRIPTION ADDRESS:
Carl T. Hartmann, Guest Editor
4907 Allison Drive Same
Lansing, Michigan 48910

PUBLISHED: Monthly (except Jan., CIRCULATION : 200
          July)
COST: 1 yr.—$5.00 (includes membership in Horatio Alger Society).

CONTENTS: Articles on and about Horatio Alger; occasional reproductions of photographs, newspaper clippings, and illustrations; news and notes on special events, book sales to Horatio Alger Society members; letters and comments from members; miscellaneous items concerning Horatio Alger.

UNSOLICITED MSS. WELCOME? Yes, if they pertain to Alger; submissions acknowledged.
SPECIFICALLY WELCOMED: Articles that defend the good name of Horatio Alger, Jr. and that make accurate the date of Alger's birth year. Any articles on or about Alger—good or bad.
MS. LENGTH: No limit stated; submit ONE copy.
COPYRIGHT: Horatio Alger Society.
EDITOR'S DECISION: 60 days.
FROM ACCEPTANCE TO PUBLICATION: 60 days.
PAYMENT/OFFPRINTS: Up to 5 free copies.
REJECTED MSS.: Returned.
GENERAL: First issue, 1961. Usual publication length, 8 pages. The Horatio Alger Society holds annual conventions; issues an index of articles from the NEWSBOY.
BACK ISSUES: Available from the editor at $.50 each.

[Baum, L. Frank]

THE BAUM BUGLE

See the section on SPECIALIZED TOPICS AND INTERDISCIPLINARY STUDIES: POPULAR CULTURE for details.

[Burroughs, Edgar Rice]

THE BURROUGHS BULLETIN

See the section on SPECIALIZED TOPICS AND INTERDISCIPLINARY STUDIES: POPULAR CULTURE for details.

[Burroughs, Edgar Rice]

ERB-DOM and THE FANTASY COLLECTOR

See the section on SPECIALIZED TOPICS AND INTERDISCIPLINARY STUDIES: POPULAR CULTURE for details.

[Burroughs, Edgar Rice]

THE GRIDLEY WAVE

See the section on SPECIALIZED TOPICS AND INTERDISCIPLINARY STUDIES: POPULAR CULTURE for details.

[Cabell, James Branch]

THE CABELLIAN: A JOURNAL OF THE SECOND AMERICAN RENAISSANCE
(suspended publication)

EDITORIAL ADDRESS:
Julius Rothman, Editor
75 Noble Street
Lynbrook, New York 11563

SUBSCRIPTION ADDRESS:

same

PUBLISHED: Biannually (Autumn, Spring)

CIRCULATION: 300

CONTENTS: Scholarly, critical, and biographical articles on James Branch Cabell (1879-1958); occasionally articles on 20th century American literary Renaissance period; biographical information; checklists; book reviews and other commentary on publications; photographs; poetry; information about the Cabell Society; occasional photographs of or about Cabell.

COPYRIGHT: The Cabell Society.
GENERAL: First issue, November, 1968; final issue, Vol. 4, No. 2, Spring, 1972. Usual length of publication, 50 pages. Indexed by volume.

BACK ISSUES: Available from Kraus Reprint Company. Kraus has reprinted Volume 1 paperbound and clothbound and is planning to reprint Volume 2.

[Cabell, James Branch]
KALKI: STUDIES IN JAMES BRANCH CABELL

EDITORIAL ADDRESS:
William L. Godshalk, Editor
Department of English
University of Cincinnati
Cincinnati, Ohio 45221

SUBSCRIPTION ADDRESS:
Paul Spencer, Secretary-Treasurer
James Branch Cabell Society
665 Lotus Avenue
Oradell, New Jersey 07649

PUBLISHED: Quarterly
COST: 1 yr.—$5.00.

CIRCULATION: 250

CONTENTS: Scholarly essays on all phases of the novels, essays, poems, and one-act play of James Branch Cabell, his life and the influence of his contemporaries; occasional drawings; notes and information about conventions, events of the James Branch Cabell Society; reprints of formerly out-of-print critiques of Cabell.

UNSOLICITED MSS. WELCOME? Yes; submissions acknowledged.
SPECIFICALLY WELCOMED: Critical articles about James Branch Cabell's writings; biographical studies.
STYLE REQUIREMENTS: MLA STYLE SHEET advised, but not mandatory; all ordinary footnotes (such as titles of books, journals, and page references) to be run directly into text inside brackets.
COPYRIGHT: James Branch Cabell Society.
EDITOR'S DECISION: 4-6 weeks.
FROM ACCEPTANCE TO PUBLICATION: 10-12 months.
PAYMENT/OFFPRINTS: Two copies of issue.
REJECTED MSS.: Returned; some criticism.
GENERAL: First issue, 1967. Usual publication length, 30-40 pages.
BACK ISSUES: From Vol. II, No. 4, available from subscription address at $2.00 each. Vol. I is out of print. Johnson Reprint Corporation will be reprinting issues on microfilm or microfiche. Those desiring a complete run should write directly to Johnson Reprint.

[Cather, Willa]

WILLA CATHER PIONEER MEMORIAL AND EDUCATIONAL FOUNDATION NEWSLETTER

EDITORIAL ADDRESS:
Bernice Slote, Editor
201 Andrews Hall
University of Nebraska
Lincoln, Nebraska 68508

SUBSCRIPTION ADDRESS:
Willa Cather Pioneer Memorial and Education Foundation
Red Cloud, Nebraska 68970

PUBLISHED: Biannually   CIRCULATION: 6,000
COST: 1 yr.—$5.00 (25.00, sustaining membership; $100.00, life membership).

CONTENTS: Reprints of early interviews, reviews, and notes about Willa Cather's works; reprints of her early journalistic writings; bibliographical items; information concerning the Willa Cather Pioneer Memorial Foundation (financial and conference reports, occasional news of Willa Cather's friends); photographs of new museum items, Cather country, and her home.

UNSOLICITED MSS. WELCOME? Yes.
SPECIFICALLY WELCOMED: Original brief notes, observations, explications, or short critical articles.
COPYRIGHT: Willa Cather Pioneer Memorial and Educational Foundation.
GENERAL: First issue, 1957. Usual publication length, 4 pages. Aim of newsletter is "to perpetuate an interest throughout the world in the work of Willa Cather."
BACK ISSUES: Inquire at subscription address.

[Chaney, William H.]

THE CHANEY CHRONICAL

EDITORIAL ADDRESS:
David H. Schlottmann, Editor
929 South Bay Road
Olympia, Washington 98506

SUBSCRIPTION ADDRESS:

same

PUBLISHED: Irregularly   CIRCULATION: 50
COST: Single copy—$.50.

CONTENTS: Bibliographies, articles, and reprints of material written by, and/or about William H. Chaney (1821-1903) who is generally believed to be the father of Jack London; an editorial each issue entitled "The Rattling Chane"; news items.

UNSOLICITED MSS. WELCOME? Yes; submission acknowledged by publication.
SPECIFICALLY WELCOMED: Anything concerning William H. Chaney.

MS. LENGTH: No limit.
STYLE REQUIREMENTS: No specific style.
COPYRIGHT: Author.
EDITOR'S DECISION: Immediate.
FROM ACCEPTANCE TO PUBLICATION: Very irregular.
PAYMENT/OFFPRINTS: Copies if desired.
REJECTED MSS.: Returned.
GENERAL: First issue, October, 1972. Usual publication length, 4-10 pages. This is a companion publication to WHAT'S NEW ABOUT LONDON, JACK?
BACK ISSUES: Available from editorial address at $.50 each. If not available, can be xeroxed at $.10 per page.

[Clemens, Samuel]

THE MARK TWAIN JOURNAL

EDITORIAL ADDRESS:
Cyril Clemens, Editor-in-Chief
Kirkwood
Missouri 63122

SUBSCRIPTION ADDRESS:

same

PUBLISHED: Biannually
COST: 1 yr.—$3.00.

CIRCULATION: 10,000

CONTENTS: Book reviews with emphasis on Mark Twain; critical articles on Twain's works; biographical articles; some poems—original and occasional unpublished poems of great authors; occasional photographs of old letters from people to 'Mark Twain' and copies of letters sent by Samuel Clemens. Example: "Mark Twain's Bitter Duality."

UNSOLICITED MSS. WELCOME? Yes; submissions acknowledged.
SPECIFICALLY WELCOMED: Articles on the works of Samuel Clemens and how they influenced later great writers; some essays on other American and English authors.
PAYMENT/OFFPRINTS: Payment by arrangement; free offprints.
GENERAL: First issue, 1936. Usual publication length, 20 pages.
BACK ISSUES: First twelve volumes have been published by Kraus Reprint Corporation. Others available from editorial address at $1.00 each.

[Clemens, Samuel]

MARK TWAIN MEMORIAL NEWSLETTER

EDITORIAL ADDRESS:
Editor
351 Farmington Avenue
Hartford, Connecticut 06105

SUBSCRIPTION ADDRESS:

same

PUBLISHED: Quarterly CIRCULATION: 1,000
COST: Free to members and selected libraries.

CONTENTS: Information concerning the events of the Mark Twain Memorial (annual meeting, birthday party, guest speakers, annual report, Women's Committee affairs, acquisitions of library and museum, new memberships, restoration of the Mark Twain house, miscellaneous news dealing with Mark Twain, his family and friends).

[Clemens, Samuel]

THE TWAINIAN

EDITORIAL ADDRESS:
Chester L. Davis, Executive Secretary
Mark Twain Research Foundation, Inc.
Perry, Missouri 63462

SUBSCRIPTION ADDRESS:

same

PUBLISHED: Bimonthly CIRCULATION: 400
COST: 1 yr.—$5.00 membership (minimum).

CONTENTS: Material heretofore unpublished (usually by Mark Twain or by his family, friends, or associates) during his lifetime until date of issue, and usually once each year selected abstracts of Mark Twain items published elsewhere.

UNSOLICITED MSS. WELCOME? No, unless newly discovered original material not generally known; submissions not acknowledged.
SPECIFICALLY WELCOMED: Only NEWLY DISCOVERED material, minimum criticism and opinions, since most of the MEMBERS are themselves capable of their own analysis and evaluation.
MSS. LENGTH: Not to exceed 12 pages.
COPYRIGHT: Mark Twain Research Foundation and/or The Mark Twain Estate.
EDITOR'S DECISION: 30 days.
FROM ACCEPTANCE TO PUBLICATION: Not definite.
PAYMENT/OFFPRINTS: No payment, but on occasion reimburse writer's actual out-of-pocket expenses if directed or necessary. Reasonable number of gratis offprints available, not to be resold.
REJECTED MSS.: Returned.

GENERAL: First issue, 1939 or 1942. Usual publication length, 4 pages.
BACK ISSUES: Available only for members that are colleges, universities, and public libraries, and then ONLY by extending back their membership to the year desired; quotation upon request, subject to available issues and the needs of other members. The usual price is the annual membership dues for the back years desired.

[Cooper, James Fenimore, and others]

NATTY BUMPO REVIEW

EDITORIAL ADDRESS: SUBSCRIPTION ADDRESS:
Jefferson Swanson, Editor
175 West Jackson, Suite 414   same
Chicago, Illinois 60604

PUBLISHED: Quarterly, as possible

CONTENTS: Articles, stories, poems, fillers concerning Eastern American Indians, James Fenimore Cooper, H. E. G. Dukes, pioneer times; photographs of Indian historical markers and statues.

UNSOLICITED MSS. WELCOME? Yes.
MS. LENGTH: Short; 1,000 word maximum; submit ONE copy.
EDITOR'S DECISION: 2 weeks.
FROM ACCEPTANCE TO PUBLICATION: Varies.
REJECTED MSS. Returned.

[Crane, Stephen]

STEPHEN CRANE NEWSLETTER

EDITORIAL ADDRESS: SUBSCRIPTION ADDRESS:
Dr. Joseph Katz, Editor
Department of English   same
University of South Carolina
Columbia, South Carolina 29208

PUBLISHED: Quarterly   CIRCULATION: 300
COST: 1 yr.—$2.00; $3.00 invoiced.

CONTENTS: Critical essays on the short stories, novel of Stephen Crane; reviews of books about Crane; notes; newly uncovered Crane letters; unpublished writings of Crane; biographical material; works in progress; checklists (including one of Crane's influence outside the world of literary scholarship).

UNSOLICITED MSS. WELCOME? Yes; submissions acknowledged.
SPECIFICALLY WELCOMED: Articles offering a new light on the works or life of Stephen Crane.
MS. LENGTH: 6 pages; submit ONE copy.
STYLE REQUIREMENTS: See recent SCN issue.
COPYRIGHT: Joseph Katz.
EDITOR'S DECISION: 3 months.
FROM ACCEPTANCE TO PUBLICATION: 3 months.
PAYMENT/OFFPRINTS: Five copies of issue.
REJECTED MSS.: Returned.
GENERAL: First issue, 1966. Usual publication length, 10-12 pages.
BACK ISSUES: Available from editor.

[Curwood, James Oliver]

THE CURWOOD COLLECTOR

EDITORIAL ADDRESS:
Ivan A. Conger, Editor
1825 Osaukie Road
Owosso, Michigan 48867

SUBSCRIPTION ADDRESS:

same

PUBLISHED: 3 to 4 times yearly   CIRCULATION: 175
COST: $2.00 for 4 issues of current volume; subscription to be renewed each 4 issues.

CONTENTS: Articles about James Oliver Curwood, as novelist and conservationist; some short stories written by Curwood; articles on the many movie productions of Curwood; reproductions of old newspaper clippings, movie advertisements, and some of Curwood's letters; photographs.

UNSOLICITED MSS. WELCOME? Yes; submissions acknowledged.
SPECIFICALLY WELCOMED: Curwood related articles—comparisons with other contemporary authors; related pictures (and/or negatives).
MS. LENGTH: Up to 4 or 5 pages
COPYRIGHT: Editor; writers may retain rights.
EDITOR'S DECISION: Up to 30 days.
FROM ACCEPTANCE TO PUBLICATION: Up to 6 months.
PAYMENT/OFFPRINTS: Several free copies; larger quantities may be purchased at one half the subscription rate.
REJECTED MSS.: Returned if requested.
GENERAL: First issue, January, 1972. Usual publication length, 8 pages; future issues, 12-16 pages.
BACK ISSUES: Available from editorial office at $2.00 per volume (4 issues).

[Dickinson, Emily]

EMILY DICKINSON BULLETIN

EDITORIAL ADDRESS:
Frederick L. Morey, Editor
4508—38th Street
Brentwood, Maryland 20722

SUBSCRIPTION ADDRESS:

same

PUBLISHED: Biannually (June, Dec.)   CIRCULATION: 200
COST: 1 yr.—$5.00 cash, $10.00 invoiced because of switching to letterpress.

CONTENTS: Researched essays about some theme, image, or issue in the poetry of Emily Dickinson or about her life and her relationship with her contemporaries; notes and queries; occasional illustrations and reprints of old newspaper items on Emily Dickinson; listing of major and minor ED holdings of libraries on the U.S. eastern seaboard; reviews of books about Emily Dickinson; bibliographical checklists (poems and letters, criticism and scholarship, collections in foreign countries, translations of criticism in English); announcements about the Emily Dickinson house.

UNSOLICITED MSS. WELCOME? Yes; submissions acknowledged.
SPECIFICALLY WELCOMED: Scholarly essays about the poetry of Emily Dickinson; checklists; bibliographies; reviews.
MS. LENGTH: 10 pages (500-4,000 words); submit ONE copy.
STYLE REQUIREMENTS: MLA STYLE SHEET; footnotes follow essay.
COPYRIGHT: Author.
EDITOR'S DECISION: 2-4 weeks.
FROM ACCEPTANCE TO PUBLICATION: 1-2 years.
PAYMENT/OFFPRINTS: Copy of issue plus any and all available tearsheets. Offprints at cost—$2.00 per copy.
REJECTED MSS.: Returned.
GENERAL: First issue, January, 1968. Usual publication length, 40-50 pages. Triennial subscription in advance entitles one to membership in the Emily Dickinson Society and receipt of all publications of Higginson Press, which includes the semiannual HIGGINSON JOURNAL OF POETRY.
BACK ISSUES: Available from editorial address at $10.00 for entire calendar year.

[Dickinson, Emily; Higginson, T. W.]

HIGGINSON JOURNAL OF POETRY

EDITORIAL ADDRESS:
Frederick L. Morey, Editor
4508—38th Street
Brentwood, Maryland 20722

SUBSCRIPTION ADDRESS:

same

PUBLISHED: Biannually (June, December) CIRCULATION: 200
COST: 1 yr.—$5.00 cash; $10.00 invoiced. Triennial option mentioned in EMILY DICKINSON BULLETIN information, workable with either/both journals.

CONTENTS: Popular overflow of Emily Dickinson material; plays, poems about her; other interests of Col. T. W. Higginson, her mentor, such as women's lib, black studies, prosody. Units of poems, biography, pictures, of contemporary poets.

UNSOLICITED MSS. WELCOME? Yes; submissions acknowledged.
SPECIFICALLY WELCOMED: Articles related to Emily Dickinson and to the interests of Col. T. W. Higginson.
MS. LENGTH: 10 pages (500-4,000 words); submit ONE copy.
STYLE REQUIREMENTS: MLA STYLE SHEET; footnotes follow essay.
COPYRIGHT: Author.
EDITOR'S DECISION: 2-4 weeks.
FROM ACCEPTANCE TO PUBLICATION: 1-2 years.
PAYMENT/OFFPRINTS: Copy of issue plus any and all available tearsheets. Offprints at $2.00 per copy.
REJECTED MSS. Returned.
GENERAL: First issue, October, 1971. Quarterly through 1972. Biannual beginning in 1973. Usual publication length, 25 to 50 pages, depending on frequency; 100 pages annual minimum.
BACK ISSUES: Available from editorial office for $10.00 per year (1971-1972 count as one issue).

[Dreiser, Theodore]

THE DREISER NEWSLETTER

EDITORIAL ADDRESS: SUBSCRIPTION ADDRESS:
Richard W. Dowell and Robert P.
Saalbach, Editors
English Department same
Indiana State University
Terre Haute, Indiana 47809

PUBLISHED: Biannually CIRCULATION: 250
COST: 2 yrs.—$2.50; $3.50 overseas; single copy—$.75; $1.00 overseas.

CONTENTS: Articles of a bibliographical nature; checklists, library holdings of manuscripts, interviews with scholars; occasional illustrations and photographs; notes and information on annual meetings; "Dreiser News & Notes"; reviews of books about Theodore Dreiser's novels and poetry. Example: "The Rocking Chair Structure of SISTER CARRIE."

UNSOLICITED MSS. WELCOME? Yes, but many are solicited; submissions acknowledged.

SPECIFICALLY WELCOMED: Articles dealing with the life and works of Theodore Dreiser; critical articles welcomed but priority given to material of bibliographical nature.
MS. LENGTH: 1,000-1,500 words; submit ONE copy.
STYLE REQUIREMENTS: MLA STYLE SHEET.
COPYRIGHT: THE DREISER NEWSLETTER; individual rights returned to author on request.
EDITOR'S DECISION: Usually less than 30 days.
FROM ACCEPTANCE TO PUBLICATION: 1 year.
PAYMENT/OFFPRINTS: Copies of issue; additional copies available. No off-prints.
REJECTED MSS.: Returned.
GENERAL: First issue, 1970. Usual publication length, 20-24 pages. THE DREISER NEWSLETTER is "dedicated to stimulating, coordinating and reporting Dreiser scholarship."
BACK ISSUES: Available from editorial office at $.75 each. Index for Vols. I-III also available.

[Emerson, Thoreau, and the Concord School]

ESQ: A JOURNAL OF THE AMERICAN RENAISSANCE
(formerly EMERSON SOCIETY QUARTERLY)

EDITORIAL ADDRESS:
G. R. Thompson, Editor
Department of English
Washington State University
Pullman, Washington 99163

SUBSCRIPTION ADDRESS:
Washington State University Press
Pullman, Washington 99163

PUBLISHED: Quarterly (Jan., April, July, Oct.)
COST: 1 yr.—$10.00.

CIRCULATION: 600-700

CONTENTS: Study of nineteenth-century American literature, with particular emphasis on Romanticism and on the reciprocal relations of European and American literatures during the century; critical studies; source and influence studies; biographical and bibliographical studies of all figures; studies in Romantic theory and the history of ideas; essays on the Romantic transcendental tradition emanating out of New England in all its literary, religious, philosophical, and historical aspects, of which Emerson is a principal figure. Example: "Charles Brocken Brown and the Uses of Gothicism: A Reassessment."

UNSOLICITED MSS. WELCOME? Yes, submissions acknowledged.
SPECIFICALLY WELCOMED: Scholarly essays about the American Renaissance in literature.
MS. LENGTH: 10-30 pages; submit ONE OR MORE copies.
STYLE REQUIREMENTS: MLA STYLE SHEET; footnotes follow essay.
COPYRIGHT: Not copyrighted.

EDITOR'S DECISION: 2-4 months.
FROM ACCEPTANCE TO PUBLICATION: 1 year or less.
PAYMENT/OFFPRINTS: One copy of journal. 25 offprints of article.
REJECTED MSS.: Returned.
GENERAL: First issue, January, 1972 (in present format); founded 1955 by Kenneth W. Cameron. Usual publication length, 70-80 pages.
BACK ISSUES: Issues before 1972 available from Kenneth W. Cameron, Box 1080, Hartford, Connecticut, others from Washington State University Press, at $2.50 each.

[Faulkner, William]

FAULKNER CONCORDANCE NEWSLETTER

EDITORIAL ADDRESS: SUBSCRIPTION ADDRESS:
Robert H. Moore, Executive Secretary
Department of English Language   same
and Literature
University of Maryland
College Park, Maryland 20742

PUBLISHED: Occasionally   CIRCULATION: 300
COST: Free.

CONTENTS: Material of interest to students of American English and American Literature who are interested in the work connected with the Faulkner Concordance project; information on the developing Faulkner collection at the United States Military Academy (the central depository for all materials associated with the project); list of locations of Faulkner Concordance volumes.

UNSOLICITED MSS. WELCOME? Not at present.
GENERAL: First issue, December, 1972. Usual publication length, 4-8 pages.
BACK ISSUES: Available free from the editor.

[Faulkner, William]

FAULKNER STUDIES (Suspended publication)

EDITORIAL ADDRESS:
Jules Chametzky and Marianne Halley,
Last Editors (Minnesota)
Originally published by James R. Baker,
John R. Marvin, & Tom E. Francis, Editors
(Colorado)

PUBLISHED: Quarterly

CONTENTS: Book reviews; critical articles and biographical information focusing on William Faulkner; bibliography of Faulkner criticism; ideas and queries; news and comments. Examples: "Genealogy as Symbol in GO DOWN, MOSES"; "Gavin Stevens: From Rhetoric to Dialectic."

GENERAL: First issue, Spring, 1952. Usual publication length, 20-30 pages.
BACK ISSUES: Xerox copies of the first three volumes (1952-54) available from: Alderman Library, Division of Rare Books, University of Virginia, Charlottesville, Virginia 22901. Inquire about cost.

[Faust, Frederick]

THE FAUST COLLECTOR

See the section on SPECIALIZED TOPICS AND INTERDISCIPLINARY STUDIES: POPULAR CULTURE for details.

[Fitzgerald, F. Scott/Hemingway, Ernest]

FITZGERALD/HEMINGWAY ANNUAL (formerly FITZGERALD NEWSLETTER)

EDITORIAL ADDRESS:
Matthew J. Bruccoli and C. E. Frazer Clark, Jr., Editors
Department of English
University of South Carolina
Columbia, South Carolina 29208

SUBSCRIPTION ADDRESS:
NCR/Microcard Editions
901—26th Street, N.W.
Washington, D. C. 20037

PUBLISHED: Annually
CIRCULATION: 3,000
COST: 1969 volume—$10.00; 1970 volume ISBN 0-910972-03-6—$12.00; 1971 volume—$15.00; 1972 volume—$15.00.

CONTENTS: Critical essays about F. Scott Fitzgerald and Ernest Hemingway; newly found manuscripts and reviews; reminiscences by friends and relatives of the authors; interviews; reviews of books about Fitzgerald and Hemingway; articles about these authors' relationship to one another and with their contemporaries. Editorial bias is bibliographical and biographical.

UNSOLICITED MSS. WELCOME? Yes; submissions acknowledged.
SPECIFICALLY WELCOMED: Scholarly articles concerning the writings of Fitzgerald and Hemingway and the influence of their time.
MS. LENGTH: No preferences; submit ONE copy.
STYLE REQUIREMENTS: MLA STYLE SHEET; footnotes follow essay.
COPYRIGHT: Negotiable.
EDITOR'S DECISION: 1 week.
FROM ACCEPTANCE TO PUBLICATION: 1 year.

PAYMENT/OFFPRINTS: 50 offprints.
REJECTED MSS. Returned.
GENERAL: First issue, 1969. Usual publication length, 360 pages. Submit all articles to Matthew J. Bruccoli.
BACK ISSUES: Available from NCR/Microcard Editions at list price.

[Fitzgerald, F. Scott]

FITZGERALD NEWSLETTER (suspended publication)

EDITORIAL ADDRESS:
Dr. Matthew J. Bruccoli, Editor
Department of English
University of South Carolina
Columbia, South Carolina 29208

SUBSCRIPTION ADDRESS:

none

PUBLISHED: Quarterly

CIRCULATION: 500

CONTENTS: Critical articles on F. Scott Fitzgerald's short stories and novels; reviews of books about Fitzgerald and his life during the twenties and early thirties; emphasis on bibliographical scholarship.

GENERAL: First issue, Spring, 1958. Usual publication length, 3-4 pages. FITZGERALD NEWSLETTER was superseded in 1969 by the FITZGERALD/HEMINGWAY ANNUAL.
BACK ISSUES: Revised edition of this quarterly published from 1958 to 1968, now issued as one unit of 327 pages, can be obtained from NCR/Microcard Editions, 901-26th Street, N.W., Washington, D. C. 20037 at $9.95, payment with order, or $10.95, invoiced.

[Frederic, Harold]

THE FREDERIC HERALD (suspended publication)

EDITORIAL ADDRESS:
Thomas F. O'Donnell, Editor
Department of English
State University College
Brockport, New York 14420

SUBSCRIPTION ADDRESS:

same

PUBLISHED: Tri-annually
(Apr., Sept., Jan.)
COST: Free, on request.

CIRCULATION: 400

CONTENTS: Short critical, bibliographical, and biographical articles and notes about Harold Frederic and his work; mixture of whimsy (fake advertisements, phoney news stories, bulletins, "inside" Frederic jokes); photographs of people, places, and things related to Frederic's work.

UNSOLICITED MSS. WELCOME? Yes; submissions acknowledged.
SPECIFICALLY WELCOMED: Both serious and whimsical articles about Harold Frederic.
MS. LENGTH: 500 words maximum; submit ONE copy.
COPYRIGHT: No copyright.
EDITOR'S DECISION: 2 weeks.
FROM ACCEPTANCE TO PUBLICATION: Varies.
PAYMENT/OFFPRINTS: Five copies; more by arrangement.
REJECTED MSS.: Returned.
GENERAL: First issue, April, 1967. Usual publication length, 6-8 pages. Periodical suspended publication after the 9th issue (Jan. 1970). Editor plans to revive it—possibly in new format—in fall, 1973. Communications, suggestions, and requests invited.
BACK ISSUES: Free, while available, from editorial address.

[Grey, Zane]
THE ZANE GREY COLLECTOR

EDITORIAL ADDRESS:
G. M. Farley, Editor
P. O. Box 167
Williamsport, Maryland 21795

SUBSCRIPTION ADDRESS:

same

PUBLISHED: Quarterly
COST: 1 yr.—$2.00.

CIRCULATION: 300

CONTENTS: Always has an out-of-print or unpublished story or article by Zane Grey; articles about Grey by various writers; page on "How to Tell First Editions of Z. G. Books"; detailed description of a different book in each issue; occasional biographical sketches of other Western writers; reviews of new books and articles about Z. G.; photographs.

UNSOLICITED MSS. WELCOME? Yes; submissions acknowledged.
SPECIFICALLY WELCOMED: Almost anything about Zane Grey, particularly in-depth articles.
MS. LENGTH: 1,500 words; submit ONE copy.
STYLE REQUIREMENTS: None.
COPYRIGHT: G. M. Farley.
EDITOR'S DECISION: 1 month.
FROM ACCEPTANCE TO PUBLICATION: 1 month to 1 year.
PAYMENT/OFFPRINTS: Payment in copies only. Offprints if requested in advance of publication.
REJECTED MSS.: Returned.

GENERAL: First issue, April, 1967. Usual publication length, 16 pages. Writer should send a query before submitting anything about Zane Grey or related subjects.
BACK ISSUES: Available from editorial office at $.40 each.

[Harris, George Washington]

THE LOVINGOOD PAPERS (suspended publication)

EDITORIAL ADDRESS:
Ben Harris McClary, Editor
Humanities Division
Middle Georgia College
Cochran, Georgia

SUBSCRIPTION ADDRESS:
The University of Tennessee Press
Publications Building
Knoxville, Tennessee 37916

PUBLISHED: Annually

CONTENTS: Reprints of writings of George Washington Harris; review of his publications; critical and biographical articles on Harris; contributors' notes and letters; editorial notes; frequent drawings. Examples: "Sut's Speech: The Dialect of a 'Nat'ral Borned' Mountaineer"; "The Harris Harvest Year: A Review of 1965 Publications."

COPYRIGHT: University of Tennessee Press.
GENERAL: First issue, 1961. Usual publication length, 70-75 pages. The Sut Society ended THE LOVINGOOD PAPERS in December, 1967.
BACK ISSUES: Available from the University of Tennessee Press: 1962; 1963—paper, $2.00 (68 pp.); 1964—paper, $2.00 (52 pp.); 1965—paper, $2.00 (76 pp.). Also available from Xerox University Microfilms.

[Hartmann, Sadakichi]

SADAKICHI HARTMANN NEWSLETTER

EDITORIAL ADDRESS:
George Knox, Editor
Department of English
University of California
At Riverside
Riverside, California 92502

SUBSCRIPTION ADDRESS:
Richard Tuerk
Department of Literature
and Languages
East Texas State University
Commerce, Texas 75428

PUBLISHED: Tri-annually
COST: 1 yr.—$2.50 for individuals and libraries; free to all correspondents who were acquainted with Hartmann or who are engaged in Hartmann research.

CONTENTS: Essays and recollections about the writings and life of Sadakichi Hartmann as Symbolist poet and dramatist, art historian and critic, essayist; correspondence between Hartmann and relatives and literary acquaintances; reviews of books that discuss Hartmann; biographical articles; checklists of all materials by or about SH (writings, drawings, and illustrations); notes and queries; many photographs of SH, his friends, and relatives; occasional drawings; essays on Hartmann's contemporaries. Example: "The Ezra Pound Correspondence: Letters to a Member of the Lost Legion."

UNSOLICITED MSS. WELCOME? Yes; submissions acknowledged.
SPECIFICALLY WELCOMED: Letters, research, illustrations about or by Sadakichi Hartmann.
MS. LENGTH: 5-10 pages.
STYLE REQUIREMENTS: Footnotes follow essay.
COPYRIGHT: Wistaria Hartmann Linton.
EDITOR'S DECISION: 3 months maximum.
FROM ACCEPTANCE TO PUBLICATION: 3-4 months.
PAYMENT/OFFPRINTS: Ten copies of issue in which contribution appears.
REJECTED MSS.: Returned.
GENERAL: First issue, Fall, 1969. Usual publication length, 8-12 pages.
BACK ISSUES: Available from editorial address at $.50 each.

[Hawthorne, Nathaniel]

NATHANIEL HAWTHORNE JOURNAL

EDITORIAL ADDRESS:
C. E. Frazier Clark, Jr., Editor
1490 Sodon Lake Drive
Bloomfield Hills, Michigan 48013

SUBSCRIPTION ADDRESS:
NCR/Microcard Editions
901—26th Street, N.W.
Washington, D. C. 20037

PUBLISHED: Annually
COST: 1971 volume—$13.00; 1972 volume—$15.00.

CONTENTS: Scholarly essays about the short stories and novels of Nathaniel Hawthorne; heretofore unpublished letters of NH; literary correspondence; biographical accounts; reprints of Hawthorne works; reprints of old newspaper articles about NH.

UNSOLICITED MSS. WELCOME? Yes; submissions acknowledged.
SPECIFICALLY WELCOMED: Researched articles about the works of Nathaniel Hawthorne, particularly biographical, bibliographical, and textual material.
MS. LENGTH: 20 pages; submit ONE copy.
STYLE REQUIREMENTS: MLA STYLE SHEET.
COPYRIGHT: NCR/Microcard Editions, with reprint rights to contributor.
EDITOR'S DECISION: 2 weeks.
FROM ACCEPTANCE TO PUBLICATION: 5-9 months.

PAYMENT/OFFPRINTS: Payment for assigned articles. 25 offprints to contributors.
REJECTED MSS.: Returned.
GENERAL: First issue, 1971. Usual publication length, 300 pages.
BACK ISSUES: Available from subscription address at published price.

[Hemingway, Ernest]

HEMINGWAY NOTES

EDITORIAL ADDRESS:
Taylor Alderman and Kenneth Rosen, Editors
Department of English
Dickinson College
Carlisle, Pennsylvania 17013

SUBSCRIPTION ADDRESS:

same

PUBLISHED: Biannually (Spring, Fall)   CIRCULATION: 120
COST: 1 yr.—$3.00; 2 yrs.—$5.00.

CONTENTS: An extensive bibliography in each issue; reviews of all book-length works related to Ernest Hemingway; brief items of interest to Hemingway buffs; short notes of explication, scholarship, criticism (3 or 4 each issue); illustrations. Examples: "Hemingway & Surrealism: A Note on the Twenties"; " 'Between Grief and Nothing': Hemingway and Faulkner."

UNSOLICITED MSS. WELCOME? Yes; submissions acknowledged.
SPECIFICALLY WELCOMED: Just about anything relating more-or-less directly to the literary career of Hemingway.
MS. LENGTH: 2,000 words maximum; submit TWO copies.
STYLE REQUIREMENTS: MLA STYLE SHEET; footnotes follow article.
COPYRIGHT: Taylor Alderman and Kenneth Rosen.
EDITOR'S DECISION: 3 months.
FROM ACCEPTANCE TO PUBLICATION: 6 months maximum.
PAYMENT/OFFPRINTS: Three copies of journal. No offprints.
REJECTED MSS.: Returned.
GENERAL: First issue, Spring, 1971. Usual publication length, 24 pages.
BACK ISSUES: Available from editorial address at $1.50 each.

[Howard, Robert E.]

THE HOWARD COLLECTOR

See the section on SPECIALIZED TOPICS AND INTERDISCIPLINARY STUDIES: POPULAR CULTURE for details.

[Jeffers, Robinson]

ROBINSON JEFFERS NEWSLETTER

EDITORIAL ADDRESS:
Dr. Robert J. Brophy, Editor
Department of English
California State College at Long Beach
6101 E. 7th Street
Long Beach, California 90801

SUBSCRIPTION ADDRESS:
ROBINSON JEFFERS NEWSLETTER
Library
1600 Campus Road
Occidental College
Los Angeles, California 90041

PUBLISHED: Quarterly
COST: 1 yr.—$4.00.

CIRCULATION: 350

CONTENTS: Reports on acquisitions, reviews of books, recordings, exhibits, festivals; abstracts of articles, dissertations, and masters theses; short articles; explications; scholarly notes; short memoirs; notice of short films, radio and TV readings, dramatic productions (media); reports on work in progress, coming publications, books in print; news of meetings.

UNSOLICITED MSS. WELCOME? Yes; submissions acknowledged.
SPECIFICALLY WELCOMED: Memoirs, especially by artists and scholars who knew Jeffers; short articles and notes on Jeffers' poetry or scholarly resources.
MS. LENGTH: 2-10 pages; submit TWO copies.
STYLE REQUIREMENTS: MLA STYLE SHEET or reasonable approximation; footnotes follow article.
COPYRIGHT: Occidental College.
EDITOR'S DECISION: 1 month.
FROM ACCEPTANCE TO PUBLICATION: 1-4 months.
PAYMENT/OFFPRINTS: Offprints on request. Supply limited.
REJECTED MSS.: Returned.
GENERAL: First issue, November, 1962. Usual publication length, 15 pages. Seven-page index to numbers 1-25 published Summer, 1970.
BACK ISSUES: Available in xerox form from subscription address at $25.00. No volume cumulations.

[Lewis, Sinclair]

SINCLAIR LEWIS NEWSLETTER

EDITORIAL ADDRESS:
James Lundquist, Editor
English Department
St. Cloud State College
St. Cloud, Minnesota 56301

SUBSCRIPTION ADDRESS:

same

PUBLISHED: Annually
COST: 1 yr.—$1.00

CIRCULATION: 500

CONTENTS: Articles of a critical or biographical nature relating to Sinclair Lewis and writers whose lives and work bear relationship to him (Menchen, Cabell, London, Fitzgerald, Anderson, and others); occasional book review, such as "Oedipus and Lewis: A Review." Example articles: "A Whartonian Woman in DODSWORTH"; " 'Vulgar Barnyard Illustrations' in ELMER GANTRY."

UNSOLICITED MSS. WELCOME? Yes, submissions acknowledged.
SPECIFICALLY WELCOMED: Critical articles, biography, memoribilia.
MS. LENGTH: 3,000 words and under.
STYLE REQUIREMENTS: MLA STYLE SHEET.
COPYRIGHT: Author.
EDITOR'S DECISION: 6 months.
FROM ACCEPTANCE TO PUBLICATION: 6 months.
PAYMENT/OFFPRINTS: Eight copies of newsletter. Extra copies sent out.
REJECTED MSS.: Returned.
GENERAL: First issue, Spring, 1969. Usual publication length, 20 pages.
BACK ISSUES: Available from editorial office at $1.00 each.

[London, Jack, and Stuart, Jesse]

JACK LONDON NEWSLETTER

EDITORIAL ADDRESS:
Hensley C. Woodbridge, Editor
Southern Illinois University Library
Carbondale, Illinois 62901

SUBSCRIPTION ADDRESS:

same

PUBLISHED: Tri-annually (Jan.-Apr., May-Aug., Sept.-Dec.)
COST: 1 yr.—$5.00

CIRCULATION: 350

CONTENTS: Critical, bibliographical, and biographical studies of Jack London and Jesse Stuart; book reviews; articles; notes; translations of materials on London. Examples: "The Ghost Dog, A Motif in THE CALL OF THE WILD"; "The Significance of Upward Mobility in MARTIN EDEN."

UNSOLICITED MSS. WELCOME? Yes; submissions acknowledged.
SPECIFICALLY WELCOMED: Critical articles.
MS. LENGTH: Up to 5,000 words.
STYLE REQUIREMENTS: Prefer MLA STYLE SHEET.
COPYRIGHT: No copyright.
EDITOR'S DECISION: 2 weeks.
FROM ACCEPTANCE TO PUBLICATION: Usually next issue.
PAYMENT/OFFPRINTS: Extra copies sold at reduced rate.
REJECTED MSS.: Returned.
GENERAL: First issue, July-Dec., 1967. Usual publication length varies from 44-94 pages.

BACK ISSUES: Most are out of stock and not available. Cost $1.00 per issue where available.

[London, Jack]
THE LONDON COLLECTOR

EDITORIAL ADDRESS:
Richard Weiderman, Frank Girard and
James E. Sisson, Editors
1420 Pontiac Road S.E.
Grand Rapids, Michigan 49506

SUBSCRIPTION ADDRESS:

same

PUBLISHED: Irregularly—about twice yearly

CIRCULATION: 150

COST: Single copy—$.50, except for special issues which vary in price depending on printing costs.

CONTENTS: Articles of interest to collectors and fans of Jack London. Each issue is devoted to one topic only, such as his poetry, science fiction, contribution to his high school paper, and the recent revival of interest in London.

UNSOLICITED MSS. WELCOME? Yes; submissions acknowledged.
SPECIFICALLY WELCOMED: Items of interest to collectors and fans—in preference to the scholar.
MS. LENGTH: No preference; submit ONE copy.
STYLE REQUIREMENTS: Clarity.
COPYRIGHT: Publishers.
EDITOR'S DECISION: Immediate.
FROM ACCEPTANCE TO PUBLICATION: 6 months to 1 year.
PAYMENT/OFFPRINTS: 12 copies of periodical.
REJECTED MSS.: Returned.
GENERAL: First issue, June, 1970. Usual publication length, 25 pages.
BACK ISSUES: Available from publishers at $2.00 each for #3 and $.50 each for #4.

[London, Jack]
WHAT'S NEW ABOUT LONDON, JACK?

EDITORIAL ADDRESS:
David H. Schlottmann, Editor
929 South Bay Road
Olympia, Washington 98506

SUBSCRIPTION ADDRESS:

same

PUBLISHED: 10-12 times yearly   CIRCULATION: 70
COST: Single copy—$.50; 10 issues—$5.00.

CONTENTS: Editorial each issue entitled "Wolf's Den"; annotated and bibliographic description of books, magazine and newspaper articles, and ephemera dealing in whole or in part with Jack London; news of any events of interest to Jack London fans; an occasional special feature.

UNSOLICITED MSS. WELCOME? Yes; submissions acknowledged by publication unless otherwise requested.
SPECIFICALLY WELCOMED: Anything of Jack London interest.
STYLE REQUIREMENTS: No specific style.
COPYRIGHT: Author can have title to his materials.
EDITOR'S DECISION: Immediate.
FROM ACCEPTANCE TO PUBLICATION: Irregular; 3 days to 1 month.
PAYMENT/OFFPRINTS: Copies of issue if requested.
REJECTED MSS.: Returned.
GENERAL: First issue, July, 1971. Usual publication length, 8-10 pages. This is a cooperative venture between editor and subscribers; subscribers inform editor of any new material they come across so all can share in the news via this paper.
BACK ISSUES: Available from editorial address. Most are out of print but can be xeroxed at $.10 per page.

[MacDonald, John D.]

THE JOHN D. MACDONALD BIBLIOPHILE

See the Section on SPECIALIZED TOPICS AND INTERDISCIPLINARY STUDIES: POPULAR CULTURE for details.

[Markham, Edwin, and others]

THE MARKHAM REVIEW

EDITORIAL ADDRESS: SUBSCRIPTION ADDRESS:
Joseph W. Slade, Editor
Horrmann Library   same
Wagner College
Staten Island, New York 10301

PUBLISHED: Tri-annually (Sept.,   CIRCULATION: 2,000
Feb., May)
COST: Free, at present.

CONTENTS: Articles dealing with American literature 1865-1940, Edwin Markham, and especially minor writers and figures on social and political scene; occasionally publishes original manuscript by one of these, e.g. previously unpublished essay by Bret Harte; photographs, e.g. of Christopher Morley, Ring Lardner. Examples: "Stephen Crane's 'The Monster' as Christian Allegory"; "The American Railroad Novel."

UNSOLICITED MSS. WELCOME? Yes; submissions acknowledged.
SPECIFICALLY WELCOMED: Anything that conforms to contents description.
MS. LENGTH: Less than 6,000 words; submit TWO copies.
STYLE REQUIREMENTS: MLA STYLE SHEET; footnotes follow article.
COPYRIGHT: Author.
EDITOR'S DECISION: 4 weeks
FROM ACCEPTANCE TO PUBLICATION: 6 months to 1 year.
PAYMENT/OFFPRINTS: 24 copies of issue in which article appears.
REJECTED MSS.: Returned.
GENERAL: First issue, February, 1968. Usual publication length, 20 pages.
BACK ISSUES: Available from Xerox University Microfilms.

[Melville, Herman]

EXTRACTS/AN OCCASIONAL NEWSLETTER
(formerly THE MELVILLE SOCIETY NEWSLETTER)

EDITORIAL ADDRESS:
Hennig Cohen, Secretary/Treasurer
Department of English
University of Pennsylvania
Philadelphia, Pennsylvania 19104

SUBSCRIPTION ADDRESS:

same

PUBLISHED: Three or more times yearly
CIRCULATION: 600
COST: 1 yr.—$5.00 for membership dues in Melville Society of America (includes publication).

CONTENTS: News of Herman Melville of interest to scholars and enthusiasts; short scholarly notes, reviews, verse; news of activities of Melville Society; illustrations.

UNSOLICITED MSS. WELCOME? Yes; submissions acknowledged.
SPECIFICALLY WELCOMED: Verse on Melville and his works; short news items and scholarly notes.
MS. LENGTH: Up to 900 words; submit ONE copy.
STYLE REQUIREMENTS: Terse writing; documentation incorporated into text.
COPYRIGHT: Not copyrighted.
PAYMENT/OFFPRINTS: Reasonable number of offprints on request.
REJECTED MSS.: Returned.

GENERAL: First issue, June 20, 1969. Usual publication length, 8-16 legal size pages.
BACK ISSUES: Available from editorial address at $2.00 each.

[Mencken, H. L.]

MENCKENIANA

EDITORIAL ADDRESS:
Richard Hart, Editor
Enoch Pratt Free Library
400 Cathedral Street
Baltimore, Maryland 21201

SUBSCRIPTION ADDRESS:
Publications Department
same

PUBLISHED: Quarterly (Spring, Summer, Fall, Winter)
COST: 1 yr.—$2.00.

CIRCULATION: 300

CONTENTS: Selections from the unpublished writings of H. L. Mencken; articles on him, his contemporaries and other subjects, with the central focus on Mencken; bibliographic checklists. Example: "Baltimore: Source and Sustainer of Mencken's Values."

UNSOLICITED MSS. WELCOME? Not at the present time.
SPECIFICALLY WELCOMED: Articles concerning H. L. Mencken's work or life.
MS. LENGTH: Up to 5,000 words; submit ONE copy.
STYLE REQUIREMENTS: See recent issue.
COPYRIGHT: Not copyrighted.
EDITOR'S DECISION: Varies.
FROM ACCEPTANCE TO PUBLICATION: Varies.
PAYMENT/OFFPRINTS: Copies of the periodical. No offprints.
REJECTED MSS.: Returned.
GENERAL: First issue, Spring, 1962. Usual publication length, 16 pages.
BACK ISSUES: Available from subscription address at $.50 each. Some are out of print.

[Miller, Henry]

HENRY MILLER LITERARY SOCIETY NEWSLETTER
(suspended publication)

EDITORIAL ADDRESS:
Edward P. Swartz, Society Founder
1521 Hennepin Avenue
Minneapolis, Minnesota 55403

SUBSCRIPTION ADDRESS:

none

PUBLISHED: Irregularly

CONTENTS: Twelve issues of reminiscences of meeting Henry Miller; brief articles about his works; reprints of news articles about Miller's novels, such as "TROPIC Ban Upset By Massachusetts Court"; radio transcription of interview with Miller ("Miller on Censorship"). The original intention of this newsletter was to get Miller published in his own country.

GENERAL: Issued from 1957 to 1964. The Henry Miller Literary Society was disbanded years ago. Contact E. P. Swartz who has a file of the newsletters.

[Miller, Henry]

THE INTERNATIONAL HENRY MILLER LETTER (suspended publication)

EDITORIAL ADDRESS:
Henk van Gelre, Editor
(The Netherlands)

PUBLISHED: From time to time
COST: Single copy—$1.00.

CONTENTS: Serious studies of Henry Miller; letters and articles by Henry Miller heretofore unpublished in English; souvenirs of Henry Miller by his friends.

GENERAL: Seven numbers issued from June, 1961, to March, 1966. For possibility of securing xerox copies, write to Richard Centing, Ohio State University Libraries, 1858 Neil Avenue, Columbus, Ohio 43210.

[Neihardt, John G.]

THE NEIHARDT FOUNDATION NEWSLETTER

EDITORIAL ADDRESS:
Lyle B. Egerman, President
John G. Neihardt Foundation, Inc.
Bancroft, Nebraska 68004

SUBSCRIPTION ADDRESS:

same

PUBLISHED: Annually

CIRCULATION: 300 memberships, 3,000 copies are printed for visitors at the Sioux Prayer Garden.

COST: 1 yr.—$5.00 (supporting membership).

CONTENTS: Up-to-date news of major events during the year; reports of John G. Neihardt's health, his progress on the books he is writing; news of progress in other fields of endeavor, Dr. Neihardt's and many, many others'.

UNSOLICITED MSS. WELCOME? Not at the present time.
GENERAL: First issue, 1969. Usual publication length, 4 pages.
BACK ISSUES: Available from editorial address at $1.00 each.

[Nin, Anaïs, and her circle]

UNDER THE SIGN OF PISCES: ANAIS NIN AND HER CIRCLE

EDITORIAL ADDRESS:
Richard Centing, Editor
Ohio State University Libraries
1858 Neil Avenue
Columbus, Ohio 43210

SUBSCRIPTION ADDRESS:
Publications Committee
same

PUBLISHED: Quarterly
COST: 1 yr.—$2.00.

CIRCULATION: 500

CONTENTS: Biographical and bibliographical information on Anaïs Nin and her literary circle (Henry Miller, ET AL); illustrations; essays, such as "Anaïs Nin and 'The Fall of the House of Usher.'"

UNSOLICITED MSS. WELCOME? Yes; submissions acknowledged.
SPECIFICALLY WELCOMED: Personal reports on Nin's public appearances; checklists of Nin's writings; and criticism of her writings in foreign countries.
MS. LENGTH: 500 words; submit ONE copy.
STYLE REQUIREMENTS: None.
COPYRIGHT: Author.
EDITOR'S DECISION: 1 month.
FROM ACCEPTANCE TO PUBLICATION: 6 months.
PAYMENT/OFFPRINTS: Copy of newsletter in which writer's work appears.
REJECTED MSS.: Returned.
GENERAL: First issue, Winter, 1970. Usual publication length, 16 pages. Submit all manuscripts to Mr. Centing. Photographs can be used to illustrate articles.
BACK ISSUES: Available from The Ohio State University Libraries at normal subscription rate of $2.00 per year.

[O'Connor, Flannery]

THE FLANNERY O'CONNOR BULLETIN

EDITORIAL ADDRESS:
Rosa Lee Walston, Editor
Box 608
Georgia College
Milledgeville, Georgia 31061

SUBSCRIPTION ADDRESS:

same

PUBLISHED: Annually
COST: 1 yr.—$2.00.

CIRCULATION: 1,200

CONTENTS: Articles on the life, thoughts and works of Flannery O'Connor; reviews of books about Miss O'Connor; reflections by those who knew her; library surveys of O'Connor collections; occasional photographs. Example: "Freaks in a Circus Tent: Flannery O'Connor's Christ-Haunted Characters."

UNSOLICITED MSS. WELCOME? Yes; submissions acknowledged.
SPECIFICALLY WELCOMED: Scholarly, well-written, significant essays about Flannery O'Connor.
MS. LENGTH: 8-12 pages; submit ONE copy.
STYLE REQUIREMENTS: Prefer University of Chicago's A MANUAL OF STYLE; footnotes follow article.
COPYRIGHT: THE FLANNERY O'CONNOR BULLETIN.
EDITOR'S DECISION: Varies.
PAYMENT/OFFPRINTS: Ten copies of issue.
REJECTED MSS.: Returned.
GENERAL: First issue, Autumn, 1972. Usual publication length, 60 pages minimum.
BACK ISSUES: Available from editorial address at $2.00 each.

[Poe, Emerson, Thoreau, Hawthorne, Melville,
Whitman, and their contemporaries]

AMERICAN TRANSCENDENTAL QUARTERLY

EDITORIAL ADDRESS:
Kenneth W. Cameron, Editor
Drawer 1080
Hartford, Connecticut 06101

SUBSCRIPTION ADDRESS:

same

PUBLISHED: Quarterly
COST: 1 yr.—$14.00 (foreign subscribers add $1.00).

CONTENTS: Studies in American literature of the American Renaissance; critical essays; explication; aids to research; bibliography; reprints of scarce tracts. Focus is on Dickinson, Hawthorne, Melville, Whitman, Poe, Emerson, Thoreau, Clemens, Longfellow, Whittier, Holmes, Bryant, Irving, and Cooper. Subject area in addition to neglected single works of those that need reappraisal include Myths and Mythologies of, Religion and Literature of, Historians of Minor Poets of, Travel Literature during, American Folklore in the Literature of, and Woman Writers of the American Renaissance, to name a few.

MS. LENGTH: 12-20 pages.
GENERAL: First issue, January, 1969. Editor reserves the right to assign article to ATQ or the EMERSON SOCIETY QUARTERLY depending on which one will have space first. ATQ is under the patronage of the Emerson Society as a complement to the EMERSON SOCIETY QUARTERLY, but it is not included in the Society's membership fee.

[Poe, Edgar Allan]

THE POE MESSENGER

EDITORAL ADDRESS: SUBSCRIPTION ADDRESS:
Virginia Page Chichester, Editor
Edgar Allan Poe Museum same
1914 East Main Street
Richmond, Virginia 23223

PUBLISHED: Biannually CIRCULATION: 600
COST: Published for the members of the Edgar Allan Poe Museum.

CONTENTS: Articles about Edgar Allan Poe's life and writing; reviews of current books about Poe; reports about Old Stone House restoration; officers' reports; photographs; reproductions of book plates.

UNSOLICITED MSS. WELCOME? Yes.
SPECIFICALLY WELCOMED: Poe material; current book reviews.
MS. LENGTH: Brief.
GENERAL: First issue, Fall, 1969. Usual publication length, 8 pages.
BACK ISSUES: Available from editorial address at $1.00 each.

[Poe, Edgar Allan]

POE STUDIES (formerly POE NEWSLETTER)

EDITORIAL ADDRESS:
G. R. Thompson, Editor
Department of English
Washington State University
Pullman, Washington 99163

SUBSCRIPTION ADDRESS:
Washington State University Press
Pullman, Washington 99163

PUBLISHED: Biannually
COST: 1 yr.—$3.00.

CIRCULATION: 1,000

CONTENTS: Articles about Edgar Allan Poe, the man and writer; critical analyses; biographical studies; source notes; history of ideas studies; bibliographical reviews. Example: "The Scornful Grin: A Study of Poesque Humor"; "Black Cat and White Cat: Richard Wright's Debt to Edgar Allan Poe."

UNSOLICITED MSS. WELCOME? Yes; submissions acknowledged.
SPECIFICALLY WELCOMED: Scholarly critical analyses.
MS. LENGTH: Under 500 words; submit TWO copies.
STYLE REQUIREMENTS: MLA STYLE SHEET; footnotes follow article.
COPYRIGHT: Not copyrighted.
EDITOR'S DECISION: 2-4 months.
FROM ACCEPTANCE TO PUBLICATION: 1 yr.
PAYMENT/OFFPRINTS: Ten copies of issues minimum.
REJECTED MSS.: Returned.
GENERAL: First issue, April, 1968. Usual publication length, 20-30 double-columned 8 x 11½ pages.
BACK ISSUES: Can be obtained from the Washington State University Press—$2.00 each.

[Pound, Ezra]

PAIDEUMA: A JOURNAL DEVOTED TO EZRA POUND SCHOLARSHIP

EDITORIAL ADDRESS:
Carroll F. Terrell, Managing Editor
225 Stevens Hall
University of Maine
Orono, Maine 04473

SUBSCRIPTION ADDRESS:

same

PUBLISHED: 2 or 3 times yearly as material is available.
COST: Single issue—$3.00; 2 years (5 issues)—$10.00 in U.S. and Canada, $12.50 in other countries.

CONTENTS: Critical articles; short but complete notes annotating obscure passages in the "Canto"; biographical material, including sketches of people Pound knew and mentions in his work; documentation; explication solving minor references or correcting misinformation or errors presently in print; unpublished Pound materials; notes and queries; illustrations. Example: "Pound and Erigena."

UNSOLICITED MSS. WELCOME? Yes; submissions acknowledged.
SPECIFICALLY WELCOMED: Essays from Pound scholars only about the life and works of Ezra Pound.
MS. LENGTH: 1-20 pages; submit TWO copies.
STYLE REQUIREMENTS: MLA STYLE SHEET.
COPYRIGHT: The National Poetry Foundation, Inc.
EDITOR'S DECISION: 2-3 months.
FROM ACCEPTANCE TO PUBLICATION: Varies.
PAYMENT/OFFPRINTS: Several copies of current issue.
REJECTED MSS.: Returned.
GENERAL: First issue, Spring and Summer, 1972. Usual publication length, 140 pages.
BACK ISSUES: Can be obtained from the editorial office. Presently only subscriptions for the first two years, with which back copies are provided, are accepted.

[Pound, Ezra]

THE POUND NEWSLETTER (suspended publication)

EDITORIAL ADDRESS:
John Edwards, Editor

PUBLISHED: Quarterly (Jan., Apr., July, Oct.)

CONTENTS: The stated purpose of this newsletter:"To collect, establish and record such fact and opinion as will contribute to the welfare of future Pound studies and related areas of literary interest." It contains brief critical pieces; notes and queries; work in progress; letters to the editor; world survey, a collection of published opinions from the international press; bibliography of newly published works by Pound and secondary materials concerning Pound, including reviews; additions and corrections to the PRELIMINARY CHECKLIST OF THE WRITINGS OF EZRA POUND.

GENERAL: Issued January, 1954, to June, 1956 (10 issues), with an Index to the complete set in Issue #10. Copies are housed in the Indiana University (Bloomington) Library. Write to the library for possibility of xerox copies.

[Rank, Otto]

THE JOURNAL

EDITORIAL ADDRESS:
Virginia P. Robinson and Anita J. Faatz,
Editors
The Otto Rank Association
58 East Court Street
Doyleston, Bucks County,
Pennsylvania 18901

SUBSCRIPTION ADDRESS:

same

PUBLISHED: Biannually (June, Dec.)   CIRCULATION: 600
COST: Four issues—$10.00.

CONTENTS: Interest is psychological, especially to explore the conceptions of Otto Rank (1884-1939); literary articles that have psychological value, such as " 'Excuse Me, It Was All a Dream': The Diary of Anaïs Nin: 1944-1947"; review articles, such as "The Relativity Novel."

UNSOLICITED MSS. WELCOME? Yes; submissions acknowledged.
MS. LENGTH: 12-20 pages; submit TWO copies.
COPYRIGHT: Editors copyright the entire journal.
EDITOR'S DECISION: Within 30 days.
FROM ACCEPTANCE TO PUBLICATION: 6 months.
PAYMENT/OFFPRINTS: No payment. Authors may order offprints if they wish.
REJECTED MSS.: Returned.
GENERAL: First issue, Fall, 1966. Usual publication length, 100-110 pages.
BACK ISSUES: Available from editorial address at $2.50 each or special price on all back issues.

[Steinbeck, John]

STEINBECK QUARTERLY (formerly STEINBECK NEWSLETTER)

EDITORIAL ADDRESS:
Tetsumaro Hayashi, Editor-in-Chief
English Department
Ball State University
Muncie, Indiana 47306

SUBSCRIPTION ADDRESS:
Editor's Secretary
English Department
Ball State University
Muncie, Indiana 47306

PUBLISHED: Quarterly   CIRCULATION: 350
COST: Single issue—$1.50 for non-members; 1 yr.—$6.00 membership dues.

CONTENTS: Critical essays on John Steinbeck and his work; bibliographical checklists; recent publications, conference news, research projects; works in progress; dissertations and theses. Example: "Steinbeck's EAST OF EDEN and Milton's PARADISE LOST."

UNSOLICITED MSS. WELCOME? Yes, after 1974; submissions acknowledged.
SPECIFICALLY WELCOMED: Original critiques of Steinbeck (not biographical ones).
MS. LENGTH: 5-8 pages; submit TWO copies.
COPYRIGHT: Editor.
PAYMENT/OFFPRINTS: Five copies of issue. No offprints.
REJECTED MSS.: Returned.
GENERAL: First issue, February, 1968. Usual publication length, 32 pages. Volumes are indexed.
BACK ISSUES: Can be obtained from the subscription office or from Kraus Reprint Co. for usually $1.50 each; inquire.

[Stevens, Wallace]

THE WALLACE STEVENS NEWSLETTER

EDITORIAL ADDRESS:
W. T. Ford, Editor
The University Library
Northwestern University
Evanston, Illinois 60201

SUBSCRIPTION ADDRESS:

same

PUBLISHED: Biannually (Oct., Apr.)
COST: 2 yrs.—$4.00.

CONTENTS: Informal essays, reviews, bibliographical notes, and news items relating to Wallace Stevens; book reviews; work in progress; occasional photograph. Example essays: "When Half-Gods Go: Stevens' Spiritual Odyssey"; "Wallace Stevens and Turkish Poetry."

UNSOLICITED MSS. WELCOME? Yes.
COPYRIGHT: W. T. Ford.
GENERAL: First issue, October, 1969. Usual publication length, 8 double-column pages.

[Thoreau, Henry David]

THE CONCORD SAUNTERER

EDITORIAL ADDRESS:
Editor
The Thoreau Foundation, Inc.
The Thoreau Lyceum
156 Belknap Street
Concord, Massachusetts 01742

SUBSCRIPTION ADDRESS:

same

COST: 1 yr.—$3.00 (membership in The Thoreau Lyceum).

CONTENTS: Essays on the works of Thoreau; books received; news and notes; occasional photograph (e.g., Thoreau notebook page); calendar of Thoreau Lyceum Lecture Series. Examples: "Thoreau's 'Indian Notebooks' and the Composition of WALDEN"; "A Note on Henry David Thoreau's Literary Nationalism."

GENERAL: First issue, 1965. Usual publication length, 14 pages. Address inquiries about The Thoreau Lyceum Annual Membership and related matters to Mrs. Thomas W. McGrath, Curator.

[Thoreau, Henry David]

THOREAU JOURNAL QUARTERLY

EDITORIAL ADDRESS; SUBSCRIPTION ADDRESS:
M. P. Sherwood, Managing Editor
P. O. Box 551 same
Old Town, Maine 04468

PUBLISHED: Quarterly CIRCULATION: 400
COST: 1 yr.—$4.00 to members; $6.00 to subscribing libraries.

CONTENTS: A montage of serious longer articles, to one-page ones; poetry; miscellaneous items; Thoreau quotes. Examples; "Thoreau as Limnologist"; "The Metaphysical Strain in Thoreau."

UNSOLICITED MSS. WELCOME? Yes; submissions, at least large articles, usually acknowledged.
SPECIFICALLY WELCOMED: Articles. All original material must be about Thoreau or his interests, which include ecology, American Indians, natural history, a little philosophy and social conscience. No emphasis on civil disobedience, though a worthwhile article on the subject would be considered.
MS. LENGTH: Maximum 10 pages; submit ONE copy.
STYLE REQUIREMENTS: None; just good grammar, popular to professional.
COPYRIGHT: Not copyrighted.
EDITOR'S DECISION: Usually 3 months.
FROM ACCEPTANCE TO PUBLICATION: From 3 months to 1 year.
PAYMENT/OFFPRINTS: Two complimentary copies for longer articles, one for smaller ones and for poems.
REJECTED MSS. Returned.
GENERAL: First issue, January, 1969. Usual publication length, 28-34 pages. A newsletter goes out with each TJQ.
BACK ISSUES: TJQ available from editorial office at $1.00 each or $2.00 for 1969 issues, $3.00 for 1970 and 1971, $4.00 for 1972 and 1973. Back issues of newsletter available at $.10 each, plus $.08 postage per every four.

[Thoreau, Henry David]

THE THOREAU SOCIETY BULLETIN

EDITORIAL ADDRESS:
Walter Harding, Secretary-Treasurer
State University College
Geneseo, New York 14454

SUBSCRIPTION ADDRESS:

same

PUBLISHED: Quarterly
COST: 1 yr.—$2.00

CIRCULATION: 1,000

CONTENTS: News, information, scholarly essays, and bibliography about Henry David Thoreau; notes and queries. Example: "Hawthorne on Thoreau: 1853-1857."

UNSOLICITED MSS. WELCOME? Yes; submissions acknowledged.
SPECIFICALLY WELCOMED: Only material about Thoreau.
MS. LENGTH: Short; 4,000 word maximum; submit ONE copy.
STYLE REQUIREMENTS: MLA STYLE SHEET.
COPYRIGHT: Not copyrighted.
EDITOR'S DECISION: 2 weeks.
FROM ACCEPTANCE TO PUBLICATION: 3-6 months.
PAYMENT/OFFPRINTS: 5-10 free copies.
REJECTED MSS.: Returned.
GENERAL: First issue, 1941. Usual publication length, 8 pages.
BACK ISSUES: Those in print can be obtained from the editorial office at $.25 each.

[Whitman, Walt]

CALAMUS: AN INTERNATIONAL WHITMAN QUARTERLY

EDITORIAL ADDRESS:
William L. Moore, Editor
Toho Gakuen University of Music
Chofu-Shi
Tokyo, Japan

SUBSCRIPTION ADDRESS;

same

PUBLISHED: Tri-annually
COST: 1 yr.—$3.00 (US$ or equivalent).

CIRCULATION: 600

CONTENTS: Commentaries on Whitman literature; surveys of Whitman interest within nations; biographies of eminent native scholars and teachers of Whitman; experiences and methods of teaching Whitman; translations of national milestones in Whitman studies; poems relating to Whitman; dramas built upon his life. Example: "Walt Whitman and William Jones."

UNSOLICITED MSS. WELCOME? Yes; submissions acknowledged.

MS. LENTTH: 18 pages maximum; submit ONE copy.
STYLE REQUIREMENTS: None; the fewer footnotes the better.
COPYRIGHT: Author.
EDITOR'S DECISION: Immediately
FROM ACCEPTANCE TO PUBLICATION: One or two issues.
PAYMENT/OFFPRINTS: An artistic Japanese calligraphic symbol of a Whitman motif of contributor's choice. Offprints, if paid for by contributor.
REJECTED MSS.: Returned.
GENERAL: First issue, 1970. Usual publication length, 50 pages. Articles are published in English. Quarterly will gladly reprint material submitted to it and allow other journals to reprint its articles.
BACK ISSUES: Most are available from the editorial office for $1.00 each.

[Whitman, Walt]

WALT WHITMAN BIRTHPLACE BULLETIN (suspended publication)

SUBSCRIPTION ADDRESS:
(Huntington Station
Long Island, New York)

GENERAL: The Bulletin was published for 16 numbers between October, 1957, and July, 1961, when its editor Verne Dyson retired and moved. Consult the Birthplace for possibility of securing back numbers. Also, William White (American Studies Program, Wayne State University, Detroit, Michigan 48202) has a file of these issues.

[Whitman, Walt]

WALT WHITMAN REVIEW (formerly WALT WHITMAN NEWSLETTER)

EDITORIAL ADDRESS:
William White and Charles E. Feinberg,
Editors
American Studies Program
Wayne State University
Detroit, Michigan 48202

SUBSCRIPTION ADDRESS:
Wayne State University Press
Detroit, Michigan 48202

PUBLISHED: Quarterly (Mar., June, Sept., Dec.)
CIRCULATION: 1,000
COST: 1 yr.—$4.00; 2 yrs.—$7.00; 3 yrs.—$10.00; add $.60 per year for postage for Canadian subscriptions and $.75 per year for all others outside of U.S.

CONTENTS: Critical essays on Walt Whitman's works; book reviews about Whitman, his contemporaries and his time; reprints of old newspaper articles concerning Whitman; biographical information; current bibliography; notes; back cover reproductions of portions of Whitman's manuscripts; commentary on Whitman's reputation as poet and essayist; occasional unpublished writings of Whitman; new interpretations of his poetry. Example: "Sociality and Seclusion in the Poetry of Walt Whitman."

UNSOLICITED MSS. WELCOME? Yes (except book reviews); submissions acknowledged.
SPECIFICALLY WELCOMED: Scholarly essays about Whitman's works.
MS. LENGTH: 500-2,000 words; submit ONE copy.
STYLE REQUIREMENTS: Modified MLA STYLE SHEET.
COPYRIGHT: Wayne State University Press—authors may reprint their own material free; others with permission of the WSU Press and author—pay $10.00 a page, shared by author and Press.
EDITOR'S DECISION: Few days.
FROM ACCEPTANCE TO PUBLICATION: 1-2 years.
PAYMENT/OFFPRINTS: Three copies of issue in which contribution appears.
REJECTED MSS.: Returned with some criticism.
GENERAL: First issue, 1955—WALT WHITMAN NEWSLETTER, 1959—WALT WHITMAN REVIEW. Usual publication length, 30 to 35 pages.
BACK ISSUES: Can be obtained from the subscription office for $1.00 each.

[Whittier, John Greenleaf]

WHITTIER NEWSLETTER

EDITORIAL ADDRESS:
John B. Pickard, Editor
Department of English
University of Florida
Gainesville, Florida 32601

SUBSCRIPTION ADDRESS:

same

PUBLISHED: Annually
COST: Free

CIRCULATION: 500

CONTENTS: Bibliography for year; notes and queries; occasional book review; research in progress; Whittier Libraries and Club activities. Special issues contain full book reviews and accounts of libraries with significant Whittier collections; illustrations.

UNSOLICITED MSS. WELCOME? Yes, small (400 to 500 word) notes; submissions acknowledged.
SPECIFICALLY WELCOMED: Brief notes, biographic and bibliographic information.
MS. LENGTH: Not over 500 words, submit ONE copy.
STYLE REQUIREMENTS: None
COPYRIGHT: WHITTIER NEWSLETTER.

EDITOR'S DECISION: 1 week.
FROM ACCEPTANCE TO PUBLICATION: A few months.
PAYMENT/OFFPRINTS: None
REJECTED MSS.: Returned.
GENERAL: First issue, 1966. Usual publication length, 4 pages.
BACK ISSUES: Can be obtained free from Donald C. Freeman, 65 Chadwick Rd., Bradford, Massachusetts.

EUROPEAN

[Arthur, King]

BIBLIOGRAPHICAL BULLETIN OF THE INTERNATIONAL ARTHURIAN SOCIETY

EDITORIAL ADDRESS:
Lewis Thorpe, Editor
The University
Nottingham NG7 2RD, England

SUBSCRIPTION ADDRESS:
American Secretary-Treasurer
Professor John L. Grigsby
Box 1077
Washington University
St. Louis, Missouri 63130

PUBLISHED: Annually
COST: 1 yr.—$5.00.

CIRCULATION: 1,200

CONTENTS: Details of the officials in all countries of the Society; full bibliography of books, articles and reviews on the Arthurian romances published in the previous calendar year, listed under countries; author and subject indexes to those bibliographies; two or more short articles on the Arthurian romances; Arthurian news and notices; obituaries of members who died during previous year; membership list with addresses. Example: "The Invention of Tintagel."

UNSOLICITED MSS. WELCOME? Yes, from members of the Society, or, exceptionally, from non-members; submissions acknowledged.
SPECIFICALLY WELCOMED: Short articles directly concerned with matière de Bretagne up to 1600.
MS. LENGTH: Short: 2,000-3,000 words; submit ONE copy.
STYLE REQUIREMENTS: Consult back issues.
COPYRIGHT: The International Arthurian Society; authors always permitted to reprint their articles.
PAYMENT/OFFPRINTS: 12 offprints.
REJECTED MSS.: Returned.
GENERAL: First issue, 1949. Usual publication length, 300 pages.
BACK ISSUES: Available from Professor Cedric E. Pickford, International Treasurer of the Arthurian Society, Department of French, The University, Hull, England, at $5.00 each. Also from Swets & Zeitlinger, Keizersgracht 471 & 487, Amsterdam, The Netherlands, at $9.00 per volume.

[Bacon, Francis]

BACONIANA (formerly BACON SOCIETY JOURNAL)

EDITORIAL ADDRESS:
Noel Fermor, Chairman
Canonbury Tower
Islington
London N1, England

SUBSCRIPTION ADDRESS:

same

PUBLISHED: Annually

COST: 1 yr.—$5.00 (£ sterling); includes membership in The Francis Bacon Society.

CONTENTS: Articles on Francis Bacon's philosophy and life, his influence on his own and succeeding times, the tendencies and results of his writing, and the evidence, including ciphers, of his sponsorship of the Shakespeare plays; editorials; book reviews; illustrations; correspondence. Examples: "Francis Bacon After His Fall"; "The Death of Falstaff."

UNSOLICITED MSS. WELCOME? Yes; submissions acknowledged.
SPECIFICALLY WELCOMED: Materials about Francis Bacon.
MS. LENGTH: 1,000-4,000 words; submit TWO OR THREE copies.
STYLE REQUIREMENTS: Best literary style.
COPYRIGHT: Francis Bacon Society, Inc.
EDITOR'S DECISION: 1 month.
FROM ACCEPTANCE TO PUBLICATION: Up to 1 year.
PAYMENT/OFFPRINTS: No payment.
REJECTED MSS.: Returned.
GENERAL: First issue, December, 1886. Usual publication length, 80-100 pages.
BACK ISSUES: Available from the Francis Bacon Society. Cost varies according to date, rarity, and size of order.

[Blake, William]

BLAKE NEWSLETTER: AN ILLUSTRATED QUARTERLY

EDITORIAL ADDRESS:
Morton D. Paley, Executive Editor
Department of English
University of California
Berkeley, California 94720

SUBSCRIPTION ADDRESS:
Morris Eaves, Managing Editor
Department of English
University of New Mexico
Albuquerque, New Mexico 87106

PUBLISHED: Quarterly
CIRCULATION: 500
COST: 1 yr.—$5.00, special rate for individuals—$3.00; overseas by air—$8.00; single copy—$2.00.

CONTENTS: Reviews of books and critiques about William Blake; news and notes; checklist of Blake scholarship (bibliography, catalogues, new and revised books, articles and sections of books, reviews, films and videotapes, tapes and phonograph records, theater, musical scores); commentary; essays about art and poetry of Blake; photographs of Blake's prints and engravings. Example: "Two Blake Prints and Two Fuseli Drawings."

UNSOLICITED MSS. WELCOME? Yes; submissions acknowledged.
SPECIFICALLY WELCOMED: Articles that are new to the Blake specialists who are aware of published scholarship about Blake.
MS. LENGTH: Short notes to 25 pages; submit TWO copies.
STYLE REQUIREMENTS: MLA STYLE SHEET.

COPYRIGHT: Morton D. Paley and Morris Eaves.
EDITOR'S DECISION: 2 weeks to 2 months.
FROM ACCEPTANCE TO PUBLICATION: 3-6 months.
PAYMENT/OFFPRINTS: Four copies of issue in which essay appears. Offprints available to writer at cost.
REJECTED MSS. Returned with criticism.
GENERAL: First issue, February, 1967. Usual publication length, 58-60 pages. The photo-offset process on enamel paper enables the editors to include as many reproductions of Blake's art as is necessary for an illustrated article.
BACK ISSUES: Can be obtained from the managing editor beginning with issue #14 at $2.00 per issue, except for #17 and #18 which is a combined issue for $5.00. Reprint of other back issues is in preparation.

[Blake, William]

BLAKE STUDIES

EDITORIAL ADDRESS: SUBSCRIPTION ADDRESS:
Kay Parkhurst Easson and
Roger R. Easson, Editors same
Department of English
Illinois State University
Normal, Illinois 61761

PUBLISHED: Biannually
COST: 1 yr.—$7.50; $8.50 outside U.S. and Canada; single copy—$4.00.

CONTENTS: Critical articles about William Blake, his contemporaries, and age; scholarly essays, notes, book reviews; reproductions of Blake's art. Example: "Blake and the Age of Reason: Spectres in the NIGHT THOUGHTS."

UNSOLICITED MSS. WELCOME? Yes; submissions acknowledged.
SPECIFICALLY WELCOMED: Critical essays about the art and poetry of William Blake.
MS. LENGTH: 12-20 pages; submit TWO copies.
STYLE REQUIREMENTS: MLA STYLE SHEET; footnotes follow essay.
COPYRIGHT: Kay Parkhurst Easson and Roger R. Easson.
EDITOR'S DECISION: 8 weeks.
FROM ACCEPTANCE TO PUBLICATION: 1 year.
PAYMENT/OFFPRINTS: Two copies of the issue in which work appears. As many offprints as author requests and pays for.
REJECTED MSS.: Returned.
GENERAL: First issue, 1968. Usual publication length, 96-128 pages.
BACK ISSUES: Vol. 1, No. 1 is out-of-print. Others can be obtained from the editorial office for $4.50 each.

[Brecht, Bertolt]

BRECHT HEUTE/BRECHT TODAY

EDITORIAL ADDRESS:
John Fuegi, Editor
Department of Comparative
Literature
University of Wisconsin—Milwaukee
Milwaukee, Wisconsin 53201

SUBSCRIPTION ADDRESS:
Athenaum Verlag Gmbh
6000 Frankfurt am Main
Germany

PUBLISHED: Annually
COST: Student—$7.00; regular—$10.00; senior—$18.00; sustaining—$25.00; institutional—$25.00 (also includes tri-annually published newsletter, COMMUNICATIONS).

CONTENTS: Essays and studies on Brechtian theory and practice; an attempt to combine contributions of Germanists, drama scholars and persons in the practical theater; book reviews. Examples: "Marx, Engels and Brecht's Galileo"; "The Morality of Combat: Brecht's Search for a Sparring Partner."

UNSOLICITED MSS. WELCOME? Yes; submissions acknowledged.
SPECIFICALLY WELCOMED: Essays and interviews.
MS. LENGTH: 6,000-15,000 words; submit TWO copies.
STYLE REQUIREMENTS: MLA STYLE SHEET.
COPYRIGHT: Athenaum Verlag Gmbh, Frankfurt am Main.
EDITOR'S DECISION: 3-5 weeks.
FROM ACCEPTANCE TO PUBLICATION: 9-12 months.
PAYMENT/OFFPRINTS: Twenty offprints provided without cost.
REJECTED MSS.: Returned.
GENERAL: First issue, 1971. Usual publication length, 200-240 pages. Essays and articles in German, English, or French may be submitted.
BACK ISSUES: Can be obtained from the editorial office at the current prices.

[Brecht, Bertolt]

COMMUNICATIONS—THE BRECHT NEWSLETTER

EDITORIAL ADDRESS:
Gisela E. Bahr, Editor
Department of German and Russian
Miami University
Oxford, Ohio 45056

SUBSCRIPTION ADDRESS:
International Brecht Society
Department of Comparative
Literature
University of Wisconsin
Milwaukee, Wisconsin 53201

PUBLISHED: Tri-annually

CIRCULATION: 300-400

COST: 1 yr.—$6.00 students; $10.00 active; $18.00 senior; $25.00 sustaining; $18.00 institutional (subject to change). Includes membership in The International Brecht Society and yearbook BRECHT TODAY.

CONTENTS: Information on activities pertaining to the work of Bertolt Brecht, primarily in, but not restricted to, the fields of literature and theater; reports on Brecht seminars, symposia, and other meetings, on theater productions, research, and publications. Regular section: work in progress; dissertations; recent and forthcoming publications.

UNSOLICITED MSS. WELCOME? Yes; submissions acknowledged.
SPECIFICALLY WELCOMED: Anything of an informative, reflective, and/or critical nature considered of interest to persons involved in some aspect of the work of Bertolt Brecht.
MS. LENGTH: 1-2 pages; submit ONE copy.
STYLE REQUIREMENTS: None.
COPYRIGHT: Contributor.
EDITOR'S DECISION: About 4 weeks.
FROM ACCEPTANCE TO PUBLICATION: Usually published in next issue.
PAYMENT/OFFPRINTS: No payment. A number of issues can be requested from the editor or Milwaukee office.
REJECTED MSS.: Returned.
GENERAL: First issue, December, 1971. Usual publication length, 10-12 pages. Reports and items may be submitted in English or German. Deadlines: for November issue—October 15; for February issue—January 15; for May issue—April 15. The aim of this publication is the dissemination of up-to-date information to the readers (primarily IBS members); more substantial contributions should be submitted to the editors of the yearbook, BRECHT HEUTE/BRECHT TODAY, Milwaukee office.
BACK ISSUES: Available from International Brecht Society in Milwaukee. Complimentary at present.

[Brontë, Charlotte, Emily, Anne]

BRONTË SOCIETY TRANSACTIONS

EDITORIAL ADDRESS:
Charles Lemon, Editor
159 Andrewes House
Barbican, London EC 2 Y8 BA
England

SUBSCRIPTION ADDRESS:
(for Americans and Canadians)
The Brontë Society
Mrs. Diane McGuire, Hon.
American Representative
Long Pasture Road
Little Compton, Rhode Island 02837

PUBLISHED: Annually
COST: 1 yr.—$3.00; £1 in England (payable January 1st); life membership—$26.00.

CONTENTS: Articles about the works, critics, and translators of the Brontës; reprints of reminiscences of people who had known the Brontës; photographs of Brontë letters purchased by the Brontë Society; essays about formerly unpublished articles on the works by the Brontës; notes about the origin of the Brontë name; a bibliography of books, reprints, articles, sections of books about the Brontës; reviews of books about Charlotte, Emily, or Anne Brontë; information about Brontë films; record of the annual meeting and officers' reports; list of gifts and additions to the museum and library. Example: "Early Critics and Translators of JANE EYRE in France."

UNSOLICITED MSS. WELCOME? Yes; submissions acknowledged.
SPECIFICALLY WELCOMED: Any articles that add to readers' knowledge of the Brontës and their works or that discuss an aspect of them in a fresh and stimulating way; biographical studies.
MS. LENGTH: 1-10 pages; submit ONE copy.
STYLE REQUIREMENTS: Footnotes, if necessary, are listed at bottom of page, not at end of the article.
COPYRIGHT: The Brontë Society.
EDITOR'S DECISION: 1 month.
FROM ACCEPTANCE TO PUBLICATION: 8 months.
PAYMENT/OFFPRINTS: Two to three copies of issue in which article appears. No offprints are made of specific articles.
REJECTED MSS. Returned.
GENERAL: First issue, 1895. Usual publication length, 80-90 pages. There is a Brontë Publication called ANALYTICAL INDEX OF ALL ARTICLES IN TRANSACTIONS (1895-1967) by the archivist, Miss Amy Foster, at a nominal price. A prize of £25 or $60.00 is awarded annually to the best paper submitted. All articles should be submitted by April 30th. Membership and subscriptions for those outside of the U.S.A. and Canada should write to: Mr. N. Raistrick, Brontë Parsonage Museum, Haworth, Keighley, Yorks BD22 8DR, England.
BACK ISSUES: Volumes 1-9, in reprint, available at $12.00 per paper bound volume; parts 50-56, in reprint, at $2.40 per paper bound part; parts 60, 61, 65-71, in reprint, at $3.00 per paper bound part. (Prices do not include postage costs.)

[Browning, Robert and Elizabeth Barrett]
BROWNING INSTITUTE STUDIES

EDITORIAL ADDRESS: SUBSCRIPTION ADDRESS:
William S. Peterson, Editor
Box 2011   same
Princeton, New Jersey 08540

PUBLISHED: Annually   CIRCULATION: 1,000
COST: Free to all members paying dues of $15.00 or more.

CONTENTS: Biographical, critical and bibliographical articles about Robert and Elizabeth Barrett Browning and their circle, with particular emphasis upon the Victorian Anglo-Florentine community with which they were associated; annotated bibliography of Browning scholarship; review essay on several recent books by or about the Brownings; annual report by President of the Institute; list of members; illustrations; index. Example: "The Influence of Robert Browning on the Art of William Wetmore Story."

UNSOLICITED MSS. WELCOME? Yes; submissions acknowledged.
SPECIFICALLY WELCOMED: Studies on Robert and Elizabeth Barrett Browning and their contemporaries.
MS. LENGTH: No set requirement but prefer long items, 8,000-10,000 words; submit ONE copy.
STYLE REQUIREMENTS: MLA STYLE SHEET.
COPYRIGHT: Browning Institute.
EDITOR'S DECISION: 1 month.
FROM ACCEPTANCE TO PUBLICATION: 12 months.
PAYMENT/OFFPRINTS: 25 offprints.
REJECTED MSS. Returned
GENERAL: First issues, June, 1973. Usual publication length, 250 pages.

[Browning, Robert and his circle]

BROWNING SOCIETY NOTES

EDITORIAL ADDRESS:
A. N. Kincaid, Editor
29 Southmoor Road
Oxford OX2 6RF
England

SUBSCRIPTION ADDRESS:
R. E. Holton
9 Lakenheath
Southgate
London N. 14
England

PUBLISHED: Tri-annually
CIRCULATION: 200
COST: 1 yr.—$4.00; £1.25 in U.K. Subscription runs by volume, which follows calendar year.

CONTENTS: Biographical and critical articles on Robert and Elizabeth Barrett Browning and (less frequently) their families and associates; hitherto unpublished letters by and to the Brownings; reviews of recent books on the Brownings; reviews or notices of dramatic representations of their works; research notes and queries; reports on Browning sites; London Browning Society news; reports of research in progress, primarily in the United Kingdom. Example: "A Book of Browning's and His 'Essay on Chatterton.' "

UNSOLICITED MSS. WELCOME? Yes; submissions acknowledged.

SPECIFICALLY WELCOMED: Biographical and critical articles on Robert and Elizabeth Barrett Browning presented so as to interest not only the Victorian specialist but also the more general literary scholar/enthusiast; reports of research in progress in the U.K.
MS. LENGTH: 10-20 pages (in case of the most interesting and original article of the century, have gone up to 40 pages); submit ONE copy.
STYLE REQUIREMENTS: MLA STYLE SHEET without publisher's name; minimize and incorporate footnotes where possible.
COPYRIGHT: Author (would appreciate, if all or part of any article BSN publishes is reprinted, the statement "Reprinted from BSN" and date of issue).
EDITOR'S DECISION: 2 weeks.
FROM ACCEPTANCE TO PUBLICATION: 8 months to 1 year.
PAYMENT/OFFPRINTS: None.
REJECTED MSS. Returned (author advised to retain copy since articles needing revision are retained).
GENERAL: First issue, June, 1970. Usual publication length, 30 pages. Editorial Consultant: Dr. Park Honan, University of Birmingham. Book Reviews Editor: Dr. Isobel Armstrong, University of Leicester.
BACK ISSUES: Available from editorial office at £1.25 or $3.50 per volume or 50p or $1.30 per single issue of Vols. I and II; $4.00 per volume or $1.50 per single issue of Vol. III.

[Browning, Robert and Elizabeth Barrett]

THE NEW YORK BROWNING SOCIETY, INC. BULLETIN

EDITORIAL ADDRESS: SUBSCRIPTION ADDRESS:
Editor
Box 2983 same
Grand Central Station
New York, New York 10017

PUBLISHED: Biannually CIRCULATION: 200
COST: Free to members of the New York Browning Society; a few copies are available upon request to non-members.

CONTENTS: Proceedings and transactions of the New York Browning Society with abstracts of monthly lectures; reports about Casa Guidi, Florentine residence of Robert and Elizabeth Barrett Browning. Examples: "Browning: The Existential Stance"; "The Brownings: Aspects of Research."

UNSOLICITED MSS. WELCOME? No.
COPYRIGHT: The New York Browning Society.
GENERAL: First issue, 1932. Usual publication length, 16 pages.
BACK ISSUES: Unobtainable at present. Scheduled for reprint in 1974 (available upon request at a small fee).

[Browning, Robert and Elizabeth Barrett]

STUDIES IN BROWNING AND HIS CIRCLE
(formerly THE BROWNING NEWSLETTER)

EDITORIAL ADDRESS:
Jack W. Herring, Editor
Box 6336
Baylor University
Waco, Texas 76706

SUBSCRIPTION ADDRESS:
Productions Editor
same

PUBLISHED: Biannually (Fall, Spring)   CIRCULATION: 300
COST: 1 yr.—$5.00.

CONTENTS: Scholarly articles on Robert and Elizabeth Barrett Browning and their circle; book reviews (solicited); notes and queries; unpublished letters or photographs; research in progress; dissertations in progress; desiderata for Browning research; reviews of each year's research; bibliographies; illustrations. Examples: "Money, Metaphor, and the Machine: Some Remarks on A BIBLIOGRAPHY OF ELIZABETH BARRETT BROWNING"; "Robert Browning and Mrs. Humphry Ward."

UNSOLICITED MSS. WELCOME? Yes; submissions acknowledged.
SPECIFICALLY WELCOMED: Scholarly essays (critical, expository, etc.).
MS. LENGTH: No limit (within reason); submit ONE copy.
STYLE REQUIREMENTS: MLA STYLE SHEET.
COPYRIGHT: Armstrong Browning Library.
EDITOR'S DECISION: 30-60 days.
FROM ACCEPTANCE TO PUBLICATION: Less than 6 months.
PAYMENT/OFFPRINTS: Authors of articles receive 10 copies of issue; book reviewers, 5 copies.
REJECTED MSS.: Returned.
GENERAL: First issue, October, 1968. Usual publication length, 60-70 pages. Screening of manuscripts is done by an editorial board of Browning scholars.
BACK ISSUES: Available (except issues #1 and #2) from Armstrong Browning Library, Baylor University, Waco, Texas 76706 at $1.50 each.

[Burke, Edmund]

STUDIES IN BURKE AND HIS TIME
(formerly THE BURKE NEWSLETTER)

EDITORIAL ADDRESS:
Steven R. Phillips, Editor
Department of English
College of Liberal Arts
Alfred University
Alfred, New York 14802

SUBSCRIPTION ADDRESS:
same

PUBLISHED: Tri-annually CIRCULATION: 600-700
(Fall, Winter, Spring)
COST: 1 yr.—$7.00; 2 yrs.—$12.00; 3 yrs.—$15.00.

CONTENTS: Inter-disciplinary articles and essays on Edmund Burke's life, thought, continuing influence, and milieu, on ideas that support or oppose Burke and on other major figures or issues of the period 1750-1800 in America, Great Britain, and Europe; book reviews. Example: "Samuel Johnson's Response to Beauty."

UNSOLICITED MSS. WELCOME? Yes; submissions acknowledged.
MS. LENGTH: 12-25 pages; submit TWO copies.
STYLE REQUIREMENTS: Conform to style of previous issues.
COPYRIGHT: Author.
EDITOR'S DECISION: 2-3 months.
FROM ACCEPTANCE TO PUBLICATION: 1 year.
PAYMENT/OFFPRINTS: Twenty free offprints; more at cost.
REJECTED MSS.: Returned.
GENERAL: First issue, Fall, 1959. Usual publication length, 100 pages.
BACK ISSUES: Available from editorial office at current subscription rates.

[Burns, Robert]

BURNS CHRONICLE

EDITORIAL ADDRESS:	SUBSCRIPTION ADDRESS:
James Veitch, Editor	Robert W. Morrison, Hon. Secretary
c/o The Burns Society of the City of New York	The Burns Society of the City of New York
281 Park Avenue South	281 Park Avenue South
New York, New York 10010	New York, New York 10010

PUBLISHED: Annually CIRCULATION: 2,500
COST: Single copy—40p paper bound; 65p cloth bound for members; 50p paper bound; 75p cloth bound for non-members.

CONTENTS: Critical essays; tributes; translations of works on Robert Burns; "Junior Burns Chronicle" section for school children; book reviews; poetry; sermons and conference speeches about Burns; lists of officials, districts, members of The Burns Federation; minutes of the Annual Conference; constitution; club notes; occasional photographs. Example: "James Currie's ROBERT BURNS: The Beginning."

UNSOLICITED MSS. WELCOME? Yes.
SPECIFICALLY WELCOME: Scholarly essays about Burns' works.
GENERAL: First issue, 1892. Usual publication length, 170-200 pages. Published in Kilmarnock, Scotland, but members purchase CHRONICLE through their district club and non-members through the Society's Hon. Secretary.
BACK ISSUES: Available from the Hon. Secretary.

[Carleton, William]

CARLETON NEWSLETTER

EDITORIAL ADDRESS:
Eileen Sullivan, Editor
Department of Comprenensive Logic
330 Little Hall
University of Florida
Gainesville, Florida 32611

SUBSCRIPTION ADDRESS:
Same

PUBLISHED: Quarterly (Jan., Apr., July, Oct.)
COST: 1 yr.—$2.00.

CIRCULATION: 250

CONTENTS: Critical articles on William Carleton's fiction; notes about Carleton scholars and their activities; bibliographic entries from Irish American academic libraries. Example: "THE TITHE PROCTOR—A Revaluation."

UNSOLICITED MSS. WELCOME? Yes; submissions acknowledged.
MS. LENGTH: 10 pages; submit ONE copy.
STYLE REQUIREMENTS: MLA STYLE SHEET.
EDITOR'S DECISION: 1 month.
FROM ACCEPTANCE TO PUBLICATION: 3-6 months.
PAYMENT/OFFPRINTS: Five to 10 copies of issue.
REJECTED MSS.: Returned.
GENERAL: First issue, July 4, 1970. Usual publication length, 8 pages.
BACK ISSUES: Available from editorial address at $.50 each.

[Chaucer, Geoffrey, and others]

THE CHAUCER REVIEW: A JOURNAL OF MEDIEVAL STUDIES AND LITERARY CRITICISM

EDITORIAL ADDRESS;
Robert W. Frank, Jr., Editor
117 Burrowes Building
The Pennsylvania State University
University Park, Pennsylvania 16802

SUBSCRIPTION ADDRESS:
The Pennsylvania State
University Press
215 Wagner Building
University Park, Pennsylvania 16802

PUBLISHED: Quarterly
COST: 1 yr.—$7.50; 2 yrs.—$14.00; 3 yrs.—$20.50 in U.S.; 1 yr.—$8.00; 2 yrs.—$15.00; 3 yrs.—$22.00 in Canada and Pan American Postal Union; 1 yr.—$8.50; 2 yrs.—$16.00; 3 yrs.—$23.50 in other countries; single issue—$2.50.

CIRCULATION: 1,350

CONTENTS: Scholarly and critical articles primarily on Chaucer and his work but also on all of medieval English literature (Old English and Middle English) and on Continental medieval literature. Example: "Chaucerian Irony and the Ending of the TROILUS."

UNSOLICITED MSS. WELCOME? Yes; submissions acknowledged.
SPECIFICALLY WELCOMED: Scholarly and critical articles; translations of medieval Latin, French, and Italian works but not of Old or Middle English; no fiction or poetry.
MS. LENGTH: Under 30 pages; submit ONE or TWO copies.
STYLE REQUIREMENTS: MLA STYLE SHEET.
COPYRIGHT: Pennsylvania State University Press.
EDITOR'S DECISION: 3 months.
FROM ACCEPTANCE TO PUBLICATION: 9 months to 1 year.
PAYMENT/OFFPRINTS: 25 free offprints. Additional complete issue for $1.00.
REJECTED MSS. Returned.
GENERAL: First issue, Summer, 1966. Usual publication length, 64-80 pages. Indexed by volume.
BACK ISSUES: Available from Pennsylvania State University Press at prices quoted above.

[Claudel, Paul]

CLAUDEL STUDIES (formerly CLAUDEL NEWSLETTER)

EDITORIAL ADDRESS:
Harold A. Waters and Moses M. Nagy, Editors-in-Chief

SUBSCRIPTION ADDRESS:
Moses M. Nagy, Managing Editor
Department of French
University of Dallas Station
Irving, Texas 75060

PUBLISHED: Biannually
COST: 1 yr.—$3.00; $3.50 for foreign subscribers; $4.00 for subscription and membership in the Paul Claudel Society; single copy—$2.00.

CONTENTS: Critical articles, monographs, notes, and reviews in English or French relating directly or indirectly to Paul Claudel. Example: "Presentation Motifs in the Prologue of Claudel's L'ANNONCE FAITE A MARIE."

UNSOLICITED MSS. WELCOME? Yes, if on Claudel; submissions acknowledged.
SPECIFICALLY WELCOMED: Scholarly essays about Claudel; reviews about his work and about his critics and contemporaries, with an English language leaning.
MS. LENGTH: 15-20 pages; submit ONE copy.
STYLE REQUIREMENTS: MLA STYLE SHEET.
COPYRIGHT: CLAUDEL STUDIES.
EDITOR'S DECISION: 6 weeks.
FROM ACCEPTANCE TO PUBLICATION: 6 months.
PAYMENT/OFFPRINTS: None.
REJECTED MSS. Returned with criticism.

GENERAL: First issue, April, 1968, as CLAUDEL NEWSLETTER; 1972, as CLAUDEL STUDIES. Usual publication length, 64-74 pages. Articles may be submitted in either French or English.
BACK ISSUES: Available from the subscription address at $3.00 each.

[Collier, John; Munro; Bramah]

PRESENTING MOONSHINE (for John Collier and Others)

EDITORIAL ADDRESS:
Charles E. Yenter, Editor
1015 South Steele Street
Tacoma, Washington 98405

SUBSCRIPTION ADDRESS:

same

PUBLISHED: Irregularly (about 8 times yearly)
COST: Free to interested collectors.

CIRCULATION: 100

CONTENTS: Bibliographical notes, some reprinted articles and stories; miscellaneous notes and articles of local interest for collectors of John Collier, H. H. Munro and other masters of the short story, essay, and novel; occasional illustrations. Example: "Bramah in Periodicals: Bibliographical Addenda."

UNSOLICITED MSS. WELCOME? Yes; submissions not acknowledged.
SPECIFICALLY WELCOMED: Bibliographical notes; checklists of collected authors.
MS. LENGTH: No limit.
STYLE REQUIREMENTS: None.
COPYRIGHT: Not copyrighted.
PAYMENT/OFFPRINTS: None.
GENERAL: First issue, July, 1969. Usual publication length, 30 pages.
BACK ISSUES: Available free from editorial office or from Fox Book Co., 1140 Broadway, Tacoma, Washington 98405. Number is limited; a few out of stock.

[Conrad, Joseph]

CONRADIANA: A JOURNAL OF JOSEPH CONRAD

EDITORIAL ADDRESS:
David Leon Higdon and
Donald W. Rude, Editors
Box 4530
Texas Tech University
Lubbock, Texas 79409

SUBSCRIPTION ADDRESS:

same

PUBLISHED: Tri-annually

CIRCULATION: 900

COST: 1 yr.—$5.00.

CONTENTS: Critical essays on all aspects and periods of Joseph Conrad's life and art; reviews of works about Conrad; illustrations of Conrad's letters; continuing checklist bibliography. Examples: "The Ironic Allusive Texture of LORD JIM: Coleridge, Crane, Milton, and Melville"; "Jungian and Oriental Symbolism in Joseph Conrad's VICTORY."

UNSOLICITED MSS. WELCOME? Yes; submissions acknowledged.
MS. LENGTH: 5,000 words maximum; 300 word abstract; submit TWO copies.
STYLE REQUIREMENTS: MLA STYLE SHEET; citation of Conrad's work should appear within text.
COPYRIGHT: CONRADIANA.
EDITOR'S DECISION: 2 months.
FROM ACCEPTANCE TO PUBLICATION: 2 years.
PAYMENT/OFFPRINTS: Five free offprints; additional copies available at $.50 each.
REJECTED MSS.: Returned.
GENERAL: First issue, 1968. Usual publication length, 75 pages. Editorial board of 49 members includes special translation, regional, and national (27 countries) editors. The "News, Notes, & Queries" section will be deleted from CONRADIANA and placed in the new CONRADIANA NEWSLETTER, William J. Cook, Jr., Editor, Auburn University, Montgomery, Alabama 36104.
BACK ISSUES: Vol. I available by direct correspondence from University Microfilms, Inc. Others from editorial address at $2.50 each.

[Conrad, Joseph]

CONRADIANA NEWSLETTER

EDITORIAL ADDRESS:
William J. Cook, Jr., Editor
Auburn University
Montgomery, Albama 36104

SUBSCRIPTION ADDRESS:

same

CONTENTS: The "News, Notes, & Queries" section of non-scholarly items of interest were deleted from CONRADIANA and placed in this new periodical.

GENERAL: This periodical had not arrived by the time the entry went to press. Potential subscribers, contributors, or collectors will have to write the editor to see whether the journal still exists, and if so, to inquire about details of manuscript submission, style, back issues, and the like.

[Dante Alighieri]

DANTE STUDIES (with the Annual Report of the Dante Society)

EDITORIAL ADDRESS:
Anthony L. Pellegrini, Editor
Department of Romance Languages
and Literatures
State University of New York at Binghamton
Binghamton, New York 13901

SUBSCRIPTION ADDRESS:
State University of New York Press
99 Washington Avenue
Albany, New York 12210

PUBLISHED: Annually
COST: $5.00 per copy

CIRCULATION: 550 (incl. libraries)

CONTENTS: Critical essays about Dante's poetry; notes; articles about other writers' assessment of Dante's work and life; articles about new editions of Dante manuscripts; an American Dante bibliography for the previous year including translations; studies; reviews; annual report of the Dante Society including membership list; the Dante prize news; secretary's report. Example: "Narrator and Landscape in the COMMEDIA: An Approach to Dante's Earthly Paradise."

UNSOLICITED MSS. WELCOME? Yes; submissions acknowledged.
SPECIFICALLY WELCOMED: Scholarly essays devoted to illuminating some aspect of Dante's work or life.
MS. LENGTH: 16-20 pages; submit ONE copy.
STYLE REQUIREMENTS: MLA STYLE SHEET; footnotes follow essay.
COPYRIGHT: The Dante Society of America.
EDITOR'S DECISION: Varies; up to 1 month.
FROM ACCEPTANCE TO PUBLICATION: Depends on when submitted.
PAYMENT/OFFPRINTS: No payment. Offprints are available at a modest price.
REJECTED MSS.: Returned.
GENERAL: First issue, 1881—ANNUAL REPORT OF THE DANTE SOCIETY; 1966—DANTE STUDIES. Usual publication length, 200-230 pages. Send membership inquiries to: Secretary of the Dante Society, Boylston Hall, Harvard University, Cambridge, Massachusetts 02138.
BACK ISSUES: Available from the State University of New York Press. Back issues to 1961—$1.00 each; to 1965—$2.00 each; to 1968—$4.00 each; 1969 on—$5.00 each. Supplementary publications are also available.

[Dickens, Charles]

BROADSTAIRS DICKENS FESTIVAL PROGRAMME

EDITORIAL ADDRESS:
J. B. Reed, Editor
48 Lanthorne Road
Broadstairs, Kent CT10 3NA
England

SUBSCRIPTION ADDRESS:

same

PUBLISHED: Annually
COST: 10 n p

CONTENTS: Programme of festival events; special feature writings of Dickensian interest. Also an illustrated edition of "Our English Watering Place" (cost, 50np). Example: "Children and Dickens."

UNSOLICITED MSS. WELCOME? No.
COPYRIGHT: Broadstairs Branch of Dickens Fellowship.
GENERAL: First issue, 1950. Usual publication length, 30 pages.
BACK ISSUES: None.

[Dickens, Charles]

THE DICKENSIAN

EDITORIAL ADDRESS:
Michael Slater, Hon. Editor
Birkbeck College
Malet Street
London WC1E 7HX

SUBSCRIPTION ADDRESS:
The Dickens House
48 Doughty Street
London WC1N 2LF
England

PUBLISHED: Tri-annually
(Jan., May, Sept.)

CIRCULATION: 2,500

COST: 1 yr.—$6.50, inclusive of annual index (preferential rates for members of The Dickens Fellowship). Subscription rate about to be reviewed.

CONTENTS: Illustrated articles on all aspects of Dickens' life, works and influence and reputation; reviews of all new books on Dickens plus (annually in September issue) a survey of all articles on Dickens in learned journals; reports of special meetings, conferences, lectures arranged by The Dickens Fellowship or others; reviews of stage and screen adaptations of Dickens; exhibitions related to his work. Example: "BLEAK HOUSE: the Agitating Women."

UNSOLICITED MSS. WELCOME? Yes; submissions acknowledged.
SPECIFICALLY WELCOMED: All scholarly work on Dickens, with a preference for biographical or historical studies, illustrated.
MS. LENGTH: 2,000-3,000 words; submit ONE copy.
STYLE REQUIREMENTS: Style sheet sent on request to would-be contributors.

COPYRIGHT: Author.
EDITOR'S DECISION: 4-6 weeks.
FROM ACCEPTANCE TO PUBLICATION: 12-18 months.
PAYMENT/OFFPRINTS: 25 offprints with covers supplied gratis; more can be purchased.
REJECTED MSS.: Returned.
GENERAL: First issue, January, 1905. Usual publication length, 68 pages.
BACK ISSUES: Complete run available from Kraus Reprint, 9491 Nendeln, Liechtenstein, at $14 for Vols. 1-14, 24-33 (paperbound); $10 for Vols. 15-23, 34-47 (paperbound); $8.00 for Vols. 48-64.

[Dickens, Charles]

DICKENS STUDIES ANNUAL

EDITORIAL ADDRESS:
Robert B. Partlow, Jr., Editor
Department of English
Southern Illinois University
Carbondale, Illinois 62901

SUBSCRIPTION ADDRESS:
Southern Illinois University Press
Carbondale, Illinois 62901

PUBLISHED: Annually
COST: Varies per volume

CIRCULATION: 1,500

CONTENTS: Critical essays about the novels of Charles Dickens, his life, and his age.

UNSOLICITED MSS. WELCOME? Yes; submissions acknowledged.
SPECIFICALLY WELCOMED: Scholarly essays in depth concerning Dickens' publications, his relation with his times and contemporaries.
MS. LENGTH: Only longer essays from 20-100 pages; submit RIBBON copy only.
STYLE REQUIREMENTS: MLA STYLE SHEET and American usages; footnotes at end of essay on separate page; quote from the Oxford illustrated Dickens edition.
COPYRIGHT: Southern Illinois University Press.
EDITOR'S DECISION: 3 months.
FROM ACCEPTANCE TO PUBLICATION: 12 months.
PAYMENT/OFFPRINTS: None.
REJECTED MSS. Returned.
GENERAL: First issue, 1970. Usual publication length, 300 pages. Last possible day for receipt of manuscripts is November 1st.
BACK ISSUES: Available from the Southern Illinois University Press. Inquire cost of press.

[Dickens, Charles]

DICKENS STUDIES NEWSLETTER

EDITORIAL ADDRESS:
Lionel Stevenson, General Editor
Department of English
University of Houston
Houston, Texas 77004

SUBSCRIPTION ADDRESS:
Robert B. Partlow, Jr.,
Production Editor
Southern Illinois University at Carbondale
Carbondale, Illinois 62901

PUBLISHED: Quarterly

CIRCULATION: 1,000 (100 libraries subscribing)

COST: 1 yr.—$5.00; free to members of the Dickens Society.

CONTENTS: Critical essays about Charles Dickens' work; reviews of books about Dickens and the Victorian era; reviews of paperback editions of Dickens' novels; letters to the editor; notes and queries; a bibliography checklist of Dickens' works and secondary sources of book and magazine articles, play, stage, and television adaptions, recordings and films. Example: "Dickens' Romanticism Domesticated."

UNSOLICITED MSS. WELCOME? Yes; submissions acknowledged.
SPECIFICALLY WELCOMED: Critical articles on Dickens; scholarly reviews of books relating to Dickens; reviews of important articles; notes and queries about specific details of Dickens' life and works and related details of Victorian thought and life.
MS. LENGTH: Critical articles—10 pages; reviews—4 pages; submit TWO copies.
STYLE REQUIREMENTS: MLA STYLE SHEET; footnotes follow essay.
COPYRIGHT: Author.
EDITOR'S DECISION: 2 weeks.
FROM ACCEPTANCE TO PUBLICATION: 4-6 months.
PAYMENT/OFFPRINTS: 12 copies of journal.
REJECTED MSS. Returned with criticism.
GENERAL: First issue, March, 1970. Usual publication length, 30 pages.
BACK ISSUES: Vol. I, Nos. 1, 2, 3 (1970) and Vol. II, Nos. 1 and 2 (1971) available from the Production Editor at $1.25 each.

[Dostoevsky, Fedor Mikhailovich]

INTERNATIONAL DOSTOEVSKY SOCIETY BULLETIN

EDITORIAL ADDRESS:
Rudolf Neuhäuser, Editor
Department of Russian Studies
The University of Western Ontario
London 72, Ontario
Canada

SUBSCRIPTION ADDRESS:
Nadine Natov, Executive Secretary
Department of Slavic Languages and Literature
George Washington University
Washington, D.C. 20006

PUBLISHED: Biannually
COST: Single copy—$2.00.

CONTENTS: Exchange of information on: Dostoevsky studies; scholarly meetings and conferences; exhibits; exchanges of professors; guest lectures and addresses (also on radio and TV); dramatizations (theatre and film), new editions, translations, reprints of Dostoevsky's works; books and articles, major review articles relating to Dostoevsky; and any other information pertaining to Dostoevsky scholarship. Examples of resumes of papers read at the Symposium: "The Concept of Beauty in Dostoevsky and Mishima"; "The Unity of Imagery and Ethical Idea in Dostoevsky's Works."

UNSOLICITED MSS. WELCOME? Yes; submissions acknowledged.
SPECIFICALLY WELCOMED: Information on Dostoevsky scholarship.
MS. LENGTH: 1-2 pages; submit TWO copies.
STYLE REQUIREMENTS: MLA STYLE SHEET.
COPYRIGHT: The BULLETIN.
EDITOR'S DECISION: Depends upon the date of submission.
FROM ACCEPTANCE TO PUBLICATION: The next issue.
PAYMENT/OFFPRINTS: Author will receive one additional copy of the BULLETIN if desired.
REJECTED MSS.: Not returned.
GENERAL: First issue, February, 1972. Usual publication length, 50-60 pages. The International Dostoevsky Society is a non-profit scholarly organization. Collaboration in the BULLETIN is on a voluntary basis—without compensation. Donations will be welcome. Notes and resumes appear in several languages.
BACK ISSUES: Available from Professor Nadine Natov at $2.00 each.

[Doyle, Arthur Conan]

THE BAKER STREET JOURNAL

See the section on SPECIALIZED TOPICS AND INTERDISCIPLINARY STUDIES: POPULAR CULTURE for details.

[Doyle, Arthur Conan]

THE COMMONPLACE BOOK

See the section on SPECIALIZED TOPICS AND INTERDISCIPLINARY STUDIES: POPULAR CULTURE for details.

[Doyle, Arthur Conan]

THE HOLMESIAN OBSERVER

See the section on SPECIALIZED TOPICS AND INTERDISCIPLINARY STUDIES: POPULAR CULTURE for details.

[Doyle, Arthur Conan]

THE HURLSTONE PAPERS

See the section on SPECIALIZED TOPICS AND INTERDISCIPLINARY STUDIES: POPULAR CULTURE for details.

[Doyle, Arthur Conan]

THE SHERLOCK HOLMES JOURNAL

See the section on SPECIALIZED TOPICS AND INTERDISCIPLINARY STUDIES: POPULAR CULTURE for details.

[Erasmus, Desiderius]

ERASMUS IN ENGLISH

EDITORIAL ADDRESS:
R. Schoeffel, Editor
University of Toronto Press
Toronto 5, Ontario
Canada

SUBSCRIPTION ADDRESS:
same

PUBLISHED: Annually, unless there is need for more frequent publication.
COST: Free
CIRCULATION: 2,700

CONTENTS: Articles and bibliographies related to Erasmus and his period, as well as information about the publication by the University of Toronto Press of the collected works of Erasmus in translation. Example: "On Erasmus' THE GODLY FEAST."

UNSOLICITED MSS. WELCOME? Yes, if they are suitable; submissions acknowledged.
MS. LENGTH: No preference; submit TWO copies

STYLE REQUIREMENTS: MLA STYLE SHEET.
COPYRIGHT: University of Toronto Press.
EDITOR'S DECISION: 1 month.
FROM ACCEPTANCE TO PUBLICATION: 1 year.
PAYMENT/OFFPRINTS: None.
REJECTED MSS.: Returned.
GENERAL: First issue, 1970. Usual publication length, 28 pages.
BACK ISSUES: Available free, unless xeroxes must be made, from the editor. Early issues are out of print.

[Galdós, Benito Perez]

ANALES GALDOSIANOS

EDITORIAL ADDRESS:
Rodolfo Cardona, Editor
Batts Hall, 112
The University of Texas
Austin, Texas 78712

SUBSCRIPTION ADDRESS:

same

PUBLISHED: Annually
CIRCULATION: 450
COST: 1 yr.—$3.00 ($2.40 for dealer's discount).

CONTENTS: Literary articles on the works, life, and times of Don Benito Galdós; book reviews; documents and articles dealing with the theoretical problems of the realist novel; also a descriptive bibliography on Galdós. Examples: "Galdós and the Humoristic Tradition"; "Religion in the Spanish Novel."

UNSOLICITED MSS. WELCOME? Yes; submissions acknowledged.
MS. LENGTH: Maximum 25 pages; submit ONE clean copy.
STYLE REQUIREMENTS: MLA STYLE SHEET.
COPYRIGHT: Authors.
EDITOR'S DECISION: 1-3 months.
FROM ACCEPTANCE TO PUBLICATION: 1-3 months.
PAYMENT/OFFPRINTS: No payment. Authors must pay for offprints.
REJECTED MSS.: Returned, with comments.
GENERAL: First issue, 1966. Usual publication length, 175 pages. Articles may be written in Spanish or English.
BACK ISSUES: All issues except for the ANEJO (supplement to Vol. III) available from editorial office at $3.00 each for Vols. III-VII; $6.00 for Vol. II; $4.00 for Vol. I. The ANEJO must be ordered from Libreria Insula, Carmen, 9, Madrid, 13, Spain.

[Gissing, George and his circle]

THE GISSING NEWSLETTER

EDITORIAL ADDRESS:
Pierre Coustillas, Editor
10, rue Gay-Lussac
59110 La Madeleine
France

SUBSCRIPTION ADDRESS:
C. C. Kohler
141 High Street
Dorking, Surrey
England

PUBLISHED: Quarterly
COST: 1 yr.—£1 for individuals; £1.50 for libraries.

CIRCULATION: 250

CONTENTS: Articles about George Gissing's works and his circle; book reviews; bibliographies; recent publications. Example: "The Revision of THYRZA."

UNSOLICITED MSS. WELCOME? Yes; submissions acknowledged.
SPECIFICALLY WELCOMED: Anything on George Gissing and his circle.
MS. LENGTH: 3,000 words; submit ONE copy.
STYLE REQUIREMENTS: MLA STYLE SHEET; footnotes follow article.
COPYRIGHT: Not copyrighted.
EDITOR'S DECISION: 2 weeks.
FROM ACCEPTANCE TO PUBLICATION: 3-9 months.
PAYMENT/OFFPRINTS: None.
REJECTED MSS.: Returned.
GENERAL: First issue, January, 1965. Usual publication length, 20 pages.
BACK ISSUES: Available from subscription address at £1.50 per annum.

[Goethe, Johann Wolfgang von]

PUBLICATIONS OF THE ENGLISH GOETHE SOCIETY: NEW SERIES

EDITORIAL ADDRESS:

SUBSCRIPTION ADDRESS:
Hon. Secretary
c/o Department of German
University College
Gower Street
London W. C. 1
England

PUBLISHED: Annually

CONTENTS: Papers read before the English Goethe Society; studies of Goethe's work and thought, as well as other fields of German Literature. Examples: "Thomas Mann and the Problematic Self"; "Herder, Goethe, and the Natural 'Type.' "

GENERAL: First issue of New Series, 1924. Usual publication length, 180 pages.

BACK ISSUES: Available from Dawsons of Pall Mall, 16 Pall Mall, London S.W. 1, England, at £2.10.0 each for Vols. 1-18, 22, in reprint, paper bound; £1.10.0 each for Vols. 19-21, 23-26, 29, 31-34, in original, paper bound.

[Graves, Robert]

FOCUS ON ROBERT GRAVES

EDITORIAL ADDRESS: SUBSCRIPTION ADDRESS:
Ellsworth Mason, Editor
Director of Libraries same
University of Colorado
Boulder, Colorado 80302

COST: Free to libraries, scholars, and collectors.

CONTENTS: Record of where important materials on Graves are now located (censuses of inscribed copies of titles, summaries of collections); tentative, as well as finished, articles on Graves—articles that seek verification of their material from readers and collectors; record of prices in the current Graves market; list of new publications about and by Graves; list of Graves scholars. Example: "History and Fantasy in the Claudius Novels."

UNSOLICITED MSS. WELCOME? No, articles are solicited.
SPECIFICALLY WELCOMED: Scholarly essays on Graves' works and his critics.
MS. LENGTH: 6-12 pages.
STYLE REQUIREMENTS: MLA STYLE SHEET; footnotes follow essay.
COPYRIGHT: University of Colorado Library.
PAYMENT/OFFPRINTS: Twenty copies of the periodical.
GENERAL: First issue, January, 1972. Usual publication length, 16-20 pages. In exchange for this periodical, recipient must inform the editor of the nature of his interest in Robert Graves. If a collector, list the highlights of your collection. If a scholar, state whether you teach Graves in any course, and whether you have written on him or plan to write on him.
BACK ISSUES: Available from the editorial office.

[Hardy, Thomas; the Powys family; Barnes, William]

THE THOMAS HARDY YEARBOOK

EDITORIAL ADDRESS:
J. Stevens Cox and
G. Stevens Cox, Editors
The Toucan Press
Mt. Durand, St. Peter Port
Guernsey, C. I. via Britain

SUBSCRIPTION ADDRESS:

same

PUBLISHED: Annually
COST: Single issue—$1.32.

CIRCULATION: 3,000

CONTENTS: Articles and essays on the life, times, and works of Thomas Hardy and his contemporaries; about the writer's environment, both physical and cultural; and about Dorset writers, especially those of the 19th century; many photographs, illustrations; lists of forthcoming books, recent essays about Hardy work in progress. Example: "A Note on Bell-Ringing in Thomas Hardy's DESPERATE REMEDIES."

UNSOLICITED MSS. WELCOME? Yes; submission acknowledged.
SPECIFICALLY WELCOMED: Essays on the life, times, and works of Thomas Hardy, the Powys family, and William Barnes.
MS. LENGTH: 1,000-20,000 words; submit ONE copy.
STYLE REQUIREMENTS: Footnotes follow article.
COPYRIGHT: Author and James and Gregory Stevens Cox.
EDITOR'S DECISION. 2 days.
FROM ACCEPTANCE TO PUBLICATION: 1 year.
PAYMENT/OFFPRINTS: Complimentary copies of relevant issue.
REJECTED MSS.: Returned.
GENERAL: First issue, 1970. Usual publication length, 108 pages.
BACK ISSUES: Available from Toucan Press at $2.50 for #1 and #2, $1.32 for #3.

[Johnson, Samuel; Defoe; Richardson; Smollett]

JOHNSONIAN NEWS LETTER

EDITORIAL ADDRESS:
James L. Clifford and
John H. Middendorf, Co-editors
610 Philosophy Hall
Columbia University
New York, New York 10027

SUBSCRIPTION ADDRESS:

same

PUBLISHED: Quarterly (Mar., June, Sept., Dec.)
COST: 1 yr.—$3.00 in U.S.; $3.50 elsewhere.

CIRCULATION: 1,100

CONTENTS: Articles on 18th-century life and literature, chiefly British, including Samuel Johnson, Daniel Defoe, Samuel Richardson, and Tobias Smollett; reviews of new books; lists of articles; scholarly news items; news of scholarly conferences.

UNSOLICITED MSS. WELCOME? Yes; submissions acknowledged.
SPECIFICALLY WELCOMED: Eighteenth century discoveries, news, etc.
MS. LENGTH: Short—400 words or less; submit ONE copy.
STYLE REQUIREMENTS: No specific requirements.
COPYRIGHT: Author.
EDITOR'S DECISION: Quick.
PAYMENT/OFFPRINTS: None.
REJECTED MSS.: Returned.
GENERAL: First issue, December, 1940. Usual publication length, 12 pages.
BACK ISSUES: Available from editorial office at $1.00 each. Facsimiles of first 30 years (in five-year gatherings) obtainable from Johnson Reprint Company.

[Johnson, Samuel]

THE NEW RAMBLER: JOURNAL OF THE JOHNSON SOCIETY OF LONDON

EDITORIAL ADDRESS:　　　　　　SUBSCRIPTION ADDRESS:
James H. Leicester, M.A., Editor
Broadmead　　　　　　　　　　　　same
Eynsford Road
Farningham, Kent
England

PUBLISHED: Biannually

CONTENTS: Papers read to the Johnson Society of London; scholarly essays on the works of Samuel Johnson and on his relationship with other writers of his time. Examples: "Johnson, Goldsmith, and THE TRAVELLER"; "Johnson's Use of English Names in the Periodical Essays."

UNSOLICITED MSS. WELCOME? Yes.
MS. LENGTH: Up to 3,000 words; submit TWO copies.
STYLE REQUIREMENTS: MLA STYLE SHEET.
PAYMENT/OFFPRINTS: Copy of issue.
GENERAL: First issue, 1941. Usual publication length, 52 pages.

[Joyce, James]

JAMES JOYCE QUARTERLY

EDITORIAL ADDRESS:
Thomas F. Staley, Editor
600 South College
The University of Tulsa
Tulsa, Oklahoma 74104

SUBSCRIPTION ADDRESS:
Charlotte Stewart, Managing Editor
The University of Tulsa
Tulsa, Oklahoma 74104

PUBLISHED: Quarterly (Spring, Summer, Autumn, Winter)

CIRCULATION: 1,115

COST: 1 yr.—$5.00 for individuals and libraries in U.S. and Canada; single copy—$1.50.

CONTENTS: Critical, biographical, or bibliographical articles; reviews of books dealing with Joyce; work in progress section; notes, reminiscences by those who knew Joyce; poetry inspired by Joyce's writings; photographs of Joyce critics, followers, and contemporaries; artistic sketches. Example: "James Joyce and Trieste."

UNSOLICITED MSS. WELCOME? Yes, but many are solicited; submissions acknowledged.
SPECIFICALLY WELCOMED: Academic criticism of Joyce's works and of his critics; book reviews; notes; occasional reminiscences; material related to Joyce and the Irish Renaissance and his relationship with writers of his time.
MS. LENGTH: Short notes to 25 pages; submit ONE copy.
STYLE REQUIREMENTS: MLA STYLE SHEET; references to Joyce's writings and Richard Ellmann's biography should be cited parenthetically within body of essay, using abbreviations listed in JJQ.
COPYRIGHT: University of Tulsa.
EDITOR'S DECISION: 6 weeks to 2 months.
FROM ACCEPTANCE TO PUBLICATION: 6-9 months.
PAYMENT/OFFPRINTS: No payment. Offprints available upon request.
REJECTED MSS.: Returned with criticism.
GENERAL: First issue, October, 1963. Usual publication length, 100 pages.
BACK ISSUES: All except current volume available from Swets & Zeitlinger, Front and Erickson, Essington, Pennsylvania 19029 and from Swets & Zeitlinger, Keizersgracht 471 & 487, Amsterdam, The Netherlands, at $17.00 per volume.

[Joyce, James]

THE JAMES JOYCE REVIEW (suspended publication)

EDITORIAL ADDRESS:
Edmund L. Epstein, Editor
Department of English
Southern Illinois University
Carbondale, Illinois 62901

BACK ISSUES:
Sales and Promotion Manager
Gotham Book Mart
New York, New York

CONTENTS: Critical essays on the works of Joyce; reviews of new editions of Joyce's writings and of books about Joyce; notes.

GENERAL First issue, February, 1957. Usual publication length, 50 pages.
BACK ISSUES: Vol. 1, no. 1 (February 2, 1957)—vol. 3, no. ½ (1959) available from Gotham Book Mart.

[Joyce, James]

A WAKE NEWSLITTER: STUDIES OF JAMES JOYCE'S FINNEGANS WAKE

EDITORIAL ADDRESS:
Clive Mart and Fritz Senn, Editors
Department of Literature
University of Essex
Wivenhoe Park
Colchester, Essex CO4 3SQ
England

SUBSCRIPTION ADDRESS:

same

PUBLISHED: 6 times yearly
(Feb., Apr., June, Aug., Oct., Dec.)
COST: 1 yr.—$5.00.

CIRCULATION: 600

CONTENTS: Articles, notes, and queries about FINNEGANS WAKE; occasional pieces on Joyce's other books; some reviews. Example: "Chronology of the Buffalo Notebooks."

UNSOLICITED MSS. WELCOME? Yes, submissions acknowledged.
SPECIFICALLY WELCOMED: Specific elucidation of cruces.
MS. LENGTH: 100-2,000 words, submit TWO copies.
STYLE REQUIREMENTS: Oxford rules.
COPYRIGHT: A WAKE NEWSLITTER.
EDITOR'S DECISION: 1 week.
FROM ACCEPTANCE TO PUBLICATION: 1-3 months.
PAYMENT/OFFPRINTS: Two copies (air mail) of the complete issue; more on request.
REJECTED MSS.: Returned.
GENERAL: First issue, March, 1962. Usual publication length, 16, 24, or 32 pages.

BACK ISSUES: Available from editorial office at cost at publication ($2.00 to $5.00 per volume).

[Keats; Shelley; Byron; and their circles]

KEATS-SHELLEY JOURNAL

EDITORIAL ADDRESS:
Rae Ann Nager, Editor
Houghton Library
Harvard University
Cambridge, Massachusetts 02138

SUBSCRIPTION ADDRESS:
Donald H. Reiman, Treasurer
Keats-Shelley Association of America
Room 815, 41 East 42nd Street
New York, New York 10017

PUBLISHED: Annually
COST: 1 yr.—$7.50 (subject to change).

CIRCULATION: 800

CONTENTS: Scholarly articles and reviews concerning Keats, Shelley, Byron, Hunt, Hazlitt, and their circles (Godwin, Peacock, Mary Shelley, Thomas Moore).

UNSOLICITED MSS. WELCOME? Yes; submissions acknowledged.
SPECIFICALLY WELCOMED: Scholarly articles only (no fiction or poetry).
MS. LENGTH: 15-20 pages; submit ONE copy.
STYLE REQUIREMENTS: MLA STYLE SHEET (with some modifications).
COPYRIGHT: Keats-Shelley Association of America, Inc.
EDITOR'S DECISION: 6 months.
FROM ACCEPTANCE TO PUBLICATION: 1-2 years.
PAYMENT/OFFPRINTS: Two copies of the JOURNAL containing his work. No offprints.
REJECTED MSS.: Returned.
GENERAL: First issue, 1952. Usual publication length, 140 pages.
BACK ISSUES: Available from Kraus Reprint Company at $7.50 each.

[Keats; Shelley; Byron; Hunt; Hazlitt]

THE KEATS-SHELLEY MEMORIAL BULLETIN

EDITORIAL ADDRESS:
Dorothy Hewlett, Honorary Editor
Longfield Cottage
Longfield Drive
Sheen Common, S. W. 14
England

SUBSCRIPTION ADDRESS:

same

PUBLISHED: Annually
COST: 1 yr.—£1.25 (£1 to Friends of the Association).

CIRCULATION: 2,000

CONTENTS: Essays about the Romantic poets who lived in Italy—Keats, Shelley, Byron, and Leigh Hunt—and contemporary associates; illustrations. Example: "Hellenism in Byron and Keats."

UNSOLICITED MSS. WELCOME? Yes; submissions acknowledged.
SPECIFICALLY WELCOMED: Biographical essays; criticism, with a new aspect.
MS. LENGTH: Up to 10 pages.
STYLE REQUIREMENTS: Clarity.
COPYRIGHT: None.
EDITOR'S DECISION: Varies.
FROM ACCEPTANCE TO PUBLICATION: About 6 months.
PAYMENT/OFFPRINTS: Ten free copies of issue. Another ten at £1.25 each.
REJECTED MSS.: Returned.
GENERAL: First issue, 1910; next issue in 1913; published annually since 1953.
BACK ISSUES: Available from William Dawson & Sons Ltd., Cannon House, Folkestone, Kent, England at £1.25 each; set of Vols. 1 to 20 at £29.75. Monographs also available from editor or from Dawson & Sons, Ltd.

[Kipling, Rudyard]

THE KIPLING JOURNAL

EDITORIAL ADDRESS:
Roger Lancelyn Green, Hon. Editor
c/o The Kipling Society
J. R. Dunlap, U.S. Secretary and Treasurer
420 Riverside Drive, 7D
New York, New York 10025

SUBSCRIPTION ADDRESS:
Lt. Col. A. E. Bagwell Purefoy,
Hon. Secretary
18, Northumberland Avenue
London WC 2N 5BJ
England

PUBLISHED: Quarterly   CIRCULATION: Up to 1,000
COST: By subscription to Kipling Society: $6.00, or £1.75.

CONTENTS: Articles, notes, letters, reviews concerning the life and works of Rudyard Kipling, and other topics of closely relevant interest. Example: "Kipling in New Zealand."

UNSOLICITED MSS. WELCOME? Yes; submissions acknowledged.
MS. LENGTH: Up to 3,000 words; submit ONE copy.
STYLE REQUIREMENTS: Scholarly, but suitable for average literary reader.
COPYRIGHT: Author.
EDITOR'S DECISION: 3 months.
FROM ACCEPTANCE TO PUBLICATION: 6 months.
PAYMENT/OFFPRINTS: None.
REJECTED MSS.: Returned.
GENERAL: First issue, March, 1927. Usual publication length, 16-32 pages.
BACK ISSUES: Available from subscription address. Cost varies.

[Lamb, Charles; Coleridge; DeQuincey]

THE CHARLES LAMB BULLETIN: THE JOURNAL OF THE CHARLES LAMB SOCIETY

EDITORIAL ADDRESS:
Mr. Basil Savage, Editor
46 Brookfield
Highgate West Hill
London N6 6AT
England

SUBSCRIPTION ADDRESS:
Miss Frieda Parsons,
Honorary Treasurer
32 Carmel Court
King's Drive
Wembley Park
Middlesex, HA9 9JE
England

PUBLISHED: Quarterly   CIRCULATION: 400
COST: 1 yr.—$3.50 for individuals, $4.50 for institutions, in dollar countries; £1.50 for individuals, £2.00 for institutions, in London; £1.00 for individuals, £1.50 for institutions, in England and overseas (membership included with subscription); single copy—40p.

CONTENTS: Non-academic literary essays on the Charles Lamb Circle including all the old Romantics (not Keats, Shelley, Byron); book reviews and news. Examples: "DeQuincey and THE LONDON MAGAZINE"; "Charles Lamb and S. T. Coleridge."

UNSOLICITED MSS. WELCOME? Yes; submissions acknowledged.
SPECIFICALLY WELCOMED: Essays on Charles Lamb and his circle.
MS. LENGTH: 3,000-5,000; submit ONE copy.
STYLE REQUIREMENTS: None.
COPYRIGHT: The Charles Lamb Society.
EDITOR'S DECISION: 1 month.
FROM ACCEPTANCE TO PUBLICATION: 6-9 months.
PAYMENT/OFFPRINTS: Up to 12 copies; more supplied by arrangement. No offprints.
REJECTED MSS.: Returned.
GENERAL: First issue, 1935; new series started January, 1973.
BACK ISSUES: Available from subscription address at 40p each.

[Lawrence, D. H.]

THE D. H. LAWRENCE REVIEW

EDITORIAL ADDRESS:
James C. Cowan, Editor
Box 1799
University of Arkansas
Fayetteville, Arkansas 72701

SUBSCRIPTION ADDRESS:
Carol Lindquist, Business Manager
same

PUBLISHED: Tri-annually (Spring, Summer, Winter)

COST: 1 yr.—$5.00 in U.S., Canada, and countries in the Pan American Union; $6.00 elsewhere; single copies—$2.00.

CONTENTS: Forum for criticism, historical scholarship, reviews, and bibliography (including lists of doctoral dissertations on D. H. Lawrence) of Lawrence and his circle; announcements of colloquia and seminars; occasional special numbers devoted to particular aspects of Lawrence's work, influences, or associations or to particular critical issues in modern literature. Example: "D. H. Lawrence's LAST POEMS."

UNSOLICITED MSS. WELCOME? Yes; submissions acknowledged.
SPECIFICALLY WELCOMED: Critical essays on Lawrence's poetry, novels, and relationship to the period in which he wrote; reviews of books including Lawrence and his circle, research in progress on Lawrence.
MS. LENGTH: Up to 20-25 pages; short notes rarely published; submit TWO copies.
STYLE REQUIREMENTS: MLA STYLE SHEET; include references in text when possible and footnotes on separate page at end.
COPYRIGHT: THE D. H. LAWRENCE REVIEW.
EDITOR'S DECISION: 3 months.
FROM ACCEPTANCE TO PUBLICATION: 1 year.
PAYMENT/OFFPRINTS: Two copies of the issue. 20 to 25 offprints.
REJECTED MSS. Returned.
GENERAL: First issue, 1968. Usual publication length, 85-100 pages.
BACK ISSUES: Available from the Business Manager at $2.00 each.

[Lessing, Gotthold Ephraim]

LESSING YEARBOOK

EDITORIAL ADDRESS:
Jerry Glenn, Editor
German Department
University of Cincinnati
Cincinnati, Ohio 45221

SUBSCRIPTION ADDRESS:
American Lessing Society
same

PUBLISHED: Annually
COST: 1 yr.—$9.00.

CIRCULATION: 1,000

CONTENTS: Articles on various aspects of eighteenth-century German literature and intellectual history, especially G. E. Lessing as critic and dramatist.

UNSOLICITED MSS. WELCOME? Yes; submissions acknowledged.
SPECIFICALLY WELCOMED: Articles on eighteenth-century German literature and intellectual history.
MS. LENGTH: 12-30 pages; submit ONE copy.
STYLE REQUIREMENTS: MLA STYLE SHEET.

COPYRIGHT: Publisher (Hueber, Munich); permission automatically given to reprint.
EDITOR'S DECISION: 4-8 weeks.
FROM ACCEPTANCE TO PUBLICATION: 1 year.
PAYMENT/OFFPRINTS: 35 free offprints; additional at cost.
REJECTED MSS.: Returned.
GENERAL: First issue, 1969. Usual publication length, 240-300 pages. Articles may be written in English or German.
BACK ISSUES: Available from American Lessing Society; Vols. I-III, $7.50 each; Vol. IV, $9.00 each.

[Lewis, C. S.]

THE BULLETIN OF THE NEW YORK C. S. LEWIS SOCIETY

EDITORIAL ADDRESS:
Eugene McGovern, Editor
9 Bradshaw Drive
Ossining, New York 10562

SUBSCRIPTION ADDRESS:
Mrs. Hope Kirkpatrick, Secretary
466 Orange Street
New Haven, Connecticut 06511

PUBLISHED: Monthly
COST: 1 yr.—$7.00.

CIRCULATION: 240

CONTENTS: Critical essays about the work of C. S. Lewis; short articles related to Lewis and his times; reviews of books about C. S. Lewis; letters; notices. Example: "Lewis CONTRA Freud."

UNSOLICITED MSS. WELCOME? Yes; submissions acknowledged.
SPECIFICALLY WELCOMED: Essays that increase knowledge and understanding of the works of C. S. Lewis.
MS. LENGTH: 500-10,000 words; submit ONE copy.
STYLE REQUIREMENTS: Standard.
COPYRIGHT: New York C. S. Lewis Society.
EDITOR'S DECISION: 2 weeks.
FROM ACCEPTANCE TO PUBLICATION: 3 months.
PAYMENT/OFFPRINTS: Five copies, more if requested.
REJECTED MSS.: Returned.
GENERAL: First issue, November, 1969. Usual publication length, 8 pages.
BACK ISSUES: Available from subscription office for $.60 to $1.00, depending on issue.

[Lorca, Garcia]

GARCIA LORCA REVIEW

EDITORIAL ADDRESS:
Grace Alvarez-Alman, Editor
State University of New York
Brockport, New York 14420

SUBSCRIPTION ADDRESS:

same

COST: $1.50 per issue.

CONTENTS: Articles on all aspects of the life and works of Garcia Lorca; book reviews.

GENERAL: First issue, September, 1973. Back issues available at $2.00 each.

[Lovecraft, H. P.]

NYCTALOPS

See the section on SPECIALIZED TOPICS AND INTERDISCIPLINARY STUDIES: POPULAR CULTURE for details.

[Machen, Arthur]

ARTHUR MACHEN SOCIETY OCCASIONAL

EDITORIAL ADDRESS:
Bob L. Mowery, President
Arthur Machen Society
Thomas Library
Wittenberg University
Springfield, Ohio 45501

SUBSCRIPTION ADDRESS:

same

PUBLISHED: Irregularly
COST: Free to members of the Arthur Machen Society.

CONTENTS: Critical essays about the writings of Arthur Machen; unpublished speeches and reminiscences about Machen as author, actor, and journalist; reprints of rare copies of Machen's work. Example: "Arthur Machen and TOM O'BEDLAM'S SONG."

UNSOLICITED MSS. WELCOME? Yes; submissions acknowledged.
SPECIFICALLY WELCOMED: Articles illuminating the life of Machen; critical essays on Machen's writing.
MS. LENGTH: Short.

COPYRIGHT: Author.
EDITOR'S DECISION: Within a month.
FROM ACCEPTANCE TO PUBLICATION: Varies.
PAYMENT/OFFPRINTS: Copy of issue.
REJECTED MSS.: Returned.
GENERAL: First issue, 1967. Usual publication length, 17-18 pages.

[Malraux, André]

MALRAUX MISCELLANY (MELANGES)

EDITORIAL ADDRESS:
Walter G. Langlois, Editor
French Department
1015 Office Tower
University of Kentucky
Lexington, Kentucky 40506

SUBSCRIPTION ADDRESS:

same

PUBLISHED: Biannually (Autumn, Spring)
CIRCULATION: 300 (including 60 major research libraries in the U.S. and Europe)
COST: 2 yrs.—$4.00; one year subscriptions not available.

CONTENTS: Critiques of works by André Malraux; bibliographical checklists devoted to a single work of Malraux; critical essays on a single image or a theme of Malraux (every third year); abstracts of studies now on microfilm; news of the Malraux Society; index of previous years' MALRAUX MISCELLANY contents in every third Autumn issue; discussions of Malraux's literary friendships; reviews of books and essays about Malraux. Example: "A Literary Friendship: André Malraux and Georges Gabory."

UNSOLICITED MSS. WELCOME? Yes; submissions acknowledged.
SPECIFICALLY WELCOMED: Critical essays focusing on some aspect of the writing and life of Malraux; historical or biographical essays relating to Malraux.
MS. LENGTH: 8-15 pages; submit ONE copy.
STYLE REQUIREMENTS: MLA STYLE SHEET; footnotes follow article.
COPYRIGHT: Walter G. Langlois, Editor, for Malraux Society.
EDITOR'S DECISION: 1 month, except during summer.
FROM ACCEPTANCE TO PUBLICATION: 6 months.
PAYMENT/OFFPRINTS: 10 free copies; others at half price.
REJECTED MSS. Returned, often with criticism.
GENERAL: First issue, Spring, 1969. Usual publication length, 32-35 pages. Articles may be submitted in either French or English. Periodical contains essays in both languages.
BACK ISSUES: Available from editor at $1.00 each. A few sets are available for those who wish a complete run of the review.

[Mill, John Stuart]

THE MILL NEWS LETTER

EDITORIAL ADDRESS:
John M. Robson and Michael Laine, Editors
Department of English
Victoria College
University of Toronto
Toronto, Ontario M5S 1K7
Canada

SUBSCRIPTION ADDRESS:

same

PUBLISHED: Biannually (Spring, Fall)   CIRCULATION: 550-600
COST: Free.

CONTENTS: Articles and notes concerning John Stuart Mill and his circle; publication and bibliographic information. Examples: "What Did Mill Mean to Poe?"; " 'Bentham' and 'Coleridge': Mill's 'Completing Counterparts.' "

UNSOLICITED MSS. WELCOME? Yes.
MS. LENGTH: Necessarily varied; submit ONE copy.
COPYRIGHT: Author.
EDITOR'S DECISION: 1-2 months.
FROM ACCEPTANCE TO PUBLICATION: 6-12 months.
PAYMENT/OFFPRINTS: None.
REJECTED MSS.: Returned.
GENERAL: First issue, Fall, 1965. Usual publication length, 24 pages.
BACK ISSUES: Available free, on request, from editorial address.

[Milton, John]

MILTON QUARTERLY (formerly MILTON NEWSLETTER)

EDITORIAL ADDRESS:
Roy C. Flannagan, Editor
Department of English
Ohio University
Athens, Ohio 45701

SUBSCRIPTION ADDRESS:

same

PUBLISHED: Quarterly (Mar., May, Oct., Dec.)
COST: 1 yr.—$4.00 ($5.00, libraries); 3 yrs.—$10.00 ($13.00, libraries); 5 yrs.—$15.00 ($20.00, libraries). $1.00 charged for invoicing; $.50 per year added for mailing outside U.S.

CONTENTS: Scholarly essays about John Milton's poetry and his life, and his position in the seventeenth century; articles about sources for Milton's works; notes; reviews of books about Milton and his era; articles of related interest; checklist of recently completed dissertations about Milton; abstracts of articles in other journals; #4 each year contains an index to that volume; occasional photographs of plaques, buildings, frescos, mosaics related to Milton or his books. Example: "Analogues and Sources for Milton's 'Great Task Master.'"

UNSOLICITED MSS. WELCOME? Essays, yes; reviews and abstracts may be solicited from authorities in various areas, but they remain anonymous— Editor assumes responsibility for their content; submissions acknowledged.
SPECIFICALLY WELCOMED: Critical essays about the poetry and career of John Milton.
MS. LENGTH: 2-10 pages; submit ONE copy.
STYLE REQUIREMENTS: MLA STYLE SHEET; footnotes follow article.
COPYRIGHT: Roy C. Flannagan.
EDITOR'S DECISION: 2 weeks to 6 months.
FROM ACCEPTANCE TO PUBLICATION: 1 year.
PAYMENT/OFFPRINTS: Five copies of the issue. Contributor should request offprints from the printer.
REJECTED MSS. Returned with criticism.
GENERAL: First issue, March, 1967, as MILTON NEWSLETTER; March, 1970, as MILTON QUARTERLY. Usual publication length, 18-25 pages. The cover often features a reproduction of a famous etching, portrait, or engraving illustrating "Adam and Eve" or some feature related to the poetry or life of Milton.
BACK ISSUES: MN and MQ available from editorial address at $1.00 each. Microfilm from University Microfilms; microfiche from Johnson Associates.

[Milton, John]

MILTON SOCIETY OF AMERICA

SUBSCRIPTION ADDRESS:
William B. Hunter, Jr., Secretary
Department of English
Hamilton-Smith Hall
University of New Hampshire
Durham, New Hampshire 03824

PUBLISHED: Annually   CIRCULATION: 450
COST: $2.00 annual dues for members; $25.00 for life membership.

CONTENTS: List of publications of the Milton scholar honored at the annual dinner and meeting; bibliography of works in progress about John Milton; constitution of The Milton Society of America; list of members.

SPECIFICALLY WELCOMED: Brief description and title of current research about Milton or his period.
GENERAL: First issue, 1948. Usual publication length, 46-50 pages.
BACK ISSUES: Available from Secretary of The Milton Society of America at $2.00 each.

[Milton, John]

MILTON STUDIES

EDITORIAL ADDRESS:
James D. Simmonds, Editor
Department of English
University of Pittsburgh
Pittsburgh, Pennsylvania 15213

SUBSCRIPTION ADDRESS:
Sales and Promotion Manager
University of Pittsburgh Press
Pittsburgh, Pennsylvania 15213

Overseas orders to: Henry M. Snyder and Co., Inc.
440 Park Avenue South
New York, New York 10016 U.S.A.

PUBLISHED: Annually
COST: $9.95 per volume.

CONTENTS: Articles and essays dealing with John Milton's work, thought, life, or historical and cultural background. Example: "Eve's Dream and the Paradox of Fallible Perfection."

UNSOLICITED MSS. WELCOME? Yes; submissions acknowledged.
SPECIFICALLY WELCOMED: Critical essays about Milton's work and life.
MS. LENGTH: 3,000 words and up; submit ONE copy.
STYLE REQUIREMENTS: MLA STYLE SHEET; footnotes follow article.
COPYRIGHT: University of Pittsburgh Press.
EDITOR'S DECISION: 3-4 months.
FROM ACCEPTANCE TO PUBLICATION: 1-2 years.
PAYMENT/OFFPRINTS: Author receives one copy of volume. No offprints.
REJECTED MSS.: Returned.
GENERAL: First issue, 1969. Usual publication length, 230 pages.
BACK ISSUES: Available from Sales and Promotion Manager at $9.95 per volume.

[More, Thomas]

MOREANA: A BILINGUAL QUARTERLY

EDITORIAL ADDRESS:
Germain Marc'hadour, Editor
29 rue Volney
49000 Angers
France

SUBSCRIPTION ADDRESS:
Amici Thomae Mori
B. P. 858
49005 Angers Cedex
France

PUBLISHED: Quarterly
CIRCULATION: 1,100
COST: 1 yr.—$10.00 ($20.00 for libraries).

CONTENTS: Articles in French and English on Thomas More as statesman and author and about his world; news and book reviews. Example: "Roper's LIFE OF MORE."

UNSOLICITED MSS. WELCOME? Yes; submissions acknowledged.
SPECIFICALLY WELCOMED: Any material about Thomas More.
MS. LENGTH: 4-20 pages; submit ONE copy.
STYLE REQUIREMENTS: Footnotes follow article.
EDITOR'S DECISION: 2 months.
FROM ACCEPTANCE TO PUBLICATION: Within 1 year.
PAYMENT/OFFPRINTS: Twenty free offprints given to authors.
REJECTED MSS.: Returned.
GENERAL: First issue, September, 1963. Usual publication length, 120 pages. MOREANA is the bulletin of an association but welcomes all subscribers. It goes to 40 countries.
BACK ISSUES: Available from subscription address at $20.00 per volume (4 issues).

[Morris, William]

JOURNAL OF THE WILLIAM MORRIS SOCIETY

SUBSCRIPTION ADDRESS:
R. C. H. Briggs, Esq.,
Hon. Secretary
William Morris Society
25 Lawn Crescent
Kew, Surrey
England

CONTENTS: Articles concerning the works of William Morris as poet and artist, and the times in which he lived.

GENERAL: First issue, 1961. U.S. Secretary and Treasurer: J. R. Dunlap, 420 Riverside Drive, 7D, New York, New York 10025, handles the Society's dollar accounts but does not distribute the publication. This periodical had not arrived by the time the entry went to press. Potential subscribers, contributors, or collectors will have to write to the editor to see whether the journal still exists, and if so, to inquire about details of manuscript submission, style, back issues, and the like.

[Morris, William]

NEWS FROM ANYWHERE

EDITORIAL ADDRESS:
Barbara and Joseph Dunlap, Editors
420 Riverside Drive, 7D
New York, New York 10025

SUBSCRIPTION ADDRESS:

. same

PUBLISHED: Annually   CIRCULATION: 160
COST: Included with membership in the William Morris Society which entitles members to all publications; $7.00—individual; $10.00—institution.

CONTENTS: Notes and brief articles about William Morris as poet, artist, and socialist; reviews of new editions of works by Morris; news of Morris appearing in other publications, including art books and travelguides; reprints of articles about Morris and his contemporaries that had been printed before 1900; news of the members of the William Morris Society; reminiscences of trip to Morris country; reviews of books about Morris.

UNSOLICITED MSS. WELCOME? Articles and notes are chiefly written by the editors; others are welcome; submissions acknowledged.
SPECIFICALLY WELCOMED: Notes, news items, insights, interpretations relating to William Morris, his aims, works, associates, influence, and times.
MS. LENGTH: 1 page; submit TWO copies.
STYLE REQUIREMENTS: Clarity.
COPYRIGHT: Not copyrighted.
EDITOR'S DECISION: 2 weeks.
FROM ACCEPTANCE TO PUBLICATION: As irregular as the date of publication.
PAYMENT/OFFPRINTS: No payment. Extra copies of the issue are usually available.
REJECTED MSS. Returned.
GENERAL: First issue, 1959. Usual publication length, 20-32 pages.
BACK ISSUES: Available from editors at $.50 each.

[Petronius, Gaius]

THE PETRONIAN SOCIETY NEWSLETTER

EDITORIAL ADDRESS:
Gareth Schmeling, Editor
Department of Classics
University of Florida
Gainesville, Florida 32601

SUBSCRIPTION ADDRESS:

same

PUBLISHED: Biannually (June, December)
COST: Free.

CIRCULATION: 200

CONTENTS: Up-to-date bibliography of works including articles on Petronius and his Satyricon; reviews at length of major monographs and articles on Petronius (by recognized Petronian scholars); reviews of dissertations on Petronius; record of all contemporary references and influences of Petronius on modern literature; short articles.

UNSOLICITED MSS. WELCOME? Yes; submissions acknowledged.
SPECIFICALLY WELCOMED: Short notes on Petronius.
MS. LENGTH: Less than 3,000 words; submit ONE copy.
STYLE REQUIREMENTS: MLA STYLE SHEET.
COPYRIGHT: THE PETRONIAN SOCIETY NEWSLETTER.
EDITOR'S DECISION: 2 months.
FROM ACCEPTANCE TO PUBLICATION: 6 months.
PAYMENT/OFFPRINTS: No payment. All copies at cost.
REJECTED MSS.: Returned.
GENERAL: First issue, June, 1970. Usual publication length; 6-8 double column pages.
BACK ISSUES: Available free from the editor.

[Pirandello, Luigi]

PIRANDELLO STUDIES

EDITORIAL ADDRESS:
Editor
Pirandello Society
45 Fifth Avenue
New York, New York 10003

SUBSCRIPTION ADDRESS:

same

PUBLISHED: Annually

CONTENTS: Society supports Pirandello productions in English and Italian.

GENERAL: First issue, 1969. This periodical had not arrived by the time the entry went to press. Potential subscribers, contributors, or collectors will have to write the editor to see whether the journal still exists, and if so, to inquire about details of manuscript submission, style, back issues, and the like.

[Pons, Solar; Holmes, Sherlock]

THE PONTINE DOSSIER

See the section on SPECIALIZED TOPICS AND INTERDISCIPLINARY STUDIES: POPULAR CULTURE for details.

[Pope, Swift, and Circle]

THE SCRIBLERIAN AND THE KIT-CATS

EDITORIAL ADDRESS:
Peter A. Tasch, Arthur J. Weitzman,
Roy S. Wolper, Editors
Department of English
Temple University
Philadelphia, Pennsylvania 19122

SUBSCRIPTION ADDRESS:

same

PUBLISHED: Biannually (Autumn, Spring)
COST: 1 yr.—$3.00.

CIRCULATION: 1,400

CONTENTS: Reviews and notes on 18th century Scriblerians (Pope, Bolingbroke, Swift, Gay, Arbuthnot, and Harley) and on Kit-Cats (Addison, Steele, Congreve, Vanbrugh, Dryden, and others). Example: "The Case for Mr. Addison."

UNSOLICITED MSS. WELCOME? Yes; submissions acknowledged.
SPECIFICALLY WELCOMED: Original ms. Intelligent and urbane notes, queries, out-of-the-way items, unusual illustrations.
MS. LENGTH: 500-1,500 words; submit ONE copy.
STYLE REQUIREMENTS: MLA STYLE SHEET.
COPYRIGHT: Individual authors and editors.
EDITOR'S DECISIONS: 6 weeks.
FROM ACCEPTANCE TO PUBLICATION: 5 months.
PAYMENT/OFFPRINTS: Two issues of journal.
REJECTED MSS.: Returned.
GENERAL: First issue, Autumn, 1968. Usual publication length, 72 pages.
BACK ISSUES: Vol. I available from Johnson Reprint Corp.; Vol. II from editorial address at $1.50 each.

[Proust, Marcel]

PROUST RESEARCH ASSOCIATION NEWSLETTER

EDITORIAL ADDRESS:
J. Theodore Johnson, Jr., Editor
Department of French and Italian
University of Kansas
Lawrence, Kansas 66044

SUBSCRIPTION ADDRESS:

same

PUBLISHED: Irregularly; normally biannually (Fall and Spring)
CIRCULATION: 250
COST: Free to active Proust scholars concerned with the more technical or heuristic aspects of current research on Marcel Proust.

CONTENTS: News items and reports of work in progress on dissertations, books and public lectures; reports of conferences on Proust; checklists of Proust manuscripts; notes regarding problems in Proust research; abstracts of recently defended dissertations, forthcoming articles, recently published works, and the like; reviews; bibliography of Proust texts, catalogs, books, articles, reviews.

UNSOLICITED MSS. WELCOME? Yes; submissions acknowledged.
SPECIFICALLY WELCOMED: Abstracts of works in progress about Marcel Proust; notes or brief commentary about problems relating to current research, particularly with the manuscripts.
MS. LENGTH: 1-5 pages; submit ONE copy.
STYLE REQUIREMENTS: MLA STYLE SHEET.
COPYRIGHT: Contributor.
EDITOR'S DECISION: 1 week.
FROM ACCEPTANCE TO PUBLICATION: 1 to 5 months.
PAYMENT/OFFPRINTS: Maximum of 5 copies of the issue.
REJECTED MSS.: Returned.
GENERAL: First issue, March, 1969. Usual publication length, 30-40 pages. Because PRAN simply serves as a forum for the discussion of technical problems that face active Proust scholars, authors of articles deserving a wider exposure are encouraged to submit these articles to the more general or widely circulated journals of the profession. Submissions may be written in either French or English.
BACK ISSUES: Free, if available, from the editor.

[Rohmer, Sax]

THE ROHMER REVIEW

See the section on SPECIALIZED TOPICS AND INTERDISCIPLINARY STUDIES: POPULAR CULTURE for details.

[Shakespeare, William]

FOLGER LIBRARY NEWSLETTER

EDITORIAL ADDRESS:
Betty Ann Kane, Editor
Folger Shakespeare Library
201 East Capitol Street, S. E.
Washington, D.C. 20003

SUBSCRIPTION ADDRESS:

same

PUBLISHED: 5 times yearly (Oct., Dec., Feb., Apr., June)
COST: Free

CIRCULATION: 8,000

CONTENTS: Reports on additions to the Library that holds the world's largest collection of Shakespeare materials, such as the earliest record of purchase of a Shakespeare work; occasional photographs; reports of the Folger Theatre Group.

GENERAL: First issue, October, 1969. Usual publication length, 4 pages. Particularly useful to collectors and researchers.
BACK ISSUES: Available free from editorial address.

[Shakespeare, William]

SHAKESPEAREAN RESEARCH AND OPPORTUNITIES

EDITORIAL ADDRESS:
W. R. Elton, Editor
English Department
Graduate Center
City University of New York
33 West 42nd Street
New York, New York 10036

SUBSCRIPTION ADDRESS:

same

PUBLISHED: Annually
COST: 1 yr.—$5.00; 3 yrs.—$12.00 (institutions—1 yr.—$10.00 or 3 yrs.—$25.00).

CONTENTS: Scholarly papers that were read at the MLA Conference; a bibliographical international Shakespearean "work in progress" section (articles, dissertation, books, new editions); notes on collations of texts of a single play; special checklists, such as English prose jestbooks; tributes to Shakespearean scholars; notes and queries; annual selective, annotated list pertaining to Shakespeare's Renaissance intellectual milieu (economic-social contexts, educational, ethical, historical, humanist-classical, iconographical, legal, linguistic-rhetorical, military, musical, philosophical, political, psychological, renaissance, scientific (and pre-scientific), theatrical, theological, TOPOI, reference tools).

UNSOLICITED MSS. WELCOME? Yes; submit TWO copies.
SPECIFICALLY WELCOMED: Materials devoted to Shakespeare directly, as well as bibliographical and other research tools of Renaissance contextual relevance.
STYLE REQUIREMENTS: MLA STYLE SHEET.
EDITOR'S DECISION: 1 month.
GENERAL: First issue, 1965. Usual publication length, 200 pages.

[Shakespeare, William]

SHAKESPEARE-JAHRBUCH

EDITORIAL ADDRESS:
Dr. Gunther Klotz, Managing Editor
102 Berlin 2
Berolinastrasse 9
D.D.R.

SUBSCRIPTION ADDRESS:

same

PUBLISHED: Annually
COST: 1 yr.—28,-M

CONTENTS: Studies of Shakespeare's work, life, contemporaries, and of his reception today; reviews of theatrical productions and of publications; international annual Shakespeare bibliography.

UNSOLICITED MSS. WELCOME? Yes.
SPECIFICALLY WELCOMED: Critical, analytical articles.
MS. LENGTH: 15-30 pages; submit TWO copies.
EDITOR'S DECISION: 6 weeks.
PAYMENT/OFFPRINTS: 12,-M per printed page.
REJECTED MSS.: Returned.
GENERAL: First issue, 1864. Usual publication length, 320 pages. Articles may be in German or English.
BACK ISSUES: Available from publisher: Hermann Böhlaüs Naclef, 53 Weimar, Meyerstrasse 50a, D.D.R.

[Shakespeare, William]

THE SHAKESPEARE NEWSLETTER

EDITORIAL ADDRESS:
Louis Marder, Editor
Department of English
University of Illinois at
Chicago Circle
Chicago, Illinois 60680

SUBSCRIPTION ADDRESS:

same

PUBLISHED: 6 times yearly (Feb., April, May, Sept., Nov., Dec.)
COST: 1 yr.—$2.00; $2.25 for Canadian and foreign subscriptions. Subscriptions taken on a two year basis.

CONTENTS: Articles about Shakespearean theatres, productions, festivals, translations, bibliographies; abstracts of dissertations on some aspect of Shakespeare and his plays; brief notes about audiences, different interpretations of Shakespearean drama; abstracts of scholarly articles on Shakespeare in other periodicals; book reviews; abstracts of lectures; news of the Shakespearean world, scholarly trends, meetings; digests of "Landmarks of Criticism."

UNSOLICITED MSS. WELCOME? Prefer inquiry first; submissions acknowledged.
SPECIFICALLY WELCOMED: Very short articles concerning Shakespeare and the drama, society, and historical events that illuminate his life and works.
MS. LENGTH: 300-1,000 words; submit ONE copy.
STYLE REQUIREMENTS: Include reference sources within text, if possible.
COPYRIGHT: Louis Marder, Editor and Publisher.
EDITOR'S DECISION: 1-2 months.
PAYMENT/OFFPRINTS: Five copies of issue; by-line. Offprints available upon request.
REJECTED MSS.: Usually returned; with criticism.
GENERAL: First issue, 1951. Usual publication length, 8 to 12 pages. Before sending manuscript, mail a brief description of article to Editor.
BACK ISSUES: Available from Editor at $.60 each or $3.50 per year, plus postage.

[Shakespeare, William]

THE SHAKESPEARE OXFORD SOCIETY NEWS-LETTER

EDITORIAL ADDRESS:
Richard C. Horne, Jr., Editor
918 F Street, N.W.
Room 612
Washington, D.C. 20004

PUBLISHED: 3 to 4 times yearly   CIRCULATION: 150-200
COST: Only sent to members of the Society and/or a few reference libraries.

CONTENTS: Analyses and discussions of topics uppermost in the Shakespearean followers' current debates and publications, such as a new "Shakespeare" signature or the speculation that Shakespeare's plays were authored by Francis Bacon, Christopher Marlowe, or Edward de Vere; reproductions of articles published in the original SHAKESPEARE FELLOWSHIP QUARTERLY; articles challenging published essays; news of the Shakespeare Birthplace; occasional book reviews; news of the Folger Shakespeare Library; announcements of articles to appear in national magazines.

UNSOLICITED MSS. WELCOME? No.
GENERAL: Society incorporated, 1957. Usual publication length, 11-18 pages.
BACK ISSUES: No longer available.

[Shakespeare, William]

SHAKESPEARE QUARTERLY

EDITORIAL ADDRESS:
Dr. R. J. Schoeck, Editor
Folger Shakespeare Library
Washington, D.C. 20003

SUBSCRIPTION ADDRESS:
Patricia R. Lyles, SHAKESPEARE QUARTERLY, Assistant
same

PUBLISHED: Quarterly (Winter, Spring, Summer, Autumn)
CIRCULATION: 3,000
COST: 1 yr.—$10.00; $12.00 outside of U.S.; single copy—$3.00.

CONTENTS: Scholarly essays about the plays of William Shakespeare; comparisons of his work to other major writers' work; exploration of questions arising from Shakespeare's drama; articles about Shakespeare's time and about his life; articles about the influences on Shakespeare's writing; analyses of his poetry; queries and notes; reviews of books of criticism about Shakespeare and of bibliographical sources; reproductions of illustrated pages of poetry in the 16th century. Example: "Coriolanus and Alceste: A Study in Misanthropy."

UNSOLICITED MSS. WELCOME? Yes; submissions acknowledged.
SPECIFICALLY WELCOMED: Critical essays about the works of William Shakespeare, his theatre, and his contemporaries.
MS. LENGTH: 12-20 pages; submit ONE copy.
STYLE REQUIREMENTS: MLA STYLE SHEET; identify quoted lines from plays within text of article.
COPYRIGHT: The Shakespeare Association of America, Inc.
EDITOR'S DECISION: 3-6 months.
FROM ACCEPTANCE TO PUBLICATION: 2 years.
PAYMENT/OFFPRINTS: Five free copies for articles; 3 for notes; 1 for reviews.
REJECTED MSS.: Returned.
GENERAL: First issue, 1950. Usual publication length, 125-130 pages. Summer issue regularly features the Shakespeare World Bibliography for the year; fall issue regularly features reviews of Shakespeare summer festivals; each volume is indexed.
BACK ISSUES: Available from AMS Press, Inc. Inquire cost of AMS.

[Shakespeare, William]

SHAKESPEARE'S PROCLAMATION

EDITORIAL ADDRESS: SUBSCRIPTION ADDRESS:
R. Thad Taylor, Editor
Shakespeare Society of America, Inc.   same
1107 N. Kings Rd.
Los Angeles, California 90069

PUBLISHED: Quarterly (Apr., Aug., Oct., Dec.)
COST: 1 yr.—$5.00 for students and out-of-state members; $10.00 for active members; $100.00 for patron members (publication included with society membership).

CONTENTS: Biographical articles on Shakespeare's life and career as playwright; articles about Shakespeare's life in legend; descriptions of the Swan theater and others; many photographs and sketches of Shakespearean characters, actors, and costumes; "in the wings" section about rehearsals of upcoming productions; short notices or critiques of certain actresses or actors in a specific Shakespearean role.

UNSOLICITED MSS. WELCOME? Yes; submissions acknowledged.
SPECIFICALLY WELCOMED: Biographical detail about Shakespeare and about his contemporaries if it sheds light on Shakespearean drama; news about forthcoming production.
MS. LENGTH: No limit; submit ONE copy.
STYLE REQUIREMENTS: None.
COPYRIGHT: Shakespeare Society of America, Inc.
EDITOR'S DECISION: 30 days.
FROM ACCEPTANCE TO PUBLICATION: 3 months.
PAYMENT/OFFPRINTS: Extra copies of issue.
REJECTED MSS.: Not returned.
GENERAL: First issue, October, 1968. Usual publication length, 10-16 pages. Membership in the Shakespeare Society of America includes 6 productions, Shakespearean Library, working copies for students, fund raising concerts, school of dancing.
BACK ISSUES: Available from editorial office at $.50 each.

[Shakespeare, William]

SHAKESPEARE STUDIES [Japan]

EDITORIAL ADDRESS: SUBSCRIPTION ADDRESS:
Jiro Ozu, Editor   The Secretary
18 Nakamachi   The Shakespeare Society of Japan
Shinjuku-ku, Tokyo 162   same
Japan

PUBLISHED: Annually   CIRCULATION: 700
COST: 1 yr.—$10.00 (Membership dues; a subscriber should be a member of The Shakespeare Society of Japan.)

CONTENTS: Articles on Shakespeare and the various aspects of Elizabethan, Jacobean, and Caroline drama. Examples: "Cleopatra and Volumia"; "Theology in Shakespeare"; "The Comic Sense in Marlowe Reconsidered."

UNSOLICITED MSS. WELCOME? Inquire; submissions acknowledged.
MS. LENGTH: 20-30 pages; submit TWO copies.
STYLE REQUIREMENTS: MLA STYLE SHEET.
COPYRIGHT: The writer.
EDITOR'S DECISION: 3 months.
FROM ACCEPTANCE TO PUBLICATION: 6-12 months.
PAYMENT/OFFPRINTS: 20 offprints.
REJECTED MSS.: Returned.
GENERAL: First issue, 1962. Usual publication length, 70-80 pages.
BACK ISSUES: Available from The Shakespeare Society of Japan. Some are out of stock; inquire.

[Shakespeare, William]

SHAKESPEARE STUDIES: AN ANNUAL GATHERING OF RESEARCH, CRITICISM, AND REVIEWS.

EDITORIAL ADDRESS: SUBSCRIPTION ADDRESS:
J. Leeds Barroll, Editor   University of South Carolina Press
Department of English   Columbia, South Carolina 29208
University of South Carolina
Columbis, South Carolina 29208

PUBLISHED: Annually   CIRCULATION: 1,200
COST: $14.95 (20% discount given to individuals who send in their check with their orders).

CONTENTS: Essays, articles, and reviews of books dealing with scholarship, criticism, and stage history of Shakespeare, his life, and his times. Emphasis is upon detailed and thorough presentations of research or critical methodology.

UNSOLICITED MSS. WELCOME? Yes; submissions acknowledged.
MS. LENGTH: No limit; submit TWO copies.
STYLE REQUIREMENTS: MLA STYLE SHEET.
COPYRIGHT: SHAKESPEARE STUDIES.
EDITOR'S DECISION: 1 month.
FROM ACCEPTANCE TO PUBLICATION: 15 months.
PAYMENT/OFFPRINTS: 25 offprints for articles; 10 for reviews.
REJECTED MSS.: Returned.

GENERAL: First issue, 1965. Usual publication length, 450 pages. Volume VII contains a composite index for Vols. I-VI; with the publication of VII in the fall of 1973, each SHAKESPEARE STUDIES will contain an index thereafter. The South Carolina Shakespeare Monographs: Studies in Renaissance Bibliography is a related series under the same editorial supervision and published over the same imprint.
BACK ISSUES: Available from University of South Carolina Press at $14.95 each.

[Shakespeare, William]

SHAKESPEARE SURVEY

EDITORIAL ADDRESS:
Kenneth Muir, Editor
Cambridge University Press
American Branch
32 East 57th Street
New York, New York 10022

SUBSCRIPTION ADDRESS:
Cambridge University Press
32 East 57th Street
New York, New York 10022

PUBLISHED: Annually
CIRCULATION: 5,000
COST: $12.50 per volume. No subscriptions.

CONTENTS: A collection of articles based around a different general theme covering all aspects of Shakespeare studies and a special section at the end covering the year's work in Shakespeare studies; illustrations. Examples: "Faith and Fashion in MUCH ADO ABOUT NOTHING"; "The Queen Mab Speech in ROMEO AND JULIET."

UNSOLICITED MSS. WELCOME? Yes.
SPECIFICALLY WELCOMED: Essays related to general theme of the year, such as the recent theme "Shakespeare's Early Tragedies."
MS. LENGTH: Up to 5,000 words.
STYLE REQUIREMENTS: Style sheet available on request; leave generous margins.
COPYRIGHT: Cambridge University Press.
PAYMENT/OFFPRINTS: Up to 20 offprints.
GENERAL: First issue, 1948. Usual publication length, 185 pages plus introduction and plates. Send contributions along with brief summary of article to: Editor, Department of English Literature, University of Liverpool, P.O. Box 147, Liverpool L69 3BX, England.
BACK ISSUES: Available from Cambridge University Press at $12.50 each.

[Shaw, George Bernard]

THE INDEPENDENT SHAVIAN: JOURNAL OF NEW YORK SHAVIANS, INC.

EDITORIAL ADDRESS:
Vera Scriabine, Editor
New York Shavians, Inc.
14 Washington Place, Apt. 5E
New York, New York 10003

SUBSCRIPTION ADDRESS:

same

PUBLISHED: Tri-annually CIRCULATION: 200
COST: 1 yr.—$3.00 in U.S., $3.10 in Canada and Mexico, $3.50 elsewhere; single copy—$1.00.

CONTENTS: Articles about George Bernard Shaw, his circles, and his contemporaries; notes; book and theater reviews (solicited from members of New York Shavians, Inc.); photographs and pen sketches. Example: "Bernard Shaw and the American Theater: A Projected Study."

UNSOLICITED MSS. WELCOME? Occasionally; submissions acknowledged.
SPECIFICALLY WELCOMED: Original items by Shaw and fugitive items about him.
MS. LENGTH: Up to 1,800 words; submit ONE copy.
STYLE REQUIREMENTS: MLA STYLE SHEET.
COPYRIGHT: New York Shavians, Inc.
EDITOR'S DECISION: A couple of weeks.
FROM ACCEPTANCE TO PUBLICATION: 6 months.
PAYMENT/OFFPRINTS: None.
REJECTED MSS.: Returned.
GENERAL: First issue, 1962. Usual publication length, 16-20 pages.
BACK ISSUES: Available from Kraus Reprint Co. at $1.00 each. Microfilm available from Xerox University Microfilms.

[Shaw, George Bernard]

THE SHAVIAN

EDITORIAL ADDRESS:
Eric F. J. Ford, Secretary
High Orchard 125 Markyate Rd.
Dagenham Essex RM8 2LB
England

SUBSCRIPTION ADDRESS:

same

PUBLISHED: 1 or 2 yearly CIRCULATION: 600
COST: 1 yr.—$3.50 (includes subscription and membership in The Shaw Society).

CONTENTS: Reviews articles on George Bernard Shaw and his contemporaries and influences.

UNSOLICITED MSS. WELCOME? Yes; submissions acknowledged.
MS. LENGTH: 3,000 words; submit TWO copies.
STYLE REQUIREMENTS: See current issue.
COPYRIGHT: Author unless assents publisher.
EDITOR'S DECISIONS: 3 months.
FROM ACCEPTANCE TO PUBLICATION: 6 months.
PAYMENT/OFFPRINTS: Up to 6 free copies.
REJECTED MSS.: Returned.
GENERAL: First issue, 1953. Usual publication length, 30 pages.
BACK ISSUES: Available from editorial office at 60p each, plus postage.

[Shaw, George Bernard]

THE SHAW REVIEW

EDITORIAL ADDRESS: SUBSCRIPTION ADDRESS:
Stanley Weintraub, Editor
S-234 Burrowes Building   same
The Pennsylvania State University
University Park, Pennsylvania 16802

PUBLISHED: Tri-annually   CIRCULATION: 600-800
COST: 1 yr.—$5.00

CONTENTS: Articles on the life, times, and work of Bernard Shaw; book reviews; checklists of Shaviana. Example: "The Underside of Undershaft: A Wagnerian Motif in MAJOR BARBARA."

UNSOLICITED MSS. WELCOME? Yes; submissions acknowledged.
SPECIFICALLY WELCOMED: Research and criticism that add to or alter our understanding of George Bernard Shaw and his milieu.
MS. LENGTH: Under 5,000 words; submit ONE copy.
STYLE REQUIREMENTS: MLA STYLE SHEET.
COPYRIGHT: THE SHAW REVIEW.
EDITOR'S DECISION: 2 months.
FROM ACCEPTANCE TO PUBLICATION: 1 year.
PAYMENT/OFFPRINTS: Ten copies of issue in which contribution appears. Inquire about offprints.
REJECTED MSS. Returned.
GENERAL: First issue, 1951. Usual publication length, 44 pages.
BACK ISSUES: Available from editorial office at $1.75 each.

[Spenser, Edmund]

SPENSER NEWSLETTER

EDITORIAL ADDRESS:
A. Kent Hieatt, Elizabeth Bieman,
David Kaula, Co-editors
Department of English
University of Western Ontario
1151 Richmond Street
London, Ontario N6A 3K7
Canada

SUBSCRIPTION ADDRESS:
Circulation Manager
same

PUBLISHED: Tri-annually   CIRCULATION: 400
COST: 1 yr.—$2.00 for individuals ($3.00 when invoiced) or 2 yrs.—$3.00.

CONTENTS: Reviews and notices of books pertaining to Spenser or providing matter of interest to Spenserian scholars; abstract of articles pertaining to Spenser; notices of reviews of books in the field which have appeared in other scholarly journals; news of work in progress; news of conferences; dissertation abstracts; occasional queries.

UNSOLICITED MSS. WELCOME? Yes, offprints of pertinent articles and reviews are welcome; news of work in progress is solicited; submissions acknowledged.
SPECIFICALLY WELCOMED: Articles; reviews. To date, the editors have not included any original notes on Spenser, although such a policy is not precluded. Nothing more than a page in length could be considered.
MS. LENGTH: 1 page.
EDITOR'S DECISION: 6 weeks.
FROM ACCEPTANCE TO PUBLICATION: Varies.
PAYMENT/OFFPRINTS: No payment.
REJECTED MSS. Returned.
GENERAL: First issue, Winter, 1970. Usual publication length, 16 pages.
BACK ISSUES: Available from editorial office at subscription rate.

[Tennyson, Alfred Lord]

TENNYSON RESEARCH BULLETIN

EDITORIAL ADDRESS:
R. F. Smith, F.L.A., Secretary
Tennyson Society at the Tennyson
Research Center
The City Library
Free School Lane
Lincoln
England

SUBSCRIPTION ADDRESS:

same

PUBLISHED: Annually
COST: 1 yr.—$4.50 for individuals; $6.00 for institutions (includes TENNYSON RESEARCH BULLETIN, the Tennyson Society monographs, and other publications during the subscription year).

CONTENTS: Articles and notes on Tennyson and the Victorian period; record of research in progress; publications; reviews; photographs. Example: "Tennyson: Mind and Method."

UNSOLICITED MSS. WELCOME? Yes; submissions acknowledged.
SPECIFICALLY WELCOMED: Tennysoniana.
MS. LENGTH: Up to 4,000 words; submit TWO copies.
STYLE REQUIREMENTS: Footnotes follow article.
COPYRIGHT: The Tennyson Society.
EDITOR'S DECISION: Varies.
PAYMENT/OFFPRINTS: Six free copies; more at reduced price, normally 50%.
REJECTED MSS.: Returned.
GENERAL: First issue, 1967. Usual publication length, 30-36 pages. Indexed by volume.
BACK ISSUES: Available from editorial office at $2.40 each ($1.80 to members).

[Tolkien, J. R. R.: Lewis, C. S.; Williams, Charles]

MYTHLORE

See the section on SPECIALIZED TOPICS AND INTERDISCIPLINARY STUDIES: POPULAR CULTURE for details.

[Tolkien, J. R. R.; Lewis, C. S.; Williams, Charles]

MYTHPRINT

See the section on SPECIALIZED TOPICS AND INTERDISCIPLINARY STUDIES: POPULAR CULTURE for details.

[Tolkien, J. R. R.]

NIEKAS

See the section on SPECIALIZED TOPICS AND INTERDISCIPLINARY STUDIES: POPULAR CULTURE for details.

[Vergil]

VERGILIAN SOCIETY NEWSLETTER

EDITORIAL ADDRESS:
Howard T. Easton, Secretary
The Vergilian Society, Inc.
12 Pleasant View Drive
Exeter, New Hampshire 03833

SUBSCRIPTION ADDRESS:

same

PUBLISHED: Annually (usually)
COST: Free to members.

CIRCULATION: 1,700

CONTENTS: Matters pertaining to society activities and members; resumes of books published under the aegis of the society; news of annual Classical Summer School and of annual essay contest.

UNSOLICITED MSS. WELCOME? Yes, if brief.
MS. LENGTH: Short paragraph; submit TWO copies.
EDITOR'S DECISION: 4 weeks.
FROM ACCEPTANCE TO PUBLICATION: 4 weeks.
PAYMENT/OFFPRINTS: None.
GENERAL: First issue, February, 1961. Usual publication length, 4 pages.
BACK ISSUES: Available free from the Society Secretary.

[Vergil]

VERGILIUS

EDITORIAL ADDRESS:
J. A. S. Evans, Editor
Department of Classics
University of British Columbia
Vancouver 8, British Columbia, Can.

SUBSCRIPTION ADDRESS:
The Vergilian Society
Charles Twichell, Treasurer
The Choate School
Wallingford, Connecticut 06492

PUBLISHED: Annually
COST: 1 yr.—$3.50 (includes membership in Vergilian Society).

CIRCULATION: Over 1,500

CONTENTS: Articles on Vergilian studies, ancient history, archeology of Italy; Vergilian bibliography; book reviews; occasional photographs. Example: "Amata: Vergil's Other Tragic Queen."

UNSOLICITED MSS. WELCOME? Yes; submissions acknowledged.
SPECIFICALLY WELCOMED: Augustan literature.
MS. LENGTH: 2,000 words; submit ONE copy.
STYLE REQUIREMENTS: MLA STYLE SHEET; footnotes follow article.
COPYRIGHT: Editor who will release it to authors on request.
EDITOR'S DECISION: 1 month.
FROM ACCEPTANCE TO PUBLICATION: 1 year.

PAYMENT/OFFPRINTS: Six copies of issue. More at discount.
REJECTED MSS.: Returned.
GENERAL: First issue, 1954. Usual publication length, 56 pages.
BACK ISSUES: Available from Charles Twichell, Treasurer, at $3.50 each.

[Voltaire, François]

STUDIES ON VOLTAIRE AND THE EIGHTEENTH CENTURY

See the section on BIBLIOGRAPHICAL AND LIBRARY RESOURCES for details.

[Wallace, Edgar]

EDGAR WALLACE SOCIETY NEWSLETTER

See the section on SPECIALIZED TOPICS AND INTERDISCIPLINARY STUDIES: POPULAR CULTURE for details.

[Waugh, Evelyn]

EVELYN WAUGH NEWSLETTER

EDITORIAL ADDRESS: SUBSCRIPTION ADDRESS:
Paul A. Doyle, Editor
English Department   same
Nassau Community College
State University of New York
Garden City, New York 11530

PUBLISHED: Tri-annually   CIRCULATION: 200
(Spring, Autumn, Winter)
COST: 1 yr.—$2.00.

CONTENTS: Critical analyses and notes about Evelyn Waugh's novels and other books; biographical data; unpublished letters by and about Waugh; extensive bibliographies of works by and about Waugh; book reviews; studies of influences of books and writers on his work; Waugh's relationships with and attitudes toward other writers; European views and critiques of Waugh and his reputation; notes on latest reprints and reference to Waugh in media; published for the first time a movie scenario by Waugh.

UNSOLICITED MSS. WELCOME? Yes; submissions acknowledged.

SPECIFICALLY WELCOMED: Critical analyses and notes on Waugh's novels and other books; notes on any phase of books or biography.
MS. LENGTH: 200-800 words; submit ONE copy.
STYLE REQUIREMENTS: MLA STYLE SHEET.
COPYRIGHT: Author.
EDITOR'S DECISION: 2-3 weeks.
FROM ACCEPTANCE TO PUBLICATION: 1-2 years.
PAYMENT/OFFPRINTS: Three offprints given to author.
REJECTED MSS: Returned.
GENERAL: First issue, Spring, 1967. Usual publication length, 10 pages.
BACK ISSUES: Available from editorial office for $.90 each or $2.50 per year. Volumes for 1970, 1971, and 1972 are still in print, although remaining copies for 1970 are few. Issues for 1967, 1968, and 1969 are now collectors' items; no back issues are available.

[Wollstonecraft, Mary, and other women writers]

MARY WOLLSTONECRAFT NEWSLETTER

EDITORIAL ADDRESS: SUBSCRIPTION ADDRESS:
Janet M. Todd, Editor
Department of English   same
University of Puerto Rico
Mayaguez, Puerto Rico 00708

PUBLISHED: Irregularly   CIRCULATION: 75, plus libraries
COST: First volume—$4.00; others—$2.00.

CONTENTS: Exchange of ideas on women writers of the 18th and 19th centuries, as well as the presentation of women by male writers during this period; articles clarifying the position of many of the women writers who seem on the border between literature and history; checklists of work in progress on Mary Wollstonecraft; reviews; notes. Example: "Jane Austen as a Political Novelist: Class Consciousness in EMMA."

UNSOLICITED MSS. WELCOME? Yes; submission acknowledged.
SPECIFICALLY WELCOMED: Literary and historical studies of women writers; general topics concerning women.
MS. LENGTH: 3,000-5,000 words.
STYLE REQUIREMENTS: None.
COPYRIGHT: MARY WOLLSTONECRAFT NEWSLETTER.
EDITOR'S DECISION: 1 month.
FROM ACCEPTANCE TO PUBLICATION: Varies.
PAYMENT/OFFPRINTS: No payment. Offprints provided if requested.
REJECTED MSS.: Returned.
GENERAL: First issue, July, 1972. Usual publication length, 30 pages.
BACK ISSUES: Available from editorial office at prices stated above.

[Woolf, Virginia]

VIRGINIA WOOLF QUARTERLY: A SCHOLARLY, CRITICAL, AND LITERARY JOURNAL

EDITORIAL ADDRESS:
Suzanne Henig, Editor
6762 Cibola Road
San Diego, California 92120

SUBSCRIPTION ADDRESS:
San Diego State Foundation
5402 College Avenue
San Diego, California 92115

PUBLISHED: Quarterly
COST: 1 yr.—$10.00; 2 yrs.—$20.00.

CONTENTS: Literary scholarship, criticism, memoirs related to Virginia Woolf, the Bloomsbury Group, their friends, associates, and the times in which they lived; bibliographies. Example: "The Evolution of the Interludes in THE WAVES."

UNSOLICITED MSS. WELCOME? Yes.
STYLE REQUIREMENTS: MLA STYLE SHEET.
COPYRIGHT: VIRGINIA WOOLF QUARTERLY.
GENERAL: First issue, Fall, 1972. Usual publication length, 155 pages. "With every two year subscription there will be included gratis the limited first edition of an unpublished work by Virginia Woolf."

[Wordsworth, Coleridge, Hazlitt, et al]

THE WORDSWORTH CIRCLE

EDITORIAL ADDRESS:
Marilyn Gaull, Editor
Department of English
Temple University
Philadelphia, Pennsylvania 19122

SUBSCRIPTION ADDRESS:

same

PUBLISHED: Quarterly
COST: 1 yr.—$4.00; 2 yrs.—$7.00; 3 yrs.—$9.00.

CIRCULATION: 600

CONTENTS: Essays; brief notes; queries; abstracts of papers; reports on meetings; conference proceedings; research in progress; auctions; exhibitions; library collections; special events; advance notices of works to be published; suggestions for projects; book reviews. Example: "Fact, Fiction, and the Introductions to the Waverly Novels."

UNSOLICITED MSS. WELCOME? Yes, but only articles from subscribers will be considered; submissions acknowledged.

SPECIFICALLY WELCOMED: Materials pertaining to writings and times of the first generation English romantics: Wordsworth, Coleridge, Hazlitt, DeQuincey, Lamb, Southey, the minor poets and popular writers.
MS. LENGTH: 20 pages or less; submit TWO copies.
STYLE REQUIREMENTS: University of Chicago's A MANUAL OF STYLE; footnotes follow essay.
COPYRIGHT: Marilyn Gaull.
EDITOR'S DECISION: 1-2 months.
FROM ACCEPTANCE TO PUBLICATION: 3-4 months.
PAYMENT/OFFPRINTS: Three complimentary copies of issue in which work is printed. Single copies available at $1.00 each.
REJECTED MSS.: Returned.
GENERAL: First issue, Winter, 1970. Usual publication length, 48 pages. Indexed by volume. United Kingdom subscriptions should be sent to: Basil Savage, The Lime Tree Bower Press, 46 Brookfield, Highgate West Hill, London N6, England.
BACK ISSUES: Available from editorial address at $1.00 each.

[Wordsworth, William]

THE WORDSWORTH SOCIETY: TRANSACTIONS (1882-1887)

William Knight, Editor

GENERAL: First issue, 1882.
BACK ISSUES: Two-volume facsimile reprint of TRANSACTIONS is available for $35.30 from : Dawson Reprint, Dawsons of Pall Mall, 16 Pall Mall, London, S. W. 1, England.

[Yeats, William Butler]

YEATS STUDIES: AN INTERNATIONAL JOURNAL

EDITORIAL ADDRESS:
Robert O'Driscoll and
Lorna Reynolds, Editors

SUBSCRIPTION ADDRESS:
Irish University Press
81 Merrion Square
Dublin 2
Ireland

PUBLISHED: Annually
COST: 1 yr.—$5.30 (£2.25) postpaid.

CONTENTS: Scholarly articles relating to William Butler Yeats, his work, his relatives, and those who knew him. Each issue centers around a theme, such as Yeats and the 1890s, Theatre and the Visual Arts, a centenary celebration of John M. Synge and Jack B. Yeats, Yeats and the Theatre, John Butler Yeats, and Yeats and the Occult; unpublished letters; illustrations. Examples: "Yeats, Synge and the Tragic Understanding"; "Poet and Designer: W. B. Yeats and Althea Gyles."

COPYRIGHT: Irish University Press.
GENERAL: First issue, 1971. Usual publication length, 140-210 pages.
BACK ISSUES: Available from Irish University Press.

II
AGE
AND/OR
NATIONALITY

COMPREHENSIVE

IN

SCOPE

ARIEL: A REVIEW OF INTERNATIONAL ENGLISH LITERATURE

EDITORIAL ADDRESS:
George Wing, Editor
University of Calgary
Calgary, Alberta T2N 1N4
Canada

SUBSCRIPTION ADDRESS:
Secretary
ARIEL
University of Calgary
2920—24 Avenue N.W.
Calgary, Alberta T2N 1N4
Canada

PUBLISHED: Quarterly (Jan., Apr., July, Oct.)
COST: 1 yr.—$6.00; single issue—$1.50.

CIRCULATION: 1,200

CONTENTS: Critical articles on literature in English from any country and any period; translations; book reviews; poetry. Example: "Tabula Rasa: Shelley's Metaphor of the Mind"; "Mordecai Richler as Satirist."
UNSOLICITED MSS. WELCOME? Yes; submissions acknowledged.
SPECIFICALLY WELCOMED: Scholarly essays.
MS. LENGTH: 2,500-4,000 words; submit ONE copy.
STYLE REQUIREMENTS: MLA STYLE SHEET; footnotes follow article.
COPYRIGHT: Author, if ARIEL is acknowledged in any reprint.
EDITOR'S DECISION: 2-3 months.
FROM ACCEPTANCE TO PUBLICATION: Less than 1 year, at present.
PAYMENT/OFFPRINTS: Poems normally paid $15.00. Eight complimentary copies of journal.
REJECTED MSS.: Returned.
GENERAL: First issue, January, 1970. Usual publication length, 100-110 pages.
BACK ISSUES: Available from the subscription address. Volumes 1 and 2—$10.00 each; Volume 3—$12.00; singles issues of Volumes 1 and 2—$2.50 each; single issues of Volume 3—$3.00 each.

THE ARYAN PATH

See the section on GENERAL REVIEW for details.

BOOKS ABROAD: AN INTERNATIONAL LITERARY QUARTERLY

EDITORIAL ADDRESS:
Ivar Ivask, Editor
1000 Asp Avenue, Room 214
Norman, Oklahoma 73069

SUBSCRIPTION ADDRESS:
Circulation Department
University of Oklahoma Press
1005 Asp Avenue
Norman, Oklahoma 73069

PUBLISHED: Quarterly (Jan.,   CIRCULATION: 3,000
Apr., July, Oct.)
COST: 1 yr.—$8.00 (institutions—$15.00); 2 yrs.—$14.50 (institutions—$25.00); single copy—$2.50.

CONTENTS: Articles on contemporary world literature plus reviews of current publications in belles-lettres in some 60 languages; often article section is devoted to a special symposium (for example, the Winter 1973 issue contained a symposium on "The Writer as Critic of His Age"); photographs of authors.

UNSOLICITED MSS. WELCOME? Unsolicited articles welcome only if they concentrate on current belles-lettres; no unsolicited reviews welcome; submissions acknowledged.
SPECIFICALLY WELCOMED: Critical articles on current authors and/or their works, and articles on literary movements.
MS. LENGTH: 12 pages maximum; submit ONE copy.
COPYRIGHT: University of Oklahoma Press.
EDITOR'S DECISION: 1 month.
FROM ACCEPTANCE TO PUBLICATION: 1 to 2 years.
PAYMENT/OFFPRINTS: Authors of articles receive 3 copies of issue in which work appears; authors of articles appearing in symposia issues receive (if bound offprints exist) 12 bound offprints of whole article section; authors of "Commentary" articles (4-8 pages) appearing in symposia issues receive (if bound offprints exist) 2 bound offprints of whole article section; authors of articles appearing in varia issues (no bound offprints) receive 25 offprints of their individual article stapled into offprint covers; authors of "Commentary" articles appearing in varia issues receive 10 offprints of their individual article stapled into offprint covers; reviewers receive one clipping of each review published.
REJECTED MSS.: Returned.
GENERAL: First issue, January, 1927. Usual publication length, 180 pages.
BACK ISSUES: Recent issues (not older than 2 years) available from University of Oklahoma Press at $2.50 each. Others from Kraus Reprint Company; consult it for cost of older issues.

CLA JOURNAL: OFFICIAL QUARTERLY PUBLICATION OF THE COLLEGE LANGUAGE ASSOCIATION

EDITORIAL ADDRESS: SUBSCRIPTION ADDRESS:
Therman B. O'Daniel, Editor
Morgan State College   same
Baltimore, Maryland 21239

PUBLISHED: Quarterly (Sept.,   CIRCULATION: 1,000
Dec., Mar., June)
COST: 1 yr.—$6.00 in U.S.A.; $6.50 in Canada; $7.00 elsewhere; single copy—$2.00; special issue—$2.50.

CONTENTS: Scholarly articles on literary authors; all types of literature; literary bibliographies; in any language; some attention to methodology in language and literature; some linguistic studies; and some attention to African, Caribbean, and Black Studies; book reviews. Examples: "Caribbean French Literature in Proper Perspective"; "The Achievement of Gwendolyn Brooks."

UNSOLICITED MSS. WELCOME? Yes; submissions acknowledged.
SPECIFICALLY WELCOMED: Scholarly treatment of any language or literature.
MS. LENGTH: At present, 10-12 pages; submit TWO copies.
STYLE REQUIREMENTS: MLA STYLE SHEET, but prefer footnotes at bottom of page.
COPYRIGHT: The College Language Association.
EDITOR'S DECISION: At present, because of backlog, 3-6 months.
FROM ACCEPTANCE TO PUBLICATION: About 1 year.
PAYMENT/OFFPRINTS: No payment. Offprints are supplied by printer at author's cost.
REJECTED MSS.: Returned.
GENERAL: First issue, 1957. Usual publication length, 124-148 pages.
BACK ISSUES: Available, at present, from the Editor at $5.00, if available, except for the very rare issues ($10.00 each) in Vol. I. Later, back issues may be handled by a reprint company.

COMPARATIVE LITERATURE

EDITORIAL ADDRESS:
Thomas R. Hart, Editor
c/o Department of Romance Languages
University of Oregon
Eugene, Oregon 97403

SUBSCRIPTION ADDRESS:

same

PUBLISHED: Quarterly
CIRCULATION: 2,150
COST: 1 yr.—$4.50; single copy—$1.25; special rates to members of American Comparative Literature Association and Canadian Comparative Literature Association.

CONTENTS: Four or 5 articles and 8 to 12 book reviews addressed to specialists in comparative literature; selected list of books received from publishers; occasional announcements concerning the American, Canadian, and International Comparative Literature Associations, and CL itself; contributions are most frequently in English, French, German, or Spanish, but are welcomed in other languages as well.

UNSOLICITED MSS. WELCOME? Yes, but editor prefers to solicit book reviews; submissions acknowledged.

SPECIFICALLY WELCOMED: Theoretical or analytical literary studies dealing with authors/works in two different languages, from the earliest times to the present; particularly welcome are longer studies on comprehensive topics and on problems of literary criticism.
MS. LENGTH: 3,500-15,000 words; submit the ORIGINAL.
STYLE REQUIREMENTS: MLA STYLE SHEET.
COPYRIGHT: University of Oregon, but permission to reprint granted by Editor of CL.
EDITOR'S DECISION: 1-4 weeks.
FROM ACCEPTANCE TO PUBLICATION: 6 months.
PAYMENT/OFFPRINTS: Five free copies of issue in which work appears. Contributors may buy offprints in additional 100's.
REJECTED MSS. Returned, by 1st class mail.
GENERAL: First issue, Winter, 1949. Usual publication length, 96 pages. CL carries no advertising, does not publish translations, and cannot provide complimentary or examination copies. CL requires exclusive submission; a xerox or carbon copy will not be considered without author's assurance that the article is not being submitted simultaneously to another journal, and will not be, until a decision has been reached by CL.
BACK ISSUES: Available from editorial address at $1.25 each.

COMPARATIVE LITERATURE STUDIES

EDITORIAL ADDRESS:
Alfred Owen Aldridge, Editor
383 Lincoln Hall
University of Illinois
2054 Foreign Language Building
Urbana, Illinois 61801

SUBSCRIPTION ADDRESS:
University of Illinois Press
Urbana, Illinois 61801

PUBLISHED: Quarterly (Mar., June, Sept., Dec.)
CIRCULATION: 800
COST: 1 yr.—$7.50, $8.00 outside U.S.; single copy—$2.00, except for special issues.

CONTENTS: Articles on literary history and the history of ideas, with particular emphasis on European literary relations with both North and South America.

UNSOLICITED MSS. WELCOME? Yes; submissions acknowledged.
MS. LENGTH: No preference; submit the ORIGINAL.
STYLE REQUIREMENTS: MLA STYLE SHEET.
COPYRIGHT: University of Illinois.
EDITOR'S DECISION: 6 months.
PAYMENT/OFFPRINTS: Contributor receives 25 free offprints and 2 copies of journal.
REJECTED MSS.: Returned.

GENERAL: First issue, 1963. Usual publication length, 100-125 pages. Occasionally articles and reviews written in French are accepted.
BACK ISSUES: Available from University of Illinois Press.

CRITIQUE: STUDIES IN MODERN FICTION

EDITORIAL ADDRESS:
James Dean Young, Editor
Department of English
Georgia Institute of Technology
Atlanta, Georgia 30332

SUBSCRIPTION ADDRESS:

same

PUBLISHED: Tri-annually CIRCULATION: 1,200-1,300
COST: 1 yr.—$7.50 in U.S.; $8.00 elsewhere; single copy—$3.00.

CONTENTS: Critical essays on fiction of contemporary writers of all countries; principal interest in essays on writers who are alive and without great reputations; issues often devoted to one or two authors; occasional checklists of primary and secondary works of individual authors (books, short fiction, plays, non-fiction, uncollected stories, articles and reviews, biography and criticism, tapes and discs, bibliographies, interviews). Example: "Pattern and Structure in Robbe-Grillet's LA MAISON DE RENDEZ-VOUS."

UNSOLICITED MSS. WELCOME? Yes; submissions not acknowledged.
SPECIFICALLY WELCOMED: Critical essays about the fiction of American, English, European, African, and Asian authors, particularly those writing today.
MS. LENGTH: 4,000-6,000 words; submit ONE copy.
STYLE REQUIREMENTS: MLA STYLE SHEET; footnotes follow essay.
COPYRIGHT: CRITIQUE.
EDITOR'S DECISION: 4-6 months.
FROM ACCEPTANCE TO PUBLICATION: Less than 1 year.
PAYMENT/OFFPRINTS: Five free copies of issue in which essay appears. 25 free offprints.
REJECTED MSS.: Returned, frequently criticized.
GENERAL: First issue, 1956. Usual publication length, 112 pages. All quotations in other languages should be translated into English.
BACK ISSUES: Available from editorial address at $2.50 each. Reprint of Vols. 1-10 available from Kraus Reprint Company. Microfiche of Vols. 1-12 available from NCR/Microcard Editions, 365 South Oak Street, West Salem, Wisconsin 54669.

THE EMPORIA STATE RESEARCH STUDIES

EDITORIAL ADDRESS:
William H. Seiler, Charles E. Walton, and Green D. Wyrick, Editors
The School of Graduate and Professional Studies
Kansas State Teachers College
1200 Commercial Street
Emporia, Kansas 66801

SUBSCRIPTION ADDRESS:

same

PUBLISHED: Quarterly (Sept., Dec., Mar., June)
COST: Free.

CIRCULATION: 1,500

CONTENTS: Generally a long critical paper, frequently about one author and his works, such as "Daylight and Darkness, Dream and Delusion: The Works of Truman Capote."

UNSOLICITED MSS. WELCOME? No. "Papers published in this periodical are written by faculty members of the Kansas State Teachers College of Emporia and by either undergraduate or graduate students whose studies are conducted in residence under the supervision of a faculty member of the college."
COPYRIGHT: Author may copyright if he so desires.
PAYMENT/OFFPRINTS: Ten free copies; additional copies at $1.00 each.
GENERAL: First issue, September, 1952. Usual publication length, 50 pages. Write editor for subjects of back issues.
BACK ISSUES: Available from editorial address at $1.00 each.

THE EXPLICATOR

EDITORIAL ADDRESS:
J. Edwin Whitesell, Managing Editor
Virginia Commonwealth University
901 West Franklin Street
Richmond, Virginia 23220

SUBSCRIPTION ADDRESS:

same

PUBLISHED: Monthly except July and August (no issues those months)
COST: 1 yr.—$3.00.

CIRCULATION: 2,600

CONTENTS: Short articles of explication de texte—any literature in any language—but articles must be written in English.

UNSOLICITED MSS. WELCOME? Yes; submissions acknowledged.
SPECIFICALLY WELCOMED: Strictly explication de texte.
MS. LENGTH: Under 1,500 words; submit TWO copies.
STYLE REQUIREMENTS: MLA STYLE SHEET, except no footnotes.
COPYRIGHT: THE EXPLICATOR.

EDITOR'S DECISION: 6-8 months.
FROM ACCEPTANCE TO PUBLICATION: 1 year or less.
PAYMENT/OFFPRINTS: Ten complimentary offprints.
REJECTED MSS.: Returned.
GENERAL: First issue, October, 1942. Usual publication length, 16 pages.
BACK ISSUES: Unbound issues for most of the last five volumes available from Managing Editor at $.50 each. Volumes available from Kraus-Thomson Organization, Ltd., at $8.50 each.

FAR-WESTERN FORUM

EDITORIAL ADDRESS: SUBSCRIPTION ADDRESS:
Elie R. Vidal, Editor
20 Poppy Lane
Berkeley, California 94708

PUBLISHED: Tri-annually.
COST: 1 yr.—$6.00; single copy—$2.25.

CONTENTS: Scholarly essays, articles, and book reviews concerning ancient and modern literatures of all genres.

UNSOLICITED MSS. WELCOME? Yes.
SPECIFICALLY WELCOMED: Thorough, original analyses of significant aspects of literature.
STYLE REQUIREMENTS: MLA STYLE SHEET.
GENERAL: First issue, February, 1974. Articles may be written in English and other languages.

THE INTERNATIONAL FICTION REVIEW

See the section on GENRES.

THE LITERARY HALF-YEARLY

See the section on LITERARY REVIEWS for details.

MODERN FICTION STUDIES

See the section on GENRES.

MOSAIC: A JOURNAL FOR THE COMPARATIVE STUDY OF LITERATURE AND IDEAS

EDITORIAL ADDRESS:
R. G. Collins and Kenneth McRobbie,
Editors
Room 208 Tier Building
The University of Manitoba
Winnipeg R3T 2N2
Canada

SUBSCRIPTION ADDRESS:
Subscription Manager
same

PUBLISHED: Quarterly   CIRCULATION: 1,400
COST: 1 yr.—$8.00; 2 yrs.—$14.00; single copy—$2.25.

CONTENTS: Articles by scholars of international reputation, from several countries, and from practicing writers, on various aspects of world literature, with perspective on the humanities, ideas, problems of form and authorship.

UNSOLICITED MSS. WELCOME? Yes; submissions acknowledged.
SPECIFICALLY WELCOMED: Articles.
MS. LENGTH: 5,000 words; submit ONE copy.
STYLE REQUIREMENTS: MLA STYLE SHEET.
COPYRIGHT: University of Manitoba Press.
EDITOR'S DECISION: Up to 3 months.
FROM ACCEPTANCE TO PUBLICATION: 9 months.
PAYMENT/OFFPRINTS: Honoraria by special arrangement with practicing authors. 25 free offprints; extra by arrangement.
REJECTED MSS.: Returned.
GENERAL: First issue, Fall, 1967. Usual publication length, 170 pages.
BACK ISSUES: Available from editorial office at $1.75 and $2.25 each (with volume five).

THE NEW YORK REVIEW OF BOOKS

EDITORIAL ADDRESS:
Editor
250 West 57th Street
New York, New York 10019

SUBSCRIPTION ADDRESS:
Subscriber Service
P. O. Box 1161, Ansonia Station
New York, New York 10023

PUBLISHED: Biweekly   CIRCULATION: 100,000
COST: 1 yr. (22 issues)—$10.00 (plus $2 postage, Canada and PAU; $4 elsewhere); single copy—$.60.

CONTENTS: Critical reviews by well known writers who "deal with the whole intellectual and cultural setting of the books under scrutiny." Examples: William Gass on Gertrude Stein; Stephen Spender on Orwell; Norman Mailer on LAST TANGO IN PARIS.

GENERAL: First issue, 1963.

THE NEW YORK TIMES BOOK REVIEW

EDITORIAL ADDRESS: SUBSCRIPTION ADDRESS:
Editor
229 West 43rd Street same
New York, New York 10036

PUBLISHED: Weekly
COST: 1 yr.—$13.00; Canada, $14.65; other foreign countries, $16.25.

CONTENTS: Critiques, reviews of 25-30 books, such as COLLECTED POEMS OF JOHN WHEELWRIGHT or THE GREAT AMERICAN NOVEL; features, such as "Writer as Wretch and Rat"; departments, such as Best Seller List, Criminals at Large, For Young Readers, New and Recommended; illustrated.

UNSOLICITED MSS. WELCOME? No.
COPYRIGHT: The New York Times Co.
GENERAL: First issue, 1895. Usual publication length, 32-40 pages.

NOTES ON CONTEMPORARY LITERATURE

EDITORIAL ADDRESS: SUBSCRIPTION ADDRESS:
W. S. Doxey and Ben W. Griffith,
Editors same
550 North White
Carrollton, Georgia 30117

PUBLISHED: 5 times yearly (Jan., Mar., CIRCULATION: 200
May, Sept., Nov.)
COST: 1 yr.—$3.50 in U.S. and Canada; elsewhere by arrangement.

CONTENTS: Short articles about literature, all types, all languages, since 1940. Example: "Poe's PYM and Nabokov's PALE FIRE."

UNSOLICITED MSS. WELCOME? Yes; submissions not acknowledged.
SPECIFICALLY WELCOMED: Notes on Post-World War II prose, fiction, poetry, drama.
MS. LENGTH: Up to 1,000 words; submit ONE copy.
STYLE REQUIREMENTS: Prefer MLA STYLE SHEET.
COPYRIGHT: William S. Doxey and Ben W. Griffith, but will assign on request.
EDITOR'S DECISION: 8 weeks.
FROM ACCEPTANCE TO PUBLICATION: 8 weeks or less.
PAYMENT/OFFPRINTS: Two copies of issue.
REJECTED MSS.: Returned.
GENERAL: First issue, January, 1971. Usual publication length, 16 pages.
BACK ISSUES: Some available from editorial office at $1.00 each; $5.00 per volume.

OUTLOOK: A MAGAZINE OF LITERARY CRITICISM

EDITORIAL ADDRESS:
Shikai Dojin, Editor
Kyoto University
Faculty of Letters
Yoshidahonmachi, Sakyo-ku
Kyoto
Japan

SUBSCRIPTION ADDRESS:

same

GENERAL: This periodical had not arrived by the time the entry went to press. Potential subscribers, contributors, or collectors will have to write the editor to see whether the journal still exists, and if so, to inquire about details of manuscript submission, style, back issues, and the like.

PMLA: PUBLICATIONS OF THE MODERN LANGUAGE ASSOCIATION OF AMERICA

EDITORIAL ADDRESS:
William D. Schaefer, Editor
Modern Language Association
62 Fifth Avenue
New York, New York 10011

SUBSCRIPTION ADDRESS:

same

PUBLISHED: Six times yearly (Jan., Mar., May, Sept., Oct., Nov.)
CIRCULATION: 34,000
COST: 1 yr.—$25, U.S. and Canada; $18, foreign; $7, student; $35, joint husband-and-wife (MLA membership dues include subscription).

CONTENTS: Four quarterly issues of scholarship on the modern languages and literatures, including a Forum section of controversy and debate; forthcoming meetings and conferences, professional notes and comment. Also, a Directory issue of professional information and a Program issue detailing the MLA Annual Convention. Example: "Blake: A Crisis of Love and Jealousy."

UNSOLICITED MSS. WELCOME? Yes, but only by member of the MLA; submissions acknowledged.
MS. LENGTH: 2,500-12,500 words; submit ORIGINAL only.
STYLE REQUIREMENTS: MLA STYLE SHEET.
COPYRIGHT: Modern Language Association.
EDITOR'S DECISION: 60 days.
FROM ACCEPTANCE TO PUBLICATION: At present, 30 months; in 1975, 9-12 months.
PAYMENT/OFFPRINTS: 25 "offprints" prepared by stapling articles together; authors can purchase at cost professionally prepared offprints from the printer.
REJECTED MSS.: Returned.
GENERAL: First issue, 1884. Publication length varies. Articles appear in English, French, and other modern languages. Submit with article an abstract.

BACK ISSUES: Available from Kraus Reprint; inquire cost. Also available from Xerox University Microfilm.

RACKHAM LITERARY STUDIES

EDITORIAL ADDRESS:
Sheryl Pearson, Editor
4019 Modern Language Building
The University of Michigan
Ann Arbor, Michigan 48104

SUBSCRIPTION ADDRESS:

same

PUBLISHED: Biannually (Fall, Spring)   CIRCULATION: 1,000
COST: 1 yr.—$3.00.

CONTENTS: Articles and notes on language, literature, and criticism; short translations; reviews. Articles published in the following fields: American and European literatures, Near and Far Eastern literatures, Latin American literature, Classical Studies, Slavic literatures, Comparative literature; RLS is presently published by graduate students in literature at The University of Michigan; however, contributors need not be graduate students. Examples: "Ben Jonson's Prosody"; "Myth, Folklore, and Literature: A Bibliography."

UNSOLICITED MSS. WELCOME? Yes; submissions acknowledged.
SPECIFICALLY WELCOMED: Articles (10-35 pp.), notes, short translations, reviews.
MS. LENGTH: 3-30 pages; submit TWO xeroxes.
STYLE REQUIREMENTS: MLA STYLE SHEET, English only.
COPYRIGHT: "Editors and Editorial Board of RLS."
EDITOR'S DECISION: 6-12 weeks.
FROM ACCEPTANCE TO PUBLICATION: 2-6 months.
PAYMENT/OFFPRINTS: Three complimentary copies of issue.
REJECTED MSS. Not returned.
GENERAL: First issue, Fall, 1971. Usual publication length, 110-140 pages. RLS contains the regular department "Doctoral Dissertations in Progress at the University of Michigan"; illustrations are provided by the University of Michigan Museum of Art collections.
BACK ISSUES: Limited supply available from editorial address.

REVIEW OF NATIONAL LITERATURES

EDITORIAL ADDRESS:
Anne Paolucci, Editor
Perboyre Hall
St. John's University
Jamaica, New York 11432

SUBSCRIPTION ADDRESS:
Robert A. Rosenbaum,
Managing Editor
same

PUBLISHED: Biannually   CIRCULATION: 3,000
COST: 1 yr.—$5.00 in U.S., $6.00 elsewhere; 3 yrs.—$13.00 in U.S.; $16.00 elsewhere; single copy—$2.50.

CONTENTS: Essays on a national culture, a representative theme, author, literary movement or critical tendency for comparative study. Example: "Racial Terms for Africans in Elizabethan Usage."

UNSOLICITED MSS. WELCOME? No; people well known in the particular field about which RNL is writing are contacted; submissions acknowledged.
MS. LENGTH: 18 pages; submit TWO copies.
COPYRIGHT: REVIEW OF NATIONAL LITERATURES.
FROM ACCEPTANCE TO PUBLICATION: Months.
PAYMENT/OFFPRINTS: Payment varies (per printed page) per issue. Six free copies of book, plus discount on reprints.
REJECTED MSS.: Returned.
GENERAL: First issue, 1970. Usual publication length, 200-300 pages.
BACK ISSUES: Available from editorial address at $2.50 for Vol. I, 1; $3.00 for Vol. I, 2; $3.50 for Vol. II, 1; $4.00 for Vol. II, 2 and Vol. III, 1; $4.50 for Vol. III, 2.

REVUE DE LITTÉRATURE COMPARÉE

EDITORIAL ADDRESS:
J. Body, Editor
3, rue des Tanneurs
Université de Tours
37041 Tours, France

SUBSCRIPTION ADDRESS:
Librairie Didier
15, rue Cujas
75005 Paris
France

PUBLISHED: Quarterly
COST: 80 French Francs

CONTENTS: Articles; notes and documents; book reviews; reports. Examples: " 'God's Country': Man and the Land in the Canadian Novel"; "Wilhelm Wetz: A Neglected Comparatist of the Turn of the Century."

UNSOLICITED MSS. WELCOME? Yes; submissions acknowledged.
SPECIFICALLY WELCOMED: Comparative works.
MS. LENGTH: Short and compact.
STYLE REQUIREMENTS: None.
COPYRIGHT: Librairie Didier.
EDITOR'S DECISION: 6 months.
FROM ACCEPTANCE TO PUBLICATION: One year.
PAYMENT/OFFPRINTS: 15-30 offprints.
REJECTED MSS.: Not returned.
GENERAL: First issue, 1921. Usual publication length, 160 pages. Articles may be written in French or English.
BACK ISSUES: Available from Librairie Didier.

STUDIA MONASTICA

EDITORIAL ADDRESS:
Rev. Josep Massot Muntañer
Abadia de Montserrat
Barcelona
Spain

SUBSCRIPTION ADDRESS:
Publicacions de l'Abadia de Montserrat
Apartat 244
Barcelona
Spain

PUBLISHED: Biannually
CIRCULATION: 800
COST: 1 yr.—400 pts. in Spain; $10.00 elsewhere.

CONTENTS: Articles concerning monastic history and literary works of all ages and all countries; bibliographic articles; author and subject bibliographies.

UNSOLICITED MSS. WELCOME? Yes; submissions acknowledged.
SPECIFICALLY WELCOMED: Scientific and unpublished articles.
MS. LENGTH: No preference; submit ONE copy.
COPYRIGHT: Author.
EDITOR'S DECISION: A few days.
FROM ACCEPTANCE TO PUBLICATION: At least 6 months.
PAYMENT/OFFPRINTS: 25 free offprints.
REJECTED MSS. Returned.
GENERAL: First issue, 1959. Usual publication length, 225 pages. Articles may be written in English, Spanish, French, Italian, and other European languages.
BACK ISSUES: Available from subscription address at $5.00 each.

STUDIES IN THE 20TH CENTURY

See the section on AGE/OR NATIONALITY: EUROPEAN.

STYLE

See the section on SPECIALIZED TOPICS AND INTERDISCIPLINARY STUDIES: THEORY OF LITERATURE for details.

SYMPOSIUM: A QUARTERLY JOURNAL IN MODERN FOREIGN LITERATURES

EDITORIAL ADDRESS:
J. H. Matthews, Editor
210 H. B. Crouse Hall
Syracuse University
Syracuse, New York 13210

SUBSCRIPTION ADDRESS:
Syracuse University Press
Box 8, University Station
Syracuse, New York 13210

PUBLISHED: Quarterly
COST: 1 yr.—$8.00; single copy—$2.25; double issues—$4.50.

CIRCULATION: 1,000

CONTENTS: Scholarly essays about modern FOREIGN languages and literature. (Essays concerning exclusively American or British literature are not acceptable.) Since Fall-Winter, 1969, special numbers have alternated with general issues. Example: "Claude Simon's LE PALACE: A Paradigm of Otherness."

UNSOLICITED MSS. WELCOME? Yes; submissions acknowledged if decision is delayed.
SPECIFICALLY WELCOMED: Literate contributions.
MS. LENGTH: 25-30 pages; submit ONE copy.
STYLE REQUIREMENTS: MLA STYLE SHEET.
COPYRIGHT: Syracuse University Press.
EDITOR'S DECISION: 1 week.
FROM ACCEPTANCE TO PUBLICATION: Up to 1 year.
PAYMENT/OFFPRINTS: Five complimentary copies of issue. No offprints.
REJECTED MSS.: Returned.
GENERAL: First issue, November, 1946. Usual publication length since Spring, 1969, 96 pages. Articles may be written in English, French, German, Italian, Portuguese, or Spanish.
BACK ISSUES: Available from Syracuse University Press. Consult press about prices.

TAMKANG REVIEW: A JOURNAL MAINLY DEVOTED TO COMPARATIVE STUDIES BETWEEN CHINESE AND FOREIGN LITERATURES

See the section on AGE/OR NATIONALITY: ASIAN for details.

TEXAS STUDIES IN LITERATURE AND LANGUAGE: A JOURNAL OF THE HUMANITIES

EDITORIAL ADDRESS:
Ernest J. Lovell, Jr.
Executive Editor
University Station, Box 7577
Austin, Texas 78712

SUBSCRIPTION ADDRESS:
Periodicals Manager
University of Texas Press
P. O. Box 7819
Austin, Texas 78712

PUBLISHED: Quarterly
CIRCULATION: 950
COST: 1 yr.—$8.00, individual; $10.00, institution; single copy—$2.75.

CONTENTS: Articles concerning all areas of literature, linguistics, philosophy, social studies, and non-technical science. Examples: "The Darkening Sun of Tess Durbeyfield"; "Carew Redivivus."

UNSOLICITED MSS. WELCOME? Yes, but no book reviews or brief notes; submissions acknowledged.
MS. LENGTH: No limit; submit ONE copy.
STYLE REQUIREMENTS: Generally MLA STYLE SHEET; footnotes numbered consecutively and at end of article.
COPYRIGHT: TSLL.
EDITOR'S DECISION: 3 months.
FROM ACCEPTANCE TO PUBLICATION: 6 months.
PAYMENT/OFFPRINTS: 50 free bound copies of all published articles.
REJECTED MSS.: Returned.
GENERAL: First issue, 1911. Usual publication length, over 500 pages. Send an abstract of 200 words or less with article.
BACK ISSUES: Available from Johnson Reprint Co. at $3.25 each.

THE TIMES LITERARY SUPPLEMENT

EDITORIAL ADDRESS:
Arthur Crook, Editor
Nestor House
Printing House Square
London EC4P 4DE
England

SUBSCRIPTION ADDRESS:
Subscription Department
same

PUBLISHED: Weekly
CIRCULATION: 40,000
COST: 12p.

CONTENTS: Anonymous reviews of academic books, fiction, and children's books from all languages and on many subjects; a few 'signed articles' on literary or closely related subjects. Some "Second Strings" articles have been on "Milton as a Political Theorist," "Michelangelo's Poetry," "Alexander Pope as a Gardener," and "Lewis Carroll as a Logician."

UNSOLICITED MSS. WELCOME? Articles of general literary interest are, but unsolicited reviews are not; submissions acknowledged.
MS. LENGTH: 800-900 words; submit ONE copy.
STYLE REQUIREMENTS: None.
COPYRIGHT: Times Newspapers Ltd.
EDITOR'S DECISION: Within 1 month.
FROM ACCEPTANCE TO PUBLICATION: Within 6 months.
PAYMENT/OFFPRINTS: £12 per 1,000 words.
REJECTED MSS. Returned.
GENERAL: First issue, January, 1902. Usual publication length, 28 pages.
BACK ISSUES: Available from Subscription Department Times Newspapers. Price varies according to age.

TWENTIETH CENTURY LITERATURE

EDITORIAL ADDRESS: SUBSCRIPTION ADDRESS:
William E. Grant, Editor
2021 North Western Avenue same
Los Angeles, California 90027

PUBLLSHED: Quarterly CIRCULATION: 2,150
COST: 1 yr.—$6.00 (individuals), $8.00 (institutions) in U.S.; $7.00 (individuals), $9.00 (institutions) elsewhere; single copy—$2.00, plus $.50 for foreign orders.

CONTENTS: Scholarly and critical articles on all aspects of modern and contemporary literature, including articles in English on writers in other languages.

UNSOLICITED MSS. WELCOME? Yes, except brief notes and book reviews; submissions acknowledged.
SPECIFICALLY WELCOMED: Analyses of modern literature.
MS. LENGTH: No limit; submit ONE copy.
STYLE REQUIREMENTS: MLA STYLE SHEET; footnotes, numbered consecutively, follow article.
COPYRIGHT: Immaculate Heart College Press.
EDITOR'S DECISION: 10-12 weeks.
FROM ACCEPTANCE TO PUBLICATION: Within the year.
PAYMENT/OFFPRINTS: 25 free offprints; additional ones available at cost.
REJECTED MSS.: Returned.
GENERAL: First issue, April, 1955. Usual publication length, 80 pages.
BACK ISSUES: Available from Kraus Reprint Co. and Xerox University Microfilms. Consult above companies about prices.

TWENTIETH CENTURY STUDIES

EDITORIAL ADDRESS:
Guido Almansi, Editor
Eliot College
University of Kent
Canterbury
England

SUBSCRIPTION ADDRESS:
Scottish Academic Press
25 Perth Street
Edinburgh EH3 5DW
Scotland
United Kingdom

PUBLISHED: Biannually
COST: 1 yr.—$5.50.

CIRCULATION: 250

CONTENTS: Articles that cross the barriers between different subjects in the "Humanities" (with authors from Europe, U.S.A., and elsewhere). Subjects of past volumes include: national tradition and European heritage; treatment of sexual themes in the modern novel; structuralism; Ireland; culture and ideology in Post-war Italy; directions in the nouveau roman; Russian formalism. Example essays: "Claude Simon: the narrator and his double"; "Poetry in Northern Ireland."

UNSOLICITED MSS. WELCOME? Query before submitting article.
SPECIFICALLY WELCOMED: Articles concerning the history of ideas, literary criticism, and cultural affairs since 1900.
MS. LENGTH: 5,000 words.
PAYMENT/OFFPRINTS: 12 offprints of author's article.
GENERAL: First issue, 1968. Usual publication length, 140 pages. Articles may be written in English, French, German, Italian, Spanish.
BACK ISSUES: Available from Scottish Academic Press at $2.75 each.

THE VIRGINIA QUARTERLY REVIEW: A NATIONAL JOURNAL OF LITERATURE AND DISCUSSION

EDITORIAL ADDRESS:
Charlotte Kohler, Editor
One West Range
Charlottesville, Virginia 22903

SUBSCRIPTION ADDRESS:
Circulation Manager
same

PUBLISHED: Quarterly
COST: 1 yr.—$7.00; single copy—$2.00.

CONTENTS: Articles on literature of any age or area; articles discussing a wide range of topics.

UNSOLICITED MSS. WELCOME? Yes; submissions not acknowledged.
MS. LENGTH: 3,000-7,000 words; submit ONE copy.
COPYRIGHT: Copyright will be transferred to author on request.
EDITOR'S DECISION: 2 weeks to 2 months.
PAYMENT/OFFPRINTS: $5 per printed page of 350 words, payable on publication. Printer will provide offprints at a price.

REJECTED MSS.: Returned.
GENERAL: First issue, April, 1925.
BACK ISSUES: 1925-1960 available from Kraus Thompson Reprint Co.: 1960—from editorial office.

YEARBOOK OF COMPARATIVE AND GENERAL LITERATURE

EDITORIAL ADDRESS:　　　　　　SUBSCRIPTION ADDRESS:
Horst Frenz, Editor-in-Chief
Comparative Literature Office　　　　　same
Ballantine Hall 402
Indiana University
Bloomington, Indiana 47401

PUBLISHED: Annually　　　　　　CIRCULATION: 1,800
COST: 1 yr.—$5.00 (20% discount for individual members of ACLA, MLA, or NCTE and book dealers).

CONTENTS: Literary essays dealing with methods, problems, and theories of comparative literature and/or criticism; reviews of recent translations and professional works; the annual comprehensive list of literary works translated into English and published in the United States; "News and Notes." Occasionally, proceedings of conferences and symposia are included. Examples: "Aesthetic Gothic Horror"; "Islam in World Literature."

UNSOLICITED MSS. WELCOME? Yes; submissions acknowledged.
MS. LENGTH: 8-14 pages (double columns); submit at least TWO copies.
STYLE REQUIREMENTS: MLA STYLE SHEET.
COPYRIGHT: Editorial Committee of the YEARBOOK.
EDITOR'S DECISION: 3 months.
FROM ACCEPTANCE TO PUBLICATION: 1 year.
PAYMENT/OFFPRINTS: 5 to 10 complimentary offprints; additional copies may be ordered at cost.
REJECTED MSS.: Returned.
GENERAL: First issue, 1953. Usual publication length, 150-200 pages.
BACK ISSUES: Volumes I-XI are reprints and may be obtained from Russell and Russell, Inc., 122 East 42nd Street, New York, N.Y. 10017, at $8.50 per volume. Volumes XII-XXII may be ordered from the Comparative Literature Office at $5.00 list price, with 20% discount for book dealers and individual members of ACLA, MLA, or NCTE.

AMERICAN

AMERICAN HUNGARIAN REVIEW

See the section on AGE AND/OR NATIONALITY: EUROPEAN.

AMERICAN LITERARY REALISM: 1870-1910

EDITORIAL ADDRESS:
Clayton L. Eichelberger, Editor
Department of English
The University of Texas
at Arlington
Arlington, Texas 76010

SUBSCRIPTION ADDRESS:

same

PUBLISHED: Quarterly (Winter—Feb., Spring—May, Summer—Sept., Fall—Nov.)
COST: 1 yr.—$5.00 in U.S; $6.00 elsewhere; single copy—$1.50 in U.S.; $2.00 elsewhere.

CONTENTS: Bibliographic essays about the works of American authors writing between 1870-1910; bibliographies of primary materials (separate publications of poems, novels, stories, plays; periodical contributions; newspaper contributions; anthology selections from separate publications; manuscripts and letters) and secondary materials (major dissertations and theses; major biographical and critical articles; book reviews) of individual authors; reviews of books about American authors; photographs of authors; previously unpublished manuscripts and letters. Example: "Charles Farrar Browne (1834-1867, pseud. Artemus Ward)."

UNSOLICITED MSS. WELCOME? Yes, if of bibliographical or textual nature; many articles are solicited; submissions acknowledged.
SPECIFICALLY WELCOMED: Bibliographical and textual articles about the works of American authors from 1870-1910; occasional critical studies.
MS. LENGTH: 15-20 pages; submit TWO copies.
STYLE REQUIREMENTS: ALR Style.
COPYRIGHT: Department of English, The University of Texas at Arlington.
EDITOR'S DECISION: 3 weeks.
FROM ACCEPTANCE TO PUBLICATION: Under 1 year.
PAYMENT/OFFPRINTS: Two copies of issue; 5 to 10 tearsheets. Additional copies at cost.
REJECTED MSS.: Returned.
GENERAL: First issue, Fall, 1967. Usual publication length, 90-100 pages. Subscriptions are by calendar year only.
BACK ISSUES: Available from editorial address at $2.00 each.

AMERICAN LITERARY SCHOLARSHIP: AN ANNUAL

EDITORIAL ADDRESS:
J. Albert Robbins, Editor
Department of English
Indiana University
Bloomington, Indiana 47401

PURCHASE ADDRESS:
Duke University Press
6697 College Station
Durham, North Carolina 27708

PUBLISHED: Annually
COST: Inquire of Duke University Press.

CONTENTS: In evaluative essays, 18 scholar specialists review the year's work in their fields, both articles and books, to describe and judge the merit of individual pieces, give a sense of trends in scholarship and criticism, and suggest areas for fruitful research. Major authors are treated in separate chapters; other authors and topics are organized by genre and period. Examples: "Emerson, Thoreau, and Transcendentalism"; "Nineteenth-Century Poetry."

UNSOLICITED MSS. WELCOME? No. ALS contributors are chosen by invitation of the editor. Authors of articles and books are urged to send review copies to the editor.
COPYRIGHT: Duke University Press.
GENERAL: First issue, 1963. Usual publication length, 425-450 pages. ALS 1968-1972 (edited by J. Albert Robbins); ALS 1963-1967 (edited by James L. Woodress). All are in print. All volumes indexed. Paperback copies distributed free to dues-paid members of American Literature Section of the Modern Language Association.
BACK ISSUES: Available from Duke University Press at $7.00 each for 1963-1968 volumes; $8.75 each for 1969-1970 volumes.

AMERICAN LITERATURE: A JOURNAL OF LITERARY HISTORY, CRITICISM, & BIBLIOGRAPHY

EDITORIAL ADDRESS:
Arlin Turner, Editor
Duke University Press
6667 College Station
Durham, North Carolina 27708

SUBSCRIPTION ADDRESS:

same

PUBLISHED: Quarterly (Nov., Jan., Mar., May)
CIRCULATION: 6,000
COST: 1 yr.—$7.00 in U.S.; Canada and Pan-American countries add $.40 postage; all others add $.75; $3.50 for students.

CONTENTS: Critical essays about the works of American authors; notes and queries; reviews of books about American literature; research in progress (dissertations on individual authors, on topics of a general nature; other research; articles on American literature appearing in current periodicals); brief mention of books and bibliographies recently published. Example: "REDBURN and the Failure of Myth Criticism."

UNSOLICITED MSS. WELCOME? Yes; submissions acknowledged.
SPECIFICALLY WELCOMED: Scholarly essays about American literature.
MS. LENGTH: 12-20 pages; submit TWO copies.
STYLE REQUIREMENTS: MLA STYLE SHEET; University of Chicago's A MANUAL OF STYLE.
COPYRIGHT: Duke University Press.
EDITOR'S DECISION: 2-3 months.
FROM ACCEPTANCE TO PUBLICATION: 6 months.
PAYMENT/OFFPRINTS: Fifty free offprints and 2 copies of issue in which article appears. Book review offprints not given. Additional offprints at cost.
REJECTED MSS.: Returned, sometimes criticized.
GENERAL: First issue, 1929. Usual publication length, 200-250 pages.
BACK ISSUES: Available from Duke University Press at $15.00 for each year; $3.50 for each issue.

AMERICAN LITERATURE ABSTRACTS: A REVIEW OF
CURRENT SCHOLARSHIP IN THE FIELD OF AMERICAN LITERATURE

See the section on BIBLIOGRAPHICAL AND LIBRARY RESOURCES for details.

AMERICAN NOTES & QUERIES

EDITORIAL ADDRESS:
Lee Ash, Editor
31 Alden Road
New Haven, Connecticut 06515

SUBSCRIPTION ADDRESS:

same

GENERAL: First issue, 1962. This periodical had not arrived by the time the entry went to press. Potential subscribers, contributors, or collectors will have to write the editor to see whether the journal still exists, and if so, to inquire about details of manuscript submission, style, back issues, and the like.

AMERICAN QUARTERLY

EDITORIAL ADDRESS:
Hennig Cohen, Editor
Box 30
Bennett Hall
University of Pennsylvania
Philadelphia, Pennsylvania 19104

SUBSCRIPTION ADDRESS:

same

PUBLISHED: 5 times yearly
COST: 1 yr.—$8.00; single copy—$1.60.

CIRCULATION: 4,500

CONTENTS: Critical interdisciplinary articles on American life (literary, historical, mass cultural topics, for example) from colonial times to present; essays on teaching and research techniques in the American civilization field; book reviews; Summer issue devoted to bibliography; illustrations.

UNSOLICITED MSS. WELCOME? Yes.
MS. LENGTH: 15-20 pages.
STYLE REQUIREMENTS: MLA STYLE SHEET.
COPYRIGHT: AMERICAN QUARTERLY.
PAYMENT/OFFPRINTS: Copy of journal.
GENERAL: First issue, 1949.

AMERICAN STUDIES

EDITORIAL ADDRESS:
Stuart Levine, Editor
University of Kansas
1135 Maine Street
Lawrence, Kansas 66044

SUBSCRIPTION ADDRESS:

same

PUBLISHED: Biannually
COST: 1 yr.—$4.00; $2.50 for students; $6.00 for libraries.

CIRCULATION: 1,000

CONTENTS: Articles read by specialists in the various disciplines concerned with American culture: history, literature, political science, sociology, anthropology, art, architecture, and music. Example: "The Southern Agrarians: H. L. Mencken, and the Quest for Southern Identity." Editor accepts articles by people in these fields when the work which they have to report is clearly of interest to Americanists in general.

UNSOLICITED MSS. WELCOME? Yes; submissions acknowledged.
SPECIFICALLY WELCOMED: Those which use literature to reach sociocultural conclusions. AS does not accept articles which deal primarily with aesthetics or with literary history.
MS. LENGTH: 10-20 pages; submit TWO ribbon copies.
STYLE REQUIREMENTS: MLA STYLE SHEET, but with footnotes doublespaced at the end of article.

COPYRIGHT: AMERICAN STUDIES.
EDITOR'S DECISION: 1-9 months.
FROM ACCEPTANCE TO PUBLICATION: Within 1 year.
PAYMENT/OFFPRINTS: No payment. $25.00 for first 100 offprints. Must have requests for offprints before press time.
REJECTED MSS.: Returned.
GENERAL: First issue, 1960. Usual publication length, 110 pages. Bulk orders for classroom adoption are available for most issues at a reduced price which is generally cheaper than paperback anthologies.
BACK ISSUES: Available from editorial address at $4.00 each. All copies are currently available.

AMERICAN STUDIES: AN INTERNATIONAL NEWSLETTER

EDITORIAL ADDRESS:
Ronald J. Fonte, Editor
2101 Constitution Avenue, N.W.
Washington, D.C. 20418

SUBSCRIPTION ADDRESS:
same

PUBLISHED: Tri-annually (Oct., Dec., May)
CIRCULATION: 13,000

COST: Free of charge to American Studies scholars.

CONTENTS: Bibliographical essays in American studies; essays, letters and news items on American studies abroad; occasional photographs. Examples: "American Studies in Yugoslavia"; "Autobiography and American Culture."

UNSOLICITED MSS. WELCOME? Discouraged; most essays solicited; submissions acknowledged.
SPECIFICALLY WELCOMED: Items of interest from and about American studies programs, especially abroad.
MS. LENGTH: Essays, 2,000-3,000 words; letters, 300-400 words; submit ONE copy.
STYLE REQUIREMENTS: University of Chicago's A MANUAL OF STYLE preferred; Sage acceptable.
COPYRIGHT: Public Domain.
EDITOR'S DECISION: 2 months.
FROM ACCEPTANCE TO PUBLICATION: 9 months.
PAYMENT/OFFPRINTS: $100 to $200. 25 copies of magazine.
REJECTED MSS.: Returned.
GENERAL: First issue, August, 1962, as AMERICAN STUDIES NEWS: AN INTERNATIONAL NEWSLETTER; May, 1970, as AS: AIN. Usual publication length, 58 pages.
BACK ISSUES: Available from editorial address free, if in print; 5 cents per page, if out of print.

AMERICAN TRANSCENDENTAL QUARTERLY: JOURNAL OF NEW ENGLAND WRITERS

See the section on SINGLE AND MULTIPLE AUTHOR FOCUS: AMERICAN for details.

AMERICAN WEST

EDITORIAL ADDRESS:
Donald E. Bower, Editor
American West Publishing Company
599 College Avenue
Palo Alto, California 94306

SUBSCRIPTION ADDRESS:
same

PUBLISHED: 6 times yearly (Jan., Mar., May, July, Sept., Nov.)
COST: 1 yr.—$9.00; single copy—$2.00.

CIRCULATION: 30,000

CONTENTS: Researched articles about the western scene: its past, present, and future; pictorial features; book reviews; essays.

UNSOLICITED MSS. WELCOME? Yes; submissions acknowledged.
SPECIFICALLY WELCOMED: Non-fiction articles on the West. Editors are particularly interested in 1,000-word articles about unusual people, places, or events of the Old West.
MS. LENGTH: 3,000-4,000 words; submit ONE copy.
STYLE REQUIREMENTS: Popular, non-annotated, but good research.
COPYRIGHT: Publisher.
EDITOR'S DECISION: 4 weeks.
FROM ACCEPTANCE TO PUBLICATION: 3-6 months.
PAYMENT/OFFPRINTS: $150 to $300. Two complimentary copies of the magazine issue in which work appears.
REJECTED MSS.: Returned.
GENERAL: First issue, Winter, 1964. Usual publication length, 64 pages.
BACK ISSUES: Available from the Publisher at $2.50 each.

AMERIKASTUDIEN (formerly JAHRBUCH FÜR AMERIKASTUDIEN)

EDITORIAL ADDRESS:
Martin Christadler, Editor
Amerika-Institut der Universität
6000 Frankfurt
Kettenhofweg 130
Germany

SUBSCRIPTION ADDRESS:
J. B. Metzlersche Verlagsbuchhandlung
7000 Stuttgart 1
Kernerstr. 43, Postfach 529
Germany

PUBLISHED: Biannually CIRCULATION: 500
COST: 1 yr.—DM 42.- (DM 30.-for students and members of the German Association for American Studies).

CONTENTS: Articles in all fields of American Studies, especially interdisciplinary studies. Contents of some numbers: The Fifties; After the New Criticism—recent approaches to literature in the United States; History & Historiography in the United States, etc.—articles concerning the theory and method of American Studies and their further development; all aspects of teaching American Studies.

UNSOLICITED MSS. WELCOME? Yes; submissions acknowledged.
MS. LENGTH: 20 pages maximum (30 ms. pages); submit TWO copies.
STYLE REQUIREMENTS: MLA STYLE SHEET; MS. 1½-space typed; abstract of 200 words.
COPYRIGHT: J. B. Metzler, Stuttgart, for 1 year after publication, then author.
EDITOR'S DECISION: 5-6 weeks.
FROM ACCEPTANCE TO PUBLICATION: 10-12 months.
PAYMENT/OFFPRINTS: DM 200.- per 16 pages. 20 offprints free; additional offprints at author's own expense.
REJECTED MSS.: Returned.
GENERAL: First issue, 1956. Usual publication length, 200 pages.
BACK ISSUES: Available from Carl Winter Universitätsverlag, 6900 Heidelberg 1, Lutherstr. 59, Postfach 1866, Germany.

ARIZONA AND THE WEST

EDITORIAL ADDRESS: SUBSCRIPTION ADDRESS:
Harwood P. Hinton, Editor
Library 308 same
University of Arizona
Tucson, Arizona 85721

PUBLISHED: Quarterly CIRCULATION: 1,200
COST: 1 yr.—$7.50; single copy—$2.00. No discount. All foreign subscriptions add $.50.

CONTENTS: Each issue dedicated to an outstanding figure in Western Belles Lettres; articles dealing with the history of the Trans-Mississippi West; one edited document or a bibliography; book reviews and book notes. Maps and pictures included when appropriate.

UNSOLICITED MSS. WELCOME? Yes; submissions acknowledged.
SPECIFICALLY WELCOMED: Scholarly articles, with footnotes, on new material or new interpretations.
MS. LENGTH: 25-30 pages; submit ONE copy.
STYLE REQUIREMENTS: The Turabian MANUAL FOR WRITERS OF TERM PAPERS, THESES AND DISSERTATIONS.

COPYRIGHT: Arizona Board of Regents.
EDITOR'S DECISION: 1-2 months.
FROM ACCEPTANCE TO PUBLICATION: 3 months to 1 year.
PAYMENT/OFFPRINTS: 25 free offprints in covers; additional ones at $10.00 per 25.
REJECTED MSS.: Returned.
GENERAL: First issue, Spring, 1959. Usual publication length, 120 pages.
BACK ISSUES: Vol. V to date available from editorial office at $1.50 each through Vol. XV, or $5.00 per volume; Vol. XVI onward at $2.00 each, or $7.50 per volume. Vols. I-IV from used book stores such as Guidon Books, Main Street, Scottsdale, Arizona, or Overland Book Shop, Hedrick Dr., Tucson, Arizona.

THE BILINGUAL REVIEW/LA REVISTA BILINGÜE

EDITORIAL ADDRESS:
Gary Keller, Editor
Department of Romance Languages
City College of the City
University of New York
New York, New York 10011

SUBSCRIPTION ADDRESS:

same

PUBLISHED: Tri-annually.
COST: 1 yr.—$6.00; 2 yrs.—$11.00; 3 yrs.—$15.00.

CONTENTS: Articles concerning linguistics and literature of English-Spanish bilingualism in the United States.

UNSOLICITED MSS. WELCOME? Yes.
SPECIFICALLY WELCOMED: Material about research, scholarly, critical, and creative fiction dealing with Hispanic life in the United States.
GENERAL: First issue, October, 1973.

CALIFORNIA QUARTERLY

EDITORIAL ADDRESS:
Elliot Gilbert, Editor
100 Sproul Hall
University of California
Davis, California 95616

SUBSCRIPTION ADDRESS:

same

PUBLISHED: Quarterly (Summer, Fall, Winter, Spring)
CIRCULATION: 800
COST: 1 yr.—$5.00 or £2.00; single copy—$1.50 or 60p.

CONTENTS: Fiction; poetry; translations, book reviews, interviews, and original critical essays; graphic art and b&w photography. Example: "Interview: Herbert Gold."

UNSOLICITED MSS. WELCOME? Yes; submissions not acknowledged.
SPECIFICALLY WELCOMED: Works by West coast writers and material about West coast, but primary interest is quality writing.
MS. LENGTH: Up to 8,000 words, fiction and articles; submit ONE copy.
STYLE REQUIREMENTS: Emphasis on quality; no particular style requirements.
COPYRIGHT: Reverts to author.
EDITOR'S DECISION: 4-8 weeks.
FROM ACCEPTANCE TO PUBLICATION: 3-6 months.
PAYMENT/OFFPRINTS: Two copies of journal and year's subscription.
REJECTED MSS.: Returned.
GENERAL: First issue, Summer, 1971. Usual publication length, 80-85 pages.
BACK ISSUES: Available from editorial address at $1.00 for #1, $1.50 each for #2-#4, or at yearly rate for #1-#4.

THE CANADIAN REVIEW OF AMERICAN STUDIES

EDITORIAL ADDRESS:
Robert L. White, Editor
Stong College
York University
Downsview 463, Ontario
Canada

SUBSCRIPTION ADDRESS:
Department of English
York University
Downsview, Ontario
Canada

PUBLISHED: Biannually (Spring, Fall)
COST: 1 yr.—$8.00 (includes membership in Canadian Association for American Studies); $5.00, institutions.

CONTENTS: Scholarly articles centered on the interplay between the cultures of Canada and the United States, both past and present; essays on American society and intellectual history; review essays. Examples: "Sexual Longing in Richard Henry Dana, Jr.'s American Victorian Diary"; "Form in Salinger's Short Fiction."

UNSOLICITED MSS. WELCOME? Yes.
MS. LENGTH: 3,000-5,000 words; submit TWO copies.
STYLE REQUIREMENTS: MLA STYLE SHEET.
GENERAL: First issue, 1970. Usual publication length, 55-75 pages.

CEAA NEWSLETTER

EDITORIAL ADDRESS:
M. J. Bruccoli, Director
CEAA, Editor
Department of English
University of South Carolina
Columbia, South Carolina 29208

SUBSCRIPTION ADDRESS:

same

PUBLISHED: Annually
COST: Free.

CIRCULATION: 750

CONTENTS: Material relating to the Center for Editions of American Authors and editorial problems.

UNSOLICITED MSS. WELCOME? Yes; submissions acknowledged.
SPECIFICALLY WELCOMED: Bibliographical, textual, editorial notes and queries.
MS. LENGTH: 300 words; submit ONE copy.
STYLE REQUIREMENTS: MLA STYLE SHEET.
COPYRIGHT: No copyright.
EDITOR'S DECISION: 1 week.
PAYMENT/OFFPRINTS: Five copies of issue.
REJECTED MSS.: Returned.
GENERAL: First issue, 1968. Usual publication length, 12 pages.
BACK ISSUES: Out of print.

COLBY LIBRARY QUARTERLY

EDITORIAL ADDRESS:
Richard Cary, Editor
Colby College
Waterville, Maine 04901

SUBSCRIPTION ADDRESS:
Kenneth P. Blake, Librarian
same

PUBLISHED: Quarterly (Mar., June, Sept., Dec.)
COST: 1 yr.—$3.00.

CIRCULATION: 700

CONTENTS: Biographical and critical essays about Maine authors, such as Sarah Orne Jewett, Edwin Arlington Robinson, Jacob Abbott, Edna St. Vincent Millay, and Kenneth Roberts; some essays about authors from other countries and states, such as Sean O'Casey, who are well represented by special collections in the Colby College Library; essays about others who touch on Maine life, letters, and arts; bibliographical checklists (books, proof sheets and periodicals inscribed by presentation copies of books and periodicals to, manuscripts and letters written by, and sent to, and about an author in the library collection); occasional picture of handwritten manuscript.

UNSOLICITED MSS. WELCOME? Yes; submissions not acknowledged.

SPECIFICALLY WELCOMED: Essays about Maine authors.
MS. LENGTH: 20 pages; submit ONE copy.
STYLE REQUIREMENTS: None specific.
COPYRIGHT: Not copyrighted.
EDITOR'S DECISION: 3 weeks.
FROM ACCEPTANCE TO PUBLICATION: 1 year or so.
PAYMENT/OFFPRINTS: Ten copies of issue in which essay appears; more at cost on request.
REJECTED MSS.: Returned.
GENERAL: First issue, January, 1943. Usual publication length, 50-60 pages.
BACK ISSUES: Available from editorial address at $.85 each; also from Xerox University Microfilms, Inc.

CONTEMPORARY LITERARY SCENE

EDITORIAL ADDRESS: SUBSCRIPTION ADDRESS:
David Madden, Editor
614 Park Boulevard   same
Baton Rouge, Louisiana 70806

PUBLISHED: Annually

CONTENTS: Articles about events during the year in the areas of theater, film, short story, novel, poetry, and television in the United States; general articles on the same subjects; interviews; lists; chronology of year's literary events; book lists.

UNSOLICITED MSS. WELCOME? Yes; submissions not acknowledged.
MS. LENGTH: 2,000-3,000 words; submit original.
STYLE REQUIREMENTS: Excellence; non-academic style; lively reportage, personalized (but not breezy) essays.
COPYRIGHT: Author, after one year.
EDITOR'S DECISION: 1 month or less.
FROM ACCEPTANCE TO PUBLICATION: About 6 months.
PAYMENT/OFFPRINTS: About $200; One hardcover copy of annual.
REJECTED MSS.: Returned.
GENERAL: First issue, February, 1974. Usual publication length, **400 pages.**

EARLY AMERICAN LITERATURE

EDITORIAL ADDRESS: SUBSCRIPTION ADDRESS:
Everett Emerson, Editor
Bartlett Hall   same
University of Massachusetts
Amherst, Massachusetts 01002

PUBLISHED: Tri-annually
COST: 1 yr.—$5.00; 3 yrs.—$14.00; membership in group included; library subscriptions same but do not include group membership.

CONTENTS: Critical essays about the works of American writers from 1600-1820; reviews of books about early American authors and their books, pamphlets, and essays; occasional issues in tribute to an Honored Scholar of the Early American Literature Group with a bibliography of that scholar's writings (books, editions, articles); occasional photographs. Example: "Freneau's 'Indian Burial Ground' and Keats' 'Grecian Urn.' "

UNSOLICITED MSS. WELCOME? Yes; submissions acknowledged.
SPECIFICALLY WELCOMED: Researched and critical essays about early American authors, intellectual and literary history.
MS. LENGTH: 4-40 pages; submit ONE copy.
STYLE REQUIREMENTS: MLA STYLE SHEET; footnotes follow article; should include abstract.
COPYRIGHT: Early American Literature Group.
EDITOR'S DECISION: 3 months.
FROM ACCEPTANCE TO PUBLICATION: 15 months.
PAYMENT/OFFPRINTS: Twelve offprints; more by order.
REJECTED MSS.: Returned.
GENERAL: First issue, 1966. Usual publication length, 96-110 pages. Started out in 1966 as a newsletter by the MLA Conference on Colonial Literature.
BACK ISSUES: Available from editorial office at $5.00 per volume.

ESQ: A JOURNAL OF THE AMERICAN RENAISSANCE
(formerly the EMERSON SOCIETY QUARTERLY founded
by Kenneth W. Cameron)

See the section on SINGLE AND MULTIPLE AUTHOR FOCUS: AMERICAN for details.

THE GREAT LAKES REVIEW: A JOURNAL OF MIDWEST CULTURE

EDITORIAL ADDRESS:　　　　　　　SUBSCRIPTION ADDRESS:
Gerald Nemanic and Gregory
Singleton, Co-editors　　　　　　　　　same
Northeastern Illinois University
Chicago, Illinois 60625

PUBLISHED: Biannually
COST: 1 yr.—$4.00 ($8.00 for libraries, other institutions).

CONTENTS: Scholarly essays on various aspects of Midwest culture, e.g., history, literature, fine arts, sociology, folklore; reviews of books dealing with Midwest culture; interviews; bibliographies; some poetry and fiction.

UNSOLICITED MSS. WELCOME? Yes.
SPECIFICALLY WELCOMED: Personal essays, fiction or poetry dealing with the Midwest; scholarly essays on Midwest literature; bibliographies of Midwest writers.
MS. LENGTH: Under 40 pages; submit ONE or TWO copies.
STYLE REQUIREMENTS: MLA STYLE SHEET.
PAYMENT/OFFPRINTS: Payment in subscriptions.
GENERAL: First issue, December, 1973. Usual publication length, 100 pages.
BACK ISSUES: Available from editorial address.

HAWAII REVIEW

EDITORIAL ADDRESS:
Dana Naone, Editor
Hemenway Hall
University of Hawaii
Honolulu, Hawaii 96822

SUBSCRIPTION ADDRESS:
c/o Managing Editor
same

PUBLISHED: Biannually   CIRCULATION: 2,500
COST: 1 yr.—$3.00; 2 yrs.—$5.00; single copy—$1.50.

CONTENTS: Fiction and poetry by young writers in Hawaii as well as elsewhere. Expansion to include criticism; interviews; reviews; other items of special interest; occasional photographs.

UNSOLICITED MSS. WELCOME? Yes; submissions acknowledged.
SPECIFICALLY WELCOMED: Fiction; poetry; reviews; interviews; criticism; particularly interested in presenting the work of young writers against a backround of more established writers in America and other cultures.
MS. LENGTH: Variable; submit ONE copy.
STYLE REQUIREMENTS: All styles acceptable.
COPYRIGHT: University of Hawaii unless otherwise specified by contributors.
EDITOR'S DECISION: 2-4 weeks.
FROM ACCEPTANCE TO PUBLICATION: Usually 3 months.
PAYMENT/OFFPRINTS: $30 per fiction piece; $10 per page or poem. Each contributor receives 3 copies.
REJECTED MSS.: Returned.
GENERAL: First issue, Winter, 1973. Usual publication length, 88 pages.
BACK ISSUES: Available from Managing Editor at $1.50 each.

THE HOLLINS CRITIC

EDITORIAL ADDRESS:
John Rees Moore, Editor
Box 9538
Hollins College, Virginia 24020

SUBSCRIPTION ADDRESS:

same

PUBLISHED: 5 times yearly (Feb., Apr., June, Oct., Dec.)
COST: 1 yr.—$2.00; $3.00 foreign.

CIRCULATION: 900-1,000

CONTENTS: Essay on particular work of one author; several poems. Examples: "The Artificial Demon: Joyce Carol Oates and the Dimensions of the Real"; "The Promised End: Bernard Malamud's THE TENANTS."

UNSOLICITED MSS. WELCOME? No; submissions acknowledged.
SPECIFICALLY WELCOMED: Poems.
MS. LENGTH: 4,500 words; submit ONE copy.
STYLE REQUIREMENTS: No footnotes.
COPYRIGHT: HOLLINS CRITIC; copyright transferred when an author publishes a book.
EDITOR'S DECISION: 2 months.
FROM ACCEPTANCE TO PUBLICATION: Within 1 year.
PAYMENT/OFFPRINTS: $100 for essayist; $20 each for poets. No offprints.
REJECTED MSS.: Returned.
GENERAL: First issue, February, 1964. Usual publication length, 12-16 pages.
BACK ISSUES: Available from editorial address at $.45 each in U.S. ($.65 xerox); $.70 each foreign ($1.25 xerox).

INDIAN JOURNAL OF AMERICAN STUDIES

EDITORIAL ADDRESS:
Sylvan Schendler, Editor
American Studies Research Centre
Hyderabad 500007
India

SUBSCRIPTION ADDRESS:

same

PUBLISHED: Biannually
COST: 1 yr.—$4.00 in U.S. and Canda; single copy—$2.00.

CIRCULATION: 1,500

CONTENTS: Scholarly articles and bibliography on the history, institutions, literature, and culture of the U.S.A.

UNSOLICITED MSS. WELCOME? Yes; submissions acknowledged.
SPECIFICALLY WELCOMED: Textual analyses; comparative studies.
MS. LENGTH: 20 pages; submit TWO copies.
STYLE REQUIREMENTS: MLA STYLE SHEET; University of Chicago's A MANUAL OF STYLE.

COPYRIGHT: American Studies Research Centre.
EDITOR'S DECISION: 2 months.
FROM ACCEPTANCE TO PUBLICATION: 3-4 months.
PAYMENT/OFFPRINTS: 25 offprints.
REJECTED MSS.: Returned.
GENERAL: First issue, July, 1969. Usual publication length, 100-130 pages.
IJAS REVIEWS, a book review supplement to the JOURNAL, is free to all subscribers of the Journal.
BACK ISSUES: Available from editorial address at $2.00 each.

JOURNAL OF AMERICAN FOLKLORE

See the section on FOLKLORE for details.

JOURNAL OF AMERICAN STUDIES

EDITORIAL ADDRESS:
Dennis Welland, Editor
Department of American Studies
University of Manchester
Manchester M13 9PL
England

SUBSCRIPTION ADDRESS:
Cambridge University Press
Bentley House, 200 Euston Road
London NW1 2DB, England
or
32 East 57th Street
New York, New York 10022

PUBLISHED: Tri-annually (Apr., Aug., Dec.)
COST: 1 yr.—£6.00.

CONTENTS: Articles by specialists of any nationality on American history, literature, politics, geography, and related subjects. Articles crossing the conventional lines of those disciplines are welcomed, as also are comparative studies of American and other cultures. Reviews and review articles are also published.

UNSOLICITED MSS. WELCOME? Yes; submissions acknowledged.
SPECIFICALLY WELCOMED: Scholarly and critical articles.
MS. LENGTH: 5,000 words; submit ONE copy.
STYLE REQUIREMENTS: See inside back cover of any issue.
COPYRIGHT: Cambridge University Press on behalf of the author.
EDITOR'S DECISION: 6-8 weeks.
FROM ACCEPTANCE TO PUBLICATION: Up to 1 year.
PAYMENT/OFFPRINTS: 25 free offprints; additional copies may be purchased.
REJECTED MSS. Returned, if international reply coupons sent.
GENERAL: First issue, April, 1967. Usual publication length, 128 pages.
BACK ISSUES: Available from subscription address. Apply to publisher for cost.

JOURNAL OF MODERN LITERATURE

EDITORIAL ADDRESS:
Maurice Beebe, Editor
Temple University
Philadelphia, Pennsylvania 19122

SUBSCRIPTION ADDRESS:
Motria Kushnir, Circulation Manager
same

PUBLISHED: 5 times yearly
COST: 1 yr.—$8.00; single copy—$2.00.

CIRCULATION: 2,000

CONTENTS: Research-based scholarly studies of the literature of the past century with main emphasis on major writers of the Modernist period from about 1885 to 1950; miscellany numbers alternate with special numbers devoted to individual writers or topics; an Annual Review supplement; photographs; occasional drawing.

UNSOLICITED MSS. WELCOME? Yes; submissions acknowledged.
SPECIFICALLY WELCOMED: Literary history and other forms of "hard scholarship" as opposed to top-of-the-head critical interpretation.
MS. LENGTH: Notes to monographs; submit ONE copy.
STYLE REQUIREMENTS: MLA STYLE SHEET.
COPYRIGHT: Temple University.
EDITOR'S DECISION: 5-8 weeks.
FROM ACCEPTANCE TO PUBLICATION: 1-2 years.
PAYMENT/OFFPRINTS: Varying honorarium for articles, notes, and essay-reviews. Free clippings of published articles.
REJECTED MSS. Returned; no criticism.
GENERAL: First issue, 1970. Usual publication length, 150-175 pages.

BACK ISSUES: Available from Circulation Manager at $2.00 each. Special charter rate—$5.00 a volume for orders beginning with Volume I, Number 1, and addressed to individual persons rather than to institutions. All subscriptions must begin with the first issue of a volume, and retroactive subscriptions will be accepted as long as copies remain available.

KANSAS QUARTERLY

EDITORIAL ADDRESS:
Harold Schneider and W. R. Moses, Editors
Department of English
Kansas State University
Manhattan, Kansas 66502

SUBSCRIPTION ADDRESS:
Business Manager
same

PUBLISHED: Quarterly
COST: 1 yr.—$7.50; single copy—$2.00 (in U.S., Canada, and Latin America); other countries add $.50.

CIRCULATION: 1,500

CONTENTS: Articles that explore and expose the culture, history, life-style, art, and writing of Mid-America; short stories; poems. Issues focus on a theme, such as Comedy and Satire in the Novel; Indians of the Mid-Plains; Writers and their Religions; Film. The Contemporary Theatre issue included such articles as "Modern Tragicomedy: Genre, Vision, Myth?" and "Harold Pinter—Past and Present."

UNSOLICITED MSS. WELCOME? Yes, but consult editor first.
MS. LENGTH: 15 pages.
STYLE REQUIREMENTS: MLA STYLE SHEET.
COPYRIGHT: KANSAS QUARTERLY.
EDITOR'S DECISION: 3 months.
PAYMENT/OFFPRINTS: Copy of issue.
GENERAL: First issue, 1872, as KANSAS MAGAZINE; 1968 as KQ.
BACK ISSUES: Available from Business Manager at $1.00 each for back numbers of KANSAS MAGAZINE (1947, 1950-1960, 1962-68); $2.00 each for those of KANSAS QUARTERLY.

THE LITERARY CRITERION

See the section on AGE AND/OR NATIONALITY: ENGLISH AND BRITISH COMMONWEALTH for details.

LITERATUR IN WISSENSCHAFT UND UNTERRICHT

See the section on AGE AND/OR NATIONALITY: EUROPEAN.

LOST GENERATION JOURNAL

EDITORIAL ADDRESS:
Tom Wood, Editor
547 South Gary Place, Apt. 1
Tulsa, Oklahoma 74104

SUBSCRIPTION ADDRESS:
same

PUBLISHED: Tri-annually (Jan., May, Sept.)
COST: 1 yr.—$5.00; single copy—$2.00.

CIRCULATION: 1,000

CONTENTS: Articles of great diversity that expand the examination of the Lost Generation era (1919-39) to include the graphic and performing arts. Editors are interested in more than a few writers and wish to examine them on a very broad plane and invite economists, sociologists, psychologists, historians, literary people to help in depth scrutiny of the people and events surrounding the lives of creative people who began their rise while in Europe during the years mentioned. For instance, Hemingway, who had first success in Europe, would be a primary figure to LGJ; Eugene O'Neill and F. Scott Fitzgerald (famous when they went to Europe) would be welcome, but secondary—unless tied to a primary person.

UNSOLICITED MSS. WELCOME? Yes; submissions acknowledged.
SPECIFICALLY WELCOMED: Little interest in plain bibliographical approaches; criticism is ordinarily confined to the book review section. However, criticism that spurns the esoteric and is documented beyond the author's skull can be very acceptable.
MS. LENGTH: 1,500-5,000 words; 1,500-3,000 words perferred; submit THREE copies.
STYLE REQUIREMENTS: MLA STYLE SHEET or Turabian's MANUAL preferred.
COPYRIGHT: LOST GENERATION JOURNAL through Literary Enterprises Inc.
EDITOR'S DECISON: 3-6 weeks.
FROM ACCEPTANCE TO PUBLICATION: 3-6 months, usually less.
PAYMENT/OFFPRINTS: Three copies of the issue. Offprints could be arranged in advance.
REJECTED MSS. Returned, at present.
GENERAL: First issue, May, 1973. Usual publication length, 40-60 pages.
BACK ISSUES: Available from editorial address at $2.00 each.

THE MARKHAM REVIEW

See the section on SINGLE AND MULTIPLE AUTHOR FOCUS: AMERICAN for details.

MIDAMERICA

EDITORIAL ADDRESS:
David D. Anderson, Editor
240 Ernst Bessey Hall
Michigan State University
East Lansing, Michigan 48824

SUBSCRIPTION ADDRESS:
Society for the Study of
Midwestern Literature
same

PUBLISHED: Annually
COST: 1 yr.—$5.00 (Price to members—$3.50).

CONTENTS: Scholarly essays on Midwestern writers and writing by members of the society.

UNSOLICITED MSS. WELCOME? Yes, by SSML members.
GENERAL: First issue, Fall, 1973.

THE MISSISSIPPI QUARTERLY:
THE JOURNAL OF SOUTHERN CULTURE

EDITORIAL ADDRESS:
Peyton W. Williams, Jr., Editor
Box 5272
Mississippi State, Mississippi 39762

SUBSCRIPTION ADDRESS:
Business Manager
Box 23
Mississippi State, Mississippi 39762

PUBLISHED: Quarterly
CIRCULATION: 600
COST: 1 yr.—$6.00 in U.S.; $3.00 for students; $7.00 foreign.

CONTENTS: Scholarly articles, notes, queries, and documents, and reviews of books on subjects dealing with the culture of the American South.

UNSOLICITED MSS. WELCOME? Yes; submissions acknowledged.
MS. LENGTH: Up to 4,000 words; submit TWO copies.
STYLE REQUIREMENTS: MLA STYLE SHEET.
COPYRIGHT: THE MISSISSIPPI QUARTERLY. Authors have complete freedom, on request, to publish their materials elsewhere; TMQ grants permission to others to reprint only with the written consent of the author, and remits to the author all payments received for such reprinting.
EDITOR'S DECISION: 1-3 months.
FROM ACCEPTANCE TO PUBLICATION: 3-18 months.
PAYMENT/OFFPRINTS: At least 15 bound offprints gratis; author may order others from printer.
REJECTED MSS. Returned.
GENERAL First issue, December, 1948. Usual publication length, 100-124 pages. Quarterly does not publish fiction, verse, or other creative materials.
BACK ISSUES: Limited quantities of some back files available from Business Manager at $1.50 each. Vols. X to date available from Xerox University Microfilms.

MOJO NAVIGATOR (E)

See section on LITERARY REVIEWS for details.

NATTY BUMPO REVIEW

See the section on SINGLE AND MULTIPLE AUTHOR FOCUS: AMERICAN for details.

THE NEW ENGLAND QUARTERLY

EDITORIAL ADDRESS:
Herbert Brown, Editor
Hubbard Hall
Bowdoin College
Brunswick, Maine 04011

SUBSCRIPTION ADDRESS:
Managing Editor
same

PUBLISHED: Quarterly (Mar., June, Sept., Dec.)
COST: 1 yr.—$8.00.

CIRCULATION: 2,000

CONTENTS: Articles on New England life and letters; literary history; criticism of major authors; memoranda and documents; essays on political and social topics; book reviews.

UNSOLICITED MSS. WELCOME? Yes; submissions acknowledged.
SPECIFICALLY WELCOMED: Literary criticism and history of New England.
MS. LENGTH: 20-25 pages; submit TWO copies.
STYLE REQUIREMENT: Consult any issue.
COPYRIGHT: The NEQ.
EDITOR'S DECISION: 6 weeks.
FROM ACCEPTANCE TO PUBLICATION: At least 1 year.
PAYMENT/OFFPRINTS: A year's complimentary subscription. 25 offprints.
REJECTED MSS.: Returned.
GENERAL: First issue, 1928. Usual publication, 164 pages.
BACK ISSUES: Available from Managing Editor's office at $2.50 each. First 40 volumes from AMS Reprint House.

THE NEWS-LETTER OF THE SOCIETY FOR THE STUDY OF SOUTHERN LITERATURE

EDITORIAL ADDRESS:

SUBSCRIPTION ADDRESS:
Louis D. Rubin, Jr.,
Secretary-Treasurer
Greenlaw 218
University of North Carolina
Chapel Hill, North Carolina 27514

PUBLISHED: Biannually
COST: 1 yr.—$1.00.

CONTENTS: News and notes of the S.S.S.L.; checklists of essays and articles on Southern literature; news about forthcoming publications.

GENERAL: First issue, 1968. Usual publication length, 10 pages.

NOTES ON MISSISSIPPI WRITERS

EDITORIAL ADDRESS:
Hilton Anderson, Editor
Box 433
Southern Station
Hattiesburg, Mississippi 39401

SUBSCRIPTION ADDRESS:

same

PUBLISHED: Tri-annually
COST: 1 yr.—$2.00; single copy—$1.00.

CIRCULATION: 200-300

CONTENTS: Articles on and interviews with Mississippi authors; bibliographies; notes; literary map of Mississippi on cover. Examples: "The Folk Humor of Joseph B. Cobb"; "Faulkner's Archaic Titles and the SECOND SHEPHERD'S PLAY."

UNSOLICITED MSS. WELCOME? Yes; submissions acknowledged.
SPECIFICALLY WELCOMED: Any material about Mississippi authors.
MS. LENGTH: Up to 2,000 words; submit ONE copy.
STYLE REQUIREMENTS: MLA STYLE SHEET; footnotes follow article.
COPYRIGHT: Not copyrighted.
EDITOR'S DECISION: 2-6 months.
FROM ACCEPTANCE TO PUBLICATION: 2 months to 1 year.
PAYMENT/OFFPRINTS: Ten free copies of issue.
REJECTED MSS.: Returned.
GENERAL: First issue, Spring, 1968. Usual publication length, 25-35 pages.
BACK ISSUES: Available from editorial office at $1.00 each.

OHIOANA QUARTERLY

EDITORIAL ADDRESS:
Bernice Williams Foley,
Managing Editor
The Martha Kinney Cooper Ohioana
Library Association
1109 Ohio Departments Building
Columbus, Ohio 43215

SUBSCRIPTION ADDRESS:

same

PUBLISHED: Quarterly (Fall, Winter, Spring. Summer)

CIRCULATION: 3,000

COST: 1 yr.—$7.50 for individuals (membership fee); $5.00 for libraries and schools.

CONTENTS: Literary—Ohio book reviews; articles relating to Ohio authors and their works; photographs. Example: "Professional Poetry in Ohio"; "Notes on Six Wittenberg Authors."

UNSOLICITED MSS. WELCOME? Only if they pertain to Ohio authors and their works; submissions acknowledged.
SPECIFICALLY WELCOMED: Ohio articles.
MS. LENGTH: 500-1,000 words; submit TWO copies.
STYLE REQUIREMENTS: Typewritten manuscript which OQ reserves the right to edit.
COPYRIGHT: Ohioana Library.
EDITOR'S DECISION: 1 month.
FROM ACCEPTANCE TO PUBLICATION: Uncertain.
PAYMENT/OFFPRINTS: One copy and any others on request ($.50 each for extras).
REJECTED MSS.: Returned.
GENERAL: First issue, 1958. Usual publication length, 48 pages.
BACK ISSUES: When available, from editorial address at $.50 each plus second class postage.

ORBIS LITTERARUM: INTERNATIONAL REVIEW OF LITERARY STUDIES

See the section on AGE AND/OR NATIONALITY: EUROPEAN.

PHILOLOGICAL QUARTERLY

See the section on AGE AND/OR NATIONALITY: EUROPEAN.

PLAYERS: THE MAGAZINE OF AMERICAN THEATRE

See the section on GENRES: THEATRE for details.

RESOURCES FOR AMERICAN LITERARY STUDY

EDITORIAL ADDRESS:
M. Thomas Inge, Maurice Duke,
Jackson R. Bryer, Editors
Department of English
Virginia Commonwealth University
Richmond, Virginia 23220

SUBSCRIPTION ADDRESS:
Business Office
Department of English
University of Maryland
College Park, Maryland 20740

PUBLISHED: Biannually (Spring, Autumn)
COST: 1 yr.—$8.00.

CIRCULATION: 400

CONTENTS: Primary materials for the study of American literature: 1) Annotated and evaluative checklists of critical and biographical scholarship on the significant works (prose, poetry, and drama) of major authors, or the total work of minor authors; 2) Evaluative bibliographical essays on major authors, works, genres, trends, and periods; 3) Informative accounts or catalogues of significant collections of research materials of literary and cultural interest available in archives and libraries, with special attention to recent acquisitions; 4) Edited correspondence, personal papers, unpublished materials, and other documents and essays of interest to literary scholars and cultural historians. Examples: "William Carlos Williams: A Review of Research and Criticism"; "The Background of the Hawthorne-Thoreau Relationship."

UNSOLICITED MSS. WELCOME? Yes; submissions acknowledged.
SPECIFICALLY WELCOMED: Checklists of criticism; edited previously-unpublished letters and mss.; bibliographical essays; catalogues of library collections.
MS. LENGTH: Up to 50 pages; submit TWO copies.
STYLE REQUIREMENTS: MLA STYLE SHEET (rev. ed.).
COPYRIGHT: Resources for American Literary Study, Inc.
EDITOR'S DECISION: 8 weeks.
FROM ACCEPTANCE TO PUBLICATION: 1 year.
PAYMENT/OFFPRINTS: No payment; reprints available at $1.00 each.
GENERAL: First issue, Spring, 1971. Usual publication length, 128 pages.
BACK ISSUES: Available from Business Office at $4.00 each.

SOCIETY FOR THE STUDY OF MIDWESTERN LITERATURE NEWSLETTER

EDITORIAL ADDRESS
David D. Anderson, Editor
240 Ernst Bessey Hall
Michigan State University
East Lansing, Michigan 48823

SUBSCRIPTION ADDRESS:

same

PUBLISHED: Tri-annually (Fall, Spring, Summer)

CIRCULATION: 350

COST: 1 yr.—$1.00 (includes membership in the Society for the Study of Midwestern Literature).

CONTENTS: Checklists (of Midwestern literary magazines, of current publications); book reviews; short essays, work in progress, notes, queries about Midwestern literature.

UNSOLICITED MSS. WELCOME? Yes, by members; submissions acknowledged.
SPECIFICALLY WELCOMED: Book reviews, short essays.
MS. LENGTH: 200-500 words; submit ONE copy.
STYLE REQUIREMENTS: MLA STYLE SHEET.
COPYRIGHT: Society for the Study of Midwestern Literature.
EDITOR'S DECISION: 2 weeks.
FROM ACCEPTANCE TO PUBLICATION: 3 months.
PAYMENT/OFFPRINTS: No payment. Offprints on request.
REJECTED MSS.: Returned.
GENERAL: First issue, Spring, 1971. Usual publication length, 12 pages.
BACK ISSUES: Available from editorial office at $2.00 per volume.

SOUTHERN LITERARY JOURNAL

EDITORIAL ADDRESS: SUBSCRIPTION ADDRESS:
Louis D. Rubin, Jr., and
C. Hugh Holman, Editors same
University of North Carolina
Department of English
Chapel Hill, North Carolina 27514

PUBLISHED: Biannually CIRCULATION: 575
COST: 1 yr.—$5.00 in U.S. and Canada; $5.50 elsewhere.

CONTENTS: Scholarly essays, reviews of books, and occasional transcriptions of discussions on Southern literature. Examples: "Simms' Indebtedness to Folk Tradition in 'Sharp Snaffles' "; "Ebenezer Cooke's THE SOT-WEED FACTOR: The Structure of Satire."

UNSOLICITED MSS. WELCOME? Yes; submissions not acknowledged.
SPECIFICALLY WELCOMED: Essays.
MS. LENGTH: 3,000-4,000 words; submit ONE copy.
STYLE REQUIREMENTS: MLA STYLE SHEET.
COPYRIGHT: SOUTHERN LITERARY JOURNAL.
EDITOR'S DECISION: 4 weeks.
FROM ACCEPTANCE TO PUBLICATION: 6 months.
PAYMENT/OFFPRINTS: $5.00 per printed page. Provide offprints at cost.
REJECTED MSS.: Returned.
GENERAL: First issue, Fall, 1969. Usual publication length, 120 pages. Volumes I and II (1968-1969, 1969-1970) indexed.

BACK ISSUES: Available from editorial address at $2.50 each and from Xerox University Microfilms.

THE SOUTHERN REVIEW

EDITORIAL ADDRESS: SUBSCRIPTION ADDRESS:
Donald E. Stanford and
Lewis P. Simpson, Editors   same
Drawer D
University Station
Baton Rouge, Louisiana 70803

PUBLISHED: Quarterly (Jan.,   CIRCULATION: 3,000-3,500
Apr., July, Oct.)
COST: 1 yr.—$5.00; 2 yrs.—$9.00; 3 yrs.—$13.00; single copy—$1.50.

CONTENTS: Poetry; fiction; critical essays. Examples: "The Place and Relevance of George Santayana"; "Robert Penn Warren's Promised Land."

UNSOLICITED MSS. WELCOME? Yes, but not book reviews; submissions not acknowledged.
SPECIFICALLY WELCOMED: Contemporary literature and essays dealing with the culture of the South.
MS. LENGTH: Prose, 4,000-8,000 words; poetry, 1 to 6 pages; submit ONE copy.
STYLE REQUIREMENTS: High literary merit.
COPYRIGHT: Copyright transferred free to author.
EDITOR'S DECISION: 4 weeks.
FROM ACCEPTANCE TO PUBLICATION: 6 months.
PAYMENT/OFFPRINTS: Poetry, $20.00 per page; prose, 3¢ a word. Contributor may purchase offprints.
REJECTED MSS. Returned.
GENERAL: Original Series, 1935-1942; New Series, January, 1965. Usual publication length, 240-300 pages.
BACK ISSUES: Original series available from Kraus Reprint Co.; New Series from editorial office at $1.50 each. Abstracts of essays and reviews, beginning with Vol. IV, No. 1, are on file at the MLA Abstract Office.

SOUTHWESTERN AMERICAN LITERATURE

EDITORIAL ADDRESS: SUBSCRIPTION ADDRESS:
Helen L. Leath, Editor
P.O. Box 13646 North Texas Station   same
Denton, Texas 76203

PUBLISHED: Tri-annually   CIRCULATION: 200-250
COST: 1 yr.—$3.00; single copy—$1.00.

CONTENTS: Articles and book reviews on Southwestern literature and folklore; illustrations and photographs. Examples: "Frontier and Region in Western Literature"; "The Recent Southwestern Novel."

UNSOLICITED MSS. WELCOME? Yes; submissions acknowledged.
SPECIFICALLY WELCOMED: Scholarly pieces about Southwestern writing and writers.
MS. LENGTH: Articles, 15-20 pages; book reviews, 2 to 3 pages; submit ONE copy.
STYLE REQUIREMENTS: MLA STYLE SHEET; footnotes follow articles.
COPYRIGHT: SOUTHWESTERN AMERICAN LITERATURE.
EDITOR'S DECISION: 60 days.
FROM ACCEPTANCE TO PUBLICATION: 1 year.
PAYMENT/OFFPRINTS: Two copies of issue in which work appears. Any extras at regular prices.
REJECTED MSS.: Returned.
GENERAL: First issue, January, 1971. Usual publication length, 55-65 pages. Indexed by volume.
BACK ISSUES: Available from editorial address at $1.00 each.

STUDI AMERICANI

EDITORIAL ADDRESS:
Edizioni di Storia e Letteratura
Via Lancellotti 18
Rome, Italy

SUBSCRIPTION ADDRESS:

same

PUBLISHED: Annually
COST: Varies from issue to issue.

CIRCULATION: 1,000

CONTENTS: Articles concerning the literature, arts, and history of America. Examples: "Will and Power in American Literature"; " 'Rappaccini's Daughter': the Gothic as a Catalyst for Hawthorne's Imagination."

UNSOLICITED MSS. WELCOME? Submissions acknowledged.
MS. LENGTH: 20 pages.
COPYRIGHT: Edizioni di Storia e Letteratura.
EDITOR'S DECISION: Varies.
FROM ACCEPTANCE TO PUBLICATION: Varies.
REJECTED MSS.: Returned.
GENERAL: First issue, 1955. Usual publication length, 400-500 pages. Articles may be written in English and Italian.
BACK ISSUES: Available from Edizioni di Storia e Letteratura at current issue price.

STUDIES IN AMERICAN FICTION

See the section on GENRES.

STUDIES IN THE 20TH CENTURY

See the section on AGE AND/OR NATIONALITY: EUROPEAN.

VENTURE: BI-ANNUAL REVIEW OF ENGLISH LANGUAGE AND LITERATURE

See the section on AGE AND/OR NATIONALITY: ASIAN for details.

WESTERN AMERICAN LITERATURE

EDITORIAL ADDRESS:
J. Golden Taylor, Editor
Western Literature Association
English Department
Colorado State University
Fort Collins, Colorado 80521

SUBSCRIPTION ADDRESS:

same

PUBLISHED: Quarterly (May, Aug., Nov., Feb.)
CIRCULATION: 745
COST: $6.00 per volume; single copy—$1.75.

CONTENTS: Literary history, criticism, bibliography, and book reviews on literature written in and/or about the American West. Example: "BLACK ELK SPEAKS: and So Does John Neihardt."

UNSOLICITED MSS. WELCOME? Yes; submissions acknowledged.
SPECIFICALLY WELCOMED: Articles about American West authors and their writing.
MS. LENGTH: 15 pages; submit TWO copies.
STYLE REQUIREMENTS: MLA STYLE SHEET: footnotes on a separate page at end of essay.
COPYRIGHT: WESTERN AMERICAN LITERATURE, except for special arrangements.
EDITOR'S DECISION: 3 months.
FROM ACCEPTANCE TO PUBLICATION: 18 months.
PAYMENT/OFFPRINTS: Three free copies of issue. 100 free offprints.
REJECTED MSS.: Returned.

GENERAL: First issue, May, 1966. Usual publication length, 76-80 pages. Quarterly is indexed by volume.
BACK ISSUES: Available from editorial office at $1.75 each.

AMERICAN AND ENGLISH
(sometimes including Continental)

AMERICAN JOURNAL OF PHILOLOGY

EDITORIAL ADDRESS:
Editor
John Hopkins Press
Homewood
Baltimore, Maryland 21218

SUBSCRIPTION ADDRESS:

same

PUBLISHED: Quarterly

GENERAL: First issue, 1880. This periodical had not arrived by the time the entry went to press. Potential subscribers, contributors, or collectors will have to write the editor to see whether the journal still exists, and if so, to inquire about details of manuscript submission, style, back issues, and the like.

ARCHIV FUR DAS STUDIUM DER NEUEREN SPRACHEN UND LITERATUREN

See the section on AGE AND/OR NATIONALITY: CONTINENTAL.

BOOKS AND BOOKMEN

EDITORIAL ADDRESS:
Frank Granville Barker, Editor
Artillery Mansion
75 Victoria Street
London SW1H OJQ
England

SUBSCRIPTION ADDRESS:
Hansom Books
same

PUBLISHED: Monthly
COST: 1 yr.—$14.00.

CONTENTS: Mainly reviews and feature articles covering literary personalities. Examples: "Philip Larkin's 20th Century Verse"; "Beckett and Pinter"; "Harold Clurman's Theatre"; "Edmund Wilson and the Russian Novel."

UNSOLICITED MSS. WELCOME? No. Commissioned work only.
COPYRIGHT: The author or his agent.
GENERAL: First issue, 1955. Usual publication length, 150/160 pages. Sample issues can be supplied to would be subscribers.
BACK ISSUES: Available from subscription address at 45p. each. Very limited numbers available; most are out of print.

CONTEMPORARY LITERATURE (formerly Wisconsin Studies in Contemporary Literature)

EDITORIAL ADDRESS:
L. S. Dembo, Editor
University of Wisconsin
Department of English
Helen C. White Building
Madison, Wisconsin 53706

SUBSCRIPTION ADDRESS:
Journals Department
The University of Wisconsin Press
Box 1379
Madison, Wisconsin 53701

PUBLISHED: Quarterly
CIRCULATION: 1,800
COST: 1 yr.—$5.50 (prepaid) for individuals; $8.00 for institutions.

CONTENTS: Scholarly essays about literature and literary criticism since 1914; reviews of books about modern authors; issues devoted to a single topic, such as Italian Literature or Modern Criticism. Example: "The Literary Criticism of Friedrich Gundolf."

UNSOLICITED MSS. WELCOME? Yes; submissions acknowledged.
SPECIFICALLY WELCOMED: Critical essays.
MS. LENGTH: 10-35 pages; submit ONE copy.
STYLE REQUIREMENTS: MLA STYLE SHEET.
COPYRIGHT: Regents of the University of Wisconsin.
EDITOR'S DECISION: 2-3 months.
FROM ACCEPTANCE TO PUBLICATION: 6-18 months.
PAYMENT/OFFPRINTS: No monetary payment, unless commissioned. Ten to 25 free offprints; others at cost.
REJECTED MSS.: Returned.
GENERAL: First issue, 1960. Usual publication length, 450-475 pages.
BACK ISSUES: Available from Journals Department.

THE CRITICAL QUARTERLY

EDITORIAL ADDRESS:
C. B. Cox and A. E. Dyson, Editors
The University
Manchester M13 9PL
England

SUBSCRIPTION ADDRESS:
Manchester University Press
316-324 Oxford Road
Manchester M13 9NR
England

PUBLISHED: Quarterly (Mar., June, Sept., Dec.)
CIRCULATION: 5,000
COST: 1 yr.—$4.00 (or £1.50); single copy—$1.00.

CONTENTS: Scholarly essays about British, European, and American literature of the 20th century; one bibliographical issue each spring; new poetry; general articles on pre-1900 British literature. Example: "Muriel Spark's Fingernails"; "Class, Power and Charlotte Brontë."

UNSOLICITED MSS. WELCOME? Yes; submissions acknowledged.

SPECIFICALLY WELCOMED: Literary criticism of highest standard.
MS. LENGTH: 500-6,000 words; submit ONE copy.
STYLE REQUIREMENTS: MLA STYLE SHEET.
COPYRIGHT: THE CRITICAL QUARTERLY.
EDITOR'S DECISION: 6-8 weeks.
FROM ACCEPTANCE TO PUBLICATION: 6 months.
PAYMENT/OFFPRINTS: Five to 10 offprints.
REJECTED MSS.: Returned.
GENERAL: First issue, 1959. Usual publication length, 96 pages. Indexed by volume.
BACK ISSUES: Available from Manchester University Press at $1.00 or 40p each.

THE CRITICAL REVIEW: MELBOURNE

EDITORIAL ADDRESS:
S. L. Goldberg, Editor
Department of English
The University of Melbourne
Parkville, Victoria 3052
Australia

SUBSCRIPTION ADDRESS:
The Bookroom
University of Melbourne
Parkville, Victoria 3052
Australia

PUBLISHED: Annually
COST: 1 yr.—US$2.00.

CIRCULATION: 1700

CONTENTS: Critical articles on English, American, and some European literature; also some more general articles, e.g. review-articles, commentaries on cultural matters related to literature, teaching, etc. Examples: "Dickens and Individualism"; "Milton: Poet as God."

UNSOLICITED MSS. WELCOME? Yes; submissions acknowledged.
MS. LENGTH: Up to 8,000 words; submit TWO copies.
STYLE REQUIREMENTS: No footnotes. Style as per RULES FOR PRINTERS & COMPOSITORS (O.U.P.).
COPYRIGHT: Author.
EDITOR'S DECISION: 2 months.
FROM ACCEPTANCE TO PUBLICATION: Articles accepted are published in that year's issue.
PAYMENT/OFFPRINTS: Six free offprints.
REJECTED MSS.: Returned, if reply coupons included.
GENERAL: First issue, 1958. Usual publication length, 132 pages.
BACK ISSUES: Nos. 1-8 available from Johnson Reprint; Nos. 9-13 (1970) out of print. Price varies.

CRITICISM: A QUARTERLY FOR LITERATURE AND THE ARTS

EDITORIAL ADDRESS:
Alva A. Gay, Editor
Department of English
Wayne State University
Detroit, Michigan 48202

SUBSCRIPTION ADDRESS:
Wayne State University Press
5980 Cass Avenue
Detroit, Michigan 48202

PUBLISHED: Quarterly (Winter, Spring, Summer, Fall)

CIRCULATION: 1,100

COST: 1 yr.—$8.00; 2 yrs.—$14.50; 3 yrs.—$20.00. Add $.60 a year for Canada; $.75 abroad. Single copy—$2.50.

CONTENTS: Articles that study the literatures and the arts of all periods and nations either individually or in their interrelationships and the critical theory regarding them; scholarly analysis and evaluation of artists and their works.

UNSOLICITED MSS. WELCOME? Yes; submissions acknowledged.
SPECIFICALLY WELCOMED: Interdisciplinary or inter-arts articles, critical theory, literary criticism. Formal aesthetics and the more technical studies in philology and linguistics are not included.
MS. LENGTH: 15-20 pages; submit ONE copy.
STYLE REQUIREMENTS: MLA STYLE SHEET.
COPYRIGHT: Wayne State University Press.
EDITOR'S DECISION: 2-3 months.
FROM ACCEPTANCE TO PUBLICATION: 8-10 months.
PAYMENT/OFFPRINTS: 25 free offprints.
REJECTED MSS.: Returned.
GENERAL: First issue, 1959. Usual publication length, 88-100 pages.
BACK ISSUES: Vol. 1-10 available from Kraus Periodicals, Inc.; recent issues from Wayne State University Press at $2.50 each.

EIGHTEENTH-CENTURY STUDIES: AN INTERDISCIPLINARY JOURNAL

EDITORIAL ADDRESS:
Robert Hopkins and Donald Greene, Editors
Department of English
University of California
Davis, California 95616

SUBSCRIPTION ADDRESS:
University of California Press
Periodicals Department
2223 Fulton Street
Berkeley, California 94720

PUBLISHED: Quarterly (Sept., Dec., Mar., June)

CIRCULATION: 2,000

COST: 1 yr.—$9.00 for individuals in U.S., Canada, and Pan-American countries; $12.00 for institutions; other countries add $1.00 for postage; single copies—$2.50 for individuals; $3.25 for institutions.

CONTENTS: Critical essays about literature, the arts and the cultural history of the 18th century; reviews of articles and books about the 18th century; section of news for members of American Society for Eighteenth-Century Studies; occasional photographs and illustrations.

UNSOLICITED MSS. WELCOME? Yes; submissions acknowledged.
SPECIFICALLY WELCOMED: Articles that present new information about the 18th century, or new interpretations, of potential value to students in more than one discipline.
MS. LENGTH: Up to 6,500 words; submit TWO copies.
STYLE REQUIREMENTS: MLA STYLE SHEET; must be in English; abstract around 200 words accompanying article.
COPYRIGHT: The Regents of the University of California.
EDITOR'S DECISION: 4 months.
FROM ACCEPTANCE TO PUBLICATION: 12-16 months.
PAYMENT/OFFPRINTS: Three copies of issue. Offprints available at minimum cost.
REJECTED MSS. Returned; criticized.
GENERAL: First issue, 1967. Usual publication length, 145-150 pages. ECS will not publish highly technical and specialized articles on narrowly limited subjects in a single field.
BACK ISSUES: Available on microfilm or xerograph facsimile from University Microfilms, Inc.

ELH

EDITORIAL ADDRESS:
Earl R. Wasserman, Senior Editor
English Department
The John Hopkins University
Baltimore, Maryland 21218

SUBSCRIPTION ADDRESS:
Periodicals Manager
The John Hopkins University Press
Baltimore, Maryland 21218

PUBLISHED: Quarterly (Mar., June, Sept., Dec.)
CIRCULATION: 1,500
COST: 1 yr.—$8.00 (individuals); $12.00 (institutions); single copy—$1.00.

CONTENTS: Scholarly essays about English and American literature on varied topics from medieval to modern times. Example: "Vanity and Vacuity: A Reading of Johnson's Verse Satires."

UNSOLICITED MSS. WELCOME? Yes; submissions acknowledged.
SPECIFICALLY WELCOMED: Essays on English literature that make a critical contribution.
MS. LENGTH: No criteria; submit ONE copy.
STYLE REQUIREMENTS: MLA STYLE SHEET.
COPYRIGHT: John Hopkins University Press.
EDITOR'S DECISION: 30 days.
FROM ACCEPTANCE TO PUBLICATION: Within a year.

PAYMENT/OFFPRINTS: Ten free offprints are given with an option to purchase more.
REJECTED MSS.: Returned.
GENERAL: First issue, 1933. Usual publication length, 160 pages.
BACK ISSUES: Available from John Hopkins University Press at $5.00 each.

ENGLISH LANGUAGE NOTES

EDITORIAL ADDRESS:
Charles L. Proudfit, Editor
Hellems 101 D
University of Colorado
Boulder, Colorado 80302

SUBSCRIPTION ADDRESS:

same

PUBLISHED: Quarterly (Sept., Dec., Mar., June)
CIRCULATION: 1,000-1,100
COST: 1 yr.—$7.00, plus $1.00 for mailing outside of U.S. and Canada; $12.00 for institutions, plus $1.00 for mailing outside of U.S. and Canada; single copy—$2.00.

CONTENTS: Short articles and scholarly notes pertaining to English and American language and literature; reviews of current scholarly books in the field of English and American language and literature. Ordinarily explication unsupported by biographical, historical, or bibliographical evidence will not be accepted.

UNSOLICITED MSS. WELCOME? Articles and notes, yes; reviews, no; submissions acknowledged.
SPECIFICALLY WELCOMED: Short articles and notes, preferably revealing or discussing the implications of new evidence in the field of English or American literature.
MS. LENGTH: Less than 12 pages; submit ONE copy.
STYLE REQUIREMENTS: MLA STYLE SHEET.
EDITOR'S DECISION: 3 to 6 months.
FROM ACCEPTANCE TO PUBLICATION: 6 months.
PAYMENT/OFFPRINTS: No payment. Offprints available for authors.
REJECTED MSS. Returned.
GENERAL: First issue, September, 1963. Usual publication length, 80-88 pages.
BACK ISSUES: Those of current year available from editorial office at $2.00 each; others from AMS Press, Inc. at $5.00 each or $20.00 per volume.

ENGLISH STUDIES: A JOURNAL OF ENGLISH LANGUAGE AND LITERATURE

EDITORIAL ADDRESS:
Professor R. Derolez, Editor
Rozier 44
9000 Gent, Belgium

SUBSCRIPTION ADDRESS:
Swets & Zeitlinger B.V.
Publishing Department
347b, Heereweg
Lisse, The Netherlands

PUBLISHED: 6 times yearly
COST: Dutch guilders 47.50.

CIRCULATION: 2,000

CONTENTS: Articles on English language and English and American literature; reviews of books in these fields; surveys of 'Recent Literature': criticism and biography, new writing, commonwealth literature; points of modern English syntax; surveys of books and periodicals received. Examples: "Key Perspective, the Tonality of Tense in Some Poems of Wordsworth"; "Reality in Fiction: NO LAUGHING MATTER."

UNSOLICITED MSS. WELCOME? Yes; submissions acknowledged.
SPECIFICALLY WELCOMED: Only scholarly contributions.
MS. LENGTH: Articles: 2,000-6,000 words; reviews: 500-1,500 words; submit ONE copy.
STYLE REQUIREMENTS: See "English Studies: A Style Sheet" (Vol. 52, 1971, p. 103) that agrees largely with MLA STYLE SHEET and with instructions for yearbook ANGLO-SAXON ENGLAND, ed. Peter Clemols.
COPYRIGHT: Swets & Zeitlinger, publishers.
EDITOR'S DECISION: Maximum 2 months.
FROM ACCEPTANCE TO PUBLICATION: 1-2 years.
PAYMENT/OFFPRINTS: 20 free offprints; additional ones at author's expense.

REJECTED MSS.: Returned only if international reply coupons are added.
GENERAL: First issue, 1919. Usual publication length, 96 pages.
BACK ISSUES: Available from Swets & Zeitlinger B.V., Backsets Department at US $20.00 per single volume; US $1,072.00 per complete set, Vols. 1-53.

ENLIGHTENMENT ESSAYS

EDITORIAL ADDRESS:
Michael Morrisroe, Jr.,
Managing Editor
1126 W. Granville Avenue
Suite 26
Chicago, Illinois 60660

SUBSCRIPTION ADDRESS:

same

PUBLISHED: Quarterly
COST: 1 yr.—$9.00.

CIRCULATION: 1,500

CONTENTS: Interdisciplinary articles on 17th and 18th century philosophy, literature, and history of the American, British, and Continental Enlightenment; book reviews; rebuttals to articles and reviews. Example: "Robinson Crusoe's Island and the Restoration TEMPEST."

UNSOLICITED MSS. WELCOME? Yes; submissions acknowledged.
SPECIFICALLY WELCOMED: Interdisciplinary scholarly articles.
MS. LENGTH: 5,000-8,000 words; submit TWO copies.
STYLE REQUIREMENTS: MLA STYLE SHEET; minimum documentation; notes at end of article.
COPYRIGHT: ENLIGHTENMENT ESSAYS with rights to reprint to author.
EDITOR'S DECISION: 30 days.
FROM ACCEPTANCE TO PUBLICATION: 5 months.
PAYMENT/OFFPRINTS: $50 for one article; $5 for reviews. Copies provided.
REJECTED MSS.: Returned.
GENERAL: First issue, Spring, 1970. Usual publication length, 92 pages.
BACK ISSUES: Available from editorial address at $3.00 each.

THE ERASMUS REVIEW

SUBSCRIPTION ADDRESS:
Joel Rubin Publishers Limited
23-45 Bell Boulevard
Bayside, New York 11360

PUBLISHED: 5 issues yearly   CIRCULATION: 1,000
COST: 1 yr.—$12.00, individuals; $15.00, libraries.

CONTENTS: Critical essays on English and American literature.

UNSOLICITED MSS WELCOME? Yes; submissions acknowledged.
SPECIFICALLY WELCOMED: Critical essays on English and American literature.
MS. LENGTH: No qualifications; submit ONE copy.
STYLE REQUIREMENTS: MLA STYLE SHEET.
COPYRIGHT: Publisher.
EDITOR'S DECISION: 3-6 months.
FROM ACCEPTANCE TO PUBLICATION: 6-12 months.
PAYMENT/OFFPRINTS: Two copies and "tear sheets."
REJECTED MSS.: Returned.
GENERAL: First issue, September, 1971. Usual publication length, 150 pages.
BACK ISSUES: From publisher at $4.00 each.

ESSAYS IN CRITICISM: A QUARTERLY JOURNAL OF LITERARY CRITICISM

EDITORIAL ADDRESS:
Stephen Wall, Editor
(Keble College, Oxford, England)
Christopher Ricks, Editor
(Bristol University, Bristol, England)

SUBSCRIPTION ADDRESS:
F. W. Bateson, Editor
Brill
Aylesbury
England

PUBLISHED: Quarterly (Jan., Apr., July, Oct.)
COST: 1 yr.—$9.00 post free.

CIRCULATION: 2,500

CONTENTS: Articles and reviews on literary criticism, mainly English and American literature.

UNSOLICITED MSS. WELCOME? Yes; submissions acknowledged.
SPECIFICALLY WELCOMED: Critical articles—non-linguistic.
MS. LENGTH: 4,000-7,000 words; submit ONE copy.
COPYRIGHT: Journal retains 50% of anthology payments.
EDITOR'S DECISION: 4 weeks.
FROM ACCEPTANCE TO PUBLICATION: 1 year to 15 months.
PAYMENT/OFFPRINTS: 12 offprints of articles; extra offprints if paid for.
REJECTED MSS. Returned, if international coupon enclosed.
GENERAL: First issue, January, 1951. Usual publication length, 120 pages.
BACK ISSUES: Volumes from 1951 to 1971, reprinted by photo-offset, available from Swets & Zeitlinger, Keizersgracht 471 & 487, Amsterdam, Holland. Inquire about cost. Elaborate cumulative index, 1951-65, obtainable from F.W. Bateson at $1.50 post free; payment must accompany order.

ESSAYS IN LITERATURE

EDITORIAL ADDRESS:
James P. Nelson, Editor
University of Denver
University Park
Denver, Colorado 80210

SUBSCRIPTION ADDRESS:

same

PUBLISHED: Tri-annually
COST: 1 yr.—$5.00; single copy—$2.00.

CIRCULATION: 500

CONTENTS: Critical essays in the broad range of English and American literature, with a preference for subjects and authors prior to World War II.

UNSOLICITED MSS. WELCOME? Yes; submissions not acknowledged.
SPECIFICALLY WELCOMED: Any, although specifically designed for graduate manuscripts.
MS. LENGTH: 15-25 pages; submit ONE copy.

STYLE REQUIREMENTS: MLA STYLE SHEET preferred.
COPYRIGHT: Author.
EDITOR'S DECISION: 2-3 months.
FROM ACCEPTANCE TO PUBLICATION: 2-3 months.
PAYMENT/OFFPRINTS: Three copies of issue in which essay appears. No offprints available.
REJECTED MSS.: Returned.
GENERAL: First issue, January, 1973. Usual publication length, 65-70 pages.
BACK ISSUES: Limited number available from editorial address at $.75 each until 1974, then $2.00 each.

ESSAYS IN LITERATURE

EDITORIAL ADDRESS:
John E. Hallwas, Editor
Department of English
Western Illinois University
Macomb, Illinois 61455

SUBSCRIPTION ADDRESS:

same

PUBLISHED: Biannually
COST: 1 yr.—$3.00 (institutions—$4.00); 3 yrs.—$8.00.

CONTENTS: Studies concerning the literature in the British and American traditions and the modern European languages, and of any literary period, figure, genre, or works. No book reviews.

UNSOLICITED MSS. WELCOME? Yes.
SPECIFICALLY WELCOMED: Scholarly essays written in English; all material quoted in a foreign language must be accompanied by a translation in the text of the paper.
MS. LENGTH: 2,000-8,000 words.
STYLE REQUIREMENTS: MLA STYLE SHEET; footnotes placed at end of essay.
GENERAL: First issue, Spring, 1974.

ÉTUDES ANGLAISES (GRANDE-BRETAGNE—ETATS-UNIS)

EDITORIAL ADDRESS:
Louis Bonnerot, Editor
129, Avenue du General de Gaulle
92170 Vanves
France

SUBSCRIPTION ADDRESS:
Publisher
Librairie Marcel Didier
15, Rue Cujas
75005 Paris
France

PUBLISHED: Quarterly
COST: About 65 Francs.

CIRCULATION: 1,300-1,600

CONTENTS: Articles on literature, usually; book reviews; a chronicle, dealing with theses, symposiums and general information; section devoted to "Revue des Revues."

UNSOLICITED MSS. WELCOME? Yes, but submitted to editorial board for decision; submissions acknowledged.
SPECIFICALLY WELCOMED: "Diversity," ranging from Old English to modern subjects covering literature, linguistics, civilization (such as the arts, sociology).
MS. LENGTH: About 15 pages of printed text; submit ONE copy.
STYLE REQUIREMENTS: Scholarly without excess.
COPYRIGHT: ETUDES ANGLAISES.
EDITOR'S DECISION: About 1 month.
FROM ACCEPTANCE TO PUBLICATION: Varies; long waiting list.
PAYMENT/OFFPRINTS: Each contributor receives 25 free offprints for his article.
REJECTED MSS. Preferably not returned.
GENERAL: First issue, 1936; discontinued during the war; revived 1952. Usual publication length, 128 pages.
BACK ISSUES: Available from the Librairie M. Didier after explication to the Editor. No price fixed.

FICTION INTERNATIONAL

See the section on GENRES.

THE HUNTINGTON LIBRARY QUARTERLY: A JOURNAL FOR THE HISTORY AND INTERPRETATION OF ENGLISH AND AMERICAN CIVILIZATION

See the section on BIBLIOGRAPHICAL AND LIBRARY RESOURCES for details.

THE INDIAN JOURNAL OF ENGLISH STUDIES

EDITORIAL ADDRESS:
B. Das, Editor

SUBSCRIPTION ADDRESS:
Orient Longman, Ltd.
17 Chittaranjan Avenue
Calcutta 13
India

COST: Single copy—Rs. 7.50.

CONTENTS: Articles on American and English literature. Examples: "A Study of J. D. Salinger's 'Teddy' "; "Crystallizing the Amorphous: Virginia Woolf's Theory of the Creative Process"; "Aestheticism and Oscar Wilde's Style."

UNSOLICITED MSS. WELCOME? Yes, by writers from India.
COPYRIGHT: The Indian Association for English Studies.
GENERAL: First issue, 1959.
BACK ISSUES: Available from subscription address.

THE JOURNAL OF NARRATIVE TECHNIQUE

See the section on GENRES.

LITERARY SKETCHES

EDITORIAL ADDRESS:
Mary Lewis Chapman, Editor
P.O. Box 711
Williamsburg, Virginia 23185

SUBSCRIPTION ADDRESS:
same

PUBLISHED: Monthly
(11 issues yearly)
COST: 1 yr.—$1.50.

CIRCULATION: 500-700

CONTENTS: Reviews; interviews; biographical sketches of writers; illustrations. Issues have centered on Hawthorne, Twain, Lewis Carroll, Pepys, Mencken, Cary, "Saki," Shirley Jackson, Kipling, Jesse Stuart, Dylan Thomas, Goldsmith, etc.

UNSOLICITED MSS. WELCOME? Yes, but size permits only one "bought" manuscript a month; submissions not acknowledged.
SPECIFICALLY WELCOMED: Biographical sketches of little known or unusual aspect of a writer's life.
MS. LENGTH: Up to 1,000 words; submit ONE copy.
STYLE REQUIREMENTS: Informal.
EDITOR'S DECISION: 1 month.
FROM ACCEPTANCE TO PUBLICATION: Varies.
PAYMENT/OFFPRINTS: ½¢ per word.
REJECTED MSS.: Returned.
GENERAL: First issue, June, 1961. Usual publication length, 8-12 pages.
BACK ISSUES: Available from editorial address at $.10 each.

MLN

EDITORIAL ADDRESS:
Editor
John Hopkins Press
Baltimore, Maryland 21218

SUBSCRIPTION ADDRESS:

same

PUBLISHED: 6 times yearly

GENERAL: First issue, 1886. This periodical had not arrived by the time the entry went to press. Potential subscribers, contributors, or collectors will have to write the editor to see whether the journal still exists, and if so, to inquire about details of manuscript submission, style, back issues, and the like.

MODERN LANGUAGE QUARTERLY

EDITORIAL ADDRESS:
William H. Matchett, Editor
Parrington Hall
University of Washington
Seattle, Washington 98195

SUBSCRIPTION ADDRESS:

same

PUBLISHED: Quarterly (Mar., June, Sept., Dec.)
COST: 1 yr.—$6.00; single copy—$1.75.

CONTENTS: Critical articles on literature and languages; book reviews; books received section. Example: "The Private Life: Dororthy Wordsworth's Journals."

MS. LENGTH: 4,000-5,000 words.
STYLE REQUIREMENTS: MLA STYLE SHEET.
GENERAL: First issue, 1940. Usual publication length, 120 pages.

NINETEENTH-CENTURY FICTION

EDITORIAL ADDRESS:
G. B. Tennyson, Editor
Department of English
2319 Rolfe Hall
University of California
at Los Angeles
Los Angeles, California 90024

SUBSCRIPTION ADDRESS:
Periodicals Department
University of California Press
2223 Fulton Street
Berkeley, California 94720

PUBLISHED: Quarterly (June, Sept., Dec., Mar.)

CIRCULATION: 2,250

COST: 1 yr.—$8.00 in North America; $9.00 elsewhere; $10.00 for institutions in N.A.; $11.00 elsewhere; single copy—$2.25 in N.A.; $2.75 elsewhere; $5.00 for students with status certificate from faculty member.

CONTENTS: Articles and notes of a critical and scholarly character on all types of English-language fiction of the nineteenth century; reviews of current scholarly and critical works in the field of nineteenth-century fiction. Example: "WUTHERING HEIGHTS: The Binding of Passion."

UNSOLICITED MSS. WELCOME? Yes; submissions acknowledged.
MS. LENGTH: 20-25 pages; submit the ORIGINAL.
STYLE REQUIREMENTS: MLA STYLE SHEET.
COPYRIGHT: Regents of the University of California.
EDITOR'S DECISION: 3-4 months.
FROM ACCEPTANCE TO PUBLICATION: 1-2 years.
PAYMENT/OFFPRINTS: 25 gratis offprints to authors of articles plus one copy of journal. Additional offprints at $.50 each without covers for articles.
REJECTED MSS.: Returned.
GENERAL: First issue, 1945. Usual publication length, 128 pages. Title page and table of contents—free to subscribers.
BACK ISSUES: Volumes XX through XVI available from A.M.S. Reprint Company. Microfilm and Xerograph available from Xerox University Microfilms. Consult above companies for prices.

NOTES AND QUERIES

EDITORIAL ADDRESS:　　　　　　SUBSCRIPTION ADDRESS:
J. C. Maxwell and E. G. Stanley,
Editors　　　　　　　　　　　　　　same
Oxford University Press
Ely House
Dover Street
London W. 1
England

PUBLISHED: Monthly

GENERAL: First issue, 1849. This periodical had not arrived by the time the entry went to press. Potential subscribers, contributors, or collectors will have to write the editor to see whether the journal still exists, and if so, to inquire about details of manuscript submission, style, back issues, and the like.

NOTRE DAME ENGLISH JOURNAL

EDITORIAL ADDRESS:
Carl T. Berkhout, Editor
Department of English
University of Notre Dame
Notre Dame, Indiana 46556

SUBSCRIPTION ADDRESS:
Secretary, Notre Dame
English Association
P.O. Box 91
Notre Dame, Indiana 46556

PUBLISHED: Biannually (Fall, Spring)
CIRCULATION: 350-400
COST: One volume—$2.50; single copy—$1.25.

CONTENTS: Critical articles and book reviews in all areas of English and American literature. Example: " 'A High-Toned Old Christian Woman': Wallace Stevens' Parable of Supreme Fiction."

UNSOLICITED MSS. WELCOME? Yes (but book reviews are assigned); submissions acknowledged.
SPECIFICALLY WELCOMED: Original, carefully-written articles, of any critical persuasion, which address the specialist but are of interest or value to the nonspecialist as well.
MS. LENGTH: Under 5,000 words; submit TWO copies.
STYLE REQUIREMENTS: MLA STYLE SHEET; double-spacing of endnotes and indented quotations.
COPYRIGHT: Notre Dame English Association; reassignment liberally granted.
EDITOR'S DECISION: 5-8 weeks.
FROM ACCEPTANCE TO PUBLICATION: Usually less than 1 year.
PAYMENT/OFFPRINTS: Five copies of issue. 10 to 15 offprints.
REJECTED MSS. Returned.
GENERAL: First issue, 1962. Usual publication length, 70-80 pages. Volume numbers follow the academic year (no. 1 in the fall, no. 2 in the spring); beginning with 1972-73 issues, pagination is continuous through each volume.
BACK ISSUES: Available from subscription address at $1.25 each. Supply before 1972 limited.

PAPERS ON LANGUAGE AND LITERATURE

EDITORIAL ADDRESS:
Editor
Southern Illinois University
Edwardsville, Illinois 62025

SUBSCRIPTION ADDRESS:
Business Manager
same

PUBLISHED: Quarterly
CIRCULATION: 975
COST: 1 yr.—$7.00; single copy of current year—$2.00.

CONTENTS: Longer papers dealing with literature in several languages but with the emphasis on British and American letters; a section of Brief Notes; a Review Essay, usually dealing with recent scholarship and criticism concerning a modern who does not write in English.

UNSOLICITED MSS. WELCOME? Yes, but review essays are usually solicited; submissions acknowledged.
SPECIFICALLY WELCOMED: Both longer essays and brief notes.
MS. LENGTH: 5-25 pages; submit TWO copies.
STYLE REQUIREMENTS: University of Chicago's A MANUAL OF STYLE.
COPYRIGHT: Board of Trustees, Southern Illinois University.
EDITOR'S DECISION: 2 weeks to 6 months.
FROM ACCEPTANCE TO PUBLICATION: 12-18 months.
PAYMENT/OFFPRINTS: Two copies of issue. 10 free offprints.
REJECTED MSS.: Returned.
GENERAL: First issue, 1964. Usual publication length, 112 pages.
BACK ISSUES: Available from Business Manager at $2.50 each.

PAPERS OF THE MMLA (suspended publication)

EDITORIAL ADDRESS:
Robert Scholes, Editor
311 English/Philosophy Building
University of Iowa
Iowa City, Iowa 52240

PUBLISHED: Annually   CIRCULATION: 2,070

CONTENTS: PAPERS, No. 1—"Poetic Theory/Poetic Practice" ed. Robert Scholes—Select papers presented at the annual meeting of MMLA in Cincinnati, Ohio, October, 1968. PAPERS, No. 2—"Criticism and Culture" ed. Sherman Paul—Select papers presented at the annual meeting of MMLA in St. Louis, Missouri, October, 1969.

GENERAL: First issue, June 1969. Usual publication length, 100-120 pages. Publication suspended with No. 2, fall of 1972.
BACK ISSUES: Available from Midwest Modern Language Association, editorial address, at $4.00 for one year (single issue); $7.50 for two years (two issues).

PROCEEDINGS OF THE COMPARATIVE LITERATURE SYMPOSIUM

EDITORIAL ADDRESS:
Wolodymyr T. Zyla and
Wendell M. Aycock, Editors
Library
P. O. Box 4079
Lubbock, Texas 74709

SUBSCRIPTION ADDRESS:
Mary Gordon, Exchange Librarian
same

PUBLISHED: Annually
CIRCULATION: 1,250
COST: PROCEEDINGS is an exchange publication which is placed in 662 libraries throughout the world. It may be purchased at $4.00 from the Exchange Librarian.

CONTENTS: Comparative literature articles that cover the theme of the Annual Comparative Literature Symposium. For example, Vol. V, MODERN AMERICAN FICTION: INSIGHTS AND FOREIGN LIGHTS, covered the Fifth Annual Comparative Literature Symposium that offered specific, rather than comprehensive, reflections on the international state of American letters.

UNSOLICITED MSS. WELCOME? No; submissions acknowledged.
SPECIFICALLY WELCOMED: Only literary works contributing to the symposium theme.
MS. LENGTH: 35 or more pages; submit THREE copies.
STYLE REQUIREMENTS: MLA STYLE SHEET.
COPYRIGHT: Author retains copyright on materials published, but should use special acknowledgement form. Inquire.
EDITOR'S DECISION: 2-3 months.
FROM ACCEPTANCE TO PUBLICATIONS: 6 months.
PAYMENT/OFFPRINTS: The writer who comes to the symposium receives his airplane fare, food, and motel. Three free copies of PROCEEDINGS and 25 offprints.
REJECTED MSS.: Returned.
GENERAL: First issue, July, 1968. Usual publication length, 200 pages. The 1975 symposium will be devoted to arid and semi-arid lands literature. Editors would like to center on two or three writers or poet who were raised and educated in the arid and semi-arid lands, or who depicted in their works these types of conditions.
BACK ISSUES: Available from Exchange Librarian at cost of xerox copies plus labor for Vols. I and II and at $4.00 each for Vols III, IV, and V.

QUARTERLY CHECK-LIST OF LITERARY HISTORY: INTERNATIONAL INDEX OF CURRENT BOOKS, MONOGRAPHS, BROCHURES AND SEPARATES

See the section on BIBLIOGRAPHICAL AND LIBRARY RESOURCES for details.

RECOVERING LITERATURE: A JOURNAL OF CONTEXTUALIST CRITICISM

EDITORIAL ADDRESS:
The Editors
c/o W. K. Buckley, Jr.
Box 672
La Jolla, California 92037

SUBSCRIPTION ADDRESS:

same

PUBLISHED: Tri-annually
COST: 1 yr.—$4.50.

CIRCULATION: 65

CONTENTS: Nineteenth- and twentieth-century literature—discussions of novels in terms of Lawrentian (D.H.), Dewey, and other criticisms, including Wayne Burn's THE PANZAIC PRINCIPLE and contextualist criticism as defined by Stephen Pepper in his book THE BASIS OF CRITICISM IN THE ARTS.

UNSOLICITED MSS. WELCOME? Yes; submissions acknowledged.
MS. LENGTH: Not stated; submit TWO or ONE copy.
COPYRIGHT: Gerald J. Butler and W. K. Buckley.
EDITOR'S DECISION: 1 month.
FROM ACCEPTANCE TO PUBLICATION: 2 or 3 months.
PAYMENT/OFFPRINTS: No payment. Xerox copies at 5¢ per page.
REJECTED MSS.: Returned.
GENERAL: First issue, Spring, 1972. Usual publication length, 70 pages.
BACK ISSUES: Available from editorial address at $2.00 each.

RENASCENCE: ESSAYS ON VALUES IN LITERATURE

EDITORIAL ADDRESS:
John D. McCabe, Editor
Marquette University
Milwaukee, Wisconsin 53233

SUBSCRIPTION ADDRESS:
Executive Secretary
Catholic Renascence Society, Inc.
Viterbo College
LaCrosse, Wisconsin 54601

PUBLISHED: Quarterly
CIRCULATION: 700
COST: 1 yr.—$6.00 in U.S.; $7.00 elsewhere; subscription with membership in Catholic Renascence Society—$8.00.

CONTENTS: Critical and scholarly essays that explore questions of humane and religious values in literature. Primary critical attention is given to modern and contemporary American and British Literature, with some attention to continental literature, especially French. Examples: "Hemingway and the Christian Paradox"; "O'Connor and Teilhard de Chardin: The Problem of Evil."

UNSOLICITED MSS. WELCOME? Yes; submissions acknowledged.
MS. LENGTH: 5,000 words; submit ONE copy.
STYLE REQUIREMENTS: MLA STYLE SHEET.
COPYRIGHT: Catholic Renascence Society.

EDITOR'S DECISION: 2-3 months.
FROM ACCEPTANCE TO PUBLICATION: 1 year.
PAYMENT/OFFPRINTS: Five free copies of issue. 50 offprints at $10.00.
REJECTED MSS.: Returned.
GENERAL: Usual publication length, 56 pages.
BACK ISSUES: Vols I-IV available only through Johnson Reprint Corp. Others available from editorial office at $3.00 each for Vols V-VI; $2.50 each for Vols. VII-XIV; $2.00 each for Vols. XV-XXIV, if available; $1.75 each for current issue; $1.00 for index for Vols. I-IV.

ROCKY MOUNTAIN MODERN LANGUAGE ASSOCIATION BULLETIN

EDITORIAL ADDRESS:
James K. Folsom, Editor
Rocky Mountain Modern
Language Association
409 Woodbury Hall
University of Colorado
Boulder, Colorado 80302

SUBSCRIPTION ADDRESS:

same

PUBLISHED: Quarterly, plus supplementary program issue.
COST: 1 yr.—$6.00.

CIRCULATION: 600-750

CONTENTS: Articles of scholarly and pedagogical interest primarily concerned with research and teaching in English and foreign languages.

UNSOLICITED MSS. WELCOME? Yes, from members of the RMMLA; submissions acknowledged.
MS. LENGTH: 2,000-5,000 words; submit TWO copies.
STYLE REQUIREMENTS: MLA STYLE SHEET.
COPYRIGHT: The BULLETIN.
EDITOR'S DECISION: 6-8 weeks.
FROM ACCEPTANCE TO PUBLICATION: 3-6 months.
PAYMENT/OFFPRINTS: No payment. Offprints available at cost.
REJECTED MSS.: Returned.
GENERAL: Usual publication length, 30-36 pages.
BACK ISSUES: Available from editorial address. Cost depends on the issue. Not all are obtainable, unless xeroxed.

SEVENTEENTH-CENTURY NEWS (including THE NEO-LATIN NEWS)

EDITORIAL ADDRESS:
J. Max Patrick and
Harrison T. Meserole, Editors
Department of English
117 Burrowes Building
Penn State University
University Park, Pennsylvania 16802

SUBSCRIPTION ADDRESS:

same

PUBLISHED: Quarterly CIRCULATION: 1,100
COST: 1 yr.—$2.00; 2 yrs.—$3.50; 3 yrs.—$5.00; 5 yrs.—$8.00.

CONTENTS: Short articles and reviews on all aspects of seventeenth-century culture, English, American, and European, with emphasis on literature and history. It enables specialists to keep abreast of new books and articles about Donne, Milton, and Dryden; Bacon, Brown, and Burton; the dramatists (except Shakespeare); the most recent work on the Metaphysicals and Cavaliers; Meditative poetry and Mannerism; the Baroque and Scientific Movements; and all other aspects of seventeenth-century life and thought.

UNSOLICITED MSS. WELCOME? Yes; submissions acknowledged.
SPECIFICALLY WELCOMED: Reviews; short articles; contributions to bibliographies; abstracts of important books and essays; reports of conferences.
MS. LENGTH: 3,000 words; submit TWO copies.
STYLE REQUIREMENTS: MLA STYLE SHEET.
COPYRIGHT: Author.
EDITOR'S DECISION: 1-2 months.
FROM ACCEPTANCE TO PUBLICATION: 9-15 months.
PAYMENT/OFFPRINTS: Six copies of issue in which work appears.
REJECTED MSS.: Returned.
GENERAL: First issue, 1941. Usual publication length, 28-32 pages.
BACK ISSUES: Available from Johnson Reprint Corp.

SOUTH ATLANTIC BULLETIN: A QUARTERLY JOURNAL
DEVOTED TO RESEARCH AND TEACHING IN THE
MODERN LANGUAGES AND LITERATURE

EDITORIAL ADDRESS;
Frank M. Duffey, Editor
Box 638
Chapel Hill, North Carolina 27514

SUBSCRIPTION ADDRESS:
Box 8410 U. T. Station
Knoxville, Tennessee 37916

PUBLISHED: Quarterly (Jan., May, Sept., Nov.)
CIRCULATION: 3,800
COST: 1 yr.—$5.00 (including membership in SAMLA).

CONTENTS: Scholarly research and criticism on English and modern foreign language and literature. Examples: "The Magazine and the Short Story in the Ante-Bellum Period"; "Memory and Desire in Eliot's 'Preludes.' "

UNSOLICITED MSS. WELCOME? Yes, from members of SAMLA; submissions acknowledged.
MS. LENGTH: 4,000 word maximum; submit ONE copy.
STYLE REQUIREMENTS: MLA STYLE SHEET.
COPYRIGHT: Author.
EDITOR'S DECISION: 6 months.
FROM ACCEPTANCE TO PUBLICATION: 12-18 months.
PAYMENT/OFFPRINTS: A limited number of offprints provided free.
REJECTED MSS.: Returned.
GENERAL: First issue, 1935. Usual publication length, 104 pages.
BACK ISSUES: Available from editor. Cost varies.

THE SOUTH CENTRAL BULLETIN

EDITORIAL ADDRESS:
Patrick G. Hogan, Jr., Editor
South Central Modern
Language Association
Department of English
University of Houston
Houston, Texas 77004

SUBSCRIPTION ADDRESS:
Business Manager
same

PUBLISHED: Quarterly   CIRCULATION: 2,300
COST: 1 yr.—$6.00 (SCMLA membership fee which includes subscription); library, $5.00.

CONTENTS: March, May, October issues include annual program, abstracts of papers read at annual SCMLA meeting, reviews of books written or edited by SCMLA members, announcements and reports of other regional and national meetings of interest to teachers of English, American, and foreign languages and literature, minutes and reports of executive committee meetings. The winter issue STUDIES is devoted to scholarly articles written by SCMLA members. Example: "The Structure of Laughter in Molière's L'AVARE."

UNSOLICITED MSS. WELCOME? Yes, if written by SCMLA members; submissions acknowledged.
SPECIFICALLY WELCOMED: Literary history, criticism, language, and linguistics—the full range of scholarship appropriate to the language and literature disciplines.
MS. LENGTH: 10-20 pages; submit TWO copies.
STYLE REQUIREMENTS: For manuscripts, in general those of the MLA STYLE SHEET.
COPYRIGHT: Author.
EDITOR'S DECISION: 6-8 months.
FROM ACCEPTANCE TO PUBLICATION: 6 months.

PAYMENT/OFFPRINTS: Tearsheets sent to author upon publication.
REJECTED MSS.: Returned.
GENERAL: First issue, 1940. Usual publication length, 50-60 pages.
BACK ISSUES: Available from the Office of the Executive Secretary, SCMLA, Rice University, Houston, Texas 77001, at usually $1.00 each for those available (recent years).

STUDIES IN ENGLISH

EDITORIAL ADDRESS:
John Pilkington, Editor
English Department
University of Mississippi
University, Mississippi 38677

SUBSCRIPTION ADDRESS:

same

PUBLISHED: Annually
COST: 1 yr.—$2.00.

CIRCULATION: 400-500

CONTENTS: Essays on literature, such as "The Evolution of the Rose: From Form to Flame"; occasional bibliographies, such as "An Annotated Bibliography of William Faulkner, 1967-1970."

UNSOLICITED MSS. WELCOME?No. Only contributions from the University of Mississippi Faculty and students are accepted.
GENERAL: First issue, 1959. Usual publication length, 99 pages.
BACK ISSUES: Available from editorial address at $2.00 each.

STUDIES IN ENGLISH LITERATURE/EIBUNGAKU KENKYU

EDITORIAL ADDRESS:
Yoshiaki Fuhara, Editor
The English Literary
Society of Japan
18 Nakamachi
Shinjuku-ku
Tokyo, 162
Japan

SUBSCRIPTION ADDRESS:
Secretary
same

PUBLISHED: Tri-annually
CIRCULATION: 3,000
COST: 1 yr.—3,000 yen, or its equivalent in any currency; single copy—1,000 yen.

CONTENTS: Articles concerning English and American literature and language, and reviews of recent publications, home and abroad. Examples: "The Sea in BEOWULF"; "The Archetype and Ectypes of Belial in Milton's Epic Poems."

UNSOLICITED MSS. WELCOME? Yes, but only from members of the Society (no particular qualification to membership); submissions acknowledged.
MS. LENGTH: 8,000-10,000 words; submit TWO copies.
STYLE REQUIREMENTS: MLA STYLE SHEET.
COPYRIGHT: The English Literary Society of Japan.
EDITOR'S DECISION: 4 months.
FROM ACCEPTANCE TO PUBLICATION: Less than 1 year.
PAYMENT/OFFPRINTS: 20 free offprints.
REJECTED MSS.: Returned.
GENERAL: First issue, February, 1920. Usual publication length, 200 pages. Articles and reviews may be written in English or Japanese. Annual English Number contains English only.
BACK ISSUES: Available from Secretary at 600 yen each (1965-1970); 700 yen each (1970-1972); 1,000 yen each from 1973.

STUDIES IN THE HUMANITIES

See the Section on SPECIALIZED TOPICS AND INTERDISCIPLINARY STUDIES: INTERDISCIPLINARY for details.

STUDIES IN THE LITERARY IMAGINATION

EDITORIAL ADDRESS:
Paul G. Blount, Editor
Department of English
Georgia State University
33 Gilmer Street, S.E.
Atlanta, Georgia 30303

SUBSCRIPTION ADDRESS:
James D. Wilson, Managing Editor
same

PUBLISHED: Biannually   CIRCULATION: 3,000
COST: Distributed free of charge to selected institutions, libraries and individuals upon request. May go on charge basis in Fall, 1974.

CONTENTS: Each issue is a special issue with a consulting editor and focuses on a particular author or theme in English and American literature, such as The Legacy of Francis Bacon, James Joyce in the Seventies, Creativity in Southern Folklore, and American Romanticism: Hawthorne and Melville. Only critical and scholarly essays are printed.

UNSOLICITED MSS. WELCOME? No, all essays are solicited by consulting editor; submissions acknowledged.
MS. LENGTH: 5,000-8,000 words; submit ONE copy.
STYLE REQUIREMENTS: MLA STYLE SHEET.
COPYRIGHT: Department of English, Georgia State University.
EDITOR'S DECISION: 2 months.
FROM ACCEPTANCE TO PUBLICATION: 6 months.

PAYMENT/OFFPRINTS: None.
REJECTED MSS.: Returned.
GENERAL: First issue, 1968. Usual publication length, 175 pages.
BACK ISSUES: Available from Managing Editor at no charge at present.

TENNESSEE STUDIES IN LITERATURE

EDITORIAL ADDRESS:
Richard M. Kelly, Editor
McClung Tower 306
University of Tennessee
Knoxville, Tennessee 37916

SUBSCRIPTION ADDRESS:
University of Tennessee Press
Communications Building
University Station
Knoxville, Tennessee 37916

PUBLISHED: Annually
COST: Inquire of published.

CIRCULATION: 800-1,000

CONTENTS: Critical, researched essays on American and English literature of any period. Example: "A Terrible Beauty: Medusa in Three Victorian Poets"; "The Short Stories of Tennessee Williams: Nucleus for His Drama."

UNSOLICITED MSS. WELCOME? Yes; submissions acknowledged.
MS. LENGTH: 12-16 pages; submit TWO copies.
STYLE REQUIREMENTS: MLA STYLE SHEET; footnotes follow essay.
COPYRIGHT: University of Tennessee Press.
EDITOR'S DECISION: 3-6 months.
FROM ACCEPTANCE TO PUBLICATION: 1-2 years.
PAYMENT/OFFPRINTS: 50 offprints.
REJECTED MSS.: Returned.
GENERAL: First issue, 1956. Usual publication length, 130 pages. Submit abstract of essay with manuscript.
BACK ISSUES: Available from University of Tennessee Press. Request price list.

THOTH

EDITORIAL ADDRESS:
Peter Lane Stambler and John W. Ferstel, Executive Editors
Department of English
Syracuse University
Syracuse, New York 13210

SUBSCRIPTION ADDRESS:

same

PUBLISHED: Tri-annually (Fall, Winter, Spring)
COST: 1 yr.—$3.00; 2 yrs.—$5.00.

CIRCULATION: 200-250

CONTENTS: Critical papers on American and British literature (all subjects, all approaches, all critical biases); an annual Stephen Crane bibliography. Example: "Glory, Jest, and Riddle: The Three Deaths of Falstaff."

UNSOLICITED MSS. WELCOME? Yes, but only from graduate students at accredited institutions; submissions acknowledged.
SPECIFICALLY WELCOMED: Scholarly essays.
MS. LENGTH: Up to 7,500 words; submit ONE copy.
STYLE REQUIREMENTS: MLA STYLE SHEET.
COPYRIGHT: THOTH.
EDITOR'S DECISION: About 4 months.
FROM ACCEPTANCE TO PUBLICATION: 4-6 months.
PAYMENT/OFFPRINTS: Six copies of issue. No offprints.
REJECTED MSS.: Returned.
GENERAL: First issue, 1959. Usual publication length, 50 pages. Indexed by volume.
BACK ISSUES: Vols. 1-3 available from Johnson Reprint Corp. Soon Johnson Associates will have all back issues (Vols. 1-12) in microfiche.

TULANE STUDIES IN ENGLISH

EDITORIAL ADDRESS:
Purvis E. Boyette, Editor
Department of English
Tulane University
New Orleans, Louisiana 70118

SUBSCRIPTION ADDRESS:

same

PUBLISHED: Annually
COST: 1 yr.—$4.50.

CIRCULATION: 800

CONTENTS: Scholarly and critical articles on English and American literature from BEOWULF to the present.

UNSOLICITED MSS. WELCOME? No.
GENERAL: First issue, 1949. Usual publication length, 160 pages.
BACK ISSUES: Available from editorial address at $4.50 each.

ZEITSCHRIFT FÜR ANGLISTIK UND AMERIKANISTIK

EDITORIAL ADDRESS:
Dr. Helmut Findeisen, Editor
VEB Verlag Enzyklopädie
DDR-701 Leipzig 1
German Democratic Republic
Gerichtsweg 26

SUBSCRIPTION ADDRESS:
Buchexport, DDR-701 Leipzig
Leninstrasse 16
or publishers: VEB Verlag
Enzyklopädie
DDR-701 Leipzig 1
Gerichtsweg 26

PUBLISHED: Quarterly
COST: 1 yr.—M48.; single copy—M12.

CIRCULATION: 1,500

CONTENTS: Articles on English and American language and literature and sociology; reviews of books relevant to these fields. Example: "SUNSHINE AND SHADOW and the Structure of Chartist Fiction."

UNSOLICITED MSS. WELCOME? Yes, within limits; submissions acknowledged.
SPECIFICALLY WELCOMED: Critical studies in English and American literature.
MS. LENGTH: About 20 pages; submit TWO copies.
STYLE REQUIREMENTS: Academic.
COPYRIGHT: Publishers.
EDITOR'S DECISION: 2 months.
PAYMENT/OFFPRINTS: M 15.-to M 20.-per printed page. 20 free offprints.
REJECTED MSS.: Returned.
GENERAL: First issue, July, 1953. Usual publication length, 112 pages.
BACK ISSUES: Available from publishers, VEB Verlag Enzyklopädie, at M 12.- each.

ENGLISH and BRITISH COMMONWEALTH

THE ABERDEEN UNIVERSITY REVIEW

EDITORIAL ADDRESS:
E. E. Morrison, Editor
Department of Mathematics
King's College
Old Aberdeen AB9 2UB
Scotland

SUBSCRIPTION ADDRESS:

same

PUBLISHED: Biannually   CIRCULATION: 1,500-1,600
COST: 1 yr.—£1.50 postage free (payable in advance); single copy—£0.75.

CONTENTS: Articles of general interest; book reviews and poems generally about Aberdeen and other parts of Scotland; news about activities of Aberdeen graduates; occasional illustrations. Example of literary article: "Writers and the Creative Process in Modern Russia."

UNSOLICITED MSS. WELCOME? Yes; submissions acknowledged.
SPECIFICALLY WELCOMED: General articles, provided that they have some specific relation to the cultural interests of this area.
MS. LENGTH: Around 4,000 words; submit ONE copy.
STYLE REQUIREMENTS: None of a specific nature.
COPYRIGHT: THE ABERDEEN UNIVERSITY REVIEW.
EDITOR'S DECISION: 1 month.
FROM ACCEPTANCE TO PUBLICATION: 1 year or more.
PAYMENT/OFFPRINTS: 12 free offprints; more supplied upon payment.
REJECTED MSS.: Returned.
GENERAL: First issue, October, 1913. Usual publication length, 96-112 pages. All queries are welcome and should be addressed to the editor.
BACK ISSUES: Available from the editor at price prevailing at time of issue. Supplies limited, but specific articles will be photocopied on request.

ALBERTA ENGLISH

See the section on TEACHING ABOUT LITERATURE for details.

ANGLO-WELSH REVIEW

EDITORIAL ADDRESS:
Roland Mathias, Editor
Deffrobani
Maescelyn
Brecon, S. Wales,
United Kingdom

SUBSCRIPTION ADDRESS:
W. S. Smith
Tynewydd
1 Lodge Hill
Caerleon
Newport Mon NP6 1DA
United Kingdom

PUBLISHED: Tri-annually CIRCULATION: 1,500
COST: 1 yr.—$5.00.

CONTENTS: Essays about the literature, life, and culture of Welshmen; any literature (poems, stories, articles, reviews) about Wales and the Welsh; works written by Welsh people or people of Welsh origins or by people living in Wales or who have visited Wales. Examples: "Notes on Modern Literature in Breton"; "George Powell—Swinburne's 'Friend of Many a Season.' "

UNSOLICITED MSS. WELCOME? Yes; submissions not acknowledged.
SPECIFICALLY WELCOMED: Anything of high quality by or about Welsh people.
MS. LENGTH: 1,000-3,000 words; submit ONE copy.
COPYRIGHT: Author.
EDITOR'S DECISION: 2 months.
FROM ACCEPTANCE TO PUBLICATION: Variable.
PAYMENT/OFFPRINTS: Two copies of issue and payment according to length.
REJECTED MSS.: Returned.
GENERAL: First issue, 1949. Usual publication length, 250 pages. This is the only magazine of its kind in Wales with a history of nearly 25 years.
BACK ISSUES: Available from William Dawson & Sons Ltd., Back Issues Department, Cannon House, Folkestone, Kent, United Kingdom, at $3.00 if in print; special reprints available.

AUMLA: A JOURNAL OF LITERARY CRITICISM, PHILOLOGY AND LINGUISTICS

EDITORIAL ADDRESS:
R. T. Sussex, Editor
James Cook University of
North Queensland
Townsville 4810
Australia

SUBSCRIPTION ADDRESS:
James Cook University of
North Queensland
Post Office
Douglas 4811
Qld Australia

PUBLISHED: Biannually CIRCULATION: 1,200
COST: 1 yr.—$4.00; single copy—$2.00.

CONTENTS: Critical articles on the literature and languages of Australia and of many tongues situated around the world; book reviews.

UNSOLICITED MSS. WELCOME? Yes; submissions acknowledged.
SPECIFICALLY WELCOMED: Scholarly criticism; reviews.
MS. LENGTH: 8,000 words; submit ONE copy.
STYLE REQUIREMENTS: MLA STYLE SHEET or near approach; footnotes follow article.
EDITOR'S DECISION: 2-3 months.
FROM ACCEPTANCE TO PUBLICATION: 2-6 months.
PAYMENT/OFFPRINTS: 15 free offprints to contributors of articles.

REJECTED MSS.: Returned.
GENERAL: First issue, 1953. Usual publication length, 148 pages. Contributions may be written in English, French, or German.
BACK ISSUES: #35 available from University of Canterbury, Christchurch, New Zealand at $2.00 each. #1-#34 available from Kraus Reprints, Nendeln, Liechtenstein; see Kraus catalogue for prices.

AUSTRALIAN LITERARY STUDIES

EDITORIAL ADDRESS:
L. T. Hergenhan & E. Stokes, Editors
University of Tasmania
Department of English
Box 252c, G. P. O.
Hobart, Tasmania 7001
Australia

SUBSCRIPTION ADDRESS:
Secretary
AUSTRALIAN LITERARY STUDIES
same

PUBLISHED: Biannually (May, Oct.)   CIRCULATION: 1,100
COST: 1 yr.—$(Aus) 3.00 in Australia and New Zealand; $(Aus)4.50 elsewhere; single copy—$(Aus)1.50; $(Aus)2.25 elsewhere; includes postage.

CONTENTS: Articles on Australian literature, past and present; predominantly critical, but some are biographical, historical; notes and documents (e.g. checklists, biographical notes, notes on literary influences, original letters); reviews of recent books (biographies, critical studies); Annual Bibliography of Studies in Australian Literature (in May); list of "Research in Progress in Australian Literature" every two years. Example: "The Imagination of John Shaw Neilson."

UNSOLICITED MSS. WELCOME? Yes; submissions acknowledged.
SPECIFICALLY WELCOMED: Articles on Australian literary history and its connections with social and cultural history.
MS. LENGTH: 3,000-5,000 words; submit TWO copies.
STYLE REQUIREMENTS: MLA STYLE SHEET (except single inverted commas used for quotations).
COPYRIGHT: Authors.
EDITOR'S DECISION: 4 weeks.
FROM ACCEPTANCE TO PUBLICATION: 6-18 months.
PAYMENT/OFFPRINTS: $5 to $50 depending on length (articles generally about $30). Copies of issue supplied; offprints not available.
REJECTED MSS.: Returned.
GENERAL: First issue, June, 1963. Usual publication length, 112 pages. Indexed by volume.
BACK ISSUES: Available from subscription address at $(Aus)2.50 each for Vols. 1, 2, 3, 4; $(Aus)2.25 each for Vol. 5.

BOOKS IN CANADA

EDITORIAL ADDRESS: SUBSCRIPTION ADDRESS:
Val Clery, Editor
6 Charles Street East same
Toronto, Ontario
Canada

PUBLISHED: Monthly CIRCULATION: 41,000
COST: 1 yr.—$9.95; distribution free through book stores.

CONTENTS: Editorial on publishing of Canadian books; reviews of books.

UNSOLICITED MSS. WELCOME? Yes; submissions acknowledged.
SPECIFICALLY WELCOMED: Literary reviews.
MS. LENGTH: 500-1,000 words; submit TWO copies.
COPYRIGHT: BOOKS IN CANADA.
EDITOR'S DECISION: 1 week.
FROM ACCEPTANCE TO PUBLICATION: 1-2 months.
PAYMENT/OFFPRINTS: Usually $25.00 and one magazine.
REJECTED MSS.: Returned.
GENERAL: First issue, Sept./Oct., 1972. Usual publication length, 32 pages. The only nationally distributed book review magazine in Canada.
BACK ISSUES: Available from editorial address at $1.00 each.

CANADIAN LITERATURE/LITTERATURE CANADIENNE: A QUARTERLY OF CRITICISM AND REVIEW

EDITORIAL ADDRESS: SUBSCRIPTION ADDRESS:
George Woodcock, Editor Circulation Manager
University of British Columbia same
Vancouver 8, British Columbia
Canada

PUBLISHED: Quarterly CIRCULATION: 2,300
COST: 1 yr.—$5.50; single copy—$2.00.

CONTENTS: Articles on Canadian writers and writing; reviews and review articles on current Canadian books. Examples: "Notes on the Canadian Imagination"; "The Occasions of Irving Layton."

UNSOLICITED MSS. WELCOME? Yes.
MS. LENGTH: Up to 5,000 words; submit ONE copy.
STYLE REQUIREMENTS: Sound English; no American spelling.
COPYRIGHT: CL asks first serial rights and nothing beyond.
EDITOR'S DECISION: 3 weeks.
FROM ACCEPTANCE TO PUBLICATION: Minimum of 1 year.
PAYMENT/OFFPRINTS: $10 a thousand words.
REJECTED MSS.: Returned.

GENERAL: First issue, 1959. Usual publication length, 128 pages.
BACK ISSUES: Available from editorial address at $2.00 each plus postage.

THE CANADIAN MODERN LANGUAGE REVIEW

EDITORIAL ADDRESS: SUBSCRIPTION ADDRESS:
Editor
194 Dawlish Avenue   same
Toronto 317
Canada

GENERAL: First issue, 1944. This periodical had not arrived by the time the entry went to press. Potential subscribers, contributors, or collectors will have to write the editor to see whether the journal still exists, and if so, to inquire about details of manuscript submission, style, back issues, and the like.

THE CANADIAN REVIEW OF AMERICAN STUDIES

See the section on AGE AND/OR NATIONALITY: AMERICAN for details.

THE DUBLIN MAGAZINE: IRELAND'S QUARTERLY OF LITERATURE AND ART

EDITORIAL ADDRESS: SUBSCRIPTION ADDRESS:
John Ryan, Editor
'Elstow'   same
Knapton Road
Dun Laoire, County Dublin
Republic of Ireland

PUBLISHED: Quarterly   CIRCULATION: 1,200
COST: 1 yr.—$6.00; single copy—$1.50.

CONTENTS: Short stories; poetry; critical essays; book reviews. Frequently featured: articles on English literature and Anglo-Irish literature including drama. Articles and studies devoted to prominent Irish writers viz: G. B. Shaw, James Joyce, J. M. Synge, W. B. Yeats, William Carleton, Patrick Kavanagh are particularly welcome.

UNSOLICITED MSS. WELCOME? Yes; submissions acknowledged.
SPECIFICALLY WELCOMED: Essays and articles on prominent Anglo-Irish or American-Irish poets, novelists, and playwrights.
MS. LENGTH: 3,000-7,000 words; submit ONE copy.

COPYRIGHT: Author.
EDITOR'S DECISION: 8-12 weeks.
FROM ACCEPTANCE TO PUBLICATION: 8-12 weeks.
PAYMENT/OFFPRINTS: Six copies of magazine with the author's work.
REJECTED MSS.: Returned.
GENERAL: First issue, 1961. Usual publication length, 125 pages.
BACK ISSUES: Available from editorial address at $2.40 each (post free).

ÉIRE-IRELAND: A JOURNAL OF IRISH STUDIES

EDITORIAL ADDRESS: SUBSCRIPTION ADDRESS:
Lawrence O'Shaughnessy, Seán
McMahon, Eóin McKiernan, Editors same
Box 5026
The College of St. Thomas
St. Paul, Minnesota 55105

PUBLISHED: Quarterly CIRCULATION: 3,900
COST: 1 yr.—$10.00 (includes membership in Irish American Cultural Institute).

CONTENTS: Original critiques on a wide spectrum of Irish-interest events, ideas, persons, or subjects; book reviews; music; commentary and a report on the Irish language movement. Examples: "Liam O'Flaherty: Literary Ecologist"; "Synge's Concept of The Tramp."

UNSOLICITED MSS. WELCOME? Yes; submissions acknowledged.
SPECIFICALLY WELCOMED: Criticism; interpretation; exposition.
MS. LENGTH: 2,000-5,000 words; submit ONE copy.
STYLE REQUIREMENTS: MLA STYLE SHEET.
COPYRIGHT: ÉIRE-IRELAND.
EDITOR'S DECISION: 2 months.
FROM ACCEPTANCE TO PUBLICATION: 6-9 months.
PAYMENT/OFFPRINTS: Six copies of complete issue.
REJECTED MSS.: Returned.
GENERAL: First issue, January, 1966. Usual publication length, 160 pages. Articles are written in English and Irish. Journal goes to 26 countries.
BACK ISSUES: Available from editorial office at $2.50 each.

ELIZABETHAN BIBLIOGRAPHIES SUPPLEMENTS

See the section on BIBLIOGRAPHICAL AND LIBRARY RESOURCES for details.

ENGLISH

EDITORIAL ADDRESS:
Margaret Willy, Editor
7 Brockmere
43 Wray Park Road
Reigate, Surrey
England

SUBSCRIPTION ADDRESS:
Oxford University Press
Neasden, London N.W. 10.
England

PUBLISHED: Tri-annually
COST: 1 yr.—£1.50, post free; single copy—52½p, post free.

CONTENTS: Articles of literary criticism intended for university-level and academic readership; book reviews (commissioned); poetry.

UNSOLICITED MSS. WELCOME? Articles and poetry, yes; not book reviews; submissions not acknowledged.
MS. LENGTH: 3,000-5,000 words; submit ONE copy.
STYLE REQUIREMENTS: Footnotes at foot of page, not at the end.
COPYRIGHT: Author.
EDITOR'S DECISION: Variable.
FROM ACCEPTANCE TO PUBLICATION: Up to 2 years.
PAYMENT/OFFPRINTS: Roughly at the rate of £1 per page. Contributors referred to the printer for quotation of cost of offprints.
REJECTED MSS.: Returned if accompanied by reply coupon.
GENERAL: First issue, 1936. Usual publication length, 48 pages.
BACK ISSUES: Available from 29 Exhibition Rd., London SW7 2AS, England at 52½p. each.

ENGLISH LITERARY RENAISSANCE

EDITORIAL ADDRESS:
Arthur F. Kinney, Editor
Department of English
University of Massachusetts
Amherst, Massachusetts 01002

SUBSCRIPTION ADDRESS:
Business Manager
same

PUBLISHED: Tri-annually (Feb., May, Nov.) plus INDEX AND ABSTRACTS (annual) and occasional SUPPLEMENTS
CIRCULATION: 610
COST: 1 yr.—10.00 (£4.07), individuals; $15.00 (£6.10), institutions and libraries; single copy—$4.50 (£1.83).

CONTENTS: Critical essays; newly printed mss. and rare texts, and annotated bibliographies of the literary achievement of Tudor and Stuart England, 1485-1674; contemporary illustrations whenever appropriate (including ms. pages). Examples: "Structure and Meaning in THE COURTIER"; "The Alexandrian Allusion in Shakespeare's HENRY V."

UNSOLICITED MSS. WELCOME? Yes; submissions acknowledged.
SPECIFICALLY WELCOMED: Thoroughly researched critical essays about writers during 1485-1674; edited texts retaining original spelling (include introduction, stemms, variants, transcriptions, translations).
MS. LENGTH: 15-50 pages; submit ORIGINAL ribbon only; xeroxes and carbons not acceptable.
STYLE REQUIREMENTS: MLA STYLE SHEET.
COPYRIGHT: ENGLISH LITERARY RENAISSANCE.
EDITOR'S DECISION: 1-3 months.
FROM ACCEPTANCE TO PUBLICATION: Within 1 year.
PAYMENT/OFFPRINTS: Two gratis copies of the issue. Contributors order offprints at cost at galle y-proof stage.
REJECTED MSS.: Returned.
GENERAL: First issue, Winter, 1971. Usual publication length, 116-216 pages. ELR has a number of other publications; see back cover of most recent issue for those still available.
BACK ISSUES: Available from business office at $4.50 (£1.83) each during the volume year; thereafter, $7.00 (£3.85) each or $20.00 (£8.13) per volume.

ENGLISH LITERATURE IN TRANSITION: 1880-1920

EDITORIAL ADDRESS:
Helmut E. Gerber, Editor
Department of English
Arizona State University
Tempe, Arizona 85281

SUBSCRIPTION ADDRESS:

same

PUBLISHED: 4 times yearly
at irregular intervals
COST: 1 yr.—$3.00 in U.S.; $4.00 elsewhere; single copy—$1.00 in U.S.; $1.50 elsewhere.

CIRCULATION: 800-850

CONTENTS: Critical articles, annotated secondary bibliographies, primary checklists on British authors publishing mainly between 1880 and 1920; reviews; notes; brief unpublished letters and primary material with commentary; informal news and notes on scholarly activities.

UNSOLICITED MSS. WELCOME? Articles, yes; for bibliographies and reviews, inquire; submissions acknowledged.
SPECIFICALLY WELCOMED: Any kind, but preferably not classroom explicatory exercises; work on minor authors are of particular interest.
MS. LENGTH: No set limits; submit TWO copies.
STYLE REQUIREMENTS: Consult issues; footnotes follow articles.
COPYRIGHT: ENGLISH LITERATURE IN TRANSITION; but author always given permission to reprint.
EDITOR'S DECISION: 6-8 weeks.
FROM ACCEPTANCE TO PUBLICATION: About 9 months.
PAYMENT/OFFPRINTS: Two free copies of whole issue. Purchase of offprints and additional full copies at special rate.

REJECTED MSS.: Returned.
GENERAL: First issue, 1957. Usual publication length, 60-70 pages.
BACK ISSUES: Volume 12 (1969) to present, in short supply, available from editorial address at $1.00 each ($1.50 foreign). Back issues of Vols. 1-11 (1957/58-1968) available from Kraus Reprint Co.

ENGLISH MISCELLANY: A SYMPOSIUM OF HISTORY, LITERATURE AND THE ARTS

EDITORIAL ADDRESS:
Mario Praz, Editor
Via Zanardelli 1
00186 Rome
Italy

SUBSCRIPTION ADDRESS:
Edizioni di Storia e Letteratura
same

PUBLISHED: Annually
COST: Varies from issue to issue (L. 6.000 and up).

CONTENTS: Scholarly articles on literature, arts, and history; some illustrations. Examples: "The Voice of Water: Lawrence's 'The Virgin and the Gipsy' "; "Wycherley's 'The Plain Dealer' and the Limits of Wit."

UNSOLICITED MSS. WELCOME? Yes; submissions acknowledged.
MS. LENGTH: Up to 20 pages.
COPYRIGHT: Edizioni di Storia e Letteratura.
EDITOR'S DECISION: Varies.
FROM ACCEPTANCE TO PUBLICATION: Varies.
REJECTED MSS.: Returned.
GENERAL: First issue, 1950. Usual publication length, 300-380 pages. Articles may be written in English, Italian, or German. French and Spanish also considered.
BACK ISSUES: Available from Edizioni di Storia e Letteratura. Price is same as for current issues.

ENGLISH STUDIES IN AFRICA: A JOURNAL OF THE HUMANITIES

EDITORIAL ADDRESS:
Dr. B. D. Cheadle, Editor
Witwatersrand University Press
Jan Smuts Avenue
Johannesburg
South Africa

SUBSCRIPTION ADDRESS:
The Publications Officer
same

PUBLISHED: Biannually
CIRCULATION: 500
COST: 1 yr.—R3,00; single copy—R1,50; 25% discount to booksellers; no discount to libraries.

CONTENTS: Articles devoted to the promotion of English Studies and of the humanities; academic literary criticism; book reviews. Example: "Irony and Attitude in George Eliot and D. H. Lawrence."

UNSOLICITED MSS. WELCOME? Yes, but book reviews are commissioned; submissions acknowledged.
SPECIFICALLY WELCOMED: Critical academic works related to English/humanities studies in Africa; NO creative writing (stories, plays).
MS. LENGTH: Not more than 20-25 pages; submit TWO copies.
STYLE REQUIREMENTS: Write for a list; use Oxford Press Style; footnotes on separate sheet.
COPYRIGHT: Witwatersrand University Press (publisher).
EDITOR'S DECISION: 3-4 months.
FROM ACCEPTANCE TO PUBLICATION: 1-6 months.
PAYMENT/OFFPRINTS: 12 free offprints; more (if required) at cost; notify editor before publication.
REJECTED MSS.: Returned.
GENERAL: First issue, 1958. Usual publication length, 55-60 pages.
BACK ISSUES: Available from Publications Officer at R1,50 each for single numbers; R2,00 each for double numbers.

ENGLISH SYMPOSIUM PAPERS

EDITORIAL ADDRESS:
Douglas H. Shepard, General Editor
Department of English
State University College
Fredonia, New York 14063

SUBSCRIPTION ADDRESS:

same

PUBLISHED: Annually
COST: Free.

CIRCULATION: 250

CONTENTS: Festschrift based on previous Symposium topic. Examples: "Two Ways of Talking about Prose Texts"; "Lyric and Lyrical in the Works of Chaucer."

UNSOLICITED MSS. WELCOME? No.
COPYRIGHT: Held for unlimited use by original authors.
GENERAL: First issue, 1970. Usual publication length, 100 pages.
BACK ISSUES: Free from editorial address.

EXPLORATIONS: A JOURNAL OF LITERARY CRITICISM

See the section on AGE AND/OR NATIONALITY: ASIAN for details.

INDEX TO AUSTRALIAN BOOK REVIEWS

See the section on BIBLIOGRAPHICAL AND LIBRARY RESOURCES for details.

IRISH UNIVERSITY REVIEW: A JOURNAL OF IRISH STUDIES

EDITORIAL ADDRESS:
Maurice Harmon, Editor
Department of English
University College—Belfield
Dublin 4
Ireland

SUBSCRIPTION ADDRESS:
Irish University Press
81 Merrion Square
Dublin 2
Ireland

PUBLISHED: Biannually (Autumn, Spring)
COST: 1 yr.—£2.50; single copy—£1.25.

CIRCULATION: 1,000

CONTENTS: Studies of Anglo-Irish literature and its contexts—history, folklore, mythology; annual Anglo-Irish "Bibliography Bulletin." Example: "Identifying the Irish Printed Sources for FINNEGANS WAKE"; "Old Irish Myth and Modern Irish Literature."

UNSOLICITED MSS. WELCOME? Yes; submissions acknowledged.
MS. LENGTH: 5,000-6,000 words; submit ONE copy.
STYLE REQUIREMENTS: MLA STYLE SHEET.
COPYRIGHT: Varies.
EDITOR'S DECISION: 3 months.
FROM ACCEPTANCE TO PUBLICATION: 1 year.
PAYMENT/OFFPRINTS: None.
REJECTED MSS.: Returned.
GENERAL: First issue, Autumn, 1970. Usual publication length, 126-150 pages.
BACK ISSUES: Available from Irish University Press.

ISLANDS: A NEW ZEALAND QUARTERLY OF ARTS AND LETTERS

EDITORIAL ADDRESS:
Robin Dudding, Editor
15 Barnes Road
Christchurch 5
New Zealand

SUBSCRIPTION ADDRESS:

same

PUBLISHED: Quarterly
COST: 1 yr.—$5.50; single copy—$1.50 in New Zealand ($7.50 overseas; single copy—$2.00 in New Zealand currency).

CIRCULATION: 1,500

CONTENTS: Fiction; poems; literary and art cirticism; reviews of books, theatre exhibitions, architecture. Sociological comment of various kinds. Material basically for and by New Zealanders and immediate Pacific area. Art illustrations.

UNSOLICITED MSS. WELCOME? Yes, but chances of publication of work other than by New Zealanders or about New Zealand limited; submissions acknowledged after consideration.
SPECIFICALLY WELCOMED: Fiction, poems—abstract and probable outline suggested before submitting other material.
MS. LENGTH: No limit; submit ONE copy.
STYLE REQUIREMENTS: Type on quarto paper—references in full.
COPYRIGHT: ISLANDS and author (shared).
EDITOR'S DECISION: Varies—up to 2 months.
FROM ACCEPTANCE TO PUBLICATION: Varies.
PAYMENT/OFFPRINTS: Varies. Approximately $1,200 (NZ) shared annually among contributors.
REJECTED MSS.: Returned.
GENERAL: First issue, September, 1972. Usual publication length, 112 pages. Indexed every 20 numbers.
BACK ISSUES: Available from editorial address at $1.50 (in New Zealand) or $2.00 (overseas) each—New Zealand currency.

JOURNAL OF CANADIAN STUDIES/REVUE D'ÉTUDES CANADIENNES

EDITORIAL ADDRESS:
Denis Smith, Editor
Trent University
Peterborough, Ontario K9J7B8
Canada

SUBSCRIPTION ADDRESS:

same

PUBLISHED: Quarterly (Feb., May, Aug., Nov.)
CIRCULATION: 1,300
COST: 1 yr.—$6.00, individuals; $10.00, institutions; 2 yrs.—$11.00, individuals; $15.00, institutions.

CONTENTS: Scholarly articles, comment, and reviews covering the whole range of studies relating to Canada. Example: "Teaching the Canadian mythology: a poet's view."

UNSOLICITED MSS. WELCOME? Yes; submissions acknowledged.
SPECIFICALLY WELCOMED: Articles about some aspect of Canadian society or history.
MS. LENGTH: 2,000-10,000 words; submit ONE copy.
COPYRIGHT: JOURNAL OF CANADIAN STUDIES.
PAYMENT/OFFPRINTS: $10 per printed page. Up to 50 offprints.
REJECTED MSS.: Returned.
GENERAL: First issue, May, 1966. Usual publication length, 64 pages. Articles may be written in English or French.

BACK ISSUES: Available from editorial office at $3.00 each.

JOURNAL OF COMMONWEALTH LITERATURE

EDITORIAL ADDRESS:
Arthur Ravenscroft, Editor
School of English
University of Leeds
Leeds LS2 9JT
England

SUBSCRIPTION ADDRESS:
Subscription Department
Oxford University Press
Press Road
Neasden, London NW10 0DD
England

PUBLISHED: Tri-annually
COST: 1 yr.—£3.00.

CONTENTS: December issue contains "Annual Bibliography of Commonwealth Literature" covering the previous calendar year, in 14 country or area divisions, each listing bibliographies, poetry, drama, fiction, non-fiction, anthologies, translations, criticism, journals. Other issues publish critical and scholarly articles on literature in English from Commonwealth countries and Pakistan and South Africa, and reviews.

UNSOLICITED MSS. WELCOME? Yes; submissions acknowledged.
SPECIFICALLY WELCOMED: Critical and scholarly articles.
MS. LENGTH: Not over 5,000 words; submit TWO copies.
STYLE REQUIREMENTS: Oxford.
COPYRIGHT: Oxford University Press, but permission for republication readily given.
EDITOR'S DECISION: About 2 months.
FROM ACCEPTANCE TO PUBLICATION: 1½ to 2 years.
PAYMENT/OFFPRINTS: Articles: £4.00 per 1,000 words; reviews: £3.00 per 1,000 words. No offprints.
REJECTED MSS.: Returned if international reply coupon sent.
GENERAL: First issue, September, 1965. Usual publication length, 88 pages (twice) and 144 pages.
BACK ISSUES: Nos. 1-8 (1965-1969) available from Swets & Zeitlinger, Amsterdam, Holland; Nos. 9-10 and Vols. VI onwards (1970—) from Oxford University Press.

KOVAVE: JOURNAL OF NEW GUINEA LITERATURE

EDITORIAL ADDRESS:
Ulli Beier, Editor
Jacaranda Press Pty. Ltd.
46 Douglas Street
Milton, Queensland 4064, Australia

SUBSCRIPTION ADDRESS:
Jacaranda Press Pty. Ltd.
46 Douglas Street
Milton, Queensland 4064, Australia

PUBLISHED: Biannually   CIRCULATION: 900
COST: 1 yr.—Australian $2.00; single copy—Australian $1.00.

CONTENTS: Selections of poetry, prose, drama, criticism and reviews by indigenous writers of Papua New Guinea.

GENERAL: First issue, November, 1969. Usual publication length, 60 pages.
BACK ISSUES: Available from Jacaranda Press Pty. Ltd. at Australian $1.00, plus postage.

THE LITERARY CRITERION

EDITORIAL ADDRESS:
C. D. Narasimhaiah, Editor
Professors' Quarters
Mysore 9
India

SUBSCRIPTION ADDRESS:
Popular Prakashan
35/C Tardeo Road
Bombay-34 WB
India

PUBLISHED: Biannually   CIRCULATION: 500
COST: 1 yr.—$2.50; single issue—$1.25.

CONTENTS: Scholarly essays about the works of American, Commonwealth and English authors, and Indian authors writing in English. Examples: "An Introduction to West African Novels in English"; "The Book Review as a Literary Factor in Britain."

UNSOLICITED MSS. WELCOME? Yes; submissions not acknowledged.
SPECIFICALLY WELCOMED: Close analysis of texts together with value judgments which have a relevance to our times.
MS. LENGTH: 2,000-3,000 words; submit TWO copies.
STYLE REQUIREMENTS: MLA STYLE SHEET; include footnotes within text.
COPYRIGHT: Author.
EDITOR'S DECISION: 2 months.
FROM ACCEPTANCE TO PUBLICATION: 3-6 months.
PAYMENT/OFFPRINTS: Ten offprints.
REJECTED MSS.: Not returned.
GENERAL: First issue, 1952. Usual publication length, 100 pages.
BACK ISSUES: Available from editorial office at $1.25 each. Johnson Reprint Corporation will microfilm Volumes I to IV.

THE MARY WOLLSTONECRAFT NEWSLETTER

See the section on SINGLE AND MULTIPLE AUTHOR FOCUS: EUROPEAN for details.

OLD ENGLISH NEWSLETTER

EDITORIAL ADDRESS:
Stanley J. Kahrl, Editor
Center for Medieval and
Renaissance Studies
The Ohio State University
320 Main Library, 1858 Neil Avenue
Columbus, Ohio 43210

SUBSCRIPTION ADDRESS:

same

PUBLISHED: Biannually
COST: Free to individuals; $3.00 per volume for institutions.

CONTENTS: News of general interest, such as a report of a survey on teaching introductory Old English in the U.S. and Canada; Old English bibliography (miscellaneous literary, linguistic, historical and cultural, individual authors and titles, reviews, work forthcoming and in progress, dissertations in progress).

GENERAL: First issue, 1966. Usual publication length, 40-50 pages.
BACK ISSUES: Available from editorial address.

PROCEEDINGS OF THE BRITISH ACADEMY

EDITORIAL ADDRESS:
The Secretary
The British Academy
Burlington House
Picadilly
London W1V ONS
England

SUBSCRIPTION ADDRESS:
Oxford University Press
Press Road
Neasden
London N.W. 10
England

PUBLISHED: Annually
COST: Price varies: Last issue, 1971—£8.00.

CIRCULATION: 1,500

CONTENTS: Lectures on philosophy, literature, history, archaeology, social anthropology, economics; memoirs of deceased fellows of the British Academy; annual report and accounts; presidential address.

UNSOLICITED MSS. WELCOME? No; contributions by invitation only.
STYLE REQUIREMENTS: Oxford University Press House Rules.
COPYRIGHT: The British Academy.
GENERAL: First issue, 1903-04. Publication length varies; recent issue, 564 pages and 40 plates.
BACK ISSUES: Available from Oxford University Press. Price varies.

QUEEN'S QUARTERLY: A CANADIAN REVIEW

EDITORIAL ADDRESS:
Kerry McSweeney, Editor
Queen's University
Kingston, Ontario
Canada

SUBSCRIPTION ADDRESS:

same

PUBLISHED: Quarterly
COST: 1 yr.—$6.00; 3 yrs.—$15.00; single copy—$1.50.

CIRCULATION: 1,700

CONTENTS: Articles on politics, literature, history of ideas, etc.—particularly Canadian; some poetry and fiction.

UNSOLICITED MSS. WELCOME? Yes; submissions not acknowledged.
SPECIFICALLY WELCOMED: Articles of general interest; non-specialist in style.
MS. LENGTH: Up to 20 pages; submit TWO copies.
COPYRIGHT: Author.
EDITOR'S DECISION: 3 weeks.
FROM ACCEPTANCE TO PUBLICATION: 9 months or less.
PAYMENT/OFFPRINTS: $3 per printed page. Fifty offprints at $1.50 per printed page; 100 at $1.75 per printed page.
REJECTED MSS.: Returned.
GENERAL: First issue, 1893. Usual publication length, 160 pages.
BACK ISSUES: Available from editorial address, Vols. I through X from Johnson Reprint Corporation. Cost varies.

RENAISSANCE DRAMA

See the section on AGE AND/OR NATIONALITY: CONTINENTAL—CLASSICAL, MEDIEVAL, AND RENAISSANCE for details.

A REVIEW OF ENGLISH STUDIES: A QUARTERLY JOURNAL OF ENGLISH LITERATURE AND THE ENGLISH LANGUAGE

EDITORIAL ADDRESS:
J. B. Bamborough, Editor
The Clarendon Press
Oxford
England

SUBSCRIPTION ADDRESS:
Oxford University Press
Press Road
Neasden, London NW10 ODD
England

PUBLISHED: Quarterly
COST: 1 yr.—$12.25 (£4.50); single copy—$4.75 net (£1.75).

CIRCULATION: 2,300

CONTENTS: Articles, short notes, and reviews of books concerned with topics and authors from all periods of English Literature; interest is in historical scholarship rather than interpretative criticism. In addition, each number includes a summary of recent periodical literature. Example: "Scott, the Romantic Past and the Nineteenth Century."

UNSOLICITED MSS. WELCOME? Yes; submissions acknowledged.
SPECIFICALLY WELCOMED: Scholarly articles and notes concerned with English Language and Literature.
MS. LENGTH: 6,000-7,000 words; submit ONE copy.
STYLE REQUIREMENTS: Style sheets can be supplied.
COPYRIGHT: Contributors, but applications for permission to reprint should be addressed to The Clarendon Press.
EDITOR'S DECISION: 1 month.
FROM ACCEPTANCE TO PUBLICATION: 6-12 months.
PAYMENT/OFFPRINTS: Articles, 25 free offprints; notes, 8; reviews and short notices, 6; extra copies can be bought.
REJECTED MSS.: Returned.
GENERAL: First issue, 1925. Usual publication length, 125-150 pages.
BACK ISSUES: Inquiries for all volumes except the current one and the 5 previous to it should be sent to Messrs. Wm. Dawson & Sons, 16 West Street, Farnham, Surrey.

REVUE DES LANGUES VIVANTES, TIJDSCHRIFT VOOR LEVENDE TALEN

See the section on AGE AND/OR NATIONALITY: EUROPEAN.

SCOTTISH INTERNATIONAL REVIEW

EDITORIAL ADDRESS:
Tom Buchan, Editor
23 George Square
Edinburgh EH8 9LD
Scotland

SUBSCRIPTION ADDRESS:
Dave Morgan, Circulation Department
same

PUBLISHED: 10 times yearly (Aug.-May)
CIRCULATION: 2,300
COST: 1 yr.—£1.50; $4.00 in U.S. and Canada; single copy—15p ($.40).

CONTENTS: News of the arts; poetry, such as "Poems in Shetlandic and Scots"; short stories; Scotland's current affairs; social and literary history; book and theatre reviews; photographs.

UNSOLICITED MSS. WELCOME? Yes; submissions not acknowledged.

SPECIFICALLY WELCOMED: Material relating to Scotland.
MS. LENGTH: 1,000-4,000 words; submit ONE copy.
COPYRIGHT: Scottish International Review Ltd.
EDITOR'S DECISION: 2 months.
FROM ACCEPTANCE TO PUBLICATION: 2 months.
PAYMENT/OFFPRINTS: £4 per 1,000 words prose; minimum £2.20 per poem. Author receives one free copy of magazine.
REJECTED MSS.: Returned.
GENERAL: First issue, January, 1968. Usual publication length, 40 pages. Index in preparation; No. 11 (Nov., 1970) contains checklist of first 10 issues. SIR incorporates FEEDBACK of which only two issues appeared: Vol. 1, No. 1, May, 1966—25 p. (65¢); Vol. 1, No. 2, Spring, 1967—12½p. (33¢).
BACK ISSUES: Available from Scottish International Review Ltd. at the following prices: Nos. 1-10 (quarterly Jan. '68 to May '70—60 pp.) 20p. (55¢) each; nos. 11-13 (quarterly Aug. '70 to Feb. '71—60 pp.) 25p (65¢) each; May '71 onwards (monthly—40pp.) 15p. (40¢) each.

SCOTTISH STUDIES

EDITORIAL ADDRESS:
John MacQueen, Editor
School of Scottish Studies
University of Edinburgh
27 George Square
Edinburgh EH8 9LD
Scotland

SUBSCRIPTION ADDRESS:
same

PUBLISHED: One annual volume in two parts (June and October)
COST: 1 yr.—£2.00; $6.00 in U.S. and Canada.

CIRCULATION: 800

CONTENTS: Articles and notes of research on topics concerning Scottish ethnology and history, folklore and music, and related subjects.

UNSOLICITED MSS. WELCOME? Yes; submissions acknowledged.
SPECIFICALLY WELCOMED: Articles concerning Scottish history, culture.
MS. LENGTH: 5,000-8,000 words; submit ONE copy.
COPYRIGHT: School of Scottish Studies.
EDITOR'S DECISION: 6 weeks.
FROM ACCEPTANCE TO PUBLICATION: Varies.
PAYMENT/OFFPRINTS: 25 free offprints; more at charge.
REJECTED MSS.: Returned.
GENERAL: First issue, 1957. Usual publication length, 210 pages per volume.
BACK ISSUES: Vols. 1-11 (inclusive) available from Swets & Zeitlinger, Heereweg 347b, Lisse, Holland; price varies. Vols. 12 onwards from the School of Scottish Studies at subscription rate to subscribers—£1.25 for stock issues.

SOUTH AUSTRALIANA: A JOURNAL FOR THE PUBLICATION AND STUDY OF SOUTH AUSTRALIAN HISTORICAL AND LITERARY MANUSCRIPTS

EDITORIAL ADDRESS:
Archives
Libraries Board of South Australia
Box 419 GPO
Adelaide 5001
Australia

SUBSCRIPTION ADDRESS:
State Library of South Australia
same

PUBLISHED: Biannually (March, September)

CIRCULATION: 350

COST: 1 yr.—$2.25 (Aust.) including postage to U.S.A.

CONTENTS: Transcripts of South Australian historical and literary manuscripts; articles of South Australian historical interest; lists of government archives, other manuscripts and South Australian publications received in the State Library of South Australia. Example: "THE RETURN OF ROBERT WASTERTON: William Hay's Comedy of Australian Manners."

UNSOLICITED MSS. WELCOME? Yes; submissions acknowledged.
SPECIFICALLY WELCOMED: Scholarly studies of South Australian historical interest.
MS. LENGTH: 5,000-10,000 words; submit ONE or TWO copies.
STYLE REQUIREMENTS: Sources mentioned in the text or footnotes should be cited fully. People mentioned should be identified if possible by full names and dates of birth and death.
COPYRIGHT: Libraries Board of South Australia.
EDITOR'S DECISION: A few weeks.
FROM ACCEPTANCE TO PUBLICATION: A few months.
PAYMENT/OFFPRINTS: Six copies of the issue containing the article.
REJECTED MSS.: Returned.
GENERAL: First issue, 1962. Usual publication length, 50 pages.
BACK ISSUES: Available from the State Library of S.A. at $2.25 (Aust.) per volume.

SOUTHERLY: A QUARTERLY REVIEW OF AUSTRALIAN LITERATURE

EDITORIAL ADDRESS:
Prof. G. A. Wilkes, Editor
English Department
The University of Sydney
Sydney 2006
Australia

SUBSCRIPTION ADDRESS:
Walter Stone, Business Manager
The Wentworth Press
48 Cooper Street
Surry Hills 2010
Australia

PUBLISHED: Quarterly

CIRCULATION: 1,000

CONTENTS: Literary criticism; reviews; short stories; poems.

UNSOLICITED MSS. WELCOME? Yes; submissions acknowledged.
SPECIFICALLY WELCOMED: Australian literary criticism.
MS. LENGTH: Up to 15 pages; submit ONE copy.
STYLE REQUIREMENTS: MLA STYLE SHEET.
COPYRIGHT: Author.
EDITOR'S DECISION: As soon as possible.
FROM ACCEPTANCE TO PUBLICATION: 6 months.
PAYMENT/OFFPRINTS: See recent periodical for payment rates. No offprints.
GENERAL: First issue, 1939. Usual publication length, 104 pages.
BACK ISSUES: Available from subscription address at $.80 each.

STUDIES IN ENGLISH LITERATURE: 1500-1900

EDITORIAL ADDRESS: SUBSCRIPTION ADDRESS:
Carroll Camden, Editor
Rice University same
P. O. Box 1892
Houston, Texas 77001

PUBLISHED: Quarterly CIRCULATION: 1,750
COST: 1 yr.—$8.00 for individuals; $10.00 for U.S. and Canadian libraries; $8.60 for U.S. library with agency discount; $9.10 for Canadian library with agency discount; $8.00 for overseas subscription.

CONTENTS: Historical and critical studies; each issue is devoted to one of four fields; Winter—English Renaissance, Spring—Elizabethan and Jacobean Drama, Summer—Restoration and Eighteenth Century, Autumn—Nineteenth Century.

UNSOLICITED MSS. WELCOME? Yes; submissions acknowledged.
SPECIFICALLY WELCOMED: Scholarly studies of English literature from 1,500-1,900.
MS. LENGTH: 12-24 pages; submit ORIGINAL only.
STYLE REQUIREMENTS: MLA STYLE SHEET.
COPYRIGHT: William Marsh Rice University.
EDITOR'S DECISION: 1 to 2 months.
FROM ACCEPTANCE TO PUBLICATION: 2 years.
PAYMENT/OFFPRINTS: 25 free offprints; additional requested ones at low fee.
REJECTED MSS.: Returned.
GENERAL: First issue, 1967. Usual publication length, 200 pages. Manuscripts submitted to the Editor; should be accompanied by a sufficient number of UNATTACHED stamps for return of manuscript.
BACK ISSUES: Available from editorial address at $3.00 each; from Johnson Reprint Corp.; and from University Microfilms.

STUDIES IN SCOTTISH LITERATURE

EDITORIAL ADDRESS:
G. Ross Roy, Editor
Department of English
University of South Carolina
Columbia, South Carolina 29208

SUBSCRIPTION ADDRESS:

same

PUBLISHED: Quarterly
COST: 1 yr.—$5.00; 3 yrs.—$12.00; single copy—$1.95.

CIRCULATION: 500

CONTENTS: Critical and interpretive articles on Scottish literature; notes and documents; reviews of books pertaining to Scottish literature. Examples: "Bridie's Concept of the Master Experimenter"; "James Macpherson's First Epic."

UNSOLICITED MSS. WELCOME? Yes; submissions acknowledged.
SPECIFICALLY WELCOMED: Articles on any phase of Scottish literature.
MS. LENGTH: 5,000-8,000 words; submit TWO copies.
STYLE REQUIREMENTS: None.
COPYRIGHT: Editor.
EDITOR'S DECISION: 6 months.
FROM ACCEPTANCE TO PUBLICATION: 3-6 months.
PAYMENT/OFFPRINTS: Articles—20 free offprints; notes & documents—10; reviews—5.
REJECTED MSS.: Returned.
GENERAL: First issue, July, 1963. Usual publication length, 65 pages.
BACK ISSUES: Available from The USC Press, Columbia, S.C. 29208 at $1.95 each.

UNIVERSITY OF TORONTO QUARTERLY: A CANADIAN JOURNAL OF THE HUMANITIES

EDITORIAL ADDRESS:
W. F. Blissett, Editor
University of Toronto Press
Toronto 181, Canada

SUBSCRIPTION ADDRESS:

same

PUBLISHED: Quarterly (Oct., Jan., Apr., July)
COST: 1 yr.—$8.00; single copy—$2.00.

CONTENTS: Learned but not minutely specialized articles. Example: "The Aristotle-Coleridge Axis." Summer issue is largely devoted to an annual survey of "Letters in Canada"—reviews of fiction, poetry, literary studies, etc., published in the previous year in English, French, and other languages in Canada or by Canadians.

UNSOLICITED MSS. WELCOME? Yes; submissions acknowledged.
SPECIFICALLY WELCOMED: Learned articles in the humanities.

MS. LENGTH: 20-25 pages; submit ONE copy.
STYLE REQUIREMENTS: Good writing; documentation, as necessary, in standard form.
COPYRIGHT: University of Toronto Press.
EDITOR'S DECISION: 2-3 months.
FROM ACCEPTANCE TO PUBLICATION: 1-2 years.
PAYMENT/OFFPRINTS: $50.00. Up to 50 offprints may be purchased.
REJECTED MSS.: Returned.
GENERAL: First issue, 1931. Usual publication length, 15 pages.
BACK ISSUES: Some available from University of Toronto Press.

VENTURE: BI-ANNUAL REVIEW OF ENGLISH LANGUAGE AND LITERATURE

See the section on AGE AND/OR NATIONALITY: ASIAN for details.

THE VICTORIAN NEWSLETTER

EDITORIAL ADDRESS:　　　　　SUBSCRIPTION ADDRESS:
William E. Buckler, Editor
East Building　　　　　　　　　　same
New York University
Washington Square
New York, New York 10003

PUBLISHED: Biannually (Spring, Fall)
COST: 1 yr.—$3.00; 2 yrs.—$5.00.

CONTENTS: Scholarly essays on Victorian authors and their works; notes; selected lists of recent publications. Examples: "Mrs. Gamp as the Great Mother: A Dickensian Use of the Archetype"; "John Ruskin and the Nature of Manliness."

UNSOLICITED MSS. WELCOME? Yes.
MS. LENGTH: Up to 7,000 words.
STYLE REQUIREMENTS: MLA STYLE SHEET; footnotes follow essay.
GENERAL: First issue, 1952. Usual publication length, 32 pages.
BACK ISSUES: Available from editorial address.

VICTORIAN PERIODICALS NEWSLETTER

EDITORIAL ADDRESS:
Hans De Groot and
Peter Morgan, Editors
English Department
University College
University of Toronto
Toronto, Ontario
Canada

SUBSCRIPTION ADDRESS:

same

PUBLISHED: Quarterly   CIRCULATION: 900
COST: 1 yr.—$3.00 ($5.00 for institutions or libraries).

CONTENTS: Articles ON (not merely utilizing) Victorian periodicals of all sorts; reviews of books on 19th-century British journalism and journals; descriptions of the activities of the Research Society for Victorian Periodicals, and its research committees and projects; notes and queries from scholars using Victorian periodicals; bibliographies, check lists, and union lists of holding dealing with Victorian periodicals. Example: "The Unitarian View of Fifteen Periodicals in 1834."

UNSOLICITED MSS. WELCOME? Yes; submissions usually acknowledged.
SPECIFICALLY WELCOMED: Only scholarly articles and items.
MS. LENGTH: From brief note to 20 pages; submit ONE copy.
STYLE REQUIREMENTS: MLA STYLE SHEET; footnotes follow article.
COPYRIGHT: Not copyrighted.
EDITOR'S DECISION: 2 months.
FROM ACCEPTANCE TO PUBLICATION: 3-6 months.
PAYMENT/OFFPRINTS: No payment. Small charge for extra issues.
REJECTED MSS.: Returned.
GENERAL: First issue, January, 1968. Usual publication length, 40 pages.
BACK ISSUES: Available from editorial address at $1.25 each plus $.15 postage (except for issues 9 and 17 which are $3.00 each).

VICTORIAN POETRY: A CRITICAL JOURNAL OF VICTORIAN LITERATURE

EDITORIAL ADDRESS:
John Stasny, Editor
129 Armstrong Hall
West Virginia University
Morgantown, West Virginia 26506

SUBSCRIPTION ADDRESS:
WVU Book Store
Morgantown, West Virginia 26506

PUBLISHED: Quarterly   CIRCULATION: 1,300
COST: 1 yr.—$8.00 (prices due to rise soon); subscriptions on a yearly basis (Jan. to Dec.) only.

CONTENTS: Scholarly essays, brief articles and notes, and reviews of books concerning Victorian literature. Examples: "Emblematic Tendencies in the Works of Christina Rossetti"; "Hardy's Skylark and Shelley's."

UNSOLICITED MSS. WELCOME? Yes; submissions acknowledged.
MS. LENGTH: Less than 25 pages; submit TWO copies.
STYLE REQUIREMENTS: MLA STYLE SHEET, plus the VP supplement.
COPYRIGHT: VICTORIAN POETRY.
EDITOR'S DECISION: 3 months.
FROM ACCEPTANCE TO PUBLICATION: 1 year.
PAYMENT/OFFPRINTS: Five free issues; offprints in attractive cover at cost.
REJECTED MSS.: Returned.
GENERAL: First issue, 1963. Usual publication length, 100 pages. Articles ten pages or more must include an abstract of 200 words maximum.
BACK ISSUES: Available from WVU Book Store; also from Bell & Howell microfilm division.

VICTORIANS INSTITUTE JOURNAL

EDITORIAL ADDRESS:
Conrad Festa, Editor
Arts and Letters Building
Old Dominion University
Norfolk, Virginia 23508

SUBSCRIPTION ADDRESS:
same

PUBLISHED: Annually
COST: 1 yr.—$2.00.

CONTENTS: Papers read at annual meetings; essays on the literature, art, and history of the Victorian era. Issues have centered on Dickens and on the Pre-Raphaelites. Essay examples: "Swinburne and Mazzini: The Origin of Swinburne's Imperialism"; "Tennyson in Xanadu."

UNSOLICITED MSS. WELCOME? Yes, but note theme of the forthcoming meeting of the Institute.
SPECIFICALLY WELCOMED: Manuscripts treating aspects of Victorian culture.
STYLE REQUIREMENTS: MLA STYLE SHEET.
GENERAL: First issue, 1971. Usual publication length, 72 pages.

VICTORIAN STUDIES

EDITORIAL ADDRESS:
Martha Vicinus, Editor
Ballantine Hall
Indiana University
Bloomington, Indiana 47401

SUBSCRIPTION ADDRESS:

same

PUBLISHED: Quarterly (Sept., Dec., Mar., June)
COST: 1 yr.—$7.00 for individuals; $12.00 for institutions.

CIRCULATION: 2,870

CONTENTS: Interdisciplinary, with essays on the literature, history, history of science, history of art, and philosophy of Nineteenth Century Britain; approximately 15 to 20 book reviews in each issue, and an occasional review essay, discussing recent trends in the field; annual bibliography. Example: "Trollope: Artist and Moralist."

UNSOLICITED MSS. WELCOME? Yes; submissions acknowledged.
SPECIFICALLY WELCOMED: Scholarly, interdisciplinary essays.
MS. LENGTH: 20-30 pages; submit TWO copies.
STYLE REQUIREMENTS: MLA STYLE SHEET.
COPYRIGHT: VICTORIAN STUDIES—The Indiana University Board of Trustees.
EDITOR'S DECISION: 2-3 months.
FROM ACCEPTANCE TO PUBLICATION: 8-12 months.
PAYMENT/OFFPRINTS: Two complimentary copies of issue. $15 for 50; $25 for 100 offprints.
REJECTED MSS.: Returned.
GENERAL: First issue, September, 1957. Usual publication length, 124 pages, except June issue (with annual bibliography) with about 172 pages.
BACK ISSUES: Those of past two years available from editorial address at $2.00 each; $2.50 for June issue. Others available from Kraus Reprint Co. at $24.00 per volume.

WLWE: WORLD LITERATURE WRITTEN IN ENGLISH
(incorporating CBCL NEWSLETTER)

EDITORIAL ADDRESS:
Robert E. McDowell, Editor
Department of English
The University of Texas
at Arlington
Arlington, Texas 76010

SUBSCRIPTION ADDRESS:

same

PUBLISHED: Biannually (April, Nov.)
COST: 1 yr.—$2.00; single copy—$1.00; available to libraries on exchange basis (for exchange, write Gifts & Exchanges, The Library, University of Texas, Austin, Texas 78712).

CIRCULATION: 600

CONTENTS: Studies in English writing outside England and the United States; interviews, book reviews, bibliographies, essays which treat "Commonwealth" literature. Each issue focuses on the literature of one country.

UNSOLICITED MSS. WELCOME? Yes; submission acknowledged within 30 days.
SPECIFICALLY WELCOMED: Single author bibliographies; genre bibliographies.
MS. LENGTH: 1,500-4,500 words; submit ONE copy.
STYLE REQUIREMENTS: MLA STYLE SHEET; footnotes follow article.
COPYRIGHT: WLWE and the author.
EDITOR'S DECISION: 30 days.
FROM ACCEPTANCE TO PUBLICATION: 1 year.
PAYMENT/OFFPRINTS: Two copies of journal; extra copies available on request.
REJECTED MSS.: Returned.
GENERAL: First issue, April, 1962. Usual publication length, 120 pages. First 17 issues of WLWE were Newsletters (12-16 pages each). A few complete sets ($10.00) remain available.
BACK ISSUES: Available from editorial office (only most recent issues) at $1.00 each.

CONTINENTAL
(SOMETIMES INCLUDING ENGLISH)

CLASSICAL

ARETHUSA

EDITORIAL ADDRESS:
John P. Sullivan, Editor
Department of Classics
390 Hayes Hall
Administration Road
State University of New York
Buffalo, New York 14214

SUBSCRIPTION ADDRESS:

same

PUBLISHED: Biannually (Spring, Fall)   CIRCULATION: 274
COST: 1 yr.—$6.00 in U.S.; $6.50 elsewhere; $7.50 for all institutions and libraries; single copy—$3.50 plus $.25 handling charge to all countries.

CONTENTS: Scholarly essays about the literature of ancient Greece or Rome; miscellaneous issues are interspersed with thematic issues centering on such topics as "Politics and Art in Augustan Literature" and "Women in Antiquity."

UNSOLICITED MSS. WELCOME? Yes; submissions acknowledged.
SPECIFICALLY WELCOMED: Critical essays about ancient literature.
MS. LENGTH: 20 pages; submit ONE copy.
COPYRIGHT: ARETHUSA.
EDITOR'S DECISION: 1-3 months.
FROM ACCEPTANCE TO PUBLICATION: 9 months.
PAYMENT/OFFPRINTS: Twenty offprints free; more at $9.00 for first batch of 25; $7.00 for subsequent batches.
REJECTED MSS.: Returned.
GENERAL: First issue, 1968. Usual publication length, 80-100 pages. Articles must be accompanied with synopsis, plus short statement of conclusion reached. Greek passages are printed with translation immediately following.
BACK ISSUES: Available from editorial address at subscription rate and from Xerox University Microfilms.

ARION: A JOURNAL OF HUMANITIES AND THE CLASSICS

EDITORIAL ADDRESS:
William Arrowsmith and
D. S. Carne-Ross,
Editors-in-Chief
Boston University
270 Bay State Rd., Rm. 512
Boston, Massachusetts 02215

SUBSCRIPTION ADDRESS:

same

PUBLISHED: Quarterly   CIRCULATION: 900
COST: $6.00 per volume in U.S. and Canada; $7.00 abroad; single copy—$1.75 in U.S.; $2.00 abroad.

CONTENTS: Scholarly essays about and translations of ancient literature; reviews of books about the classical era. Example: "Four Levels of Reality, in Plato, Spinoza, and Blake."

UNSOLICITED MSS. WELCOME? Yes; submissions acknowledged.
SPECIFICALLY WELCOMED: Researched essays about the literature of ancient Greece and Rome.
MS. LENGTH: 5-30 pages; submit ONE copy.
STYLE REQUIREMENTS: MLA STYLE SHEET; University of Chicago's A MANUAL OF STYLE.
COPYRIGHT: Trustees of Boston University.
EDITOR'S DECISION: 6-12 months.
FROM ACCEPTANCE TO PUBLICATION: 1-2 years.
PAYMENT/OFFPRINTS: No payment. Offprints available on request at moderate cost.
REJECTED MSS.: Returned.
GENERAL: First issue, 1962. Usual publication length, 150-160 pages. ARION, beginning April, 1973, will be first in a new series published by Boston University.
BACK ISSUES: Available from editorial address at $2.00 or more each.

THE CLASSICAL BULLETIN

EDITORIAL ADDRESS:
Chauncey E. Finch, Editor
Department of Classical Languages
St. Louis University
221 North Grand Boulevard
St. Louis, Missouri 63103

SUBSCRIPTION ADDRESS:

same

PUBLISHED: Monthly (Nov. through Apr.)
CIRCULATION: 2,500
COST: 1 yr.—$2.00; $1.60 through the Secretary-Treasurer of the organizations ACL, CAAS, CAMWS, CANE, CAPS and CCA; single copy $.40.

CONTENTS: Essays on the literature and language of ancient Greece and Rome; articles on classical art, history; list of books recently published about some area of classical antiquity. Example: "Senecan Tragedy: Patterns of Irony and Art."

UNSOLICITED MSS. WELCOME? Yes; submissions acknowledged.
SPECIFICALLY WELCOMED: Researched essays about the literature and all other phases of classical Greece and Rome.
MS. LENGTH: 1,000-3,000 words; submit ONE copy.
STYLE REQUIREMENTS: Consult issues; footnotes follow essay.
COPYRIGHT: Not copyrighted.
EDITOR'S DECISION: 1 month.
FROM ACCEPTANCE TO PUBLICATION: 1 year or more.
PAYMENT/OFFPRINTS: Five free copies of issue; others at $.40 each.

REJECTED MSS.: Returned, criticized if requested.
GENERAL: First issue, 1923. Usual publication length, 16 pages.
BACK ISSUES: Available from editorial address at $.50 each.

THE CLASSICAL JOURNAL

See the section on TEACHING ABOUT LITERATURE for details.

CLASSICAL PHILOLOGY

EDITORIAL ADDRESS:
R. T. Bruère, Editor
Box 1 Faculty Exchange
970 East 58th Street
Chicago, Illinois 60637

SUBSCRIPTION ADDRESS:
The University of Chicago Press
5801 Ellis Avenue
Chicago, Illinois 60637

PUBLISHED: Quarterly   CIRCULATION: 1,700-2,000
COST: Individuals: 1 yr.—$8.00; 2 yrs.—$15.00; 3 yrs.—$22.00; institutions: 1 yr.—$12.00; 2 yrs.—$23.00; 3 yrs.—$34.00; Abroad, $1.00 more per year. Single copy—$3.00 for individuals; $3.75 for institutions.

CONTENTS: Research in the languages, literatures, history, and life of classical antiquity: major articles, notes, and discussions, critical book reviews; books received. Example articles: "The Virgilian Background of Lucan's Fourth Book"; "Aristotle, Horace, and the Ironic Man." Review article: "New Perspectives in Euripidean Criticism."

UNSOLICITED MSS. WELCOME? Yes, but not book reviews; submission acknowledged.
MS. LENGTH: Varies; submit ONE copy.
STYLE REQUIREMENTS: Generally, the University of Chicago's A MANUAL OF STYLE.
COPYRIGHT: The University of Chicago.
EDITOR'S DECISION: 6 weeks.
FROM ACCEPTANCE TO PUBLICATION: 18-24 months.
PAYMENT/OFFPRINTS: Offprints provided free; minimum number available for ordering 50, minimum charge $7.00.
REJECTED MSS.: Returned.
GENERAL: First issue, 1906. Usual publication length, 80 pages.
BACK ISSUES: Vols. 1965 on available from University of Chicago Press; Vols. I-LVI from Johnson Reprint Corp.; volumes in microfilm and microfiche listed, along with prices, on the inside cover of current issue.

GREEK, ROMAN AND BYZANTINE STUDIES

EDITORIAL ADDRESS:
William H. Willis, Editor
Department of Classical Studies
Duke University
Durham, North Carolina 27706

SUBSCRIPTION ADDRESS:

same

PUBLISHED: Quarterly.

GENERAL: First issue, 1958. This periodical had not arrived by the time the entry went to press. Potential subscribers, contributors, or collectors will have to write the editor to see whether the journal still exists, and if so, to inquire about details of manuscript submission, style, back issues, and the like.

HESPERIA: JOURNAL OF THE AMERICAN SCHOOL OF CLASSICAL STUDIES AT ATHENS

EDITORIAL ADDRESS:
Marian H. McAllister, Editor
American School of Classical
Studies at Athens
c/o Institute for Advanced Study
Princeton, New Jersey 08540

SUBSCRIPTION ADDRESS:

same

PUBLISHED: Quarterly   CIRCULATION: 970
COST: 1 yr.—$15.00 in U.S. and Canada; $16.00 elsewhere; single copy (current)—$3.75 in U.S. and Canada; $4.00 elsewhere.

CONTENTS: Reports of the School excavations, studies of the material from them, and researches of the members of the School in Ancient and Mediaeval Greek Studies. Articles in English or ancient Greek.

UNSOLICITED MSS. WELCOME? Yes, if submitted by alumni of the School; submissions acknowledged.
MS. LENGTH: 30-40 pages; submit ONE copy.
STYLE REQUIREMENTS: Style Sheet (Information for Authors) is available.
COPYRIGHT: All rights reserved by the School.
EDITOR'S DECISION: Publications Committee takes 6 months.
FROM ACCEPTANCE TO PUBLICATION: 1 year.
PAYMENT/OFFPRINTS: 25 free offprints; additional copies at cost.
REJECTED MSS.: Returned.
GENERAL: First issue, March, 1932. Usual publication length, 120-130 pages, 24 plates. Useful to Classical Studies literary scholars for consulting purposes.
BACK ISSUES: Available from editorial address; price quoted on request.

NEO-HELLENIKA: ANNUAL PUBLICATION OF THE CENTER FOR NEO-HELLENIC STUDIES

EDITORIAL ADDRESS:
George G. Arnakis, Editor
Center for Neo-Hellenic Studies
1010 West 22nd Street
Austin, Texas 78705

SUBSCRIPTION ADDRESS:

same

PUBLISHED: Annually
COST: Price varies according to size of volume.

CONTENTS: Original articles on Greece of the post-1204 period, in English and other widely used European languages; subjects in the humanities and the social sciences. Example: "Solomos and the Britannic Muses."

UNSOLICITED MSS. WELCOME? Yes; submissions acknowledged.
SPECIFICALLY WELCOMED: Literary criticism ref. modern Greek authors (late Byzantine, i.e. 1204-1453) are included.
MS. LENGTH: 10-16 printed pages; submit TWO copies.
STYLE REQUIREMENTS: MLA STYLE SHEET adjusted for languages other than English.
COPYRIGHT: For Vol. I, A. M. Hakkert, Publisher; for subsequent volumes, C.N.H.S. and Hakkert.
EDITOR'S DECISION: 2-3 months.
FROM ACCEPTANCE TO PUBLICATION: 1 year.
PAYMENT/OFFPRINTS: One copy of journal; 100 offprints.
REJECTED MSS.: Returned.
GENERAL: First issue, 1970. Usual publication length, 150-350 pages.
BACK ISSUES: Available from Center for Neo-Hellenic Studies or A. M. Hakkert, Herengracht 73, Amsterdam, Holland; Vol. I—$13.50.

PHILOLOGICAL QUARTERLY: A JOURNAL DEVOTED TO SCHOLARLY INVESTIGATION OF THE CLASSICAL AND MODERN LANGUAGES AND LITERATURES

See the section on AGE AND/OR NATIONALITY: EUROPEAN.

PHOENIX: JOURNAL OF THE CLASSICAL ASSOCIATION OF
CANADA/REVUE DE LA SOCIÉTÉ CANADIENNE
DES ÉTUDES CLASSIQUES

EDITORIAL ADDRESS:
T. M. Robinson, Editor
Trinity College
Toronto, Ontario M5S 1H8
Canada

SUBSCRIPTION ADDRESS:
P. S. Derow
University College
Toronto, Ontario M5S 1A1
Canada

PUBLISHED: Quarterly
COST: 1 yr.—$10.00.

CIRCULATION: 1,200

CONTENTS: Articles, notes, and book reviews on ancient Greek and Roman literature, history, philosophy, art, archaeology—in short, classical antiquity. Example: "Some Observations on the Narrative Technique of Petronius."

UNSOLICITED MSS. WELCOME? Yes; submissions acknowledged.
SPECIFICALLY WELCOMED: Original scholarly articles and notes on the subjects listed above.
MS. LENGTH: Average of 5,000-7,000 words; submit ONE copy.
STYLE REQUIREMENTS: Style Sheet, PHOENIX Vol. 27, No. 1 (Spring, 1973) 1-3.
COPYRIGHT: Jointly held by author and journal.
EDITOR'S DECISION: 3-4 months.
FROM ACCEPTANCE TO PUBLICATION: 18-24 months.
PAYMENT/OFFPRINTS: 25 free offprints; additional copies available at cost, i.e. $.20-$.40 per copy, depending on length.
REJECTED MSS.: Returned.
GENERAL: First issue, 1946. Usual publication length, 420 pages per year.
BACK ISSUES: Available from editorial address; details on application.

QUARTERLY CHECK-LIST OF CLASSICAL STUDIES

See the section on BIBLIOGRAPHICAL AND LIBRARY RESOURCES for details.

TRADITIO: STUDIES IN ANCIENT AND MEDIEVAL HISTORY,
THOUGHT, AND RELIGION

EDITORIAL ADDRESS:
Rev. Edwin A. Quain, S. J.,
Senior Editor
Fordham University
Bronx, New York 10458

SUBSCRIPTION ADDRESS:
Fordham University Press
Box L, Fordham University
Bronx, New York 10458

PUBLISHED: Annually

CIRCULATION: 1,300

COST: Current volume $17.50, prepaid subscription.

CONTENTS: Critical editions; magisterial studies; bibliographical studies and surveys; antiquity to end of the Middle Ages.

UNSOLICITED MSS. WELCOME? Yes; but only at beginning of March in each year; submissions acknowledged.
SPECIFICALLY WELCOMED: Critical editions, multi-disciplinary studies.
MS. LENGTH: No preference; submit ONE copy.
STYLE REQUIREMENTS: TRADITIO style sheet.
COPYRIGHT: Author.
EDITOR'S DECISION: By October.
FROM ACCEPTANCE TO PUBLICATION: 1 year.
PAYMENT/OFFPRINTS: Free copy of volume. 25 free offprints.
GENERAL: First issue, 1943. Usual publication length, 500 pages.
BACK ISSUES: Available from Fordham University Press at $25.00 each.

MEDIEVAL AND RENAISSANCE

ANNUALE MEDIAEVALE

EDITORIAL ADDRESS:
Herbert H. Petit, Editor
Department of English
Duquesne University
Pittsburgh, Pennsylvania 15219

SUBSCRIPTION ADDRESS:
Humanities Press, Inc.
450 Park Avenue South
New York, New York 10016

PUBLISHED: Annually
COST: 1 yr.—$10.00.

CONTENTS: Critical articles on Medieval literature and language (not limited to English). Generally, anything embraced by the broad term philology.

UNSOLICITED MSS. WELCOME? Yes; submissions acknowledged.
SPECIFICALLY WELCOMED: Scholarly and critical articles on Medieval literature.
MS. LENGTH: 20-25 pages; submit TWO copies.
STYLE REQUIREMENTS: MLA STYLE SHEET.
COPYRIGHT: Publisher.
EDITOR'S DECISION: 3 months.
FROM ACCEPTANCE TO PUBLICATION: 1 year.
PAYMENT/OFFPRINTS: 25 free copies.
REJECTED MSS.: Returned.
GENERAL: First issue, 1960. Usual publication length, 150 pages.
BACK ISSUES: Available from AMS Press, Inc. at $10.00 per library bound volume.

ARCHIV FÜR DAS STUDIUM DER NEUEREN SPRACHEN UND LITERATUREN

EDITORIAL ADDRESS:
Dr. Rudolf Sühnel, Editor
Anglistisches Seminar
der Universität
D-69 Heidelberg
West Germany

SUBSCRIPTION ADDRESS:
Georg Westermann Verlag
Westermann Allee
D-33 Braunschweig
West Germany

PUBLISHED: Biannually
COST: 1 yr.—DM 72.—.

CIRCULATION: 820

CONTENTS: Articles, notes, book reviews concerning general philology and literary history. Example: "PARADISE LOST and the Misery of the Human Condition."

UNSOLICITED MSS. WELCOME? Inquiry preferable; submissions acknowledged.
SPECIFICALLY WELCOMED: Research rather than general education.
MS. LENGTH: Up to 16 pages; submit ONE copy.

STYLE REQUIREMENTS: MLA STYLE SHEET.
COPYRIGHT: Publisher.
EDITOR'S DECISION: Up to 3 months.
FROM ACCEPTANCE TO PUBLICATION: 1 year.
PAYMENT/OFFPRINTS: 30 offprints, unless more are expressly required.
REJECTED MSS.: Returned.
GENERAL: First issue, 1845. Usual publication length, 240 pages. Articles written in several languages.
BACK ISSUES: Vols. 1-50 available from Johnson Reprint Corp.; others from subscription address.

BULLETIN OF THE COMEDIANTES

EDITORIAL ADDRESS:
James A. Parr, Editor
Department of Spanish and Portuguese
University of Southern California
Los Angeles, California 90007

SUBSCRIPTION ADDRESS:
Karl C. Gregg, Business Manager
Department of Romance Languages
University of Arizona
Tucson, Arizona 85721

PUBLISHED: Biannually
(Spring, Fall)

CIRCULATION: 500

COST: 1 yr.—$2.50 for individuals; $3.00 for libraries.

CONTENTS: Researched essays about the COMEDIA, Spanish drama from the CELESTINA through Calderón, roughly 1500-1700; annual bibliography of foreign publications on the drama of this period; Mentidero de Comediantes. Example: "The Grotesque Vision of Rojas Zorilla."

UNSOLICITED MSS. WELCOME? Yes; submissions acknowledged.
SPECIFICALLY WELCOMED: Scholarly essays about the drama of Spain from 1500-1700.
MS. LENGTH: 4-12 pages; submit ONE copy.
STYLE REQUIREMENTS: MLA STYLE SHEET; footnotes follow essay.
COPYRIGHT: Author.
EDITOR'S DECISION: 1 month.
FROM ACCEPTANCE TO PUBLICATION: 18 months.
PAYMENT/OFFPRINTS: Twenty copies of issue.
REJECTED MSS.: Returned.
GENERAL: First issue, 1948. Founded by Everett W. Hesse. Usual publication length, 30 pages per issue, 60 pages per volume. Articles may be in either English or Spanish.
BACK ISSUES: 1949-64, bound in one volume, available from Johnson Reprint Corporation at approximately $50.00. 1965 to date available from Business Manager. (Volume 23 contains index for 1949-1970.)

CHRONICA

EDITORIAL ADDRESS:
James J. Murphy, Editor
Rhetoric Department
University of California at Davis
Davis, California 95616

SUBSCRIPTION ADDRESS:

same

PUBLISHED: Biannually
COST: 1 yr.—$4.00.

CIRCULATION: 500

CONTENTS: Medieval studies; it is the newsletter of the Medieval Association of the Pacific; methods of organizing medieval studies programs.

UNSOLICITED MSS. WELCOME? No. All are solicited. Submissions not acknowledged.
SPECIFICALLY WELCOMED: Methods of organizing medieval studies programs.
MS. LENGTH: 2,000-2,500 words; submit ONE copy.
STYLE REQUIREMENTS: MLA STYLE SHEET.
COPYRIGHT: Not copyrighted.
EDITOR'S DECISION: 2 weeks.
FROM ACCEPTANCE TO PUBLICATION: 1-2 months.
PAYMENT/OFFPRINTS: No payment or offprints.
REJECTED MSS.: Not returned.
GENERAL: First issue, Fall, 1967. Usual publication length, 24 pages.
BACK ISSUES: Available from editorial address at $.50 each.

COMITATUS

EDITORIAL ADDRESS:
T. G. Hahn, Editor
Department of English
University of California
405 Hilgard Avenue
Los Angeles, California 90024

SUBSCRIPTION ADDRESS:

same

PUBLISHED: Annually
COST: 1 yr.—$2.50 (institutions—$4.00).

CIRCULATION: 300

CONTENTS: Medieval literary studies including criticism, texts of short works, bibliographies. Articles may deal with any European literature.

UNSOLICITED MSS. WELCOME? Yes (although many are solicited); submissions acknowledged.
SPECIFICALLY WELCOMED: Those with fresh and provocative viewpoints.
MS. LENGTH: No preference; submit ONE copy.
STYLE REQUIREMENTS: MLA STYLE SHEET.
COPYRIGHT: Author.

EDITOR'S DECISION: 3 months.
FROM ACCEPTANCE TO PUBLICATION: 1 year.
PAYMENT/OFFPRINTS: No payment. Offprints at nominal cost according to length (average $.25 each).
REJECTED MSS.: Returned.
GENERAL: First issue, December, 1970. Usual publication length, 112 pages. No book reviews. Articles need not be written in English.
BACK ISSUES: Available from editorial address at $2.00 for Vol. I; regular price for subsequent volumes (i.e., $2.50 for individuals, $4.00 for institutions).

ITALICA

See the section on TEACHING ABOUT LITERATURE for details.

THE JOURNAL OF MEDIEVAL AND RENAISSANCE STUDIES

EDITORIAL ADDRESS:
Marcel Tetel, Editor
Duke Station 4666
Durham, North Carolina 27706

SUBSCRIPTION ADDRESS:
Duke University Press
6697 College Station
Durham, North Carolina 27708

PUBLISHED: Biannually
COST: 1 yr.—$10.00.

CIRCULATION: 700

CONTENTS: Scholarly articles on any matters pertinent to the processes of change observable in late medieval and Renaissance culture; articles that examine general problems as well as specific issues and accomplishments in art, history, literature, music, philosophy, and theology.

UNSOLICITED MSS. WELCOME? Yes; submissions acknowledged.
SPECIFICALLY WELCOMED: Interdisciplinary or comparative studies of thought, expressions, and institutions; articles on more limited topics or on particular figures which throw light on the problem of transition.
MS. LENGTH: 25-30 pages; submit ONE copy.
STYLE REQUIREMENTS: MLA STYLE SHEET.
COPYRIGHT: Duke University Press.
EDITOR'S DECISION: 6-8 weeks.
FROM ACCEPTANCE TO PUBLICATION: 1 year.
PAYMENT/OFFPRINTS: 25 free offprints.
REJECTED MSS.: Returned.
GENERAL: First issue, Spring, 1971. Usual publication length, 130-150 pages.
BACK ISSUES: Available from subscription address at $8.00 each or $16.00 per volume.

LA CORÓNICA

EDITORIAL ADDRESS:
John Lihani, Editor
Department of Spanish and Italian
University of Kentucky
Lexington, Kentucky 40506

SUBSCRIPTION ADDRESS:

same

PUBLISHED: Biannually
COST: 1 yr.—$1.00.

CIRCULATION: 300

CONTENTS: Feature stories; bibliography, book reviews; dissertations completed and in progress; personalia; conferences; conventions; symposiums; employment opportunities in the medieval field; necrologies. In general: items of current interest to Hispanic medievalists. Example: "Research Possibilities for the Hispanic Medievalist in the Roman Libraries."

UNSOLICITED MSS. WELCOME? Yes; submissions acknowledged.
SPECIFICALLY WELCOMED: Topics dealing with Hispanic medieval research and its problems; abstracts of papers presented at medievalist meetings and conventions.
MS. LENGTH: Paragraph to a few pages; submit ORIGINAL.
STYLE REQUIREMENTS: Less formal and more relaxed than MLA style.
COPYRIGHT: Spanish 1 of MLA.
EDITOR'S DECISION: 2 weeks.
FROM ACCEPTANCE TO PUBLICATION: 6 months.
PAYMENT/OFFPRINTS: No payment. Ten copies for $3.00.
REJECTED MSS.: Returned.
GENERAL: First issue, December (Fall) 1972. Usual publication length, 20 pages. Primary purpose of publication is to serve as newsletter dedicated to the dissemination of news of interest to Hispanic medievalists in America and abroad.
BACK ISSUES: Available from editorial address at $.50 each.

MEDIAEVAL STUDIES

EDITORIAL ADDRESS:
J. Reginald O'Donnell, Editor
Pontifical Institute of Mediaeval
Studies
59 Queen's Park Crescent East
Toronto, Ontario M5S 2C4
Canada

SUBSCRIPTION ADDRESS:
J. P. Morro, C.S.B. Director of
Publications
same

PUBLISHED: Annually
COST: $12.00 per volume.

CIRCULATION: 1,100

CONTENTS: Articles on research concerning the Middle Ages. The fields are for the most part on literature, theology, philosophy, history with special emphasis on the edition of new texts. Example: "The Literal and the Allegorical: Jean de Meun and the DE PLANCTU NATURAE."

UNSOLICITED MSS. WELCOME? Yes; submissions acknowledged.
SPECIFICALLY WELCOMED: Edition of texts and studies on unedited material.
MS. LENGTH: 25 printed pages; submit ONE copy.
STYLE REQUIREMENTS: MLA STYLE SHEET with a supplementary style sheet of MS.
COPYRIGHT: Pontifical Institute of Mediaeval Studies.
EDITOR'S DECISION: Several months.
FROM ACCEPTANCE TO PUBLICATION: 1-2 years.
PAYMENT/OFFPRINTS: 50 free offprints.
REJECTED MSS.: Returned.
GENERAL: First issue, 1939. Usual publication length, 350-400 pages. Ten percent discount to subscription agencies.
BACK ISSUES: Available from Director of Publications at $12.00 per volume.

MEDIEVALIA ET HUMANISTICA: STUDIES IN MEDIEVAL AND RENAISSANCE CULTURE

EDITORIAL ADDRESS:
Paul M. Clogan, Editor
P. O. Box 13348
North Texas Station
Denton, Texas 76203

SUBSCRIPTION ADDRESS:

same

PUBLISHED: Annually   CIRCULATION: 20,000
COST: 1 yr.—$10.95; 10% discount on all standing orders for individuals, institutions and libraries.

CONTENTS: Significant scholarship, criticism, and reviews in all areas of medieval and Renaissance culture: literature, art, history, law, music, philosophy and science. Review articles examine significant recent publications, and contributing editors report on the progress of medieval and Renaissance studies in the United States and Canada. Examples: "The Social Significance of Twelfth-Century Chivalric Romance"; "Medieval Poems and Medieval Society."

UNSOLICITED MSS. WELCOME? Yes; submissions acknowledged.
SPECIFICALLY WELCOMED: Interdisciplinary, critical and historical studies which make significant contribution to knowledge or understanding in the field of medieval or Renaissance studies. M&H encourages the individual scholar to examine the relationship of his discipline to other disciplines and to relate his study in a theoretical or practical way to its cultural and historical content.
MS. LENGTH: 15-25 pages; submit ONE copy.

STYLE REQUIREMENTS: Attractive, clear and concise style; footnotes follow MLA STYLE SHEET.
COPYRIGHT: Medieval and Renaissance Society.
EDITOR'S DECISION: 2 months.
FROM ACCEPTANCE TO PUBLICATION: 11-12 months.
PAYMENT/OFFPRINTS: 25 offprints gratis and 40% discount on volume in which his article appears.
REJECTED MSS.: Returned.
GENERAL: First issue, 1943. Usual publication length, about 300 pages. M&H is sponsored by the Medieval Interdepartmental Section of the MLA, and publication in the series is open to contributions from all sources. Prospective authors should read the Editorial Note printed in each volume of the New Series for MS information and guidance.
BACK ISSUES: The entire stock of back issues, Fasciculi I-XVII (1943-1966) of the original series and Nos. 1-3 (1970-1972) of the New Series, is available from the editorial address at $8.00 each for the original series; $10.95 each for the New Series.

MEDIUM AEVUM

EDITORIAL ADDRESS:
J. A. W. Bennett, Editor
Magdalene College
Cambridge
England

SUBSCRIPTION ADDRESS:
Basil Blackwell & Mott Ltd.
108 Cowley Road
Oxford OX4 1JF
England

PUBLISHED: Tri-annually
CIRCULATION: 950
COST: 1 yr.—£4.50 to non-members; £3.50 to members.

CONTENTS: Scholarly essays about Medieval literature and about Medieval languages; review of books. Example: "A Comparison of two Episodes in the Prose LANCELOT."

UNSOLICITED MSS. WELCOME? Yes; submissions acknowledged.
MS. LENGTH: See current issue; submit ONE copy.
STYLE REQUIREMENTS: See current issue.
EDITOR'S DECISION: 3 months.
FROM ACCEPTANCE TO PUBLICATION: 2-3 years.
PAYMENT/OFFPRINTS: 12 free copies.
REJECTED MSS.: Returned.
GENERAL: First issue, 1932. Usual publication length, 100 pages.
BACK ISSUES: Available from publishers at £1.80 each.

MODERN PHILOLOGY: A JOURNAL DEVOTED TO RESEARCH IN MEDIEVAL AND MODERN LITERATURE

EDITORIAL ADDRESS:
Gwin J. Kolb and Edward W.
Rosenheim, Jr., Editors
The University of Chicago
1050 East 59th Street
Chicago, Illinois 60637

SUBSCRIPTION ADDRESS:
University of Chicago Press
5801 Ellis Avenue
Chicago, Illinois 60637

PUBLISHED: Quarterly (Aug., Nov., Feb., May)

CIRCULATION: 1,900

COST: Individuals: 1 yr.—$8.00, 2 yrs.—$15.00; 3 yrs.—$22.00; Institutions: 1 yr.—$12.00, 2 yrs.—$23.00, 3 yrs.—$34.00; Student: 1 yr.—$5.00 (letter from professor); outside U.S., add $1.00 per year.

CONTENTS: Materials dealing with the literatures, medieval and modern, of Britain and America and, to a lesser extent, of France, Germany, Italy, and Spain; major articles; notes and documents; review articles; and reviews. Example: "Donne's Epic Venture in the METEMPSYCHOSIS."

UNSOLICITED MSS. WELCOME? Articles and notes or documents, yes; review articles or reviews, no; submissions acknowledged.
SPECIFICALLY WELCOMED: Studies in bibliography, various aspects of literary history, analysis, and criticism, but editors discourage "new readings" unless they are not only persuasive and readable but demonstrably useful.
MS. LENGTH: 4-50 pages; submit ONE copy.
STYLE REQUIREMENTS: University of Chicago's A MANUAL OF STYLE.
COPYRIGHT: University of Chicago Press.
EDITOR'S DECISION: 1-3 months.
FROM ACCEPTANCE TO PUBLICATION: 18-24 months.
PAYMENT/OFFPRINTS: Complimentary copies of issue to all; 50 free offprints to authors (except reviews). Extra offprints or offprints of reviews may be purchased in groups of 50.
REJECTED MSS.: Returned.
GENERAL: First issue, 1903. Usual publication length, 112 pages.
BACK ISSUES: Vols. 1-62 available from Johnson Reprint Corp. Subsequent issues from University of Chicago Press at $4.00 each to individuals; $4.50 each to institutions; $13.00 per volume. Microfilm from Xerox University Microfilms; microfiche from J. S. Canner & Co.

NEOPHILOLOGUS

EDITORIAL ADDRESS:
P. J. E. Hyams, Editorial Secretary
Engels Seminarium
Herengracht 330
Amsterdam-C
The Netherlands

SUBSCRIPTION ADDRESS:
Wolters-Noordhoff N.V.
Groningen
The Netherlands

PUBLISHED: Quarterly CIRCULATION: 900
COST: Hfl. 50,—(excluding postage).

CONTENTS: Scholarly articles devoted to the study of modern and medieval language and literature, but usually no Dutch literature or language; articles on general linguistics; literary theory; comparative literature articles. Examples: "The Unity of 'The Dream of the Rood' "; "THE CORRIDA and FOR WHOM THE BELL TOLLS."

UNSOLICITED MSS. WELCOME? Yes, most articles unsolicited; reviews are allotted; submissions acknowledged.
MS. LENGTH: 8,000 words or less—excess page charge is imposed on contributions which exceed 16 printed pages (including footnotes) of Hfl. 50,—; submit ONE copy.
STYLE REQUIREMENTS: MLA STYLE SHEET basically.
COPYRIGHT: Editors and publisher.
EDITOR'S DECISION: About 6 months.
FROM ACCEPTANCE TO PUBLICATION: Varies according to subject; usually 1-2 years.
PAYMENT/OFFPRINTS: 25 free offprints, unlimited number at cost; 5 for reviews.
REJECTED MSS.: Returned.
GENERAL: First issue, 1916. Usual publication length, 100 pages or so. The usual languages published are English, French, German, Italian, and Spanish, but articles in other languages may also be submitted for consideration.
BACK ISSUES: Available from subscription address and Johnson Reprint Corp.

NEUPHILOLOGISCHE MITTEILUNGEN: BULLETIN OF THE MODERN LANGUAGE SOCIETY

See the section on AGE AND/OR NATIONALITY: EUROPEAN.

NOTTINGHAM MEDIAEVAL STUDIES

EDITORIAL ADDRESS: SUBSCRIPTION ADDRESS:
Prof. Lewis Thorpe, Editor
The University same
Nottingham NG7 2RD
England

PUBLISHED: Annually (Sept.) CIRCULATION: 600
COST: 1 yr.—$3.00 (trade price: $2.50).

CONTENTS: Articles on the literature, history, fine art, music, and other aspects of the Middle Ages.

UNSOLICITED MSS. WELCOME? Yes; submissions acknowledged.
SPECIFICALLY WELCOMED: Serious articles on the Middle Ages.
MS. LENGTH: 12,000 words; submit ONE copy.
STYLE REQUIREMENTS: MLA STYLE SHEET.
COPYRIGHT: Nominally the editor; inquire about reprinting.
EDITOR'S DECISION: Up to 6 months.
FROM ACCEPTANCE TO PUBLICATION: Up to 6 months.
PAYMENT/OFFPRINTS: 50 free offprints.
REJECTED MSS.: Returned.
GENERAL: First issue, September, 1957. Usual publication length, 20-24 pages.
BACK ISSUES: Volumes I-II (1957-1958) are out of print. Volumes III-XVI (1958-1972) available from editor at $3.00 per volume, post free.

QUARTERLY CHECK-LIST OF MEDIEVALIA

See the Section on BIBLIOGRAPHICAL AND LIBRARY RESOURCES for details.

RENAISSANCE AND MODERN STUDIES

EDITORIAL ADDRESS:
J. T. Boulton and R. S. Smith, Editors
University of Nottingham
Nottingham NG7
England

SUBSCRIPTION ADDRESS:
Sisson & Parker Ltd.
Wheeler Gate
Nottingham NG7
England

PUBLISHED: Annually
COST: 1 yr.—£1.75.

CIRCULATION: 500

CONTENTS: Humanities, Renaissance and after; English and historical studies predominate.

UNSOLICITED MSS. WELCOME? No. Contributors must have connection with University of Nottingham.
SPECIFICALLY WELCOMED: Longish articles on topics within field described above.
MS. LENGTH: 10,000-20,000 words; submit ONE copy.
STYLE REQUIREMENTS: Modified Oxford University Press.
COPYRIGHT: Author.
EDITOR'S DECISION: 1-2 months.
FROM ACCEPTANCE TO PUBLICATION: 6-12 months.
PAYMENT/OFFPRINTS: 25 free copies. Additional at 15p. each.
REJECTED MSS.: Returned.
GENERAL: First issue, 1957. Usual publication length, 150 pages.
BACK ISSUES: Available from subscription address at £1.75 per volume.

RENAISSANCE AND REFORMATION

EDITORIAL ADDRESS:
J. A. Molinaro, Editor
Department of Italian and
Hispanic Studies
University of Toronto
Toronto 5, Ontario
Canada

SUBSCRIPTION ADDRESS:
Leslie T. McCormick, Business
Manager
Erindale College
3359 Mississauga Road
Clarkson, Ontario
Canada

PUBLISHED: Tri-annually (Sept. through June)
COST: 1 yr.—$3.00.

CIRCULATION: 500-600

CONTENTS: Articles of historical and literary interest in a broad field; bibliographical materials; essays concerning the history of ideas; research which breaks new ground; book reviews. Example: "Montaigne and Socrates."

UNSOLICITED MSS. WELCOME? Yes; submissions acknowledged.
SPECIFICALLY WELCOMED: Research articles of historical or aesthetic interest.
MS. LENGTH: 20 pages; submit ONE copy.
STYLE REQUIREMENTS: MLA STYLE SHEET; footnotes follow article.
COPYRIGHT: Journal.
EDITOR'S DECISION: 4-6 weeks.
FROM ACCEPTANCE TO PUBLICATION: 6 months to 1 year.
PAYMENT/OFFPRINTS: No payment. Offprints may be ordered by author at his expense.
REJECTED MSS.: Returned.
GENERAL: First issue, Fall, 1964. Usual publication length, 44 pages.
BACK ISSUES: Available from Business Manager at $1.25 each; $3.75 per volume.

RENAISSANCE DRAMA

EDITORIAL ADDRESS:
S. Schoenbaum, Editor
Northwestern University
617 Foster Street
Evanston, Illinois 60201

SUBSCRIPTION ADDRESS:
Northwestern University Press
1735 Benson Avenue
Evanston, Illinois 60201

PUBLISHED: Annually
COST: 1 yr.—$10.00.

CONTENTS: Scholarly articles on drama, not limited to any one theatre, during the Renaissance; articles on later authors' use of Renaissance themes; some articles about predecessors of the era; review articles, such as "The Stage in the Time of Shakespeare: A Survey of Major Scholarship." Example essay: "TAMBURLAINE in the Theatre: Tartar, Grand Guignol, or Janus?" Volume V is principally on the theory and practice of comedy.

UNSOLICITED MSS. WELCOME? Yes.
SPECIFICALLY WELCOMED: "Essays that are exploratory in nature, that are concerned with critical or scholarly methodology, that raise new questions or embody fresh approaches to perennial problems."
STYLE REQUIREMENTS: MLA STYLE SHEET; for quotations from Shakespeare, use Alexander edition.
COPYRIGHT: Northwestern University Press.
GENERAL: First issue of New Series, 1968. Usual publication length, 250 pages.
BACK ISSUES: Available from Northwestern University Press.

RENAISSANCE PAPERS

EDITORIAL ADDRESS:
Dennis G. Donovan, Editor
English Department
University of North Carolina
Chapel Hill, North Carolina 27510

SUBSCRIPTION ADDRESS:
402 Allen Building
Duke University
Durham, North Carolina 27706

PUBLISHED: Annually
COST: 1 yr.—$3.00.

CIRCULATION: 500

CONTENTS: A selection of papers read at the annual Southeastern Renaissance Conference held in April. Example: "Herrick and the Ceremony of Death."

UNSOLICITED MSS. WELCOME? No.
STYLE REQUIREMENTS: MLA STYLE SHEET (generally).
PAYMENT/OFFPRINTS: 25 free offprints.
GENERAL: First issue, 1954. Usual publication length, 60-80 pages.
BACK ISSUES: Available from subscription address.

RENAISSANCE QUARTERLY (formerly RENAISSANCE NEWS)

EDITORIAL ADDRESS:
Elizabeth S. Donno and
James V. Mirollo, Editors
Renaissance Society of America
1161 Amsterdam Avenue
New York, New York 10027

SUBSCRIPTION ADDRESS:

same

PUBLISHED: Quarterly   CIRCULATION: 3,260
COST: Distributed to Society members: individual membership per calendar year—$12.50; institutional membership—$16.00.

CONTENTS: Short articles, book reviews, and a bibliography on all aspects of the Renaissance period (1399-1660); conference news. Example: "Two Emblems in Brutus' Orchard."

UNSOLICITED MSS. WELCOME? Yes; submissions acknowledged.
SPECIFICALLY WELCOMED: Short articles of interdisciplinary interest which reveal new information or clarify previous understanding; no interest in notes, translations only, or critical explications of single works.
MS. LENGTH: Up to 20 pages; submit ONE copy.
STYLE REQUIREMENTS: MLA STYLE SHEET; footnotes follow article.
COPYRIGHT: Renaissance Society of America.
EDITOR'S DECISION: 1-2 months.
FROM ACCEPTANCE TO PUBLICATION: 1 year.
PAYMENT/OFFPRINTS: No payment. Offprints may be ordered at cost.
REJECTED MSS.: Returned.
GENERAL: First issue, 1948 (RENAISSANCE NEWS). Title changed beginning with Vol. 20, 1967. Usual publication length, 125-150 pages.
BACK ISSUES: Vols. 1-24 available from Kraus Reprint Company; Vol. 24 and later from Renaissance Society of America. Apply to above addresses for information on price and microfilm availability.

RESEARCH OPPORTUNITIES IN RENAISSANCE DRAMA

EDITORIAL ADDRESS: SUBSCRIPTION ADDRESS:
David M. Bergelon, Editor
Department of English   same
Louisiana State University
in New Orleans
New Orleans, Louisiana 70122

PUBLISHED: Annually   CIRCULATION: 1,300-1,500
COST: Free.

CONTENTS: Report of Modern Language Association Seminars on Renaissance Drama and on Medieval Drama; articles dealing with research opportunities or providing research tools; works in progress; art reproductions. Examples: "Iconography and Renaissance Drama: Ethical and Mythological Themes"; "Spenser: Some Uses of the Sea and the Storm-tossed Ship."

UNSOLICITED MSS. WELCOME? Yes; submissions acknowledged.
SPECIFICALLY WELCOMED: Materials specifically related to research opportunities, e.g. checklist bibliographies.
MS. LENGTH: No preference; submit ONE copy.
STYLE REQUIREMENTS: MLA STYLE SHEET.

COPYRIGHT: Editor of journal.
EDITOR'S DECISION: 1-2 months.
FROM ACCEPTANCE TO PUBLICATION: 1 year.
PAYMENT/OFFPRINTS: None.
REJECTED MSS.: Returned.
GENERAL: First issue, 1963. Usual publication length, 100 pages.
BACK ISSUES: Available free, as long as supply lasts, from the editor; early numbers have been reprinted.

SPECULUM: A JOURNAL OF MEDIAEVAL STUDIES

EDITORIAL ADDRESS:
Paul Meyvaert, Editor
1430 Massachusetts Avenue
Cambridge, Massachusetts 02138

SUBSCRIPTION ADDRESS:
Mediaeval Academy of America
same

PUBLISHED: Quarterly (Jan., Apr., July, Oct.)
CIRCULATION: 5,400
COST: 1 yr.—$18.00. Subscriptions accepted on calendar year basis only. No discounts available. Members of the Academy receive SPECULUM upon payment of minimum annual dues ($15 per yr.).

CONTENTS: Articles concerned with mediaeval architecture, armor, fine arts, geography, heraldry, history, law, literature, music, numismatics, philosophy, science, social and economic institutions, and all other aspects of the civilization of the Middle Ages (500-1500 A.D.); book reviews. Example: "Edward III and the Alliterative MORTE ARTHURE."

UNSOLICITED MSS. WELCOME? Yes; submissions acknowledged.
SPECIFICALLY WELCOMED: Scholarly articles concerned with mediaeval studies.
MS. LENGTH: No preference; submit ONE or TWO copies.
STYLE REQUIREMENTS: MLA STYLE SHEET.
COPYRIGHT: Mediaeval Academy of America.
EDITOR'S DECISION: Approximately 6 months.
FROM ACCEPTANCE TO PUBLICATION: Approximately 12 months.
PAYMENT/OFFPRINTS: No payment. Offprints (100 minimum) available to author at cost.
REJECTED MSS.: Returned.
GENERAL: First issue, 1926. Usual publication length, 200 pages.
BACK ISSUES: Available from Mediaeval Academy of America at $22.00 per volume for Vols. 1-45 (1926-1970); $20.00 per volume for Vols. 46 and 47 (1971-1972); $18.00 for Vol. 48 (1973).

STUDIES IN THE RENAISSANCE

EDITORIAL ADDRESS:
Richard Harrier, Editor
Renaissance Society of America
1161 Amsterdam Avenue
New York, New York 10027

SUBSCRIPTION ADDRESS:

same

PUBLISHED: Annually
CIRCULATION: 3,260
COST: 1 yr.—$12.50 for individuals; $16.00 for institutions; distributed to members of the Society.

CONTENTS: Scholarly articles on all aspects (literature, history, philosophy, art, etc.) of the Renaissance period (1399-1600).

UNSOLICITED MSS. WELCOME? Yes; submissions acknowledged.
SPECIFICALLY WELCOMED: Preference is given to articles which relate two or more fields of Renaissance culture.
MS. LENGTH: 20 or more pages; submit ONE copy.
STYLE REQUIREMENTS: MLA STYLE SHEET; footnotes follow articles.
COPYRIGHT: Renaissance Society of America.
EDITOR'S DECISION: 1-3 months.
FROM ACCEPTANCE TO PUBLICATION: 1 year.
PAYMENT/OFFPRINTS: No payment. Offprints may be ordered at cost.
REJECTED MSS.: Returned.
GENERAL: First issue, 1954. Usual publication length, 200-250 pages.
BACK ISSUES: Vols. 1-18 available from Kraus Reprint Co.; Vol. 19 from editorial address. Apply to above addresses for information on prices and microfilm availability.

VIATOR: MEDIEVAL AND RENAISSANCE STUDIES

EDITORIAL ADDRESS:
Lynn White, Jr., Editor
Center for Medieval and
Renaissance Studies, UCLA
Los Angeles, California 90024

SUBSCRIPTION ADDRESS:
University of California Press
2223 Fulton Street
Berkeley, California 94720

PUBLISHED: Annually
COST: 1 yr.—$15.00.

CONTENTS: Essays on all aspects of the period between late Antiquity and A.D. 1600; primary, but not exclusive, focus on intercultural and interdisciplinary research; concerned with problems internal to the West and with relations among the West, Byzantium, the Slavs, Jewish and smaller Christian groups. Example: "The Literary Magic of WIO FAERSTICE."

UNSOLICITED MSS. WELCOME? Yes; submissions acknowledged.

SPECIFICALLY WELCOMED: Intercultural and interdisciplinary items are preferred, but more specialized studies of medieval and Renaissance literature are also acceptable.
MS. LENGTH: Any length up to 150 pages.
STYLE REQUIREMENTS: Accordance with the style sheet at back of each volume.
COPYRIGHT: University of California.
EDITOR'S DECISION: 6 weeks.
FROM ACCEPTANCE TO PUBLICATION: 12-24 months.
PAYMENT/OFFPRINTS: 75 free offprints.
REJECTED MSS.: Returned.
GENERAL: First issue, 1970. Usual publication length, 450 pages.
BACK ISSUES: Vols. 1, 2, & 3 available from University of California Press at $12.00 each.

EUROPEAN: POST-RENAISSANCE THROUGH CONTEMPORARY

AMERICAN HUNGARIAN REVIEW

EDITORIAL ADDRESS:
Leslie Konnyu, Editor
5410 Kerth Road
St. Louis, Missouri 63128

SUBSCRIPTION ADDRESS:

same

PUBLISHED: Quarterly
COST: 1 yr.—$5.00.

CIRCULATION: 1,000

CONTENTS: Articles on literature, art, science, bibliography.

UNSOLICITED MSS. WELCOME? Yes; submissions acknowledged.
SPECIFICALLY WELCOMED: Articles on American Hungarian cultural relations.
MS. LENGTH: 5-10 pages; submit ONE copy.
STYLE REQUIREMENTS: Literary.
COPYRIGHT: Magazine.
EDITOR'S DECISION: 1-2 weeks.
FROM ACCEPTANCE TO PUBLICATION: 3-6 months.
PAYMENT/OFFPRINTS: Returned.
REJECTED MSS.: Returned.
GENERAL: First issue, January, 1963. Usual publication length, 32 pages.
BACK ISSUES: Available from editorial address at $1.25 each.

THE AMERICAN-SCANDINAVIAN REVIEW

EDITORIAL ADDRESS:
Erik J. Friis, Editor
127 East 73rd Street
New York, New York 10021

SUBSCRIPTION ADDRESS:
American-Scandinavian Foundation
same

PUBLISHED: Quarterly
COST: 1 yr.—$7.50.

CIRCULATION: 7,000

CONTENTS: All aspects of Scandinavian life and letters, arts, and sciences, past and present.

UNSOLICITED MSS. WELCOME? Yes; submissions usually acknowledged.
SPECIFICALLY WELCOMED: Solid articles about Scandinavian topics.
MS. LENGTH: 2,500 words; submit ONE copy.
COPYRIGHT: THE AMERICAN-SCANDINAVIAN REVIEW.
EDITOR'S DECISION: 3 weeks.
FROM ACCEPTANCE TO PUBLICATION: 6 months.
PAYMENT/OFFPRINTS: $75.00. Offprints at author's cost.
REJECTED MSS.: Returned.
GENERAL: First issue, January, 1913. Usual publication length, 112 pages.
BACK ISSUES: Available from subscription address at $2.00 each.

ARCHIV FÜR DAS STUDIUM DER NEUEREN SPRACHEN UND LITERATUREN

See the section on AGE AND/OR NATIONALITY: CONTINENTAL—CLASSICAL, MEDIEVAL AND RENAISSANCE for details.

BULLETIN OF HISPANIC STUDIES

EDITORIAL ADDRESS:
Geoffrey Ribbans, Editor
School of Hispanic Studies
P. O. Box 147
University of Liverpool
Liverpool L69 3BX
England

SUBSCRIPTION ADDRESS:
Liverpool University Press
123 Grove Street
Liverpool L7 7AF
England

PUBLISHED: Quarterly
(Jan., Apr., July, Oct.)
COST: 1 yr.—£4.00, $10.00, or 700 pesetas.

CIRCULATION: 1,000

CONTENTS: Articles, reviews of books; reviews of reviews (Apr. and Oct.); concerned primarily with Spanish, Portuguese, Catalan, and Latin-American language and literature, and to some extent with related history and culture. Example: "Don Quixote as Magus: the rhetoric of interpolation."

UNSOLICITED MSS. WELCOME? Yes; submissions acknowledged.
SPECIFICALLY WELCOMED: Scholarly articles on literature and language of Spain, Portugal, and Latin America.
MS. LENGTH: 6,000-8,000 words; submit TWO copies.
STYLE REQUIREMENTS: Consult recent issue.
COPYRIGHT: Editor.
EDITOR'S DECISION: Approximately 2 months, but may vary greatly.
FROM ACCEPTANCE TO PUBLICATION: 2 years.
PAYMENT/OFFPRINTS: 25 free offprints of articles.
REJECTED MSS.: Returned.
GENERAL: First issue, 1923. Usual publication length, 108 pages. Indexed by volume.
BACK ISSUES: Vols. 1-61 available from Kraus Reprint Co. (U.S. and Canada) and from Scientific Periodicals Establishment, P.O. Box 34377, Vaduz, Liechtenstein (for rest of world). Vols. 42 onwards available from Liverpool University Press.

COMPARATIVE LITERATURE STUDIES

See the section on AGE AND/NATIONALITY: COMPREHENSIVE IN SCOPE for details.

DIMENSION: CONTEMPORARY GERMAN ARTS AND LETTERS

EDITORIAL ADDRESS:
A. Leslie Willson, Editor
Department of Germanic Languages
University of Texas
P. O. Box 7819
Austin, Texas 78712

SUBSCRIPTION ADDRESS:
University of Texas Press
P. O. Box 7819
Austin, Texas 78712

PUBLISHED: Tri-annually   CIRCULATION: 650
COST: 1 yr.—$6.00 in U.S.; $7.00 elsewhere; single copy—$2.50 in U.S.; $2.75 elsewhere.

CONTENTS: Prose and poetry of today's German, Swiss, and Austrian authors written in German with the English translation on the adjacent page; occasional critical essay about the works of German authors.

UNSOLICITED MSS. WELCOME? Occasionally; submissions acknowledged.
SPECIFICALLY WELCOMED: Translations of contemporary German authors, preferably of material not yet in print.
MS. LENGTH: 5-20 pages; submit ONE copy.
STYLE REQUIREMENTS: MLA STYLE SHEET.
COPYRIGHT: DIMENSION/The Department of Germanic Languages.
EDITOR'S DECISION: 2 weeks.
FROM ACCEPTANCE TO PUBLICATION: 1 year.
PAYMENT/OFFPRINTS: Twenty free offprints; others at cost.
REJECTED MSS.: Returned; sometimes criticized.
GENERAL: First issue, 1968. Usual publication length, 200-300 pages.
BACK ISSUES: Available from University of Texas Press at $2.50 each. Out-of-print issues from Xerox University Microfilms.

EUROPEAN STUDIES REVIEW

EDITORIAL ADDRESS:
Dr. J. H. Shennan, Editor
Department of History
University of Lancaster
Bailrigg, Lancaster LA1 4YG
United Kingdom

SUBSCRIPTION ADDRESS:
MacMillan Journals Ltd.
Subscription Department
Brunel Road
Basingstoke, Hampshire RG21 2XX
United Kingdom

PUBLISHED: Quarterly (Jan., Apr., July, Oct.)
COST: 1 yr.—£6.50; $17.70, U.S.A. and Canada, including postage; single copy—£2.00.

CONTENTS: Articles on European history, literature in an historical context, social and political thought over the period c.1500-1945. Review articles and book reviews lay some stress on books published in European languages other than English. Example: "Woman's Vital Statistics on the Modern French Stage."

UNSOLICITED MSS. WELCOME? Yes; articles may be submitted in any European language for translation; submissions acknowledged.
SPECIFICALLY WELCOMED: Articles within the above area and period of interest, of an original and academic nature.
MS. LENGTH: 10,000-12,000 words; submit TWO copies.
STYLE REQUIREMENTS: Articles should conform to Hart's RULES FOR COMPOSITORS AND READERS (Oxford University Press, 1967).
COPYRIGHT: Author.
EDITOR'S DECISION: A few weeks to a few months.
FROM ACCEPTANCE TO PUBLICATION: 18 months.
PAYMENT/OFFPRINTS: 25 free offprints of articles and review articles and 5 of reviews. Extra offprints may be ordered.
REJECTED MSS.: Returned.
GENERAL: First issue, January, 1971. Usual publication length, 96 pages. This is the first British journal to present an interdisciplinary study of Europe.
BACK ISSUES: Available from subscription address.

FORUM ITALICUM: A QUARTERLY OF ITALIAN STUDIES

EDITORIAL ADDRESS:
M. Ricciardelli, Editor
221 Crosby Hall
State University of New York
Buffalo, New York 14214

SUBSCRIPTION ADDRESS:
same

PUBLISHED: Quarterly (Mar., June, Sept., Dec.)
CIRCULATION: 750
COST: 1 yr.—$4.00; $3.00, students; $4.75, foreign; single copy—$1.25.

CONTENTS: Contains critical and informative articles on the language, literature, and culture of Italy and of other countries in relation to Italy; poetry; translations; fiction; book reviews; news of literary prizes; bibliography; biographical information on outstanding writers and their works. Example: "Rococo Motives in Settecento Literature."

UNSOLICITED MSS. WELCOME? Yes; submissions acknowledged.
MS. LENGTH: 4-12 pages; submit ONE copy.
STYLE REQUIREMENTS: MLA STYLE SHEET.
COPYRIGHT: Author and editor.
EDITOR'S DECISION: 3 weeks.
FROM ACCEPTANCE TO PUBLICATION: 6 months.
PAYMENT/OFFPRINTS: Offprints may be obtained.
REJECTED MSS.: Returned.
GENERAL: First issue, March, 1967. Usual publication length, 150 pages. Articles may be written in English or Italian. Contributions in French, Portuguese, or Spanish also considered.
BACK ISSUES: Available from editorial address at cost of recent issues.

FRENCH NOTES & QUERIES

EDITORIAL ADDRESS:
Peter Hoy, Editor
97 Holywell Street
Oxford
England

SUBSCRIPTION ADDRESS:

same

GENERAL: This periodical had not arrived by the time the entry went to press. Potential subscribers, contributors, or collectors will have to write the editor to see whether the journal still exists, and if so, to inquire about details of manuscript submission, style, back issues, and the like.

THE FRENCH REVIEW

EDITORIAL ADDRESS:
Jacques Hardré, Editor
P. O. Box 771
University of North Carolina
Chapel Hill, North Carolina 27514

SUBSCRIPTION ADDRESS:
F. W. Nachtmann, Executive Secretary
American Association of Teachers of French
59 East Armory Avenue
Champaign, Illinois 61820

PUBLISHED: 6 yearly (Oct., Dec., Feb., Mar., Apr., May)

CIRCULATION: 13,400

COST: 1 yr.—$10.00 in U.S. and Canada; $11.00 elsewhere for American Association of Teachers of French membership; $5.00 for student membership; includes free copy of THE FRENCH REVIEW.

CONTENTS: Literary criticism of French and francophone literature (all periods); articles on civilization and pedagogy; book reviews; association news; dissertations in progress. Example: "A Case for Black Literature in the French Classroom."

UNSOLICITED MSS. WELCOME? Only from members of AATF; submissions acknowledged.
SPECIFICALLY WELCOMED: Articles on French and francophone literature, all periods.
MS. LENGTH: Maximum 6,000 words; submit ONE copy.
STYLE REQUIREMENTS: MLA STYLE SHEET.
COPYRIGHT: The American Association of Teachers of French.
EDITOR'S DECISION: 3 months.
FROM ACCEPTANCE TO PUBLICATION: 12-18 months.
PAYMENT/OFFPRINTS: No payment. Offprints paid for and ordered by author from press.
REJECTED MSS.: Returned.
GENERAL: First issue, November, 1927. Usual publication length, 200-250 pages. The May issue contains the Directory and Index for the year's publication. Articles may be written in English or French.

BACK ISSUES: Complete series available from F. W. Nachtmann, Executive Secretary. Request price list.

FRENCH STUDIES: A QUARTERLY REVIEW

EDITORIAL ADDRESS:
L. J. Austin, General Editor
Taylor Institution
Oxford OX1 3NA
England

SUBSCRIPTION ADDRESS:
Basil Blackwell & Mott Ltd.
108 Cowley Road
Oxford OX4 1JF
England

PUBLISHED: Quarterly   CIRCULATION: 1,500
COST: 1 yr.—£6.50 for non-members of Society for French Studies; £5.00 for members (including subscription to Society).

CONTENTS: Scholarly articles on French language and literature of all periods; reviews of scholarly books on French language, literature, history, art and institutions; varia (obituaries of scholars associated with the journal, notices, lists of books received). Example: "Some Uses of SENTENTIAE in Ronsard's love-sonnets."

UNSOLICITED MSS. WELCOME? Articles, yes; submissions acknowledged. Reviews are commissioned and not acknowledged.
SPECIFICALLY WELCOMED: Scholarly articles on French language and literature from the origins to the present day.
MS. LENGTH: 5,000-6,000 words; submit ONE copy.
STYLE REQUIREMENTS: MHRA Style Book.
COPYRIGHT: The Editorial Board of FRENCH STUDIES.
EDITOR'S DECISION: Approximately 3 months.
FROM ACCEPTANCE TO PUBLICATION: 12-15 months.
PAYMENT/OFFPRINTS: Free offprints of articles, 12 of reviews. Further copies may be ordered at a charge.
REJECTED MSS.: Returned.
GENERAL: First issue, January, 1947. Usual publication length, 128 pages.
BACK ISSUES: Available from Basil Blackwell & Mott Ltd. Inquire about cost.

GERMANIC NOTES

EDITORIAL ADDRESS:
A. Wayne Wonderley, Editor
Department of Germanic Languages and Literatures
1055 Patterson Tower
University of Kentucky
Lexington, Kentucky 40506

SUBSCRIPTION ADDRESS:
Erasmus Press
225 Culpepper
Lexington, Kentucky 40502

PUBLISHED: 8 times yearly

COST: 1 yr.—$4.00 in U.S. and Canada; $5.00 elsewhere.

CONTENTS: Notes, queries, and critical reviews of scholarly reference works; annotated lists of reference works which are basic to research libraries embracing advanced studies of aspects of the culture of past or present German or Germanic areas of Europe; articles on German literature, language, folklore and history; book reviews. Example: "The Ritual Execution of Don Carlos."

UNSOLICITED MSS. WELCOME? Yes.
SPECIFICALLY WELCOMED: Critical reviews on scholarly Germanic reference works.
MS. LENGTH: Articles, up to 6 pages, reviews, up to 3 pages; submit TWO copies.
STYLE REQUIREMENTS: Publication's style; footnotes follow article.
COPYRIGHT: Not copyrighted.
PAYMENT/OFFPRINTS: Ten free offprints; more at minimum rate of $15 per 100 copies.
GENERAL: First issue, January, 1970. Usual publication length, 8 pages. Articles may be written in English or German.
BACK ISSUES: Available from publisher.

THE GERMANIC REVIEW: DEVOTED TO STUDIES DEALING WITH THE GERMANIC LANGUAGES AND LITERATURES

EDITORIAL ADDRESS:
Joseph Bauke, Editor
319 Hamilton Hall
Columbia University
New York, New York 10027

SUBSCRIPTION ADDRESS:
Columbia University Press
Periodicals Department
136 South Broadway
Irving-on-Hudson, New York 10533

PUBLISHED: Quarterly
(Jan., Mar., May, Nov.)

CIRCULATION: 1,400

COST: 1 yr.—$7.50 in U.S.; $7.80 foreign; single copy—$2.00 in U.S.; $2.15 foreign.

CONTENTS: Scholarly studies of the Germanic languages and literatures; book reviews. Example: "The Genesis and Development of Friedrich Spee's Love-Imagery in the TRUTZNACHTIGALL."

UNSOLICITED MSS. WELCOME? Yes; submissions acknowledged.
SPECIFICALLY WELCOMED: Critical articles giving basically new information.
MS. LENGTH: 5,000-7,000 words; submit ONE copy.
STYLE REQUIREMENTS: MLA STYLE SHEET; footnotes on separate sheet.
COPYRIGHT: Columbia University Press
EDITOR'S DECISION: 4-6 weeks.
FROM ACCEPTANCE TO PUBLICATION: 1 year.
PAYMENT/OFFPRINTS: Ten free copies of issue to authors of articles; two to authors of reviews.

REJECTED MSS.: Returned.
GENERAL: First issue, 1926. Usual publication length, 80 pages. Manuscripts should be written in English except in the most unusual cases.
BACK ISSUES: Available from Columbia University Press. Price varies.

GERMAN LIFE AND LETTERS: A QUARTERLY REVIEW

EDITORIAL ADDRESS:
Leonard Forster, Editor
Germanic Institute
29 Russell Square
London W.C.1.
England

SUBSCRIPTION ADDRESS:
Basil Blackwell Publisher
5 Alfred Street
Oxford
England

PUBLISHED: Quarterly (Oct., Jan., Apr., July)

CONTENTS: Scholarly articles, almost exclusively in English, on German literature and culture.

UNSOLICITED MSS. WELCOME? Yes, preferably after previous inquiry; submissions acknowledged.
SPECIFICALLY WELCOME: Critical essays.
MS. LENGTH: 5,000 words or less; submit ONE copy.
STYLE REQUIREMENTS: MHRA Style Book.
COPYRIGHT: Basil Blackwell Publisher.
EDITOR'S DECISION: 5-6 weeks.
FROM ACCEPTANCE TO PUBLICATION: 18 months or more.
PAYMENT/OFFPRINTS: 20 free offprints of all articles.
REJECTED MSS.: Returned.
GENERAL: First issue, 1947/48.

THE GERMAN QUARTERLY

EDITORIAL ADDRESS:
William A. Little, Editor
University of Virginia
Cocke Hall
Charlottesville, Virginia 22903

SUBSCRIPTION ADDRESS:
American Association of Teachers of German
339 Walnut Street
Philadelphia, Pennsylvania 19106

PUBLISHED: Quarterly (Jan., Mar., May, Nov.)

CIRCULATION: 9,500

COST: 1 yr.—$7.50; single copy—$2.00; AATG membership dues—$10.00 per year and includes subscriptions to THE GERMAN QUARTERLY, DIE UNTERRICHTSPRAXIS, AATG NEWSLETTER, and AATG MEMBERSHIP DIRECTORY.

CONTENTS: Literary criticism of works of German literature; articles on topics connected with German linguistics and pedagogy; book reviews; annual "Bibliography Americana Germanica." Examples: "Shoemaking as a Mystic Symbol in Nelly Sachs' Mystery Play ELI"; "The Poetic Language of Gerd Gaiser."

UNSOLICITED MSS. WELCOME? Yes; submissions acknowledged.
SPECIFICALLY WELCOMED: Critical articles on German literature, linguistics.
MS. LENGTH: Around 30 pages; submit ONE copy.
STYLE REQUIREMENTS: MLA STYLE SHEET; footnotes follow article.
COPYRIGHT: American Association of Teachers of German.
EDITOR'S DECISION: Around 3 months.
FROM ACCEPTANCE TO PUBLICATION: 1 year.
PAYMENT/OFFPRINTS: No payment. Offprints available from printer.
REJECTED MSS.: Returned, criticized.
GENERAL: First issue, 1928. Usual publication length, 200-250 pages. Articles are accepted in either English or German. Original typescripts preferred. "Bibliography Americana Germanica," printed annually in TGQ September number, may be secured from E. F. Bauer, Haverford College, Haverford, Pennsylvania 19041 at $3.00. Quarterly is indexed by volume.
BACK ISSUES: Available from AATG at $3.00 each.

HISPANIC REVIEW

EDITORIAL ADDRESS:
Arnold G. Reichenberger and
Russell P. Sebold, Editors
Williams Hall
University of Pennsylvania
Philadelphia, Pennsylvania 19104

SUBSCRIPTION ADDRESS:
Mrs. Edith Seiver
same

PUBLISHED: Quarterly
COST: 1 yr.—$9.50; single copy—$2.50.
CIRCULATION: 1,400

CONTENTS: Researched essays concerning Hispanic languages and literatures; book reviews.

UNSOLICITED MSS. WELCOME? Seldom; submissions acknowledged.
SPECIFICALLY WELCOMED: Scholarly articles pertaining primarily to Spanish literatures and language.
MS. LENGTH: 1,000-1,500 words; submit ONE copy.
STYLE REQUIREMENTS: MLA STYLE SHEET.
COPYRIGHT: Not copyrighted.
EDITOR'S DECISION: 3-4 weeks.
FROM ACCEPTANCE TO PUBLICATION: 2-3 years.
PAYMENT/OFFPRINTS: Fifteen free offprints for reviews; 10 for articles.
REJECTED MSS.: Returned; sometimes criticized.

GENERAL: First issue, 1933. Usual publication length, 100-120 pages. Will only accept original articles—no carbon or xerox accepted. Articles may be written in English or Spanish.
BACK ISSUES: Vol. 1-37 Philadelphia 1933-1969 (partly in the original edition) available from Johnson Reprint Corporation at $750.00 cloth bound; $600 paper bound.

HISPANOFILA

See the section on AGE AND/OR NATIONALITY: AFRICAN, CARIBBEAN, LATIN AMERICAN, NEAR EASTERN for details.

ITALIAN QUARTERLY

EDITORIAL ADDRESS:
Gian Piero Barricelli, Editor
Library South 4139
University of California
Riverside, California 92502

SUBSCRIPTION ADDRESS:

same

PUBLISHED: Tri-annually   CIRCULATION: 700
COST: 1 yr.—$6.00; 2 yrs.—$11.00; 3 yrs.—$17.00; single copy—$1.50; double issue—$2.50.

CONTENTS: Scholarly articles dealing primarily with Italian literature but also with Italian culture, language, history, politics, art, and music. Regular sections, such as "Essays," "Trends," "Reviews," and "Items" are supplemented from time to time by features, such as the "Translation Workshop," the "Dante Shelf," and the "Bookshelf." On occasion, an issue is devoted to an individual author or to a special topic. Examples: "Symbol and Structure in THE LEOPARD"; "Luigi Pirandello in search of a Total Theatre."

UNSOLICITED MSS. WELCOME? Yes; submissions acknowledged.
SPECIFICALLY WELCOMED: Various kinds of literary contributions—including analyses of single works or comparative studies; many critical points of view have been represented in the past.
MS. LENGTH: Maximum 25 pages, including notes; submit ONE copy.
STYLE REQUIREMENTS: MLA STYLE SHEET.
EDITOR'S DECISION: 1 to 2 months.
FROM ACCEPTANCE TO PUBLICATION: 15 to 18 months.
PAYMENT/OFFPRINTS: Authors of essays automatically receive 25 free offprints.
REJECTED MSS.: Returned.
GENERAL: First issue, Spring, 1957. Usual publication length, 100-120 pages. An index to Vols. I-XV (1957-1971) is available at $2.10 per copy.

BACK ISSUES: Available from editorial address at $1.75 each for single issues; $3.50 each for double issues.

ITALICA

See the section on TEACHING ABOUT LITERATURE for details.

JOURNAL OF ENGLISH AND GERMANIC PHILOLOGY: A QUARTERLY DEVOTED TO THE ENGLISH, GERMAN, AND SCANDINAVIAN LANGUAGES AND LITERATURES

EDITORIAL ADDRESS:
Editor
107 English Building
University of Illinois
Urbana, Illinois 61801

SUBSCRIPTION ADDRESS:

same

PUBLISHED: Quarterly

GENERAL: First issue, 1897. The annual "Anglo-German Literary Bibliography," ed. John R. Frey, appears in the July issue. A single copy, $2.25, may be purchased from University of Illinois Press, Urbana, Illinois 61801. This periodical had not arrived by the time the entry went to press. Potential subscribers, contributors, or collectors will have to write the editor to see whether the journal still exists, and if so, to inquire about details of manuscript submission, style, back issues, and the like.

JOURNAL OF MODERN LITERATURE

See the section on AGE AND/OR NATIONALITY: AMERICAN for details.

JOURNAL OF SPANISH STUDIES: TWENTIETH CENTURY

EDITORIAL ADDRESS:
Vicente Cabrera and Luis
Gonzáles-del-Valle, Editors
Department of Modern Languages
Kansas State University
Manhattan, Kansas 66506

SUBSCRIPTION ADDRESS:

same

PUBLISHED: Tri-annually (Spring,   CIRCULATION: 800
Fall, Winter)
COST: 1 yr.—$6.00; 2 yrs.—$11.00; 3 yrs.—$15.00.

CONTENTS: Scholarly articles on the literatures of Spain and Spanish America in the 20th century (from modernismo and generation of 1898 to the ever changing present) with emphasis on the aesthetic characteristics of literary works; essays on literary criticism. Example: "Self-Creation and Alienation in the Novels of Azorín."

UNSOLICITED MSS. WELCOME? Yes; submissions acknowledged.
MS. LENGTH: 12-25 pages; submit ORIGINAL, two copies, and abstract.
STYLE REQUIREMENTS: MLA STYLE SHEET; footnotes follow article.
COPYRIGHT: JOURNAL OF SPANISH STUDIES.
EDITOR'S DECISION: 4-8 weeks.
FROM ACCEPTANCE TO PUBLICATION: 6 months.
PAYMENT/OFFPRINTS: No payment. Authors pay modest charge for offprints.
REJECTED MSS.: Returned.
GENERAL: First issue, June, 1973. Usual publication length, 110 pages. Essays may be written in English or Spanish.
BACK ISSUES: Available from editorial address at subscription price, plus $1 service charge.

KENTUCKY ROMANCE QUARTERLY

EDITORIAL ADDRESS: SUBSCRIPTION ADDRESS:
John E. Keller, Editor
University of Kentucky   same
1115 Office Tower
Lexington, Kentucky 40506

PUBLISHED: Quarterly   CIRCULATION: 425
COST: 1 yr.—$5.00 in U.S.; $6.50 elsewhere.

CONTENTS: Scholarly articles on interpretive, historical, linguistic, folkloric areas of foreign literatures.

UNSOLICITED MSS. WELCOME? Yes; submissions acknowledged.
SPECIFICALLY WELCOMED: Linguistic, historical, interpretive, folkloric areas of foreign literature.
MS. LENGTH: 15-20 pages; submit TWO copies.
STYLE REQUIREMENTS: MLA STYLE SHEET.
COPYRIGHT: University of Kentucky.
EDITOR'S DECISION: For acceptance, 2 evaluations by one on-campus and one off-campus specialist are required. Often revision is required of authors.
FROM ACCEPTANCE TO PUBLICATION: 1 year.
PAYMENT/OFFPRINTS: None.
REJECTED MSS.: Returned.

GENERAL: First issue, 1967, as KRQ (formerly FOREIGN LANGUAGE QUARTERLY). Usual publication length, 100-150 pages.
BACK ISSUES: Available from editorial address at $2.00 each; $8.00 per volume in U.S.; $2.25 each; $9.00 per volume elsewhere.

L'ESPRIT CRÉATEUR

EDITORIAL ADDRESS:　　　　SUBSCRIPTION ADDRESS:
John D. Erickson, Editor
P.O. Box 222　　　　　　　　　　same
Lawrence, Kansas 66044

PUBLISHED: Quarterly　　　　CIRCULATION: 1,250
COST: 1 yr.—$4.00.

CONTENTS: Substantially articles of a critical nature on French and Francophone literature and book reviews of critical works. Features appearing irregularly are review articles (on French criticism), and interviews with contemporary French and Francophone authors and critics. Example: "Apollinaire's Use of Arthurian Legend."

UNSOLICITED MSS. WELCOME? Yes; submissions acknowledged.
SPECIFICALLY WELCOMED: Critical articles focusing on French literary texts.
MS. LENGTH: Maximum 4,000 words; submit TWO copies.
STYLE REQUIREMENTS: MLA STYLE SHEET; few footnotes.
COPYRIGHT: L'ESPRIT CRÉATEUR.
EDITOR'S DECISION: 3-6 months.
FROM ACCEPTANCE TO PUBLICATION: Up to 6 months.
PAYMENT/OFFPRINTS: Five copies of journal. Offprints available; size of article determines cost.
REJECTED MSS.: Returned; sometimes criticized.
GENERAL: First issue, Spring, 1961. Usual publication length, 90-100 pages.
BACK ISSUES: Available from publisher at $1.25 each ($3.50 for Vol. XI, No. 2) except for Vols. L-LV, 1961-1964, which are available in microfilm or enlarged editions from Xerox University Microfilms.

LITERATURE, MUSIC, FINE ARTS: A REVIEW OF GERMAN-LANGUAGE RESEARCH CONTRIBUTIONS ON LITERATURE, MUSIC, AND FINE ARTS

EDITORIAL ADDRESS:　　　　SUBSCRIPTION ADDRESS:
Dr. J. Hohnholz, Editor
German Studies　　　　　　　　same
Landhausstr. 18
74 Tübingen, West Germany

PUBLISHED: Biannually   CIRCULATION: 2,200
COST: 1 yr.—DM20.— or $5.00 (postage extra); single copy—DM10.— or $2.50.

CONTENTS: Book reviews; bibliographies of new books and articles in the fields of literature, music, and fine arts, confined to German research contribution.

UNSOLICITED MSS. WELCOME? No; submissions acknowledged.
SPECIFICALLY WELCOMED: After invitation, book reviews.
MS. LENGTH: 1-8 pages; submit TWO copies.
EDITOR'S DECISION: 1 month.
FROM ACCEPTANCE TO PUBLICATION: Depends.
PAYMENT/OFFPRINTS: Review copy.
REJECTED MSS.: Returned.
GENERAL: First issue, 1968. Usual publication length, 128-144 pages.
BACK ISSUES: Available from subscription address at recent prices.

LITERATUR IN WISSENSCHAFT UND UNTERRICHT

EDITORIAL ADDRESS: SUBSCRIPTION ADDRESS:
Horst Kruse, Peter Nicolaisen,   Walter R. Rix, Managing Editor
Paul G. Buchloh, Dietrich Jäger, Editors   same
Department of English
University of Kiel, 2300 Kiel
Olshausenstrasse 40-60
West Germany

PUBLISHED: Quarterly (Mar., June,   CIRCULATION: 2,500
Sept., Dec.)
COST: 1 yr.—$4.00.

CONTENTS: Essays on the literature of America, England, France, and Germany; researched articles on works of authors from these four lands; book reviews, special emphasis on explication de texte. Examples: "Thom Gunn's 'Black Jackets': An Interpretation"; "The Contemporary Novel of the American West."

UNSOLICITED MSS. WELCOME? Yes; submissions acknowledged.
SPECIFICALLY WELCOMED: Explication de texte.
MS. LENGTH: 4,000-7,000 words; submit ONE copy.
STYLE REQUIREMENTS: MLA STYLE SHEET.
COPYRIGHT: Arranged individually, generally editors.
EDITOR'S DECISION: 6 months.
FROM ACCEPTANCE TO PUBLICATION: 6 months.
PAYMENT/OFFPRINTS: Twenty offprints.
REJECTED MSS.: Returned.
GENERAL: First issue, 1968. Usual publication length, 64-75 pages. Articles may be submitted in English, French, and German.
BACK ISSUES: Available from Managing Editor at $4.00 for 4 back issues.

MODERN AUSTRIAN LITERATURE

EDITORIAL ADDRESS:
Donald G. Daviau, Editor
Department of German and Russian
University of California at Riverside
Riverside, California 92502

SUBSCRIPTION ADDRESS:
William H. Snyder
Secretary-Treasurer, I.A.S.R.A.
Department of Germanic Languages
and Literature
State University of New York
Binghamton, New York 13901

PUBLISHED: Quarterly
CIRCULATION: 1,000
COST: 1 yr.—$5.00; associate membership—$3.00; students—$3.00; single copy—$1.50.

CONTENTS: Studies; articles of interpretation and literary historical focus; book reviews; bibliographies; lectures; letters and other primary material; reports of Austrian literary meetings. Example: "Musical Structure and Meaning in Arthur Schnitzler's ZWISCHENSPIEL."

UNSOLICITED MSS. WELCOME? Yes; submissions acknowledged.
SPECIFICALLY WELCOMED: Material relating to Modern Austrian literature and culture of the 19th and 20th centuries.
MS. LENGTH: 20-25 pages; submit ONE copy.
STYLE REQUIREMENTS: MLA STYLE SHEET.
COPYRIGHT: International Arthur Schnitzler Research Association.
EDITOR'S DECISION: Approximately 6 months.
FROM ACCEPTANCE TO PUBLICATION: 1½ years.
PAYMENT/OFFPRINTS: Five complimentary copies of journal; offprints available at cost.
REJECTED MSS.: Returned.
GENERAL: First issue, 1962, as JOURNAL OF THE INTERNATIONAL ARTHUR SCHNITZLER RESEARCH ASSOCIATION; 1968, as MAL. Articles may be written in English or German. Usual publication length, 200 pages.
BACK ISSUES: Available from Secretary-Treasurer at $1.50 each.

THE MODERN LANGUAGE REVIEW

EDITORIAL ADDRESS:
C. P. Brand, General Editor
Department of Italian
University of Edinburgh
David Hume Tower, George Square
Edinburgh EH8 9JX
Scotland

SUBSCRIPTION ADDRESS:
R.A. Wisbey, Treasurer MHRA
Department of German
King's College, Strand
London WC2R 2LS
England

PUBLISHED: Quarterly (Jan., Apr., July, Oct.)
CIRCULATION: 3,000
COST: 1 yr.—£3.00 ($7.50) to members of the Modern Humanities Research Association; £8.50 ($26.50) otherwise.

CONTENTS: Original articles (in English) on all aspects of modern European languages and literature (including English); reviews of books on these subjects.

UNSOLICITED MSS. WELCOME? Articles, yes; submissions acknowledged. All reviews are by invitation only.
SPECIFICALLY WELCOMED: Any article dealing, in scholarly fashion, with a topic with the general province of MLR.
MS. LENGTH: Up to 10,000 words; submit ONE copy.
STYLE REQUIREMENTS: All contributions follow the MHRA STYLE BOOK.
COPYRIGHT: The Modern Humanities Research Association.
EDITOR'S DECISION: 1-3 months.
FROM ACCEPTANCE TO PUBLICATION: 1-2 years.
PAYMENT/OFFPRINTS: 20 free offprints of articles; 10 of reviews; extra copies may be paid for.
REJECTED MSS.: Returned.
GENERAL: First issue, 1905. Usual publication length, 240 pages. General indexes are available for Vols. 11-20, 21-30, 31-50, 51-60.
BACK ISSUES: Vols. 57-68 (current year) available from subscription address at £10.00 ($31.00) per volume. Vols. 1-56 and general indexes from Wm. Dawson and Sons Ltd., Cannon House, Park Farm Road, Folkestone, England.

MODERN PHILOLOGY: A JOURNAL DEVOTED TO RESEARCH IN
MEDIEVAL AND MODERN LITERATURE

See the section on AGE AND/OR NATIONALITY: CONTINENTAL—CLASSICAL, MEDIEVAL AND RENAISSANCE for details.

MONATSHEFTE: A JOURNAL DEVOTED TO THE STUDY OF
GERMAN LANGUAGE AND LITERATURE

EDITORIAL ADDRESS:
Valters Nollendorfs, Editor
Department of German
810 Van Hise Hall
University of Wisconsin
Madison, Wisconsin 53706

SUBSCRIPTION ADDRESS:
Journals Department
University of Wisconsin Press
Box 1379
Madison, Wisconsin 53701

PUBLISHED: Quarterly (Mar., June, Sept., Dec.)

CIRCULATION: 1,500

COST: 1 yr.—$7.50 (individuals); $20.00 (institutions); single copy—$3.00 (individuals); $6.00 (institutions).

CONTENTS: Articles of general interest dealing with the language and literature of the German-speaking countries, and with cultural matters which have linguistic, literary, or pedagogical significance; book reviews; annual listing of German Departments in the U.S.A. and Canada including staff members by rank, promotions, changes of affiliation, visiting professors, and completed dissertations. Example: "Carl Sternheim: Satirist or Creator of Modern Heroes?"

UNSOLICITED MSS. WELCOME? Articles, yes; book reviews, no; submissions acknowledged.
SPECIFICALLY WELCOMED: Papers dealing with literature.
MS. LENGTH: 15-20 pages; submit ONE copy.
STYLE REQUIREMENTS: MLA STYLE SHEET.
COPYRIGHT: The Regents of the University of Wisconsin.
EDITOR'S DECISION: 2 months or more.
FROM ACCEPTANCE TO PUBLICATION: 2 years.
PAYMENT/OFFPRINTS: 10 copies gratis. More available at cost.
REJECTED MSS.: Returned.
GENERAL: First issue, 1899. Usual publication length, 112 pages. Articles may be written in English or German, but English is preferred.
BACK ISSUES: Available from subscription address at $6.00 each. Out of print issues from Kraus Reprint Co.

NEOPHILOLOGUS: A QUARTERLY DEVOTED TO THE STUDY OF THE MODERN LANGUAGES AND THEIR LITERATURES

See the section on AGE AND/OR NATIONALITY: CONTINENTAL—CLASCAL, MEDIEVAL AND RENAISSANCE for details.

NEUPHILOLOGISCHE MITTEILUNGEN:
BULLETIN OF THE MODERN LANGUAGE SOCIETY

EDITORIAL ADDRESS:
Matti Rissanen, Editorial Secretary
Porthania
The University
00100 Helsinki 10
Finland

SUBSCRIPTION ADDRESS:
Kari Sajavaara, Hon. Secretary
of the Society
Torpankuja 5 C 14
40740 Jyväskylä 74
Finland

PUBLISHED: Quarterly
COST: 1 yr.—US$8.00.

CIRCULATION: 1,200

CONTENTS: Articles and reviews on English, German, and Romance languages and literatures. Examples: "The Knights of Malta in Renaissance Drama"; "Revenge and Reward as Recurrent Motives in BEOWULF"; "Chatterton's Minor Satirical Poems."

UNSOLICITED MSS. WELCOME? Yes; submissions not acknowledged.
MS. LENGTH: 10 pages maximum; submit ONE copy.
STYLE REQUIREMENTS: MLA STYLE SHEET.
COPYRIGHT: The publisher (Modern Language Society, Helsinki).
EDITOR'S DECISION: Varies.
FROM ACCEPTANCE TO PUBLICATION: Varies.
PAYMENT/OFFPRINTS: Fifty free offprints.
REJECTED MSS.: Returned.
GENERAL: First issue, 1899. Usual publication length, 192 pages. "Middle English Research in Progress," annually in NM; reprint $.25 preordered from R. H. Robbins, ed., Rte. 1, Box 87, Saugerties, N.Y. 12477.
BACK ISSUES: Available from subscription address at $8.00 per volume (single issues not normally sold).

THE NEW HUNGARIAN QUARTERLY

EDITORIAL ADDRESS:
Iván Bolizsár, Editor
17 Rákóczi út
1088 Budapest
Hungary

SUBSCRIPTION ADDRESS:
KULTURA Hungarian Trading
Company for Books and Newspapers
1376 Budapest, P.O.B. 149
Hungary

PUBLISHED: Quarterly
COST: 1 yr.—$8.00; single copy—$2.00 or 80p.

CIRCULATION: 5,000

CONTENTS: History, politics, economy, literature, surveys, the arts; illustrations and plates. Example: "Janus Pannonius: Poet of the Hungarian Renaissance."

SPECIFICALLY WELCOMED: Articles on Hungarian literature.
MS. LENGTH: 8 pages; submit TWO copies.
COPYRIGHT: Editorial office.
EDITOR'S DECISION: 10 weeks.
FROM ACCEPTANCE TO PUBLICATION: 6 months.
REJECTED MSS.: Returned.
GENERAL: First issue, 1960. Usual publication length, 224 pages. Enclose check or remit the subscription price to the account: KULTURA 024/7, Hungarian National Bank, 1850 Budapest, Hungary. U.S.A. distributors: Stechert-Hafner, Inc., 31 East 10th Street, New York, New York 10021; Center of Hungarian Literature, Inc., 1538 Second Avenue, New York, New York 10028; FAM Book Service, 69 Fifth Avenue, New York, New York 10003
BACK ISSUES: Available at $2.00 each from KULTURA Hungarian Trading Company for Books and Newspapers, 1376 Budapest, P. O. B. 149, Hungary.

NINETEENTH-CENTURY FRENCH STUDIES

EDITORIAL ADDRESS:
Thomas H. Goetz, Editor
Department of Foreign Languages
State University College
Fredonia, New York 14063

SUBSCRIPTION ADDRESS:

same

PUBLISHED: Quarterly (Nov., Feb., May, Sept.)

CIRCULATION: 600

COST: 1 yr.—$4.00 in U.S.; $4.50 elsewhere; current single copy—$1.25 in U.S.; $1.50 elsewhere.

CONTENTS: Studies of nineteenth-century French literature from a philosophical, psychological, sociological, anthropological, cultural, historical, or other critical standpoint; book reviews; notes and news. Example: "The Entanglement of Sexuality and Aesthetics in Gautier and Mallarmé."

UNSOLICITED MSS. WELCOME? Yes; submissions acknowledged.
SPECIFICALLY WELCOMED: New approaches, new points of view; comparative studies.
MS. LENGTH: 15-30 pages; submit the ORIGINAL.
STYLE REQUIREMENTS: MLA STYLE SHEET; footnotes on separate page at end of article.
COPYRIGHT: T. H. Goetz.
EDITOR'S DECISION: 1-4 months.
FROM ACCEPTANCE TO PUBLICATION: 3 months.
PAYMENT/OFFPRINTS: 8 to 10 free offprints. Author may order and pay for offprints desired.
REJECTED MSS.: Returned.
GENERAL: First issue, November, 1972. Usual publication length, 50-70 pages. Articles may be written in English or French.
BACK ISSUES: Available from editorial address at $1.50 each.

NOTTINGHAM FRENCH STUDIES

EDITORIAL ADDRESS:
Prof. Lewis Thorpe, Editor
The University
Nottingham NG7 2RD
England

SUBSCRIPTION ADDRESS:

same

PUBLISHED: Biannually (May, Oct.)   CIRCULATION: 600
COST: 1 yr.—$5.00 (trade price, $4.50), post free.

CONTENTS: Articles on French literature from 1600 to present.

UNSOLICITED MSS. WELCOME? Yes; submissions acknowledged.

SPECIFICALLY WELCOMED: Articles of some 6,000 words in French or English literature (1600-now).
MS. LENGTH: Some 6,000 words; submit ONE copy.
COPYRIGHT: Nominally editor; inquire about reprinting.
EDITOR'S DECISION: Up to 6 months.
FROM ACCEPTANCE TO PUBLICATION: Up to 6 months.
PAYMENT/OFFPRINTS: 50 free offprints.
REJECTED MSS.: Returned.
GENERAL: First issue, May, 1962. Usual publication length, 12 pages.
BACK ISSUES: Available from editor at $2.50 each or $5.00 per volume. All are in print.

ORBIS LITTERARUM: INTERNATIONAL REVIEW OF LITERARY STUDIES

EDITORIAL ADDRESS:
Morte Nojgaard, Editor
Munksgaard A.S.
35 Nørre Søgade
DK-1370 Copenhagen K
Denmark

SUBSCRIPTION ADDRESS:
Munksgaard Publishers
35 Nørre Søgade
DK-1370 Copenhagen K
Denmark

PUBLISHED: Quarterly
CIRCULATION: 500
COST: 1 yr.—D.kr. 138, plus postage D.kr.12 (US$24.75; £9.90; DM 70.50).

CONTENTS: Articles concerning the theory of literature and all sorts of methods of literary criticism; articles on European and American literature in English, German, and French, especially articles that illustrate, on the basis of single analyses, important general critical problems or essential problems in the works of the greatest authors of Western Europe.

UNSOLICITED MSS. WELCOME? Yes; submissions acknowledged.
SPECIFICALLY WELCOMED: Essays on the theory of literature, on the methods of literary criticism, analysis of works with discussion of general methodological problems.
MS. LENGTH: 10-20 pages; submit ONE copy.
STYLE REQUIREMENTS: See the cover page of the review.
COPYRIGHT: Author.
EDITOR'S DECISION: 2-4 months.
FROM ACCEPTANCE TO PUBLICATION: 6-12 months.
PAYMENT/OFFPRINTS: 30 free offprints.
REJECTED MSS.: Returned.
GENERAL: First issue, 1943. Usual publication length, 80 pages.
BACK ISSUES: Available from Munksgaard Publishers.

PHILOLOGICA PRAGENSIA (including ČASOPIS PRO MODERNÍ FILOLOII)

EDITORIAL ADDRESS:
Zdeněk Vančura, Chief Editor
Liliová 13
116 45 Praha 1
Czechoslovakia

SUBSCRIPTION ADDRESS:
John Benjamins N.V.
Periodical Trade
Warmoesstraat 54
Amsterdam
Holland

PUBLISHED: Quarterly
COST: 1 yr.—Dutch Glds. 30,—; in Czechoslovakia—Kčs 32.—.

CIRCULATION: 1,000

CONTENTS: Articles, news and book reviews in Germanic and Romance linguistics, literary history and criticism. Example: "Topic, Focus, and the Ordering of Elements of Semantic Representations."

UNSOLICITED MSS. WELCOME? Yes; submissions acknowledged on request.
SPECIFICALLY WELCOMED: Studies in Anglo-Germanic and Romance literary history and criticism (monographic or comparative).
MS. LENGTH: Up to 20 pages; submit ONE OR TWO copies.
STYLE REQUIREMENTS: None specific.
COPYRIGHT: Academia [Publishing House], Vodičkova 40, 112 29 Praha 1.
EDITOR'S DECISION: 2-6 months.
FROM ACCEPTANCE TO PUBLICATION: About 3 months.
PAYMENT/OFFPRINTS: Payment possible only in Czechoslovak currency. 50 offprints maximum after publication.
REJECTED MSS.: Preferably not returned.
GENERAL: First issue, 1958. Usual publication length, 256 pages. Contributions are generally published in English, German, French, Spanish. From 1972 on, each odd number includes a Czech supplement (32 pages per annum) ČASOPIS PRO MODERNÍ FILOLOGII, which has hitherto appeared as a separate journal.
BACK ISSUES: Available either on an exchange basis from Ústav pro českou a světovou literaturu knihovna at editorial address or from subscription address. Cost depends on number and publishing date.

PHILOLOGICAL QUARTERLY

EDITORIAL ADDRESS:
Curt A. Zimansky, Editor
Department of English
University of Iowa
Iowa City, Iowa 52242

SUBSCRIPTION ADDRESS:
Department of Publications
University of Iowa
Iowa City, Iowa 52242

PUBLISHED: Quarterly (Jan., Apr., July, Oct.)
COST: 1 yr.—$7.50; 2 yrs.—$14.00; 3 yrs.—$20.00.

CIRCULATION: 2,000

CONTENTS: Scholarly and critical articles and notes on the classical and modern languages and literatures. Examples: "The Progress of the Hoard in BEOWULF"; "Misconceptions in Current Thoreau Criticism."

UNSOLICITED MSS. WELCOME? Yes; submissions acknowledged.
MS. LENGTH: Under 8,000 words; submit ONE copy.
STYLE REQUIREMENTS: MLA STYLE SHEET.
COPYRIGHT: The University of Iowa.
EDITOR'S DECISION: 1-2 months.
FROM ACCEPTANCE TO PUBLICATION : 2½ years.
PAYMENT/OFFPRINTS: No payment. Editor supplies offprint order form with galley proofs.
REJECTED MSS.: Returned.
GENERAL: First issue, January, 1921. Usual publication length, 160 pages (July issue runs about 300 pages). Articles may be written in English, French, German, Italian, or Spanish.
BACK ISSUES: Volumes 1 to 40 available from Walter J. Johnson, Inc. Vol. 41 on available from subscription address at $2.00 each except for special issues.

RENAISSANCE AND MODERN STUDIES

See the section on AGE AND/OR NATIONALITY: CONTINENTAL—CLASSICAL, MEDIEVAL AND RENAISSANCE for details.

REVISTA DE ESTUDIOS HISPÁNICOS

See the section on AGE AND/OR NATIONALITY: AFRICAN, CARIBBEAN, LATIN AMERICAN, NEAR EASTERN for details.

REVUE DES LANGUES VIVANTES/TIJDSCHRIFT VOOR LEVENDE TALEN

EDITORIAL ADDRESS:
Pierre Michel, Editor
Université de Liège, 3 place
Cockerill, 4000 Liège
Belgique

SUBSCRIPTION ADDRESS:
Editions Marcel Didier
14, rue des Comédiens
1000 Bruxelles
Belgique

PUBLISHED: 6 times yearly
COST: 1 yr.—325 Belgian francs.

CIRCULATION: 850

CONTENTS: Articles on modern literatures and languages (all major European languages); pure and applied linguistics; etymology; methodology of modern languages. Example: "The Overpopulated Wasteland: Myth in Anthony Burgess' THE WANTING SEED."

UNSOLICITED MSS. WELCOME? Yes; submissions acknowledged.
SPECIFICALLY WELCOMED: Criticism, research surveys.
MS. LENGTH: 10-20 pages; submit ONE copy.
STYLE REQUIREMENTS: MLA STYLE SHEET.
COPYRIGHT: Editor.
EDITOR'S DECISION: 1 month.
FROM ACCEPTANCE TO PUBLICATION: 10 months.
PAYMENT/OFFPRINTS: 50 free offprints.
REJECTED MSS.: Returned.
GENERAL: First issue, 1935. Usual publication length, 96 pages.
BACK ISSUES: Available from subscription address.

RIVISTA DI LETTERATURE MODERNE E COMPARATE

EDITORIAL ADDRESS:
G. C. Sansoni, Editor
Viale Mazzini, 46
50132 Florence
Italy

SUBSCRIPTION ADDRESS:
LI. CO.SA.
via Lamarmora, 45
50129 Florence
Italy

PUBLISHED: Quarterly
COST: 1 yr.—$17.00.

CIRCULATION: 1,000

CONTENTS: Articles on modern literatures and comparative literature; notes. Essay example: "Bergson and Pirandello's 'Il Giuoco delle Parti.' "

UNSOLICITED MSS. WELCOME? Unsolicited articles are accepted for examination; submissions not acknowledged.
MS. LENGTH: 20 pages; submit ONE copy.
COPYRIGHT: Publishers.
EDITOR'S DECISION: 3 months.
FROM ACCEPTANCE TO PUBLICATION: 4-5 months.
PAYMENT/OFFPRINTS: 20 offprints.
REJECTED MSS.: Not returned.
GENERAL: First issue, 1947. Usual publication length, 80 pages.
BACK ISSUES: Available from subscription address at about $6.00 each.

ROMANCE NOTES

EDITORIAL ADDRESS:
George B. Daniel, Editor
Department of Romance Languages
Dey Hall
University of North Carolina
Chapel Hill, North Carolina 27514

SUBSCRIPTION ADDRESS:

same

PUBLISHED: Tri-annually (Autumn, Winter, Spring)
CIRCULATION: 700
COST: 1 yr.—$8.00 (20% discount to agencies); $4.00 for students.

CONTENTS: Articles dealing with all areas of the Romance Languages and Literatures.

UNSOLICITED MSS. WELCOME? Yes; submissions acknowledged.
MS. LENGTH: 6-12 pages; submit ONE copy.
STYLE REQUIREMENTS: MLA STYLE SHEET.
EDITOR'S DECISION: 2-3 months.
FROM ACCEPTANCE TO PUBLICATION: 1-2 years.
PAYMENT/OFFPRINTS: No payment. Authors may pay costs for offprints, in lots of 50.
REJECTED MSS.: Returned.
GENERAL: First issue, Autumn, 1959. Usual publication length, 100-200 pages. Articles may be written in English, French, Italian, Portuguese, and Spanish.
BACK ISSUES: Available from editorial address at following prices: Vols. 1-5, $2.25 per issue; Vols. 6-9, $2.75 per issue; Vols. 10-14, $3.00 per issue; Index Vols. 1-5, $2.50; Index Vols. 6-10, $3.50.

ROMANCE PHILOLOGY

EDITORIAL ADDRESS:
Yakov Malkiel, Editor
Room 2321, Dwinelle Hall
University of California
Berkeley, California 94720

SUBSCRIPTION ADDRESS:
Periodicals Division
University of California Press
2223 Fulton Street
Berkeley, California 94720

PUBLISHED: Quarterly
CIRCULATION: 1,200
COST: 1 yr.—$13.00 ($18.00 for institutions).

CONTENTS: Scholarly articles, review articles, notes, book reviews of varying length, necrologies, editorial comments, bearing on older Romance culture—in particular, its literary and linguistic facet.

UNSOLICITED MSS. WELCOME? No; submissions acknowledged.
SPECIFICALLY WELCOMED: Typically, monographic or critical, occasionally essayistic contributions.
MS. LENGTH: Up to 30 pages; submit TWO copies.

STYLE REQUIREMENTS: Academic.
COPYRIGHT: Regents of the University of California.
EDITOR'S DECISION: 2 weeks to 2 months.
FROM ACCEPTANCE TO PUBLICATION: 9-24 months.
PAYMENT/OFFPRINTS: From 10 to 100 offprints; varies with length and category of item.
REJECTED MSS.: Returned.
GENERAL: First issue, August, 1947. Usual publication length, 150 pages. Each volume is indexed. Articles may be written in English or the romance languages.
BACK ISSUES: Available from subscription address and Xerox University Microfilms. Request price list.

THE ROMANIC REVIEW

EDITORIAL ADDRESS:
Michael Riffaterre, General Editor
518 Philosophy Hall
Columbia University
New York, New York 10027

SUBSCRIPTION ADDRESS:
Columbia University Press
Periodicals Department
136 South Broadway
Irving-on-Hudson, New York 10533

PUBLISHED: Quarterly (Feb., Apr., Oct., Dec.)
COST: 1 yr.—$7.50 in U.S.; $7.80 elsewhere.

CIRCULATION: 1,200

CONTENTS: Studies of Romance literatures; poetics; many book reviews. Example: "Metaphor and Ambiguity in Rimbaud's 'Memoire.'"

UNSOLICITED MSS. WELCOME? Yes; submissions acknowledged.
MS. LENGTH: 10-25 pages; submit ONE copy.
STYLE REQUIREMENTS: MLA STYLE SHEET.
COPYRIGHT: Columbia University Press.
EDITOR'S DECISION: 2 months.
FROM ACCEPTANCE TO PUBLICATION: 12-18 months.
PAYMENT/OFFPRINTS: No payment. Offprints can be purchased.
REJECTED MSS.: Returned.
GENERAL: First issue, 1909. Usual publication length, 80 pages. Articles may be written in English or a prominent Romance language.
BACK ISSUES: Available from Columbia University Press at $2.00 each.

SCANDINAVIAN STUDIES: THE JOURNAL OF THE SOCIETY FOR THE ADVANCEMENT OF SCANDINAVIAN STUDY

EDITORIAL ADDRESS:
Harold Naess, Editor
Department of Scandinavian Studies
University of Wisconsin
Madison, Wisconsin 53706

SUBSCRIPTION ADDRESS:
James E. Cathey, Secretary
Department of Germanic Languages
Herter Hall
University of Massachusetts
Amherst, Massachusetts 01002

PUBLISHED: Quarterly (Winter, Spring, Summer, Autumn)
CIRCULATION: 800
COST: 1 yr.—$25.00 for institutions; $15.00 for member of Society for the Advancement of Scandinavian Study (includes membership dues); $7.50 for students.

CONTENTS: Scholarly articles and reviews on the literatures of Denmark, The Faeroes, Finland, Iceland, Norway, and Sweden; articles concerning philology, linguistics, history, and social studies. Example: "The Machine Theme in Sonie Poems by Lars Gustafsson."

UNSOLICITED MSS. WELCOME? Yes, except reviews; submissions acknowledged.
SPECIFICALLY WELCOMED: Articles by competent scholars; NO translations, NO contributions of a general nature.
MS. LENGTH: Up to 25-30 pages; submit TWO copies.
STYLE REQUIREMENTS: MLA STYLE SHEET.
COPYRIGHT: SCANDINAVIAN STUDIES.
EDITOR'S DECISION: 2-3 months.
FROM ACCEPTANCE TO PUBLICATION: 2 months to 1 year.
PAYMENT/OFFPRINTS: Five free offprints.
REJECTED MSS.: Returned.
GENERAL: First issue, 1912. Usual publication length, 110 pages. North American contributors to SS must be members of SASS. Only those papers based on material examined in the original language will be considered.
BACK ISSUES: Available from The Allen Press, 1041 New Hampshire Street, Lawrence, Kansas. Consult Allen Press about price.

STUDIES IN PHILOLOGY

EDITORIAL ADDRESS:
Ernest W. Talbert, Editor
Department of English
The University of North Carolina
Chapel Hill, North Carolina 27514

SUBSCRIPTION ADDRESS:
University of North Carolina
Box 2288
Chapel Hill, North Carolina 27514

PUBLISHED: 5 times yearly (Jan., Apr., July, Oct., Dec.)
COST: 1 yr.—$10.00.

CIRCULATION: 2,000-2,100

CONTENTS: Studies of classical, medieval, and modern literature, with emphasis upon the Middle Ages and the Renaissance.

UNSOLICITED MSS. WELCOME? Yes; submissions acknowledged.
MS. LENGTH: 15-25 pages; submit ONE copy.
STYLE REQUIREMENTS: University of Chicago's A MANUAL OF STYLE or MLA STYLE SHEET.
COPYRIGHT: University of North Carolina Press.
EDITOR'S DECISION: 1-3 months.
FROM ACCEPTANCE TO PUBLICATION: 18 months.
PAYMENT/OFFPRINTS: 20 free offprints.
REJECTED MSS.: Returned.
GENERAL: First issue, 1906. Usual publication length, 11-20. Agents for Great Britain and Continent: Cambridge University Press, Bentley House, 200 Euston Road, London N. W. 1, England.
BACK ISSUES: Available from University of North Carolina Press; runs from Johnson Reprint Corp. Price varies.

STUDIES IN ROMANTICISM

EDITORIAL ADDRESS:
W. H. Stevenson, Editor
Boston University
236 Bay State Road
Boston, Massachusetts 02215

SUBSCRIPTION ADDRESS:

same

PUBLISHED: Quarterly (Winter, Spring, Summer, Autumn)
COST: 1 yr.—$6.50; 2 yrs.—$12.00; 3 yrs.—$16.00.

CIRCULATION: 1,250

CONTENTS: Scholarly articles on all aspects of the Romantic period—literature, art, music, social science, philosophy; book reviews. Example: "The Politics of Blithedale: the Dilemma of the Self."

UNSOLICITED MSS. WELCOMED? Yes; submissions acknowledged.
SPECIFICALLY WELCOMED: Anything dealing with the Romantic period.
MS. LENGTH: 6,000 words; submit ORIGINAL.
STYLE REQUIREMENTS: MLA STYLE SHEET; keep footnotes to minimum.
COPYRIGHT: Studies in Romanticism.
EDITOR'S DECISION: 2 months.
FROM ACCEPTANCE TO PUBLICATION: 18 months.
PAYMENT/OFFPRINTS: Four free copies of issue. Authors may purchase offprints.
REJECTED MSS.: Returned.
GENERAL: First issue, Fall, 1961. Usual publication length, 92 pages. Cumulative index for first ten volumes available for $1.00. Contributions must be in English; but quoted matter may be in any of the major modern European languages.

BACK ISSUES: Complete bound volumes available from A.M.S. Press at $25.00 each. Scattered issues available from editorial address at $1.75 each; $6.50 per volume.

STUDIES IN THE 20TH CENTURY

EDITORIAL ADDRESS:
Stephen H. Goode, Editor
P. O. Box 12
Troy, New York 12181

SUBSCRIPTION ADDRESS:

same

PUBLISHED: Biannually
COST: 1 yr.—$4.00.

CIRCULATION: 300

CONTENTS: Scholarly and critical articles surrounding the literary and art movements of the 20th century, particularly their philosophies. Example: "Galsworthy's Apple Tree and The Longus Tradition."

UNSOLICITED MSS. WELCOME? Yes; submissions not acknowledged.
SPECIFICALLY WELCOMED: Critical articles involving, for example, trends in recent French avant-garde theater—as opposed to, e.g. light-dark motif in Faulkner, etc.
MS. LENGTH: Fairly long, 4,000-9,500 words; submit ONE copy.
STYLE REQUIREMENTS: MLA STYLE SHEET.
COPYRIGHT: Stephen H. Goode.
EDITOR'S DECISION: 2 weeks.
FROM ACCEPTANCE TO PUBLICATION: 1 year.
PAYMENT/OFFPRINTS: Three copies of issue; 25 free offprints.
REJECTED MSS.: Returned.
GENERAL: First issue, 1968. Usual publication length, 100 pages.
BACK ISSUES: Available from editorial office at $2.50 to $3.00 each.

STUDIES ON VOLTAIRE AND THE EIGHTEENTH CENTURY

See the section on BIBLIOGRAPHICAL AND LIBRARY RESOURCES for details.

YALE FRENCH STUDIES

EDITORIAL ADDRESS:
Philip H. Solomon, Editor
Yale University
New Haven, Connecticut 06520

SUBSCRIPTION ADDRESS:
The YFS Office
323 William L. Harkness Hall
Yale University
New Haven, Connecticut 06520

PUBLISHED: Biannually CIRCULATION: 1,500
COST: 1 yr.—$3.00; 2 yrs.—$5.00; single copy—$1.50.

CONTENTS: Studies of French literature and culture in the light of modern theories; often contains interdisciplinary investigations as well as material relating to other national literatures but relevant to French and France; illustrations. Each issue is devoted to a specific theme, author, subject. Example: "Ronsard as Apollo: Myth, Poetry and Experience in a Renaissance Sonnet-cycle."

UNSOLICITED MSS. WELCOME? Usually not; submissions acknowledged.
SPECIFICALLY WELCOMED: Scholarly essays.
MS. LENGTH: 15 pages; submit ONE copy.
STYLE REQUIREMENTS: MLA STYLE SHEET.
COPYRIGHT: YALE FRENCH STUDIES.
PAYMENT/OFFPRINTS: 25 free offprints. More at cost.
REJECTED MSS.: Returned.
GENERAL: First issue, 1948. Usual publication length, 200 pages.
BACK ISSUES: Available from YFS office at $1.50 each. Also from Kraus Reprint Co.

BALTIC AND SLAVIC

AAASS NEWSLETTER

EDITORIAL ADDRESS:
Linda B. Bowers, Editor
Room 254
190 West 19th Avenue
The Ohio State University
Columbus, Ohio 43210

SUBSCRIPTION ADDRESS:
American Association for the
Advancement of Slavic Studies
same

PUBLISHED: 6 times yearly   CIRCULATION: 2,500
COST: 1 yr.—$4.00 for non-members; newsletter is received by all members of the Association for the Advancement of Slavic Studies.

CONTENTS: News of the association and professional activities of scholars in the Slavic field; brief articles; news of institutions and libraries; announcements of fellowships, honors, awards; calendar of international and national meetings; announcements of opportunities of support for Slavic scholars; list of appointments and staff changes in the field.

UNSOLICITED MSS. WELCOME? Yes.
MS. LENGTH: Up to 2,000 words.
PAYMENT/OFFPRINTS: Up to 10 offprints.
GENERAL: First issue, 1960. Usual publication length, 8 pages. Useful as a scholar's reference source. Articles may be written in English, French, German, and Slavic languages.
BACK ISSUES: Available from subscription address at $1.00 each.

ÅRSBOK SLAVISKA INSTITUTIONEN VID LUNDS UNIVERSITET

EDITORIAL ADDRESS:
Editor
Slaviska Institutionen
Finngatan 12-14
S-223 62 Lund
Sweden

SUBSCRIPTION ADDRESS:

same

PUBLISHED: Irregularly   CIRCULATION: 400
COST: Varies.

CONTENTS: Articles on Baltic and Slavic philology published in Baltic, English, French, German, or Slavic languages.
UNSOLICITED MSS. WELCOME? No. (Only materials from persons within the institute are published.)
COPYRIGHT: Slavic Institute or author.
GENERAL: First issue, 1951 (Arsbok 1948-49). Publication length varies from 70-200 pages.
BACK ISSUES: Available from editorial address at 10:-(Swedish cr.)-20:- each.

BALKAN STUDIES

EDITORIAL ADDRESS:
Prof. K. Mitsakis, Editor
Institute for Balkan Studies
4 Vas. Sophia St
Thessaloniki
Greece

SUBSCRIPTION ADDRESS:

same

PUBLISHED: Biannually
COST: 1 yr.—$12.00; single copy—$7.00.

CONTENTS: Scholarly articles devoted to the affairs of South-Eastern Europe (history, literature, folklore, economy, geography, comparative studies). Example: "Romanticism in the Interpretation of the Greek Tragedy on the Roumanian Stage."

UNSOLICITED MSS. WELCOME? Yes; submissions acknowledged.
SPECIFICALLY WELCOMED: Articles concerning Greece and the Balkan countries and literary relations between Europe and the Balkans.
MS. LENGTH: 5-32 pages; submit ONE copy.
COPYRIGHT: The Institute for Balkan Studies.
EDITOR'S DECISION: 6 months.
FROM ACCEPTANCE TO PUBLICATION: 6 months to 1 year.
PAYMENT/OFFPRINTS: 50 offprints of the published article.
REJECTED MSS.: Returned.
GENERAL: First issue, 1961. Usual publication length, 200 pages.
BACK ISSUES: Available from the Institute for Balkan Studies at $7.00 each; $12.00 for two issues of the same year.

BULGARIAN REVIEW

SUBSCRIPTION ADDRESS:
Foyez Bulgare
Caixa Postal 21007
Rio de Janeiro, GB
Brazil

PUBLISHED: Annually
COST: 1 yr.—US$10.00.

CIRCULATION: 1,000

CONTENTS: Historical truth about Bulgaria: history, literature, economics; memories; book review.

UNSOLICITED MSS. WELCOME? Yes; submissions acknowledged.
SPECIFICALLY WELCOMED: Articles regarding Bulgaria.
MS. LENGTH: 5-15 pages maximum; submit ONE copy.
STYLE REQUIREMENTS: Any style.
COPYRIGHT: BULGARIAN REVIEW.

EDITOR'S DECISION: 1 month.
FROM ACCEPTANCE TO PUBLICATION: Until usual time of publication: end of each year.
PAYMENT/OFFPRINTS: 50 free offprints.
REJECTED MSS.: Not returned.
GENERAL: First issue, 1961. Usual publication length, 80-90 pages. The magazine is published by Bulgarian political refugees. Articles may be written in English or French.
BACK ISSUES: Available from subscription address. Price to be determined on occasion.

CANADIAN SLAVONIC PAPERS—REVUE CANADIENNE DES SLAVISTES

EDITORIAL ADDRESS:
John W. Strong, Editor
256 Paterson Hall
Carleton University
Ottawa K1S 5B6
Canada

SUBSCRIPTION ADDRESS:

same

PUBLISHED: Quarterly   CIRCULATION: 1,100
COST: 1 yr.—$12.00 (Canadian). Also includes annual journal SLAVIC AND EAST EUROPEAN STUDIES.

CONTENTS: Interdisciplinary articles on Soviet and East European studies in the fields of history, political science, economics, literature, linguistics, religion, sociology; many book reviews. Example: "The Intellectual's Dilemma: The Hero in the Modern Czech Novel."

UNSOLICITED MSS. WELCOME? Yes; submissions acknowledged.
SPECIFICALLY WELCOMED: Restricted to literature of the Soviet Union and East Europe.
MS. LENGTH: 20-25 pages; submit TWO copies.
STYLE REQUIREMENTS: MLA STYLE SHEET.
COPYRIGHT: CANADIAN SLAVONIC PAPERS.
EDITOR'S DECISION: 2-3 months.
FROM ACCEPTANCE TO PUBLICATION: 6-8 months.
PAYMENT/OFFPRINTS: 25 free offprints to author of article.
REJECTED MSS.: Returned.
GENERAL: First issue, 1956. Usual publication length, 150-200 pages. Articles may be written in English or French.
BACK ISSUES: Available from editorial address at $3.00 each; $12.00 per volume.

EAST SLAVIC LANGUAGES AND LITERATURES

EDITORIAL ADDRESS:
Charles Schlacks, Jr., Editor
University Center for International Studies
G7A Social Science Building
University of Pittsburgh
Pittsburgh, Pennsylvania 15213

SUBSCRIPTION ADDRESS:

same

PUBLISHED: 2-4 times yearly

GENERAL: First issue, 1972. This periodical had not arrived by the time the entry went to press. Potential subscribers, contributors, or collectors will have to write the editor to see whether the journal still exists, and if so, to inquire about details of manuscript submission, style, back issues, and the like.

INTERNATIONAL JOURNAL OF SLAVIC LINGUISTICS AND POETICS

EDITORIAL ADDRESS:
Dean S. Worth, Editor
Department of Slavic Languages
University of California
Los Angeles, California 90024

SUBSCRIPTION ADDRESS:
Mouton and Company
P. O. Box 1132
The Hague
The Netherlands

PUBLISHED: Annually

CIRCULATION: 500

CONTENTS: Articles on linguistics and poetics of the Balkans, Baltic Area, Eastern Europe, Russia.

UNSOLICITED MSS. WELCOME? Yes, but not book reviews; submissions usually acknowledged.
SPECIFICALLY WELCOMED: Poetics only.
MS. LENGTH: 10-25 pages; submit ONE copy.
COPYRIGHT: Mouton and Company.
EDITOR'S DECISION: 1-2 months.
FROM ACCEPTANCE TO PUBLICATION: Variable.
PAYMENT/OFFPRINTS: 25 free offprints; more at cost.
REJECTED MSS.: Returned.
GENERAL: First issue, 1959. Articles may be written in any Slavic language, English, French, or German.
BACK ISSUES: Available from subscription address.

JOURNAL OF BALTIC STUDIES (formerly BULLETIN OF BALTIC STUDIES)

EDITORIAL ADDRESS:
Arvids Ziedonis, Jr., Editor
Muhlenberg College
Allentown, Pennsylvania 18104

SUBSCRIPTION ADDRESS:
Mr. Janis Gaigulis
AABS Executive Office
366 86th Street
Brooklyn, New York 11209

PUBLISHED: Quarterly
CIRCULATION: 1,200
COST: 1 yr.—$12.00 (AABS membership includes subscription); students—$6.00; libraries—$15.00.

CONTENTS: Interdisciplinary scholarly articles about social sciences and humanities; review articles, reviews, bibliographical notes, news on conferences, research in progress, professional news. The journal concentrates on the Baltic area, especially Estonia, Latvia, and Lithuania, and related area, and events.

UNSOLICITED MSS. WELCOME? Yes; submissions acknowledged.
SPECIFICALLY WELCOMED: Articles of research and evaluation.
MS. LENGTH: 12-30 pages; submit TWO copies.
STYLE REQUIREMENTS: MLA STYLE SHEET. (Publ. name, pl. date, pp.).
COPYRIGHT: Association for the Advancement of Baltic Studies.
EDITOR'S DECISION: 5-6 weeks.
FROM ACCEPTANCE TO PUBLICATION: 3 months.
PAYMENT/OFFPRINTS: Two gratis copies of articles; one of reviews. Offprints available if requested.
REJECTED MSS.: Returned.
GENERAL: First issue, March, 1970 (as BULLETIN OF BALTIC STUDIES); 1972, present title. Usual publication length, 100 pages.
BACK ISSUES: Available from AABS Executive Office at $2.50 each for BULLETIN OF BALTIC STUDIES and $4.00 each for JOURNAL OF BALTIC STUDIES; also from University Microfilms, Inc.

KRITIKON LITTERARUM: INTERNATIONAL BOOK REVIEW FOR AMERICAN, ENGLISH, ROMANCE, AND SLAVIC STUDIES

EDITORIAL ADDRESS:
Edward Jayne, Editor
Department of English
University of Massachusetts
Amherst, Massachusetts 01003

SUBSCRIPTION ADDRESS:
Thesen Verlag Vowinckel & Co.
D6100 Darmstadt
Dreibrunnenstrausse 3
West Germany

PUBLISHED: Quarterly
CIRCULATION: 600
COST: Vol. I: DM44,—; single copy—DM 15,—; Vol. II: DM 58,—; single copy—DM 20,—.

CONTENTS: Critical reviews of recent publications in literary criticism in German, French, English, and slavic languages. Emphasis is upon theory but editors are also interested in its practical applications in explication.

UNSOLICITED MSS. WELCOME? No, but editors accept offers to review particular books.
SPECIFICALLY WELCOMED: Exclusively book reviews.
MS. LENGTH: 1,000-1,500 words; submit ONE copy.
STYLE REQUIREMENTS: Clarity and sympathetic iconoclasm.
COPYRIGHT: First year after publication, publisher; afterwards, author of review.
EDITOR'S DECISION: 1 week.
FROM ACCEPTANCE TO PUBLICATION: Next issue.
PAYMENT/OFFPRINTS: 20 copies by surface mail from Germany.
REJECTED MSS.: Returned.
GENERAL: First issue, March, 1972. Usual publication length, 80 pages. Review articles are written only in the language of the field of study, irrespective of the reviewer's own native language.
BACK ISSUES: Available from publisher at original cost.

LITUANUS: THE LITHUANIAN QUARTERLY

EDITORIAL ADDRESS:
Antanas Klimas, Ignas K. Skrupskelis, and Thomas Remeikis, General Editors
P. O. Box 9318
Chicago, Illinois 60690

SUBSCRIPTION ADDRESS:
same

PUBLISHED: Quarterly (Spring, Summer, Fall, Winter)
COST: 1 yr.—$8.00; single copy—$2.00.

CIRCULATION: 4,102 in 97 countries.

CONTENTS: Interdisciplinary articles; book reviews; comments; art reproductions; documentary materials; BELLES LETTRES. Examples: "The Assertion of Identity via Myth and Folklore in Soviet Lithuanian Literature"; "Lithuanian Cultural Imagery in Recent German Literature."

UNSOLICITED MSS. WELCOME? Yes; submissions acknowledged.
SPECIFICALLY WELCOMED: Articles and essays on Baltic States of Lithuania, Latvia, and Estonia, as well as on the general problems of Eastern Europe and the Soviet Union.
MS. LENGTH: No preference; submit TWO copies.
STYLE REQUIREMENTS: University of Chicago's A MANUAL OF STYLE.
COPYRIGHT: Lituanus Foundation, Inc.
EDITOR'S DECISION: 2 months.
FROM ACCEPTANCE TO PUBLICATION: 5 months.
PAYMENT/OFFPRINTS: Several copies of issue where article appears.
REJECTED MSS.: Returned, if requested.
GENERAL: First issue, November, 1954. Usual publication length, 86 pages.

BACK ISSUES: Available from editorial address or University Microfilms.

MELBOURNE SLAVONIC STUDIES

EDITORIAL ADDRESS:
Nina Christesen and Zd.
Oliverius, Editors
University of Melbourne
Parkville 3052
Australia

SUBSCRIPTION ADDRESS:
Russian Department
same

PUBLISHED: Annually
COST: 1 yr.—$3.50.

CIRCULATION: 350-400

CONTENTS: Articles on Russian language and literature; all subjects related to the study of Slavonic languages and literatures; book reviews.

UNSOLICITED MSS. WELCOME? Yes; submissions acknowledged.
SPECIFICALLY WELCOMED: Hitherto unpublished material on Russian literature and language.
MS. LENGTH: 2,000-3,000 words; submit TWO copies.
COPYRIGHT: The author, but Journal must be acknowledged on republication.
EDITOR'S DECISION: 2-3 months; special delays in 1972-1973.
FROM ACCEPTANCE TO PUBLICATION: 3-4 months.
PAYMENT/OFFPRINTS: Six complimentary copies of magazine and 10 offprints.
REJECTED MSS.: Returned.
GENERAL: First issue, 1967. Usual publication length, 100 pages. Articles may be written in English or Russian.
BACK ISSUES: Available from subscription address at $3.50 each.

NEW WORLD REVIEW

EDITORIAL ADDRESS:
Jessica Smith, Editor
Suite 308, 156 Fifth Avenue
New York, New York 10010

SUBSCRIPTION ADDRESS:
same

PUBLISHED: Quarterly. Beginning with 1974, it will be bi-monthly.
COST: 1 yr.—$4.00; 2 yrs.—$7.00; 3 yrs.—$10.00. Canada and Foreign, respectively, $5, $9, and $13. Bi-monthly subscription will be the same.

CONTENTS: Factual articles reporting the life and thought of the USSR and other socialist countries in all its main aspects, the relations of these countries with the United States and the rest of the world; by both U.S. and other English speaking and native writers of the countries covered; creative writing and poetry. Also articles about Third World countries and national liberation movements everywhere and all movements opposing aggressive wars; hard-to-find documents; book reviews; art work. Examples: "Soviet Children and the Art of the Possible"; "Esthetics and Culture: National and International."

UNSOLICITED MSS. WELCOME? Only if pertinent to subject matter, factually reliable, and well-written; submissions usually acknowledged.
SPECIFICALLY WELCOMED: Creative writing and poetry from socialist countries.
MS. LENGTH: 1,000-3,000 words; submit ONE copy.
COPYRIGHT: Material is not copyrighted.
EDITOR'S DECISION: 1 week to 1 month.
FROM ACCEPTANCE TO PUBLICATION: Extremely variable.
REJECTED MSS.: Returned.
GENERAL: First issue, 1951 (its predecessor, SOVIET RUSSIA TODAY, began in 1932). Publication length varies.
BACK ISSUES: Available from subscription office at above address. Cost varies according to date and availability.

OBZOR: BULGARIAN QUARTERLY REVIEW OF LITERATURE AND THE ARTS

EDITORIAL ADDRESS:
Lilyana Stephanova, Editor-in-Chief
Committee for Friendship and Cultural Relations with Foreign Countries
Union of Bulgaria Writers
39 Dondukov Blvd.
Sofia
Bulgaria

SUBSCRIPTION ADDRESS:
Y. Shoulhov, Managing Editor
same

(or subscription agents)

PUBLISHED: Quarterly
COST: 1 yr.—US$3.20.

CIRCULATION: 30,000

CONTENTS: Review of Bulgarian literature and the arts, Bulgarian poetry, fiction, and nonfiction exclusively; articles and book reviews on the same range of problems.

UNSOLICITED MSS. WELCOME? Seldom; submissions not acknowledged.
SPECIFICALLY WELCOMED: Articles concerning Bulgarian literature and art.
MS. LENGTH: Up to 10 pages; submit THREE copies.
STYLE REQUIREMENTS: Literary.
COPYRIGHT: Author.
PAYMENT/OFFPRINTS: According to the existing copyright law in Bulgaria in Bulgarian currency. Five copies of issue.
REJECTED MSS.: Not returned.

GENERAL: First issue, 1967. Usual publication length, 112 pages and art supplement. Articles may be written in English or French.
BACK ISSUES: All of them available from subscription address at current price.

POLISH LITERATURE/LITTERATURE POLONAISE

EDITORIAL ADDRESS:
Michal Rusinek, Editor-in-Chief
Krucza Street 46/64
00-509 Warsaw
Poland

SUBSCRIPTION ADDRESS:
Agencja Autorska
ul. Hipoteczna 2
Post Box 133
00-950 Warsaw
Poland

PUBLISHED: Quarterly
COST: 1 yr.—U.S. $4.00; single copy—$1.00.

CONTENTS: Critical reviews about new publications in fiction and popular science; notes about authors of works reviewed in the issue and extensive chronicle; photographs of authors. Examples: "Marek Nowakowski's Short Stories"; "The New Traditionalism (On the Writing of Bohdan Czesko)."

MS. LENGTH: 1-2 pages.
GENERAL: First issue, 1968. Printed in English with French translation.

POLISH PERSPECTIVES

EDITORIAL ADDRESS:
Stefan Arski, Editor-in-Chief
Polish Institute of International Affairs
Warsaw 1 Warecka 1a
Poland

SUBSCRIPTION ADDRESS:
Stechert-Hafner, Inc.
31 East 10th Street
New York, New York 10003

PUBLISHED: Monthly
COST: 1 yr.—$5.50.

CIRCULATION: 5,300

CONTENTS: Articles on all aspects of Polish life and thought; book reviews. Article example: "Literature: National or Universal."

UNSOLICITED MSS. WELCOME? Query.
MS. LENGTH: 5-12 pages.
GENERAL: First issue, May, 1958. Usual publication length, 90 pages. PERSPECTIVES POLONAISES (French ed.) and POLNISCHE PERSPEKTIVEN (German ed.) published simultaneously with English edition.
BACK ISSUES: Available free from editorial address.

THE POLISH REVIEW

EDITORIAL ADDRESS:
Ludwik Krzyzanowski, Editor
59 East 66th Street
New York, New York 10021

SUBSCRIPTION ADDRESS:
Business Manager
same

PUBLISHED: Quarterly
(Feb., May, Aug., Nov.)
COST: 1 yr.—$8.00.

CIRCULATION: 2,000

CONTENTS: Scholarly articles concerning political and social contemporary affairs, history, economics, creative and critical literature, theater, Polish American ethnicity; book reviews; bibliography (materials written in English on Poland and items by Polish authors). Examples: "Remarks on the Poetry of Tadeusz Różewicz"; "The Betrayer as Intellectual: Conrad's 'Under Western Eyes.' "

UNSOLICITED MSS. WELCOME? Yes; submissions acknowledged.
SPECIFICALLY WELCOMED: Critical articles, translations, comparative literature.
MS. LENGTH: 10-15 pages; submit TWO copies.
STYLE REQUIREMENTS: MLA STYLE SHEET.
COPYRIGHT: THE POLISH REVIEW.
EDITOR'S DECISION: 3 months.
FROM ACCEPTANCE TO PUBLICATION: 6 months.
PAYMENT/OFFPRINTS: No payment. Arrange for offprints with printer.
REJECTED MSS.: Returned.
GENERAL: First issue, 1956. Usual publication length, 128 pages. Indexed (1956-1966) (1967-1970).
BACK ISSUES: Available from the editorial office at $2.00 each.

REVUE DES ÉTUDES SUD-EST EUROPÉENNES

EDITORIAL ADDRESS:
Mihai Berza, Editor
Strada I. C. Frimu nr. 9
Bucharest
Romania

SUBSCRIPTION ADDRESS:
Rompresfilatelia
Calea Grivitei, 64-66
P. O. Box 2001
Bucharest, Romania

PUBLISHED: Quarterly
COST: 1 yr.—$12.00.

CONTENTS: Articles, reviews, short bibliographical notes concerning history, linguistics, history of culture, art history, history of law, economics, sociology.

UNSOLICITED MSS. WELCOME? Yes; submissions acknowledged.
SPECIFICALLY WELCOMED: Comparative studies.
MS. LENGTH: 20 pages; submit TWO copies.

EDITOR'S DECISION: 1-3 months.
FROM ACCEPTANCE TO PUBLICATION: 6 months-1 year.
PAYMENT/OFFPRINTS: Payment depends on length of typescript; 45 free offprints.
REJECTED MSS.: Returned.
GENERAL: First issue, 1963. Usual publication length, 200-300 pages. Articles accepted in French, as well as English, German, Italian, and Russian.
BACK ISSUES: Available from the editor.

ROMANIAN REVIEW

EDITORIAL ADDRESS:
Nicolae Moraru, Editor
Foreign Languages Press
Strade Ion Ghica 5
Bucharest
Rumania

SUBSCRIPTION ADDRESS:

same

PUBLISHED: Quarterly   CIRCULATION: 12,000
COST: 1 yr.—US$3.00 for each edition (English, French, German, Russian).

CONTENTS: Romanian poetry and prose, classical and contemporary; literary criticism and history of literature; studies and essays on philosophy, sociology, aesthetics; theatre, fine arts, films, music; cultural relations between Romania and other countries; reviews of Romanian books on literature and the arts and of books about Romania; art reproductions. Examples: "New Generations of Romanian Fiction Writers"; "What Do Young People Demand from the Theatre?"; "Convergences and Divergences in the Poetics of Generations."

UNSOLICITED MSS. WELCOME? From case to case; submissions acknowledged.
MS. LENGTH: No preference; submit one copy.
COPYRIGHT: By agreement.
PAYMENT/OFFPRINTS: Romanian royalty regulations.
REJECTED MSS.: Returned if requested.
GENERAL: First issue, Spring, 1946. Usual publication length, 125 pages.
BACK ISSUES: Available from subscription address at $1.00 each.

RUMANIAN STUDIES

EDITORIAL ADDRESS:
Keith Hitchins, Editor
Department of History
University of Illinois
Urbana, Illinois 61801

SUBSCRIPTION ADDRESS:
E. J. Brill
Oude R1JN 33a
Leiden
The Netherlands

PUBLISHED: Annually CIRCULATION: 400
COST: 1 yr.—$10.00 (subscription price may increase because of the devaluation of the dollar).

CONTENTS: Literary history and criticism; history and civilization.

UNSOLICITED MSS. WELCOME? Yes; submissions acknowledged.
SPECIFICALLY WELCOMED: History and criticism.
MS. LENGTH: 25-30 pages; submit TWO copies.
STYLE REQUIREMENTS: MLA STYLE SHEET.
COPYRIGHT: Publisher.
EDITOR'S DECISION: 2 months.
FROM ACCEPTANCE TO PUBLICATION: 6 months to 1 year.
PAYMENT/OFFPRINTS: 25 free offprints.
REJECTED MSS.: Returned.
GENERAL: First issue, 1970. Usual publication length, 225 pages.
BACK ISSUES: Available from subscription address at about $10.00 each.

RUSSIAN LITERATURE TRIQUARTERLY: A JOURNAL OF TRANSLATION AND CRITICISM

SUBSCRIPTION ADDRESS:
Ardis Publishers
615 Watersedge
Ann Arbor, Michigan 48105

PUBLISHED: Tri-annually
COST: 1 yr.—$15.00; students—$12.00; institutions—$19.00.

CONTENTS: Previously unpublished texts, letters, essays, documents, photographs related to Russian literature; new translations; biography. Major articles on and translations of Mandelstam, Akhmatova, Bulgakov, Pasternak, Solzhenitsyn, Zamyatin, Babel, Zoshchenko, and others. Issues focus on such topics as "Acmeism; Brodsky; Stylistics," "Prose of the Twenties; The Serapions," "Romanticism; Nabokov," "Symbolism," "Contemporary Russian Literature," "The Russian Theater."

UNSOLICITED MSS. WELCOME? Yes.
GENERAL: First issue, October, 1971. Usual publication length, 422-542 pages.

THE RUSSIAN REVIEW: AN AMERICAN QUARTERLY DEVOTED TO RUSSIA PAST AND PRESENT

EDITORIAL ADDRESS:
Dimitri von Mohrenschildt, Editor
The Hoover Institution
Stanford, California 94305

SUBSCRIPTION ADDRESS:

same

PUBLISHED: Quarterly
(Jan., Apr., June, Oct.)
COST: 1 yr.—$9.00; 2 yrs.—$16.00.

CIRCULATION: 2,000

CONTENTS: Articles, review articles, and book reviews, notes and documents on Russia, particularly on pre-revolutionary and Soviet periods. Philosophy, religious studies, folklore, history of ideas, philosophy of history, and other cultural aspects. Example: "Anarchism and Bolshevism in the Works of Boris Pilnyak."

UNSOLICITED MSS. WELCOME? Occasionally.
SPECIFICALLY WELCOMED: Contributions on literary history and criticism, theatre and drama.
MS. LENGTH: 12-20 pages; submit ONE copy.
STYLE REQUIREMENTS: University of Chicago's A MANUAL OF STYLE.
COPYRIGHT: THE RUSSIAN REVIEW.
EDITOR'S DECISION: 1 month.
FROM ACCEPTANCE TO PUBLICATION: 6 months to 1 year.
PAYMENT/OFFPRINTS: $75.00 to free-lance writers; members of academic profession receive no payment. 25 free offprints.
REJECTED MSS.: Returned.
GENERAL: First issue, November, 1941. Usual publication length, 128 pages.
BACK ISSUES: Available from editorial address at $2.50 each; also from Kraus Reprint Co.

SLAVIC AND EAST EUROPEAN JOURNAL

EDITORIAL ADDRESS:
Frank Y. Gladney, Editor
Department of Slavic Languages
and Literatures
University of Illinois at
Urbana-Champaign
Urbana, Illinois 61801

SUBSCRIPTION ADDRESS:
Joe Malik, Jr., Secretary
Department of Russian
Modern Languages 340
University of Arizona
Tucson, Arizona 85721

PUBLISHED: Quarterly (Mar., June, Sept., Dec.)
COST: 1 yr.—$15.00 for individuals; $7.50 for students for a maximum of three years; $17.50 for libraries and institutions.

CIRCULATION: 2,200

CONTENTS: Articles on Slavic and East European languages, literatures, and language pedagogy; book reviews. It does not publish translations or article-length reviews of new literary productions, nor is it an outlet for large amounts of purely documentary material, such as collections of texts or glossaries. Example: "Elements of Light in the Fiction of Korolenko."

UNSOLICITED MSS. WELCOME? Yes; submissions acknowledged.
SPECIFICALLY WELCOMED: Analytical or synthesizing studies which contain their own documentation and demonstrate a command of the basic materials of scholarship in the original languages.
MS. LENGTH: 20 pages of pica typescript; maximum 7,000 words; submit ONE copy.
STYLE REQUIREMENTS: MLA STYLE SHEET; footnotes follow article.
COPYRIGHT: AATSEEL of the U.S., Inc.
EDITOR'S DECISION: 2 months.
FROM ACCEPTANCE TO PUBLICATION: 1 year.
PAYMENT/OFFPRINTS: One free copy of issue. Authors of articles receive 25 free offprints; authors of reviews, 12.
REJECTED MSS.: Returned.
GENERAL: First issue, 1957. Usual publication length, 135 pages. Articles must be in English; Cyrillic may be used for quotations which are too long to be given in transliteration and for citations of four or more lines of verse.
BACK ISSUES: Pre-1972 issues available from University of Wisconsin Press, Journals Department, Box 1379, Madison, Wisconsin 53701. Subsequent issues available from subscription address at $4.50 each.

SLAVIC REVIEW: AMERICAN QUARTERLY OF SOVIET AND EAST EUROPEAN STUDIES (formerly THE AMERICAN SLAVIC AND EAST EUROPEAN REVIEW)

EDITORIAL ADDRESS:
Donald W. Treadgold, Editor
503 Thomson Hall
University of Washington
Seattle, Washington 98195

SUBSCRIPTION ADDRESS:
Leon Twarog, Executive Secretary
190 West Nineteenth Avenue
The Ohio State University
Columbus, Ohio 43210

PUBLISHED: Quarterly (Mar., June, Sept., Dec.)
CIRCULATION: 3,800
COST: 1 yr.—$20.00, foreign and domestic postage included (AAASS membership: $15.00 regular; $7.50 student); current single copy—$5.25.

CONTENTS: Scholarly contributions on Russia and Eastern Europe, past and present; articles; notes and comment; review articles; reviews; news of the profession; books received. Examples: "Multilingualism and Ranges of Tone in Nabokov's BEND SINISTER"; "The Ukrainian Literary Scene Today."

UNSOLICITED MSS. WELCOME? Yes.
SPECIFICALLY WELCOMED: Scholarly articles on the literature of Russia and Eastern Europe.

MS. LENGTH: 25 pages; submit TWO copies.
STYLE REQUIREMENTS: University of Chicago's A MANUAL OF STYLE.
COPYRIGHT: SLAVIC REVIEW.
EDITOR'S DECISION: 2 months.
FROM ACCEPTANCE TO PUBLICATION: About 8 or 9 months.
PAYMENT/OFFPRINTS: One copy of the issue; 15 copies of article; more available at cost.
REJECTED MSS.: Returned.
GENERAL: First issue, 1941. Usual publication length, 248 pages. Indexed by volume. Members receive an annual AMERICAN BIBLIOGRAPHY OF SLAVIC AND EAST EUROPEAN STUDIES.
BACK ISSUES: Available from subscription address at $5.00 each.

SLOVAKIA

EDITORIAL ADDRESS:
Joseph Pauco, Editor
313 Ridge Avenue
Middletown, Pennsylvania 17057

SUBSCRIPTION ADDRESS:
Slovak League of America
same

PUBLISHED: Annually
CIRCULATION: 2,500
COST: 1 yr.—$3.00 in U.S.; $4.00 elsewhere.

CONTENTS: Articles on history, politics, culture of Slovaks in the United States and in Slovakia; book reviews. Essay example: "The Renaissance of the Slovak American Literature."

UNSOLICITED MSS. WELCOME? Yes; submissions acknowledged.
SPECIFICALLY WELCOMED: Articles related to Slovak people.
MS. LENGTH: 10-15 pages; submit ONE copy.
STYLE REQUIREMENTS: On academic level.
COPYRIGHT: Slovak League of America.
EDITOR'S DECISION: By November.
FROM ACCEPTANCE TO PUBLICATION: 4-6 months.
PAYMENT/OFFPRINTS: $3.00 per page.
REJECTED MSS.: Returned.
GENERAL: First issue, 1951. Usual publication length, 200 pages.
BACK ISSUES: Available from Slovak League of America at $10.00 each (1951-1959); $6.00 each (1960-1972).

SOUTH SLAVIC AND BALKAN LANGUAGES AND LITERATURES

EDITORIAL ADDRESS;
Charles Schlacks, Jr., Editor
University Center for International
Studies
G7A Social Science Building
University of Pittsburgh
Pittsburgh, Pennsylvania 15213

SUBSCRIPTION ADDRESS:

same

PUBLISHED: 2-4 times yearly

GENERAL: First issue, 1972. This periodical had not arrived by the time the entry went to press. Potential subscribers, contributors, or collectors will have to write the editor to see whether the journal still exists, and if so, to inquire about details of manuscript submission, style, back issues, and the like.

SOVIET FILM (AN ILLUSTRATED MONTHLY MAGAZINE)

See the section on FILM for details.

SOVIET JEWISH AFFAIRS: A JOURNAL ON JEWISH PROBLEMS IN THE USSR AND EASTERN EUROPE

EDITORIAL ADDRESS:
Lukasz Hirszowicz, Editor
Institute of Jewish Affairs
13-16 Jacob Well Mews
George Street
London WIH 5PD
England

SUBSCRIPTION ADDRESS:
F. Muller, Circulation Manager
same

PUBLISHED: Biannually   CIRCULATION: 1,500-2,000
COST: 1 yr.—$5.00 or £2.00 (airmail surcharge £1.50 or $4.00); single copy—$2.50 or £1.05.

CONTENTS: Scholarly articles on the history, culture, political, and legal problems of Jews living in the USSR and Eastern Europe, and on relevant topics, e.g. religion and nationality problems in those countries; reviews on books in the field; documents of interest; short notices on books received from publishers; a chronicle of events for previous six-month period; letters. Examples: "Heroes and Jews in Byelorussian Literature"; "Politics and Linguistics in the Standardization of Soviet Yiddish."

UNSOLICITED MSS. WELCOME? Yes; submissions acknowledged.

SPECIFICALLY WELCOMED: Scholarly articles on relevant topics. Historical articles: 20th century preferred; in certain cases, 19th century accepted.
MS. LENGTH: 5,000-10,000 words; submit TWO copies.
STYLE REQUIREMENTS: Manuscripts submitted double-spacing, all dates: day, month, year.
COPYRIGHT: Institute of Jewish Affairs.
EDITOR'S DECISION: 2 weeks.
FROM ACCEPTANCE TO PUBLICATION: 5-6 months.
PAYMENT/OFFPRINTS: £6.00 per 1,000 words. Twelve offprints plus copy free of charge. Additional offprints at small charge on request.
REJECTED MSS.: Returned.
GENERAL: First issue, 1960, as BULLETIN ON SOVIET AND EAST EUROPEAN JEWISH AFFAIRS: 1971, as SOVIET JEWISH AFFAIRS. Usual publication length, 144 pages.
BACK ISSUES: Available from circulation manager at £1.05 or $2.50 each. Six issues of BULLETIN ON SOVIET AND EAST EUROPEAN JEWISH AFFAIRS were published. #1 and #3 out of print, but photocopies supplied at special request. Price for complete set (surface mail, including postage) would be US$17.50 or £7. Single copies of #2, 4, 5, 6 at US$1.80 or 70p. each.

SOVIET LITERATURE

EDITORIAL ADDRESS:
Savva Dangulov, Editor-in-chief
1/7 Kutuzovsky Prospekt
Moscow 121248
U.S.S.R.

SUBSCRIPTION ADDRESS:

same

PUBLISHED: Monthly
COST: 1 yr.—$5.00.

CONTENTS: The best of Soviet fiction and poetry; literary criticism; art criticism. Examples: "New Trends in Soviet Poetry"; "Soviet Prose at the Beginning of the Seventies."

UNSOLICITED MSS. WELCOME? Yes; submissions acknowledged.
SPECIFICALLY WELCOMED: Any material of general interest.
MS. LENGTH: Article—12 pages; short note—2-5 pages; submit TWO copies.
STYLE REQUIREMENTS: Vivid and expressive style.
COPYRIGHT: SOVIET LITERATURE.
EDITOR'S DECISION: 10-15 days.
FROM ACCEPTANCE TO PUBLICATION: About 2 months.
PAYMENT/OFFPRINTS: Royalties depend on whether the material is reprinted or is an original one. No offprints are provided, but contributor may order a copy of the magazine.
REJECTED MSS.: Not returned.

GENERAL: First issue, June, 1948. Usual publication length, 185 pages. U.S. firms that accept subscription orders: Four Continent Book Corp., 156 Fifth Ave., N.Y. 10; Imported Publications and Products, 1 Union Square, Rm. 809, N.Y. 3; Znanie Bookstore, 5237 Geary Blvd., San Francisco 18, Ca.; Imported Publications, Inc., 1730 Arcade Place, Chicago, Ill. 60612.
BACK ISSUES: Not available.

SOVIET STUDIES IN LITERATURE

EDITORIAL ADDRESS:
Bernard Koten and A. J. Hollander, Editors
International Arts and Sciences Press
901 North Broadway
White Plains, New York 10603

SUBSCRIPTION ADDRESS:

same

PUBLISHED: Quarterly
COST: 1 yr.—$15.00 (institutions—$60.00).

CONTENTS: Translations of the best articles in literary criticism, esthetics and current literary controversy. The journal seeks to reflect all important new developments which are of most interest to students concerned with this field.
UNSOLICITED MSS. WELCOME? No. Articles are selected by the editors from various Soviet publications.
COPYRIGHT: SOVIET STUDIES IN LITERATURE.
GENERAL: First issue, Winter, 1964-65. Usual publication length, 100 pages.
BACK ISSUES: Available from editorial address at subscription price.

VIATOR: MEDIEVAL AND RENAISSANCE STUDIES

See the section on AGE/OR NATIONALITY: CONTINENTAL.

WEST SLAVIC LANGUAGES AND LITERATURE

EDITORIAL ADDRESS:
Charles Schlacks, Jr., Editor
University Center for
International Studies
G7A Social Science Building
University of Pittsburgh
Pittsburgh, Pennsylvania 15213

SUBSCRIPTION ADDRESS:

same

PUBLISHED: 2-4 times yearly

GENERAL: First issue, 1972. This periodical had not arrived by the time the entry went to press. Potential subscribers, contributors, or collectors will have to write the editor to see whether the journal still exists, and if so, to inquire about details of manuscript submission, style, back issues, and the like.

ASIAN

ASIAN AFFAIRS: JOURNAL OF THE ROYAL CENTRAL ASIAN SOCIETY

EDITORIAL ADDRESS:
Peter Howard, Editor
42 Devonshire Street
London W1N 1LN
England

SUBSCRIPTION ADDRESS:

same

PUBLISHED: Tri-annually
COST: 1 yr.—£4.00.

CIRCULATION: 3,250

CONTENTS: Articles on current Asian affairs: politics, international relations, culture, society, economics; reviews of books. Essay example: "Orwell of the Burma Police."

UNSOLICITED MSS. WELCOME? Yes; submissions acknowledged.
MS. LENGTH: 4,000 words; submit TWO copies.
COPYRIGHT: Royal Central Asian Society.
EDITOR'S DECISION: 4-6 weeks.
PAYMENT/OFFPRINTS: 12 free offprints.
REJECTED MSS.: Not returned.
GENERAL: First issue, 1904. Usual publication length, 128 pages.
BACK ISSUES: Available from Kraus Reprint Co., FL-9491, Nendeln, Liechtenstein.

ASIAN FOLKLORE STUDIES

See the section on FOLKLORE for details.

ASIAN THEATRE BULLETIN

See the section on GENRES: THEATRE for details.

CHINESE LITERATURE/LITTERATURE CHINOISE

EDITORIAL ADDRESS:
Foreign Languages Press
Yu Chou Hung
Peking 37
People's Republic of China

SUBSCRIPTION ADDRESS:
Guozi Shudian
Box 399
Peking
China

PUBLISHED: Monthly
COST: 1 yr.—US$4.00; 2 yrs.—US$6.00; 3 yrs.—US$8.00; single copy—$.40.

CONTENTS: Essays; short stories; poems; tales; drama. Regular features include "Notes on Literature and Arts," "Cultural Exchange," "Chronicle"; plates of Chinese paintings, many in color. Example article: "Home of Folk-Songs."

GENERAL: First issue, 1951. Usual publication length, 100-138 pages. Published monthly in English and quarterly in French.
BACK ISSUES: Available from subscription address; on microfilm from AMS at $420.00 for Vols. 1-21 (1951-1970), 21 reels.

DHARA: A QUARTERLY REVIEW OF INDIAN LITERATURE IN ENGLISH LANGUAGE

EDITORIAL ADDRESS:
R. S. Yadav, Editor
Dhara Publications
37D, Gupta Colony
Delhi 9
India

SUBSCRIPTION ADDRESS:

same

PUBLISHED: Quarterly
COST: 1 yr.—$5.00; single copy—$1.25.

CIRCULATION: 1,000

CONTENTS: Critical articles; short stories; poems; literary surveys; international writing; book reviews; information about writers and journals in Indian languages. Example: "Mask and Reality: A Note on Oriya Literature in the Fifties and the Sixties."

UNSOLICITED MSS. WELCOME? Yes; submissions acknowledged.
SPECIFICALLY WELCOMED: English original compositions and translations from India and abroad on above topics plus on culture, art and traditions of various regions.
MS. LENGTH: 10 pages maximum; submit ONE copy only.
STYLE REQUIREMENTS: Relevance to literary journals.
COPYRIGHT: Author.
EDITOR'S DECISION: 1 month.
FROM ACCEPTANCE TO PUBLICATION: 3-4 months.
PAYMENT/OFFPRINTS: 4 offprints.
REJECTED MSS.: Returned.
GENERAL: First issue, October, 1969. Usual publication length, 64 pages.
BACK ISSUES: Available from editorial address at $2.00 each paid in advance.

EXPLORATIONS: A JOURNAL OF LITERARY CRITICISM

EDITORIAL ADDRESS:
Siddiq Kalim, Editor
Government College
Department of English
Language and Literature
Lahore
Pakistan

SUBSCRIPTION ADDRESS:
Department of English
Government College
Lahore
Pakistan

PUBLISHED: Quarterly
CIRCULATION: 1,000
COST: Rupees 5,000, but varies according to the market condition.

CONTENTS: Research and critical articles on English literature and language; research and critical articles on Urdu and Panjabi language and literature; translations of Urdu and Panjabi poetry (by mostly the members of the Faculty of the Government College). Example: "Archetypes of the Collective Unconscious in Literature."

UNSOLICITED MSS. WELCOME? Yes; submissions acknowledged.
MS. LENGTH: 5-30 pages; submit ONE copy.
STYLE REQUIREMENTS: Modern English prose style.
COPYRIGHT: EXPLORATIONS.
EDITOR'S DECISION: 1 month.
FROM ACCEPTANCE TO PUBLICATION: 3-6 months.
PAYMENT/OFFPRINTS: No payment. Offprints arranged with its own press.
REJECTED MSS.: Returned.
GENERAL: First issue, January-March, 1969. Usual publication length, 100-125 pages.
BACK ISSUES: Available free from subscription address.

HARVARD JOURNAL OF ASIATIC STUDIES

EDITORIAL ADDRESS:
John L. Bishop, Editor
2 Divinity Avenue
Cambridge, Massachusetts 02138

SUBSCRIPTION ADDRESS:
same

PUBLISHED: Annually
CIRCULATION: 1,200
COST: $10.00 per volume.

CONTENTS: Scholarly articles primarily concerned with the languages, literatures, cultures, and histories of the countries of Eastern and Central Asia and dealing with modern scholarship and publication on these subjects but not with contemporary political and social matters.

UNSOLICITED MSS. WELCOME? Yes; submissions acknowledged.
SPECIFICALLY WELCOMED: Historical, critical studies, translations if annotated, of East Asian literatures based primarily on original language sources.

MS. LENGTH: 20-80 pages; submit ONE copy.
STYLE REQUIREMENTS: HJAS Style Sheet available.
COPYRIGHT: Not copyrighted.
EDITOR'S DECISION: 3-12 months.
FROM ACCEPTANCE TO PUBLICATION: 1-2 years.
PAYMENT/OFFPRINTS: 50 free offprints for articles; 25 for reviews.
REJECTED MSS.: Returned.
GENERAL: First issue, 1936. Usual publication length, 300 pages.
BACK ISSUES: Vols. 1-20 (1936-1957) and Vols. 21-24 (1958-1963) now out of print and available only in reprint form from Johnson Reprint Corp.; request price list. Vols. 25-32 (1964-1972) available from publisher at original prices.

INDIAN LITERATURE

EDITORIAL ADDRESS:
Editor
Sahitya Akademi
Rabindra Bhavan
35 Ferozeshah Road
New Delhi-1
India

SUBSCRIPTION ADDRESS:

same

PUBLISHED: Quarterly
CIRCULATION: 1,000
COST: 1 yr.—$4.00 or Rs.8/-; single copy—$1.00 or Rs.2/-.

CONTENTS: Informative material about literary activities in twenty Indian languages; English translations of poems and stories from Indian languages; special features on various forms of writing; articles on authors; book reviews; bibliographies; articles on languages and comparative literature, research material. Example: "The Age of Sri Aurobindo."

UNSOLICITED MSS. WELCOME? Yes, but the magazine contains mostly commissioned writing; submissions generally acknowledged.
MS. LENGTH: 1,000-2,000 words; submit TWO copies.
STYLE REQUIREMENTS: None in particular.
COPYRIGHT: Contributor, but the Akademi retains concurrent reproduction rights.
EDITOR'S DECISION: 1 month.
FROM ACCEPTANCE TO PUBLICATION: 1 year.
PAYMENT/OFFPRINTS: Rs.100/- per article; Rs.25/- per poem; Rs. 25/- per book review. 20 free offprints.
REJECTED MSS.: Returned.
GENERAL: First issue, October, 1957; biannual until 1965, quarterly since 1966. Usual publication length, 100 pages.
BACK ISSUES: Available from Publisher, Sahitya Akademi, at $1.00 or Rs.2/- each.

THE INDIAN REVIEW: DEVOTED TO THE DISCUSSION OF ALL TOPICS OF INTEREST

EDITORIAL ADDRESS:
M. C. Subrahmanyam, Editor
2-A Cathedral Road, Madras-86
Tamilnad
India

SUBSCRIPTION ADDRESS:

same

PUBLISHED: Monthly   CIRCULATION: 2,500
COST: 1 yr.—$5.00; single copy—Rupee one (Re. 1/-).

CONTENTS: Academic articles devoted to an objective discussion of political, economic, social, cultural, philosophic and literary problems.

UNSOLICITED MSS. WELCOME? Yes; submissions acknowledged.
SPECIFICALLY WELCOMED: All subjects reflecting the creative endeavor of man in pursuit of his evolution to a higher plane.
MS. LENGTH: 800-1,500 words; submit TWO copies.
STYLE REQUIREMENTS: Simple, clear and therefore effective.
COPYRIGHT: Author.
EDITOR'S DECISION: 1 month.
FROM ACCEPTANCE TO PUBLICATION: 1 month.
PAYMENT/OFFPRINTS: From Rs. 50 to Rs. 100/-. Offprints will be supplied if required.
REJECTED MSS.: Returned.
GENERAL: First issue, 1900-1967; 1970+. Usual publication length, 80 pages.
BACK ISSUES: Supplied if available from editorial address at 50% extra.

INDIAN WRITING TODAY

EDITORIAL ADDRESS:
Sadanand G. Bhatkal and
Probhakar Padhye, Editors
Nirmala-Sadanand Publishers
35c Tardeo Road
Bombay 34 WB
India

SUBSCRIPTION ADDRESS:
Care Popular Book Depot
Dr. Bhadkamkar Road
Bombay 400 007 WB
India

PUBLISHED: Quarterly   CIRCULATION: 1,100
COST: 1 yr.—$5.00; 2 yrs.—$8.00; 3 yrs.—$10.00.

CONTENTS: Articles devoted to Indian literature by well-known authors in all the Indian languages; reviews; short stories; poems. Examples: "New Horizon in the Tamil Drama"; "Literature of Social Protest in Telugu."

UNSOLICITED MSS. WELCOME? Only articles about Indian languages; submissions acknowledged.
MS. LENGTH: Above 2,000 words; submit TWO copies.

COPYRIGHT: INDIAN WRITING TODAY.
EDITOR'S DECISION: 2 months.
FROM ACCEPTANCE TO PUBLICATION: 3 months or more.
PAYMENT/OFFPRINTS: Some remuneration. Offprints or copies of the journal if required.
REJECTED MSS.: Returned.
GENERAL: First issue, March, 1967. Usual publication length, 80 pages. Articles are in English.
BACK ISSUES: Available from subscription address at $2.00 each. #1 and #14 are out of print.

JOURNAL OF THE AMERICAN ORIENTAL SOCIETY

EDITORIAL ADDRESS:
Ernest Bender, Editor

SUBSCRIPTION ADDRESS:
Secretary-Treasurer
American Oriental Society
329 Sterling Memorial Library
Yale Station
New Haven, Connecticut 06520

PUBLISHED: Quarterly

GENERAL: Usual publication length, 150 pages. The Society was founded in 1842. For further information, contact the secretary-treasurer.

THE JOURNAL OF INDIAN WRITING IN ENGLISH

EDITORIAL ADDRESS:
Dr. G. S. Balarama Gupta, Editor
Department of English
Post-Graduate Centre
Gulbarga-2, Mysore State
India

SUBSCRIPTION ADDRESS:

same

PUBLISHED: Biannually (Jan., July)   CIRCULATION: 1,000
COST: 1 yr.—$3.00, 25 shillings, or Rs.10 by sea (postage included); single copy—$2.00, 10 shillings, or Rs.5 by sea.

CONTENTS: Creative writing (poems, stories, playlets) in English by Indians; critical articles on Indian writing in English (including reviews) by Indians as well as foreign scholars.

UNSOLICITED MSS. WELCOME? Yes; submissions acknowledged.
MS. LENGTH: Short pieces preferred; submit TWO copies.
STYLE REQUIREMENTS: MLA STYLE SHEET; footnotes follow the essay. For reviews, send two copies of the book.

COPYRIGHT: Not settled yet.
EDITOR'S DECISION: 1 month.
FROM ACCEPTANCE TO PUBLICATION: 6 months to 1 year.
PAYMENT/OFFPRINTS: Up to 20 free offprints.
REJECTED MSS.: Returned.
GENERAL: First issue, January, 1973. Usual publication length, 100-120 pages.
BACK ISSUES: Available from editorial address at $3.00 each by air or $2.00 each by sea.

JOURNAL OF SOUTH ASIAN LITERATURE (formerly MAHFIL: A QUARTERLY OF SOUTH ASIAN LITERATURE)

EDITORIAL ADDRESS:
Carlo Coppola, Surjit Dulai, and
C. M. Naim, Editors
Box 39, Foster Hall
University of Chicago
Chicago, Illinois 60637

SUBSCRIPTION ADDRESS:
Asian Studies Center
Center for International Programs
Michigan State University
East Lansing, Michigan 48823

PUBLISHED: Quarterly
CIRCULATION: 200
COST: 1 yr.—$5.00 in U.S. and Canada; $6.00 elsewhere; single copy—$1.50; double issue—$3.00.

CONTENTS: Dissemination of the best of South Asian literature in English translation, including literature of India, Pakistan, Bangladesh, and Ceylon; poetry, short stories, essays, plays, novellas, and selections from novels of all periods—classical, medieval, modern, and contemporary; book reviews; critical studies; and bibliographies on and about South Asian literature.

UNSOLICITED MSS. WELCOME? Yes; submissions acknowledged.
SPECIFICALLY WELCOMED: Poetry, short stories, essays, review articles, plays, critical studies.
MS. LENGTH: Not stated; submit ONE copy.
STYLE REQUIREMENTS: None.
COPYRIGHT: JOURNAL OF SOUTH ASIAN LITERATURE.
EDITOR'S DECISION: 6 weeks.
FROM ACCEPTANCE TO PUBLICATION: Varies.
PAYMENT/OFFPRINTS: One copy of issue; two offprints.
REJECTED MSS.: Returned.
GENERAL: First issue, Summer, 1963. Usual publication length, 100-125 pages.
BACK ISSUES: Available from Asian Studies Center at original cost. Out-of-print issues can be obtained from Xerox University Microfilms.

THE LITERARY CRITERION

See the section on AGE AND/OR NATIONALITY: ENGLISH, AND BRITISH COMMONWEALTH for details.

LITERARY STUDIES: A QUARTERLY REVIEW OF LITERATURE AND CRITICISM FROM THE PANJAB (suspended publication)

EDITORIAL ADDRESS:
B. M. Razdan, Editor
Razdan House
Sirhindi Darwaza
Patiala (Punjab)
India

PUBLISHED: Quarterly   CIRCULATION: 2,000

CONTENTS: Poetry; drama; fiction; critical essays and reviews from writers of various countries.

GENERAL: Usual publication length, from 150-175 pages.
BACK ISSUES: Available from editor at $2.50 per single copy (air mail postage extra) or $5.00 each for double issues (air mail postage extra).

LITERATURE EAST AND WEST

EDITORIAL ADDRESS: SUBSCRIPTION ADDRESS:
Roy E. Teele, Editor
Box 8107, University Station   same
Austin, Texas 78712

PUBLISHED: Quarterly   CIRCULATION: 500
COST: 1 yr.—$8.00.

CONTENTS: Translations of poetry, drama, fiction, and criticism from Far East, Near East, South Asia, Africa; critical articles dealing with those literatures and their relations with European and American literatures; book reviews; bibliographies. Examples: "Conformity and Originality in the Poetry of Tu Mu (803-852)"; "Rhythm in M. Malgonkar's THE PRINCES."

UNSOLICITED MSS. WELCOME? Yes; submissions acknowledged.
SPECIFICALLY WELCOMED: Translations and critical articles.
MS. LENGTH: Under 20 pages; submit ONE copy.
STYLE REQUIREMENTS: MLA STYLE SHEET.
COPYRIGHT: Literature East & West, Inc.
EDITOR'S DECISION: 6 months.

FROM ACCEPTANCE TO PUBLICATION: 1 to 2 years.
PAYMENT/OFFPRINTS: Two copies of issue in which work appears. 25 offprints.
REJECTED MSS.: Returned.
GENERAL: First issue, 1954. Usual publication length, 120 pages.
BACK ISSUES: Those published before 1968 available from Johnson Reprint Corporation. Subsequent issues available from editorial address at $2.00 each if single issue; $4.00 each if double issue.

THE PAKISTAN REVIEW

EDITORIAL ADDRESS:
M. Hasan, Editor
60-Shara-e-Quaid-e-Azam
Lahore
Pakistan

SUBSCRIPTION ADDRESS:
Ferozsons, Ltd.
same

PUBLISHED: Monthly
COST: $0-17 per issue.

CONTENTS: Cultural articles on Pakistani life and thought.

UNSOLICITED MSS. WELCOME? Yes; submissions acknowledged.
SPECIFICALLY WELCOMED: Material relating to Pakistani culture and literature.
MS. LENGTH: Articles, 2,000-2,500 words; submit ONE copy.
STYLE REQUIREMENTS: In English.
COPYRIGHT: Copyright can continue to belong to the authors.
EDITOR'S DECISION: 1 month.
FROM ACCEPTANCE TO PUBLICATION: 1 month.
PAYMENT/OFFPRINTS: Pak Rs.50/-. If prior notice is given, offprints can be provided in small quantity.
REJECTED MSS.: Returned.
GENERAL: First issue, 1953. Usual publication length, 48 pages.
BACK ISSUES: If available (rarely), from subscription address.

QUARTERLY CHECK-LIST OF ORIENTAL STUDIES

See the section on BIBLIOGRAPHICAL AND LIBRARY RESOURCES for details.

SOUTH ASIAN REVIEW: THE JOURNAL OF THE ROYAL SOCIETY FOR INDIA, PAKISTAN AND CEYLON

EDITORIAL ADDRESS:
John White, Editor
3 Temple Chambers
London EC4Y OHB
England

SUBSCRIPTION ADDRESS:
Research Publications Services Ltd.
Victoria Hall
East Greenwich
London SE 10 ORF
England

PUBLISHED: Quarterly
CIRCULATION: 1,200
COST: U.K.: 1 yr.—£2.50; 3 yrs.—£6.00; single copy—75p; India, Pakistan, Ceylon: 1 yr.—£1.50; elsewhere: 1 yr.—£3.00; 3 yrs.—£7.00; students: 1 yr.—£1.50 (prices subject to change).

CONTENTS: Area articles that cover India, Pakistan, Sri Lanka, Bangladesh, and their peripheral countries, and that are multi-disciplinary: economics, literature, history, sociology, social anthropology, politics (including commentary on current events), art, and Indology; book reviews. Example: "Social Comment in South Indian Prose Fiction."

UNSOLICITED MSS. WELCOME? Articles, yes; all book reviews are solicited; submissions acknowledged.
SPECIFICALLY WELCOMED: Work on social trends as demonstrated in vernacular writing; on specific forms of writing associated with particular cultural groups in the area; on the use of language.
MS. LENGTH: 2,000-5,000 words; submit TWO copies.
STYLE REQUIREMENTS: No stipulations.
COPYRIGHT: The Royal Society for India, Pakistan and Ceylon.
EDITOR'S DECISION: Varies.
FROM ACCEPTANCE TO PUBLICATION: 3-6 months.
PAYMENT/OFFPRINTS: £1.00 per printed page for articles (not book reviews). 40 free offprints for articles (not book reviews).
REJECTED MSS.: Returned, if requested.
GENERAL: First issue in present form, November, 1967. Usual publication length, 96 pages.
BACK ISSUES: Available from Research Publications Services Ltd. at cover price (50p.) plus postage; individual copies, 75p including postage.

TAMKANG REVIEW: A JOURNAL MAINLY DEVOTED TO COMPARATIVE STUDIES BETWEEN CHINESE AND FOREIGN LITERATURES

EDITORIAL ADDRESS:
Yen Yuan-Shu, Editor
Western Literature Research Institute
Tamkang College of Arts & Sciences
King-hua Street, Taipei, Taiwan 106
Republic of China

SUBSCRIPTION ADDRESS:

same

PUBLISHED: Biannually (Apr., Oct.)
COST: 1 yr.—US$6.00; 2 yrs.—US$11.00; 3 yrs.—US$16.00; single copy—US$3.00.

CONTENTS: Comparative studies between Chinese and foreign literature; comparative studies between Oriental and Western literatures; studies in Chinese literature with Western viewpoints or methods. Examples: "The Grass Motif in Chinese Poetry"; "Voltaire and the Cult of China"; "The Influences of Chinese Literature on Korean Literature."

UNSOLICITED MSS. WELCOME: Yes; submissions acknowledged.
SPECIFICALLY WELCOMED: Scholarly comparative articles.
MS. LENGTH: 5,000-10,000 words; submit ONE copy.
STYLE REQUIREMENTS: MLA STYLE SHEET.
COPYRIGHT: TAMKANG REVIEW, but negotiable in special cases.
EDITOR'S DECISION: 1-3 months.
FROM ACCEPTANCE TO PUBLICATION: 1-12 months.
PAYMENT/OFFPRINTS: $7.00 to $10.00 per 1,000 words. Cost of offprints deducted from honorarium.
REJECTED MSS.: Returned.
GENERAL: First issue, April, 1970. Usual publication length, 250 pages.
BACK ISSUES: Available from editorial address at US$3.00 each.

VENTURE: BI-ANNUAL REVIEW OF ENGLISH LANGUAGE AND LITERATURE

EDITORIAL ADDRESS:
S. A. Ashraf, Editor
Professor, Department of English
University of Karachi
Karachi 32, Pakistan

SUBSCRIPTION ADDRESS:

same

PUBLISHED: Biannually
(Summer, Winter)
COST: 1 yr.—$5.50 including postage; single copy—$2.50, postage extra.

CIRCULATION: 500

CONTENTS: Scholarly and critical essays on English language and literature, literature in English in other parts of the world, Canada, U.S.A., Australia, Indo-Pakistan sub-continent; articles on linguistics and language-teaching; special issues on specific subjects—either language or literature or on a special author (e.g. T. S. Eliot) or a specific area (e.g. creative writing in English in Pakistan); original poetry in English and English translation of poetry in Pakistan languages. Issues on language/linguistics and literature may be separately published or published in two separate sections.

UNSOLICITED MSS. WELCOME? Yes; submissions not acknowledged unless requested.
SPECIFICALLY WELCOMED: Any aspect of literature in English or linguistics and language-teaching (except for special issues).
MS. LENGTH: Preferably 3,000 words; 5,000 word maximum; submit ONE copy.

STYLE REQUIREMENTS: No footnotes; notes at end of article and numbered continuously, not page-wise.
COPYRIGHT: Author.
EDITOR'S DECISION: 1 month.
FROM ACCEPTANCE TO PUBLICATION: Depends on nature of article and availability of space.
PAYMENT/OFFPRINTS: No payment. Offprints, if desired, should be indicated when articles are sent, otherwise no arrangement is made.
REJECTED MSS.: Not returned.
GENERAL: First issue, March, 1960 (Quarterly 1960-62); revived, 1965 (bi-annually). Usual publication length, 70-80 pages.
BACK ISSUES: Available from editorial address at $2.50 each, postage extra.

AFRICAN, CARIBBEAN,

LATIN AMERICAN,

and

NEAR EASTERN

AFRICAN ARTS

See the section on AMERICAN ETHNIC MINORITIES for details.

AFRICAN LITERATURE TODAY: AN ANNUAL REVIEW

EDITORIAL ADDRESS:
Prof. Eldred Durosimi Jones
Department of English
Fourah Bay College
University of Sierra Leone
Freetown, Sierra Leone, West Africa

SUBSCRIPTION ADDRESS:
Africana Publishing Corporation
101 Fifth Avenue
New York, New York 10003

PUBLISHED: Annually, beginning with Vol. 5
COST: 1 yr.—$8.00 (hardback only).

CONTENTS: Critical essays about African literature with each issue centering on a particular topic, such as the novel or poetry in Africa; reviews of books about and by African writers; "Comments" section for replies to previous articles; bibliographic listings essentially of creative writings but includes critical works, reference works, and anthologies. Examples: "Language and Action in the Novels of Chinua Achebe"; "Cultural Nationalism in Modern African Creative Literature."

UNSOLICITED MSS. WELCOME? Yes; submissions acknowledged.
SPECIFICALLY WELCOMED: Scholarly essays about the works of African authors.
MS. LENGTH: 3,000 words; submit ONE copy.
STYLE REQUIREMENTS: MLA STYLE SHEET preferred.
COPYRIGHT: AFRICAN LITERATURE TODAY; but reprint permission given freely.
EDITOR'S DECISION: 3 months.
FROM ACCEPTANCE TO PUBLICATION: 1 year.
PAYMENT/OFFPRINTS: £3.3 per 1,000 words for articles; £1.1 for reviews; plus one free copy of journal. No offprints.
REJECTED MSS.: Returned.
GENERAL: First issue, 1968. Usual publication length, 150-160 pages. Title of first 4 issues was AFRICAN LITERATURE TODAY: A JOURNAL OF EXPLANATORY CRITICISM and originated as THE BULLETIN OF THE ASSOCIATION FOR AFRICAN LITERATURE IN ENGLISH. Foreign Sales Representatives: C. Hurst & Co., 40A Royal Hill, Greenwich, London SE10 8SA; and Internationaler Universitaets-Buchandel, Landwehrstrasse 37, 8 Muenchen 2. All orders from individuals must include payment.
BACK ISSUES: Available from Africana Publishing Corporation at $6.95 for combined 4 issues in paper (nos. 1-4, with index).

ALAC-ALAS PAPERS

EDITORIAL ADDRESS:
Katharine Phillips, Editor
Center for Latin American Studies
Arizona State University
Tempe, Arizona 85381

SUBSCRIPTION ADDRESS:

same

PUBLISHED: Annually
CIRCULATION: 200-400
COST: $8.00 for entire set, or $1.00 per session (introduction and 2 papers).

CONTENTS: Papers presented at the Annual Latin American Conference of Arizona Latin American Studies (ALAC-ALAS); various disciplines, all Latin American topics.

COPYRIGHT: ASU Board of Regents.
GENERAL: First issue, August, 1973. Usual publication length, 30-35 pages each session.
BACK ISSUES: Available from editorial address at $1.00 per session, $8.00 per set.

AMÉRICAS

EDITORIAL ADDRESS:
Guillermo de Zéndequi, Editor-in-Chief
Department of Information and Public Affairs
Organization of American States
Washington, D.C. 20006

SUBSCRIPTION ADDRESS:
Sales and Promotion Division
General Secretariat of the Organization of Amerian States
Washington, D.C. 20006

PUBLISHED: 10 to 12 times yearly
CIRCULATION: 100,000
COST: 1 yr.—$6.00; 2 yrs.—$10.00; 3 yrs.—$13.00.

CONTENTS: Articles on various matters relating to the Western Hemisphere; historical, cultural, literary, travel, nature and ecology, economic development; short stories; photo essays; book reviews; recent book notes; OAS news and calendar. Example: "Poet of Two Cultures."

UNSOLICITED MSS. WELCOME? Yes; submissions acknowledged.
SPECIFICALLY WELCOMED: Articles relating to the Western Hemisphere; book reviews.
MS. LENGTH: 8-10 pages; submit TWO copies.
STYLE REQUIREMENTS: Should be appropriate for an international audience of people who share an interest in the Americas.
COPYRIGHT: No copyright made unless author requests it; then it is in author's name.
EDITOR'S DECISION: 4-6 months.
FROM ACCEPTANCE TO PUBLICATION: Varies.

PAYMENT/OFFPRINTS: Maximum of $75. Offprints at author's expense; consult editors.
REJECTED MSS.: Returned.
GENERAL: First issue, 1949. Usual publication length, 48 pages plus supplement. Published in English, Spanish, and Portuguese editions.
BACK ISSUES: Available from subscription address at $.75 each; microfilm form from University Microfilms.

BLACK ACADEMY REVIEW: QUARTERLY OF THE BLACK WORLD

See the section on AMERICAN ETHNIC MINORITIES for details.

BULLETIN OF HISPANIC STUDIES

See the section on AGE AND/OR NATIONALITY: EUROPEAN.

CARIBBEAN REVIEW: A QUARTERLY JOURNAL DEDICATED TO THE CARIBBEAN, LATIN AMERICA, AND THEIR EMIGRANT GROUPS

EDITORIAL ADDRESS:
Barry B. Levine and Joseph D. Olander, Editors
G. P. O. Box C. R.
San Juan, Puerto Rico 00936

SUBSCRIPTION ADDRESS:
Fulfillment Center
Box 3335
Norland Branch
Miami, Florida 33169

PUBLISHED: Quarterly
COST: 1 yr.—$5.50; 3 yrs.—$7.50; lifetime—$25.00.

CONTENTS: Articles concerning literary, political, and social issues, such as "Chile: Poetry and Anti-Poetry"; "Recent Books" section introducing books about the Caribbean, Latin America, and their emigrant groups, such as MEXICAN-AMERICAN AUTHORS.

UNSOLICITED MSS. WELCOME? Yes; submissions not acknowledged.
SPECIFICALLY WELCOMED: Articles, essays, reprints, excerpts, translations, book reviews, poetry.
MS. LENGTH: No limit stated; submit ONE copy.
STYLE REQUIREMENTS: Good writing.
COPYRIGHT: Depends.
EDITOR'S DECISION: 6 weeks.
FROM ACCEPTANCE TO PUBLICATION: 2-3 months.
PAYMENT/OFFPRINTS: Copies of the issue are offered to the author.

REJECTED MSS.: Returned.
GENERAL: First issue, April, 1969. Usual publication length, 60 pages.
BACK ISSUES: Available from subscription address at $3.00 each for Vol. 1, #1 and Vol. 3, #1; all other back issues at $2.00 each.

CARIBBEAN STUDIES [Mexico, Central America, West Indies]

EDITORIAL ADDRESS:
Mrs. Sybil Lewis, Editor
Institute of Caribbean Studies
College of Social Sciences
University of Puerto Rico
Rio Piedras, Puerto Rico 00931

SUBSCRIPTION ADDRESS:

same

PUBLISHED: Quarterly

GENERAL: First issue, 1961. This periodical had not arrived by the time the entry went to press. Potential subscribers, contributors, or collectors will have to write the editor to see whether the journal still exists, and if so, to inquire about details of manuscript submission, style, back issues, and the like.

COMPARATIVE LITERATURE STUDIES

See the section on AGE AND/OR NATIONALITY: COMPREHENSIVE IN SCOPE for details.

FREEDOMWAYS: A QUARTERLY REVIEW OF THE FREEDOM MOVEMENT

See the section on AMERICAN ETHNIC MINORITIES for details.

HANDBOOK OF LATIN AMERICAN STUDIES

See the section on BIBLIOGRAPHICAL AND LIBRARY RESOURCES for details.

HISPANIA

See the section on TEACHING ABOUT LITERATURE for details.

HISPANIC REVIEW: A QUARTERLY JOURNAL DEVOTED TO RESEARCH IN THE HISPANIC LANGUAGES AND LITERATURES

See the section on AGE AND/OR NATIONALITY: EUROPEAN.

HISPANOFILA

EDITORIAL ADDRESS:
A. V. Ebersole, Jr., Editor
Department of Romance Languages
University of North Carolina
Chapel Hill, North Carolina 27514

SUBSCRIPTION ADDRESS:

same

PUBLISHED: Tri-annually
COST: 1 yr.—$5.50; single copy—$2.00.

CIRCULATION: 520

CONTENTS: Scholarly articles on Spanish and Spanish-American literature, culture; bibliographies; book reviews. Example: "Blasco Ibáñez and Drama."

UNSOLICITED MSS. WELCOME? Articles, yes.
STYLE REQUIREMENTS: MLA STYLE SHEET.
GENERAL: First issue, 1958. Usual publication length, 82 pages. Articles may be written in Spanish and English.
BACK ISSUES: Short supply of back issues available from editorial address.

THE INDIAN HISTORIAN

See the section on AMERICAN ETHNIC MINORITIES for details.

JOURNAL OF JEWISH STUDIES

EDITORIAL ADDRESS:
Dr. Geza Vermes, Editor
The Oriental Institute
Pusey Lane
Oxford OX1 2LE
England

SUBSCRIPTION ADDRESS:
Subscription Department
67, Great Russell Street
London WC1B 3BT
England

PUBLISHED: Biannually
COST: 1 yr.—$8.00 (£2.50).

CIRCULATION: 750-1,000

CONTENTS: Scholarly articles on Jewish history, literature, philosophy, art, religion (not contemporary issues); book reviews.

UNSOLICITED MSS. WELCOME? Yes; submissions acknowledged, if requested.
SPECIFICALLY WELCOMED: Essays.
MS. LENGTH: 5,000-10,000 words; submit TWO copies.
STYLE REQUIREMENTS: Good English prose.
COPYRIGHT: The Journal.
EDITOR'S DECISION: 2 months.
FROM ACCEPTANCE TO PUBLICATION: 12-18 months.
PAYMENT/OFFPRINTS: 25 free offprints; further copies may be ordered.
REJECTED MSS.: Returned.
GENERAL: First isue, 1948. Usual publication length, 100-120 pages.
BACK ISSUES: Available from subscription department.

JOURNAL OF NEAR EASTERN STUDIES

EDITORIAL ADDRESS:
Robert D. Biggs, Editor
Oriental Institute
University of Chicago
Chicago, Illinois 60637

SUBSCRIPTION ADDRESS:
University of Chicago Press
5801 Ellis Avenue
Chicago, Illinois 60637

PUBLISHED: Quarterly   CIRCULATION: 2,400
COST: 1 yr.—$10.00; 2 yrs.—$19.00; 3 yrs.—$28.00 (add $1.00 per year for foreign postage); students (USA only)—$7.00.

CONTENTS: Historical, archaeological, linguistic, literary studies of the ancient and medieval Near East; includes prehistory, Old Testament, Islam, Egyptian hieroglyphs, cuneiform; book reviews. Example: "An Example of Coptic Literary Influence on Ibn Isḥāq's STRAH."

UNSOLICITED MSS. WELCOME? Yes; submissions acknowledged.
SPECIFICALLY WELCOMED: Serious scholarly work.
MS. LENGTH: No preference; submit TWO copies.
STYLE REQUIREMENTS: Generally follow University of Chicago's A MANUAL OF STYLE, 12th edition.
COPYRIGHT: University of Chicago.
EDITOR'S DECISION: 1-3 weeks.
FROM ACCEPTANCE TO PUBLICATION: 1½ to 2 years.
PAYMENT/OFFPRINTS: Fifty free offprints; additional at established rates.
REJECTED MSS.: Returned.
GENERAL: First issue, 1884. Usual publication length, 72-100 pages.

BACK ISSUES: Available from The University of Chicago Press generally at $3.75 each ($5.00 each for special issues); back volumes—$9.00, available from 1968 (Vol. 27); set of back volumes (20 issues, 1968-1972, vols. 27-31)—$40.00. Single issues and reprinted volumes through 1964 available from Johnson Reprint Corp; microfilm from University Microfilms; microfiche from J. S. Canner and Co., 49-65 Landsdowne St., Boston, Mass. 02215.

JOURNAL OF THE NEW AFRICAN LITERATURE AND THE ARTS (JONALA)

See the section on AMERICAN ETHNIC MINORITIES for details.

JOURNAL OF SPANISH STUDIES: TWENTIETH CENTURY

See the section on AGE AND/OR NATIONALITY: EUROPEAN.

LA REVISTA CHICANO-RIQUEÑA

See the section on AMERICAN ETHNIC MINORITIES for details.

THE LATIN AMERICAN LITERARY REVIEW

EDITORIAL ADDRESS:
Yvette Espinosa Miller, Carlos Navarro, Edward Dudley, Editors
Department of Modern Languages
Baker Hall
Carnegie-Mellon University
Pittsburgh, Pennsylvania 15213

SUBSCRIPTION ADDRESS:

same

PUBLISHED: Biannually (Fall, Spring)
COST: 1 yr.—$7.00.

CIRCULATION: 400

CONTENTS: Essays about works of Latin American writers; reviews of books concerned with Spanish-speaking minorities in the United States and about Latin American culture; some creative writing. Examples: "The Nature of Spanish-American Literature"; "Conversation with Jorge Carrera Andrade."

UNSOLICITED MSS. WELCOME? Yes; submissions acknowledged.
SPECIFICALLY WELCOMED: Original articles; book reviews; translations.

MS. LENGTH: No preference; submit ORIGINAL and ONE photocopy.
STYLE REQUIREMENTS: Text must be in English; translations in brackets must follow Spanish quotations and titles; book reviews limited to analysis of creative works rather than literary criticism.
COPYRIGHT: Author.
EDITOR'S DECISION: About 2 months.
FROM ACCEPTANCE TO PUBLICATION: About 2 months.
PAYMENT/OFFPRINTS: Ten offprints given to each contributor.
REJECTED MSS.: Returned.
GENERAL: First issue, Fall, 1972. Usual publication length, 130-170 pages.
BACK ISSUES: Available from editorial office at $3.50 each.

LATIN AMERICAN THEATRE REVIEW

See the section on GENRES: THEATRE for details.

LITERATURE EAST AND WEST

See the section on AGE AND/OR NATIONALITY: ASIAN for details.

LUSO-BRAZILIAN REVIEW: DEVOTED TO THE CULTURE OF THE PORTUGUESE SPEAKING WORLD

EDITORIAL ADDRESS:
Lloyd Kasten, Editor
University of Wisconsin Press
Box 1379
Madison, Wisconsin 53701

SUBSCRIPTION ADDRESS:
same

PUBLISHED: Biannually   CIRCULATION: 600
COST: 1 yr.—$8.00 ($16.00 for institutions). Subscriptions annual or continuing.

CONTENTS: Articles covering the fields of economics, sociology, history, geography, anthropology, art, music, language, literature, political science, as they touch on any Portuguese-speaking area; current bibliography. Originally, a dearth of articles represented some fields, but recent contributions are expanding the representation.

UNSOLICITED MSS. WELCOME? Yes; submissions acknowledged.
SPECIFICALLY WELCOMED: As to literature, basically anything dealing with Portuguese, Brazilian, or Portuguese-African literatures.
MS. LENGTH: Around 20 pages; submit ONE copy.

STYLE REQUIREMENTS: For literature, use MLA STYLE SHEET; for others, University of Chicago's A MANUAL OF STYLE.
EDITOR'S DECISION: 2-15 weeks.
FROM ACCEPTANCE TO PUBLICATION: Varies.
PAYMENT/OFFPRINTS: No payment. Contributor arranges for offset prints.
REJECTED MSS.: Returned.
GENERAL: First issue, June, 1964. Usual publication length, 128 pages. Articles may be written in English or Portuguese.
BACK ISSUES: Available from University of Wisconsin Press at $4.00 each.

THE MASTERKEY: FOR INDIAN LORE AND HISTORY

See the section on AMERICAN ETHNIC MINORITIES for details.

MEXICO QUARTERLY REVIEW

EDITORIAL ADDRESS:
Coley Taylor and Edmund J. Robbins, Editors
University of the Americas
Apartado Postal 15
Santa Catarina Mártin
Puebla
Mexico

SUBSCRIPTION ADDRESS:

same

PUBLISHED: Quarterly   CIRCULATION: 700
COST: 1 yr.—$3.00, 35 pesos; 2 yrs.—$5.50, 65 pesos; 3 yrs.—$7.50, 90 pesos.

CONTENTS: Quality writing which expresses the editors' philosophy of "the spirit of inner tolerance" and interprets "two cultures in a manner conforming to the ideals of true responsible scholarship"; "fact articles"; researched papers; short stories; poetry; folk tales, such as "Death and the Man"; essays: "A Dialogue on Criticism."

UNSOLICITED MSS. WELCOME? Yes.
SPECIFICALLY WELCOMED: All quality writing directed to the intelligent, critical reader. Partial to a Mexican slant.
MS. LENGTH: No preference; submit one copy.
COPYRIGHT: MEXICO QUARTERLY REVIEW; permission will be given author for re-publication.
EDITOR'S DECISION: 2-4 weeks.
FROM ACCEPTANCE TO PUBLICATION: 4 months.
PAYMENT/OFFPRINTS: 5 copies of issue; additional copies of journal at cost.
REJECTED MSS.: Returned.
GENERAL: First issue, Winter, 1962. Usual publication length, 70 pages.

BACK ISSUES: Available from editorial address; cost dependent upon remaining copies. University libraries given first choice.

THE MUSLIM WORLD

See the section on SPECIALIZED TOPICS AND INTERDISCIPLINARY STUDIES: INTERDISCIPLINARY for details.

ODU: A JOURNAL OF WEST AFRICAN STUDIES

EDITORIAL ADDRESS:
D. O. O. Oyelaran, Editor
Institute of African Studies
University of Ife
Ile Ife
Nigeria

SUBSCRIPTION ADDRESS:
Oxford University Press
PMB 5142
Ibadan
Nigeria

PUBLISHED: Biannually
COST: 1 yr.—US$4.75.

CONTENTS: Articles concerning the entire spectrum of West African Studies with an emphasis on intensive local research. ODU aims at the highest level of scholarship, publishing papers which, though of a particular regional reference, may serve as source material for more comprehensive studies.

UNSOLICITED MSS. WELCOME? Yes, but writers are advised to submit outlines to the editor first; submissions acknowledged.
MS. LENGTH: No preference; submit TWO copies.
STYLE REQUIREMENTS: Notes on style available from editor.
COPYRIGHT: Writer.
PAYMENT/OFFPRINTS: 25 offprints of any article published.
REJECTED MSS.: Returned.
GENERAL: First issue, July, 1964. Usual publication length, 120 pages.
BACK ISSUES: Available from subscription address at US$2.00 each.

OROT: JOURNAL OF HEBREW LITERATURE

EDITORIAL ADDRESS:
A. Zemach, Editor
World Zionist Organization
Department of Education and
Culture in the Diaspora
Box 92
Jerusalem, Israel

SUBSCRIPTION ADDRESS:

same

PUBLISHED: Quarterly
COST: 1 yr.—$3.00; single copy—$1.00.

CIRCULATION: 1,500

CONTENTS: Current Hebrew literature and thought; reviews of books; occasional illustration. Examples: "Some Problems of Hassidic Thought"; "The Development of Hebrew."

UNSOLICITED MSS. WELCOME? Yes; submissions acknowledged.
SPECIFICALLY WELCOMED: Poetry and prose in Hebrew.
MS. LENGTH: Up to 2,000 words; submit TWO copies.
COPYRIGHT: Author and OROT.
EDITOR'S DECISION: 5 months.
FROM ACCEPTANCE TO PUBLICATION: 6 months.
PAYMENT/OFFPRINTS: Payment according to Israeli rates. Fifty copies on request.
REJECTED MSS.: Returned.
GENERAL: First issue (in its present form), 1967. Written in Hebrew with English translation.
BACK ISSUES: Available from editorial address at $1.00 each.

RESEARCH IN AFRICAN LITERATURES

See the section on AMERICAN ETHNIC MINORITIES for details.

REVISTA DE ESTUDIOS HISPANICOS

EDITORIAL ADDRESS:
Enrique Ruiz-Fornells, Editor
P. O. Box 3544
University, Alabama 35486

SUBSCRIPTION ADDRESS:
University of Alabama Press
Drawer 2877
University, Alabama 35486

PUBLISHED: Tri-annually
COST: 1 yr.—$6.00; 2 yrs.—$11.50; 3 yrs.—$17.00; single copy—$2.00.

CIRCULATION: 700

CONTENTS: Articles on literary topics which offer new ideas concerning Spanish and Spanish-American literature; book reviews. Example: "The Dramatic Perspective in Contemporary Peru."

UNSOLICITED MSS. WELCOME? Yes; submissions not acknowledged.
SPECIFICALLY WELCOMED: Any kind of Spanish and Spanish American literary contributions.
MS. LENGTH: Up to 25 pages; submit ONE copy.
STYLE REQUIREMENTS: MLA STYLE SHEET.
EDITOR'S DECISION: 2 weeks to 1 month.
FROM ACCEPTANCE TO PUBLICATION: 2-3 years.
PAYMENT/OFFPRINTS: Five free offprints; a maximum of 20 more available for $.25 each.
REJECTED MSS.: Returned.
GENERAL: First issue, May, 1967. Usual publication length, 160 pages. Articles may be written in Spanish, French, Portuguese, Italian or English. Indexed by volume.
BACK ISSUES: Available from University of Alabama Press at $2.00 each.

REVISTA INTERAMERICANA DE BIBLIOGRAFIA: INTER-AMERICAN REVIEW OF BIBLIOGRAPHY

See the section on BIBLIOGRAPHICAL AND LIBRARY RESOURCES for details.

SPECIALIA: A MULTIDISCIPLINARY JOURNAL

EDITORIAL ADDRESS;
A. W. Bork, Editor
P. O. Box 2662
Carbondale, Illinois 62901

SUBSCRIPTION ADDRESS:
Professional Productivity Associates
same

PUBLISHED: No fixed frequency, about 2 issues yearly
COST: 10 issues—$40.00.

CIRCULATION: 1,000

CONTENTS: Articles and studies of lasting interest in the area of the humanities and social sciences, literature, and other disciplines; bibliographies.

UNSOLICITED MSS. WELCOME? Yes; submissions acknowledged.
SPECIFICALLY WELCOMED: Principally research with reference to Latin America.
MS. LENGTH: 15-20 pages; submit ONE copy.
STYLE REQUIREMENTS: Standard MLA STYLE SHEET, AHA, or University of Chicago's A MANUAL OF STYLE.
COPYRIGHT: The author or institution concerned.
EDITOR'S DECISION: 2 months.

FROM ACCEPTANCE TO PUBLICATION: Varies, up to 1 year.
PAYMENT/OFFPRINTS: 25 free offprints.
REJECTED MSS.: Returned.
GENERAL: First issue, 1969. Usual publication length, 72 pages.
BACK ISSUES: Available from Professional Productivity Associates. At present, a subscription can begin with Vol. 1, No. 1.

SPECIAL STUDIES

EDITORIAL ADDRESS: SUBSCRIPTION ADDRESS:
Lewis A. Tambs, Director
Center for Latin American Studies same
Arizona State University
Tempe, Arizona 85381

PUBLISHED: 3 or 4 yearly CIRCULATION: 200-400
COST: $2.00 per copy.

CONTENTS: Special studies on any area or discipline relating to Latin America. Example: "A Bibliography of Jorge Luis Borges."

UNSOLICITED MSS. WELCOME? Yes, mss, from outside ASU welcomed; all submissions refereed and acknowledged.
SPECIFICALLY WELCOMED: Bibliographies very welcome; studies in art, history, economics, foreign languages, anthropology, sociology, political science.
MS. LENGTH: 15-40 pages; submit TWO copies.
STYLE REQUIREMENTS: MLA STYLE SHEET; end notes.
COPYRIGHT: Arizona State University Board of Regents.
EDITOR'S DECISION: 2-3 months.
FROM ACCEPTANCE TO PUBLICATION: 4-8 months.
PAYMENT/OFFPRINTS: 10 copies of published study. Offprints at cost.
REJECTED MSS.: Returned.
GENERAL: First issue, March, 1970. Usual publication length, 35 pages.
BACK ISSUES: Available from editorial address. First 10 studies are on microfilm, 16mm negative, two reels, $2.00 each.

STUDIES IN BLACK LITERATURE

See the section on AMERICAN ETHNIC MINORITIES for details.

III

GENRES

POETRY

AGENDA

EDITORIAL ADDRESS:
William Cookson, Editor
5 Cranbourne Court
Albert Bridge Road
London SW11 4PE
England

SUBSCRIPTION ADDRESS:

same

PUBLISHED: Quarterly   CIRCULATION: 2,000-3,000
COST: 1 yr.—$6.00; single copy—$1.50; double issue—$3.00.

CONTENTS: Poetry; criticism; special issues on particular writers.

UNSOLICITED MSS. WELCOME? Yes.
SPECIFICALLY WELCOMED: Poetry and criticism.
MS. LENGTH: Optional; submit ONE copy.
PAYMENT/OFFPRINTS: Poems—$1 per page. No payment for prose. No offprints.
REJECTED MSS.: Returned.
GENERAL: First issue, January, 1959. Usual publication length, 90 pages single issue; 160 pages double issue.
BACK ISSUES: Available from editorial address or, for Vols. I-IV, from Kraus Reprint, FL-9491, Nendeln, Liechtenstein. Prices vary.

THE AMERICAN POETRY REVIEW

EDITORIAL ADDRESS:
Steve Berg, Steve Parker,
Rhoda Schwartz, Editors
401 South Broad Street
Philadelphia, Pennsylvania 19147

SUBSCRIPTION ADDRESS:
Subscription Department
same

PUBLISHED: 6 times yearly   CIRCULATION: 50,000
COST: 1 yr.—$5.00; 2 yrs.—$9.00; 3 yrs.—$13.00.

CONTENTS: Poetry; literary essay; psychology; special articles on the teaching of poetry; photographs; reviews; drawings; interviews. Examples: "On Literature of Survival"; "Analysis of Depths: Dante's INFERNO."

UNSOLICITED MSS. WELCOME? Yes; submissions not acknowledged.
SPECIFICALLY WELCOMED: Poetry.
MS. LENGTH: No preference; submit ONE copy.
COPYRIGHT: Author.
EDITOR'S DECISION: 3 months.
FROM ACCEPTANCE TO PUBLICATION: 6 months.
PAYMENT/OFFPRINTS: None.
REJECTED MSS.: Returned.
GENERAL: First issue, Nov.-Dec., 1972. Usual publication length, 56 pages.

BACK ISSUES: Available from subscription address at $1.00 each.

CONCERNING POETRY

EDITORIAL ADDRESS:
L. L. Lee, Editor
Department of English
Western Washington State College
Bellingham, Washington 98225

SUBSCRIPTION ADDRESS:

same

PUBLISHED: Biannually CIRCULATION: 400-500
COST: 1 yr.—$3.00; $3.50 outside of North America.

CONTENTS: Explications of poems; general articles on poetry; reviews; original poems. Example essays: "Theodore Roethke's Proverbs"; "Andrew Marvell's 'On a Drop of Dew': A Reading and a Possible Source."

UNSOLICITED MSS. WELCOME? Yes; submissions acknowledged.
MS. LENGTH: Less than 3,000 words.
STYLE REQUIREMENTS: MLA STYLE SHEET; footnotes follow article.
COPYRIGHT: CONCERNING POETRY, but released to author on request.
EDITOR'S DECISION: 1-2 months.
FROM ACCEPTANCE TO PUBLICATION: Up to 1 year.
PAYMENT/OFFPRINTS: Copies of issue.
REJECTED MSS.: Returned.
GENERAL: First issue, Spring, 1968. Usual publication length, 85 pages.
BACK ISSUES: Available (bound) from editorial address at $2.00 each; also from Xerox University Microfilms.

CONTEMPORARY POETRY: A JOURNAL OF POETRY CRITICISM

EDITORIAL ADDRESS:
Selwyn Kittredge, Editor
Fairleigh Dickinson University
Teaneck, New Jersey 07666

SUBSCRIPTION ADDRESS:

same

PUBLISHED: Quarterly

COST: 1 yr.—$4.00 ($5.00 for libraries and other institutions).

CONTENTS: Articles on contemporary poets and interpretations of significant contemporary poems, particularly in the period from 1950 to the present; reviews of books about and of poetry. Examples: "A Hard Nut to Crack from Sylvia Plath"; "The Poet as Translator: Thomas Kinsella and the Irish Tradition."

UNSOLICITED MSS. WELCOME? Yes.

COPYRIGHT: CONTEMPORARY POETRY.
GENERAL: First issue, Spring, 1973. Usual publication length, 78 pages.

CREATIVE MOMENT

EDITORIAL ADDRESS:
Syed Amanuddin, Editor
Poetry Eastwest Publications
P.O. Box 391
Sumter, South Carolina 29150

SUBSCRIPTION ADDRESS:

same

PUBLISHED: Biannually
COST: 1 yr.—$3.00; single copy—$1.50.

CIRCULATION: 300

CONTENTS: International scene in poetry, especially poetry written in English: poetry; poetry reviews; and articles on contemporary world poetry in English. Example articles: "Avant-Gardism in Contemporary American Poetry"; "Black Poets in Australia."

UNSOLICITED MSS. WELCOME? Yes; submissions acknowledged.
SPECIFICALLY WELCOMED: Articles under 3,000 words on current poetry scene in Australia, Canada, India, Nigeria, and other countries where English is used as a medium of creative expression.
MS. LENGTH: 1,000-3,000 words; submit ONE copy.
STYLE REQUIREMENTS: No footnotes.
COPYRIGHT: Copyright reverts to author three months after publication.
EDITOR'S DECISION: 4 months for articles.
FROM ACCEPTANCE TO PUBLICATION: 6 months.
PAYMENT/OFFPRINTS: One copy of the publication. No offprints.
REJECTED MSS.: Returned.
GENERAL: First issue, Spring, 1972. Usual publication length, 40 pages.
BACK ISSUES: Available from publisher or any magazine subscription agency at $2.50 each.

DRAGONFLY: A QUARTERLY OF HAIKU HIGHLIGHTS

EDITORIAL ADDRESS:
Lorraine Ellis Harr, Editor
4102 N. E. 130th Place
Portland, Oregon 97230

SUBSCRIPTION ADDRESS:
J & C Transcripts
Box 15
Kanona, New York 14856

PUBLISHED: Quarterly
COST: 1 yr.—$4.00; single copy—$1.00.

CIRCULATION: 500

CONTENTS: Japanese haiku in English language; some senryu; some other short Oriental poetic froms; brief articles on haiku. Acts as a show case for ALL haiku poets writing in this form; holds the line at traditional/classical standards of haiku writing—rather than off-shoot innovations; distinguishes between Japanese haiku and the English language poetics that pass all too often as haiku. Example prose: "Murasaki Shikibu: THE TALE OF GENJI."

UNSOLICITED MSS. WELCOME? Yes, as long as submission shows some knowledge of haiku other than a 5-7-5 finger count; submissions not acknowledged.
SPECIFICALLY WELCOMED: Knowledgeable articles on haiku and related materials. No personal opinion pieces. No generalities. Must know haiku. 5-7-5 syllable count not essential.
MS. LENGTH: Articles, under 300 words; limited submission of 5 haiku per poet; submit ORIGINAL.
STYLE REQUIREMENTS: Poets should speak with own voice. Must know haiku.
COPYRIGHT: Copyrights revert to individual poets, writers.
EDITOR'S DECISION: Within 30 days.
FROM ACCEPTANCE TO PUBLICATION: 3-4 months.
PAYMENT/OFFPRINTS: Numerous awards, prizes and gift subscriptions, contests. Poet can purchase extra copies from J & C Transcripts.
REJECTED MSS.: Returned.
GENERAL: First issue, 1965—began as HAIKU HIGHLIGHTS (bimonthly); 1973—DRAGONFLY. Usual publication length, 60 pages. July, 1973 issue had center-fold of Alan Watts original haiku.
BACK ISSUES: Available from J & C Transcripts at $1.00 each for 1972/1973 issues; $.75 each for others (no choice).

ENGLISH SYMPOSIUM PAPERS

See the section on AGE AND/OR NATIONALITY: ENGLISH, AND BRITISH COMMONWEALTH for details.

HIRAM POETRY REVIEW

EDITORIAL ADDRESS: SUBSCRIPTION ADDRESS:
Hale Chatfield, Editor
P. O. Box 162   same
Hiram, Ohio 44234

PUBLISHED: Biannually   CIRCULATION: 500
COST: 1 yr.—$2.00; 3 yrs.—$5.00 (no institutions); lifetime—$50.00; single copy—$1.00.

CONTENTS: Original poetry; special feature articles on poetry; reviews of poetry books. Essay example: " 'The Step-Mother World': One More Reading of MOBY DICK."

UNSOLICITED MSS. WELCOME? Yes, but poetry only (reviews and special features by invitation only); submissions not acknowledged.
SPECIFICALLY WELCOMED: High quality poetry.
MS. LENGTH: No preference; submit typed ORIGINALS only.
COPYRIGHT: HIRAM POETRY REVIEW; but will assign to author on written request.
EDITOR'S DECISION: 1 month.
FROM ACCEPTANCE TO PUBLICATION: Under 6 months.
PAYMENT/OFFPRINTS: Two copies, plus one year's subscription. Contributors may purchase additional copies at 40% off.
REJECTED MSS.: Returned.
GENERAL: First issue, Fall-Winter, 1966. Usual publication length, 36 pages.
BACK ISSUES: Available from editorial address at $50 for #2, $20 for #3, $5.00 for #4, $2 for #5-#10, $1.00 thereafter (#1 out-of-print). Prices subject to change without notice. Also available from Xerox University Microfilms.

INTERNATIONAL POETRY REVIEW

EDITORIAL ADDRESS:
Henry Picola, Editor
1060 North Saint Andrews Place
Hollywood, California 90038

SUBSCRIPTION ADDRESS:

same

CIRCULATION: 5,000

COST: Sample copy available to potential contributor for $1.00.

CONTENTS: Biographical articles about poets, focusing on new material about a poet's experiences, contemporaries, or other influences on his writing; interviews; humor; poetry (all forms); photographs.

UNSOLICITED MSS. WELCOME? Inquire of editor first.
SPECIFICALLY WELCOMED: Poetry on timely issues.
MS. LENGTH: Articles—up to 1,800 words.
EDITOR'S DECISION: 1 month.
PAYMENT/OFFPRINTS: Payment for articles; occasionally prizes for poetry.
GENERAL: First issue, 1961.

THE JOURNAL OF NARRATIVE TECHNIQUE

See the section on GENRES: PROSE for details.

THE LANGUAGE OF POEMS

EDITORIAL ADDRESS:
Richard Gunter, Editor
Department of English
University of South Carolina
Columbia, South Carolina 29208

SUBSCRIPTION ADDRESS:

same

PUBLISHED: 2 or 3 times yearly (irregularly)
COST: Free.

CONTENTS: Close linguistic interpretations of poems (descriptions of the grammar and paraphrases of the meaning); occasional theoretical article about some aspect of linguistics or semantics. The whole journal has a somewhat linguistic and epistemological flavor. Its central purpose is to raise this question: What does it mean to have read a poem and to have understood it? Volume I is devoted to Gerard Manley Hopkins and Volume II to E. E. Cummings and others.

UNSOLICITED MSS. WELCOME? All articles are assigned except for short notes; submissions acknowledged.
SPECIFICALLY WELCOMED: Short notes that take exception to explications previously run, or that amplify or elaborate points in those explications.
MS. LENGTH: 100-300 words; submit ONE copy.
STYLE REQUIREMENTS: Contributor should consult "Notes and Comments" in issues already published; notes should be simple, crisp and clear.
COPYRIGHT: Editor, but will reassign it to the writer on request.
EDITOR'S DECISION: A month or so.
FROM ACCEPTANCE TO PUBLICATION: Variable.
PAYMENT/OFFPRINTS: Five free copies of issue containing contributor's work.
REJECTED MSS.: Returned.
GENERAL: First issue, January, 1972. Usual publication length, 15 pages.
BACK ISSUES: Available free from editorial office.

MODERN HAIKU

EDITORIAL ADDRESS:
Mrs. Kay Titus Mormino, Editor
414 North Orange Drive
Los Angeles, California 90036

SUBSCRIPTION ADDRESS:

same

PUBLISHED: Tri-annually
CIRCULATION: 600
COST: 1 yr.—$4.00; 2 yrs.—$7.50; 3 yrs.—$10.75; rates for multiple copies to same address.

CONTENTS: Limited to haiku, senryu, and prose related to these; book reviews, articles on aspects of writing or understanding haiku and on outstanding poets; some original art and occasional meaningful photographs.

UNSOLICITED MSS. WELCOME? Yes; submissions acknowledged.
SPECIFICALLY WELCOMED: Haiku.
MS. LENGTH: 3 lines; submit ONE copy.
STYLE REQUIREMENTS: Those pertinent to haiku. Submit only one poem on a page of paper.
COPYRIGHT: MODERN HAIKU but permission to reprint is always given.
EDITOR'S DECISION: 8 weeks.
FROM ACCEPTANCE TO PUBLICATION: 4 weeks.
PAYMENT/OFFPRINTS: No payment, but good prizes, several in cash, are awarded each issue.
REJECTED MSS.: Returned.
GENERAL: First issue, Winter, 1969. Usual publication length, 48 pages.
BACK ISSUES: Available from editorial office at $1.50 to $3.00 each. (The first two issues have become collectors' items.)

MODERN POETRY IN TRANSLATION

EDITORIAL ADDRESS:
Daniel Weissbort, Editor
10 Compayne Gardens
London NW6 3DH
England

SUBSCRIPTION ADDRESS:

same

PUBLISHED: Quarterly
CIRCULATION: 1,500-2,000
COST: 1 yr.—$6.00 in U.S.; £2 in U.K.; £2.25 elsewhere; single copy—$1.50 or 50p.

CONTENTS: Translated modern poetry; originally concentrated exclusively on presenting original material with some bio-bibliographical information; now includes reviews, interviews, essays (by poets). Recent individual issues devoted to somewhat neglected areas: e.g. Slovenia, Turkey, Czechoslovakia, Portugal.

UNSOLICITED MSS. WELCOME? Yes, but most issues are largely planned; submissions not acknowledged.
SPECIFICALLY WELCOMED: Translations of work by lesser known writers rather than re-translation of the much translated ones. Bias toward literal translation but not dogmatic here.
MS. LENGTH: No preference; submit ONE copy.
STYLE REQUIREMENTS: Not interested in "imitations."
COPYRIGHT: The translator/author.
EDITOR'S DECISION: Varies.
FROM ACCEPTANCE TO PUBLICATION: Varies.
PAYMENT/OFFPRINTS: Small payment, if anything.
REJECTED MSS.: Returned.
GENERAL: First issue, 1965. Usual publication length, 32 pages.
BACK ISSUES: Available from editorial address at $1.50 for Nos. 1, 6, 9, 10, 11, 12, 15, and 16; $1.25 for Nos. 4, 5, 8; $3.00 for Nos. 13/14; Nos. 2, 3, and 7 out of print.

MODERN POETRY STUDIES

EDITORIAL ADDRESS:
Editors
147 Capen Boulevard
Buffalo, New York 14226

SUBSCRIPTION ADDRESS:

same

GENERAL: This periodical had not arrived by the time the entry went to press. Potential subscribers, contributors, or collectors will have to write the editor to see whether the journal still exists, and if so, to inquire about details of manuscript submission, style, back issues, and the like.

PAPERS OF THE MMLA

See the section on AGE AND/OR NATIONALITY: AMERICAN AND ENGLISH for details.

PARNASSUS: POETRY IN REVIEW

EDITORIAL ADDRESS:
Herbert Leibowitz, Editor
216 West 89th Street
New York, New York 10024

SUBSCRIPTION ADDRESS:

same

PUBLISHED: Biannually (Fall/ Winter, Spring/Summer)   CIRCULATION: 750
COST: 1 yr.—$7.00; 2 yrs.—$13.00; $1.00 extra outside of U.S.; single copy—$3.50.

CONTENTS: Essays and reviews solely devoted to poetry; occasional photographs of poets. Examples: "Ashberry's Meditations"; "Latin American Poetry: Excavations of El Dorado."

UNSOLICITED MSS. WELCOME? No.
GENERAL: First issue, Fall/Winter, 1972. Usual publication length, 220 pages.
BACK ISSUES: Available from editorial address at $3.50 each.

POET AND CRITIC

EDITORIAL ADDRESS:
Richard Gustafson, Editor
210 Pearson Hall
Iowa State University
Ames, Iowa 50010

SUBSCRIPTION ADDRESS:
The Iowa State University Press
Press Building
Ames, Iowa 50010

PUBLISHED: Tri-annually
CIRCULATION: 600
COST: 1 yr.—$3.00; 2 yrs.—$5.00; $.25 extra per year for foreign subscriptions; single copy—$1.00.

CONTENTS: Poetry; comments by contributors on each others' work; articles; reviews; occasional illustration. Example article: "The Peace of a Good Line."

UNSOLICITED MSS. WELCOME? Yes; submissions not acknowledged.
SPECIFICALLY WELCOMED: Poetry.
MS. LENGTH: 3,000 words—prose; submit ONE copy.
STYLE REQUIREMENTS: MLA STYLE SHEET.
COPYRIGHT: Author.
EDITOR'S DECISION: 1 month.
FROM ACCEPTANCE TO PUBLICATION: 3 months.
PAYMENT/OFFPRINTS: Complimentary copies; discounts on extra copies. $30 for best poem in each issue.
REJECTED MSS.: Returned.
GENERAL: First issue, Fall, 1964. Usual publication length, 48 pages.
BACK ISSUES: Available from Johnson Reprint Society at Iowa State University Press. Consult Johnson Reprint Society about price.

POET LORE: A NATIONAL QUARTERLY OF WORLD POETRY

EDITORIAL ADDRESS:
John Williams Andrews, Editor-in-Chief
Literary Publications Foundations Inc.
52 Cranbury Road
Box 688
Westport, Connecticut 06880

SUBSCRIPTION ADDRESS:

same

PUBLISHED: Quarterly
CIRCULATION: 1,200-1,400
COST: 1 yr.—$8.00; 2 yrs.—$14.00.

CONTENTS: Groups of poems by single authors and poems of a group of poets, associated or working together in "Showcase for Poets"; reviews of current books of poetry; Books in Brief, Books Received sections; contributors mentioned.

UNSOLICITED MSS. WELCOME? Yes; submissions not acknowledged.
SPECIFICALLY WELCOMED: Poetry.
MS. LENGTH: No restrictions; submit ONE copy.

STYLE REQUIREMENTS: Any style as long as BEAUTY, CLARITY, PROFUNDITY are there.
COPYRIGHT: POET LORE; author retains rights.
EDITOR'S DECISION: 3-4 months.
FROM ACCEPTANCE TO PUBLICATION: 6 months.
PAYMENT/OFFPRINTS: Free copy of magazine. No offprints.
REJECTED MSS.: Returned.
GENERAL: First issue, 1889. Usual publication length, 135 pages.
BACK ISSUES: Available from editorial address at $3.00 each; special discount to libraries.

POETRY

EDITORIAL ADDRESS:
Daryl Hine, Editor
1228 N. Dearborn Parkway
Chicago, Illinois 60610

SUBSCRIPTION ADDRESS:

same

PUBLISHED: Monthly
COST: 1 yr.—$15.00; 2 yrs.—$28.00.

CIRCULATION: 9,000

CONTENTS: Original poetry; reviews of poetry books—one of the chief resources for poetry appraisals.

UNSOLICITED MSS. WELCOME? Poems, yes; submissions not acknowledged.
SPECIFICALLY WELCOMED: Poetry.
MS. LENGTH: 5 or 6 poems; submit ONE copy.
COPYRIGHT: Modern Poetry Association (publisher); released on author's request.
EDITOR'S DECISION: 6 weeks.
FROM ACCEPTANCE TO PUBLICATION: 4-6 months.
PAYMENT/OFFPRINTS: $1 per line. Two copies for each contributor.
REJECTED MSS.: Returned.
GENERAL: First issue, October, 1912. Usual publication length, 64 pages.
BACK ISSUES: Available from AMS Press, Inc.; price varies.

POETRY REVIEW

EDITORIAL ADDRESS:
Eric Mottram, Editor
21 Earls Court Square
London S. W. 5
England

SUBSCRIPTION ADDRESS:
The Poetry Society
same

PUBLISHED: Tri-annually

CIRCULATION: 2,500

COST: 1 yr.—£1.60; single copy—60p.

CONTENTS: Poems; articles of interest regarding contemporary poetry—though emphasis has been on poetry.

UNSOLICITED MSS. WELCOME? Yes; submissions not acknowledged.
SPECIFICALLY WELCOMED: Articles and poems or translations of poems.
MS. LENGTH: Flexible. Long poems not often published (maximum 30 lines, normally); submit ONE copy.
STYLE REQUIREMENTS: All considered.
COPYRIGHT: The Poetry Society.
EDITOR'S DECISION: 3 weeks.
FROM ACCEPTANCE TO PUBLICATION: Up to 3 months.
PAYMENT/OFFPRINTS: £10, regardless of number of poems accepted; one voucher copy.
REJECTED MSS.: Returned.
GENERAL: First issue, 1909. Usual publication length, 95-100 pages.
BACK ISSUES: Available from editorial address at 40 p. each plus postage.

REVIEW: A MAGAZINE OF POETRY AND CRITICISM

EDITORIAL ADDRESS: SUBSCRIPTION ADDRESS:
Ian Hamilton, Editor
72 Westbourne Terrace   same
London, W. 2
England

GENERAL: This periodical had not arrived by the time the entry went to press. Potential subscribers, contributors, or collectors will have to write the editor to see whether the journal still exists, and if so, to inquire about details of manuscript submission, style, back issues, and the like.

THE SPARROW MAGAZINE

EDITORIAL ADDRESS: SUBSCRIPTION ADDRESS:
Felix and Selma Stefanile, Editors
103 Waldron Street   same
West Lafayette, Indiana 47906

PUBLISHED: Biannually   CIRCULATION: 400
COST: 1 yr.—$2.00 for individuals; $2.50 for libraries and institutions.

CONTENTS: Modern poetry; features in-depth reviews and criticism; relevant topical comment on the poetry scene; translations. Note: poems originally appearing in SPARROW have been included in the better known anthologies, including Allen's "New American Poetry," Hall, Pack and Simpson's "New Poets of England and America," Untermeyer, and Bantam Books "Modern European Poetry."

UNSOLICITED MSS. WELCOME? Yes; submissions not acknowledged.
SPECIFICALLY WELCOMED: Anything that strikes editors' "fairly well-developed literary predilections. We are lively, and oppose pretentiousness."
MS. LENGTH: No limit; submit ONE copy.
STYLE REQUIREMENTS: Freshness, accuracy, and zest.
COPYRIGHT: Editors take first rights; release on request.
EDITOR'S DECISION: 6 weeks.
FROM ACCEPTANCE TO PUBLICATION: 6-8 months lead time.
PAYMENT/OFFPRINTS: Modest prize system ($25.00) and copies.
REJECTED MSS.: Returned.
GENERAL: First issue, April, 1954. Usual publication length, 48 pages; slowly expanding, now 52 pages. Editors also publish the Vagrom Chap Books.
BACK ISSUES: Magazine is a collector's item. First ten copies are extremely rare. Those available can be obtained from editorial office. Only #26 is sold at sample copy price of $.50. Purchaser should query prices of others. For Microfilm reprints contact Xerox University Microfilms.

TENNESSEE POETRY JOURNAL (suspended publication)

EDITORIAL ADDRESS:
Stephen Mooney, Editor

SUBSCRIPTION ADDRESS:
English Department
University of Tennessee
Martin, Tennessee 38237

PUBLISHED: Tri-quarterly
COST: All issues are $3.00 each depending on availability.

CONTENTS: Poetry; some interviews with poets; a few photographs and essays. Special issues devoted to David Ignatow, William Stafford, Robert Bly, William Matthews, Donald Hall, John Lindsey.

GENERAL: Issued Fall, 1967-Spring, 1971 (Vol. 4, #3). Ceased publication in Spring of 1971 after the death of founder-editor-publisher Stephen Mooney. Last issue was memorial to Mooney.
BACK ISSUES: Available from Stephen Mooney Memorial Fund (cash payment) or from the University of Tennessee, c/o English Department, Martin, Tennessee 38237 (money order or check), at $3.00 each. All orders are subject to what is available. Unavailable issue orders will be returned.

THE WESTIGAN REVIEW

EDITORIAL ADDRESS:
John Knapp II, Editor
Swetman Hall
State University College
Oswego, New York 13126

SUBSCRIPTION ADDRESS:

same

PUBLISHED: 1 or 2 times yearly, "occasionally"
COST: 4 issues—$2.00.

CIRCULATION: 400

CONTENTS: Contemporary poetry and comment about poetry. The first seven issues included poetry from writers in about 40 states.

UNSOLICITED MSS. WELCOME? Yes; submissions not acknowledged.
SPECIFICALLY WELCOMED: Poetry; infrequently editor accepts unsolicited comment on poetry.
MS. LENGTH: No preference; submit ONE copy.
STYLE REQUIREMENTS: Original typed manuscripts.
COPYRIGHT: THE WESTIGAN REVIEW, but reprint rights freely given.
EDITOR'S DECISION: 1-6 weeks.
FROM ACCEPTANCE TO PUBLICATION: 2 weeks to 1 year.
PAYMENT/OFFPRINTS: Copies of the issue in which work appears.
REJECTED MSS.: Returned.
GENERAL: First issue, January, 1970. Usual publication length, 32-40 pages.
BACK ISSUES: Available from editorial address. Price varies; usually original value.

THEATRE

ASIAN THEATRE BULLETIN

EDITORIAL ADDRESS:
Samuel Leiter, Editor
Department of Speech and Theater
Brooklyn College
Brooklyn, New York 11210

SUBSCRIPTION ADDRESS:
Nancy Ferrell
American Theatre Association
1317 F Street, NW
Washington, D.C. 20004

PUBLISHED: Biannually   CIRCULATION: 2,000
COST: $1.00 per issue for members of ATA, other than those whose program membership includes receipt of bulletin; $2.00 per issue to non-members.

CONTENTS: Reports on American productions of Asian plays (professional and amateur); activities of persons involved in Asian theatre research and performance; reports from Japan, Korea, India, etc. on theater activities there; book reviews; dissertation abstracts of Ph.D.'s in Asian Theater Studies; bibliographies; convention reports. Example: "Chinese Shadow Plays."

UNSOLICITED MSS. WELCOME? Yes; submissions acknowledged.
SPECIFICALLY WELCOMED: Materials relating to Asian theater activities, especially as they are connected to college and university programs.
MS. LENGTH: 800 words or less; submit ONE copy.
STYLE REQUIREMENTS: Formal and informal—newsletter style.
COPYRIGHT: American Theatre Association.
EDITOR'S DECISION: 1 month.
FROM ACCEPTANCE TO PUBLICATION: 2-6 months.
PAYMENT/OFFPRINTS: Two copies of issue.
REJECTED MSS.: Returned.
GENERAL: First issue, Spring, 1971. Usual publication length, 14-15 double-columned pages.
BACK ISSUES: Available from subscription address at $1.00 per volume or on microfiche from Professor Andrew Tsubaki, International Theatre Studies Center, University of Kansas, Lawrence, Kansas 66044.

ASTR: AMERICAN SOCIETY FOR THEATRE RESEARCH NEWSLETTER

EDITORIAL ADDRESS:
B. Beinstein, Acting Editor
Department of English
C. W. Post College
Greenvale, New York 11548

SUBSCRIPTION ADDRESS:
William Green, Secretary-Treasurer
c/o American Society for Theatre Research
Department of English
Queens College
Flushing, New York 11367

CIRCULATION: 400

CONTENTS: Theatre news; articles on books in progress or in print; what's happening this month on campuses (i.e. theatre department introducing new programs, courses, events, personnel). Examples: "Brander Matthews Dramatic Museum"; "What's Happening to the Dance Historian."

UNSOLICITED MSS. WELCOME? Yes.
SPECIFICALLY WELCOMED: Theatre news, especially from and about ASTR members; journalistic articles, snappy reviews, spicy items of speculation or information.
MS. LENGTH: Brief.
GENERAL: First issue of New Series, 1972. Usual publication length, 8 pages.

BLACK THEATRE

See the section on AMERICAN ETHNIC MINORITIES for details.

COMPARATIVE DRAMA

EDITORIAL ADDRESS:
Clifford Davidson, C. J. Gianakaris,
John H. Stroupe, Editors
Department of English
Western Michigan University
Kalamazoo, Michigan 49001

SUBSCRIPTION ADDRESS:

same

PUBLISHED: Quarterly (Spring, Summer, Fall, Winter)
CIRCULATION: 700
COST: Individuals: 1 yr.—$3.50; 2 yrs.—$6.00 (outside U.S. and Canada, add $.50 per yr.) Institutions: 1 yr.—$5.00; 2 yrs.—$10.00 (outside U.S. and Canada, add $1.00 per yr.).

CONTENTS: Critical studies of dramatic literature which are international in spirit and interdisciplinary in scope. Examples: "Kabuki Today and Tomorrow"; "Nietzsche, Georg Brandes, and Ibsen's MASTER BUILDER"; "The Theatre of the Absurd in Spanish America."

UNSOLICITED MSS. WELCOME? Yes; submissions acknowledged.
SPECIFICALLY WELCOMED: Work on drama of all nations and all periods.
MS. LENGTH: 2,000-5,000 words; submit TWO copies.
STYLE REQUIREMENTS: MLA STYLE SHEET; footnotes follow essay (incorporate into text when possible).
COPYRIGHT: Editors.
EDITOR'S DECISION: 2-4 weeks normally.
FROM ACCEPTANCE TO PUBLICATION: 6 months.
PAYMENT/OFFPRINTS: Two copies of entire issue. 20 to 40 offprints gratis.
REJECTED MSS.: Returned.

GENERAL: First issue, Spring, 1967. Usual publication length, 80-90 pages. Free sample copies are available on request. Title pages and indexes are supplied to subscribers.
BACK ISSUES: Vols. I-III available from Johnson Reprint Corp. at $15.00 per volume. Rest available from editorial address at $2.50 per issue.

DRAMA AND THEATRE (formerly FIRST STAGE)

EDITORIAL ADDRESS:
Henry F. Salerno, Editor
Department of English
State University College
Fredonia, New York 14063

SUBSCRIPTION ADDRESS:

same

PUBLISHED: Tri-annually
COST: 1 yr.—$4.50; 2 yrs.—$8.00; single copy—$1.50.

CIRCULATION: 1,500

CONTENTS: Plays; articles; interviews; book reviews; photographs. Examples: "An Interview with British Poet, Ted Hughes"; "Goering's SEESCHLACHT, a New ANTIGONE?"

UNSOLICITED MSS. WELCOME? Yes; submissions acknowledged.
SPECIFICALLY WELCOMED: New plays, long and short; articles on the contemporary theater; interviews with noted playwrights, directors, and producers.
MS. LENGTH: 3,000 words (articles); submit ONE copy.
COPYRIGHT: Author.
EDITOR'S DECISION: 2-4 months.
FROM ACCEPTANCE TO PUBLICATION: 6 months to 1 year.
PAYMENT/OFFPRINTS: Ten complimentary copies; others at a discount.
REJECTED MSS.: Returned.
GENERAL: First issue, November, 1961. Usual publication length, 68 pages.
BACK ISSUES: Available from editorial address at $1.50 each; also from Xerox University Microfilms.

EDUCATIONAL THEATRE JOURNAL

EDITORIAL ADDRESS:
Anthony Graham-White, Editor
Theatre Department
Meadows School of the Arts
Southern Methodist University
Dallas, Texas 75222

SUBSCRIPTION ADDRESS:
American Theatre Association
1317 F Street, N.W.
Washington, D.C. 20004

PUBLISHED: Quarterly (Mar., May, Oct., Dec.)

CIRCULATION: 6,410

COST: 1 yr.—$9.00 ATA members (libraries—$12.50; 2 yrs.—$23.50; 3 yrs.—$31.50); single copy $2.50 ($3.50 to non-ATA members).

CONTENTS: Articles on theatre history and dramatic literature and others relevant to college-level theatre education; book reviews; bibliographies; reviews of theatre productions; occasional photographs. Examples: "Remembering Tom Robertson (1829-1871)"; "Dramatic Multitude and Mystical Experience: W. B. Yeats."

UNSOLICITED MSS. WELCOME? Yes; submissions acknowledged.
SPECIFICALLY WELCOMED: Interviews, bibliographies, translations of critical articles and documents of theatre history.
MS. LENGTH: 5-40 pages; submit TWO copies.
STYLE REQUIREMENTS: MLA STYLE SHEET.
COPYRIGHT: American Theatre Association, unless author specifies otherwise.
EDITOR'S DECISION: 8 weeks.
FROM ACCEPTANCE TO PUBLICATION: 6 months to 1 year.
PAYMENT/OFFPRINTS: Author orders offprints from press (minimum 100).
REJECTED MSS.: Returned.
GENERAL: First issue, 1949. Usual publication length, 160 pages. Editor has three-year term (present editor, 1972-1975). Theatre review editor. Book review editor.
BACK ISSUES: Available from American Theatre Association.

HORIZON: MAGAZINE OF THE ARTS

See the section on LITERARY REVIEWS for details.

LATIN AMERICAN THEATRE REVIEW

EDITORIAL ADDRESS: SUBSCRIPTION ADDRESS:
George Woodyard, Editor
Center of Latin American Studies same
University of Kansas
Lawrence, Kansas 66045

PUBLISHED: Biannually CIRCULATION: 700
COST: 1 yr.—$4.00 for individuals; $6.00 for institutions.

CONTENTS: Scholarly articles, book reviews, and news and notes about recent theatrical activities in Latin America. Also play synopses, works in progress, materials received and bibliography, visiting theatre personnel, etc.

UNSOLICITED MSS. WELCOME? Yes; submissions acknowledged.

SPECIFICALLY WELCOMED: Histories of theatre activity in a particular city, of a single performing company or of a theatre institution; critical assessments of the works of an individual playwright or a theatrical movement; studies of the accomplishments of an actor, director, or other contributor to Latin American theatre; bibliographies.

MS. LENGTH: 15-25 pages; submit ONE copy.
STYLE REQUIREMENTS: MLA STYLE SHEET.
COPYRIGHT: LATIN AMERICAN THEATRE REVIEW.
EDITOR'S DECISION: 2-3 months.
FROM ACCEPTANCE TO PUBLICATION: 3-8 months.
PAYMENT/OFFPRINTS: 25 free offprints; no extras available.
REJECTED MSS.: Returned.
GENERAL: First issue, Fall, 1967. Usual publication length, 90-100 pages.
BACK ISSUES: Available from Center for Latin American Studies at $4.00 each.

MODERN DRAMA

EDITORIAL ADDRESS:
F. J. Marker, Editor
Graduate Centre for the
Study of the Drama
Massey College
University of Toronto
Toronto 5, Ontario
Canada

SUBSCRIPTION ADDRESS:
Alan E. Samuel
A. M. Hakkert Ltd. Publishers
554 Spadina Crescent
Toronto 179, Ontario
Canada

PUBLISHED: Quarterly (May, Sept., Dec., Feb.)
COST: 1 yr.—$4.00; single copy—$1.50.

CIRCULATION: 3,000

CONTENTS: Critical essays on drama and dramatists since Ibsen; book reviews. Examples: "Strindberg and the New Poetics"; "William Saroyan: Romantic Existentialist"; "Exorcism and Baptism in Le Roi Jones's THE TOILET."

UNSOLICITED MSS. WELCOME? Yes.
MS. LENGTH: Articles up to 4,000 words; book reviews—500 word maximum.
STYLE REQUIREMENTS: MLA STYLE SHEET.
PAYMENT/OFFPRINTS: Offprints available.
GENERAL: First issue, 1958. Usual publication length, 110 pages.
BACK ISSUES: Available from publisher at $1.50 each.

NINETEENTH CENTURY THEATRE RESEARCH

EDITORIAL ADDRESS:
L. W. Connolly and
J. P. Wearing, Editors
Department of English
University of Alberta
Edmonton T6G 2E1 Canada

SUBSCRIPTION ADDRESS:

same

PUBLISHED: Biannually (March, September)
COST: 1 yr.—$3.00 for individuals; $5.00 for institutions; single copies to individuals—$2.00, institutions—$3.00. Canadian funds or add $.50.

CONTENTS: Scholarly research into 19th century theatre of the English speaking world; book reviews; work-in-progress; notes and queries; books received. Examples: "Bunn, Byron, and MANFRED"; "Burletta and the Early Nineteenth-Century English Theatre."

UNSOLICITED MSS. WELCOME? Yes; submissions acknowledged.
SPECIFICALLY WELCOMED: Scholarly articles of high quality.
MS. LENGTH: 5,000 words, but consider any length; submit TWO copies.
STYLE REQUIREMENTS: MLA STYLE SHEET.
COPYRIGHT: Author.
EDITOR'S DECISION: 1-2 months.
FROM ACCEPTANCE TO PUBLICATION: 6 months.
PAYMENT/OFFPRINTS: 25 offprints.
REJECTED MSS.: Returned.
GENERAL: First issue, March, 1973. Usual publication length, 64 pages.
BACK ISSUES: Available from editorial address at $2.00 each (institutions—$3.00 each). Canadian funds or add $.50.

PLAYERS: THE MAGAZINE OF AMERICAN THEATRE

EDITORIAL ADDRESS:
Byron Schaffer, Jr., Editor
NIU Theatre
DeKalb, Illinois 60115

SUBSCRIPTION ADDRESS:
Circulation Department
same

PUBLISHED: 6 times yearly
COST: 1 yr.—$5.00; 2 yrs.—$8.50; foreign, $1.00 extra per year.

CIRCULATION: 8,000

CONTENTS: Articles on all aspects of the American theatre scene; interviews; photographs. Examples: "Camping Out: TINY ALICE and Susan Sontag"; "Physical Metaphor: An Acting Technique"; "Tenderness in Brutality: The Plays of Ed Bullins."

UNSOLICITED MSS. WELCOME? Yes; submissions acknowledged.
SPECIFICALLY WELCOMED: Articles on any and every aspect of American theatre.

MS. LENGTH: 4,000-6,000 words; submit ONE copy.
STYLE REQUIREMENTS: MLA STYLE SHEET; footnotes follow article.
COPYRIGHT: PLAYERS MAGAZINE.
EDITOR'S DECISION: Varies.
FROM ACCEPTANCE TO PUBLICATION: Soon.
PAYMENT/OFFPRINTS: Five free copies; any more are negotiable.
REJECTED MSS.: Returned.
GENERAL: First issue, 1924. Usual publication length, 50 pages. Indexed by volume.
BACK ISSUES: Available from Circulation Department at $1.25 each.

PLAYS AND PLAYERS (Incorporating THEATRE WORLD, ENCORE, PLAY PICTORIAL, SHOWS ILLUSTRATED)

EDITORIAL ADDRESS:
Peter Ansorge, Editor
Hansom Books at
Artillery Mansions
75 Victoria Street
London SW1H OH2
England

SUBSCRIPTION ADDRESS:
Circulation Department
same

PUBLISHED: Monthly
COST: Single copy—40p.

CONTENTS: Articles related to the theater; reviews of plays; centrefold featuring a complete text; playguide; letters; cues; books; scripts. Examples: "Images of World Theatre"; "Visconti versus Pinter."

UNSOLICITED MSS. WELCOME? Contact the editor.
COPYRIGHT: Hansom Books.
GENERAL: First issue, 1953. Usual publication length, 74 pages.

RENAISSANCE DRAMA

See the section on AGE AND/OR NATIONALITY: CONTINENTAL—CLASSICAL, MEDIEVAL AND RENAISSANCE for details.

RESEARCH OPPORTUNITIES IN RENAISSANCE DRAMA

See the section on AGE AND/OR NATIONALITY: CONTINENTAL—CLASSICAL, MEDIEVAL AND RENAISSANCE for details.

RESTORATION AND 18TH CENTURY THEATRE RESEARCH
(formerly 17TH AND 18TH CENTURY THEATRE RESEARCH)

EDITORIAL ADDRESS:
John S. Shea, Editor
English Department
Loyola University
820 North Michigan Avenue
Chicago, Illinois 60611

SUBSCRIPTION ADDRESS:

same

PUBLISHED: Biannually
COST: 1 yr.—$3.00.

CIRCULATION: 1,000

CONTENTS: Articles devoted primarily to research on the theatre itself and on all aspects of theatre activity rather than to criticism of individual plays. RECTR includes an annual bibliography (annotated) of books, articles, and dissertations concerned with Restoration and eighteenth century theatre research. Works in progress in the field are published regularly.

UNSOLICITED MSS. WELCOME? Yes; submissions acknowledged.
SPECIFICALLY WELCOMED: Bibliography, research on production of plays, actors, billing.
MS. LENGTH: Under 5,000 words; submit ONE copy.
STYLE REQUIREMENTS: MLA STYLE SHEET.
COPYRIGHT: RECTR.
EDITOR'S DECISION: 3-6 months.
FROM ACCEPTANCE TO PUBLICATION: 6-18 months.
PAYMENT/OFFPRINTS: 5 copies of issue in which author's work appears.
REJECTED MSS.: Returned.
GENERAL: First issue, 1962. Usual publication length, 64 pages.
BACK ISSUES: Some available from editorial office at $1.50 each. Bound volumes 1-3, 4-6, 7-9 available from Johnson Reprint Corporation at $17.50 per volume.

TDR: THE DRAMA REVIEW

EDITORIAL ADDRESS:
Michael Kirby, Editor
32 Washington Place, Rm. 73
New York, New York 10003

SUBSCRIPTION ADDRESS:

same

PUBLISHED: Quarterly
COST: 1 yr.—$9.50 (student—$7.50); 2 yrs.—$17.00; single copy—$3.00.

CIRCULATION: 15,000

CONTENTS: Documents; historical and contemporary trends in the full range of performing arts—theatre, music, film, TV, dance; interviews. Essay example: "Peking Drama with Contemporary Themes"; "Rock Theatricality"; "Genet's Theatre of Possession."

UNSOLICITED MSS. WELCOME? Yes; submissions acknowledged.
SPECIFICALLY WELCOMED: Essays; theory; translations of historically significant scripts.
MS. LENGTH: 10-20 pages; submit TWO copies.
COPYRIGHT: Author and magazine.
EDITOR'S DECISION: 3 months.
FROM ACCEPTANCE TO PUBLICATION: 3-6 months.
PAYMENT/OFFPRINTS: 2 cents per word. Offprints can be arranged.
REJECTED MSS.: Returned.
GENERAL: First issue, 1955. Usual publication length, 160-200 pages.
BACK ISSUES: Available from editorial address at $3.00 each; special rates for bulk orders.

THEATRE ANNUAL

EDITORIAL ADDRESS:
John V. Falconier, Editor
John Cabot International College
Viale Pola, 12
Rome
Italy

SUBSCRIPTION ADDRESS:
Hiram College
Hiram, Ohio

PUBLISHED: Annually
COST: 1 yr.—$2.00.

CIRCULATION: 600

CONTENTS: History of theatre: authors, scenography, criticism.

UNSOLICITED MSS. WELCOME? Yes; submissions acknowledged.
MS. LENGTH: 15 pages; submit ONE copy.
STYLE REQUIREMENTS: MLA STYLE SHEET.
COPYRIGHT: THEATRE ANNUAL.
EDITOR'S DECISION: 3 months.
FROM ACCEPTANCE TO PUBLICATION: 8 months.
PAYMENT/OFFPRINTS: No payment. Offprints available at author's expense.
REJECTED MSS.: Returned.
GENERAL: First issue, 1934. Usual publication length, 100 pages.
BACK ISSUES: Available from subscription address at $2.00 each.

THEATRE ARTS

EDITORIAL ADDRESS:
Bruce Bohle, Editor
Theatre Publications, Inc.
104 East 40th Street
New York, New York 10016

SUBSCRIPTION ADDRESS:

same

PUBLISHED: Monthly

CONTENTS: Interviews; plays; "Theatre Bookshelf"; photographs; essays, such as "Ghana's Young Theatre"; "Eugene O'Neill: The Tragic in Exile"; "The British National Theatre"; "The Playwright and the Contemporary World."

UNSOLICITED MSS. WELCOME? Contact editor.
COPYRIGHT: Theatre Publications, Inc.
GENERAL: First issue, 1919. Usual publication length, 80 pages.

THEATRE STUDIES: THE JOURNAL OF THE OHIO STATE UNIVERSITY THEATRE RESEARCH INSTITUTE (formerly THE OSU THEATRE COLLECTION BULLETIN)

EDITORIAL ADDRESS:
Editor
The OSU Theatre Research Institute
309 Thompson Library
1858 Neil Avenue
Columbus, Ohio 43210

SUBSCRIPTION ADDRESS:
same

PUBLISHED: Annually
COST: Free.

CIRCULATION: 1,500

CONTENTS: Scholarly research in theatre history; illustrations; reviews of dissertations.

UNSOLICITED MSS. WELCOME? No.
GENERAL: First issue, 1954. Usual publication length, 90 pages.
BACK ISSUES: Available from OSU Theatre Research Institute at $.50 handling charge per issue. Out of print issues are furnished for the cost of xeroxing.

THEATRE SURVEY: THE AMERICAN JOURNAL OF THEATRE HISTORY

EDITORIAL ADDRESS:
Attillio Favorini, Executive Editor
Department of Speech and Theatre Arts
University of Pittsburgh
Pittsburgh, Pennsylvania 15213

SUBSCRIPTION ADDRESS:
1117 CL
University of Pittsburgh
Pittsburgh, Pennsylvania 15213

PUBLISHED: Biannually (May, Nov.) with occasional special issues.
COST: 1 yr.—$5.00, $5.50 outside of U.S.; single issue—$2.50.

CIRCULATION: 950

CONTENTS: Articles, brief notes, and comments in the field of theatre history; illustrations. Examples: "Toward a Reappraisal of the Children's Troupes."

UNSOLICITED MSS. WELCOME? Yes; submissions acknowledged.
SPECIFICALLY WELCOMED: Articles, notes, comment; articles on drama interpretation are NOT considered unless they are addressed to the history of the performed drama.
MS. LENGTH: No preference; submit THREE copies.
STYLE REQUIREMENTS: University of Chicago's A MANUAL OF STYLE; footnotes follow article.
COPYRIGHT: American Society for Theatre Research, Inc.
EDITOR'S DECISION: 3 months.
FROM ACCEPTANCE TO PUBLICATION: 8 months.
PAYMENT/OFFPRINTS: 25 complimentary offprints; more at $10 for 25.
REJECTED MSS.: Returned.
GENERAL: First issue, 1960. Usual publication length, 90 pages.
BACK ISSUES: Available from subscription address at $2.50 each.

YALE/THEATRE

EDITORIAL ADDRESS:
Editors
2046 Yale Station
New Haven, Connecticut 065 20

SUBSCRIPTION ADDRESS:
Box 802
Meriden, Connecticut 06450

PUBLISHED: Tri-annually
COST: 1 yr.—$5.50; 2 yrs.—$10.50; single copy—$2.00.

CONTENTS: Articles on the theatre (drama in general, specific plays and playwrights and all other aspects); interviews; bibliographies; photographs. Themes have included: Politics and Imagination; Sex and the Single Theatre; The Living Theatre; New Playwrights; Education vs. Theatre; Film and Design; Story Theatre. Example: "Georg Büchner: History Redeemed."

UNSOLICITED MSS. WELCOME? Yes.
MS. LENGTH: 3,000-10,000 words.
STYLE REQUIREMENTS: MLA STYLE SHEET.
COPYRIGHT: yale/theatre.
GENERAL: First issue, 1968. Usual publication length, 112 pages.
BACK ISSUES: Available from subscription address at $1.50 each for Vol. 1, #2 and #3; $2.00 each for issues of Vol. 2 onward.

PROSE: FICTION AND NON-FICTION

ATHANOR

EDITORIAL ADDRESS:
Douglas Calhoun, Editor
P.O. Box 582
Clarkson, New York 14430

SUBSCRIPTION ADDRESS:

same

PUBLISHED: Biannually
COST: Four issues—$5.00; single copy—$1.50.

CIRCULATION: 500-750

CONTENTS: Poetry; fiction; critical articles; interviews; letters; graphics; checklists; occasional issue on one author (#4 was a Creeley issue, and an issue on Robert Duncan is being considered); work that is vital and contains an intensity of language in a charged field—or work about that. Examples are the works of Olson, Corman, Dorn, Duncan, Kerouac, Ginsberg, Ferlinghetti, Corso, and younger writers. Example essay: "Robert Creeley, the Domestic Muse, and Post-Modernism."

UNSOLICITED MSS. WELCOME? Yes; submissions not acknowledged.
MS. LENGTH: Brief and to the point; submit ONE copy.
STYLE REQUIREMENTS: No restrictions.
COPYRIGHT: Author.
EDITOR'S DECISION: 1 week or more.
FROM ACCEPTANCE TO PUBLICATION: Variable
PAYMENT/OFFPRINTS: Copies of issue; no offprints.
REJECTED MSS.: Returned.
GENERAL: First issue, Spring, 1971. Usual publication length, 72-84 pages.
BACK ISSUES: Available from editorial address at $5.00 for #1; $3.00 for #2; $2.00 for #3; $1.50 for current issues; and $10.00 for 1-4.

ENGLISH SYMPOSIUM PAPERS

See the section on AGE AND/OR NATIONALITY: ENGLISH, AND BRITISH COMMONWEALTH for details.

FICTION INTERNATIONAL

EDITORIAL ADDRESS:
Joe David Bellamy, Editor
Department of English
St. Lawrence University
Canton, New York 13617

SUBSCRIPTION ADDRESS:

same

PUBLISHED: Biannually
COST: 1 yr.—$4.00 (institutions, $8.00; 2 yrs.—$14.00); single copy—$2.00.

CIRCULATION: 2,000

CONTENTS: Fiction by writers seriously involved in discovering viable new forms or of working in traditional forms in fruitful new ways; contributors include Joyce Carol Oates, Robley Wilson, Jr., Ronald Sukenick. Interviews with well-known fiction writers, such as Jerzy Kosinski, Ishmael Reed, David Madden. Poetry which explores the borderline between fiction and poetry; recent contributors: Gary Gildner, William Stafford. Critiques—critical essays on or explications of difficult, important and/or ignored contemporary writers; contributors: Robert Scholes, Ihab Hassan, Raymond Federman, Jerome Klinkowitz. Short reviews usually of first collections of short fiction.

UNSOLICITED MSS. WELCOME? Yes, but not poetry; submissions not acknowledged.
SPECIFICALLY WELCOMED: Fiction; interviews; critiques; short reviews.
MS. LENGTH: Varies; submit ONE copy.
STYLE REQUIREMENTS: Check recent issues of the magazine.
COPYRIGHT: FICTION INTERNATIONAL, unless author requests reversion of copyright.
EDITOR'S DECISION: 1-2 months.
FROM ACCEPTANCE TO PUBLICATION: Varies from 1 to 5 months currently.
PAYMENT/OFFPRINTS: $5 to $150. Contributor's copies of magazine provided.
REJECTED MSS.: Returned.
GENERAL: First issue, July, 1973. Usual publication length, 130 pages. St. Lawrence Award for Fiction. FICTION INTERNATIONAL, under the auspices of St. Lawrence University and the David B. Steinman Festival of the Arts, presents an annual award—a cash prize of $1000—to the author of an outstanding first collection of short fiction published by an American publisher during that year.
BACK ISSUES: Available from editorial address at $2.00 each (individuals), $4.00 each (institutions). Microfilm and xerographic editions available from Xerox University Microfilms.

GENRE

EDITORIAL ADDRESS:
Donald E. Billiar, Edward F. Heuston, Robert Vales, Editors
Department of English
State University College
Plattsburgh, New York 12901

SUBSCRIPTION ADDRESS:

same

PUBLISHED: Quarterly
COST: 1 yr.—$5.00, individuals; $6.00, libraries; $7.00 outside of U.S. and Canada.

CIRCULATION: 550

CONTENTS: Generic criticism: theoretical discussions of the genre concept; historical studies of particular genres and genre debates; attempts to establish and define genre; interpretations of works of literature from the genre point of view; book reviews. Examples: "Form and Theme in Novels about Non-Human Characters, a Neglected Sub-Genre"; "Generic Structures in Russian Folklore."

UNSOLICITED MSS. WELCOME? Yes; submissions acknowledged.
SPECIFICALLY WELCOMED: Critical essays.
MS. LENGTH: Not important; submit TWO copies.
STYLE REQUIREMENTS: MLA STYLE SHEET with documentation minimal; notes placed after text.
COPYRIGHT: Editors.
EDITOR'S DECISION: 2-3 months.
FROM ACCEPTANCE TO PUBLICATION: Approximately 1 year.
PAYMENT/OFFPRINTS: Eight complimentary copies of issue containing article; extra copies for $.60 each.
REJECTED MSS.: Returned.
GENERAL: First issue, January, 1968. Usual publication length, 94 pages. Indexed by volume.
BACK ISSUES: Available from editorial address at $1.50 each in the U.S. and Canada, $2.00 each elsewhere, or at subscription rates for complete volumes.

THE INTERNATIONAL FICTION REVIEW

EDITORIAL ADDRESS:
S. Elkhadem, General Editor
University of New Brunswick
Fredericton, New Brunswick
Canada

SUBSCRIPTION ADDRESS:

same

PUBLISHED: Biannually
COST: 1 yr.—$6.00; 3 yrs.—$16.00.

CIRCULATION: 1,000

CONTENTS: Original research, critical essays, and reviews of modern works of fiction of European, Latin American and Oriental authors, including those national literatures which are less well-known; bibliographical notes; biographical information; reports on recent literary trends and tendencies. Examples: "The Criticism of African Fiction: Its Nature and Function"; "The Mythical Female in the Fictional Works of Pär Lagerkvist"; "Microtexts. An Aspect of the Work of Beckett, Robbe-Grillet and Nathalie Sarraute."

UNSOLICITED MSS. WELCOME? Yes; submissions acknowledged.
SPECIFICALLY WELCOMED: Reviews of recently published novels and scholarly works on fiction.
MS. LENGTH: Essays—10 pages; reviews—4 pages; short reviews—2 pages; submit ONE copy.
STYLE REQUIREMENTS: MLA STYLE SHEET.
COPYRIGHT: Writer.

EDITOR'S DECISION: 2-4 weeks.
FROM ACCEPTANCE TO PUBLICATION: 6-18 months.
PAYMENT/OFFPRINTS: Two offprints of the article or review.
REJECTED MSS.: Returned.
GENERAL: First issue, January, 1974. Usual publication length, 80-100 pages.
BACK ISSUES: Available from the General Editor at $3.00 each.

THE JOURNAL OF NARRATIVE TECHNIQUE

EDITORIAL ADDRESS:
George Perkins, General Editor
English Department
Eastern Michigan University
Ypsilanti, Michigan 48197

SUBSCRIPTION ADDRESS:
Martin L. Kornbluth,
Subscription Editor
same

PUBLISHED: Tri-annually
COST: 1 yr.—$3.00.

CIRCULATION: 400-500

CONTENTS: Scholarly essays dealing with narrative literature in English, both prose and verse, from all periods and all literary genres. In each instance, the focus of the critic is on the author's management of his narrative elements. Example: "The Martyrdom of Stephen in HARD TIMES."

UNSOLICITED MSS. WELCOME? Yes; submissions acknowledged.
SPECIFICALLY WELCOMED: Scholarly interviews and essays.
MS. LENGTH: 12-30 pages; submit ONE copy.
STYLE REQUIREMENTS: MLA STYLE SHEET; footnotes kept to minimum, in text if possible.
COPYRIGHT: Eastern Michigan University Press.
EDITOR'S DECISION: 2 weeks to 3 months.
FROM ACCEPTANCE TO PUBLICATION: 4-8 months.
PAYMENT/OFFPRINTS: Copies of the relevant issue; additional copies available at reduced rate.
REJECTED MSS.: Returned.
GENERAL: First issue, January, 1971. Usual publication length, 65 pages. This journal has an international circulation and welcomes and prints foreign submissions as well as those from the United States.
BACK ISSUES: Available from Subscription Editor at $3.00 per year. Microfilm copies available to subscribers from Xerox University Microfilms.

MODERN FICTION STUDIES

EDITORIAL ADDRESS:
Margaret Church and William T. Stafford, Editors
Department of English
Purdue University
Lafayette, Indiana 47907

SUBSCRIPTION ADDRESS:
Building D, South Campus Courts
Purdue University
West Lafayette, Indiana 47907

PUBLISHED: Quarter (Spring, Summer, Winter, Autumn)

CIRCULATION: 4,200-4,500

COST: 1 yr.—$4.00 in U.S. and Canada ($5.00 elsewhere); libraries and institutions—$5.00; single copy—$1.25 in U.S. and Canada ($1.50 elsewhere).

CONTENTS: Criticism and scholarship of and on fiction in all languages since about 1880. The Spring and Winter issues are often devoted to individual writers or groups of writers or themes. Bibliographies on the subject of these special issues are often included. Special sections of the general numbers include Notes and Discussion, Correspondence, and Recent Books on Modern Fiction; occasional photographs.

UNSOLICITED MSS. WELCOME? Yes; submissions acknowledged.
SPECIFICALLY WELCOMED: Literary criticism on scholarship about modern fiction.
MS. LENGTH: 2,000-6,000 words; submit ONE copy.
STYLE REQUIREMENTS: MLA STYLE SHEET.
COPYRIGHT: Purdue Research Foundation.
EDITOR'S DECISION: 2-3 months.
FROM ACCEPTANCE TO PUBLICATION: Up to 2 years.
PAYMENT/OFFPRINTS: Free offprints to authors.
REJECTED MSS.: Returned, sometimes criticized.
GENERAL: First issue, 1955. Usual publication length, 150-175 pages. Abstracts of articles beginning with Vol. 14, No. 1 (Spring, 1968) are on file at the MLA Abstract Office. Each volume contains author and subject indexes.
BACK ISSUES: Available from subscription address at $1.25 each.

NOVEL: A FORUM ON FICTION

EDITORIAL ADDRESS:
Edward Bloom, Senior Editor
Box 1984
Brown University
Providence, Rhode Island 02912

SUBSCRIPTION ADDRESS:

same

PUBLISHED: Tri-annually (Fall, Winter, Spring)

CIRCULATION: 1,400

COST: 1 yr.—$4.50; 2 yrs.—$7.50; 3 yrs.—$10.00; single copy—$1.50.

CONTENTS: Articles and reviews on novel theory and developments in English, American, and Continental fiction. Examples: "Community in WOMEN IN LOVE"; "Mrs. Woolf's Selfless World"; "Thematic Counterpoint in Agee."

UNSOLICITED MSS. WELCOME? Yes; submissions acknowledged.
SPECIFICALLY WELCOMED: Essays; reviews of neglected fiction or of books on fiction.
MS. LENGTH: 20 to 25 pages; submit ONE copy.
STYLE REQUIREMENTS: MLA STYLE SHEET.
COPYRIGHT: NOVEL.
EDITOR'S DECISION: 3-6 months.
FROM ACCEPTANCE TO PUBLICATION: 1 year.
PAYMENT/OFFPRINTS: $50 for articles; $35 for review essays; $10 for book reviews. Complimentary copies of issue provided.
REJECTED MSS.: Returned.
GENERAL: First issue, Fall, 1967. Usual publication length, 96 pages. Five-year cumulative index by author, subject, article and book reviews.
BACK ISSUES: Volumes 1, 2, and 3 available from Kraus Reprint Co. at $3.00 each for Vol. 1, #1 and #3, and Vol. 2, #1, #2, and #3; $5.00 for Vol. 1, #2; $1.00 each for Vol. 3, #1 and #3 (Vol. 3, #2 out of print). Volumes 4 and 5 available from editorial address at $1.50 per issue.

PROSE

EDITORIAL ADDRESS: SUBSCRIPTION ADDRESS:
Coburn Britton, Editor
Prose Publishers, Inc. same
6 St. Luke's Place
New York, New York 10014

PUBLISHED: Biannually (Spring, Fall)   CIRCULATION: 5,000
COST: 1 yr.—$3.00 in U.S.; $3.50 elsewhere; single copy—$2.00.

CONTENTS: Nonfiction only: belles lettres, essays, criticism in literature, music, and the arts, autobiography, biography, letters, philosophy. Example: "The Notion of the Absurd in Contemporary French Literature."

UNSOLICITED MSS. WELCOME? Yes; submissions not acknowledged.
SPECIFICALLY WELCOMED: Belles lettres and as described under Contents.
MS. LENGTH: 1,500-6,000 words; submit ONE copy.
STYLE REQUIREMENTS: "high" literary style; no jargon.
COPYRIGHT: Copyright reverts to author on publication of magazine.
EDITOR'S DECISION: 2 weeks.
FROM ACCEPTANCE TO PUBLICATION: 3 months to 1 year.
PAYMENT/OFFPRINTS: $500.00. Contributors may have up to 25 copies of magazine.
REJECTED MSS.: Returned.
GENERAL: First issue, Fall, 1970. Usual publication length, 224 pages.
BACK ISSUES: Available from publisher at $3.00 each.

STUDIES IN AMERICAN FICTION

EDITORIAL ADDRESS:
James Nagel, Editor
Department of English
Northeastern University
Boston, Massachusetts 02115

SUBSCRIPTION ADDRESS:

same

PUBLISHED: Biannually (Spring, Autumn)
COST: 1 yr.—$3.00 (one volume with two issues).

CIRCULATION: 1,000

CONTENTS: Articles, notes, reviews relating to the prose fiction of the United States.

UNSOLICITED MSS. WELCOME? Yes; submissions acknowledged.
SPECIFICALLY WELCOMED: Scholarly material about individual works, authors, movements, influences and other topics related to American fiction.
MS. LENGTH: 1-25 pages; submit TWO copies.
STYLE REQUIREMENTS: MLA STYLE SHEET.
COPYRIGHT: STUDIES IN AMERICAN FICTION.
EDITOR'S DECISION: 3 months.
FROM ACCEPTANCE TO PUBLICATION: 1 year.
PAYMENT/OFFPRINTS: Ten free offprints; more on payment of minimal fee.
REJECTED MSS.: Returned.
GENERAL: First issue, Spring, 1973. Usual publication length, 120 pages.
BACK ISSUES: Available from editorial address at $2.00 each.

STUDIES IN THE NOVEL

EDITORIAL ADDRESS:
James W. Lee, Editor
P. O. Box 13706, N. T. Station
North Texas State University
Denton, Texas 76203

SUBSCRIPTION ADDRESS:

same

PUBLISHED: Quarterly
COST: 1 yr.—$4.00; single copy—$1.00.

CIRCULATION: 1,800

CONTENTS: Essays on the novel and on specific novelists; book reviews on critical works; interviews (with Brian Moore, Peter DeVries, Robert Penn Warren); two general numbers and two special numbers annually; bibliographies. Examples: "The Black Revolutionary Novel: 1899-1969"; "Dreiserian Tragedy."

UNSOLICITED MSS. WELCOME? Yes; submissions acknowledged.
SPECIFICALLY WELCOMED: Scholarly essays.
MS. LENGTH: 20 pages; submit ONE copy.
STYLE REQUIREMENTS: MLA STYLE SHEET; footnotes follow essay.
COPYRIGHT: STUDIES IN THE NOVEL.

EDITOR'S DECISION: 60 days.
FROM ACCEPTANCE TO PUBLICATION: 1 year.
PAYMENT/OFFPRINTS: Offprints provided whenever possible.
REJECTED MSS.: Returned.
GENERAL: First issue, Spring, 1969. Usual publication length, 125 pages.
BACK ISSUES: Available from editorial address at $1.50 each.

STUDIES IN SHORT FICTION

EDITORIAL ADDRESS:
Frank L. Hoskins, Jr., Editor
Newberry College
Newberry, South Carolina 29108

SUBSCRIPTION ADDRESS:

same

PUBLISHED: Quarterly (Jan., Apr., July, Oct.)
CIRCULATION: 1,300
COST: 1 yr.—$8.00; single copy—$2.50.

CONTENTS: Critical articles on, notes on, and reviews of short fiction. Examples: "Obsessive Elements in Julien Green's Short Stories: Early Essays in Style"; "Rhetorical Devices in a Ming Short Story."

UNSOLICITED MSS. WELCOME? Yes; submissions acknowledged.
SPECIFICALLY WELCOMED: Scholarly articles; explications; previously unpublished short story by a master and critical apparatus.
MS. LENGTH: Articles—2,250 words, maximum 15 pages; notes—750 words; reviews—450 words; submit ONE copy.
STYLE REQUIREMENTS: Generally MLA STYLE SHEET.
COPYRIGHT: Newberry College.
FROM ACCEPTANCE TO PUBLICATION: 4-6 weeks.
PAYMENT/OFFPRINTS: No payment. Offprints sold at $15 for 50, $20 for 75, $30 for 100.
REJECTED MSS.: Returned.
GENERAL: First issue, October, 1963. Usual publication length, 110 pages.
BACK ISSUES: Copies back to Vols. 5-6 available from editorial office. Reprints of out-of-print volumes available from Johnson Reprint Corp. Cost depends on publication date.

IV

AMERICAN

ETHNIC

MINORITIES

AFRICAN ARTS

EDITORIAL ADDRESS:　　　　　SUBSCRIPTION ADDRESS:
John Povey, Managing Editor
African Studies Center　　　　　same
Bunche Hall 10377
University of California
Los Angeles, California 90024

PUBLISHED: Quarterly (Autumn,　　CIRCULATION: 4,000
Winter, Spring, Summer)
COST: 1 yr.—$12.00; 2 yrs.—$22.00; single copy—$3.50.

CONTENTS: Articles on literature, such as Southern Sesotho; essays on African sculpture, weaving, and African music; articles on recent, current, and continuing exhibitions; book reviews on art, poetry, and civilization in Black Africa; photographs of African art, sculptures, dancers, and masks.

UNSOLICITED MSS. WELCOME? Yes; submissions acknowledged.
SPECIFICALLY WELCOMED: Essays about the literature and the performing arts of Africa; articles about and illustrations of the graphic and plastic arts of Africa.
MS. LENGTH: 5,000-7,000 words; submit ONE copy.
STYLE REQUIREMENTS: University of Chicago's A MANUAL OF STYLE.
COPYRIGHT: Regents of the University of California.
EDITOR'S DECISION: 2 months.
FROM ACCEPTANCE TO PUBLICATION: Indeterminate.
PAYMENT/OFFPRINTS: $50.00 to Africans; $25.00 to non-Africans.
REJECTED MSS.: Returned, not criticized.
GENERAL: First issue, October, 1967. Usual publication length, 80-90 pages.
BACK ISSUES: Available from subscription address at $4.00 each, if available.

AFRICAN LITERATURE TODAY: AN ANNUAL REVIEW

See the section on AGE AND/OR NATIONALITY: AFRICAN for details.

AFRO-AMERICAN HISTORY AND CULTURE: NEW BOOKS
QUARTERLY CHECKLIST SERIES

See the section on BIBLIOGRAPHICAL AND LIBRARY RESOURCES for details.

AMERICAN JEWISH HISTORICAL QUARTERLY

EDITORIAL ADDRESS:
Nathan M. Kaganoff, Editor
2 Thornton Road
Waltham, Massachusetts 02154

SUBSCRIPTION ADDRESS:

same

PUBLISHED: Quarterly
COST: 1 yr.—$15.00.

CIRCULATION: 3,000

CONTENTS: Articles, book reviews, review essays, and photographs relating to the history of Jews on the American continent including their immigration to America and reasons for same.

UNSOLICITED MSS. WELCOME? Yes; submissions acknowledged.
SPECIFICALLY WELCOMED: Research articles; review essays of books; edited manuscripts.
MS. LENGTH: 10-20 pages; submit ONE copy.
STYLE REQUIREMENTS: University of Chicago's A MANUAL OF STYLE.
COPYRIGHT: The American Jewish Historical Society.
EDITOR'S DECISION: 1 month.
FROM ACCEPTANCE TO PUBLICATION: Varies, now 1 year.
PAYMENT/OFFPRINTS: 50 free offprints for articles; 10 free for book reviews; more at a fee.
REJECTED MSS.: Returned.
GENERAL: First issue, 1893, as ANNUAL PUBLICATION OF THE AMERICAN JEWISH HISTORICAL SOCIETY. Usual publication length, 96-150 pages.
BACK ISSUES: Vols. 1-50 available from Kraus Reprint Co.; also from editorial address. Price varies according to year.

AMISTAD: WRITINGS ON BLACK HISTORY AND CULTURE
(suspended publication)

EDITORIAL ADDRESS:
John A. Williams and
Charles F. Harris, Editors

SUBSCRIPTION ADDRESS:
Vintage Books
A Division of Random House
New York, New York

PUBLISHED: Annually
COST: 1 yr.—$1.95.

CONTENTS: Articles about black life and literature, past and present; interviews, such as one with Chester Himes; fiction. Examples: "Blood of the Lamb: The Ordeal of James Baldwin"; "Blueprint for Negro Literature."

GENERAL: First issue, 1970. Usual publication length, 308-338 pages.
BACK ISSUES: Available from subscription address.

AZTLÁN: CHICANO JOURNAL OF THE SOCIAL SCIENCES AND THE ARTS

EDITORIAL ADDRESS:
Juan Gómes-Quiñones, Reynaldo
Maciás, Andres Chávez,
Deluvina Hernández, Editors
Aztlán Publications
Chicano Student Center
405 Hilgard Avenue
UCLA
Los Angeles, California 90024

SUBSCRIPTION ADDRESS:

same

PUBLISHED: Biannually   CIRCULATION: 1,500-2,000
COST: Single copy—$3.00. Standing orders available.

CONTENTS: Articles in the social sciences, especially on Mexican-American affairs; essays on the arts. Example: "Library Services and Chicano Periodicals: A Critical Look at Librarianship."

UNSOLICITED MSS. WELCOME? Yes; submissions acknowledged.
SPECIFICALLY WELCOMED: Literary criticism.
MS. LENGTH: 30 pages maximum; submit THREE copies.
STYLE REQUIREMENTS: Refer to latest issue of the journal.
COPYRIGHT: Author.
EDITOR'S DECISION: 90-120 days.
FROM ACCEPTANCE TO PUBLICATION: 60-90 days.
PAYMENT/OFFPRINTS: Two copies of the journal and 10 offprints.
REJECTED MSS.: Not returned.
GENERAL: First issue, Spring, 1970. Usual publication length, 180-200 pages. AZTLÁN is a forum for scholarly writings on all aspects of the Chicano community.
BACK ISSUES: Available from editorial address at $3.00 each.

BEAU-COCOA

EDITORIAL ADDRESS:
L. Addison, Editor
P.O. Box 409
New York, New York 10035

SUBSCRIPTION ADDRESS:

same

PUBLISHED: Biannually
COST: 1 yr.—$2.00; 2 yrs.—$3.75; single copy—$1.00.

CONTENTS: Poetry; essays; fiction; have published one play, biography.

UNSOLICITED MSS. WELCOME? Yes; submissions not acknowledged.

SPECIFICALLY WELCOMED: Interested in material projecting black ethos, esthetics, and the liberation of humanity from various obstacles in pursuit of happiness—sexual, social, racial—toward democratization and human enchantment.
MS. LENGTH: Short, except poems; submit ONE copy.
STYLE REQUIREMENTS: "Polished," whatever idiom.
COPYRIGHT: BEAU-COCOA.
EDITOR'S DECISION: 1-4 weeks.
FROM ACCEPTANCE TO PUBLICATION: 4 or 5 months.
PAYMENT/OFFPRINTS: Three copies of relevant issue.
REJECTED MSS.: Returned.
GENERAL: First issue, Autumn, 1968. Usual publication length, 120 pages.
BACK ISSUES: Available from editorial address at $1.00 each.

BLACK ACADEMY REVIEW: QUARTERLY OF THE BLACK WORLD

EDITORIAL ADDRESS: SUBSCRIPTION ADDRESS:
S. Okechukwa Nezu, Editor
Black Academy Press, Inc.   same
135 University Avenue
Buffalo, New York 14214

PUBLISHED: Quarterly (Mar., June, Oct., Dec.)
COST: 1 yr.—$7.00; special student rate—$4.00; single copy—$2.00. Airmail postage extra.

CONTENTS: Critical articles on the writings of black writers; occasional interview, such as "Theme and Structure in Boles' CURLING: An Interview with the Author"; reviews of literary, social, scientific, political, and other works by black scholars and artists; articles on major issues confronting the black culture as well as semi-technical essays dealing with various facets of the black civilization in Africa, West Indies, the Americas, and elsewhere. Examples: "Passion and Poetry in the Works of Dennis Brutus"; "The Calypso Tradition in West Indian Literature."

COPYRIGHT: Black Academy Press, Inc.
GENERAL: First issue, 1970. Usual publication legnth, 80-100 pages.
BACK ISSUES: Available from University Microfilms, Inc., and from Canadian Distributors—Bellhaven House Ltd., 1145 Bellamy Road, Scarborough, Ontario, Canada.

THE BLACK ARTS MAGAZINE

EDITORIAL ADDRESS:
David Rambeau, Editor
401 E. Adams Street
Detroit, Michigan 48226

SUBSCRIPTION ADDRESS:

same

CIRCULATION: 1,000

COST: Single copy—$1.50.

CONTENTS: Short stories, essays, one act plays, TV and film scenarios.

UNSOLICITED MSS. WELCOME? Yes; submissions not acknowledged.
SPECIFICALLY WELCOMED: Any on the black arts with exception of poetry; particularly interested in short (30 minutes) plays and TV and radio scripts as well as film scenarios.
MS. LENGTH: No preference; submit ONE copy.
STYLE REQUIREMENTS: None.
COPYRIGHT: Author.
EDITOR'S DECISION: 1 month.
FROM ACCEPTANCE TO PUBLICATION: Within 3 months after royalty negotiation.
PAYMENT/OFFPRINTS: A reasonable number of offprints available to authors.
REJECTED MSS.: Returned when time permits.
GENERAL: First issue, 1970. Usual publication length, 24-48 pages.
BACK ISSUES: Not available.

BLACK BOOKS BULLETIN

EDITORIAL ADDRESS:
Don L. Lee, Editor
7848 S. Ellis Avenue
Chicago, Illinois 60619

SUBSCRIPTION ADDRESS:
Subscription Department
same

PUBLISHED: Quarterly   CIRCULATION: 10,000
COST: 1 yr.—$8.00; charter—$6.00; sustaining—$10.00; supportive—$25.00; single copy—$2.00.

CONTENTS: Literary articles; criticisms; book reviews (children and general); bibliographies; editorials; interviews; information from publishers; photographs. Example: "Frank Yerby: Golden Debunker."

UNSOLICITED MSS. WELCOME? Yes; submissions acknowledged.
SPECIFICALLY WELCOMED: Reviews of fiction, non-fiction, poetry; literary and political essays and criticisms.
MS. LENGTH: 2,500 words; submit ONE copy.
STYLE REQUIREMENTS: Scholarly.
COPYRIGHT: BLACK BOOKS BULLETIN.

EDITOR'S DECISION: 1 month.
FROM ACCEPTANCE TO PUBLICATION: 2-6 months.
PAYMENT/OFFPRINTS: 20 copies of the magazine for personal distribution.
REJECTED MSS.: Returned.
GENERAL: First issue, October, 1971. Usual publication length, 80 pages.
BACK ISSUES: Available from Subscription Department at $1.00 each.

BLACK REVIEW

EDITORIAL ADDRESS:
Mel Watkins, Editor

SUBSCRIPTION ADDRESS:
William Morrow & Company, Inc.
105 Madison Avenue
New York, New York 10016

PUBLISHED: Annually
COST: 1 yr.—$2.95.

CONTENTS: Articles by black authors about all aspects of Afro-American culture: poems, plays, and short stories by contemporary black artists; essays on black novelists, playwrights, poets, and singers; drawings. Examples: "Richard Wright: Blackness and the Adventure of Western Culture"; "Eatonville's Zora Neale Hurston: A Profile."

UNSOLICITED MSS. WELCOME? Yes.
SPECIFICALLY WELCOMED: Articles that "further the black man's independent analysis and defining of black American culture, in the hope that it be better understood and more richly developed.
COPYRIGHT: William Morrow & Company, Inc.
GENERAL: First issue, 1971. Usual publication length, 150-180 pages. According to the Editor's "Introduction" in No. 1, non-black writers' contributions will be considered if "their examination of some aspect of their own culture illuminates an interrelated aspect of black life."
BACK ISSUES: Available from William Morrow & Company, Inc. at $1.95 for No. 1; $2.95 for No. 2.

THE BLACK SCHOLAR: JOURNAL OF BLACK STUDIES AND RESEARCH

EDITORIAL ADDRESS:
Robert Chrisman, Editor
P.O. Box 908
Sausalito, California 94965

SUBSCRIPTION ADDRESS:

same

PUBLISHED: Monthly (except July, Aug.)
COST: 1 yr.—$10.00; 3 yrs.—$25.00; single copy—$1.25.

CONTENTS: Scholarly articles and research on black authors and artists, culture, attitudes, history; book reviews.

UNSOLICITED MSS. WELCOME? Inquire of editor.
COPYRIGHT: THE BLACK SCHOLAR.
GENERAL: First issue, 1970. Usual publication length, 64 pages.

BLACK THEATRE (suspended publication)

EDITORIAL ADDRESS:
Ed Bullins, Editor
2349 Seventh Avenue
Harlem, New York 10030

SUBSCRIPTION ADDRESS:
Richard Wesley, Managing Editor
same

COST: 6 issues—$2.50.

CONTENTS: Black theatre news from around the country and the world; book reviews and black theatre reviews; articles, interviews, poems, and plays concerning Afro-American culture; directory of black theatres in the black world; drawings; photographs; woodcuts. Example: "The Black Ritual Theatre: An Interview with Robert Macbeth."

SPECIFICALLY WELCOMED: Articles about the development of the black theatre, about present productions, about its impact on today's culture.
COPYRIGHT: New Lafayette Theatre Publications.
GENERAL: Usual publication length, 35-50 pages. Publication is temporarily suspended.
BACK ISSUES: Available from subscription address.

BLACK WORLD (formerly NEGRO DIGEST)

EDITORIAL ADDRESS:
John H. Johnson, Editor
Johnson Publishing Company
820 South Michigan Avenue
Chicago, Illinois 60605

SUBSCRIPTION ADDRESS:

same

PUBLISHED: Monthly
COST: 1 yr.—$5.00 in U.S.; $6.00 elsewhere.

CONTENTS: Essays on the literature of black writers; articles on all aspects of black culture; poetry; fiction; cartoon features; book reviews; notes on books, writers, artists, and the arts; current record releases; book excerpts. Example: "Thematic Patterns in Baldwin's Essays"; "Black Folk Spirit and the Shape of Black Literature."

UNSOLICITED MSS. WELCOME? Yes; submissions acknowledged.
SPECIFICALLY WELCOMED: Original fiction; critical evaluations of Black literary works by Black writers; incisive essays on culture, politics.
MS. LENGTH: 3,500 words or less; submit ONE copy.
STYLE REQUIREMENTS: Flexible.
COPYRIGHT: Johnson Publishing Company (in custody for authors).
EDITOR'S DECISION: 1-4 weeks.
FROM ACCEPTANCE TO PUBLICATION: 2-4 months.
PAYMENT/OFFPRINTS: Payment is certain; amount varies. Complimentary copies of issue provided. No offprints.
REJECTED MSS.: Returned.
GENERAL: First issue, November, 1942 (as NEGRO DIGEST). Usual publication length, 100 pages.
BACK ISSUES: Available from Johnson Publishing Co., at regular cost.

CLA JOURNAL: OFFICIAL QUARTERLY PUBLICATION OF THE COLLEGE LANGUAGE ASSOCIATION

See the section on AGE AND/OR NATIONALITY: COMPREHENSIVE IN SCOPE for details.

EL GRITO: JOURNAL OF CONTEMPORARY MEXICAN AMERICAN THOUGHT

EDITORIAL ADDRESS:
Octavio I. Romano-V. and
Herminio Ríos C., Editors
P. O. Box 9275
Berkeley, California 94709

SUBSCRIPTION ADDRESS:
Quinto Sol Publications, Inc.
P. O. Box 9275
Berkeley, California 94709

PUBLISHED: Quarterly
COST: 1 yr.—$5.00, $6.00, foreign; single copies—$1.25 to $1.50.

CONTENTS: Social science, short stories, dramatic works, art, poetry, book reviews; does not generally print literary interpretation but will consider such contributions.

UNSOLICITED MSS. WELCOME? Yes; submissions acknowledged.
SPECIFICALLY WELCOMED: Open, relating to Chicanos.
MS. LENGTH: No requirement; submit ONE copy.
STYLE REQUIREMENTS: Open.
COPYRIGHT: Quinto Sol Publications, Inc., but assigned to author upon request.
EDITOR'S DECISION: 2 months.
FROM ACCEPTANCE TO PUBLICATION: 4 months.

PAYMENT/OFFPRINTS: Works less than 4,000 words—$25 to $30; works longer than 4,000 words prorated and negotiated with author. Ten free copies of journal in which work is published.
REJECTED MSS.: Returned.
GENERAL: First issue, Fall 1967. Usual publication length, 88 pages. See Summer, 1972 issue for bibliography of the first five years of EL GRITO (1967-1972).
BACK ISSUES: Available from subscription address or from editorial office, 2150 Shattuck Avenue, Suite #606, Berkeley, California 94709, for $1.25 to $1.50 each.

FREEDOMWAYS: A QUARTERLY REVIEW OF THE FREEDOM MOVEMENT

EDITORIAL ADDRESS:
Esther Jackson, Managing Editor
799 Broadway
New York, New York 10003

SUBSCRIPTION ADDRESS:

same

PUBLISHED: Quarterly   CIRCULATION: 7,500
COST: 1 yr.—$4.50 in U.S.; $6.00 abroad; single copy—$1.25 (special issues—$1.50).

CONTENTS: Emphasis on Afro-American and African areas of political and social thought; fiction and poetry; book reviews; occasional illustrations. Examples: "Le Roi Jones and the New Black Writers of the Sixties"; "Afro-Asian Writers' Movement in its 15th Year"; "Paul Laurence Dunbar."

UNSOLICITED MSS. WELCOME? Yes; submissions not acknowledged.
MS. LENGTH: 15 pages maximum; submit TWO copies.
COPYRIGHT: FREEDOMWAYS; relinquished on request.
EDITOR'S DECISION: 4-6 weeks.
FROM ACCEPTANCE TO PUBLICATION: 3-6 months.
PAYMENT/OFFPRINTS: Contributor's copies.
REJECTED MSS.: Returned on request.
GENERAL: First issue, Spring, 1961. Usual publication length, 96 pages.
BACK ISSUES: Available from editorial address at $2.00 each; $2.50 for special back issues. Bound copies of Vols. 1-8 available from Kraus Reprint Co.; microfilm editions from University Microfilms.

THE INDIAN HISTORIAN

EDITORIAL ADDRESS:
Jeannette Henry, Editor
1451 Masonic Avenue
San Francisco, California 94117

SUBSCRIPTION ADDRESS:
American Indian Historical Society
same

PUBLISHED: Quarterly (Mar., June, Aug., Nov.)
CIRCULATION: 10,000
COST: 1 yr.—$6.00; 2 yrs.—$10.00; 3 yrs.—$15.00 (add $1.00 to foreign orders); single copy—$1.40.

CONTENTS: Articles on North and South American Indian culture, philosophy, history, literature, and language; reviews of books such as KARANKAWA BOY and THE WIND RIVER RESERVATION: YESTERDAY AND TODAY; poetry.

UNSOLICITED MSS. WELCOME? Inquire before submitting manuscript.
COPYRIGHT: American Indian Historical Society.
GENERAL: First issue, 1964. Usual publication length, 44 pages.

JOURNAL OF JEWISH STUDIES

See the section on AGE AND/OR NATIONALITY: AFRICAN, CARIBBEAN, LATIN AMERICAN, AND NEAR EASTERN for details.

JOURNAL OF THE NEW AFRICAN LITERATURE AND THE ARTS
(JONALA)

EDITORIAL ADDRESS:
Joseph Okpaku, Editor
The Third Press
444 Central Park West
New York, New York 10025

SUBSCRIPTION ADDRESS:
same

PUBLISHED: Quarterly (Jan., Apr., July, Oct.)
CIRCULATION: 3,000
COST: 1 yr.(4 issues)—$10.00; 2 yrs.(8 issues)—$18.95; single copy—$3.00.

CONTENTS: Critical essays on African (or Black) literature and the arts (literature, music, fine art, dance); fiction; drama; poetry; short stories; reviews; art reproductions. Examples: "Four Ghanian Novels"; "The Plays of Sarif Easmon."

UNSOLICITED MSS. WELCOME? Yes; submissions acknowledged.
MS. LENGTH: Reasonable; submit ONE copy.
STYLE REQUIREMENTS: Articles must be professionally sound and well-written.
COPYRIGHT: JONALA.
EDITOR'S DECISION: 6-8 weeks.
FROM ACCEPTANCE TO PUBLICATION: Around 3 months.
PAYMENT/OFFPRINTS: Free copy of issue. Offprints supplied at modest cost.
REJECTED MSS.: Returned.
GENERAL: First issue, 1966. Usual publication length, 100-150 pages.

BACK ISSUES: Available from The Third Press at $3.75 each.

LA LUZ

EDITORIAL ADDRESS: SUBSCRIPTION ADDRESS:
Dr. Philip D. Ortego, Senior Editor and
Literary Director same
360 South Monroe
Denver, Colorado 80209

PUBLISHED: Monthly CIRCULATION: 80,000
COST: 1 yr.—$10.00; new subscription—$7.50.

CONTENTS: General interest stories and features for Hispano readers; regular departments such as editorials; strong literary section; emphasis on photos.

UNSOLICITED MSS. WELCOME? Yes; submissions acknowledged.
SPECIFICALLY WELCOMED: Any sort of Hispano life and culture (Mexican-American, Chicano, Latino, Puerto Rican, Cuban, Boricua).
MS. LENGTH: 5-7 pages with pics; submit ONE copy.
STYLE REQUIREMENTS: None.
COPYRIGHT: Authors.
EDITOR'S DECISION: 2-3 months.
FROM ACCEPTANCE TO PUBLICATION: 6-8 months.
PAYMENT/OFFPRINTS: Payment in copies except for assignments. Writers order and pay for offprints.
REJECTED MSS.: Returned.
GENERAL: First issue, April, 1972. Usual publication length, 48-60 pages.
BACK ISSUES: Available from editorial address at $.50 each.

LA REVISTA CHICANO-RIQUEÑA

EDITORIAL ADDRESS: SUBSCRIPTION ADDRESS:
Nicolás Kanellos and
Luis Davila, Editors same
Indiana University Northwest
3400 Broadway
Gary, Indiana 46408

PUBLISHED: Quarterly CIRCULATION: 500
COST: 1 yr.—$5.00 (first year $2.50—2 issues).

CONTENTS: Chicano and Puerto Rican literature and art; critical articles on this type of literature; book reviews. Example: "Mexican American Literature: A Historical Perspective."

UNSOLICITED MSS. WELCOME? Yes; submissions acknowledged.
SPECIFICALLY WELCOMED: All types excluding novels.
MS. LENGTH: Flexible; submit ONE copy.
STYLE REQUIREMENTS: MLA STYLE SHEET for critical articles.
COPYRIGHT: Writers may retain copyright after published by magazine.
EDITOR'S DECISION: 2 months.
FROM ACCEPTANCE TO PUBLICATION: 3 months.
PAYMENT/OFFPRINTS: Free issue or issues of magazine.
REJECTED MSS.: Not returned unless requested.
GENERAL: First issue, April, 1973. Usual publication length, 60 pages.
BACK ISSUES: Available from editorial address at $1.50 each, unless late subscription for that year.

THE LATIN AMERICAN LITERARY REVIEW

See the section on AGE AND/OR NATIONALITY: AFRICAN, CARIBBEAN, LATI N AMERICAN, AND NEAR EASTERN for details.

MANY SMOKES

EDITORIAL ADDRESS:
Sun Bear and Wabun, Editors
P. O. Box 5895
Reno, Nevada 89503

SUBSCRIPTION ADDRESS:

same

PUBLISHED: Quarterly
COST: 1 yr.—$2.00.

CIRCULATION: 5,000-7,500

CONTENTS: Current news; history; legends; poetry; explanation of the traditional Indian way of life; book reviews. Legend example: "The Story of the Mountain Dweller."

UNSOLICITED MSS. WELCOME? Yes, but not often used; query first.
MS. LENGTH: 1,000-2,000 words.
PAYMENT/OFFPRINTS: No payment.
GENERAL: First issue, 1965. Usual publication length, 20 pages.
BACK ISSUES: Available from editorial address; price varies.

THE MASTERKEY: FOR INDIAN LORE AND HISTORY

EDITORIAL ADDRESS:
Bruce Bryan, Editor
The Southwest Museum
Highland Park
Los Angeles, California 90042

SUBSCRIPTION ADDRESS:

same

PUBLISHED: Quarterly
COST: 1 yr.—$3.50; single copy—$1.00.

CIRCULATION: 1,200

CONTENTS: Popular articles and technical papers on the American Indian (North, Central and South America): history, archaeology, anthropology, ethnology, arts and handicrafts; reviews of books concerning Indians.

UNSOLICITED MSS. WELCOME? Yes; submissions acknowledged.
SPECIFICALLY WELCOMED: Articles that focus on California and the Southwest.
MS. LENGTH: Not more than 5,000 words; submit ONE copy.
STYLE REQUIREMENTS: Legible, easy-reading English prose.
COPYRIGHT: Southwest Museum.
EDITOR'S DECISION: 2 weeks.
FROM ACCEPTANCE TO PUBLICATION: Depends on backlog; sometimes up to a year.
PAYMENT/OFFPRINTS: Six complimentary copies. No offprints.
REJECTED MSS.: Returned.
GENERAL: First issue, May, 1927. Usual publication length, 40 pages.
BACK ISSUES: Available from Southwest Museum at $1.00 each. Some earlier issues, as well as some individual numbers, are out of print. Suggest queries on issues required. No complete sets available.

NEGRO AMERICAN LITERATURE FORUM

EDITORIAL ADDRESS:
John F. Bayliss, Editor
School of Education
Indiana State University
Terre Haute, Indiana 47809

SUBSCRIPTION ADDRESS:

same

PUBLISHED: Quarterly (March, June, Sept., Dec.)
COST: 1 yr.—$4.00; single copy—$1.00.

CONTENTS: Scholarly essays about black literature and about their authors; articles on black music, leaders, contemporary issues; photographs; reviews of books by black writers; articles about black oral literature; curricular essays for the teaching of black culture in grade school through high school; occasional special issues devoted to creative work; bibliographies; reading lists. Examples: "The West Indian as an Ethnic Stereotype in Black American Literature"; "An Inquiry Model for Black Oral Literature."

UNSOLICITED MSS. WELCOME? Yes; submissions acknowledged.
SPECIFICALLY WELCOMED: Critical essays about black literature.
MS. LENGTH: 10-15 pages; submit ONE copy.
STYLE REQUIREMENTS: MLA STYLE SHEET; footnotes follow essay.
COPYRIGHT: Indiana State University.
EDITOR'S DECISION: 1-2 months.
FROM ACCEPTANCE TO PUBLICATION: 1 year.
PAYMENT/OFFPRINTS: Three copies of issue.
REJECTED MSS.: Returned, with criticism.
GENERAL: First issue, Summer, 1967. Usual publication length, 36 pages.
BACK ISSUES: Microfilm and xerox copies available from Xerox University Microfilms.

THE NEGRO HISTORY BULLETIN

EDITORIAL ADDRESS:
J. Rupert Picott, Editor
1407 Fourteenth Street, N. W.
Washington, D.C. 20005

SUBSCRIPTION ADDRESS:
Association for the Study
of Afro-American Life and History
same

PUBLISHED: Monthly
(8 times yearly)
COST: 1 yr.—$15.00.

CIRCULATION: 20,000

CONTENTS: Serious historical articles; editorials; some poetry; teacher's guides; book reviews; illustrations; and other items of general interest to teachers and the lay public. Examples: "Black, White, and Mulatto in Martin R. Delaney's BLAKE"; "The Bible and the Negro."

UNSOLICITED MSS. WELCOME? Yes; submissions acknowledged.
SPECIFICALLY WELCOMED: Largely historical articles showing role that the Black man has played in the building of civilization and history. Others.
MS. LENGTH: 10 pages or more, shorter articles used as fillers; submit TWO copies.
COPYRIGHT: The Association for the Study of Afro-American Life and History.
EDITOR'S DECISION: 4 weeks.
PAYMENT/OFFPRINTS: Payment is made in contributor's copies only. Offprints must be ordered before publication. Fees will be based on length and number of copies.
REJECTED MSS.: Returned.
GENERAL: First issue, October, 1937. Usual publication length, 24 pages.
BACK ISSUES: Available from subscription address at $1.25 to $2.25 each. Not all are available.

PHYLON: THE ATLANTA UNIVERSITY REVIEW OF RACE AND CULTURE

EDITORIAL ADDRESS:
John D. Reid, Editor
Atlanta University
223 Chestnut Street, S. W.
Atlanta, Georgia 30314

SUBSCRIPTION ADDRESS:

same

PUBLISHED: Quarterly
(Mar., June, Sept., Dec.)
COST: 1 yr.—$4.50.

CIRCULATION: 2,500

CONTENTS: Articles pertaining to race and culture: book reviews, poems, short stories. Examples: "Ralph Ellison's INVISIBLE MAN: 'It Goes a Long Way Back, Some Twenty Years' "; "Sutton E. Griggs: Militant Black Novelist."

UNSOLICITED MSS. WELCOME? Yes; submissions acknowledged.
MS. LENGTH: 20 pages; submit TWO copies.
STYLE REQUIREMENTS: University of Chicago's A MANUAL OF STYLE.
EDITOR'S DECISION: 6 months.
FROM ACCEPTANCE TO PUBLICATION: Unable to specify.
PAYMENT/OFFPRINTS: Twenty offprints.
REJECTED MSS.: Returned.
GENERAL: First issue, 1940. Usual publication length, 10 pages.
BACK ISSUES: Available from Kraus Reprint Co. at $1.50 each.

RESEARCH IN AFRICAN LITERATURES

EDITORIAL ADDRESS:
Bernth Lindfors, Editor
African and Afro-American
Research Institute
2609 University Avenue, 320
The University of Texas at Austin
Austin, Texas 78712

SUBSCRIPTION ADDRESS:
University of Texas Press
P. O. Box 7819
Austin, Texas 78712

PUBLISHED: Biannually
(Spring, Fall)

CIRCULATION: 1,500

COST: 1 yr.—$6.00; 2 yrs.—$11.00; 3 yrs.—$15.00. Free to subscribers in Africa, South & Central America, and Eastern Europe.

CONTENTS: Researched articles about the literature of Africa and about African authors; notes; research reports; abstracts of dissertations on African literature; reviews of books about Afro-Americans and Africans; information about conferences, new publications; letters to the editor; occasional drawings and photographs. Examples: "Aniceti Kitereza: A Kerebe Novelist"; "Humanitarianism and the Criticism of African Literature, 1770-1810."

UNSOLICITED MSS. WELCOME? Yes; submissions acknowledged.
SPECIFICALLY WELCOMED: Scholarly contributions on all aspects of the oral and written literatures of Africa.
MS. LENGTH: No specified length; submit TWO copies.
STYLE REQUIREMENTS: MLA STYLE SHEET; footnotes follow article.
COPYRIGHT: RESEARCH IN AFRICAN LITERATURE.
EDITOR'S DECISION: 1-3 months.
FROM ACCEPTANCE TO PUBLICATION: 8 months.
PAYMENT/OFFPRINTS: Several copies of issue in which article appears.
REJECTED MSS.: Returned, if requested.
GENERAL: First issue, Spring, 1970. Usual publication length, 112 pages. Manuscripts may be submitted in English or French. Translations, creative writing, and unanalyzed collections of folklore texts are NOT desired. Subscribers receive, free of charge, OCCASIONAL PUBLICATIONS OF THE AFRICAN & AFRO-AMERICAN RESEARCH INSTITUTE.
BACK ISSUES: Available from the University of Texas Press at $4.00 each or $20.00 for all six back issues (Vol. 1, #1, 2; Vol. 2, #1, 2; Vol. 3, #1, 2).

STUDIES IN BLACK LITERATURE

EDITORIAL ADDRESS:
Ramon K. Singh, Editor
Department of English
Mary Washington College
Box 3425
Fredericksburg, Virginia 22401

SUBSCRIPTION ADDRESS:

same

PUBLISHED: Tri-annually   CIRCULATION: 300-400
COST: 1 yr.—$4.00 (institutions—$7.00); single copy—$2.50.

CONTENTS: Critical articles on Afro-American, African, and Caribbean literatures; creative work; bibliographies. Example: "Individuality and Fraternity: The Novels of William Gardner Smith."

UNSOLICITED MSS. WELCOME? Yes; submissions not acknowledged.
SPECIFICALLY WELCOMED: Critical articles; creative work.
MS. LENGTH: 2,000-4,000 words; submit ONE copy.
STYLE REQUIREMENTS: MLA STYLE SHEET.
COPYRIGHT: STUDIES IN BLACK LITERATURE: rights reassigned on request.
EDITOR'S DECISION: 2-8 weeks.
FROM ACCEPTANCE TO PUBLICATION: 6 months.
PAYMENT/OFFPRINTS: Copies of journal.
REJECTED MSS.: Returned.
GENERAL: First issue, February, 1970. Usual publication length, 30 pages.
BACK ISSUES: Available from the Xerox Corporation.

THE WEEWISH TREE: A MAGAZINE OF INDIAN AMERICA FOR YOUNG PEOPLE

EDITORIAL ADDRESS:
Editorial Board
1451 Masonic Avenue
San Francisco, California 94117

SUBSCRIPTION ADDRESS:
American Indian Historical Society
same

PUBLISHED: 6 times yearly (Jan., Mar., May, Sept., Oct., Nov.)
COST: 1 yr.—$6.50; 2 yrs.—$11.00; 3 yrs.—$17.00.

CONTENTS: Stories; poetry; games; history; factual articles, such as "Something About Language"; brief reviews of books, such as NORTH AMERICAN INDIAN ARTS; Indian lore, such as "How Kodoyampe Created Man."

COPYRIGHT: American Indian Historical Society.
GENERAL: First issue, 1972. Usual publication length, 32 pages.

V

FOLKLORE

ARCTIC ANTHROPOLOGY

EDITORIAL ADDRESS:
Chester S. Chard, Editor
(until May 1974)*
5434 Social Science Building
Madison, Wisconsin 53706

SUBSCRIPTION ADDRESS:
Journals Department
University of Wisconsin Press
P. O. Box 1379
Madison, Wisconsin 53701

*thereafter, Catherine McClellan, same address.

PUBLISHED: Biannually   CIRCULATION: 900
COST: 1 yr.—$25.00 (special rate to individuals, $15.00).

CONTENTS: Articles devoted to all aspects of the study of man in the arctic, subarctic, and contiguous regions of the world both past and present; essays giving particular attention to circumpolar problems, to the origins and Eurasian relationships of New World peoples and cultures, and to the presentation, in translation, of Russian, Japanese, and Scandinavian contributions to our field of interest; folklore. The journal also provides an outlet for materials not readily publishable in existing media owing to nature or length, and it places useful data on record. Example: "Structural Analysis of a Koryak Incest Myth."

UNSOLICITED MSS. WELCOME? Yes; submissions acknowledged.
SPECIFICALLY WELCOMED: Scholarly articles in our field of interest.
MS. LENGTH: No requirements; submit ONE copy.
STYLE REQUIREMENTS: University of Chicago's A MANUAL OF STYLE.
COPYRIGHT: University of Wisconsin.
EDITOR'S DECISION: 2 months.
FROM ACCEPTANCE TO PUBLICATION: 1 year.
PAYMENT/OFFPRINTS: No payment. Offprints may be ordered at commercial rates.
REJECTED MSS.: Returned.
GENERAL: First issue, 1962. Usual publication length, 120 pages (occasional larger issues when subsidized).
BACK ISSUES: Available from subscription address at $13.50 each ($8.50 for individuals if remittance accompanies order) for current issues (published within last 12 months); $25.50 each for older issues. Prices include postage and handling. Volumes I-III are out of print.

ASIAN FOLKLORE STUDIES

EDITORIAL ADDRESS:
Editor
The Society for Asian Folklore
Bloomington, Indiana 47401

SUBSCRIPTION ADDRESS:

same

GENERAL: This periodical had not arrived by the time the entry went to press. Potential subscribers, contributors, or collectors will have to write the editor to see whether the journal still exists, and if so, to inquire about details of manuscript submission, style, back issues, and the like.

FABULA: JOURNAL OF FOLKTALE STUDIES

EDITORIAL ADDRESS:
Kurt Ranke, Editor
Verlag Walter de Gruyter
& Company
Genthmer Strasse 13
1 Berlin 30
West Germany

SUBSCRIPTION ADDRESS:

same

GENERAL: First issue, 1957. Articles may be written in English, French, or German. This periodical had not arrived by the time the entry went to press. Potential subscribers, contributors, or collectors will have to write the editor to see whether the journal still exists, and if so, to inquire about details of manuscript submission, style, back issues, and the like.

FOLKLORE

EDITORIAL ADDRESS:
Miss Christina Hole, Hon. Editor
292 Iffley Road
Oxford OX4 4AE
England

SUBSCRIPTION ADDRESS:
Hon. Secretary
c/o University College
Gower Street
London WC1E 6BT
England

PUBLISHED: Quarterly
COST: 1 yr.—£3.15; single copy—90 pence.

CIRCULATION: 1,000

CONTENTS: Serious articles on folklore of any country; reviews; correspondence; folklore news and announcements. Examples: "Basic Themes in Icelandic Folklore"; "The Role of Folk-Songs in Russian Folk-Plays"; "Medieval Japanese Tales."

UNSOLICITED MSS. WELCOME? Yes; submissions acknowledged.
SPECIFICALLY WELCOMED: Serious articles on folklore subjects; book reviews; letters; folklore news; reports.
MS. LENGTH: 1,000-9,000 words; submit ONE copy.
COPYRIGHT: FOLKLORE.
EDITOR'S DECISION: 3 weeks.
FROM ACCEPTANCE TO PUBLICATION: Varies.
PAYMENT/OFFPRINTS: 20 offprints free; others by arrangement.

REJECTED MSS.: Returned.
GENERAL: First issue, 1890, then called FOLK-LORE, successor to the FOLK-LORE JOURNAL. Usual publication length, 88 pages. Articles are to be in English, but not necessarily on English topics.
BACK ISSUES: Available from Wm. Glaisher, Ltd., 294. Croxted Road, Herne Hill, London S.E. 24, England.

FOLKLORE ANNUAL OF THE UNIVERSITY FOLKLORE ASSOCIATION

EDITORIAL ADDRESS: SUBSCRIPTION ADDRESS:
Editorial Board
Center of Intercultural Studies same
in Folklore and Oral History
Social Work Building, 306
University of Texas
Austin, Texas 78712

PUBLISHED: Annually (Spring) CIRCULATION: 500
COST: Free, by request.

CONTENTS: Papers by students in folklore; illustrations. Examples: "Navaho Mythmakers"; "Five Versions of the Riding-Horse Tale: A Comparative Study."
UNSOLICITED MSS. WELCOME? Yes; submissions acknowledged.
SPECIFICALLY WELCOMED: Any paper dealing with the loosely-defined subject, folklore.
MS. LENGTH: No preference; submit ONE copy.
STYLE REQUIREMENTS: American Anthropological Association style; footnotes follow essay.
COPYRIGHT: University of Texas Folklore Association.
EDITOR'S DECISION: 2 weeks.
FROM ACCEPTANCE TO PUBLICATION: Less than 1 year.
PAYMENT/OFFPRINTS: Up to 5 copies of the issue.
REJECTED MSS.: Returned.
GENERAL: First issue, 1969. Usual publication length, 60 pages. Editorial Board consists of three co-editors named for one-year terms.
BACK ISSUES: Available free from editorial office.

FOLKLORE FORUM: A COMMUNICATION FOR STUDENTS OF FOLKLORE

EDITORIAL ADDRESS: SUBSCRIPTION ADDRESS:
Janet Gilmore, Managing Editor
Folklore Institute same
504 North Fess Street
Bloomington, Indiana 47401

PUBLISHED: Quarterly (Jan., Apr., July, Oct.) plus Bibliographic and Special Series issues—usually two per year.
CIRCULATION: 260
COST: 1 yr.—$4.00; $3.50 to subscription agencies. Includes regular and Bibliographic and Special Series issues.

CONTENTS: Articles; "notes for queries"; occasional editorial comments; reviews of books, recordings, and films, that are pertinent to folklore in some way, written both by students and professionals in the field; reprints of articles that have gone out of print; translations of articles not previously translated into English. Bibliographic and Special Series issues offer specialized bibliographies, collections, and research aids in the field, and compilations of papers on special topics. Example: "An Index to the Known Oral Sources of the Child Collection."

UNSOLICITED MSS. WELCOME? Yes; submissions acknowledged.
SPECIFICALLY WELCOMED: Any contributions to the study, collection, or teaching of folklore.
MS. LENGTH: Less than 20 pages; submit ONE copy.
STYLE REQUIREMENTS: Generally MLA STYLE SHEET.
COPYRIGHT: Author or original publisher.
EDITOR'S DECISION: Less than 2 weeks.
FROM ACCEPTANCE TO PUBLICATION: About 2 months.
PAYMENT/OFFPRINTS: 3 to 5 copies of articles to authors.
REJECTED MSS.: Returned, with comments.
GENERAL: First issue, March, 1968. Usual publication length, 40 pages.
BACK ISSUES: Available from editorial address at $1.00 each for regular issues; $2.00 or more each for Bibliographic and Special Series issues.

FROM THE SOURDOUGH CROCK

EDITORIAL ADDRESS:
Barbara LaPan Rahm, Editor
Department of Anthropology
California State University
Northridge, California 91324

SUBSCRIPTION ADDRESS:

same

PUBLISHED: 4 times yearly (hopefully quarterly)
COST: 1 yr.—$1.00.

CIRCULATION: 850

CONTENTS: Announcements of meetings of professional societies in folklore and related fields; business issues before the membership; reports from the field and other research (brief); other brief materials of interest to folklorists.

UNSOLICITED MSS. WELCOME? Article length manuscripts are not solicited or accepted but should be sent to: Editor, WESTERN FOLKLORE, Folklore and Mythology, University of California, Los Angeles, California.

SPECIFICALLY WELCOMED: Short research reports.
GENERAL: First issue, September, 1960; suspended in December, 1969 (Vol. 2, No. 11); reactivated in December, 1972 (Vol. 3, No. 1). Usual publication length, 8 pages.
BACK ISSUES: Available free, up to 1973, from editorial address.

INDIANA FOLKLORE

EDITORIAL ADDRESS:
Dr. Linda Dégh, Editor
504 North Fess Street
Bloomington, Indiana 47401

SUBSCRIPTION ADDRESS:
Secretary-Treasurer
Hoosier Folklore Society
same

PUBLISHED: Biannually
CIRCULATION: 450
COST: 1 yr.—$5.00; student—$3.50; institutions—$7.00 (includes membership to Hoosier Folklore Society).

CONTENTS: Folklore and folklife of Indiana, surrounding states, and other American folklore; emphasis on legends; also material culture, tales, jokes, immigrant lore (customs, etc.) and other genres. Format is often: original texts with information on context and article analyzing. Examples: "Some Thoughts on the Ethnic-Regional Riddle Jokes"; "A Case for the Humorous Anti-Legend."

UNSOLICITED MSS. WELCOME? Yes; submissions not acknowledged.
SPECIFICALLY WELCOMED: Articles showing evidence of careful fieldwork; oral narrative texts.
MS. LENGTH: Varies; submit ONE copy.
STYLE REQUIREMENTS: University of Chicago's A MANUAL OF STYLE.
EDITOR'S DECISION: About 3 months.
FROM ACCEPTANCE TO PUBLICATION: 1 or 2 years.
PAYMENT/OFFPRINTS: 5 complimentary copies of issue; additional issues sold to author at 20% discount.
REJECTED MSS.: Returned.
GENERAL: First issue, 1968. Usual publication length, 140 pages.
BACK ISSUES: Available from subscription address at $4.00 each, except Vol. 2, No. 1 at $3.50. Volume 1 out of print and unavailable.

JOHN EDWARDS MEMORIAL FOUNDATION QUARTERLY

EDITORIAL ADDRESS:
Editor
Folklore and Mythology Center
University of California
Los Angeles, California

SUBSCRIPTION ADDRESS:
same

PUBLISHED: Quarterly   CIRCULATION: 700
COST: 1 yr.—$7.50 for individuals; $10.00 for institutions.

CONTENTS: Articles pertaining to commercially-recorded folk music and related forms; book reviews; bibliographic notes.

UNSOLICITED MSS. WELCOME? Yes; submissions acknowledged.
SPECIFICALLY WELCOMED: Articles, biographies, discographies, bibliographies dealing with country music, blues, old time, hillbilly, cowboy, bluegrass, soul, rhythm and blues, rock, and others.
MS. LENGTH: 1,000-4,000 words; submit TWO copies.
STYLE REQUIREMENTS: None.
COPYRIGHT: Author.
EDITOR'S DECISION: 1 month.
FROM ACCEPTANCE TO PUBLICATION: 3 months.
PAYMENT/OFFPRINTS: Five free copies of issue.
REJECTED MSS.: Returned.
GENERAL: First issue, 1965. Usual publication length, 55 pages.
BACK ISSUES: Available from John Edwards Memorial Foundation at $1.25 each.

JOURNAL OF AMERICAN FOLKLORE

EDITORIAL ADDRESS:
Barre Toelken, Editor
Department of English
University of Oregon
Eugene, Oregon 97403

SUBSCRIPTION ADDRESS:
The American Folklore Society
University of Texas Press
Box 7819
Austin, Texas 78712

PUBLISHED: Quarterly   CIRCULATION: 2,300
(Jan., Apr., July, Oct.)
COST: 1 yr.—$10.00 for individuals (includes membership in American Folklore Society); $12.00 for institutions.

CONTENTS: Articles on all aspects of world folklore; reviews of books and records of current interest to folklorists; notes and queries; illustrations. Example: "Focus for Conflict: Southern Mountain Medical Beliefs in Detroit."

UNSOLICITED MSS. WELCOME? Yes; submissions acknowledged.
SPECIFICALLY WELCOMED: Researched essays.
MS. LENGTH: 7,000-9,000 words; submit TWO copies.
STYLE REQUIREMENTS: MLA STYLE SHEET; University of Chicago's A MANUAL OF STYLE; JAF style sheet.
COPYRIGHT: American Folklore Society.
EDITOR'S DECISION: 2-3 months.
FROM ACCEPTANCE TO PUBLICATION: 2-4 months.
PAYMENT/OFFPRINTS: 25 free offprints of article.
REJECTED MSS.: Returned.
GENERAL: First issue, January, 1887. Usual publication length, 92 pages.

BACK ISSUES: Vols. 1-78 available from Kraus Reprint Corp. at $3.00 per issue; more recent issues from University of Texas Press.

JOURNAL OF THE FOLKLORE INSTITUTE

EDITORIAL ADDRESS:
The Fellows of the Folklore
Institute, Editors
Indiana University
504 North Fess Street
Bloomington, Indiana 47401

SUBSCRIPTION ADDRESS:
Co-Libri Distributors for Mouton
P. O. Box 482
The Hague 2076
The Netherlands

PUBLISHED: Tri-annually
COST: 1 yr.—$8.40 or Dglds. 27,--.

CIRCULATION: 800

CONTENTS: Oral traditions, such as legends, ballads, and tales (collections of these published only with commentary). Articles usually have a strong theoretical basis. Example: "The Hero of Gbaya Tradition."

UNSOLICITED MSS. WELCOME? Usually not (most accepted articles are written by professional scholars); submissions acknowledged.
SPECIFICALLY WELCOMED: Professional articles.
MS. LENGTH: 15-25 pages; submit ONE copy.
STYLE REQUIREMENTS: MLA STYLE SHEET or University of Chicago's A MANUAL OF STYLE.
COPYRIGHT: Editor.
EDITOR'S DECISION: 6-10 weeks.
FROM ACCEPTANCE TO PUBLICATION: 1-2 years.
PAYMENT/OFFPRINTS: 25 free offprints.
REJECTED MSS.: Returned.
GENERAL: First issue, 1964. Usual publication length, 75 pages.
BACK ISSUES: Available from subscription address at $4.20 or Dglds. 13,50 each; $11.20 or Dglds. 36,-- per volume.

JOURNAL OF THE FOLKLORE SOCIETY OF GREATER WASHINGTON

EDITORIAL ADDRESS:
Editor
P.O. Box 19303, 20th Street Station
Washington, D.C. 20036

SUBSCRIPTION ADDRESS:

same

PUBLISHED: 2-3 times yearly

GENERAL: This periodical had not arrived by the time the entry went to press. Potential subscribers, contributors, or collectors will have to write the editor to see whether the journal still exists, and if so, to inquire about details of manuscript submission, style, back issues, and the like.

JOURNAL OF THE GYPSY LORE SOCIETY

EDITORIAL ADDRESS:
D. E. Yates, Editor
The University Library
Liverpool
England

SUBSCRIPTION ADDRESS:

same

GENERAL: First issue, 1888. This periodical had not arrived by the time the entry went to press. Potential subscribers, contributors, or collectors will have to write the editor to see whether the journal still exists, and if so, to inquire about details of manuscript submission, style, back issues, and the like.

KENTUCKY FOLKLORE RECORD

EDITORIAL ADDRESS:
Charles S. Guthrie, Editor
Box 169
Western Kentucky University
Bowling Green, Kentucky 42101

SUBSCRIPTION ADDRESS:

same

PUBLISHED: Quarterly
COST: 1 yr.—$3.00

CIRCULATION: 350-400

CONTENTS: Articles on folklore, primarily with emphasis on Kentucky; folksongs; book reviews; some pictures used with articles. Example: "Similes from the Mammoth Cave Region with a Farm Flavor."

UNSOLICITED MSS. WELCOME? Yes; submissions acknowledged.
SPECIFICALLY WELCOMED: Articles on folktales, folksong, folk speech, folkways, folk poetry, folklore theory, folklorists; songs; book reviews; occasional record reviews.

MS. LENGTH: Articles, 600-2,000 words, longer ones may be run in installments; book reviews—variable length, depending on importance of book; submit ONE copy.
STYLE REQUIREMENTS: MLA STYLE SHEET.
COPYRIGHT: Kentucky Folklore Society, but will grant permission for reprinting.
EDITOR'S DECISION: 1 month.
FROM ACCEPTANCE TO PUBLICATION: 6 months to 1 year.

PAYMENT/OFFPRINTS: Three copies of issue containing the work.
REJECTED MSS.: Returned.
GENERAL: First issue, January-March, 1955. Usual publication length, 28 pages.
BACK ISSUES: 1960-1972 inclusive available from editorial address at $.75 each; $3.00 per volume; $28.00 for entire run, postpaid. 1955-1959 inclusive available from Johnson Reprint Corp.

KEYSTONE FOLKLORE QUARTERLY

EDITORIAL ADDRESS:
Jay Anderson, Editor
American Studies and Folklore
The Pennsylvania State University
The Capitol Campus
Middletown, Pennsylvania 17057

SUBSCRIPTION ADDRESS:
Robert H. Byington, Executive Secretary
Department of English
Point Park College
Pittsburgh, Pennsylvania 15222

PUBLISHED: Quarterly
COST: 1 yr.—$4.00 (membership in Pennsylvania Folklore Society); single copy—$1.25.

CONTENTS: Articles on folklore and folklore theory. Examples: "The Structure and Dynamics of Folklore in the Novel Form: The Case of John O. Killens"; "Charlie Parker: A Contemporary Folk Hero."

GENERAL: First issue, 1955. Usual publication length, 35-40 pages.
BACK ISSUES: Microfilm and xerox copies of back issues may be purchased from Xerox University Microfilms.

MID-SOUTH FOLKLORE

EDITORIAL ADDRESS:
William M. Clements, Editor
Division of English,
Philosophy, & Languages
Arkansas State University
State University, Arkansas 72467

SUBSCRIPTION ADDRESS:

same

PUBLISHED: Tri-annually
COST: 1 yr.—$4.00 (checks payable to Arkansas State University); single copy—$1.50.

CONTENTS: Articles dealing with folklore texts collected in Arkansas and adjacent states. Material must be annotated and be accompanied by an analysis. Examples: "Black Jack Ketchum: The Birth of a Folk Hero"; " 'The Kosciusko Bootlegger's Gripe,' A Ballad as History and Argumentation."

UNSOLICITED MSS. WELCOME? Yes; submissions acknowledged.
SPECIFICALLY WELCOMED: Articles which contribute to folklore scholarship.
MS. LENGTH: No preference; submit ONE copy.
STYLE REQUIREMENTS: MLA STYLE SHEET.
COPYRIGHT: Arkansas State University.
EDITOR'S DECISION: 1 month.
FROM ACCEPTANCE TO PUBLICATION: 6 months.
PAYMENT/OFFPRINTS: Five copies of issue in which article appears.
REJECTED MSS.: Returned.
GENERAL: First issue, Spring, 1973. Usual publication length, 40 pages.

MISSISSIPPI FOLKLORE REGISTER

EDITORIAL ADDRESS:
Jack Smith, Editor
Southern Station, Box 418
Hattiesburg, Mississippi 39401

SUBSCRIPTION ADDRESS:
Ovid S. Vickers, Secretary
Department of English
Box 697
East Central Junior College
Decatur, Mississippi 39327

PUBLISHED: Quarterly
COST: 1 yr.—$3.00.

CIRCULATION: 375

CONTENTS: Folk material of Mississippi and the South; some articles on national and international folklore; occasional bibliographies of Mississippi folklore; photographs; some book reviews; articles about the principal archives of folklore in Mississippi. Example: "The Legend of the Whiskey Bottle Gravestone."

UNSOLICITED MSS. WELCOME? Yes; submissions acknowledged.
SPECIFICALLY WELCOMED: Literary contribution related to any area of folklore.
MS. LENGTH: No requirements; submit ONE copy.
STYLE REQUIREMENTS: MLA STYLE SHEET; footnotes follow article.
COPYRIGHT: The Mississippi Folklore Society.
EDITOR'S DECISION: 1 month.
FROM ACCEPTANCE TO PUBLICATION: 3 months.
PAYMENT/OFFPRINTS: Six free offprints.
REJECTED MSS.: Returned.
GENERAL: First issue, Spring, 1967. Usual publication length, 45 pages.
BACK ISSUES: Available from subscription address at $1.00 each.

NEW YORK FOLKLORE QUARTERLY

EDITORIAL ADDRESS:
Roderick J. Roberts, Editor
Cooperstown Graduate Programs
Cooperstown, New York 13326

SUBSCRIPTION ADDRESS:
Betty Morris
The Farmers' Museum, Inc.
Cooperstown, New York 13326

PUBLISHED: Quarterly
COST: 1 yr.—$5.00; single copy—$1.25.

CIRCULATION: 900

CONTENTS: Articles concerned with folklore with special emphasis on New York material. Example: "Ballad Tragedy and the Moral Matrix: Observations on Tragic Causation."

UNSOLICITED MSS. WELCOME? Yes; submissions acknowledged.
SPECIFICALLY WELCOMED: Scholarly articles dealing with folklore and related disciplines.
MS. LENGTH: 10-25 pages; submit ONE copy.
STYLE REQUIREMENTS: MLA STYLE SHEET; footnotes follow essay.
COPYRIGHT: NEW YORK FOLKLORE QUARTERLY.
EDITOR'S DECISION: 2 months.
FROM ACCEPTANCE TO PUBLICATION: 3 months to 1 year.
PAYMENT/OFFPRINTS: Three free offprints.
REJECTED MSS.: Returned.
GENERAL: First issue, 1948. Usual publication length, 80 pages.
BACK ISSUES: Available from Betty Morris, New York State Historical Association, Cooperstown, New York 13326, at $1.25 each.

NORTH CAROLINA FOLKLORE

EDITORIAL ADDRESS:
Leonidas Betts, Editor
Department of English
North Carolina State University
Raleigh, North Carolina 27607

SUBSCRIPTION ADDRESS:

same

PUBLISHED: Regularly in May and Nov. with occasional special issues.
COST: 1 yr.—$2.00 (includes membership in North Carolina Folklore Society).

CIRCULATION: 1,000

CONTENTS: Articles on North Carolina folklore, but not exclusively; poetry; pen drawings; occasional photographs. Example: "The Vanishing Hitchhiker in Eastern North Carolina."

UNSOLICITED MSS. WELCOME? Yes; submissions acknowledged.
SPECIFICALLY WELCOMED: Any material on folklore of North Carolina.
MS. LENGTH: 1,000-2,000 words; submit ONE copy.
STYLE REQUIREMENTS: Merely good writing.
COPYRIGHT: Author.

EDITOR'S DECISION: 2-3 weeks.
FROM ACCEPTANCE TO PUBLICATION: Varies—will notify.
PAYMENT/OFFPRINTS: Three copies of issue; more upon request. No offprints.
REJECTED MSS.: Returned.
GENERAL: First issue, June, 1948. Usual publication length, 32-64 pages.
BACK ISSUES: Available from Johnson Reprint Corp. at $1.00 each.

NORTHEAST FOLKLORE (suspended publication)

EDITORIAL ADDRESS:
Editor
B Stevens Hall South
University of Maine
Orono, Maine 04473

SUBSCRIPTION ADDRESS:

same

PUBLISHED: Annually
COST: 1 yr.—$2.00.

CIRCULATION: 400

CONTENTS: Fresh, well-annotated collections of folklore material relevant to New England and the Atlantic Provinces of Canada; studies based on materials from this area.

UNSOLICITED MSS. WELCOME? Yes; submissions acknowledged.
SPECIFICALLY WELCOMED: Folklore studies focusing on the region of New England and the Canadian Atlantic Provinces.
STYLE REQUIREMENTS: MLA STYLE SHEET or AAA Style Sheet.
COPYRIGHT: Northeast Folklore Society (or arrangement).
EDITOR'S DECISION: 60 days.
FROM ACCEPTANCE TO PUBLICATION: 1-2 years.
PAYMENT/OFFPRINTS: 25 free copies of issue; more available at 40% discount.
REJECTED MSS.: Returned.
GENERAL: First issue, 1958. Usual publication length, 75 pages. (The Newsletter, not published since 1963, may start up again some time.)
BACK ISSUES: Vols. I-IV available from Johnson Reprint Corp. Others from editorial address at $2.00 each.

PENNSYLVANIA FOLKLIFE

EDITORIAL ADDRESS:
Dr. Don Yoder, Editor
Logan Hall, Box 13
University of Pennsylvania
Philadelphia, Pennsylvania 19174

SUBSCRIPTION ADDRESS:
Pennsylvania Folklife Society
Box 1053
Lancaster, Pennsylvania 17604

PUBLISHED: Quarterly   CIRCULATION: 2,000
COST: 1 yr.—$6.00; single copy—$1.50.

CONTENTS: Folklife, folklore, and historical ethnography of Pennsylvania's regional, ethnic, and sectarian cultures. Every aspect of traditional culture covered from art and architecture to cookery, costume, medicine, and witchcraft; many illustrations. Example: "Calligraphic Drawings and Pennsylvania German Fraktur."

UNSOLICITED MSS. WELCOME? Yes; submissions acknowledged.
SPECIFICALLY WELCOMED: Solid scholarly articles with critical and bibliographical apparatus; illustrations, charts, map.
MS. LENGTH: 12-20 pages; submit ONE copy.
STYLE REQUIREMENTS: University of Chicago's A MANUAL OF STYLE.
COPYRIGHT: Pennsylvania Folklife Society.
EDITOR'S DECISION: 1-2 months.
FROM ACCEPTANCE TO PUBLICATION: 4 months.
PAYMENT/OFFPRINTS: Author can purchase offprints at his expense.
REJECTED MSS.: Returned.
GENERAL: First issue, May 12, 1949, as THE PENNSYLVANIA DUTCHMAN; 1958, as PENNSYLVANIA FOLKLIFE. Usual publication length, 48 pages.

SCOTTISH STUDIES

See the section on AGE AND/OR NATIONALITY: ENGLISH, AND BRITISH COMMONWEALTH for details.

SEATTLE FOLKLORE SOCIETY JOURNAL
(formerly SEATTLE FOLKLORE SOCIETY NEWSLETTER)

EDITORIAL ADDRESS: SUBSCRIPTION ADDRESS:
Vivian Williams, Editor
Seattle Folklore Society   same
424 35th Avenue
Seattle, Washington 98122

PUBLISHED: Quarterly (Sept.,   CIRCULATION: 400
Dec., Mar., June)
COST: 1 yr.—$3.00 (includes membership in Seattle Folklore Society); $2.00 (libraries); $20 life membership available.

CONTENTS: Articles of interest to folk musicians, craftsmen, other folklore scholars and "fans"; occasional original songs, picture stories; reports of local folk music and other folklore activities; news of Seattle Folklore Society business; book and record reviews; photographs. Example: "Folkdancing and Changing Times."

UNSOLICITED MSS. WELCOME? Yes; submissions acknowledged.
SPECIFICALLY WELCOMED: Articles concerned with folk music and folklore of any degree of specialization and sophistication; opinions, riddles, jokes, recipes, helpful hints, pictures, letters, items related to folk music, folklore, "folklife."
MS. LENGTH: No preference (long articles may be run in consecutive issues); submit ONE copy.
STYLE REQUIREMENTS: None.
COPYRIGHT: Seattle Folklore Society.
EDITOR'S DECISION: 1 month.
FROM ACCEPTANCE TO PUBLICATION: Less than 3 months.
PAYMENT/OFFPRINTS: One copy of journal; more if requested. No offprints.
REJECTED MSS.: Returned.
GENERAL: First issue, September, 1969. Usual publication length, 24 to 32 pages. Volumes 1 through 3 are indexed in Vol. 3, No. 4.
BACK ISSUES: Available from editorial address at $.50 each.

SOUTHERN FOLKLORE QUARTERLY

EDITORIAL ADDRESS:
Roger M. Thompson, Editor
Anderson Hall
University of Florida
Gainesville, Florida 32601

SUBSCRIPTION ADDRESS:

same

PUBLISHED: Quarterly
COST: 1 yr.—$6.50.

CIRCULATION: 850

CONTENTS: Scholarly analysis of folklore and folklife; annual annotated bibliography of folklore publications in North and South America; book reviews. Example: "Pain and Suffering in Arabic Folklore."

UNSOLICITED MSS. WELCOME? Yes; submissions acknowledged.
SPECIFICALLY WELCOMED: Researched essays.
MS. LENGTH: Less than 50 pages; submit ONE copy.
STYLE REQUIREMENTS: MLA STYLE SHEET.
COPYRIGHT: Author.
EDITOR'S DECISION: 4-8 months.
FROM ACCEPTANCE TO PUBLICATION: 6-12 months.
PAYMENT/OFFPRINTS: No payment. Author pays for offprints.
REJECTED MSS.: Returned.
GENERAL: First issue, 1937. Usual publication length, 90 pages.
BACK ISSUES: Available from editorial address at $1.75 each; $6.50 for 4 issues. Out of print issues from Xerox University Microfilm.

SOUTHWESTERN AMERICAN LITERATURE

See the section on AGE AND/OR NATIONALITY: AMERICAN for details.

TENNESSEE FOLKLORE SOCIETY BULLETIN

EDITORIAL ADDRESS:
Ralph W. Hyde and Charles K. Wolfe, Editors
Middle Tennessee State University
Box 234
Murfreesboro, Tennessee 37130

SUBSCRIPTION ADDRESS:

same

PUBLISHED: Quarterly (Mar., June, Sept., Dec.)
CIRCULATION: 400
COST: 1 yr.—$2.00 for students; $3.00 for other individuals; $4.00 for libraries, institutions.

CONTENTS: Articles on folklore, mostly with regional orientation; book reviews; record reviews; editorial comment; announcements. Example: "The Scottish 'Tam Lin' in the Light of Other Folk Literature."

UNSOLICITED MSS. WELCOME? Yes; submissions acknowledged.
SPECIFICALLY WELCOMED: Folklore-oriented (no creative writing as such) articles, either field collections or research (folklore in literature); book reviews.
MS. LENGTH: Up to 3,000-5,000 words; submit ONE copy.
STYLE REQUIREMENTS: MLA STYLE SHEET.
COPYRIGHT: Tennessee Folklore Society; permission for use of materials is routinely given.
EDITOR'S DECISION: Usually 2 weeks.
FROM ACCEPTANCE TO PUBLICATION: 3-9 months.
PAYMENT/OFFPRINTS: Three copies of issue if article, two if review. No offprints.
REJECTED MSS.: Returned.
GENERAL: First issue, 1935. Usual publication length, 30-38 pages. A master index and the microfilm will soon be ready for sale—price to be announced.
BACK ISSUES: About two-thirds available from editorial address at $.65 each. All back issues are microfilmed.

WESTERN FOLKLORE

EDITORIAL ADDRESS:
D. K. Wilgus, Editor
Folklore and Mythology Group
University of California
Los Angeles, California 90024

SUBSCRIPTION ADDRESS:
Secretary-Treasurer
California Folklore Society
University of California Press,
Periodicals
2223 Fulton Street
Berkeley, California 94720

PUBLISHED: Quarterly (Jan., Apr., July, Oct.)
CIRCULATION: 865
COST: 1 yr.—$8.00 (includes membership in California Folklore Society); $9.00 outside of U.S., Canada, and Pan-America; institutional fees, respectively—$12.00 and $13.00; student fees—$3.00; single copy—$2.25 for individuals; $3.25 for institutions.

CONTENTS: Analysis and criticism of world folklore; short items of collectenea; notes and queries; book and record reviews; illustrations. Example: "The Social Context of a Local 'Lingo.' "

UNSOLICITED MSS. WELCOME? Yes; submissions acknowledged.
SPECIFICALLY WELCOMED: Articles about folklore of western North America. Belles lettres are not considered.
MS. LENGTH: 3,000-4,000 words; submit ONE copy.
STYLE REQUIREMENTS: University of Chicago's A MANUAL OF STYLE (12 rev. ed., 1969).
COPYRIGHT: University of California Press in the name of the Regents of the University of California.
EDITOR'S DECISION: 1 month.
FROM ACCEPTANCE TO PUBLICATION: 9 months.
PAYMENT/OFFPRINTS: 25 free offprints; others at author's expense.
REJECTED MSS.: Returned.
GENERAL: First issue, January, 1942 (as CALIFORNIA FOLKLORE QUARTERLY). Usual publication length, 76 pages.
BACK ISSUES: Through Vol. 20 available in offset from A.M.S. Reprint Co. Microfilm or xerox copies from Xerox University Microfilms. Recent single copy rate: $2.25; $3.25 for institutions; those more than a year old cost an additional $1.00.

VI

FILM

ACTION

EDITORIAL ADDRESS:
Bob Thomas, Editor
7950 Sunset Boulevard
Los Angeles, California 90046

SUBSCRIPTION ADDRESS:
Directors Guild of America
same

PUBLISHED: Bi-monthly
COST: 1 yr.—$4.00 ($6.00 foreign).

CIRCULATION: 8,400

CONTENTS: Articles and material on movies, television, nontheatrical areas, and industrial commercial areas from the viewpoint of the Directors and their assistants—useful information to film scholars for reference.

UNSOLICITED MSS. WELCOME? No.
GENERAL: First issue, September-October, 1966. Usual publication length, 22-30 pages.
BACK ISSUES: From subscription address at $2.00 each, if available.

ANDY WARHOL'S INTERVIEW

EDITORIAL ADDRESS:
Glenn O'Brien, Managing Editor
33 Union Square West
New York, New York 10003

SUBSCRIPTION ADDRESS:
same

PUBLISHED: Monthly
COST: 1 yr.—$5.00 in U.S.; $8.00 in Europe, £2.50 in U.K., $10.00 in rest of the world.

CIRCULATION: 40,000

CONTENTS: Long interviews; short analyses of films; reviews; reports on events and film personalities; illustrations.

GENERAL: First issue, 1969. Usual publication length, 40 pages.
BACK ISSUES: Available from editorial address at $1.00 postage paid.

ARGENTINE SCIENCE FICTION REVIEW

See the section on SPECIALIZED TOPICS AND INTERDISCIPLINARY STUDIES: POPULAR CULTURE for details.

AV GUIDE: THE LEARNING MEDIA MAGAZINE

EDITORIAL ADDRESS:
G. Littlefield, Managing Editor
434 South Wabash
Chicago, Illinois 60605

SUBSCRIPTION ADDRESS:

same

PUBLISHED: Monthly
COST: 1 yr.—$6.00; 2 yrs.—$10.00; 3 yrs.—$14.00.

CIRCULATION: 10,000

CONTENTS: Feature articles dealing with aspects of the contemporary AV field, especially in relation to educational use; book reviews; film reviews; filmstrip reviews; new software and hardware news; general news.

UNSOLICITED MSS. WELCOME? Yes; submissions on features acknowledged.
SPECIFICALLY WELCOMED: Feature articles dealing with contemporary aspects of the AV field.
MS. LENGTH: Features, 1,500-2,500 words; submit TWO copies.
COPYRIGHT: Educational Screen, Inc.
EDITOR'S DECISION: 3 weeks.
FROM ACCEPTANCE TO PUBLICATION: 2 months.
PAYMENT/OFFPRINTS: Offprints available free to author (250 maximum).
REJECTED MSS.: Returned.
GENERAL: First issue, 1922. Usual publication length, 32 pages.
BACK ISSUES: Available from managing editor at $1.00 each; Blue Book (December issue), $2.00 each.

CANYON CINEMANEWS

EDITORIAL ADDRESS:
Canyon Cinema Co-op
Suite 220 Industrial Center Bldg.
Sausalito, California 94965

SUBSCRIPTION ADDRESS:
P.O. Box 637
Sausalito, California 94965

PUBLISHED: Bimonthly
COST: 1 yr.—$3.00; $5.00 for airmail.

CIRCULATION: 2,000-4,000

CONTENTS: News and articles directed toward people interested in the American independent film movement.

UNSOLICITED MSS. WELCOME? Yes; submissions acknowledged.
SPECIFICALLY WELCOMED: Articles regarding Independent filmmaking.
MS. LENGTH: 500 words; submit TWO copies.
STYLE REQUIREMENTS: Open.
COPYRIGHT: Writer.
EDITOR'S DECISION: 4 weeks.
FROM ACCEPTANCE TO PUBLICATION: 8-12 weeks.
PAYMENT/OFFPRINTS: None.
REJECTED MSS.: Returned, if requested.

GENERAL: First issue, January, 1966. Usual publication length, 8-10 pages.
BACK ISSUES: Available from subscription office at $1.00 each.

CINÉASTE

EDITORIAL ADDRESS: SUBSCRIPTION ADDRESS:
Gary Crowdus, Editor
244 West 27th Street same
New York, New York 10001

PUBLISHED: Quarterly CIRCULATION: 3,000
COST: 1 yr.—$3.00; single issue—$.75.

CONTENTS: Critical essays about films, particularly those about social change; reviews of films, of books and magazines about films; interviews; special reports; photographs. Example article: "Critical Approaches Toward Film, Then and Now."
UNSOLICITED MSS. WELCOME? Yes.
SPECIFICALLY WELCOMED: Materials about political films and film makers.
MS. LENGTH: No preference; submit ONE copy.
STYLE REQUIREMENTS: None in particular; just make it readable.
COPYRIGHT: CINÉASTE; authors allowed reprint rights.
EDITOR'S DECISION: 1 month.
PAYMENT/OFFPRINTS: Payment in copies only. Extra copies and/or tearsheets provided if requested.
REJECTED MSS.: Returned.
GENERAL: First issue, 1967. Usual publication length, 48-60 pages.
BACK ISSUES: Available from editorial address at $1.00 each.

CINEMA

EDITORIAL ADDRESS: SUBSCRIPTION ADDRESS:
Paul Schrader and
Jack M. Hanson, Editors same
9667 Wilshire Boulevard
Beverly Hills, California 90212

PUBLISHED: Tri-annually CIRCULATION: 3,000
COST: 1 yr.—$5.00; 2 yrs.—$8.00; 3 yrs.—$10.00.

CONTENTS: Essays presenting films as forms of art; book reviews; notes on film magazines; many photographs; interviews.

UNSOLICITED MSS. WELCOME? Yes; submissions acknowledged.

SPECIFICALLY WELCOMED: Articles on films, generally current films, or studies of a director, studio, writer.
MS. LENGTH: Varies; submit ONE copy.
STYLE REQUIREMENTS: None.
COPYRIGHT: Spectator International, Inc.
EDITOR'S DECISION: Varies.
FROM ACCEPTANCE TO PUBLICATION: Varies.
PAYMENT/OFFPRINTS: Copies of the magazine.
REJECTED MSS.: Returned.
GENERAL: First issue, 1964. Usual publication length, 56 pages.
BACK ISSUES: Available from editorial office at $3.00 each.

CINEMA CANADA

EDITORIAL ADDRESS:
George Csaba Koller, Editor
6 Washington Avenue #3
Toronto M5S 1L2
Ontario, Canada

SUBSCRIPTION ADDRESS:

same

PUBLISHED: Bi-monthly (Jan., Mar., May, July, Sept., Nov.)
CIRCULATION: 3,500
COST: 1 yr.—$5.00 in U.S.; abroad, $6.50; institution, $10.00; student, $4.00.

CONTENTS: An intensive Film News section; Technical News; regular submissions from Canadian Society of Cinematographers, Canadian Film Editors Guild, Director's Guild of Canada, and NABET-AFC local 700; Film Book Reviews by David Beard; Opinion by Kirwan Cox; film reviews; Toronto Filmmakers' Co-op page, Le Cinema Quebecois—regular feature; plus in-depth interviews with filmmakers, and extensive coverage of festivals, panel discussions. Covers Film in Canada.

UNSOLICITED MSS. WELCOME? Yes, if concerning Canadian film; submissions acknowledged.
SPECIFICALLY WELCOMED: Coverage of Canadian film events in other parts of the country; film reviews; technical articles.
MS. LENGTH: Depends on subject; submit ONE or TWO copies.
STYLE REQUIREMENTS: None.
COPYRIGHT: Authors.
EDITOR'S DECISION: 4-6 weeks.
FROM ACCEPTANCE TO PUBLICATION: Depends on subject.
PAYMENT/OFFPRINTS: Small payment; depends on type of article.
REJECTED MSS.: Returned.
GENERAL: First issue, 1961, as CANADIAN CINEMATOGRAPHER. Revived, March, 1972.
BACK ISSUES: Available from editorial office at $5.00 each for first three issues; $2.50 each for all others.

CINEMA JOURNAL

EDITORIAL ADDRESS:
Richard Dyer MacCann, Editor
Broadcasting and Film Division
The University of Iowa
Iowa City, Iowa 52242

SUBSCRIPTION ADDRESS:
Publications Order Department
The University of Iowa
17 West College Street
Iowa City, Iowa 52242

PUBLISHED: Biannually (Nov., Apr.)
COST: 1 yr.—$4.00; single copy—$2.00.

CONTENTS: Scholarly articles on film, emphasizing film as an art and criticism of it as one of the humanities; contributions of a theoretical, historical, comparative, critical, or controversial nature concerning cinema; reviews of books about film. Examples: "Japanese Swordfighters and American Gunfighters"; "Sinclair Lewis and the Movies."

UNSOLICITED MSS. WELCOME? Yes; submissions acknowledged.
SPECIFICALLY WELCOMED: Film history and theory.
STYLE REQUIREMENTS: Serious, concise, interesting and relaxed.
COPYRIGHT: Society for Cinema Studies.
EDITOR'S DECISION: 1-3 months.
PAYMENT/OFFPRINTS: Several copies of the magazine.
REJECTED MSS.: Returned.
GENERAL: First issue, 1961. Usual publication length, 80 pages.
BACK ISSUES: Available from subscription address.

CINEMA STUDIES

EDITORIAL ADDRESS:
Gerald Noxon, Editor
The Experiment Press
10 Harborside Park
P.O. Box 266
Dennisport, Massachusetts 02639

SUBSCRIPTION ADDRESS:

same

PUBLISHED: Irregularly   CIRCULATION: 200
COST: Single issue—$2.00; $2.50, foreign.

CONTENTS: Essays comparing films with literature and with visual arts; film theory, analysis, and criticism.

UNSOLICITED MSS. WELCOME? No.
GENERAL: First issue, 1967. Usual publication length, 150 pages. There are three issues: 1967, #1 "An Analysis of 'A Diary for Timothy' "; 1968, #2 "Pictorial Origins of Cinema Narrative"; 1968, #3 "Music, Mathematics and Film." Future publication, possibly 1974.
BACK ISSUES: Available from editorial address at current prices cited above.

CLASSIC FILM COLLECTOR

EDITORIAL ADDRESS:
Samuel K. Rubin, Editor
734 Philadelphia Street
Indiana, Pennsylvania 15701

SUBSCRIPTION ADDRESS:
Contact, Inc.
Box 391
Indiana, Pennsylvania 15701

PUBLISHED: Quarterly
COST: Single copy—$1.50.

CIRCULATION: 2,000

CONTENTS: Reviews of films available for collectors; biographies and features on classic movie stars and other notables; news concerning 8, 16, 9.5, 35 mm films; reviews of movie related books, magazines, and other publications; illustrated film reviews; historical articles; news of the Society for Cinephiles, Ltd.; news clips from national and international publications. Examples: "Citizen Kane: A Character Analysis"; "The Five Chaplins."

UNSOLICITED MSS. WELCOME? Yes; submissions acknowledged.
SPECIFICALLY WELCOMED: Anything on classic movie field.
MS. LENGTH: No restrictions; submit ONE copy.
STYLE REQUIREMENTS: None.
COPYRIGHT: Author (if he wishes) or publication.
EDITOR'S DECISION: At once.
FROM ACCEPTANCE TO PUBLICATION: Indefinite.
PAYMENT/OFFPRINTS: No payment. Will supply offprints at cost.
REJECTED MSS.: Returned.
GENERAL: Usual publication length, 64-72 pages. The COLLECTOR covers the complete range of the classic field.
BACK ISSUES: Available from subscription address at $1.00 each.

COUNT DRACULA SOCIETY QUARTERLY

EDITORIAL ADDRESS:
Gordon B. Guy, Editor
Gothick Gateway
22 Canterbury Street
East Hartford, Connecticut 06118

SUBSCRIPTION ADDRESS:
The Count Dracula Society
334 West 54th Street
Los Angeles, California 90037

PUBLISHED: Quarterly
COST: Included in membership (non-members—$2.50 per year).

CONTENTS: Essays about Gothic literature and about horror films; reviews of films and books in this area; notes; illustrated.

UNSOLICITED MSS. WELCOME? Yes.
MS. LENGTH: 2,000 words, submit TWO copies.
GENERAL: First issue, 1967.

CRITIC (formerly FILM CRITICS' GUILD BULLETIN)

EDITORIAL ADDRESS:
Doré Silverman, Editor
Film Critics' Guild
9 Compayne Gardens
London N.W. 6
England

SUBSCRIPTION ADDRESS:

same

PUBLISHED: Weekly
COST: 1 yr.—£10 sterling; airmailed weekly to U.S.

CONTENTS: Brief reviews of films and of books about films; news.

UNSOLICITED MSS. WELCOME? No.
GENERAL: First issue, 1950. Usual publication length, 1 legal-size page. The CRITIC campaigns "for decency and intelligence in the treatment of the Press" (hence its exposure of actions contrary to this). Contents are factual.
BACK ISSUES: Available from editorial address. Price depends on date.

CTVD (CINEMA-TV-DIGEST)

EDITORIAL ADDRESS:
Ben Hamilton, Editor
Hampton Books
Route 1, Box 76
Newberry, South Carolina 29108

SUBSCRIPTION ADDRESS:

same

PUBLISHED: Tri-annually (Spring, Fall, Winter)
COST: 1 yr.—$3.00 in U.S.; $4.00 elsewhere.

CONTENTS: Reviews of films; translations of foreign reviews; photos of film scenes; special articles, such as "Film Making in Greece."

UNSOLICITED MSS. WELCOME? Inquire first; submissions acknowledged.
SPECIFICALLY WELCOMED: Only foreign accounts of U.S. and foreign cinema activities.
COPYRIGHT: Hampton Books.
PAYMENT/OFFPRINTS: Little, if any, payment. Six copies of magazine.
REJECTED MSS.: Returned.
GENERAL: First issue, Winter, 1962. Usual publication length, 32 pages.
BACK ISSUES: Available from editorial address at current prices.

DADA/SURREALISM

See section on SPECIALIZED TOPICS AND INTERDISCIPLINARY STUDIES: INTERDISCIPLINARY for details.

DECEMBER: A MAGAZINE OF THE ARTS AND OPINION

EDITORIAL ADDRESS:
Curt Johnson, Editor
Box 274
Western Springs, Illinois 60558

SUBSCRIPTION ADDRESS:

same

PUBLISHED: Once or twice yearly   CIRCULATION: 1,500-2,000
COST: $2.00 an issue; $7.00 for 4 issues.

CONTENTS: Poetry; fiction; some reviews of books; many reviews of movies (60-page movie section each issue, edited by Robert Wilson); articles generally about the state of literature and publishing; political articles; many photos; some graphics. Recent examples of critical essays: "A Revolutionary Art: Le Roi Jones, Ed Bullins, and the Black Revolution"; "Fantasy and Form in the Western: From Hart to Peckinpah."

UNSOLICITED MSS. WELCOME? Yes; submissions not acknowledged.
MS. LENGTH: Any length; submit ONE copy.
STYLE REQUIREMENTS: None.
COPYRIGHT: Curt Johnson.
EDITOR'S DECISION: 6-8 weeks.
FROM ACCEPTANCE TO PUBLICATION: 1 year.
PAYMENT/OFFPRINTS: Two copies of the issue.
REJECTED MSS.: Returned.
GENERAL: First issue, 1958. Usual publication length, 280 pages.
BACK ISSUES: Available from Kraus Reprint Co.

FILM

EDITORIAL ADDRESS:
Peter Cargin, Editor
British Federation of Film Societies
81, Dean Street
London W. 1V 6AA
England

SUBSCRIPTION ADDRESS:
21, Larchwood Road
Woking Surrey GU21 1XB
England

PUBLISHED: Monthly
COST: 1 yr.—$8.80.

CONTENTS: Reviews of films, festivals, and books about film; television, media, news/listings/information; general articles and interviews; illustrations.

UNSOLICITED MSS. WELCOME? No; submissions acknowledged.
SPECIFICALLY WELCOMED: Articles on contemporary visual media.
MS. LENGTH: To be agreed; submit TWO copies.
COPYRIGHT: FILM.
EDITOR'S DECISION: 1 month.
PAYMENT/OFFPRINTS: Payment can be made to overseas writers.
REJECTED MSS.: Returned.
GENERAL: First issue, 1952. Usual publication length, 28 pages.
BACK ISSUES: Available from subscription address at $1.50 each.

FILM COMMENT

EDITORIAL ADDRESS:
Richard Corliss, Editor
214 East 11th Street
New York, New York 10003

SUBSCRIPTION ADDRESS:
Box 686 Village Station
Brookline, Massachusetts 02147

PUBLISHED: Bimonthly

CIRCULATION: 10,000

COST: 1 yr.—$9.00; 2 yrs.—$17.00; 3 yrs.—$25.00. Outside of U.S., 1 yr.—$10.50. Student in U.S. only, 1 yr.—$8.00, 2 yrs.—$15.00.

CONTENTS: Interpretations and critiques of films; interviews with actors, directors, producers; reviews of new films; articles on the history of films, rereviews of old and neglected films; book reviews; photographs of film scenes. Example: "Linguistics, Structuralism, Semiology: Approaches to Cinema, with a Bibliography."

UNSOLICITED MSS. WELCOME? Yes; submissions acknowledged.
MS. LENGTH: 3,000-30,000 words; submit ONE copy.
STYLE REQUIREMENTS: MLA STYLE SHEET.
COPYRIGHT: Film Comment Publishing Company.
EDITOR'S DECISION: 4-6 weeks.
FROM ACCEPTANCE TO PUBLICATION: 1-6 months.
PAYMENT/OFFPRINTS: ½ to 1¢ a word.
REJECTED MSS.: Returned.
GENERAL: First issue, 1962. Usual publication length, 80 pages. Indexed annually.
BACK ISSUES: Available from Box 686 Village Station, Brookline, Mass. 02147 at $1.50 each, some at $.90. Available on microfilm from Xerox University Microfilms.

FILM CRITIC (formerly FILM SOCIETY REVIEW)

EDITORIAL ADDRESS:
William A. Starr, Editor
American Federation of Film Societies
333 Avenue of the Americas
New York, New York 10014

SUBSCRIPTION ADDRESS:

same

PUBLISHED: Bimonthly (Sept. through June)
CIRCULATION: 2,000
COST: 1 yr.—$5.00 (20% discount for libraries and students).

CONTENTS: Film and social criticism; articles on directors, the history of cinema, television, the press, the international film and television scene; reviews of books about films.

UNSOLICITED MSS. WELCOME? Yes; submissions acknowledged.
SPECIFICALLY WELCOMED: Sound, socially-relevant criticism.
MS. LENGTH: 750-5,000 words; submit ONE copy.
STYLE REQUIREMENTS: Standard; stylesheet available on request.
COPYRIGHT: Author.
EDITOR'S DECISION: Immediate.
FROM ACCEPTANCE TO PUBLICATION: 1-3 months.
PAYMENT/OFFPRINTS: 1¢ per word minimum. Author receives copies.
REJECTED MSS.: Returned.
GENERAL: First issue, 1965, as FILM SOCIETY REVIEW; 1972, as FILM CRITIC. Usual publication length, 80 pages.
BACK ISSUES: Available from editorial address at $.50 each for FILM SOCIETY REVIEW; $1.00 each for FILM CRITIC.

FILM CULTURE

EDITORIAL ADDRESS:
Jonas Mekas, Editor-in-Chief
G.P.O., Box 1499
New York, New York 10001

SUBSCRIPTION ADDRESS

same

PUBLISHED: Quarterly
CIRCULATION: 6,000
COST: 1 yr.—$4.00; $5.00 outside U.S.A.; single copy—$1.00.

CONTENTS: Essays on cinema; reviews; extensive interviews with film-makers; letters, documents, notes, exchanges by the Avantgarde film-makers; filmographies; photographs; specializes in American Avantgarde (Independent) Film. Occasionally entire issues devoted to work of one film-maker, such as Leni Riefenstahl, D. W. Griffith, Maya Deren, Ron Rice, Andy Warhol.

UNSOLICITED MSS. WELCOME? Yes; submissions not always acknowledged.
MS. LENGTH: No limit; submit ONE copy.
STYLE REQUIREMENTS: Double spaced. All film titles l.c., underlined.

COPYRIGHT: FILM CULTURE or the author.
EDITOR'S DECISION: 6 months.
FROM ACCEPTANCE TO PUBLICATION: 6 months to 1½ years.
PAYMENT/OFFPRINTS: Very few authors are paid; fee is low. Complimentary copies of the magazine.
REJECTED MSS.: Returned.
GENERAL: First issue, 1955. Usual publication length, 100-275 pages (single numbers-double numbers).
BACK ISSUES: Available from editorial address at from $1.50 to $4.00 each, depending on the issue.

FILM-ENGLISH/HUMANITIES JOURNAL

EDITORIAL ADDRESS
c/o Herbert Bergman
Film-English/Humanities Association
265 Ernst A. Bessey Hall
Michigan State University
East Lansing, Michigan 48823

SUBSCRIPTION ADDRESS:

same

GENERAL: This projected journal had not yet been issued at the time this entry went to press. Potential contributors should inquire for details from the editor.

FILM FACTS

EDITORIAL ADDRESS:
Ernest Parmentier, Editor
P.O. Box 213, Village Station
New York, New York 10014

SUBSCRIPTION ADDRESS:

same

PUBLISHED: Semi-monthly
COST: 1 yr.—$35.00 in U.S., Canada, and Mexico; $40.00, elsewhere.

CONTENTS: Synopses, critiques, and reviews of feature motion pictures (domestic and foreign) released in the U.S.; a complete listing of the production credits of each film; pertinent data about each film; the code ratings of MPAA: relevant background footnotes such as information on plays or novels from which screenplays have been adapted; a digest of the critical reception accorded each film by leading reviewers; a full index of any movie and the most obscure fact about it; illustrations.

UNSOLICITED MSS. WELCOME? No.
COPYRIGHT: Ernest Parmentier.
GENERAL: First issue, 1958. Publication length varies from 10-100 pages.

BACK ISSUES: Available from the editorial address in volumes only: 1958-1963—$40.00 each; 1964 and 1965—$20.00 each (incomplete); 1966-1968—$40.00 each; 1969—$25.00 (incomplete); 1970—unavailable; 1971—$40.00.

FILM FAN MONTHLY

EDITORIAL ADDRESS: SUBSCRIPTION ADDRESS:
Leonard Maltin, Editor
77 Grayson Place same
Teaneck, New Jersey 07666

PUBLISHED: Monthly
COST: 1 yr.—$4.25; $5.00 via 1st class mail; $7.00 via air mail; overseas, $4.50 3rd class mail; $6.50 1st class mail, $11.50 air mail.

CONTENTS: Articles, interviews, photos, filmographies on films and film personalities of the 1920's, 30's, and 40's. Example: "Myrna Loy Today."

UNSOLICITED MSS. WELCOME? Yes; submissions acknowledged.
SPECIFICALLY WELCOMED: Detailed, scrupulously researched material on lesser-known figures and aspects of Hollywood's past.
MS. LENGTH: 1,000-2,500 words; submit ONE copy.
STYLE REQUIREMENTS: Try to keep articles light.
COPYRIGHT: FILM FAN MONTHLY.
EDITOR'S DECISION: 3 weeks.
FROM ACCEPTANCE TO PUBLICATION: 3 months.
PAYMENT/OFFPRINTS: Extra copies of issue.
REJECTED MSS.: Returned.
GENERAL: First issue, 1961. Usual publication length, 32 pages. FFM's editorial policy is to shed light on neglected areas of film history; consequently, material appears in the magazine that is to be found nowhere else. Film scholars as well as film buffs have found it to be an invaluable research tool.
BACK ISSUES: Available from editorial address (1966 and after) at $.75 each.

FILM HERITAGE

EDITORIAL ADDRESS: SUBSCRIPTION ADDRESS:
F. Anthony Macklin, Editor
College of Liberal Arts same
Wright State University
Dayton, Ohio 45431

PUBLISHED: Quarterly CIRCULATION: 2,000
COST: 1 yr.—$2.00 in U.S., $2.50 elsewhere; 2 yrs.—$4.00 in U.S., $5.00 elsewhere.

CONTENTS: Analyses of films and rediscoveries of underrated films; occasional interviews; selected photographs from films. No reviews. Example: "Straw Dogs, Chess Men, and War Games."

UNSOLICITED MSS. WELCOME? Yes; submissions not acknowledged.
MS. LENGTH: 10 pages; submit ONE copy.
STYLE REQUIREMENTS: University of Chicago's A MANUAL OF STYLE.
COPYRIGHT: F. Anthony Macklin.
EDITOR'S DECISION: 6-8 weeks.
FROM ACCEPTANCE TO PUBLICATION: 6-9 months.
PAYMENT/OFFPRINTS: Three copies of issue in which article appears.
REJECTED MSS.: Returned.
GENERAL: First issue, Fall, 1965. Usual publication length, 40 pages.
BACK ISSUES: Available from editorial office at $3.00 for each issue of Vol. 1; $2.00 for each issue of Vols. 2 and 3; $1.00 for all others.

FILM INFORMATION

EDITORIAL ADDRESS:
Beatrice M. Rothenbuecher, Editor
Broadcasting and Film Commission
National Council of Churches
Box 500, Manhattanville Station
New York, New York 10027

SUBSCRIPTION ADDRESS:

same

PUBLISHED: Monthly
COST: 1 yr.—$6.00.

CIRCULATION: 5,000

CONTENTS: Reviews of films.

UNSOLICITED MSS. WELCOME? No.
GENERAL: First issue, 1970. Usual publication length, 6 pages. Most issues include a copy of FILM FEEDBACK, a service of the BFC NCC. FILM INFORMATION is written by leading Protestant critics—theologians, educators, communications specialists—who review approximately 300 theatrical films each year as to content, style, MPAA rating, potential audience, implicit and explicit values.
BACK ISSUES: Available from editorial address at $.50 each.

THE FILM JOURNAL

EDITORIAL ADDRESS:
Thomas R. Atkins, Editor
Box 9602
Hollins College, Virginia 24020

SUBSCRIPTION ADDRESS:

same

PUBLISHED: Quarterly   CIRCULATION: 5,000-6,000
COST: 1 yr.—$5.00 in U.S. and Canada ($7.00, foreign); 2 yrs.—$9.00 ($13.00, foreign); single copy—$1.25.

CONTENTS: Critical evaluations and original documents useful to scholars, students, teachers, and anyone seriously interested in film; book reviews (lengthy reviews, plus short capsule reviews in each issue); special features on library film collections of interest to scholars; filmographies; bibliographies; drawings; photographs; poetry related to movies. Special emphasis on relationship between movies and the humanities. Example: "Broken Blossoms: D. W. Griffith and the Making of an Unconventional Masterpiece."

UNSOLICITED MSS. WELCOME? Yes; submissions acknowledged.
SPECIFICALLY WELCOMED: All types of submissions related to film; they need not be works of film specialists. Regular contributors include poets, novelists, philosophers, graphic artists.
MS. LENGTH: 2,000-3,000 words; submit ONE copy.
STYLE REQUIREMENTS: MLA STYLE SHEET.
COPYRIGHT: THE FILM JOURNAL.
EDITOR'S DECISION: 4-6 weeks.
FROM ACCEPTANCE TO PUBLICATION: 6 months to 1 year.
PAYMENT/OFFPRINTS: Copies of the journal.
REJECTED MSS.: Returned.
GENERAL: First issue, Spring, 1971. Usual publication length, 72-88 pages. Indexed by volume.
BACK ISSUES: Available from subscription address at $3.00 each. Also available on microfilm from University Microfilms.

FILM LIBRARY QUARTERLY

EDITORIAL ADDRESS: SUBSCRIPTION ADDRESS:
William Sloan, Editor
Film Library Information Council   same
Box 348, Radio City Station
New York, New York 10019

PUBLISHED: Quarterly
COST: 1 yr.—$8.00 for non-members. Subscription included in membership in Film Library Information Council.

CONTENTS: Articles on films, film makers (experimental, educational, documentary), and film uses; reviews of new films; reviews of reference books about film; news of film organizations; interviews; photographs. Example: "Film and the Humanities."

UNSOLICITED MSS. WELCOME? Yes; submissions acknowledged.
SPECIFICALLY WELCOMED: Articles about film, video or non-print, and their relationship to public library service.
MS. LENGTH: 1,000-4,000 words; submit ONE copy.

STYLE REQUIREMENTS: None.
COPYRIGHT: Film Library Information Council.
EDITOR'S DECISION: 1 month.
FROM ACCEPTANCE TO PUBLICATION: 3 months.
PAYMENT/OFFPRINTS: Unlimited copies of the quarterly.
REJECTED MSS.: Returned.
GENERAL: First issue, 1967. Usual publication length, 56 pages.
BACK ISSUES: Available from editorial address at $2.00 each.

FILMMAKERS NEWSLETTER

EDITORIAL ADDRESS:
Suni Mallow and
H. Whitney Bailey, Editors
41 Union Square West
New York, New York 10003

SUBSCRIPTION ADDRESS:

same

PUBLISHED: Monthly   CIRCULATION: 11,000
COST: 1 yr.—$7.00 in U.S., $8.00 in Canada and Mexico, $10.00 elsewhere; 2 yrs.—$10.00 in U.S., $14.00 in Canada and Mexico, $18.00 elsewhere; single issue—$1.00 ($.75 on newsstand).

CONTENTS: Essays on 16mm and 8mm films; film reviews; news on various film festivals; in-depth studies of some topic related to filmmaking, such as technological developments, making and selling independent films, film as art, film history, dance and film, computer-made films, anthropology and film and new techniques for maximum use of equipment.

UNSOLICITED MSS. WELCOME? Yes; submissions acknowledged.
SPECIFICALLY WELCOMED: Film production stories, new equipment rundowns, observations on filmmaking economics (particularly distribution).
MS. LENGTH: 5,000 words maximum; submit ONE copy.
STYLE REQUIREMENTS: Well-typed, double-spaced manuscripts.
COPYRIGHT: FILMMAKERS NEWSLETTER unless otherwise agreed with author.
EDITOR'S DECISION: 4 weeks.
FROM ACCEPTANCE TO PUBLICATION: 1-6 months.
PAYMENT/OFFPRINTS: Will negotiate payment directly. Author must pay for printing of offprints; not less than 1,000.
REJECTED MSS.: Returned.
GENERAL: First issue, 1967. Usual publication length, 76-84 pages.
BACK ISSUES: Available from publisher. Write for price sheet.

FILMOGRAPH

EDITORIAL ADDRESS:
Murray Summers, Editor
Orlean, Virginia 22128

SUBSCRIPTION ADDRESS:

same

PUBLISHED: Quarterly
COST: 1 yr.—$7.00; single issue—$2.00.

CIRCULATION: 500

CONTENTS: Articles on all aspects of the film, current and past; emphasis is on the past. A continuing feature is an article on the career of a famous film star, usually with comments by the star himself; many film photos. Example: "Recollections of the Filming of THE WOLF MAN."

UNSOLICITED MSS. WELCOME? Yes; submissions acknowledged.
SPECIFICALLY WELCOMED: Anything relating to theatrical film.
MS. LENGTH: No preference; submit ONE copy.
STYLE REQUIREMENTS: None, since everything is edited.
COPYRIGHT: Murray Summers, Editor.
EDITOR'S DECISION: 1 week.
FROM ACCEPTANCE TO PUBLICATION: 3-6 months.
PAYMENT/OFFPRINTS: Two copies of issue in which author's work appears.
REJECTED MSS.: Returned.
GENERAL: First issue, 1970. Usual publication length, 48 pages.
BACK ISSUES: Available from editorial office at $2.00 each.

FILM QUARTERLY

EDITORIAL ADDRESS:
Ernest Callenbach, Editor
University of California Press
Berkeley, California 94720

SUBSCRIPTION ADDRESS:
Sales and Promotion Manager
same

PUBLISHED: Quarterly
COST: 1 yr.—$5.00 for individuals.

CIRCULATION: 8,000-8,500

CONTENTS: Critical essays about films, about their history; articles about new techniques in film making; studies of directors' or actors' developments throughout their careers; reviews of books about films.

UNSOLICITED MSS. WELCOME? Yes; submissions not acknowledged.
SPECIFICALLY WELCOMED: Articles, reviews, interviews, book reviews containing film criticism.
MS. LENGTH: Up to 5,000 words; submit ONE copy.
STYLE REQUIREMENTS: Journal is very specialized; writers should study it. Footnotes follow essay.
COPYRIGHT: The Regents of the University of California.
EDITOR'S DECISION: 10 days to 3 months.
FROM ACCEPTANCE TO PUBLICATION: 3 months.

PAYMENT/OFFPRINTS: About 1¢ per word, plus two gratis copies of issue.
REJECTED MSS.: Returned.
GENERAL: First issue, September, 1958. Usual publication length, 68 pages plus covers.
BACK ISSUES: Available from subscription office at $2.50 each. A.M.S. Reprint Co. can supply the out-of-print copies.

FILM REVIEW

EDITORIAL ADDRESS:
Norman Taylor, Editor
Old Court House
Old Court Place
42-70 Kensington High Street
London W.8
England

SUBSCRIPTION ADDRESS:
same

PUBLISHED: Monthly
COST: 1 yr.—£2.10; single copy—10p.

CIRCULATION: 124,000

CONTENTS: Film reviews; film studio news; star interviews; competitions; production features; collectors feature; film book reviews; record reviews; illustrated in color.
UNSOLICITED MSS. WELCOME? No.
COPYRIGHT: FILM REVIEW.
GENERAL: First issue, January, 1951. Usual publication length, 64 pages.
BACK ISSUES: Available from editorial address at 10p each. Only the last 12 months or so are still available.

FILMS AND FILMING

EDITORIAL ADDRESS:
Robin Bean, Editor
Hansom Books at Artillery Mansions
75 Victoria Street
London SW1H OH2
England

SUBSCRIPTION ADDRESS:
Circulation Department
same

PUBLISHED: Monthly
COST: 1 yr.—$14.00. Prices subject to change.

CONTENTS: Reviews of American and foreign films; articles about film making and about film actors; letters; questions and answers; interviews, such as "Intensification: François Truffaut in an interview with Gordon Gow."

COPYRIGHT: Hansom Books.

GENERAL: First issue, 1954. Usual publication length, 82 pages. Sample issues can be supplied to would be subscribers.
BACK ISSUES: Available from subscription address.

FILMS ILLUSTRATED

EDITORIAL ADDRESS: SUBSCRIPTION ADDRESS:
David Castell, Editor
First Media Press same
1121 Carney Street
Cincinnati, Ohio 45202

PUBLISHED: Monthly CIRCULATION: 15,000
COST: 1 yr.—introductory offer, $8.00; regular, $10.00; 2 yrs.—$18.00; 3 yrs.—$25.00.

CONTENTS: Reviews of films; filmographies; photographs of cinematic scenes; interviews (e.g. with Michael York, Sir Alec Guiness). Example: "Richard Chamberlain as Lord Byron."

UNSOLICITED MSS. WELCOME? Yes; submissions acknowledged.
SPECIFICALLY WELCOMED: Film reviews; interviews with actors, directors, etc.; career articles; book reviews; essays on film topics.
MS. LENGTH: Under 1,500 words; submit TWO copies.
COPYRIGHT: FILMS ILLUSTRATED.
EDITOR'S DECISION: 2 months.
FROM ACCEPTANCE TO PUBLICATION: 1 month.
PAYMENT/OFFPRINTS: Varies.
REJECTED MSS.: Returned.
GENERAL: First issue, July, 1971. Usual publication length, 42 pages.
BACK ISSUES: Available from First Media Press at $1.00 each.

FILMS IN REVIEW

EDITORIAL ADDRESS: SUBSCRIPTION ADDRESS:
Charles Phillips Reilly, Editor
210 East 68th Street same
New York, New York 10021

PUBLISHED: Monthly, October CIRCULATION: 6,500
through May; bi-monthly, June
through September
COST: 1 yr.—$8.50 in U.S., $8.75 in Canada, $9.00 elsewhere.

CONTENTS: Interpretation and reviews of new 8mm and 16mm films; interviews with actors, directors; reviews of films on TV; book reviews; letters; list of ten best English and foreign films; illustrated and indexed. Example article: "Shakespeare on Film."

UNSOLICITED MSS. WELCOME? Yes; submissions acknowledged.
SPECIFICALLY WELCOMED: Film research on history of films.
MS. LENGTH: Depends on content; submit ONE copy.
COPYRIGHT: FILMS IN REVIEW, but give authors permission to reprint.
EDITOR'S DECISION: Varies.
FROM ACCEPTANCE TO PUBLICATION: 3 months.
PAYMENT/OFFPRINTS: None.
REJECTED MSS.: Returned.
GENERAL: First issue, 1950. Usual publication length, 75 pages. Sends sample copy upon request. Written for general adult audience.
BACK ISSUES: Available from editorial address at $1.50 each.

FILM WORLD

EDITORIAL ADDRESS:
T. M. Ramachandran, Editor-in-Chief
12 Ocean View
Dumayne Road, Colaba
Bombay 400 005
India

SUBSCRIPTION ADDRESS:
Circulation Manager
same

PUBLISHED: Monthly
CIRCULATION: 25,000
COST: 1 yr.—$7.00; 2 yrs.—$12.00; 3 yrs.—$17.00; single copy—$.75.

CONTENTS: Reviews of films made in India; articles about current problems in cinema; interviews with directors and actors; pen portraits of new talent; stories about forthcoming films; illustrations. Example: "Why Double Standards in Censorship?"

UNSOLICITED MSS. WELCOME? Yes; submissions acknowledged.
SPECIFICALLY WELCOMED: Critical analyses of American films.
MS. LENGTH: 1,000 words; submit ONE copy.
STYLE REQUIREMENTS: Simple Queen's English.
COPYRIGHT: Author.
EDITOR'S DECISION: 6 weeks.
FROM ACCEPTANCE TO PUBLICATION: 6 weeks.
PAYMENT/OFFPRINTS: Due to foreign exchange restrictions in India, payment will be made in the form of gifts. Offprints can be given, but should advise quantity desired.
REJECTED MSS.: Returned, if requested.
GENERAL: First issue, 1964. Usual publication length, 56-70 pages.
BACK ISSUES: Available on microfilm from AMS Press Inc. Write to AMS Press for prices.

FOCUS! CHICAGO'S FILM JOURNAL

EDITORIAL ADDRESS:
Donald M. Druker, Editor
5811 South Ellis Avenue
Box 22
Chicago, Illinois 60637

SUBSCRIPTION ADDRESS:

same

PUBLISHED: Biannually
COST: 1 yr.—$2.00; 3 yrs.—$5.00; single copy—$1.00.

CIRCULATION: 2,500

CONTENTS: Essays and critical commentary on feature films, film history, documentary films; reviews of recent films and film books. Example: "Character, Action, and Symbol in Ingmar Bergman's THE TOUCH."

UNSOLICITED MSS. WELCOME? Yes; submissions acknowledged.
MS. LENGTH: Preferably 1,500-2,500 words; submit ONE copy.
COPYRIGHT: FOCUS!
EDITOR'S DECISION: 1 month.
PAYMENT/OFFPRINTS: None.
REJECTED MSS.: Returned.
GENERAL: First issue, 1967. Usual publication length, 48-64 pages.
BACK ISSUES: Issues #6, #7, #8, #9 available from editorial address at $1.00 each. Numbers 1, 2, 3/4, 5 available only in xeroxed form at $4.00 each.

HORIZON: MAGAZINE OF THE ARTS

See the section on LITERARY REVIEWS for details.

JOURNAL OF POPULAR FILM

EDITORIAL ADDRESS:
Sam L. Grogg, Jr., Michael T. Marsden, and John G. Nachbar, Co-Editors
The Bowling Green University
Popular Press
101 University Hall
Bowling Green State University
Bowling Green, Ohio 43403

SUBSCRIPTION ADDRESS:

same

PUBLISHED: Quarterly
COST: 1 yr.—$4.00, $2.00 for students; 3 yrs.—$10.00; single copy—$1.50.

CIRCULATION: 1,000-1,200

CONTENTS: Articles on film theory and criticism; interviews; filmographies; bibliographies; film chronologies; book reviews. Concentration is upon the commercial cinema: stars, directors, other artists working within the industry, individual films as well as genres. Editorial policy of the journal is dedicated to "popular film" in the broadest sense of that term with no esoteric distinctions between "motion pictures," "film," "cinema," or "movies," and with no limits on period or country covered. Example: "An Extraordinary Picture: The Film Criticism of Robert E. Sherwood."

UNSOLICITED MSS. WELCOME? Yes; submissions acknowledged.
MS. LENGTH: 10-15 pages; submit TWO copies.
STYLE REQUIREMENTS: Revised MLA STYLE SHEET; double-spaced; notes follow article.
COPYRIGHT: Co-editors.
EDITOR'S DECISION: 1 month.
FROM ACCEPTANCE TO PUBLICATION: 2-6 months.
PAYMENT/OFFPRINTS: Several copies of issue and 25 to 50 offprints.
REJECTED MSS.: Returned.
GENERAL: First issue, January, 1972. Usual publication length, 96 pages.
BACK ISSUES: Available from editorial address at $2.00 each, $7.00 for Volume I.

JOURNAL OF THE UNIVERSITY FILM ASSOCIATION

EDITORIAL ADDRESS:
Robert W. Wagner, Editor
Department of Photography and Cinema
156 West 19th Avenue
Ohio State University
Columbus, Ohio 43210

SUBSCRIPTION ADDRESS:
Editorial Secretary
same

PUBLISHED: Quarterly
CIRCULATION: 1,250
COST: 1 yr.—$6.00 in U.S.; $9.50 foreign (includes air mail postage); single copy—$2.00.

CONTENTS: Brief essays on the history of films; articles on film research and production; descriptive articles on film-television curricula in film institutes and universities; state-of-the-art comments on film genres, from educational to theatrical; bibliographic surveys of film at U.S. universities; photographs. Example: "The Education of the Film Maker for Tomorrow's Cinema."

UNSOLICITED MSS. WELCOME? Yes; submissions acknowledged.
MS. LENGTH: 2,500-3,000 words plus photos; submit ONE copy.
STYLE REQUIREMENTS: MLA STYLE SHEET.
COPYRIGHT: UFA JOURNAL (University Film Association).
EDITOR'S DECISION: Indefinite.
FROM ACCEPTANCE TO PUBLICATION: Indefinite.
PAYMENT/OFFPRINTS: Copies.
REJECTED MSS.: Usually returned.

GENERAL: First issue, 1948. Usual publication length, 32 pages.
BACK ISSUES: Available from Editorial Secretary at $1.00 for individual copy or $.75 each when four or more are ordered at the same time.

LITERATURE/FILM QUARTERLY

EDITORIAL ADDRESS:
Thomas L. Erskine, Editor
Box 960
Salisbury State College
Salisbury, Maryland 21801

SUBSCRIPTION ADDRESS:

same

PUBLISHED: Quarterly
(Jan., Apr., July, Oct.)

CIRCULATION: 5,000.

COST: 1 yr.—$5.00 for individuals; $4.00 for students; $6.00 for libraries; single copy—$2.00.

CONTENTS: Articles on individual movies, on different cinematic adaptations of a single literary work, on a director's style of adaptation, on theories of film adaptation, on the "cinematic" qualities of authors or works, on the reciprocal influences between film and literature, on authors' attitudes toward film and film adaptations, on the role of the screen writer, and on the teaching of film; interviews with directors, screen writers, and literary figures; reviews of current film adaptations of literary works; reviews of books concerning film and the relationship between film and literature; responses to any of the articles and reviews; photographs of film scenes.

UNSOLICITED MSS. WELCOME? Yes; submissions acknowledged.
SPECIFICALLY WELCOMED: Critical articles and interviews.
MS. LENGTH: Articles, 3,000 words; book and movie reviews, 1,500 words; submit two copies.
STYLE REQUIREMENTS: MLA STYLE SHEET; keep footnotes to a minimum; footnotes follow article.
COPYRIGHT: Salisbury State College.
EDITOR'S DECISION: 2 months.
FROM ACCEPTANCE TO PUBLICATION: 6 months.
PAYMENT/OFFPRINTS: Three offprints.
REJECTED MSS.: Returned.
GENERAL: First issue, January, 1973. Usual publication length, 96 pages.
BACK ISSUES: Available from editorial address at $2.00 each or at annual subscription rate.

MEDIA AND METHODS (formerly SCHOOL PAPERBACK JOURNAL)

EDITORIAL ADDRESS:
Frank McLaughlin, Editor
134 N. 13th Street
Philadelphia, Pennsylvania 19107

SUBSCRIPTION ADDRESS:

same

PUBLISHED: Monthly (Sept. through May)
COST: 1 yr.—$7.00.

CONTENTS: Articles on curriculum and teaching concepts, television, films, paperbacks, tapes, and other media. Examples: "Violence: Real and Mediate", (about teaching works with violence in them); "HOME FOR LIFE: A Verité Film by Gerald Remaner and Gordon Guin"; "Kitsch: A Guided Tour."

COPYRIGHT: Media and Methods Institute, Inc.
GENERAL: First issue, 1964. Usual publication length, 50 pages.

MONTHLY FILM BULLETIN

EDITORIAL ADDRESS:
Jan Dawson, Editor
British Film Institute
81 Dean Street
London W1V 6AA
England

SUBSCRIPTION ADDRESS:

same

PUBLISHED: Monthly
COST: 1 yr.—$4.75, includes postage (shortly to increase).

CONTENTS: Complete credits, accurate synopses and informed reviews of all feature films released in Great Britain and of selected short films.

UNSOLICITED MSS. WELCOME? No (except sample reviews in the magazine's format); submissions eventually acknowledged.
MS. LENGTH: Synopsis, 250 words maximum; review (single paragraph), 600 words maximum; submit ONE copy.
COPYRIGHT: The British Film Institute.
REJECTED MSS.: Returned, if requested.
GENERAL: First issue, 1934. Usual publication length, 20-24 pages.
BACK ISSUES: Available from editorial address. Cost depends on year of publication.

ON FILM

EDITORIAL ADDRESS:
Thomas W. Russell III, Editor
Cinema Ventures, Inc.
23 West 9th Street
New York, New York 10011

SUBSCRIPTION ADDRESS:

same

PUBLISHED: 6 times yearly

GENERAL: Usual publication length, 18 pages. This periodical had not arrived by the time the entry went to press. Potential subscribers, contributors, or collectors will have to write the editor to see whether the journal still exists, and if so, to inquire about details of manuscript submission, style, back issues, and the like.

PHOTON

EDITORIAL ADDRESS:
Mark Frank, Editor
801 Avenue "C"
Brooklyn, New York 11218

SUBSCRIPTION ADDRESS:

same

PUBLISHED: Quarterly   CIRCULATION: 3,000
COST: Six issues—$5.50; single copy—$1.00.

CONTENTS: Reviews of films, especially horror, fantasy and science fiction; photographs of film scenes; interviews. Example: "Fu Manchu on Film: A Historical Survey."

UNSOLICITED MSS. WELCOME? Yes; submissions acknowledged.
SPECIFICALLY WELCOMED: Film reviews; personality interviews; book reviews; television critiques; data on old and forgotten films.
MS. LENGTH: Optional; submit ONE copy.
STYLE REQUIREMENTS: Variable.
COPYRIGHT: Publisher.
EDITOR'S DECISION: 4-6 weeks.
FROM ACCEPTANCE TO PUBLICATION: 2-3 months.
PAYMENT/OFFPRINTS: Free copies in which contribution appears.
REJECTED MSS.: Returned.
GENERAL: First issue, September, 1963. Usual publication length, 48 pages.
BACK ISSUES: Available from publisher at $2.00 each.

SCREEN

EDITORIAL ADDRESS:
Sam Romdie, Editor
SEFT 63 Old Compton Street
London W1V 5PN
England

SUBSCRIPTION ADDRESS:
Society for Education in
Film and Television
same

PUBLISHED: Quarterly
COST: 1 yr.—$7.00; single copy—$1.95.

CIRCULATION: 3,000

CONTENTS: Original articles, translations, interviews (with detailed footnotes, filmographies) in the area of film criticism; film theory and film analysis with particular interest in the politics and ideology of film (to include television as well) and its analysis. Example: "Methodological Propositions for the Analysis of Film"; "Christian Metz: Bibliography."

UNSOLICITED MSS. WELCOME? Yes; submissions acknowledged.
MS. LENGTH: Up to 10,000 words; submit ONE copy.
STYLE REQUIREMENTS: To follow existing style (i.e. in terms of content and approach).
COPYRIGHT: Normally SCREEN, except on author's request.
EDITOR'S DECISION: 6 weeks.
FROM ACCEPTANCE TO PUBLICATION: 6 months; depends on issues planned.
PAYMENT/OFFPRINTS: If any, £15.
REJECTED MSS.: Returned if requested.
GENERAL: First issue, January, 1969. Usual publication length, 128 pages. Indexed by Volume.
BACK ISSUES: Available from subscription address at $2.50 each.

SIGHT AND SOUND: THE INTERNATIONAL FILM QUARTERLY

EDITORIAL ADDRESS:
Penelope Houston, Editor
British Film Institute
81 Dean Street
London W1V 6AA
England

SUBSCRIPTION ADDRESS:
Eastern News Distributors
155 West 15th Street
New York, New York 10011

PUBLISHED: Quarterly (Jan., Apr., July, Oct.)
COST: 1 yr.—$5.00, including postage; single copy—$1.50.

CIRCULATION: 31,000

CONTENTS: Critical and informational articles on all aspects of cinema, both current and historical; film reviews; news section; book reviews; guide to current films; illustrations; annual index to contributors, text, and illustrations; interviews. Example: "Time of Roses? New Cinema in Finland."

UNSOLICITED MSS. WELCOME? Yes; submissions acknowledged.
MS. LENGTH: Up to 6,000 words; submit ONE copy.
STYLE REQUIREMENTS: Should broadly conform to magazine's general style.
COPYRIGHT: SIGHT AND SOUND by The British Film Institute.
EDITOR'S DECISION: 2 weeks.
FROM ACCEPTANCE TO PUBLICATION: 2 months.
PAYMENT/OFFPRINTS: Basic rate of £10 per thousand words, plus copy of magazine.
REJECTED MSS.: Returned.
GENERAL: First issue, 1932. Usual publication length, 60-72 pages.
BACK ISSUES: Available from Publications Department at editorial address. Inquire about price.

SIGHTLINES

EDITORIAL ADDRESS:
Nadine Covert, Editor
Educational Film Library Association
17 West 60th Street
New York, New York 10023

SUBSCRIPTION ADDRESS:

same

PUBLISHED: 5 times yearly   CIRCULATION: 1,800-2,000
COST: 1 yr.—$12.00 (includes EFLA Personal Membership).

CONTENTS: News and articles on 16mm film production and utilization, and current developments in the field; listing of new releases on 16mm, 8mm filmstrips; listing of newly released film books; special subject filmographies or bibliographies.

UNSOLICITED MSS. WELCOME? Yes; submissions acknowledged.
MS. LENGTH: 3-6 pages; submit ONE copy.
COPYRIGHT: EFLA or author by agreement.
EDITOR'S DECISION: 3-6 weeks.
FROM ACCEPTANCE TO PUBLICATION: 2-6 months.
PAYMENT/OFFPRINTS: At least six free copies.
REJECTED MSS.: Returned.
GENERAL: First issue, Sept./Oct., 1967. Usual publication length, 28-32 pages.
BACK ISSUES: Available from Educational Film Library Association at $2.00 each; $3.00 each for "rarer" issues.

THE SILENT PICTURE

EDITORIAL ADDRESS:
Anthony Slide, Editor
First Media Press
1121 Carney Street
Cincinnati, Ohio 45202

SUBSCRIPTION ADDRESS:

same

PUBLISHED: Quarterly (Spring, Summer, Fall, Winter)
CIRCULATION: 1,000
COST: 1 yr.—$4.00 in U.S.; $5.00 elsewhere; 2 yrs.—$7.00 in U.S.; $8.00 elsewhere; 3 yrs.—$10.00 in U.S.; $12.00 elsewhere; single copy—$1.00.

CONTENTS: Interviews with silent film stars and technicians; critical pieces on films, such as DREAM STREET and TRUE HEART SUSIE; career articles; book reviews; photographs of film scenes and actors.

UNSOLICITED MSS. WELCOME? Yes; submissions acknowledged.
SPECIFICALLY WELCOMED: Material devoted to the art and history of the silent motion picture.
MS. LENGTH: Under 1,500 words; submit TWO copies.
COPYRIGHT: First Media Press unless otherwise arranged.
EDITOR'S DECISION: 2 months.
FROM ACCEPTANCE TO PUBLICATION: 3 months.
PAYMENT/OFFPRINTS: Varies.
REJECTED MSS.: Returned.
GENERAL: First issue, 1968. Usual publication length, 40 pages.
BACK ISSUES: Available from First Media Press at $1.00 each; microfilm editions from University Microfilms.

SOVIET FILM (AN ILLUSTRATED MONTHLY MAGAZINE)

EDITORIAL ADDRESS:
Maria Korolyova, Editor-in-Chief
v/o "Sovexportfilm"
14, Kalashny Perenlok
Moscow 103009
U.S.S.R.

SUBSCRIPTION ADDRESS:
c/o Eastern News Distributors
155 West 15th Street
New York, New York 10011

PUBLISHED: Monthly
COST: $.35 per copy on newsstands.

CONTENTS: Articles on the history of Soviet film, on film art today; profiles of and interviews with actresses, actors, directors; interpretations of films; festival reports. Examples: "The Hero and the Film"; "Soviet Films on World Screens"; "The Political Film."

UNSOLICITED MSS. WELCOME? Contact the editor.

GENERAL: First issue, 1957. Usual publication length, 28 pages. This periodical appears in Russian, English, French, German, Spanish, Arabic.
BACK ISSUES: Available from subscription address.

STUDIES IN THE HUMANITIES

See the section on SPECIALIZED TOPICS AND INTERDISCIPLINARY STUDIES: INTERDISCIPLINARY for details.

TAKE ONE

EDITORIAL ADDRESS:
Peter Lebensold, Editor
Unicorn Publishing Corporation
P.O. Box 1778, Station B
Montreal 110
Canada

SUBSCRIPTION ADDRESS:

same

PUBLISHED: Bimonthly   CIRCULATION: 20,000
COST: 12 issues—$4.50 in North America; $6.50 foreign; single copy—$.40.

CONTENTS: Reviews of films and of books about films; interviews with stars and film makers; Canadian Film Awards; letters; reports of film festivals; illustrations. Examples: "Griffith in Hollywood"; "The B-Movie as Art."

UNSOLICITED MSS. WELCOME? Yes; submissions acknowledged.
SPECIFICALLY WELCOMED: Articles on directors; interviews; reviews.
MS. LENGTH: Not stated; submit ONE copy.
STYLE REQUIREMENTS: None.
COPYRIGHT: Unicorn Publishing Corporation.
EDITOR'S DECISION: 1 month.
FROM ACCEPTANCE TO PUBLICATION: 3 months.
PAYMENT/OFFPRINTS: Payment varies widely.
REJECTED MSS.: Returned.
GENERAL: First issue, September, 1966. Usual publication length, 35-50 pages. Subscriptions sent free to individuals at prison addresses.
BACK ISSUES: Available only in microfilm editions and xerox copies from Xerox University Microfilms. Price varies from $.50 to $4.50 per issue; request price list.

UNIVERSITY VISION

EDITORIAL ADDRESS:
Paul Smith, Editor
British Universities Film Council Ltd.
Royalty House
72 Dean Street
London W2V 5HB
England

SUBSCRIPTION ADDRESS:

same

PUBLISHED: Biannually CIRCULATION: 900
COST: 1 yr.—$3.00 or £1.25, overseas (payment in sterling preferred); 43p in U.K.

CONTENTS: Articles dealing with the use, selection and production of audio-visual materials for teaching and research at university level (technical aspects of audio-visual aids are not dealt with); book reviews; conference reports; illustrations. Example: "Making an Educational Film: The Roles of Teacher and Producer."

UNSOLICITED MSS. WELCOME? Yes; submissions acknowledged.
SPECIFICALLY WELCOMED: Any articles dealing with aspects of the topics described above (descriptions of courses in which films are used; effect on pupils of audio-visual methods).
MS. LENGTH: 2,000-6,000 words; submit ONE copy.
STYLE REQUIREMENTS: See current issue; minimum footnotes (follow essay).
COPYRIGHT: British Universities Film Council Limited.
EDITOR'S DECISION: 1 month.
FROM ACCEPTANCE TO PUBLICATION: 2-3 months.
PAYMENT/OFFPRINTS: 12 free copies of issue in which article appears. If requested, first 30 offprints free, remainder at cost.
REJECTED MSS.: Returned.
GENERAL: First issue, February, 1968. Usual publication length, 44 pages.
BACK ISSUES: Available from editorial address at $1.50 or 43p. each (payment in sterling preferred).

THE VELVET LIGHT TRAP: A QUARTERLY JOURNAL OF FILM HISTORY AND CRITICISM

EDITORIAL ADDRESS:
Susan Davis and John Davis, Editors
Route 1
Cottage Grove, Wisconsin 53527

SUBSCRIPTION ADDRESS:

same

PUBLISHED: Quarterly CIRCULATION: 1,000
COST: 1 yr.—$3.00 (institutions—$8.00); single copy—$.75.

CONTENTS: Each issue is thematic; articles on film history; criticism; analyses of specialized topics (e.g. politics in film); interviews; critiques of directors, writers, etc.; book reviews; illustrations. Example: "Sydney Greenstreet: Hollywood's Heaviest Heavy."

UNSOLICITED MSS. WELCOME? Yes, if on the theme of forthcoming issue as announced in the magazine; submissions acknowledged.
SPECIFICALLY WELCOMED: Articles having to do with film and on the topic for next issue. Reviews of current films not accepted.
MS. LENGTH: 15-20 pages; submit ONE copy.
STYLE REQUIREMENTS: Well-written and interesting.
COPYRIGHT: Editors.
EDITOR'S DECISION: 1-2 months.
FROM ACCEPTANCE TO PUBLICATION: 1-2 months.
PAYMENT/OFFPRINTS: No payment at present; possibly a modest fee in the future.
REJECTED MSS.: Returned.
GENERAL: First issue, June, 1971. Usual publication length, 60 pages.
BACK ISSUES: Available from the editors at $1.50 each; very few of the first eight issues are left. Plans to have them reprinted are underway.

VIEWS & REVIEWS: QUARTERLY MAGAZINE OF THE REPRODUCED ARTS

EDITORIAL ADDRESS:
Ruth Tuska, Managing Editor
633 W. Wisconsin, Suite 1700
Milwaukee, Wisconsin 53203

SUBSCRIPTION ADDRESS:

same

PUBLISHED: Quarterly
CIRCULATION: 9,000-10,000
COST: 1 yr.—$5.00 in continental U.S.; $6.30 elsewhere.

CONTENTS: Articles devoted to the REPRODUCED arts; cinematographs; filmographies; career studies; photographs. Examples: "The Movies 100 Years from Now"; "Notes on the Establishment of a Star: Clark Gable."

UNSOLICITED MSS. WELCOME? Yes; submissions acknowledged.
SPECIFICALLY WELCOMED: First person articles by participants to the production of popular works in the mediums of film, phonograph records, popular literature or the graphics.
MS. LENGTH: Complete (quarterly serializes); submit ONE copy.
STYLE REQUIREMENTS: Accuracy.
COPYRIGHT: Depends on materials, author, payment, additional uses that quarterly or author wishes to put it to.
EDITOR'S DECISION: Rejections are quick; acceptances take 3-6 months.
FROM ACCEPTANCE TO PUBLICATION: 6-9 months.
PAYMENT/OFFPRINTS: Research articles run between $5 and $10 a printed page. First person material goes much higher depending on use and interest value of individual piece.

REJECTED MSS.: Returned.
GENERAL: First issue, 1969. Usual publication, 96-100 pages. Index (film; graphic arts; literature; music; plastic arts; illustrations) sent free on request which includes stamped, self-addressed envelope.
BACK ISSUES: Available from editorial address at $2.00 each.

WORKING PAPERS IN CULTURAL STUDIES

EDITORIAL ADDRESS: SUBSCRIPTION ADDRESS:
Editorial Group
Centre for Contemporary Cultural Studies   same
University of Birmingham
P.O. Box 363
Birmingham B15 2TT
England

PUBLISHED: Biannually (Autumn, Spring)
COST: 1 yr.—$3.50 or £1.00 (U.K.).

CONTENTS: Analyses of the modern media, their content and their effects. Example: "Ideological Analysis of the Message: a Bibliography."

UNSOLICITED MSS. WELCOME? Consult editor.

VII

SPECIALIZED TOPICS AND INTERDISCIPLINARY STUDIES

INTERDISCIPLINARY:
LITERATURE AND PSYCHOLOGY, RELIGION, POLITICS, PHILOSOPHY, SCIENCE, OR THE ARTS

AMERICAN IMAGO

EDITORIAL ADDRESS:
Harry Slochower, Editor
46 East 73rd Street
New York, New York 10021

SUBSCRIPTION ADDRESS:
Wayne State University Press
Detroit, Michigan 48202

PUBLISHED: Quarterly
COST: 1 yr.—$10.00.

CIRCULATION: 1,400

CONTENTS: Application of psychoanalysis to the humanities. Examples: "The Journeys in KING LEAR"; "Hamlet and Ressentiment."

UNSOLICITED MSS. WELCOME? Yes; submissions acknowledged.
MS. LENGTH: 5,000-10,000 words; submit TWO copies.
STYLE REQUIREMENTS: University of Chicago's A MANUAL OF STYLE.
COPYRIGHT: Association for Applied Psychoanalysis.
EDITOR'S DECISION: 1-2 months.
FROM ACCEPTANCE TO PUBLICATION: 6 months to 1 year.
PAYMENT/OFFPRINTS: None.
REJECTED MSS.: Returned.
GENERAL: First issue, 1939. Usual publication length, 100 pages.
BACK ISSUES: Volumes 23-29 available from Wayne State University Press at $3.00 each; Volumes 1-22 from Kraus Reprint Company.

THE CENTENNIAL REVIEW (formerly CENTENNIAL REVIEW OF ARTS AND SCIENCE)

EDITORIAL ADDRESS:
David Mead, Editor
110 Morrill Hall
Michigan State University
East Lansing, Michigan 48823

SUBSCRIPTION ADDRESS:

same

PUBLISHED: Quarterly
COST: 1 yr.—$3.00; 2 yrs.—$5.00; single copy—$1.00.

CIRCULATION: 1,200

CONTENTS: Articles concerned with the interrelations among the disciplines; poetry. Examples: "The Evasion of Adult Love in Fitzgerald's Fiction"; "BEND SINISTER and the Novelist as Anthropomorphic Deity."

UNSOLICITED MSS. WELCOME? Yes; submissions acknowledged.
SPECIFICALLY WELCOMED: Articles on the sciences and humanities.
MS. LENGTH: 2,000-3,000 words; submit TWO copies.
STYLE REQUIREMENTS: MLA STYLE SHEET.
COPYRIGHT: Author.
EDITOR'S DECISION: 3 months.
FROM ACCEPTANCE TO PUBLICATION: 6 months.

PAYMENT/OFFPRINTS: Extra copies of journal. One year free subscription to CENTENNIAL REVIEW.
GENERAL: First issue, 1957. Usual publication length, 100 pages.
BACK ISSUES: Available from editorial office at $1.00 each. Microfilm and microfiche of back issues available from Xerox University Microfilms.

CHRISTIANITY AND LITERATURE

EDITORIAL ADDRESS:
Arnold R. Hoffman, Editor
Department of English
Adrian College
Adrian, Michigan 49221

SUBSCRIPTION ADDRESS:
Dr. Patricia Ward
Department of French
Penn State University
University Park, Pennsylvania 16802

PUBLISHED: Quarterly
COST: $5.00 per academic year.

CIRCULATION: 275

CONTENTS: Essays, book reviews, and poetry which treat of the relationship of the theological and literary imaginations; a continuing bibliography of books and articles related to literature and theology.

UNSOLICITED MSS. WELCOME? Yes; submissions acknowledged.
SPECIFICALLY WELCOMED: Critical essays on theology and literature; some poetry.
MS. LENGTH: 2,000-3,000 words; submit ONE copy.
STYLE REQUIREMENTS: MLA STYLE SHEET.
COPYRIGHT: The journal or the author.
EDITOR'S DECISION: 2-4 months.
FROM ACCEPTANCE TO PUBLICATION: 2-4 months.
PAYMENT/OFFPRINTS: Appreciation copies.
REJECTED MSS.: Returned.
GENERAL: Usual publication length, 68-72 pages.
BACK ISSUES: Available from the editor at $.50 each.

CLIO: AN INTERDISCIPLINARY JOURNAL OF LITERATURE, HISTORY, AND THE PHILOSOPHY OF HISTORY

EDITORIAL ADDRESS:
Robert H. Canary and
Henry Kozicki, Editors
The University of Wisconsin-Parkside
Kenosha, Wisconsin 53140

SUBSCRIPTION ADDRESS:

same

PUBLISHED: Tri-annually
COST: 1 yr.—$4.50 for individuals; $12.00 for institutions and libraries.

CIRCULATION: 400

CONTENTS: Material of general interest for scholars who move about in literature, history, philosophy, and religion; essays on interdisciplinary pedagogy; reviews; review-articles; and related scholarly communications; editors solicit essays on the historical dimensions of literary works, the literary qualities of historical works, and the philosophical assumptions underlying such criticism. Example: " 'To Penshurst' and Jonson's Historical Imagination."

UNSOLICITED MSS. WELCOME? Yes; submissions acknowledged.
SPECIFICALLY WELCOMED: Scholars working as above.
MS. LENGTH: 10-50 pages.
STYLE REQUIREMENTS: MLA STYLE SHEET.
COPYRIGHT: CLIO, in standard understanding.
EDITOR'S DECISION: 2-3 months.
FROM ACCEPTANCE TO PUBLICATION: Within 1 year.
PAYMENT/OFFPRINTS: Two free copies of journal. Offprints offered at cost.
REJECTED MSS.: Returned.
GENERAL: First issue, October, 1971. Usual publication length, 100-110 pages.
BACK ISSUES: Available from editorial address at $1.75 each for individuals, $4.00 each for libraries. Also available on microfilm.

COMPUTER STUDIES IN THE HUMANITIES AND VERBAL BEHAVIOR

EDITORIAL ADDRESS:
Floyd R. Horowitz and
Sally Y. Sedelow, Editors
Department of English
University of Kansas
Lawrence, Kansas 66044

SUBSCRIPTION ADDRESS:

same

GENERAL: On good authority, we are assured that this journal does exist, though we had no response to inquiries by the time the entry went to press. Potential subscribers, contributors, or collectors will have to write the editors about details of manuscript submission, contents, and the like.

DADA/SURREALISM

EDITORIAL ADDRESS:
Mary Ann Caws, Editor
Box 85, Hunter College
695 Park Avenue
New York, New York 10021

SUBSCRIPTION ADDRESS:
Jean Schroeder
Department of Romance Languages
Queens College
Flushing, New York 11367

PUBLISHED: Annually
COST: 1 yr.—$6.00 (includes membership in Association for the Study of Dada and Surrealism); single copy—$3.00.

CONTENTS: Articles in the fields of dada and surrealism on art, film, literature and language of a thematic, linguistic, or stylistic orientation; bibliography; occasional photograph. Examples: "Surrealist Patterns in René Char's 'Eaux-mères' "; "Surrealism in DOG STAR MAN."

UNSOLICITED MSS. WELCOME? Yes.
SPECIFICALLY WELCOMED: Brief papers connected with dada and surrealism, whatever approach or attitude is taken.
STYLE REQUIREMENTS: Ms. written in English; where French quotation is used in the text, English translation should be supplied in the notes.
COPYRIGHT: Association for the study of Dada and Surrealism.
GENERAL: First issue, 1971. Usual publication length, 84 pages.
BACK ISSUES: Available from subscription address.

HARTFORD STUDIES IN LITERATURE: A JOURNAL OF INTERDISCIPLINARY CRITICISM

EDITORIAL ADDRESS:
Leonard F. Manheim, Editor
University of Hartford
200 Bloomfield Avenue
West Hartford, Connecticut 06117

SUBSCRIPTION ADDRESS:
same

PUBLISHED: Tri-annually
CIRCULATION: 500
COST: 1 yr.—$4.50 for individuals; $6.00 for agencies and institutions; foreign subscribers add 10%.

CONTENTS: Literary criticism as informed by any other art or science in the form of scholarly essays and book reviews. Example: "Fantasy and Defense in Faulkner's 'A Rose for Emily.' "

UNSOLICITED MSS. WELCOME? Yes; submissions acknowledged.
SPECIFICALLY WELCOMED: All forms of literary criticism informed by any of the arts or sciences.
MS. LENGTH: 10-30 pages; submit ONE copy.
STYLE REQUIREMENTS: MLA STYLE SHEET.
COPYRIGHT: University of Hartford.
EDITOR'S DECISION: 60-90 days.
FROM ACCEPTANCE TO PUBLICATION: 3-12 months.
PAYMENT/OFFPRINTS: Three copies of issue.
REJECTED MSS.: Returned.
GENERAL: First issue, Winter, 1969. Minimum publication length, 200 pages per year.
BACK ISSUES: Available from publisher at $2.00 each. Also available from Xerox University Microfilms.

THE INTERCOLLEGIATE REVIEW: A JOURNAL OF SCHOLARSHIP AND OPINION

EDITORIAL ADDRESS:
Robert A. Schadler, Editor
14 South Bryn Mawr Avenue
Bryn Mawr, Pennsylvania 19010

SUBSCRIPTION ADDRESS:
Barbara Leonard,
Editorial Assistant
same

PUBLISHED: Quarterly
COST: 1 yr.—$5.00.

CIRCULATION: 35,000

CONTENTS: Interdisciplinary articles of scholarship and opinion covering history, literary and social criticism, economics, politics, and international relations.

UNSOLICITED MSS. WELCOME? Yes, but not frequently published; submissions acknowledged.
SPECIFICALLY WELCOMED: Literary criticism with a social or philosophical framework.
MS. LENGTH: 10-25 pages; submit ONE OR TWO copies.
COPYRIGHT: THE INTERCOLLEGIATE REVIEW.
EDITOR'S DECISION: 2-4 months.
FROM ACCEPTANCE TO PUBLICATION: 4 months.
PAYMENT/OFFPRINTS: $100. Up to 50 copies of the journal; no offprints.
REJECTED MSS.: Returned.
GENERAL: First issue, January, 1965.
BACK ISSUES: Available from publisher, University Microfilms, Bell & Howell Microfiche, and Johnson Microfilms. Price varies.

INTERNATIONAL JOURNAL OF SYMBOLOGY

EDITORIAL ADDRESS:
R. A. Craddick and W. L. Kelly,
Editors
c/o Department of Psychology
Georgia State University
Atlanta, Georgia 30303

SUBSCRIPTION ADDRESS:

same

PUBLISHED: Tri-annually
CIRCULATION: 400
COST: 1 yr.—$20.00 ($21.00 foreign) for libraries and institutions; $11.00 dues membership to International Society for the Study of Symbols.

CONTENTS: Articles of a theoretical, empirical or historical nature dealing with symbols in art, literature, architecture, archeology, psychology, religion, music, psychotherapy, etc. Any area dealing with symbols is invited to submit articles. Example: "Goethe's Use of the Veil as a Symbol of Poetic Symbolism."

UNSOLICITED MSS. WELCOME? Yes; submissions acknowledged.
MS. LENGTH: 10 pages; submit TWO copies.

STYLE REQUIREMENTS: See recent issue of IJS for style.
COPYRIGHT: International Society for the Study of Symbols.
EDITOR'S DECISION: 1-2 months.
FROM ACCEPTANCE TO PUBLICATION: 3-5 months.
PAYMENT/OFFPRINTS: 50 gratis copies of the journal.
REJECTED MSS.: Returned.
GENERAL: First issue, August, 1969. Usual publication length, 40-50 pages.
BACK ISSUES: Available from editorial address at approximately $7.00 each.

INTERPRETATION: A JOURNAL OF BIBLE AND THEOLOGY

EDITORIAL ADDRESS:
Prof. James L. Mays, Editor
Union Theological Seminary
in Virginia
3401 Brook Road
Richmond, Virginia 23227

SUBSCRIPTION ADDRESS:

same

PUBLISHED: Quarterly
CIRCULATION: 6,500
COST: 1 yr.—$7.00 (foreign $7.70); 3 yrs.—$18.00 (foreign $20.10); single copy—$3.00.

CONTENTS: Articles; editorial; major book reviews; shorter reviews; notices; books received.

UNSOLICITED MSS. WELCOME? Yes; submissions acknowledged.
SPECIFICALLY WELCOMED: Biblical and theological articles.
MS. LENGTH: 10-15 journal pages; submit ONE copy.
STYLE REQUIREMENTS: None.
COPYRIGHT: INTERPRETATION.
EDITOR'S DECISION: 3 months.
FROM ACCEPTANCE TO PUBLICATION: 1 year.
PAYMENT/OFFPRINTS: $35.00. Authors order offprints from the printer and are billed direct.
REJECTED MSS.: Returned.
GENERAL: First issue, January, 1947. Usual publication length, 128 pages.
BACK ISSUES: Available from editorial address at $3.00 each.

JOURNAL OF BIBLICAL LITERATURE

EDITORIAL ADDRESS:
Joseph A. Fitzmyer, S. J., Editor
Fordham University
Bronx, New York 10458

SUBSCRIPTION ADDRESS:
Business Office—SBL/CSR
Society of Biblical Literature
Waterloo Lutheran University
Waterloo, Ontario N2L 3C5
Canada

PUBLISHED: Quarterly CIRCULATION: 4,604
(Mar., June, Sept., Dec.)
COST: 1 yr.—$18.00 (members of Society of Biblical Literature—$15.00; student members—$7.50); single copy—$5.00.

CONTENTS: Scholarly articles devoted to the critical study of the Bible and related subjects (history and archaeology of ancient Palestine; intertestamental literature of the Jews; Greek, Aramaic and Hebrew philological problems related to the Bible; biblical theology; hermeneutics of the Bible).

UNSOLICITED MSS. WELCOME? Yes; submissions acknowledged by card.
SPECIFICALLY WELCOMED: Critical interpretations of biblical passages; studies in biblical theology, philology, history, archaelogy.
MS. LENGTH: 20 pages; submit ONE copy.
STYLE REQUIREMENTS: Instructions for Contributors in JBL 90 (1971) 510-19.
COPYRIGHT: The Society of Biblical Literature.
EDITOR'S DECISION: About 3 months.
FROM ACCEPTANCE TO PUBLICATION: 6-9 months.
PAYMENT/OFFPRINTS: 50 offprints of articles; extra offprints available at printer's rate.
REJECTED MSS.: Returned.
GENERAL: Usual publication length, 160 pages.
BACK ISSUES: Available from subscription address.

THE JOURNAL OF INTERDISCIPLINARY HISTORY

EDITORIAL ADDRESS: SUBSCRIPTION ADDRESS:
Robert I. Rotberg and Journals Department
Theodore K. Rabb, Editors 28 Carleton Street
Department of Political Science, E53-490 Cambridge, Massachusetts 02142
Massachusetts Institute of Technology
Cambridge, Massachusetts 02139

PUBLISHED: Quarterly CIRCULATION: 1,750
COST: 1 yr.—$12.50 (institution—$16.50).

CONTENTS: Articles, review essays, research notes, reviews, and bibliographic notes promoting the exchange of information and methods between historical research and work in applied fields of the humanities and social sciences. Example: "Historians and the Evidence of Literature."

UNSOLICITED MSS. WELCOME? Yes; submissions acknowledged.
MS. LENGTH: 20-30 pages; submit TWO copies.
STYLE REQUIREMENTS: Footnotes at end of article, double-spaced.
COPYRIGHT: THE JOURNAL OF INTERDISCIPLINARY HISTORY.
EDITOR'S DECISION: 1 month.
FROM ACCEPTANCE TO PUBLICATION: 6-10 months.
PAYMENT/OFFPRINTS: 25 free offprints.

REJECTED MSS.: Returned.
GENERAL: First issue, Autumn, 1970. Usual publication length, 176 pages.
BACK ISSUES: Available from subscription address at $3.50 each (institution—$4.50 each); special issues—$5.00.

JOURNAL OF LITERARY SEMANTICS

EDITORIAL ADDRESS:
Trevor Eaton, Editor
18, Highfield Road,
Willesborough
Ashford, Kent TN24 OJJ
England

SUBSCRIPTION ADDRESS:
Co-Libri
P.O. Box 482
The Hague 2076
The Netherlands

PUBLISHED: Each issue appears as soon as sufficient good material has accrued.

CIRCULATION: Not yet known.

COST: Subscription price: df1.18 (ca. $5.60) per issue. Single issue price: df1.22 (ca. $6.85).

CONTENTS: Articles on all aspects of literary semantics; articles of a philosophical nature attempting to relate the study of literature to other disciplines such as linguistics, mathematics, psychology, neurophysiology, history; articles dealing with the educational problems inherent in the study of literature; reviews of books whose subject are germane to literary semantics. Emphasis is THEORETICAL.

UNSOLICITED MSS. WELCOME? Yes; submissions acknowledged only if delay in making decision is likely.
SPECIFICALLY WELCOMED: Articles whose approach to the problems of literature is scientific and theoretical; articles by theoretical linguists, philosophers, psychologists, mathematicians.
MS. LENGTH: No preference; submit ONE copy; author should retain a copy.
STYLE REQUIREMENTS: As for LINGUISTICS (Mouton & Co.).
COPYRIGHT: Mouton & Co.
FROM ACCEPTANCE TO PUBLICATION: 6-24 months.
PAYMENT/OFFPRINTS: 25 free offprints.
REJECTED MSS.: Returned.
GENERAL: First issue, 1972. Usual publication length, 124 pages. The Academic Headquarters of the Journal is: The Language Centre, The University of Kent at Canterbury, Kent, England.

JOURNAL OF THE WARBURG AND COURTAULD INSTITUTES

EDITORIAL ADDRESS:
D. S. Chambers, D. P. Walker,
J. B. Trapp, T. S. R. Boase,
Christopher Hohler, Frances A. Yates,
Ernst Gombrich, George Zarnecki,
Anthony Blunt, Editors

SUBSCRIPTION ADDRESS:
The Warburg Institute
University of London
Woburn Square
London WC1H OAB
England

PUBLISHED: Annually (Nov.)   CIRCULATION: 2,000
COST: £6.00 plus (at present) postage and packing, 45p. Booksellers' discount: 20%.

CONTENTS: Interdisciplinary articles on cultural history of interest to historians of art, religion, science, literature, social and political life, as well as for philosophers and anthropologists. The continuity of the classical tradition in western civilization is one theme.

UNSOLICITED MSS. WELCOME? Yes; submissions acknowledged.
SPECIFICALLY WELCOMED: Articles of up to 5,000-6,000 words; shorter notes of a miscellaneous character; a limited number of substantially longer papers, the material or treatment of which demands exceptional space; editions or transcriptions of new texts and documents (these may also be published as appendices to articles).
MS. LENGTH: Articles: up to 6,000 words; submit ONE copy for journal, one copy for author.
STYLE REQUIREMENTS: Footnotes must be numbered consecutively and typed on separate page at end of article. 'Notes for JOURNAL Contributors' is printed in each volume.
COPYRIGHT: The Warburg Institute.
FROM ACCEPTANCE TO PUBLICATION: 1 year, usually longer.
PAYMENT/OFFPRINTS: For articles, a complimentary copy of the relevant volume; 15 free offprints, plus any number at author's expense.
REJECTED MSS.: Returned.
GENERAL: First issue, July, 1937. Usual publication length, 400 pages.
BACK ISSUES: Available from The Warburg Institute at £4.00 each (plus postage, handling) for Vols. 31-33 (1968-70); £6.00 each (plus postage, handling) for Vols. 34 ff. Vols. 1-30 from Kraus Reprints (Liechtenstein); inquire cost from Kraus.

LITERATURE & IDEOLOGY

EDITORIAL ADDRESS:
Editor
The National Publications Centre
P.O. Box 727
Adelaide Station
Toronto 210
Canada

SUBSCRIPTION ADDRESS:

same

PUBLISHED: Quarterly CIRCULATION: 2,000
COST: 1 yr.—$5.00.

CONTENTS: Scholarly articles about "the political and social role of literature, art, and criticism." Examples: "Pro-Imperialist Ideas in Gabrielle Roy's TIN FLUTE"; "THE PLAGUE: Camus's Pro-Fascist Allegory."

UNSOLICITED MSS. WELCOME? Yes; submissions not acknowledged.
SPECIFICALLY WELCOMED: Marxist contributions.
MS. LENGTH: 3,000 words; submit ONE copy.
STYLE REQUIREMENTS: MLA STYLE SHEET.
COPYRIGHT: Norman Bethune Institute of Ideological Studies
EDITOR'S DECISION: 3 months.
FROM ACCEPTANCE TO PUBLICATION: Varies.
PAYMENT/OFFPRINTS: None.
REJECTED MSS.: Returned.
GENERAL: First issue, March, 1969. Usual publication length, 52-100 pages.
BACK ISSUES: Issues 1-7 are out of print; #8 and on available from National Publications Centre at $1.25 each.

LITERATURE AND PSYCHOLOGY

EDITORIAL ADDRESS: SUBSCRIPTION ADDRESS:
Morton Kaplan, Editor
Department of English same
Fairleigh Dickinson University
Teaneck, New Jersey 07666

PUBLISHED: Quarterly CIRCULATION: 1,000
COST: 1 yr.—$5.00 ($8.00 for institutions).

CONTENTS: Psychological interpretations of literary works; book reviews; notes. Example: "Aggression, Femininity, and Irony in MOLL FLANDERS."

UNSOLICITED MSS. WELCOME? Yes; submissions acknowledged.
SPECIFICALLY WELCOMED: Psychological interpretation, in-depth (psychoanalytic), of literary works.
MS. LENGTH: 15-20 pages; submit TWO copies.
STYLE REQUIREMENTS: MLA STYLE SHEET.
COPYRIGHT: Morton Kaplan.
EDITOR'S DECISION: 1-2 months.
FROM ACCEPTANCE TO PUBLICATION: 4 months.
PAYMENT/OFFPRINTS: Three free copies of issue in which work appears, plus extra copies at $1.50 each.
REJECTED MSS.: Returned.
GENERAL: First issue, 1950. Usual publication length, 40-50 pages.

BACK ISSUES: Vols. 15 to current available from editorial office at $4.00 each or $12.00 for complete volume year. Vols. 7-13 from Dr. Leonard F. Manheim, English Department, University of Hartford, 200 Bloomfield Avenue, Hartford, Connecticut 06117. Vols. 1-6 on microfilm from Xerox University Microfilms.

MIDWEST MODERN LANGUAGE ASSOCIATION BULLETIN

EDITORIAL ADDRESS: SUBSCRIPTION ADDRESS:
Gerald L. Bruns, Editor
Midwest Modern Language Association   same
311 English-Philosophy Building
University of Iowa
Iowa City, Iowa 52240

PUBLISHED: Biannually CIRCULATION: 2,150
(Spring, Fall)
COST: 1 yr.—$4.00; 3 yrs.—$10.50; single copy—$2.00.

CONTENTS: "...articles of general scholarly and professional interest. Essays on the study and teaching of language and literature, particularly in relation to political, historical, and cultural issues, are especially welcome, as are studies in critical methodology, literary history, and the theory of language."

UNSOLICITED MSS. WELCOME? Yes; submissions acknowledged.
MS. LENGTH: Not over 8,000 words; submit ONE copy.
STYLE REQUIREMENTS: MLA STYLE SHEET.
COPYRIGHT: MMLA.
EDITOR'S DECISION: 1 week.
FROM ACCEPTANCE TO PUBLICATION: No more than 6 months.
PAYMENT/OFFPRINTS: No payment. Offprints provided at current printer's costs.
REJECTED MSS.: Returned.
GENERAL: First issue, September, 1968. Usual publication length, 100-150 pages.
BACK ISSUES: Volumes 2, 3, 4, 5, and Spring issue for 1973 (Vol. 6, No. 1) are all available immediately upon request from Midwest Modern Language Association office at $2.00 per issue; single volume—$4.00; two volumes—$7.50; three volumes—$10.50. Vol. 1 is out-of-print.

THE MUSLIM WORLD

EDITORIAL ADDRESS:
Willem A. Bijlefeld,
Issa J. Boullata, Editors
The Hartford Seminary Foundation
55 Elizabeth Street
Hartford, Connecticut 06105

SUBSCRIPTION ADDRESS:

same

PUBLISHED: Quarterly
(Jan., Apr., July, Oct.)
COST: 1 yr.—$6.00.

CIRCULATION: 1,200

CONTENTS: Articles devoted to the study of Islam and of Christian-Muslim relationship in past and present; reviews of such books as ARABIC AND PERSIAN POEMS IN ENGLISH, MYTHS AND LEGENDS OF THE SWAHILI, and THE AUTHENTICITY OF THE TRADITION LITERATURE: DISCUSSIONS IN MODERN EGYPT. Theme for the January, 1973, issue was Arab literature and art.

UNSOLICITED MSS. WELCOME? Yes. No carbons or xeroxed mss. No multiple submissions. Submissions acknowledged.
SPECIFICALLY WELCOMED: Scholarly articles.
MS. LENGTH: Maximum 6,000 words; submit TWO copies preferably.
STYLE REQUIREMENTS: Scholarly, but not pedantic. Please refer to recent issues.
COPYRIGHT: Publisher.
EDITOR'S DECISION: 2 or more months.
FROM ACCEPTANCE TO PUBLICATION: At least 18 months.
PAYMENT/OFFPRINTS: Either 20 offprints or 5 complete copies of journal.
REJECTED MSS.: Returned.
GENERAL: First issue, January, 1911. Usual publication length, 80-96 pages.
BACK ISSUES: 1911-1964 available from Kraus Reprint Co.; some from publisher at $1.00 each for copies available through 1969; $1.50 each beginning in 1970 (plus postage).

PAUNCH

EDITORIAL ADDRESS:
Arthur Efron, Editor
123 Woodward Avenue
Buffalo, New York 14214

SUBSCRIPTION ADDRESS:

same

PUBLISHED: Biannually
COST: 1 yr.—$3.00 (libraries—$4.00).

CIRCULATION: 400

CONTENTS: Literary criticism emphasizing the importance of the body and sexuality, the aesthetic theories of Dewey and Pepper, and the personal experience of the work of literature. Examples: "Le Roi Jones and a Black Aesthetic"; "Bellow's HENDERSON and the Limits of Freudian Criticism."

UNSOLICITED MSS. WELCOME? Yes; submissions acknowledged.
SPECIFICALLY WELCOMED: A FEW poems with explorations of bodily experience.
MS. LENGTH: Any length; submit ONE copy.
STYLE REQUIREMENTS: Variable.
COPYRIGHT: PAUNCH.
EDITOR'S DECISION: 60 days.
FROM ACCEPTANCE TO PUBLICATION: 6 months.
PAYMENT/OFFPRINTS: Article, about $25; long article, $35; review, $15. At least 15 offprints, more if arranged prior to printing.
REJECTED MSS.: Returned.
GENERAL: First issue distributed, #21, October, 1965. Usual publication length, 80 pages.
BACK ISSUES: Available from the editor at $1.00 each for #21 through #33; $1.50 for #34 onward.

THE PENDULUM OF TIME AND THE ARTS

EDITORIAL ADDRESS:
Arthur W. Muller, Editor and Publisher
414 North Braddock Street
Winchester, Virginia 22601

SUBSCRIPTION ADDRESS:

same

PUBLISHED: Five issues yearly   CIRCULATION: 250
COST: 1 yr.—$1.50 in U.S.; $2.75 elsewhere; single copy—$.30.

CONTENTS: Brief essays on literature, the arts, philosophy; biography; reviews of general interesting articles of the past and present. (No poetry, fiction, political or controversial material.)

UNSOLICITED MSS. WELCOME? Yes; submissions acknowledged.
MS. LENGTH: Under 500 words; submit ONE copy.
COPYRIGHT: Author.
EDITOR'S DECISION: 2-3 weeks.
FROM ACCEPTANCE TO PUBLICATION: Varies.
PAYMENT/OFFPRINTS: Free copy containing author's published work.
REJECTED MSS.: Returned.
GENERAL: First issue, May, 1957. Usual publication length, 20 pages.
BACK ISSUES: Available from editor at $.30 each (only a few available).

THE PSYCHOANALYTIC REVIEW

EDITORIAL ADDRESS:
Editor
150 West 13th Street
New York, New York 10011

SUBSCRIPTION ADDRESS:
same

PUBLISHED: Quarterly
CIRCULATION: 2,100
COST: 1 yr.—$16.00 beginning with Volume 61, No. 1, 1974.

CONTENTS: Articles and reviews of books concerned with promotion of psychoanalytic study of mind and culture (including psychoanalytic interpretations of literature and of history).

UNSOLICITED MSS. WELCOME? Yes; submissions acknowledged.
MS. LENGTH: 12-30 pages; submit THREE copies.
STYLE REQUIREMENTS: Bibliographies and minimum footnotes should conform to style of journal.
COPYRIGHT: THE PSYCHOANALYTIC REVIEW.
EDITOR'S DECISION: 2-6 months.
FROM ACCEPTANCE TO PUBLICATION: Approximately 2 years.
PAYMENT/OFFPRINTS: No payment. Offprints may be ordered at author's expense.
REJECTED MSS.: Returned.
GENERAL: First issue, 1913.
BACK ISSUES: Many available directly from editorial address at $14.00 per volume.

SOUNDINGS: AN INTERDISCIPLINARY JOURNAL

EDITORIAL ADDRESS:
Sallie TeSelle, Editor
Box 6309 Station B
Vanderbilt University
Nashville, Tennessee 37235

SUBSCRIPTION ADDRESS:
Timothy F. Sedgwick,
Managing Editor
same

PUBLISHED: Quarterly (Mar., June, Sept., Dec.)
CIRCULATION: 1,900
COST: 1 yr.—$9.00; 2 yrs.—$15.00; 3 yrs.—$20.00. Student rate: $6.00. Foreign: 1 yr.—$10.00; 2 yrs.—$16.00; 3 yrs.—$21.00; single copy—$2.50.

CONTENTS: Articles that combine boldness with professional competence and that highlight those insights, findings, and issues in diverse fields of study which disclose serious humane concerns. Essay example: "Gypsies: People with a Hidden History."

UNSOLICITED MSS. WELCOME? Yes; submissions acknowledged.
SPECIFICALLY WELCOMED: Interdisciplinary essays of criticism; no poetry or fiction.

MS. LENGTH: 6,000-8,000 words; submit ONE copy.
STYLE REQUIREMENTS: MLA STYLE SHEET.
COPYRIGHT: SOUNDINGS, unless other arrangements made.
EDITOR'S DECISION: 1 month.
FROM ACCEPTANCE TO PUBLICATION: 3-6 months.
PAYMENT/OFFPRINTS: 10 free copies of issue in which article appears. At time of galleys, author receives printer's cost schedule for offprints.
REJECTED MSS.: Returned.
GENERAL: First issue, 1968. Usual publication length, 120 pages.
BACK ISSUES: Available from Managing Editor at $2.50 each.

SOUTHERN REVIEW

See the section on LITERARY REVIEWS for details.

STUDIES IN COMPARATIVE COMMUNISM: AN INTERDISCIPLINARY JOURNAL

EDITORIAL ADDRESS:
Peter Berton, Editor
University of Southern California
VKC 330
University Park
Los Angeles, California 90007

SUBSCRIPTION ADDRESS:

same

PUBLISHED: Quarterly (Spring, Summer, Autumn, Winter)
COST: 1 yr.—$10.00, foreign and domestic postage included ($16, institutions).

CONTENTS: Scholarly articles (sometimes in the form of a symposium around a given theme); review articles; research notes; documents; graduate student essays; bibliographical section. Subject matter: political, economic, social, and cultural developments in the Communist world; Communist movements in non-Communist countries; Marxist ideology; comparative Communist and cross-system studies. Recent example touching on literary scholarship is a ten-page review essay on György Lukács, political philosopher and literary critic.

UNSOLICITED MSS. WELCOME? Yes; submissions acknowledged.
SPECIFICALLY WELCOMED: Comparative and interdisciplinary studies preferred. Special interest in analyses of the divided countries (East and West Germany, North and South Vietnam, Communist and Nationalist China), as well as of Outer and Inner Mongolia and the various republics, regions, and nationalities.
MS. LENGTH: Articles, 6,000-9,000 words; research notes, 2,000-4,000 words; student essays, 3,000-6,000 words (exceptions made); submit THREE copies.
STYLE REQUIREMENTS: University of Chicago's A MANUAL OF STYLE; footnotes, references, tables, and charts on separate pages; double-space footnotes.

COPYRIGHT: School of International Relations, U.S.C.
EDITOR'S DECISION: 2-12 weeks.
FROM ACCEPTANCE TO PUBLICATION: 3-18 months.
PAYMENT/OFFPRINTS: Free issue plus 25 free offprints with covers; additional at cost.
REJECTED MSS.: Returned.
GENERAL: First issue, 1968. Usual publication length, 128 pages. Index for Vols. I-IV (1968-1972) contained in Vol. V. No. 4 (Winter 1972), pp. 465-469. Advertising section, bibliography section, documents section, cumulative index.
BACK ISSUES: First five volumes, 1968-1972, available from editorial address at $60.00.

STUDIES IN THE HUMANITIES

EDITORIAL ADDRESS:
John R. Freund, Editor
111 B Leonard Hall
Indiana University of Pennsylvania
Indiana, Pennsylvania 15701

SUBSCRIPTION ADDRESS:

same

PUBLISHED: Biannually, usually
COST: 2 issues—$3.00.

CIRCULATION: 100-125

CONTENTS: Articles in the areas of literature, philosophy, films, and language. Examples: "The Minister and the Whore: An Examination of Bernard Malamud's 'The Magic Barrel' "; "The Comedy of Johnson's RASSELAS."

UNSOLICITED MSS. WELCOME? Yes; submissions acknowledged.
SPECIFICALLY WELCOMED: Articles of a general rather than highly specialized nature, including interdisciplinary investigations.
MS. LENGTH: Under 4,000 words; submit ONE copy.
STYLE REQUIREMENTS: MLA STYLE SHEET.
COPYRIGHT: STUDIES IN THE HUMANITIES.
EDITOR'S DECISION: 6 months.
FROM ACCEPTANCE TO PUBLICATION: 2 months.
PAYMENT/OFFPRINTS: Three copies of journal. For offprints, deal directly with Park Press, 330 Locust, Indiana, Pa.
REJECTED MSS.: Returned.
GENERAL: First issue, March, 1969. Usual publication length, 40-50 pages.
BACK ISSUES: Available from editorial address at $3.00 for two numbers.

POPULAR CULTURE

ALGOL: A MAGAZINE ABOUT SCIENCE FICTION

EDITORIAL ADDRESS:
Andrew Porter, Editor
P.O. Box 4175
New York, New York 10017

SUBSCRIPTION ADDRESS:

same

PUBLISHED: Biannually
(May, November)

CIRCULATION: 1,100-1,500

COST: 4 issues for $3.00; 6 issues for $4.00; single issue—$.80. Make checks payable to Andrew Porter. UK agent: Ethel Lindsay, Courage House, 6 Langley Ave, Surbiton Surrey KT6 6QL. Australian agent: Space Age Books Ltd., 317 Swanston St., Melbourne, 3000 Victoria, Aust. German agent: Waldemar Kumming, 8 Munchen 2, Herzogspitalstr. 5, Postschekkonto 14 78 14 D, West Germany.

CONTENTS: Articles about science fiction; articles by authors explaining the why and how of their creations; regular columns by Ted White, and book reviews by Richard Lupoff, Hugo-nominee; letters from authors and readers around the world; art work. Example: "Charles Brockden Brown: The Broken-Hearted Look."

UNSOLICITED MSS. WELCOME? Yes; submissions not acknowledged.
SPECIFICALLY WELCOMED: Articles about science fiction, by people who know what they're talking about, and can write well for the mass audience.
MS. LENGTH: Minimum 1,000 words; no maximum; submit ONE copy.
STYLE REQUIREMENTS: Writing from a personal viewpoint rather than a more academic style.
COPYRIGHT: Andrew Porter; copyright may be assigned to authors.
EDITOR'S DECISION: 2-3 weeks.
FROM ACCEPTANCE TO PUBLICATION: Varies.
PAYMENT/OFFPRINTS: Payment in copies of the issue.
REJECTED MSS.: Returned.
GENERAL: First issue, November, 1963. Usual publication length, 44 pages. Effective with issue #20, ALGOL is completely typeset. ALGOL was nominated for the Hugo award in the "best Amateur publication" category by the 1973 World Science Fiction Convention.
BACK ISSUES: Available from editorial address at $1.00 each beginning with #17, #18, #19.

THE ALIEN CRITIC

EDITORIAL ADDRESS:
Richard E. Geis, Editor-Publisher
P. O. Box 11408
Portland, Oregon 97211

SUBSCRIPTION ADDRESS:

same

PUBLISHED: Quarterly

CIRCULATION: 2,000

COST: 1 yr.—$4.00; 2 yrs.—$7.00; 3 yrs.—$10.00; special school, college, public library rates: 1 yr.—$3.50; 2 yrs.—$6.25; 3 yrs.—$9.00.

CONTENTS: Articles, speeches, commentary, reviews, letters, interviews dealing with science fiction, fantasy, and writing in general. Article example: "The Literary Dreamers."

UNSOLICITED MSS. WELCOME? No, but editor will look at them; submissions not acknowledged.
SPECIFICALLY WELCOMED: Generally, inside information, revealing interviews, human interest which has valuable information about writing, writer, science fiction and fantasy.
MS. LENGTH: Open; submit ONE copy.
STYLE REQUIREMENTS: Informal, conversational.
COPYRIGHT: Richard E. Geis, but all rights returned to author, unless copyrighted in his name.
EDITOR'S DECISION: 1 week.
FROM ACCEPTANCE TO PUBLICATION: Up to 1 year.
PAYMENT/OFFPRINTS: Payment depends on value of work, author's name. $50 tops, at moment. Receive as many copies as wish, within reasonable limits.
REJECTED MSS.: Returned.
GENERAL: First issue, May, 1972, as RICHARD E. GEIS; retitled THE ALIEN CRITIC, January, 1973. Usual publication length, 68 pages.
BACK ISSUES: Available from publisher at $1.00 each. #1 through #4 out of print.

AMRA

EDITORIAL ADDRESS:
George H. Scithers, Editor
Box 8243
Philadelphia, Pennsylvania 19101

SUBSCRIPTION ADDRESS:

same

PUBLISHED: Occasionally
COST: 10 issues—$4.00; single copy—$.50.

CIRCULATION: 1,000

CONTENTS: Material ABOUT swordplay and sorcery fiction; illustrations, the strongest features of the magazine; only occasional articles on literature, such as "H. P. Lovecraft and H. S. Chamberlain."

UNSOLICITED MSS. WELCOME? Generally, no; but reasonably interested in submissions from people who are familiar with the material in the magazine; submissions acknowledged.
MS. LENGTH: Less than 10,000 words; submit ONE copy.
STYLE REQUIREMENTS: Read magazine to find out present style.
COPYRIGHT: AMRA, unless writer asks for return of rights.
EDITOR'S DECISION: Regretfully, slow.
FROM ACCEPTANCE TO PUBLICATION: Regretfully, slow.

PAYMENT/OFFPRINTS: Reasonable number of offprints supplied on request.
REJECTED MSS.: Returned.
GENERAL: First issue, April, 1956. Usual publication length, 20 pages. Be sure to consult the magazine before submitting any articles. Useful to interested popular culture scholars and collectors.
BACK ISSUES: Vol. 2, #44 through #59 available from publisher at $.50 each; no reduction for quantity.

ARGENTINE SCIENCE FICTION REVIEW

EDITORIAL ADDRESS:
Hector R. Pessina, Editor
Argentine Science Fiction
Review Publications
Casilla 3869
Correo Central
Buenos Aires
Argentina

SUBSCRIPTION ADDRESS:

same

PUBLISHED: Quarterly
CIRCULATION: 500
COST: 1 yr.—$2.00 plus postage; single copy—$.50.

CONTENTS: Articles, reviews and news about science fiction and fantasy films, stories, and surveys of science fiction and the future.

UNSOLICITED MSS. WELCOME? Yes; submissions acknowledged.
SPECIFICALLY WELCOMED: Stories, articles, and reviews of books and films.
MS. LENGTH: No limits; submit TWO copies.
STYLE REQUIREMENTS: Normal style.
COPYRIGHT: Authors.
EDITOR'S DECISION: A few weeks.
FROM ACCEPTANCE TO PUBLICATION: A few weeks.
PAYMENT/OFFPRINTS: Copies of the magazine. Offprints on request.
REJECTED MSS.: Returned.
GENERAL: First issue, September, 1972. Usual publication length, 14-32 pages.
BACK ISSUES: Available from the publisher at $1.00 each (includes postage by air).

THE ARKHAM COLLECTOR (ceased publication)

EDITORIAL ADDRESS:
August Derleth, Editor

SUBSCRIPTION ADDRESS:
General Manager
Mycroft & Moran: Publishers
Arkham House/Stanton & Lee
Sauk City, Wisconsin 53583

PUBLISHED: Biannually

CONTENTS: Bibliographical notes, poetry, short stories; brief articles on Lovecraft, the macabre and related topics; necrology.

GENERAL: First issue, 1967.
BACK ISSUES: The 10 issues (348 pages) are bound and available in limited number at $10.00. With the exception of #2, back issues are available at $.65 each.

THE ARMCHAIR DETECTIVE

EDITORIAL ADDRESS: SUBSCRIPTION ADDRESS:
Allen J. Hubin, Editor
3656 Midland   same
White Bear Lake, Minnesota 55110

PUBLISHED: Quarterly   CIRCULATION: 740
COST: 1 yr.—$6.00 in U.S., $7.00 outside of U.S.

CONTENTS: Articles, critiques, reviews, analyses, bibliographic and biographic material, relating to mystery, detective and suspense fiction; book exchange information. Example: "An Interview with Ursula Curtiss."

UNSOLICITED MSS. WELCOME? Yes; submissions usually acknowledged.
SPECIFICALLY WELCOMED: Essays, as well as fillers and special features.
MS. LENGTH: 6,000 words or less; submit ONE copy.
STYLE REQUIREMENTS: Entertaining and communicative writing; footnotes follow article.
COPYRIGHT: Allen J. Hubin, but author's copyright can be given on first page of text.
EDITOR'S DECISION: About 4 weeks.
FROM ACCEPTANCE TO PUBLICATION: 6-9 months.
PAYMENT/OFFPRINTS: One copy of issue.
REJECTED MSS.: Returned.
GENERAL: First issue, October, 1967. Usual publication length, 85 pages.
BACK ISSUES: Unavailable since all out of print.

THE BAKER STREET JOURNAL

EDITORIAL ADDRESS: SUBSCRIPTION ADDRESS:
Julian Wolff, M.D., Editor
33 Riverside Drive   same
New York, New York 10023

PUBLISHED: Quarterly   CIRCULATION: 1,200

COST: 1 yr.—$4.00.

CONTENTS: Articles about Sherlock Holmes and the Sherlockian scene; checklists; occasional photograph. Example: "A Purloined Letter: Conan Doyle from Bret Harte."

UNSOLICITED MSS. WELCOME? Yes; submissions acknowledged.
SPECIFICALLY WELCOMED: Only articles about Sherlock Holmes; preferably critical studies of the stories; no parodies.
MS. LENGTH: Up to 2,000 words; submit ONE copy.
STYLE REQUIREMENTS: None.
COPYRIGHT: THE BAKER STREET JOURNAL, but author may have rights on request.
EDITOR'S DECISION: 2-3 weeks.
FROM ACCEPTANCE TO PUBLICATION: 1 year.
PAYMENT/OFFPRINTS: Two copies of journal.
REJECTED MSS.: Returned.
GENERAL: First issue, 1946; new series, January, 1951. Usual publication length, 64 pages.
BACK ISSUES: A few recent back issues available from editorial office at $1.00 each. Reprints of Volumes 1-19 (1951 to 1959) available from AMS Press.

THE BAUM BUGLE

EDITORIAL ADDRESS:
Fred M. Meyer, Secretary
The International Wizard
of Oz Club, Inc.
220 North 11th Street
Escanaba, Michigan 49829

SUBSCRIPTION ADDRESS:

same

PUBLISHED: Tri-annually   CIRCULATION: 1,000
COST: 1 yr.—$2.50 membership fee that includes subscription.

CONTENTS: Articles, illustrations, and photographs about Oz-related subjects; usually a short story or other type of writing by L. Frank Baum; bibliographical points of Baum and Oz books; biographies of Oz authors and illustrators and Baum book illustrators; scholarly papers about different "Oz" subjects; quizzes based on the 40 Oz books in the series; information about club activities; reviews of articles about Oz and L. Frank Baum in other publications.

UNSOLICITED MSS. WELCOME? Yes; usually do not solicit material.
SPECIFICALLY WELCOMED: Material of Oz or Baum interest.
GENERAL: First issue, June, 1957. Usual publication length, 24-28 pages. Club holds conventions with displays, auctions of Baum and Oz material; gives L. Frank Baum Memorial Award for outstanding achievement; has directory of members; publishes books: ANIMAL FAIRY TALES by Baum, YANKEE IN OZ by Ruth Plumly Thompson; puts out annual OZIANA magazine of Oz stories, poems, drawings by club members, and issues quarterly "Oz Trading Post" for book exchange.

BACK ISSUES: $1.00 each or 3 for $2.50; can be obtained from Fred M. Meyer, Secretary. Not all issues are available.

THE BURROUGHS BULLETIN

EDITORIAL ADDRESS:
Vernell Coriell, Editor
House of Greystoke
6657 Locust
Kansas City, Missouri 64131

SUBSCRIPTION ADDRESS:

same

PUBLISHED: At least 4 times yearly   CIRCULATION: 500-2,000
COST: 1 yr.—$5.00 for membership dues; members receive the official club publications—THE BURROUGHS BULLETIN, THE GRIDLEY WAVE, and DUM-DUM.

CONTENTS: Critical articles on Edgar Rice Burroughs' writings; reprints of works and sketches by ERB; section called "Ad-Libs"—editorial remarks about the material included in that publication; information on ERB life; photographs of movie scenes; original work by ERB; original art.

UNSOLICITED MSS. WELCOMED? Yes; submissions acknowledged.
SPECIFICALLY WELCOMED: Material on Edgar Rice Burroughs—his life, writings, sketches.
MS. LENGTH: No preference; submit ONE copy.
STYLE REQUIREMENTS: Open.
COPYRIGHT: Edgar Rice Burroughs, Inc.
EDITOR'S DECISION: 2 months.
FROM ACCEPTANCE TO PUBLICATION: 1 year or less.
PAYMENT/OFFPRINTS: Copies of issue in which work appears.
REJECTED MSS.: Returned, not criticized.
GENERAL: First issue, 1947. Usual publication length, 19-20 pages.
BACK ISSUES: Available from editorial address at $2.00 each for black and white issues; $3.00 each when color used.

THE COMMONPLACE BOOK

EDITORIAL ADDRESS:
W. T. Rabe, Editor
Old Soldiers of Baker Street
of the Two Saults
909 Prospect
Sault Sainte Marie, Michigan 49783

SUBSCRIPTION ADDRESS:

same

PUBLISHED: Quarterly   CIRCULATION: 200
COST: 1 yr.—$3.00; 2 yrs.—$5.00; 5 yrs.—$10.00.

CONTENTS: Newspaper and magazine clippings related to Sherlock Holmes and Sir Arthur Conan Doyle. The publication is composed entirely of reprints.

UNSOLICITED MSS. WELCOME? Yes.
STYLE REQUIREMENTS: Originals or photostats; no xeroxes.
PAYMENT/OFFPRINTS: None.
GENERAL: "First issue" published from Summer, 1964, to April, 1969. Revived Summer, 1974. Usual publication length, 24 pages.
BACK ISSUES: Available from editorial office at $.50 each.

EDGAR WALLACE SOCIETY NEWSLETTER
(formerly EDGAR WALLACE CLUB NEWSLETTER)

EDITORIAL ADDRESS: SUBSCRIPTION ADDRESS:
Penelope Wallace, Editor
4 Bradmore Road same
Oxford OX2 6QW
England

PUBLISHED: Quarterly CIRCULATION: 350
COST: 1 yr.—$2.80 seamail, $4.20 airmail.

CONTENTS: Information on Edgar Wallace, including forthcoming publications and books in print; articles about Edgar Wallace; poems by and about Wallace; book mart section.

UNSOLICITED MSS. WELCOME? Yes (articles usually by Society members); submissions acknowledged.
SPECIFICALLY WELCOMED: Material relating to Edgar Wallace.
MS. LENGTH: Up to 2,000 words; short pieces welcome; submit ONE copy.
STYLE REQUIREMENTS: None.
COPYRIGHT: Author.
EDITOR'S DECISION: 2-4 weeks.
FROM ACCEPTANCE TO PUBLICATION: Up to 3 months.
PAYMENT/OFFPRINTS: Ten free copies; more at cost.
REJECTED MSS.: Returned.
GENERAL: First issue, January, 1969. Usual publication length, 4 pages plus eight page Book Mart supplement and short Edgar Wallace reprint. Sample copy of newsletter supplied free.
BACK ISSUES: Available from editorial address at $.33 each (seamail only).

THE ELLERY QUEEN REVIEW
(formerly THE QUEEN CANON BIBLIOPHILE)

EDITORIAL ADDRESS:
Rev. Robert E. Washer, Editor
82 East Eighth Street
Oneida Castle, New York 13421

SUBSCRIPTION ADDRESS:
same

PUBLISHED: Irregularly
COST: 4 issues—$3.50.

CONTENTS: Essays on Ellery Queen, his works, and development of his detective writing; checklists of his first editions; the serialization of critic Nevins' "Royal Bloodline: The Biography of the Queen Canon"; reviews of new fiction in the mystery/detective field.

UNSOLICITED MSS. WELCOME? Inquire.
GENERAL: First issue, 1968. Usual publication length, 24 pages.

ERB-DOM & THE FANTASY COLLECTOR

EDITORIAL ADDRESS:
Camille Cazedessus, Jr., Editor
Route Two, Box 119
Clinton, Louisiana 70722

SUBSCRIPTION ADDRESS:
same

PUBLISHED: 5 times yearly
COST: 1 yr.—$5.00.

CIRCULATION: 1,200

CONTENTS: Brief articles on E. R. Burroughs and ephemera; checklists; photo features; occasional index to old magazines, such as GHOST STORIES. THE FANTASY COLLECTOR, on yellow pages in the middle, advertizes and lists collectors' Western, mystery, radio, comic book materials, books, films, fanzines, and magazines.

UNSOLICITED MSS. WELCOME? Yes.
SPECIFICALLY WELCOMED: General information and speculation on ERB.
GENERAL: First issue, May, 1960. Usual publication length, 20-32 pages.
BACK ISSUES: Some are available from the editor at $.50 and $1.00 each.

EXTRAPOLATION: A JOURNAL OF SCIENCE FICTION AND FANTASY

EDITORIAL ADDRESS:
Thomas D. Clareson, Editor
Department of English
Box 3186
The College of Wooster
Wooster, Ohio 44691

SUBSCRIPTION ADDRESS:

same

PUBLISHED: Biannually
(December, May of academic yr.)
COST: 1 yr.—$3.00; 3 yrs.—$7.50; single issue—$1.75.

CIRCULATION: 1,000-1,200

CONTENTS: Historical, critical, bibliographical articles dealing with American, British, European science fiction and modern fantasy; book reviews of scholarly works in fields; some reviews of fiction. Departments include "SF in the Classroom" and Futurology; soon Cinema. Examples: "C. S. Lewis and the Fictions of 'Scientism' "; "Cosmic Imagery in A VOYAGE TO ARCTURUS."

UNSOLICITED MSS. WELCOME? Yes; submissions acknowledged.
SPECIFICALLY WELCOMED: Articles, reviews.
MS. LENGTH: 2,000-5,000 words; submit ONE or TWO copies.
STYLE REQUIREMENTS: MLA STYLE SHEET; documentation at end of article.
COPYRIGHT: EXTRAPOLATION; permissions granted freely.
EDITOR'S DECISION: 6-10 weeks.
FROM ACCEPTANCE TO PUBLICATION: 3 months to 1 year.
PAYMENT/OFFPRINTS: Provide copies of issue; 6 offprints of article on request.
REJECTED MSS.: Returned.
GENERAL: First issue, December, 1959. Usual publication length, 96 pages. Note that so long as twice yearly, the volumes coincide with the academic year, not calendrical year.
BACK ISSUES: Both microfilms and reprints available from Johnson Reprint Corp. at $24 (cloth) or $20 (paper) for Vol. 1-10; $16 (paper 1 volume) or $44 (clothbound set) or $36 (paperbound set) for Vol. 11-13.

THE FAUST COLLECTOR

EDITORIAL ADDRESS:
William J. Clark, Editor
11744½ Gateway Boulevard
Los Angeles, California 90064

SUBSCRIPTION ADDRESS:

same

PUBLISHED: Quarterly
COST: Single copy—$.60.

CONTENTS: Articles on the stories and verse of Frederick Faust, "Max Brand," "George Challis," "Evan Evans"; checklists; bibliographical commentary; reprints of Faust's work; occasional previously unpublished work by Faust, such as "The Plow and the Stars."

GENERAL: First issue, 1969. Inquiries from us received no response; thus we cannot attest that it still exists. We hope, therefore, that someone will inform us where back issues may be obtained, if it is defunct.

THE GRIDLEY WAVE

EDITORIAL ADDRESS:
Vernell Coriell, Editor
House of Greystoke
6657 Locust
Kansas City, Missouri 64131

SUBSCRIPTION ADDRESS:

same

PUBLISHED: At least 4 times yearly   CIRCULATION: 500-2,000
COST: 1 yr.—$5.00 membership dues; members receive the official club publications—THE BURROUGHS BULLETIN, THE GRIDLEY WAVE, and DUM-DUM.

CONTENTS: Book and film reviews and news on Edgar Rice Burroughs' writings; screenplays; TV information; comic art; illustrations.

UNSOLICITED MSS. WELCOME? Yes; submissions acknowledged.
SPECIFICALLY WELCOMED: All material must be on some aspect of Edgar Rice Burroughs' writings.
MS. LENGTH: Open; submit ONE copy.
STYLE REQUIREMENTS: Open.
COPYRIGHT: Edgar Rice Burroughs, Inc.
PAYMENT/OFFPRINTS: Copies of issue in which work appears.
REJECTED MSS.: Returned.
GENERAL: First issue, 1947. Usual publication length, 2-3 pages.
BACK ISSUES: Available from editorial address.

THE HOLMESIAN OBSERVER

EDITORIAL ADDRESS:
Andrew Page, Editor
3130 Irwin Avenue
Bronx, New York 10463

SUBSCRIPTION ADDRESS:

same

PUBLISHED: Biannually   CIRCULATION: 110-150
COST: 1 yr.—$1.00; single copy—$.60.

CONTENTS: Scholarly investigations into the life and times of Sherlock Holmes, Dr. Watson, and the rest of Dr. Doyle's fictional characters in the 60 tales; articles, monographs and essays dealing with material in the Holmes Canon, such as inconsistencies (Dr. Watson's wound in the shoulder in one story becomes in the following story a bullet wound "in the leg"); other serious topics have been: was Holmes bribed in "The Adventure of The Priory School"?, "Was Holmes a Racist?," "Where did Sherlock Holmes develop his philosophy on life?"; letters, criticism, and short novel ideas; editorial; pastiches of the Holmes stories (serious replicas); some parodies of the tales; occasional quiz with prizes on some facts from the Holmes Canon; essays considering the literary side of the tales—how they were written, the writing styles, concepts, the format, and viewing the actual writer, Arthur Conan Doyle, as being the most important person in all.

UNSOLICITED MSS. WELCOME? Yes; submissions acknowledged.
SPECIFICALLY WELCOMED: Material mainly on Sherlock Holmes and the Holmes tales; articles, monographs, essays, pastiches, parodies, stories, humor; articles on the life and times of Sir Doyle.
MS. LENGTH: 6-12 pages; submit ONE copy.
STYLE REQUIREMENTS: None in particular.
COPYRIGHT: Both the author and publisher (Priory School of New York).
EDITOR'S DECISION: Under 1 week.
FROM ACCEPTANCE TO PUBLICATION: 6 months to 1 year.
PAYMENT/OFFPRINTS: No payment. Small fee for offprints.
REJECTED MSS.: Returned immediately.
GENERAL: First issue, March, 1971. Usual publication length, 20-22 pages.
BACK ISSUES: Vol. 1—o.p. A few back issues of Vols. 2 and 3 are available from the editorial address at $.90 each for Vol. 2, #1 and #2; $.80 for Vol. 2, #3; $.70 for Vol. 3, #1; and $.60 for Vol. 3, #2.

THE HOWARD COLLECTOR

EDITORIAL ADDRESS:
Glenn Lord, Editor
P. O. Box 775
Pasadena, Texas 77501

SUBSCRIPTION ADDRESS:

same

PUBLISHED: Biannually
COST: 60¢ per copy.

CIRCULATION: 450

CONTENTS: Material by and about the author Robert E. Howard including book reviews.

UNSOLICITED MSS. WELCOME? Yes; submissions not acknowledged.
SPECIFICALLY WELCOMED: Articles and book reviews pertinent to the subject matter; some verse in same vein.
MS. LENGTH: Short; submit ONE copy.
STYLE REQUIREMENTS: Literate.
COPYRIGHT: Taken out in publisher's name; all rights returned to authors.

EDITOR'S DECISION: 3 weeks.
FROM ACCEPTANCE TO PUBLICATION: Varies.
PAYMENT/OFFPRINTS: Copies of issue. No offprints.
REJECTED MSS.: Returned.
GENERAL: First issue, Summer, 1961. Usual publication length, 36-40 pages.
BACK ISSUES: Not available.

THE HURLSTONE PAPERS

EDITORIAL ADDRESS:
William J. Walsh, Editor
6 Ernst Drive
Suffern, New York 10901

SUBSCRIPTION ADDRESS:

same

PUBLISHED: Irregularly
COST: No charge.

CIRCULATION: 30

CONTENTS: Short articles on Sherlock Holmes; any and all aspects of the sixty stories written by Dr. John Watson for Sir Arthur Conan Doyle may be discussed, usually with the presupposition that Holmes, Watson, ET AL did, in fact, exist. Editorials and editorial notes also may appear from time to time, as well as letters and wants and offers.

UNSOLICITED MSS. WELCOME? Most certainly; submissions acknowledged.
SPECIFICALLY WELCOMED: Generally anything having to do with Sherlock Holmes Saga. Preferably something that has not already been said. Parodies and pastiches are also welcome.
MS. LENGTH: 2-4 pages; submit ONE OR TWO copies.
STYLE REQUIREMENTS: None.
COPYRIGHT: At this time, the author.
EDITOR'S DECISION: 3 weeks.
FROM ACCEPTANCE TO PUBLICATION: 6-18 months.
PAYMENT/OFFPRINTS: An extra copy of the periodical.
REJECTED MSS.: Returned.
GENERAL: First issue, January, 1972. Usual publication length, 15-20 pages. THP is published by the Musgrave Ritualists Beta, scion society of the Baker Street Irregulars, Inc. of New York City. The Musgrave Ritualists Beta have also published A CURIOUS COLLECTION, an anthology available from the editor, above.
BACK ISSUES: None available.

IS: A QUARTERLY OF POPULAR LITERATURE AND POPULAR CULTURE

EDITORIAL ADDRESS:
Tom Collins, Editor
4305 Balcones Drive
Austin, Texas 78731

SUBSCRIPTION ADDRESS:

same

PUBLISHED: Quarterly   CIRCULATION: 600-1,000
COST: 4 issues—$6.00; single copy—$1.50.

CONTENTS: Articles on science fiction, fantasy, children's literature, horror; literary subcultures; articles from jazz to anarchism, Gothic novels to detective stories; essays; criticism; art; science; documents of the counter culture; literary discoveries, such as rare or unpublished works by London, O. Henry, and others; illustrations. Examples: "The Language of Science Fiction"; "August Derleth and the Comics."

UNSOLICITED MSS. WELCOME? Yes, but queries advised with return envelopes; submissions acknowledged.
SPECIFICALLY WELCOMED: History and criticism of popular literature; especially articles on Georgette Heyer, wierd fiction, science fantasy; substantive articles on children's literature, hitchhiking, and Piet Hein.
MS. LENGTH: Up to 5,000 words; submit ONE copy.
STYLE REQUIREMENTS: None.
COPYRIGHT: Editor; may be reassigned to author.
EDITOR'S DECISION: 1 week.
FROM ACCEPTANCE TO PUBLICATION: 2-6 months.
PAYMENT/OFFPRINTS: Payment in copies only.
REJECTED MSS.: Returned.
GENERAL: First issue, January, 1971. Usual publication length, 80-100 pages.
BACK ISSUES: #4 (August Derleth), #5 (History of SAPS Science Fiction Club), and #6 (General) available from the editorial address at $3.00, $1.50, and $1.50 respectively. Rest are out of print.

THE JOHN D. MACDONALD BIBLIOPHILE

EDITORIAL ADDRESS:
Len and June Moffatt, Editors
Box 4456
Downey, California 90241

SUBSCRIPTION ADDRESS:

same

PUBLISHED: 1 or 2 times yearly   CIRCULATION: 200
COST: $.50 a copy or letter of comment; no subscriptions.

CONTENTS: Articles, columns, and news about John D. McDonald and his writings; reviews; letters, crime and detective fiction comments in general.

UNSOLICITED MSS. WELCOME? Yes; submissions acknowledged.
SPECIFICALLY WELCOMED: Reviews of JDM books and stories, old or new.

MS. LENGTH: 500-2,000 words; submit ONE copy.
STYLE REQUIREMENTS: Literate and nonobfuscatory.
COPYRIGHT: Leonard J. Moffatt and June M. Moffatt, but rights are assigned to contributors.
EDITOR'S DECISION: 4-6 weeks.
FROM ACCEPTANCE TO PUBLICATION: 1 month to 1 year.
PAYMENT/OFFPRINTS: Reasonable number of offprints.
REJECTED MSS.: Returned.
GENERAL: First issue, March, 1964. Usual publication length, 30 pages. The "JDM Checklist," a bibliography of the works of John D. MacDonald which also features a photo and brief biography of the writer, is available from the editors at $1.00 per copy.
BACK ISSUES: Available from the editorial office at $.25 each for issues 11 through 14 and $.50 each for issues 15, 16, 17.

JOURNAL OF POPULAR CULTURE

EDITORIAL ADDRESS:
Ray B. Browne, Editor
University Hall 100
Bowling Green University
Bowling Green, Ohio 43403

SUBSCRIPTION ADDRESS:

same

PUBLISHED: Quarterly CIRCULATION: 1,800
COST: 1 yr.(effective V7:1)—$7.50 for students; $15.00 for others (includes membership in Popular Culture Association).

CONTENTS: Articles relating to the area of Popular Culture of any period or country. Examples: "The Quest of the Bourgeois Hero: An Approach to Fowles' THE MAGUS"; "Chicano Poetry: A Popular Manifesto."

UNSOLICITED MSS. WELCOME? Yes; submissions acknowledged.
SPECIFICALLY WELCOMED: Articles pertaining to Popular Culture in the broadest sense of the term.
MS. LENGTH: 10-15 pages; submit ONE copy.
STYLE REQUIREMENTS: MLA STYLE SHEET, 2nd edition.
COPYRIGHT: JOURNAL OF POPULAR CULTURE, Ray B. Browne, Editor.
EDITOR'S DECISION: 6 months.
FROM ACCEPTANCE TO PUBLICATION: Varies.
PAYMENT/OFFPRINTS: Ten to 20 free offprints.
REJECTED MSS.: Returned.
GENERAL: First issue, Summer, 1967. Usual publication length, 192-256 pages.
BACK ISSUES: Available from editorial address at $3.00 each. Microfilm copies from Xerox University Microfilms. Microfiche from 3M International Microfilms.

LOCUS

EDITORIAL ADDRESS:
Charlie and Dena Brown, Editors
3400 Ulloa Street
San Francisco, California 94116

SUBSCRIPTION ADDRESS:

same

PUBLISHED: Biweekly
COST: 12 issues—$3.00; 26 issues—$6.00; 1 yr.—$8.50 for libraries who request billing in advance.

CIRCULATION: 1,400

CONTENTS: All facets of the science fiction field; lists of forthcoming books, magazine contents, market reports; reports of conventions and other important meetings, both fan and professional; book reviews; magazine reviews; news on TV and radio and film science fiction; movie, TV, theatre reviews of SF productions; any other material of interest to the writer, publisher, or reader of science fiction; illustrations.

UNSOLICITED MSS. WELCOME? No.
GENERAL: First issue, April, 1968. Usual publication length, 10 pages.
BACK ISSUES: Available from editorial address at $.25 each or 5 for $1.00 except for several special issues at a higher price. All are still in print. List of them is published periodically in "Things for Sale" section in LOCUS.

LUNA MONTHLY

EDITORIAL ADDRESS:
Ann F. Dietz, Editor
655 Orchard Street
Oradell, New Jersey 07649

SUBSCRIPTION ADDRESS:
Franklin M. Dietz, Jr.
same

PUBLISHED: Monthly
COST: 1 yr.—$4.00, 3rd class mail; $5.00, 1st class mail (subject to adjustment with postal increase); $.50 extra for invoicing.

CIRCULATION: 800

CONTENTS: News, reviews, features, bibliography of science fiction/fantasy fiction field. Examples: "An Interview with Poul Anderson"; "The Other Derleths."

UNSOLICITED MSS. WELCOME? Yes; submissions not acknowledged.
SPECIFICALLY WELCOMED: Articles and reviews of books and films.
MS. LENGTH: 500-2,000 words; submit ONE copy.
STYLE REQUIREMENTS: Serious material, not frivolous.
COPYRIGHT: Author.
EDITOR'S DECISION: 2 weeks.
FROM ACCEPTANCE TO PUBLICATION: 2 months.
PAYMENT/OFFPRINTS: Contributors copies only. No offprints.
REJECTED MSS.: Returned.
GENERAL: First issue, June, 1969. Usual publication length, 32 pages.

BACK ISSUES: Available from publisher at following prices (to 12/31/73): #1-#13—$.75 each; #14-#37—$.50 each; #38 to current—$.40 each.

LUNA (PRIME)

EDITORIAL ADDRESS:
Franklin M. Dietz, Jr., Editor
655 Orchard Street
Oradell, New Jersey 07649

SUBSCRIPTION ADDRESS:

same

PUBLISHED: Irregularly
COST: $1.00 for 3 issues.

CIRCULATION: 500

CONTENTS: Transcripts of speeches from Science Fiction conventions.

UNSOLICITED MSS. WELCOME? No.
GENERAL: First issue, 1962. Usual publication length, 32 pages.
BACK ISSUES: Available from publisher at following prices: #3—$.20; #4—$.30; #5—$.20; #6 to #8—$1.00 each.

THE MYSTERY & DETECTION ANNUAL

EDITORIAL ADDRESS:
Donald K. Adams, General Editor
Department of English and
Comparative Literature
Occidental College
Los Angeles, California 90041

SUBSCRIPTION ADDRESS:
Publisher
152 South Clark Drive
Beverly Hills, California 90211

PUBLISHED: Annually (Autumn)
COST: 1 yr.—$15.00.

CIRCULATION: 400-500

CONTENTS: Scholarly, critical and informal articles dealing with the nature and development of the genre of mystery, Gothic, supernatural, detective, crime, pursuit and espionage fiction; authorial reminiscences; short notes; critical reviews; bibliographic essays. All material is original (no reprinting of material originally published elsewhere); original poetry, art work, and photographs are encouraged.

UNSOLICITED MSS. WELCOME? Yes; submissions acknowledged.
SPECIFICALLY WELCOMED: Scholarly articles.
MS. LENGTH: Up to 30-35 pages; submit TWO copies.
STYLE REQUIREMENTS: MLA STYLE SHEET.
COPYRIGHT: Publisher (unless specific request by author).
EDITOR'S DECISION: 1-6 months.
FROM ACCEPTANCE TO PUBLICATION: 1 year.

PAYMENT/OFFPRINTS: Complimentary copy of the annual. Up to 12 offprints.
REJECTED MSS.: Returned.
GENERAL: First issue, November, 1972. Usual publication length, 280-300 pages.
BACK ISSUES: Available from subscription address at $15.00 each.

THE MYSTERY READER'S NEWSLETTER
(formerly THE MYSTERY LOVER'S NEWSLETTER)

EDITORIAL ADDRESS:
Mrs. Lianne Carlin, Editor
P. O. Box 113
Melrose, Massachusetts 02176

SUBSCRIPTION ADDRESS:
same

PUBLISHED: Quarterly   CIRCULATION: 450-500
COST: 1 yr.—$4.00; single issue—$1.00.

CONTENTS: Articles and checklists about all facets of mystery fiction; letters section; list of current mysteries; book trading section; current news about authors; illustrations. Examples: "All Good Mysteries are Short Stories: A Polemic"; "An Interview with Howard Haycraft."

UNSOLICITED MSS. WELCOME? Yes; submissions acknowledged.
SPECIFICALLY WELCOMED: Articles (no fiction) about the genre; pertinent author checklists; films; artwork.
MS. LENGTH: 2,000 words; submit ONE copy.
STYLE REQUIREMENTS: None.
COPYRIGHT: Author.
EDITOR'S DECISION: 1 week.
FROM ACCEPTANCE TO PUBLICATION: 6 months.
PAYMENT/OFFPRINTS: ½¢ per word. Five free offprints; others at a discount.
REJECTED MSS.: Returned.
GENERAL: First issue, August, 1967. Usual publication length, 50 pages.
BACK ISSUES: Occasionally available from the editor; sometimes from other readers. Price varies from $.50 to $1.00.

THE MYSTERY TRADER

EDITORIAL ADDRESS:
Ethel Lindsay, Editor
6 Langley Avenue
Surbiton
Surrey KT6 6 QL
Great Britain

SUBSCRIPTION ADDRESS:
same

PUBLISHED: Usually 4 times yearly   CIRCULATION: 200
COST: 4 issues—$1.25 (or 50p); $2.00 airmail overseas.

CONTENTS: Articles on mystery authors and books; reviews of mystery books; letters from readers often with information for collectors; reports on dealers, other mystery magazines and organizations; lists of books for sale.

UNSOLICITED MSS. WELCOME? Yes; submissions acknowledged.
SPECIFICALLY WELCOMED: Articles on any aspect of mystery fiction.
MS. LENGTH: Short articles, but could run longer ones in installments.
STYLE REQUIREMENTS: Clarity.
COPYRIGHT: Author.
EDITOR'S DECISION: 2 weeks.
FROM ACCEPTANCE TO PUBLICATION: 2-3 months.
PAYMENT/OFFPRINTS: One free issue.
REJECTED MSS.: Returned.
GENERAL: First issue, June, 1971. Usual publication length, 20 pages. This is a duplicate magazine. Artwork would be welcome.
BACK ISSUES: Available from editorial address at rates cited above.

MYTHLORE

EDITORIAL ADDRESS:
Glen GoodKnight, Editor
334 North Robinson Avenue
Los Angeles, California 90026

SUBSCRIPTION ADDRESS:
The Mythopoeic Society
P. O. Box 4671
Whittier, California 90607

PUBLISHED: Irregularly, 2 or 3 times yearly
COST: Four issues—$3.50; single copy—$1.00.

CONTENTS: Articles on myth, fantasy, imaginative literature, especially the works of J. R. R. Tolkien, C. S. Lewis, and Charles Williams; some fiction by these authors; reviews; letters of comment; artwork. Examples: "Tolkien at Eighty: An Appreciation"; "The C. S. Lewis Collection At Wheaton College."

UNSOLICITED MSS. WELCOME? Yes; submissions acknowledged.
SPECIFICALLY WELCOMED: Articles, reviews, letters on past issues, artwork. Serious, scholarly, but may be tongue-in-cheek, treatment of material.
MS. LENGTH: Any length; submit ONE copy.
STYLE REQUIREMENTS: Nothing faanish, please; no Howard, Lovecraft, sf.
COPYRIGHT: The Mythopoeic Society, Inc.
EDITOR'S DECISION: Varies.
FROM ACCEPTANCE TO PUBLICATION: Varies.
PAYMENT/OFFPRINTS: Contributor's copy of issue. Offprints on request.
REJECTED MSS.: Returned.
GENERAL: First issue, January, 1969. Usual publication length, 30-40 offset pages reduced.
BACK ISSUES: I, II, III, V, VI, VII, VIII, and IX available from subscription address at $1.00 each. Write for order blank.

MYTHPRINT

EDITORIAL ADDRESS:
Glen GoodKnight, and Larry and
Martha Krieg, Editors
P.O. Box 24150
Los Angeles, California 90024

SUBSCRIPTION ADDRESS:
The Mythopoeic Society
P.O. Box 4671
Whittier, California 90607

PUBLISHED: Monthly
COST: Twelve issues—$3.00, payable in increments of $1.50. Subscription plus active (voting) membership in the Mythopoeic Society—$6.00 per year.

CONTENTS: Mini-reviews; artwork; reports of branch discussions of imaginative literature and the works of Tolkien, C. S. Lewis, and Charles Williams (e.g., The Ring Bearers in Tolkien's THE HOBBIT and the Trilogy; THE VOYAGE OF THE DAWN TREADER); letter column; humorous material; editorial; Society news.

UNSOLICITED MSS. WELCOME? Letters of comment, book mini-reviews, yes; submissions usually acknowledged.
MS. LENGTH: Edited to space; submit ONE copy.
STYLE REQUIREMENTS: Must be typed in column format given in magazine.
COPYRIGHT: The Mythopoeic Society, Inc.
EDITOR'S DECISION: Varies.
FROM ACCEPTANCE TO PUBLICATION: Not more than 3 months.
PAYMENT/OFFPRINTS: Contributor's copy of issue. Reviewers may secure extra copies.
REJECTED MSS.: Returned.
GENERAL: First issue, February, 1970, as MYTHPRINT (in bulletin form earlier). Usual publication length, 16-20 pages.
BACK ISSUES: Available from subscription address. Write for order blank.

MYTHRIL

EDITORIAL ADDRESS:
Nick Smith, Editor-in-Chief
214 South Wilson Avenue
Pasadena, California 91106

SUBSCRIPTION ADDRESS:
The Mythopoeic Society
P.O. Box 4671
Whittier, California 90607

PUBLISHED: Quarterly or 3 times yearly.
COST: Four issues—$2.50; single copy—$.75.

CONTENTS: Fiction, poetry, letters, artwork, reviews of fiction 'zines.

UNSOLICITED MSS. WELCOME? Yes; submissions acknowledged.
SPECIFICALLY WELCOMED: Fiction, poems, letters, reviews.
MS. LENGTH: Any length; submit ONE copy.
STYLE REQUIREMENTS: Fantasy over science fiction.
COPYRIGHT: The Mythopoeic Society, Inc.

EDITOR'S DECISION: Query editor.
FROM ACCEPTANCE TO PUBLICATION: Query editor.
PAYMENT/OFFPRINTS: Contributor's copy of issue in which piece appears.
REJECTED MSS.: Returned.
GENERAL: First issue, Fall, 1971. Usual publication length, 20 offset pages.
BACK ISSUES: Write to The Mythopoeic Society for order blank.

NIEKAS

EDITORIAL ADDRESS:
Edmund R. Meskys, Editor
Box 233
Center Harbor, New Hampshire 03226

SUBSCRIPTION ADDRESS:
same

PUBLISHED: Irregularly
COST: $1.00 per issue.

CIRCULATION: 700

CONTENTS: Reviews and discussions of fantasy and science fictions; offshoots to Georgette Heyer, Gilbert and Sullivan, and other topics of interest.

UNSOLICITED MSS. WELCOME? Yes; submissions acknowledged.
SPECIFICALLY WELCOMED: All types.
MS. LENGTH: Under 10,000 words, with exceptions; submit ONE copy.
STYLE REQUIREMENTS: None (informal preferred).
COPYRIGHT: Author.
EDITOR'S DECISION: 3 months.
FROM ACCEPTANCE TO PUBLICATION: Indefinite.
PAYMENT/OFFPRINTS: No payment. Offprints, if requested in advance.
REJECTED MSS.: Returned.
GENERAL: First issue, June, 1962. Usual publication length, 90 pages.
BACK ISSUES: Temporarily unavailable; later through Xerox Ulrich's International Periodicals Directory, irregular serials & annuals.

NOSTALGIA NEWS (formerly DALLASCON BULLETIN)

EDITORIAL ADDRESS:
Larry Herndon, Editor
P. O. Box 34305
Dallas, Texas 75234

SUBSCRIPTION ADDRESS:
same

PUBLISHED: Bimonthly
COST: 5 issues—$2.50; single copy—$.60.

CIRCULATION: 6,000

CONTENTS: Articles and features on old movies and serials, show business personalities, old comic book heroes, artists, writers, pulp magazine articles; features on big bands of the past; articles on old radio shows; interviews with personalities of the past; reports on nostalgia conventions; illustrations.

UNSOLICITED MSS. WELCOME? Yes; submissions acknowledged in many cases.
SPECIFICALLY WELCOMED: Historical or analytical articles dealing with nostalgia on old movies, stars, old radio shows and personalities, serials, comic books, pulp magazines, big bands of the 1930's and 1940's.
MS. LENGTH: Over 1,500 words; submit ONE copy.
COPYRIGHT: Nostalgia, Inc.
EDITOR'S DECISION: 2-4 weeks.
FROM ACCEPTANCE TO PUBLICATION: Varies.
PAYMENT/OFFPRINTS: Payment ranges from free copies to cash.
REJECTED MSS.: Returned.
GENERAL: First issue, Spring, 1969. Usual publication length, 32 pages. Particularly useful to popular culture scholars and collectors.
BACK ISSUES: Available from editorial address. Some are out of print. Cost depends on issue.

NYCTALOPS

EDITORIAL ADDRESS:
Harry O. Morris, Jr., Editor
500 Wellesley, S. E.
Albuquerque, New Mexico 87106

SUBSCRIPTION ADDRESS:

same

PUBLISHED: Approximately 3 times yearly.
CIRCULATION: 400
COST: 3 issues—$2.00; single copy—$.75.

CONTENTS: Articles, fiction, poetry, and art work dealing with fantasy and supernatural horror in literature. Main focus in on H. P. Lovecraft and his Cthulhu Mythos. Example article: "Eroes and the Ghoul: Necrophilia in the Prose and Poetry of Clark Ashton Smith."

UNSOLICITED MSS. WELCOME? Yes; submissions acknowledged.
SPECIFICALLY WELCOMED: Essays concerned with weird/fantasy authors and their works. Fiction-poetry in the macabre tradition.
MS. LENGTH: 1,300-13,000 words; submit ONE copy.
COPYRIGHT: All rights released to author.
EDITOR'S DECISION: Several days.
FROM ACCEPTANCE TO PUBLICATION: Several months.
PAYMENT/OFFPRINTS: One copy of issue in which work appears. Additional copies (up to 10) at ½ price.
REJECTED MSS.: Returned.
GENERAL: First issue, May, 1970. Usual publication length, 50 pages reduced type.

BACK ISSUES: Numbers 1-6 out-of-print, not available. Number 7, a 100-page tribute to Clark Ashton Smith is available from editorial address at $1.25.

PARMA ELDALAMBERON (Book of the Elven Tongues)

EDITORIAL ADDRESS:
Jim Vibber, Editor
1124 East Del Mar, Apt. C
Pasadena, California 91106

SUBSCRIPTION ADDRESS:
The Mythopoeic Society
P. O. Box 4671
Whittier, California 90607

PUBLISHED: Irregularly
COST: Four issues—$3.50 (½ comb $1.00); single copy—$1.00.

CONTENTS: Articles and letters about imaginary languages, such as Tolkien's Elvish.

UNSOLICITED MSS. WELCOME? Query editor.
SPECIFICALLY WELCOMED: Factual articles on imaginary languages and grammars, alphabets.
MS. LENGTH: Any length; submit ONE copy.
STYLE REQUIREMENTS: Serious approach.
COPYRIGHT: The Mythopoeic Society, Inc.
EDITOR'S DECISION: Query editor.
FROM ACCEPTANCE TO PUBLICATION: Query editor.
PAYMENT/OFFPRINTS: Contributor's copy of issue in which piece appears.
REJECTED MSS.: Returned.
GENERAL: First issue, Autumn, 1971. Usual publication length, 20 offset pages.
BACK ISSUES: Write to The Mythopoeic Society for order blank.

THE PONTINE DOSSIER

EDITORIAL ADDRESS:
Luther Norris, Editor
The Praed Street Irregulars
3844 Watseka Avenue
Culver City, California 90230

SUBSCRIPTION ADDRESS:

same

PUBLISHED: Annually
COST: $4.00 each.

CIRCULATION: 500

CONTENTS: Articles about Solar Pons and Sherlock Holmes, and material on all fictional detectives; verse, puzzles, and articles on detective fiction, writers, and their works; art work; photographs. Examples: "August Derleth: Pre-Romantic"; "Being an Examination of the Ponsian and Holmesian Secret Deductive Systems."

UNSOLICITED MSS. WELCOME? Yes; submissions acknowledged.
SPECIFICALLY WELCOMED: Anything and everything that will be of interest to mystery buffs. Material slanted on Holmes and Solar Pons are of greatest interest.
MS. LENGTH: 2,000 words or less; submit ONE copy.
COPYRIGHT: Author.
EDITOR'S DECISION: About 1 year.
PAYMENT/OFFPRINTS: None.
REJECTED MSS.: Returned.
GENERAL: First issue, 1971 (new series). Usual publication length, 40 pages.
BACK ISSUES: A few copies may be obtained from various dealers, but all issues are out of print.

THE PULP ERA (formerly JD-ARGASSY)

EDITORIAL ADDRESS:
Lynn A. Hickman, Editor
413 Ottokee Street
Wauseon, Ohio 43567

SUBSCRIPTION ADDRESS:

same

PUBLISHED: Quarterly
COST: 10 issues—$7.00; single copy—$.75.

CIRCULATION: 500

CONTENTS: Articles on pulp magazines, artists, and authors; indexes of same; book reviews; publishing news on reprints of the pulps; artwork, both new and reprinted from the pulps; cartoons.

UNSOLICITED MSS. WELCOME? Yes; submissions acknowledged.
SPECIFICALLY WELCOMED: Historical or analytical articles on pulp magazines, artists, and authors; satires on certain characters; book reviews.
MS. LENGTH: Any—depends on subject; submit ONE copy.
STYLE REQUIREMENTS: Good writing only.
COPYRIGHT: Publisher, but is freely given to artist or author.
EDITOR'S DECISION: 6 weeks.
FROM ACCEPTANCE TO PUBLICATION: 6 months.
PAYMENT/OFFPRINTS: Three copies of issue.
REJECTED MSS.: Returned.
GENERAL: First issue, Summer, 1951. Usual publication length, 32 pages. Particularly valuable for popular culture historians and collectors of pulp literature.
BACK ISSUES: Only 5 issues back available, from publisher, at $1.00 each.

REMEMBER WHEN

EDITORIAL ADDRESS:
Larry Herndon, Editor
1830 Highland
Carrollton, Texas 75006

SUBSCRIPTION ADDRESS:

same

PUBLISHED: Monthly
COST: $.65 per copy or 8 for $4.50.

CIRCULATION: 2,000

CONTENTS: Nostalgia articles on old radio, comic books, serials, films, show business personalities, early days of television, interviews.

UNSOLICITED MSS. WELCOME? Yes; submissions sometimes acknowledged.
SPECIFICALLY WELCOMED: Articles only, must deal with the "Popular Culture" of the 1920 to 1950 period (TV, radio, comics).
MS. LENGTH: 1,500 words or more; submit ONE copy.
COPYRIGHT: Nostalgia, Inc.
EDITOR'S DECISION: 2-4 weeks.
FROM ACCEPTANCE TO PUBLICATION: Varies.
PAYMENT/OFFPRINTS: Payment depends on article's length.
REJECTED MSS.: Returned.
GENERAL: First issue, November, 1971. Usual publication length, 32 pages.
BACK ISSUES: Available from editorial address at $.65 each.

RIVERSIDE QUARTERLY

EDITORIAL ADDRESS:
Leland Sapiro, Editor
Box 40
University Station
Regina, Saskatchewan S4S OA2
Canada

SUBSCRIPTION ADDRESS:

same

PUBLISHED: Irregularly
COST: 1 yr.—$2.00; single issue—$.60; individual copies of current issue not sold.

CIRCULATION: 1,400

CONTENTS: Critical articles on science fiction and fantasy; reviews of books, magazines, and movies in this field; poetry; illustrations. Examples: "Science Fiction as Will and Idea: The World of Alfred Bester"; "The Function of Time Travel in Vonnegut's SLAUGHTERHOUSE FIVE."

UNSOLICITED MSS. WELCOME? Yes; submissions not acknowledged.
SPECIFICALLY WELCOMED: Critical articles on the history, themes, and literary qualities of professional science fiction authors.
MS. LENGTH: No preference; submit ONE copy.
STYLE REQUIREMENTS: None.
COPYRIGHT: Editor; rights released to author.

EDITOR'S DECISION: 2 weeks.
FROM ACCEPTANCE TO PUBLICATION: 6 months.
PAYMENT/OFFPRINTS: Payment in copies. No offprints.
REJECTED MSS.: Returned.
GENERAL: First issue, August, 1964. Usual publication length, 92 pages.
BACK ISSUES: Available from editorial office at $.60 each.

THE ROHMER REVIEW

EDITORIAL ADDRESS:
Robert E. Briney, Editor
245 Lafayette Street, Apt. 3G
Salem, Massachusetts 01970

SUBSCRIPTION ADDRESS:

same

PUBLISHED: Biannually   CIRCULATION: 250
COST: $2.00 for 3 issues via 3rd class mail; $2.50 for 3 issues via first class mail; single issue—$.75.

CONTENTS: Reprints of little-known fiction, verse, and nonfiction by Sax Rohmer (Arthur Sarsfield Ward); essays, articles, and bibliographical material about Rohmer or his writings or closely related subjects; sketches and photographs.

UNSOLICITED MSS. WELCOME? Yes; submissions acknowledged.
SPECIFICALLY WELCOMED: Material about Sax Rohmer.
MS. LENGTH: Up to 3,500 words; submit TWO copies.
STYLE REQUIREMENTS: Footnotes follow article.
COPYRIGHT: Editor, but rights assigned to individual contributors.
EDITOR'S DECISION: 1 month.
FROM ACCEPTANCE TO PUBLICATION: 6 months to 1 year.
PAYMENT/OFFPRINTS: One copy of magazine plus two copies of tear-sheets.
REJECTED MSS.: Returned.
GENERAL: First issue, July, 1968. Usual publication length, 36 pages.
BACK ISSUES: Recent back issues available from editorial office at subscription rates. Early issues are out of print and unavailable.

SCIENCE-FICTION STUDIES

EDITORIAL ADDRESS:
R. D. Mullen and D. Suvin, Editors
Department of English
Indiana State University
Terre Haute, Indiana 47809

SUBSCRIPTION ADDRESS:

same

PUBLISHED: Quarterly.

CONTENTS: Articles about science fiction including utopian fiction, but not supernatural or mythological fantasy (except for purposes of comparison and contrast).

UNSOLICITED MSS. WELCOME? Yes.
MS. LENGTH: Not stated; submit TWO copies.
STYLE REQUIREMENTS: MLA STYLE SHEET; references should be made only to editions found in libraries.
GENERAL: First issue, 1973. Articles should be accompanied by an abstract of 200 words or less.

SF COMMENTARY

EDITORIAL ADDRESS:
Bruce R. Gillespie, Editor
GPO Box 5195AA
Melbourne, Victoria 3001
Australia

SUBSCRIPTION ADDRESS:
US agent:
Charles and Dena Brown
3400 Ulloa Street
San Francisco, California 94116

PUBLISHED: Approximately every 2 months
CIRCULATION: 800
COST: $4.00 for 9 issues, surface mail; $10.00 air mail.

CONTENTS: "Straight talk about science fiction"; serious criticism of science fiction, "speculative fiction," and literature on the fringes of the field; reviews; discussion of the s-f world, news of the s-f community; well-written, entertaining articles on topics of interest to the editor (recent e.g.—article on Ivan Illich).

UNSOLICITED MSS. WELCOME? Yes, if well-written; submissions acknowledged.
SPECIFICALLY WELCOMED: Serious discussion of science fiction, especially single-author monographs; serious or humorous articles about topics of interest to science fiction readers, e.g. futurology, politics; in-depth reviews of science fiction books; some science fiction film criticism.
MS. LENGTH: Not less than 500 words; submit ONE copy.
STYLE REQUIREMENTS: Journalistic rather than ultra-academic; gritty, not waffly.
COPYRIGHT: Author.
EDITOR'S DECISION: 2-4 weeks.
FROM ACCEPTANCE TO PUBLICATION: 6 months.
PAYMENT/OFFPRINTS: Published authors obtain airmailed, free copy of issue plus credit on subscriptions.
REJECTED MSS.: Returned.
GENERAL: First issue, January, 1969. Usual publication length, 50 pages. Considerable emphasis is placed on the letter column, which usually features top writers in the science fiction field. Contributors to SFC usually receive considerable informed feedback.

BACK ISSUES: Very few available. Either a "Best of . . ." collection or facsimile reprint planned.

SHERLOCK HOLMES JOURNAL

EDITORIAL ADDRESS:
The Marquis of Donegall, Editor
The Studio
39 Clabon Mews
London S.W.1
England

SUBSCRIPTION ADDRESS:

same

PUBLISHED: Biannually
COST: 1 yr.—$7.50.

CIRCULATION: 700-800

CONTENTS: Articles; comment; letters; proceedings of meetings of the Sherlock Holmes Society of London which is devoted to study of the life and work of Sherlock Holmes—not forgetting his friend Doctor J. H. Watson.

UNSOLICITED MSS. WELCOME? Yes; submissions acknowledged.
SPECIFICALLY WELCOMED: Articles on Holmes.
MS. LENGTH: 3,000 words maximum; submit ONE copy.
COPYRIGHT: Sherlock Holmes Society of London.
EDITOR'S DECISION: 2 months.
FROM ACCEPTANCE TO PUBLICATION: Up to 1 year.
PAYMENT/OFFPRINTS: Offprints by arrangement.
REJECTED MSS.: Returned.
GENERAL: First issue, May, 1952. Usual publication length, 3-5 pages. Contributors should be serious scholars of the Sherlock Holmes canon but light-hearted contributions, provided they are germane to study of the canon, are welcomed.
BACK ISSUES: Available from editorial address at $3.00 each (except Spring, 1967, double issue—$6.00).

TAMLACHT

EDITORIAL ADDRESS:
Victor Boruta, Editor
11 W. Linden Avenue
Linden, New Jersey 07036

SUBSCRIPTION ADDRESS:

same

PUBLISHED: 2 or 3 times yearly
COST: 4 issues—$1.00; single issue—$.25.

CIRCULATION: 100

CONTENTS: Articles dealing with personal opinion on the occult and literature; occasional special issues concentrating upon one individual and his work (see #12 on H. P. Lovecraft); book and record reviews; illustrations.

UNSOLICITED MSS. WELCOME? Yes; submissions acknowledged.
SPECIFICALLY WELCOMED: Articles, artwork, fiction, poetry only if exceptional.
MS. LENGTH: No preference; submit ONE copy.
STYLE REQUIREMENTS: None on written pieces; artwork must be black and white.
COPYRIGHT: Contributor.
EDITOR'S DECISION: 1-2 weeks.
FROM ACCEPTANCE TO PUBLICATION: 4 months.
PAYMENT/OFFPRINTS: Copies of the magazine; $10 for cover material artwork when accepted. Request number of desired offprints before printing.
REJECTED MSS.: Returned.
GENERAL: First issue, September, 1969. Usual publication length, 24 pages.
BACK ISSUES: Available from editorial office at $.25 for #11 and #15, $.60 for #12.

UNICORN: A MISCELLANEOUS JOURNAL

See the section on LITERARY REVIEWS for details.

VECTOR: JOURNAL OF THE BRITISH SCIENCE FICTION ASSOCIATION

EDITROIAL ADDRESS:
Malcolm Edwards, Editor
7 Dunsmore
The Hoe
Carpenders Park
Watford, Herts
United Kingdom

SUBSCRIPTION ADDRESS:
Mrs. G. T. Adams
54 Cobden Avenue
Bitterne Park
Southampton SO2 4FT
United Kingdom

PUBLISHED: Bimonthly   CIRCULATION: 500
COST: 10 issues—$6.00, outside of U.K. only; single issue—30p ($.60). Membership of B.S.F.A. Ltd.—£1.50 ($3.00) per year (includes VECTOR).

CONTENTS: Critical articles about science fiction; articles by working science fiction writers concerning their own work and the creative process; occasional humor; science fiction book and film reviews; interviews; news; letters; illustrations.

UNSOLICITED MSS. WELCOME? Yes; submissions not acknowledged.

SPECIFICALLY WELCOMED: Articles concerned with science fiction (widely defined); NO poetry.
MS. LENGTH: No preference; submit ONE copy.
STYLE REQUIREMENTS: Good English.
COPYRIGHT: Author.
EDITOR'S DECISION: 2 weeks.
FROM ACCEPTANCE TO PUBLICATION: 6 months.
PAYMENT/OFFPRINTS: No payment. Contact editor about offprints.
REJECTED MSS.: Returned.
GENERAL: First issue, 1960. Usual publication length, 40-48 pages. All checks should be payable to the British Science Fiction Association, Ltd.
BACK ISSUES: Available from Mrs. Christine Smith, 4 Lister Avenue, East Grinstead, Sussex, United Kingdom, at $.60 or 30p each.

YANDRO [Fanzine Example]

EDITORIAL ADDRESS:
Robert and Juanita Coulson, Editors
Route 3
Hartford City, Indiana 47348

SUBSCRIPTION ADDRESS:

same

PUBLISHED: Irregularly; 8 to 12 times yearly
CIRCULATION: 300
COST: 4 issues—$1.50; 12 issues—$4.00; single issue—$.40.

CONTENTS: Editorials; letter column, book reviews (primarily but not entirely science fiction); reviews of other amateur publications; one or more of the following per issue: humorous articles, humorous column, article about science fiction, sociological article, verse. Example: "Kurt Vonnegut and the Wrath of God."

UNSOLICITED MSS. WELCOME? More or less; submissions usually acknowledged.
SPECIFICALLY WELCOMED: Humor.
MS. LENGTH: Not over 1,000 words; submit ONE copy.
STYLE REQUIREMENTS: None.
COPYRIGHT: Not copyrighted except under special circumstances.
EDITOR'S DECISION: 1 week to 1 month.
FROM ACCEPTANCE TO PUBLICATION: 1 month to 2 years.
PAYMENT/OFFPRINTS: Free copy of issue in which material appears. Offprints may be negotiated.
REJECTED MSS.: Returned.
GENERAL: First issue, February, 1953. Usual publication length, 30 to 40 pages. This publication has recently been listed in a handbook for teachers of high school science fiction courses.
BACK ISSUES: Available from editorial office at current prices. Most out of print.

THEORY OF LITERATURE

CENTRUM: WORKING PAPERS OF THE MINNESOTA CENTER FOR ADVANCED STUDIES IN LANGUAGE, STYLE, AND LITERARY THEORY

EDITORIAL ADDRESS:
Martin Steinmann, Jr., Editor
Minnesota Center for Advanced
Studies in Language, Style, and
Literary Theory
202 Main Engineering Building
University of Minnesota
Minneapolis, Minnesota 55455

SUBSCRIPTION ADDRESS:

same

PUBLISHED: Biannually (Autumn, Spring)

CIRCULATION: 700

COST: $2.00 per issue ($2.50 abroad); billing upon receipt of each issue.

CONTENTS: Papers somehow bearing upon the THEORY of language, style, and literature, including computer-aided analysis of discourse, especially papers with an interdisciplinary approach; book reviews; review articles; and reviews of new journals; surveys of recent work in a field or a country; annotated bibliographies; and queries, letters, comments, squibs, rejoinders, ripostes.

UNSOLICITED MSS. WELCOME? Yes; submissions acknowledged.
SPECIFICALLY WELCOMED: No poems or stories published. See above.
MS. LENGTH: No specification; submit ONE copy.
STYLE REQUIREMENTS: Double spacing throughout (including quotations and, following the text, footnotes); any established style (MLA, e.g., or LSA).
COPYRIGHT: Minnesota Center for Advanced Studies in Language, Style, and Literary Theory but, upon request and without charge, contributors are given permission to reprint.
EDITOR'S DECISION: 1 month.
FROM ACCEPTANCE TO PUBLICATION: 1 month.
PAYMENT/OFFPRINTS: Five copies of the relevant issue.
REJECTED MSS.: Returned.
GENERAL: First issue, Spring, 1973. Usual publication length, 80 pages. Every manuscript reporting research should be prefaced by an abstract of no more than 100 words.
BACK ISSUES: When available, from subscription address at $2.00 each.

COLLEGE ENGLISH

See the section on TEACHING ABOUT LITERATURE for details.

COMPARATIVE LITERATURE

See the section on AGE AND/OR NATIONALITY: COMPREHENSIVE IN SCOPE for details.

CRITICISM: A QUARTERLY FOR LITERATURE AND THE ARTS

See the section on AGE AND/OR NATIONALITY: AMERICAN AND ENGLISH for details.

DIACRITICS: A REVIEW OF CONTEMPORARY CRITICISM

EDITORIAL ADDRESS:
David I. Grossvogel, Editor
Department of Romance Studies
278 Goldwin Smith Hall
Cornell University
Ithaca, New York 14850

SUBSCRIPTION ADDRESS:

same

PUBLISHED: Quarterly (Spring, Summer, Fall, Winter)
COST: 1 yr.—$6.00; 2 yrs.—$10.50; 3 yrs.—$15.00.

CIRCULATION: 500

CONTENTS: Articles on critical approaches to literatures and experiments in literary creation and on all the arts to which the word is central—books and book reviews, films and drama, criticism, and criticism of criticism. Example: "Sartre as Critic."

UNSOLICITED MSS. WELCOME? No; submissions acknowledged.
SPECIFICALLY WELCOMED: Critical articles on contemporary criticism.
MS. LENGTH: 15 pages; submit ONE copy.
STYLE REQUIREMENTS: MLA STYLE SHEET.
COPYRIGHT: Diacritics Inc.
EDITOR'S DECISION: 1 month or less.
FROM ACCEPTANCE TO PUBLICATION: 3-6 months.
PAYMENT/OFFPRINTS: Two free copies of issue in which work appears. Offprints at author's expense.
REJECTED MSS.: Returned.
GENERAL: First issue, September, 1971. Usual publication length, 60-70 pages.
BACK ISSUES: Available from editorial address at $2.50 each for Vol. I, issues 1 and 2; $1.75 each for all others. Subscription may be retroactive to Vol. II, #1.

HA-SIFRUT: QUARTERLY FOR THE STUDY OF LITERATURE

EDITORIAL ADDRESS:
Benjamin Hrushovski, Editor
Tel Aviv University
P.O.B. 39085
Tel-Aviv
Israel

SUBSCRIPTION ADDRESS:

same

PUBLISHED: Quarterly CIRCULATION: 1,600
COST: 1 yr.—$15.00; single copy—$4.00.

CONTENTS: Articles on the theory of literature, poetics, Hebrew literature, comparative literature.

UNSOLICITED MSS. WELCOME? Yes; submissions acknowledged.
SPECIFICALLY WELCOMED: Theory and poetics.
MS. LENGTH: No preference; submit TWO copies.
COPYRIGHT: HA-SIFRUT.
EDITOR'S DECISION: 3-4 months.
FROM ACCEPTANCE TO PUBLICATION: 9-12 months.
PAYMENT/OFFPRINTS: 50 offprints, automatically.
REJECTED MSS.: Returned whenever possible.
GENERAL: First issue, Spring, 1968. Usual publication length, 200 double-column pages. Published in Hebrew with extensive English summaries.
BACK ISSUES: Available from editorial address at $4.00 each or $15 per any 4 numbers.

JOURNAL OF AESTHETICS AND ART CRITICISM

EDITORIAL ADDRESS:
Herbert M. Schueller, Editor
Wayne State University
Detroit, Michigan 48202

SUBSCRIPTION ADDRESS:
American Society for Aesthetics
Cleveland Museum of Art
Cleveland, Ohio 44106

PUBLISHED: Quarterly CIRCULATION: 2,550
COST: Subscription included in annual membership dues of the American Society for Aesthetics.

CONTENTS: Articles on the arts; book reviews; bibliographies.

UNSOLICITED MSS. WELCOME? Contact the editor.
GENERAL: First issue, 1941.
BACK ISSUES: Available from subscription address.

LANGUAGE AND STYLE: AN INTERNATIONAL JOURNAL

EDITORIAL ADDRESS:
E. L. Epstein, Editor
Department of English
Southern Illinois University
Carbondale, Illinois 62901

SUBSCRIPTION ADDRESS:

same

PUBLISHED: Quarterly
COST: 1 yr.—$7.50, $8.00 overseas.

CIRCULATION: 500

CONTENTS: Critical and scholarly articles on the definition of style in the arts and outside the arts, in all of its social and cultural contexts. Example: "Cognitive Apparatus in DAISY MILLER, THE AMBASSADORS, and Two Works by Howells: A Comparative Study of the Epistemology of Henry James."

UNSOLICITED MSS. WELCOME? Yes; submissions acknowledged.
SPECIFICALLY WELCOMED: Any scholarly or critical contribution.
MS. LENGTH: 2,000-10,000 words; submit TWO copies.
STYLE REQUIREMENTS: MLA STYLE SHEET.
COPYRIGHT: Board of Trustees, Southern Illinois University.
EDITOR'S DECISION: 6 weeks to 2 months.
FROM ACCEPTANCE TO PUBLICATION: 1½ years.
PAYMENT/OFFPRINTS: No payment. Author must arrange for and pay for offprints.
REJECTED MSS.: Returned.
GENERAL: First issue, Winter, 1968. Usual publication length, 15-25 pages. Articles may be written in English, French, and German.
BACK ISSUES: Available from editorial address at $2.00 each.

MIDWEST MODERN LANGUAGE ASSOCIATION BULLETIN

See section on SPECIALIZED TOPICS AND INTERDISCIPLINARY STUDIES: INTERDISCIPLINARY for details.

NEOPHILOLOGUS

See the section on AGE AND/OR NATIONALITY: CONTINENTAL—CLASSICAL, MEDIEVAL AND RENAISSANCE for details.

NEW LITERARY HISTORY: A JOURNAL OF THEORY AND INTERPRETATION

EDITORIAL ADDRESS:
Ralph Cohen, Editor
Wilson Hall
University of Virginia
Charlottesville, Virginia 22903

SUBSCRIPTION ADDRESS:
Mrs. Barbara B. Smith,
Subscription Manager
same

PUBLISHED: Tri-annually (Nov., Feb., May)

CIRCULATION: 1,425

COST: 1 yr.—advance subscription, $8.00; 2 yrs.—advance subscription, $15.00; postage outside territorial United States $.65 per year, and $.25 per single issue; single copy—$3.00.

CONTENTS: Articles on theory of literature that deal with such subjects as reasons for literary change, the definitions of periods and their uses in interpretation, the evolution of styles, conventions, genres and their relationship to each other and to the periods in which they flourish, the interconnection between national literary histories, the place of evaluation in literary history; articles from other disciplines that help interpret or define the problems of literary history. Not limited to English or American literature. Example: "Some Observations on Method in Literary Studies."

UNSOLICITED MSS. WELCOME? Yes; submissions acknowledged.
SPECIFICALLY WELCOMED: Articles of a theoretical nature which fit the general description of Contents. No book reviews; no explications except as they support theoretical arguments.
MS. LENGTH: 5,000-6,000 words; submit ONE copy.
STYLE REQUIREMENTS: MLA STYLE SHEET.
COPYRIGHT: NEW LITERARY HISTORY.
EDITOR'S DECISION: 3-4 months.
FROM ACCEPTANCE TO PUBLICATION: Articles must wait for issue on specific subject.
PAYMENT/OFFPRINTS: Copy of journal in which article appears. 25 free offprints; more at $.50 each.
REJECTED MSS.: Returned.
GENERAL: First issue, Autumn, 1969. Usual publication length, 208 pages. Indexed every two years. Index sent free to subscribers of record on date of publication (September following last issue published).
BACK ISSUES: Available from Subscription Manager at $3.00 each (plus $.25 postage outside U.S.). Volume 1 issues are out of print.

POETICS: INTERNATIONAL REVIEW FOR THE THEORY OF LITERATURE

EDITORIAL ADDRESS:
Teun A. Van Dijk, Editor
University of Amsterdam
Department of General
Literary Studies
Herengracht 256
Amsterdam 1001
The Netherlands

SUBSCRIPTION ADDRESS:
Co-Libri
Distributors for Mouton
Publications
P. O. B. 482
The Hague 2076
The Netherlands

PUBLISHED: About 4 issues yearly   CIRCULATION: 800
COST: 1 yr.—D. Glds 72,—; individuals, D.Glds 50,—; single copy—D.Glds 22,—.

CONTENTS: Articles dedicated exclusively to the theory of literature and its foundations, viz. linguistics, logic and mathematics, and to the study of the relations with neighboring disciplines, such as psychology, sociology, anthropology, and ethnology. Articles contain explicit hypotheses, part of systematic theories of the structure of literary texts and communication processes. Example: "On Poetics and Metrical Theory."

UNSOLICITED MSS. WELCOME? Yes; submissions acknowledged.
SPECIFICALLY WELCOMED: Theoretical articles with example analyses only for illustration of presented hypotheses and models.
MS. LENGTH: Maximum 80 pages; submit ONE copy.
STYLE REQUIREMENTS: Consult journal.
COPYRIGHT: Mouton and Company, The Hague.
EDITOR'S DECISION: 1 month maximum.
FROM ACCEPTANCE TO PUBLICATION: 1 year maximum.
PAYMENT/OFFPRINTS: 25 free offprints.
REJECTED MSS.: Returned.
GENERAL: First issue, 1971. Usual publication length, 128 pages. Articles may be written in English, French, German.
BACK ISSUES: Available from subscription address at D.Glds 22,—.

RECOVERING LITERATURE: A JOURNAL OF CONTEXTUALIST CRITICISM

See the section on AGE AND/OR NATIONALITY: AMERICAN AND ENGLISH for details.

STYLE

EDITORIAL ADDRESS: SUBSCRIPTION ADDRESS:
James R. Bennett and
Blair Rouse, Editors same
University of Arkansas
Fayetteville, Arkansas 72701

PUBLISHED: Tri-annually CIRCULATION: 350
(Winter, Spring, Fall)
COST: 1 yr.—$5.00; $3.00 for students; single copy—$2.00.

CONTENTS: Analyses of style, particularly those which deal with literature in English and provide systematic methods of description and evaluation of style; reviews of books which contribute significantly to our understanding of style; annual bibliography of stylistic criticism and, periodically, bibliographies of criticism focusing on aspects of style; a survey of the study of style internationally through essays on various nations or regions or schools; exchange of information on teaching style. Example: "Formulaic Rhythms in FINNEGANS WAKE."

UNSOLICITED MSS. WELCOME? Yes; submissions acknowledged.
SPECIFICALLY WELCOMED: Analyses, reviews, bibliographies, critical essays.
MS. LENGTH: 20-30 pages; submit TWO copies.
STYLE REQUIREMENTS: MLA STYLE SHEET.
COPYRIGHT: STYLE (as safeguard to authors).
EDITOR'S DECISION: Uncertain.
FROM ACCEPTANCE TO PUBLICATION: Uncertain.
PAYMENT/OFFPRINTS: 15 offprints, plus two copies of issue in which essay appears; extra offprints at 10¢ each.
REJECTED MSS.: Returned.
GENERAL: First issue, Winter, 1967. Usual publication length, 100 pages.
BACK ISSUES: Available from editorial address at $2.00 each, or $5.00 per volume.

CHILDREN'S LITERATURE, SATIRE,

AND WOMEN'S STUDIES

BULLETIN OF THE CENTER OF CHILDREN'S BOOKS

See the section on BIBLIOGRAPHICAL AND LIBRARY RESOURCES for details.

CHILDREN'S LITERATURE

EDITORIAL ADDRESS:
Francelia Butler, Editor
English Department
University of Connecticut
Storrs, Connecticut 06268

SUBSCRIPTION ADDRESS:
University of Connecticut
Bookstore
Storrs, Connecticut 06268

PUBLISHED: Annually
COST: $4.25 plus $.25 postage.

CIRCULATION: 2,000

CONTENTS: Critical articles about children's literature by professors of the languages, psychology, anthropology, philosophy, history, and so on. Examples: "Aesop as Litmus: The Acid Test of Children's Literature"; "PILGRIM'S PROGRESS as Fairy Tale."

UNSOLICITED MSS. WELCOME? Yes; submissions acknowledged.
SPECIFICALLY WELCOMED: Contributions from scholars which give fresh insights into the quality of literature and its effect on children.
MS. LENGTH: 5-20 pages; submit ONE copy.
STYLE REQUIREMENTS: MLA STYLE SHEET.
COPYRIGHT: Editor.
EDITOR'S DECISION: 2 months.
FROM ACCEPTANCE TO PUBLICATION: 6 months.
PAYMENT/OFFPRINTS: One copy of the volume; 10 free offprints of the article.
REJECTED MSS.: Returned.
GENERAL: First issue, February, 1972. Usual publication length, 200 or more pages.
BACK ISSUES: Available from subscription address at $4.25 plus $.25 postage.

HORN BOOK MAGAZINE

EDITORIAL ADDRESS:
Paul Heins, Editor
585 Boylston Street
Boston, Massachusetts 02116

SUBSCRIPTION ADDRESS:

same

PUBLISHED: Bi-monthly
COST: 1 yr.—$8.50.

CIRCULATION: 27,000

CONTENTS: Articles about children's literature; reviews of current children's books; illustrations. Examples: "McLuhan, Youth, and Literature"; "Random Thoughts by a Translator of Andersen."

UNSOLICITED MSS. WELCOME? Yes; submissions acknowledged.
SPECIFICALLY WELCQMED: Articles about children's literature, their authors and illustrators, history of children's literature.
MS. LENGTH: 6-10 pages; submit ONE copy.
STYLE REQUIREMENTS: None.
COPYRIGHT: Horn Book Magazine.
EDITOR'S DECISION: 2 months.
FROM ACCEPTANCE TO PUBLICATION: 3 months.
PAYMENT/OFFPRINTS: $5 per magazine page; issues of magazine can be supplied.
REJECTED MSS.: Returned.
GENERAL: First issue, October, 1924. Usual publication length, 96 pages. Indexed by volume.
BACK ISSUES: Available from editorial address at $1.50 each.

THE MARY WOLLSTONECRAFT NEWSLETTER

See the section on SINGLE AND MULTIPLE AUTHORS FOCUS: EUROPEAN.

PUCRED

EDITORIAL ADDRESS: SUBSCRIPTION ADDRESS:
Richard R. Jesson, Jim Springer Borck,
and Charles R. Larson, Editors   same
Box 382
San Francisco, California 94101

PUBLISHED: Quarterly   CIRCULATION: 200
COST: 1 yr.—$3.50.

CONTENTS: Parodies of scholarly approaches; political satire in critical forms; humorous verse; parodies of exams, lectures, anything else writer can think of; student bloopers.

UNSOLICITED MSS. WELCOME? Yes; submissions acknowledged.
SPECIFICALLY WELCOMED: Parody and satire.
MS. LENGTH: 2-4 pages; submit ONE copy.
STYLE REQUIREMENTS: Original forms encouraged.
COPYRIGHT: Magazine and author.
EDITOR'S DECISION: 1 week.
FROM ACCEPTANCE TO PUBLICATION: 1-6 months.

PAYMENT/OFFPRINTS: A few presentation copies; free offprints.
REJECTED MSS.: Returned.
GENERAL: First issue, October, 1972. Usual publication length, 52 pages. PUCRED is not affiliated with any institution. It encourages independence—departure from "serious" scholarship—and individual participation. Subscribers are encouraged to contribute to and establish policy of the journal.
BACK ISSUES: Available from the editors at $1.00 each until reprinting is necessary.

SATIRE NEWSLETTER

EDITORIAL ADDRESS:
George A. Test, Editor
State University of
New York College
Oneonta, New York 13820

SUBSCRIPTION ADDRESS:

same

PUBLISHED: Biannually (Fall, Spring) CIRCULATION: 450-500
COST: 1 yr.—$3.00.

CONTENTS: Articles on satire; satiric fiction and poetry; book reviews; bibliographies. Example: "Satire and Word Games in Amis's ENGLISHMAN."

UNSOLICITED MSS. WELCOME? Yes; submissions acknowledged.
SPECIFICALLY WELCOMED: Anything satiric; skits, stories, short plays, poetry.
MS. LENGTH: Not over 15 pages; submit ONE copy.
STYLE REQUIREMENTS: MLA STYLE SHEET with notes at end.
COPYRIGHT: No copyright.
EDITOR'S DECISION: 1-3 months.
FROM ACCEPTANCE TO PUBLICATION: 1—1½ years.
PAYMENT/OFFPRINTS: Two copies of issue and free mailing of few additional copies (available at reduced rates).
REJECTED MSS.: Returned.
GENERAL: First issue, 1963. Usual publication length, 90-100 pages.
BACK ISSUES: Vols. I-V available from Kraus Reprint Co. Others available from editorial address at $1.50 each.

STUDIES IN CONTEMPORARY SATIRE:
A CREATIVE AND CRITICAL JOURNAL

EDITORIAL ADDRESS:
C. D. Sheraw, Editor
Department of English
Alliance College
Cambridge Springs, Pennsylvania 16403

SUBSCRIPTION ADDRESS:

same

PUBLISHED: Biannually
COST: 1 yr.—$3.00; for overseas rate add $1.00.

CONTENTS: Articles on recent satiric fiction, poetry, drama, journalistic and other nonfiction satire, and satiric graphic art.

UNSOLICITED MSS. WELCOME? Yes.
MS. LENGTH: Up to 5,000 words.
STYLE REQUIREMENTS: MLA STYLE SHEET.
COPYRIGHT: Not copyrighted.
REJECTED MSS.: Returned, if requested.
GENERAL: First issue, June, 1973.

VIII

TEACHING ABOUT LITERATURE

ALBERTA ENGLISH

EDITORIAL ADDRESS:
R. G. Martin, Editor
Department of Secondary Education
University of Alberta
Edmonton, Alberta T6G 2G5
Canada

SUBSCRIPTION ADDRESS:
Alberta Teachers' Association
11010 142 Street
Edmonton, Alberta T5N 2R1
Canada

PUBLISHED: 3 to 4 times yearly   CIRCULATION: 600
COST: 1 yr.—$5.00 (includes other publications).

CONTENTS: Material of interest to teachers of English at any level: chiefly professional articles; some poetry (both adult and student); book reviews. Comparable, on a small scale, to ENGLISH JOURNAL, plus elementary and university-level material.

UNSOLICITED MSS. WELCOME? Yes; submissions not acknowledged.
SPECIFICALLY WELCOMED: Very limited use of poetry. Literary analysis should have teaching implications.
MS. LENGTH: 1,500-2,500 words; submit ONE copy.
STYLE REQUIREMENTS: Preferably informal.
COPYRIGHT: The journal, with unrestricted rights for author.
EDITOR'S DECISION: 3 months.
FROM ACCEPTANCE TO PUBLICATION: 5 months.
PAYMENT/OFFPRINTS: Complimentary copies; no offprints.
REJECTED MSS.: Returned.
GENERAL: First issue, 1960. Usual publication length, 40 pages.
BACK ISSUES: Some available from editorial address at $2.00 (not usually available).

ARIZONA ENGLISH BULLETIN

EDITORIAL ADDRESS:
Kenneth L. Donelson, Editor
English Department
Arizona State University
Tempe, Arizona 85281

SUBSCRIPTION ADDRESS:

same

PUBLISHED: Tri-annually   CIRCULATION: 500
(Oct., Feb., Apr.)
COST: 1 yr.—$4.00; single copy—$1.50 (except for more expensive and longer issues).

CONTENTS: Each issue has a theme (e.g., films, adolescent literature, media, student teaching), but each issue is aimed at secondary English teachers with a theme to lend concentration upon one aspect of secondary English teaching. Example: "The Literary Value and Adolescent Appeal of Mary Stolz' Novels."

UNSOLICITED MSS. WELCOME? Yes, if they are on the theme of an upcoming issue. Check with editor on themes before sending mss. Submissions generally acknowledged.
MS. LENGTH: 4-10 pages; submit ONE copy.
STYLE REQUIREMENTS: Taken care of by editor before final typing by us.
COPYRIGHT: Not copyrighted.
EDITOR'S DECISION: 3 weeks.
FROM ACCEPTANCE TO PUBLICATION: Depends on issue.
PAYMENT/OFFPRINTS: Three copies of issue in which work appears. No offprint arrangements possible.
REJECTED MSS.: Returned.
GENERAL: First issue, 1958. Usual publication length, 90-130 pages.
BACK ISSUES: Available from editorial office at $1.50 each, usually.

THE CEA CRITIC

EDITORIAL ADDRESS:
Earle Labor, Editor
Centenary College
P. O. Box 4188
Shreveport, Louisiana 71104

SUBSCRIPTION ADDRESS:
Herbert V. Fackler
CEA Treasurer
University of Southwestern Louisiana
Lafayette, Louisiana 70501

PUBLISHED: 4 times yearly (Nov., Jan., Mar., May)
CIRCULATION: 2,700-3,000
COST: $10.00 yearly dues to College English Association, includes subscriptions to all CEA publications (CEA CRITIC, CEA FORUM, CHAP Books).

CONTENTS: Brief critical essays dealing with literary works taught in college English courses; creative writing, especially poems, related to literary subjects; reviews of books related to literary scholarship and criticism.

UNSOLICITED MSS. WELCOME? Yes; contributors should be members of CEA: submissions acknowledged.
SPECIFICALLY WELCOMED: Contributions should be brief, lively, readable. Critical essays should be directly usable in college English classroom.
MS. LENGTH: 1,000-2,000 words; submit TWO copies.
STYLE REQUIREMENTS: MLA STYLE SHEET; footnotes discouraged.
COPYRIGHT: CEA.
EDITOR'S DECISION: 4-6 weeks.
FROM ACCEPTANCE TO PUBLICATION: 2-12 months.
PAYMENT/OFFPRINTS: 5 to 10 tearsheets of article; 2 free copies of issue.
REJECTED MSS.: Returned.
GENERAL: First issue, September, 1939. Usual publication length, 48 pages.
BACK ISSUES: Available from editorial address at $2.00 each.

THE CEA FORUM

EDITORIAL ADDRESS:
Earle Labor, Editor
P. O. Box 4188
Centenary College
Shreveport, Louisiana 71104

SUBSCRIPTION ADDRESS:
Herbert V. Fackler
CEA Treasurer
University of Southwestern Louisiana
Lafayette, Louisiana 70501

PUBLISHED: 4 times yearly (Oct., Dec., Feb., Apr.)

CIRCULATION: 2,700-3,000

COST: $10 annual dues to College English Association, includes subscriptions to all CEA publications: THE CEA FORUM, THE CEA CRITIC, and occasional Chap Books.

CONTENTS: "News and Views" relating to the teaching of college English, along with reports of national and regional CEA activities; dialogue on timely academic issues; brief, lively articles and creative work concerned with college English.

UNSOLICITED MSS. WELCOME? Yes; contributors should be members of CEA: submissions acknowledged.
SPECIFICALLY WELCOMED: Contributions should be brief (under 1,500 words); "mini-articles" (under 250 words) are most welcome. Subjects should be provocative of dialogue.
MS. LENGTH: 250-500 words; submit TWO copies.
STYLE REQUIREMENTS: Informal and lively, but well written and free of jargon and cant.
COPYRIGHT: CEA.
EDITOR'S DECISION: 4-6 weeks.
FROM ACCEPTANCE TO PUBLICATION: 1-12 months.
PAYMENT/OFFPRINTS: 5 to 10 tearsheets of article; 2 free copies of issue.
REJECTED MSS.: Returned.
GENERAL: First issue, October, 1970. Usual publication length, 12 pages.
BACK ISSUES: Available from editorial address at $1.00 each.

THE CLASSICAL JOURNAL

EDITORIAL ADDRESS:
Roy Arthur Swanson, Editor of Literature and Philology

SUBSCRIPTION ADDRESS:
Classical Association of the Middle West and South, Inc.
Ohio University
Athens, Ohio 45701

PUBLISHED: Monthly (Oct. through May)

CONTENTS: Essays directed to the teachers of the literature, art, culture, and history of ancient Greece and Rome (no poetry).

UNSOLICITED MSS. WELCOME? Yes.
COPYRIGHT: Classical Association of Middle West and South, Inc.
GENERAL: First issue, 1905. This periodical had not arrived by the time the entry went to press. Potential subscribers, contributors, or collectors will have to write the editor to see whether the journal still exists, and if so, to inquire about details of manuscript submission, style, back issues, and the like.

COLLEGE ENGLISH

EDITORIAL ADDRESS:
Richard Ohmann, Editor
Department of English
Wesleyan University
Middletown, Connecticut 06457

SUBSCRIPTION ADDRESS:
National Council of
Teachers of English
1111 Kenyon Road
Urbana, Illinois 61801

PUBLISHED: 8 times annually (Oct.-May)
COST: 1 yr.—$12.00.

CIRCULATION: 15,000

CONTENTS: Articles concerning: (1) The working concepts of criticism: structure, genre, influence, period, myth, rhetoric. (2) The nature of critical and scholarly reasoning; implicit standards of evidence and inference; the nature of critical explanation. (3) The structure of our field; implications of the way we segment it; consequences of specializing in usual ways; the place of rhetoric and composition. (4) The relevance of current thinking and research in other fields (e.g. philosophy, history, art history, psychology, linguistics) to the study of English. (5) Curriculum, pedagogy, and educational theory. (6) Practical affairs in the profession. (7) Scholarly books, textbooks, and journals in the field. (Stated "Editorial Policy" quoted.) Also, rebuttals of articles; reviews and review articles on books of general interest to the profession. Example: "From Problem-solving to a Theory of Imagination."

UNSOLICITED MSS. WELCOME? Yes, except reviews; submissions acknowledged.
MS. LENGTH: Up to 40 pages (rebuttals—6 pages maximum); submit ONE copy.
STYLE REQUIREMENTS: MLA STYLE SHEET.
COPYRIGHT: National Council of Teachers of English.
EDITOR'S DECISION: Up to 4 months.
FROM ACCEPTANCE TO PUBLICATION: Varies.
PAYMENT/OFFPRINTS: Copies. Offprints by direct order, paid, to the printer.
REJECTED MSS.: Returned.
GENERAL: First issue, 1939. Usual publication length, 144 pages. CE no longer publishes critical articles or explications, except for those mainly calculated to have an impact on critical theory, curricular thinking, pedagogy.
BACK ISSUES: Available from subscription address.

COLLEGE LITERATURE

EDITORIAL ADDRESS:　　　　SUBSCRIPTION ADDRESS:
Bernard Oldsey, Editor
Department of English　　　　　　　same
West Chester State College
West Chester, Pennsylvania 19380

PUBLISHED: Tri-annually
COST: 1 yr.—$3.00; 2 yrs.—$5.00; single copy—$1.25.

CONTENTS: Articles; book reviews; some editorial material; comments or questions on previous articles. Each article is meant to be a VADE MECUM, a guide to one of the works that are most often taught in literature courses in American colleges and universities—works from Homer to present, works which constitute a loose canon of Western culture.

UNSOLICITED MSS. WELCOME? Yes; submissions acknowledged.
SPECIFICALLY WELCOMED: Analytical articles that make available the information and critical acumen of the scholar and critic to the college teacher for use in his or her classroom or seminar.
MS. LENGTH: 20-25 pages; submit TWO copies.
STYLE REQUIREMENTS: MLA STYLE SHEET.
COPYRIGHT: COLLEGE LITERATURE, except for special situation.
EDITOR'S DECISION: 1 month.
FROM ACCEPTANCE TO PUBLICATION: 5-6 months.
PAYMENT/OFFPRINTS: Five copies of the journal-issue; 25 tear sheets of article.
REJECTED MSS.: Returned.
GENERAL: First issue, January, 1974. Usual publication length, 85 pages.
BACK ISSUES: Available from editorial address at $1.25 each.

CONNECTICUT ENGLISH JOURNAL

EDITORIAL ADDRESS:　　　　　SUBSCRIPTION ADDRESS:
Ralph L. Corrigan, Jr., Editor　　Thomas Fitzsimmons
Sacred Heart University　　　　Puddin Lane RR 3
Bridgeport, Connecticut 06604　Willimantic, Connecticut 06226

PUBLISHED: Biannually　　　　　CIRCULATION: 500
(Fall, Spring)
COST: 1 yr.—$3.00 (includes annual membership dues); single copy—$1.00.

CONTENTS: Articles on teaching of language arts; poetry; articles at all levels on linguistics, composition and literature. Example: "Young Adult Literature: Enlarging the Frame of Reference."

UNSOLICITED MSS. WELCOME? Yes; submission acknowledged.

SPECIFICALLY WELCOMED: Essays about all genres, but practical for classroom use.
MS. LENGTH: 10 pages; submit ONE copy.
STYLE REQUIREMENTS: MLA STYLE SHEET; prefer footnotes included in text.
COPYRIGHT: Not copyrighted.
EDITOR'S DECISION: 1 month.
FROM ACCEPTANCE TO PUBLICATION: 1-6 months.
PAYMENT/OFFPRINTS: Five copies of issue.
REJECTED MSS.: Returned.
GENERAL: First issue, Fall, 1968. Usual publication length, 36 pages.
BACK ISSUES: Available from editorial address at $.50 each.

CONNECTIONS II (formerly CONNECTIONS: THE RADICAL AMERICAN STUDIES JOURNAL)

EDITORIAL ADDRESS:
Lee Chambers-Schiller and
Betsy Jameson, Editors
406 North State Street
Ann Arbor, Michigan 48104

SUBSCRIPTION ADDRESS:

same

PUBLISHED: Tri-annually
COST: 1 yr.—$3.00.

CONTENTS: Essays, letters, reports on efforts toward developing a new critical language for the analysis and laying off of American culture—much of which is literature—conceptionalizing an affirmative politics, and encouraging mutual aid among radical American Studies scholars, teachers, and students. Emphasis on literature as a separate discipline may not appear, but as an integral part of an interdisciplinary effort, insights into teaching literature about. Recent example: "Method and Teaching in American Studies."

UNSOLICITED MSS. WELCOME? Inquire first.
SPECIFICALLY WELCOMED: Contributions cluster around three themes for 1973/74: 1) The Classroom (Doris Friedensohn, Dean of Interdisciplinary Studies, Jersey City State College, Jersey City, New Jersey, is editor); 2) Therapeutic Communities/Self-Help Groups/Mutual Aid Groups/Cohorts/Energy Centers (editor for this issue is Robert Sklar, Program in American Culture, University of Michigan, Ann Arbor, Michigan 48104); 3) Cultural Revolution (editor is Robert Meredith, Chairman, American Studies, University of California, Davis, California 95616). Inquire of each coordinating editor for participating in an issue. Write the general editors (above) for themes and editors of future issues.
MS. LENGTH: 250-1,500 words; submit ONE copy.
STYLE REQUIREMENTS: None.
COPYRIGHT: Author.
PAYMENT/OFFPRINTS: None. Author is free to photocopy.
GENERAL: First issue, Fall, 1971. Usual publication length, 60-70 pages.

BACK ISSUES: If available, from editors at $.50 to $1.00 each.

DIALOGUE FOR ENGLISH TEACHERS IN WEST VIRGINIA

EDITORIAL ADDRESS:
Elaine K. Ginsberg, Editor
Department of English
West Virginia University
Morgantown, West Virginia 26506

SUBSCRIPTION ADDRESS:

same

PUBLISHED: Tri-annually
(Fall, Winter, Spring)
COST: Free.

CIRCULATION: 5,000

CONTENTS: Theoretical and pedagogical essays on the teaching of language, composition, and literature at elementary, secondary, and college levels. Example: "Teaching Black Literature."

UNSOLICITED MSS. WELCOME? Yes; submissions acknowledged.
SPECIFICALLY WELCOMED: Anything that fits into categories described in Contents.
MS. LENGTH: 3-6 pages; submit ONE copy.
STYLE REQUIREMENTS: None.
COPYRIGHT: Author.
EDITOR'S DECISION: 4 weeks.
FROM ACCEPTANCE TO PUBLICATION: 3-6 months.
PAYMENT/OFFPRINTS: Five copies of issue.
REJECTED MSS.: Returned.
GENERAL: First issue, Spring, 1968. Usual publication length, 8 pages.
BACK ISSUES: Available free from editorial address.

EDUCATIONAL THEATRE JOURNAL

See the section on GENRES: THEATRE for details.

ELEMENTARY ENGLISH

EDITORIAL ADDRESS:
Dr. Iris M. Tiedt, Editor
University of Santa Clara
Santa Clara, California 95053

SUBSCRIPTION ADDRESS:
National Council of
Teachers of English
1111 Kenyon Road
Urbana, Illinois 61801

PUBLISHED: 8 issues yearly CIRCULATION: 27,850
(Oct. through May)
COST: 1 yr.—$12.00.

CONTENTS: Articles on any aspect of teaching the language arts in the elementary school or on topics of general interest to elementary English teachers. Example: "Basic Concepts of Death in Children's Literature."

UNSOLICITED MSS. WELCOME? Yes; submissions acknowledged.
MS. LENGTH: 10-12 pages; submit TWO copies.
STYLE REQUIREMENTS: Writing directed to classroom teacher rather than pedantic style.
COPYRIGHT: National Council of Teachers of English.
EDITOR'S DECISION: 2 months.
FROM ACCEPTANCE TO PUBLICATION: 3 months to 1 year.
PAYMENT/OFFPRINTS: Two copies of issue in which article appears. Order blank for offprints sent to author with galley proof.
REJECTED MSS.: Returned.
GENERAL: First issue, 1924. Usual publication length, 168 pages.
BACK ISSUES: Available from subscription address at $1.50 each.

ENGLISH EDUCATION

EDITORIAL ADDRESS:
Oscar M. Haugh, Editor
CEE Publications
209 Bailey Hall
University of Kansas
Lawrence, Kansas 66044

SUBSCRIPTION ADDRESS:
National Council of
Teachers of English
1111 Kenyon Road
Urbana, Illinois 61801

PUBLISHED: Tri-annually CIRCULATION: 2,000
(Oct., Feb., May)
COST: 1 yr.—$5.00; single copy—$1.00. Canada and members of the Pan American Postal Union, add $.50 per year; all other foreign countries, add $1.00.

CONTENTS: Articles dealing with preparing teachers to teach English, including such subjects as accountability, certification, curriculum, methods courses, objectives, selection of teachers, student teaching, teacher education, and the teaching of composition, communication, literature. Example article on literature is "Demystifying Literature: Northrup Frye in the Classroom."

UNSOLICITED MSS. WELCOME? Yes; submissions acknowledged.
SPECIFICALLY WELCOMED: Expository articles; poetry if it relates to teaching.
MS. LENGTH: 1,000-3,000 words; submit TWO copies.
STYLE REQUIREMENTS: Footnotes of complete citations.
COPYRIGHT: National Council of Teachers of English.
EDITOR'S DECISION: 1 week to several months.

FROM ACCEPTANCE TO PUBLICATION: About 6 months.
PAYMENT/OFFPRINTS: No payment. Offprints provided at cost; about $3 per page per first 100 copies.
REJECTED MSS.: Returned.
GENERAL: First issue, October, 1969. Usual publication length, 70 or more pages.
BACK ISSUES: Available from National Council of Teachers of English at $1.00 each.

ENGLISH IN TEXAS

EDITORIAL ADDRESS:
Zenobia Verner, Editor
Department of Curriculum
and Instruction
University of Houston
Houston, Texas 77004

SUBSCRIPTION ADDRESS:
Fred Tarpley, Executive Secretary
Texas Council of Teachers
of English
East Texas Station
Commerce, Texas 75428

PUBLISHED: Quarterly
COST: 1 yr.—$5.00.

CIRCULATION: 800

CONTENTS: Articles dealing with the teaching of English language and literature. Examples: "Gulliver's Field Methods"; "Jarrell's Use of Metaphor in 'The Death of the Ball Turrett Gunner.'"

UNSOLICITED MSS. WELCOME? Yes; submissions acknowledged.
SPECIFICALLY WELCOMED: Articles dealing with the teaching of English language and literature.
MS. LENGTH: 8-10 pages; submit ONE copy.
COPYRIGHT: Texas Council of Teachers of English.
EDITOR'S DECISION: 6 weeks to 2 months.
FROM ACCEPTANCE TO PUBLICATION: 2-6 months.
PAYMENT/OFFPRINTS: Three copies of issue in which work appears.
REJECTED MSS.: Returned.
GENERAL: First issue, Fall, 1969. Usual publication length, 16-24 pages.
BACK ISSUES: Available from either editorial or subscription address at $1.00 each.

ENGLISH JOURNAL

EDITORIAL ADDRESS:
Stephen N. Judy, Editor
P. O. Box 112
East Lansing, Michigan 48823

SUBSCRIPTION ADDRESS:
National Council of
Teachers of English
1111 Kenyon Road
Urbana, Illinois 61801

PUBLISHED: Monthly, Sept. through May
CIRCULATION: 54,873
COST: 1 yr.—$12.00 (includes NCTE dues).

CONTENTS: Articles, essays, and reviews on the teaching of English and the language arts in secondary schools (grades 6-12). Articles may focus on theoretical and practical aspects of teaching, as well as current problems and trends in politics and society which may influence teachers. Example: "Gogol's Hollow Man."

UNSOLICITED MSS. WELCOME? Yes; submissions acknowledged.
SPECIFICALLY WELCOMED: Analyses of books appropriate for young people; bibliographies and reviews of such books; thematic or issue-centered bibliographies; notes on teaching literary works.
MS. LENGTH: 3,000-5,000 words; submit ONE copy.
STYLE REQUIREMENTS: Style sheet available from the Editor.
COPYRIGHT: National Council of Teachers of English.
EDITOR'S DECISION: 60 days.
FROM ACCEPTANCE TO PUBLICATION: 150 days.
PAYMENT/OFFPRINTS: Six free copies of issue. Authors may purchase offprints at time of publication.
REJECTED MSS.: Returned.
GENERAL: First issue, 1912. Usual publication length, 96-128 pages.
BACK ISSUES: Available from subscription address. Price is variable; inquire from NCTE.

ENGLISH LITERATURE, CRITICISM, TEACHING

EDITORIAL ADDRESS:
Margaret Willy, Editor
Oxford University Press
Press Road
Neasden, London N. W. 10
England

SUBSCRIPTION ADDRESS:

same

GENERAL: This periodical had not arrived by the time the entry went to press. Potential subscribers, contributors, or collectors will have to write the editor to see whether the journal still exists, and if so, to inquire about details of manuscript submission, style, back issues, and the like.

THE ENGLISH QUARTERLY

EDITORIAL ADDRESS:
John S. North, Editor
Department of English
University of Waterloo
Waterloo, Ontario N2L 3G1
Canada

SUBSCRIPTION ADDRESS:
Canadian Council of
Teachers of English
Language Study Center
155 College Street
Toronto, Ontario M5T 1P6
Canada

PUBLISHED: Quarterly
CIRCULATION: 1,200
COST: 1 yr.—$10.00 (as CCTE member); single copy—$2.50 (as non-member).

CONTENTS: Articles that acquaint teachers of English at all levels of education with developments in the teaching of English across Canada and in other parts of the world; professional and scholarly articles as well as information on curricular matters and classroom practices; book reviews; poems. Example: "The Small Town in Canadian Fiction"; "Is Riz, Some Hot, Clumb, and Other Canadianisms."

UNSOLICITED MSS. WELCOME? Yes; submissions acknowledged.
SPECIFICALLY WELCOMED: Anything of pedagogical interest.
MS. LENGTH: 1-20 pages; submit TWO copies.
STYLE REQUIREMENTS: Well-written; for book reviews, use MLA STYLE SHEET.
COPYRIGHT: THE ENGLISH QUARTERLY.
EDITOR'S DECISION: Maximum of 3 months.
FROM ACCEPTANCE TO PUBLICATION: 1 or 2 months.
PAYMENT/OFFPRINTS: Minimum of 2 copies of the periodical; other copies negotiable.
REJECTED MSS.: Returned.
GENERAL: First issue, Summer, 1968. Usual publication length, 120 pages.
BACK ISSUES: Available from editorial address at $2.50 each.

THE ENGLISH RECORD

EDITORIAL ADDRESS:
Daniel J. Casey, Editor
Department of English
State University College
Oneonta, New York 13820

SUBSCRIPTION ADDRESS:
Patrick E. Kilburn,
Executive Secretary
Union College Humanities Center
Schenectady, New York 12308

PUBLISHED: Quarterly (Fall, Winter, Spring, Summer)
CIRCULATION: 2,000
COST: 1 yr.—$10.00; single copy—$2.00.

CONTENTS: Critical articles on language, composition, rhetoric, drama; original short fiction; poetry; research in English education; book reviews. Example: "On Teaching A MODEST PROPOSAL."

UNSOLICITED MSS. WELCOME? Yes; submissions acknowledged.
SPECIFICALLY WELCOMED: Critical articles on all areas; original fiction and poetry.
MS. LENGTH: 3,000 words; submit ONE copy.
STYLE REQUIREMENTS: MLA STYLE SHEET; include documentation in text.
COPYRIGHT: THE ENGLISH RECORD.
EDITOR'S DECISION: 6 weeks.
FROM ACCEPTANCE TO PUBLICATION: 3 months.
PAYMENT/OFFPRINTS: Two copies of issue. Offprints may be purchased at cost from printer.
REJECTED MSS.: Returned.
GENERAL: First issue, Fall, 1950. Usual publication length, 106 pages.
BACK ISSUES: Available from subscription address at $2.00 each.

EXERCISE EXCHANGE: A JOURNAL FOR TEACHERS OF ENGLISH IN HIGH SCHOOLS AND COLLEGES

EDITORIAL ADDRESS:
Paul A. Escholz and
Alfred F. Rosa, Editors
English Department
University of Vermont
Burlington, Vermont 05401

SUBSCRIPTION ADDRESS:

same

PUBLISHED: Biannually (Fall and Spring)
COST: 1 yr.—$2.00, individuals (prepaid); $3.50, institutions; 2 yrs.—$3.50, individuals; $5.00, institutions.

CONTENTS: Articles on successful approaches to the teaching of language, writing and literature in high schools and colleges. Examples: "Langston Hughes: Poet Laureate of Black America"; "Research Areas in WALDEN and CIVIL DISOBEDIENCE."

UNSOLICITED MSS. WELCOME? Yes; submissions acknowledged.
MS. LENGTH: 500-4,000 words; submit ONE copy.
STYLE REQUIREMENTS: Loosely MLA STYLE SHEET.
COPYRIGHT: EXERCISE EXCHANGE.
EDITOR'S DECISION: Up to 2 months.
FROM ACCEPTANCE TO PUBLICATION: Not more than 6 months.
PAYMENT/OFFPRINTS: 2 contributor's copies; no offprints.
REJECTED MSS.: Returned.
GENERAL: First issue, Fall, 1951. Usual publication length, 30 pages.
BACK ISSUES: Available from editorial address at $1.00 each.

FLORIDA COUNCIL OF TEACHERS OF ENGLISH NEWSLETTER

EDITORIAL ADDRESS:
Mabel M. Staats, Editor
5110 San Amaro Drive
Coral Gables, Florida 33146

SUBSCRIPTION ADDRESS:

same

PUBLISHED: Tri-annually (usually Jan., May, Sept.)
COST: Subscription—$3.00; single copy—$.50.

CIRCULATION: 1,200

CONTENTS: News about county, state meetings; brief reviews of main speakers' presentations; information on future meetings, officers; short features on special people; details of annual workshops, district meetings, county council news; NCTE news.

UNSOLICITED MSS. WELCOME? Yes, a few on teaching of literature and grammar; submissions acknowledged.
SPECIFICALLY WELCOMED: Successful approaches to teaching of prose and poetry; new methods.
MS. LENGTH: Not over 3 pages; submit ONE copy.
STYLE REQUIREMENTS: Brief, concise description of procedure, specific examples. Bibliography of any reference material recommended. News article style.
COPYRIGHT: Author.
EDITOR'S DECISION: 30 days.
FROM ACCEPTANCE TO PUBLICATION: 3 months.
PAYMENT/OFFPRINTS: Three complimentary copies.
REJECTED MSS.: Returned.
GENERAL: First issue, 1965. Usual publication, 6-8 pages.
BACK ISSUES: Available (from 1970 on) from editorial address at $.50 each.

FLORIDA ENGLISH JOURNAL

EDITORIAL ADDRESS:
Arthur S. Healey, Editor
5591 S. W. 3rd Court
Plantation, Florida 33314

SUBSCRIPTION ADDRESS:

same

PUBLISHED: Biannually
COST: 1 yr.—$3.00.

CIRCULATION: 1,200

CONTENTS: All aspects of "teaching" English, as well as professional and scholarly articles.

UNSOLICITED MSS. WELCOME? Yes; submissions acknowledged.
SPECIFICALLY WELCOMED: Non-esoteric articles—of interest to high school teachers.
MS. LENGTH: Around 1,000 words; submit TWO copies.

STYLE REQUIREMENTS: Legibility coupled with common sense prose.
COPYRIGHT: The JOURNAL.
EDITOR'S DECISION: 1 month.
FROM ACCEPTANCE TO PUBLICATION: 3 months to 1 year.
PAYMENT/OFFPRINTS: At least five copies.
REJECTED MSS.: Returned.
GENERAL: First issue, 1966. Usual publication length, 28 pages.
BACK ISSUES: Available from editor at $1.00 each.

HISPANIA

EDITORIAL ADDRESS:
Donald W. Bleznick, Acting Editor
Department of Romance Languages
University of Cincinnati
Cincinnati, Ohio 45221

SUBSCRIPTION ADDRESS:
Eugene Savaiano, Secretary-Treasurer, AATSP
Wichita State University
Wichita, Kansas 67208

PUBLISHED: Quarterly (Mar., May, Sept., Dec.)
CIRCULATION: 16,500
COST: 1 yr.—$8.00, $4.00 for students (for 3 years only)—includes membership in American Association for Teachers of Spanish and Portuguese.

CONTENTS: Articles of interest to all teachers of Spanish and Portuguese concerning language, literature, culture, pedagogy, professional news; textbook information; book reviews. Example: "Horacio Quiroga and His Exceptional Protagonists."

UNSOLICITED MSS. WELCOME? Yes, but only from AATSP members; submissions acknowledged.
SPECIFICALLY WELCOMED: Research, literary history, cirticism; no creative writing.
MS. LENGTH: 12-20 pages; submit ORIGINAL.
STYLE REQUIREMENTS: HISPANIA style sheet as well as MLA STYLE SHEET.
COPYRIGHT: The AATSP, Inc.
EDITOR'S DECISION: 2-4 months.
FROM ACCEPTANCE TO PUBLICATION: 1-2 years.
PAYMENT/OFFPRINTS: No payment. Offprints can be purchased from the printer.
REJECTED MSS.: Returned.
GENERAL: First issue, November, 1917. Usual publication length, 180-200 pages. Articles may be written in English, Spanish, or Portuguese.
BACK ISSUES: Available from subscription address at $1.00 each, usually.

HORIZON [South Carolina Council of Teachers of English]

EDITORIAL ADDRESS:
Tom Parks, Editor
English Consultant
State Department of Education
1429 Senate
Columbia, South Carolina 29201

SUBSCRIPTION ADDRESS:
same

PUBLISHED: Biannually
(Fall, Spring)

CIRCULATION: 3,000

COST: Free to members of State Council of Teachers of English and others interested in English education.

CONTENTS: State news in English education; teacher and student creative writing; articles; reports; poems; interviews, such as with poet and novelist James Dickey.

UNSOLICITED MSS. WELCOME? Yes; submissions acknowledged.
SPECIFICALLY WELCOMED: Essays, articles by teachers or students, preferably on subjects of S.C. English teachers; poems on any subject, any style but not over 30 lines long; short fiction under 400 words; reports by teachers on effective classroom practices, projects, and ideas.
MS. LENGTH: 600 words or less; submit ONE copy.
STYLE REQUIREMENTS: None.
COPYRIGHT: Authors.
EDITOR'S DECISION: 1 month.
FROM ACCEPTANCE TO PUBLICATION: Always next issue.
PAYMENT/OFFPRINTS: Free copies.
REJECTED MSS.: Returned.
GENERAL: First issue, 1969. Usual publication length, 20 pages.
BACK ISSUES: Available free from editorial office.

ILLINOIS ENGLISH BULLETIN

EDITORIAL ADDRESS:
Wilmer A. Lamar, Editor
100 English Building
University of Illinois
Urbana, Illinois 61801

SUBSCRIPTION ADDRESS:
IATE Treasurer
same

PUBLISHED: 8 times yearly
(Oct. through May)
COST: 1 yr.—$5.00.

CIRCULATION: 1,800

CONTENTS: Articles on literature, grammar, and composition of interest to English teachers, such as "The Teaching of Drama in High School."

UNSOLICITED MSS. WELCOME? Yes; submission acknowledged.

SPECIFICALLY WELCOMED: Expository prose of particular interest to high school English teachers.
MS. LENGTH: Up to 8,000 words; submit ONE copy.
STYLE REQUIREMENTS: No poetry or narrative writing.
COPYRIGHT: Illinois Association of Teachers of English.
EDITOR'S DECISION: 6 months.
FROM ACCEPTANCE TO PUBLICATION: Varies.
PAYMENT/OFFPRINTS: Five complimentary issues of bulletin.
REJECTED MSS.: Returned.
GENERAL: First issue, October, 1913. Usual publication length, 24-32 pages.
BACK ISSUES: Available from editorial address. Price varies from $.50 to $.75.

INDIANA ENGLISH JOURNAL

EDITORIAL ADDRESS:　　　　　　SUBSCRIPTION ADDRESS:
Editor
Indiana Council of Teachers of English　　same
Division of Continuing Education and
Extended Services
Indiana State University
Terre Haute, Indiana 47809

PUBLISHED: Quarterly　　　　　　CIRCULATION: 1,600
COST: 1 yr.—$3.00. (Sample issues available.)

CONTENTS: Articles of interest to elementary and secondary English teachers.

UNSOLICITED MSS. WELCOME? Yes; submissions acknowledged.
MS. LENGTH: No preference; submit TWO copies.
COPYRIGHT: No copyright.
PAYMENT/OFFPRINTS: Five copies of publication.
REJECTED MSS.: Returned.

IOWA ENGLISH BULLETIN: YEARBOOK

EDITORIAL ADDRESS:　　　　　　SUBSCRIPTION ADDRESS:
Richard J. Zbaracki, Editor
Department of English　　　　　　same
Iowa State University
Ames, Iowa 50010

PUBLISHED: Annually (November)
COST: $1.50 per issue.

CONTENTS: Articles of general scholarly interest on literature, language, composition, and professional problems; occasional narrative and poetry of interest to teachers in a Midwest setting. Examples: "Intimacy in the Novels of Jane Austen"; "Heroes Never Learn: Irony in A SEPARATE PEACE"; "Graham Greene's Spiritual Lepers."

UNSOLICITED MSS. WELCOME? Yes; submissions not acknowledged.
SPECIFICALLY WELCOMED: Occasional short narratives and poems.
MS. LENGTH: Not over 5,000 words; submit ONE copy.
STYLE REQUIREMENTS: MLA STYLE SHEET.
COPYRIGHT: Editor.
EDITOR'S DECISION: 1-6 months.
FROM ACCEPTANCE TO PUBLICATION: Current year.
PAYMENT/OFFPRINTS: Two copies of issue with 10 offprints.
REJECTED MSS.: Returned.
GENERAL: First issue, 1956. Usual publication length, 50-60 pages.
BACK ISSUES: 1964 onwards available from editor at $1.50 each; those before 1964 from Kraus Reprint Co.

ITALICA

EDITORIAL ADDRESS:
Olga Ragusa, Editor
601 Casa Italiana
Columbia University
New York, New York 10027

SUBSCRIPTION ADDRESS:
Secretary-Treasurer of AATT
Department of Italian
Rutgers University
New Brunswick, New Jersey 08903

PUBLISHED: Quarterly
(Spring, Summer, Autumn, Winter)
COST: 1 yr.—$8.00 (includes membership in the American Association of Teachers of Italian).

CIRCULATION: 1,800

CONTENTS: Articles and reviews of books dealing with Italian language, literature, and the teaching of Italian; bibliographies (general, translations, linguistics, Dante, 13th and 14th centuries, 20th century, textbooks, and pedogogy). Example: "Animal Symbolism in Silone's VINO E PANE."

UNSOLICITED MSS. WELCOME? Yes; submissions sometimes acknowledged.
SPECIFICALLY WELCOMED: Scholarly articles.
MS. LENGTH: 20-25 pages; submit TWO copies.
STYLE REQUIREMENTS: MLA STYLE SHEET; footnotes follow article.
COPYRIGHT: Author.
EDITOR'S DECISION: 1 month.
FROM ACCEPTANCE TO PUBLICATION: 1-2 years.
PAYMENT/OFFPRINTS: No payment. Offprints available at author's expense.
REJECTED MSS.: Returned.
GENERAL: First issue, 1924. Usual publication length, 130 pages. Articles may be written in English or Italian.

BACK ISSUES: Available from subscription address. Price depends on availability.

JOURNAL

EDITORIAL ADDRESS:
Lois Green, Editor
711 Second Avenue
Salt Lake City, Utah 84103

SUBSCRIPTION ADDRESS:

same

PUBLISHED: Annually (September)   CIRCULATION: 300
COST: 1 yr.—$3.00 (included in membership fees for U.C.T.E.).

CONTENTS: Articles dealing with the teaching of English and the language arts. Example: "Other Voices, Other Rooms: The Ethnic Strain in American Literature."

UNSOLICITED MSS. WELCOME? Yes, but local (Utah) articles are given preference; submissions acknowledged.
SPECIFICALLY WELCOMED: Innovative approaches on all levels (primary, secondary, college).
MS. LENGTH: 2,000 words; submit ONE copy.
STYLE REQUIREMENTS: Journalistic, expository (refer to ENGLISH JOURNAL for style).
COPYRIGHT: Author.
EDITOR'S DECISION: By month of June.
FROM ACCEPTANCE TO PUBLICATION: 3 months.
PAYMENT/OFFPRINTS: None.
REJECTED MSS.: Returned.
GENERAL: First issue, September, 1972. Usual publication length, 75 pages.

JOURNAL OF AESTHETIC EDUCATION

EDITORIAL ADDRESS:
Ralph A. Smith, Editor
288B-Education
University of Illinois at
Urbana-Champaign
Urbana, Illinois 61801

SUBSCRIPTION ADDRESS:
Subscription Department
University of Illinois Press
1002 West Green Street
Urbana, Illinois 61801

PUBLISHED: Quarterly   CIRCULATION: 1,350
(Jan., April, July, Oct.)
COST: 1 yr.—$7.50 in U.S.; $8.00 foreign; single copy—$2.25.

CONTENTS: Articles devoted to an understanding of the basic problem areas of education in the arts and in the humanities (literature, music, the visual and performing arts); articles dealing with the aesthetic aspects of the art and craft of teaching in general; articles about the appreciation and understanding of the aesthetic character of other disciplines and subjects, such as the sciences; articles treating the aesthetic import and significance of the new communications media and the environmental arts in their various forms; book reviews; notes and news; occasional photographs. Example: "The Question of Relevance in Literature."

UNSOLICITED MSS. WELCOME? Yes; submissions acknowledged.
SPECIFICALLY WELCOMED: Critical essays about the arts, with educational relevance.
MS. LENGTH: 5,000-6,000 words; submit TWO copies.
STYLE REQUIREMENTS: Send for style sheet.
COPYRIGHT: University of Illinois Press, unless otherwise specified.
EDITOR'S DECISION: 2 months or less.
FROM ACCEPTANCE TO PUBLICATION: 1 month or less.
PAYMENT/OFFPRINTS: Usually no payment; special issues may be an exception.
REJECTED MSS.: Returned.
GENERAL: First issue, 1966; as a quarterly, 1968. Usual publication length, 128 pages.
BACK ISSUES: Available from subscription address at $2.25 each.

JOURNAL OF ENGLISH TEACHING TECHNIQUES

EDITORIAL ADDRESS:
R. D. Kush, Editor
Department of English
Colorado State University
Fort Collins, Colorado 80521

SUBSCRIPTION ADDRESS:
same

PUBLISHED: Quarterly
(Spring, Summer, Winter, Fall)

CIRCULATION: 300

COST: 1 yr.—$3.00; 2 yrs.—$5.50; 3 yrs.—$8.00. Through subscription agency: 1 yr.—$2.00; 2 yrs.—$4.00; 3 yrs.—$6.00.

CONTENTS: Articles on techniques with which to teach English; book reviews; occasional photographs. Example: "Teaching Blake's 'The Sick Rose.' "

UNSOLICITED MSS. WELCOME? Yes; submissions acknowledged.
SPECIFICALLY WELCOMED: English teaching techniques.
MS. LENGTH: No preference; submit TWO copies.
STYLE REQUIREMENTS: MLA STYLE SHEET.
COPYRIGHT: JOURNAL OF ENGLISH TEACHING TECHNIQUES.
EDITOR'S DECISION: 90 days.
FROM ACCEPTANCE TO PUBLICATION: 90 days.
PAYMENT/OFFPRINTS: Five copies of issue in which work appears.

REJECTED MSS.: Returned.
GENERAL: First issue, 1968. Usual publication length, 50 pages. Indexed by volume.
BACK ISSUES: Available from editorial address.

KANSAS ENGLISH

EDITORIAL ADDRESS:
Donald Stewart, Editor
Department of English
Kansas State University
Manhattan, Kansas 66506

SUBSCRIPTION ADDRESS:
Frances McKenna
1821 Burnett Road
Topeka, Kansas 66604

PUBLISHED: 3 or 4 times per academic year
COST: 1 yr.—$4.00; single copy—$1.00.

CIRCULATION: 500

CONTENTS: Fall issue features articles on the teaching of written composition; winter issue, when issued, features articles on matters professional; spring issue (Feb. or Mar.) features articles on the teaching of literature. Example: "Teaching the Short Story: An Approach to Steinbeck's 'Flight.' "

UNSOLICITED MSS. WELCOME? Yes; submissions not acknowledged.
SPECIFICALLY WELCOMED: Articles on the teaching of literature. Critical articles or explications are invited only if their purpose will have an impact on critical theory, curriculum development, or pedagogy.
MS. LENGTH: Up to 15 pages; submit ONE copy.
STYLE REQUIREMENTS: MLA STYLE SHEET; avoid footnotes whenever possible by including documentation in text.
COPYRIGHT: Author.
EDITOR'S DECISION: 2-3 weeks.
FROM ACCEPTANCE TO PUBLICATION: 1-6 months.
PAYMENT/OFFPRINTS: Payment in copies. Offprints available from printer at near cost.
REJECTED MSS.: Returned.
GENERAL: First issue, 1915. Usual publication length, 32-38 pages. NCTE is reprinting one back issue (Dec. 1970) featuring articles on Dickens. A fourth issue, "Young Kansas Writers," is given over to the work of high school and junior high school students in Kansas (Jim Penarvis and Kent Noel, Editors, Junction City High School, Junction City, Kansas 66441).
BACK ISSUES: A few available from Professor Tom Hemmens, Department of English, Kansas State College, Pittsburg, Kansas 66762, at $1.00 each.

KENTUCKY ENGLISH BULLETIN

EDITORIAL ADDRESS:
Maurice A. Hatch, Editor
Department of English
University of Kentucky
Lexington, Kentucky 40506

SUBSCRIPTION ADDRESS:
Katherine C. Lawrence
109 East Brashear Avenue
Bardstown, Kentucky 40004

PUBLISHED: Tri-annually
(Fall, Winter, Spring)
COST: 1 yr.—$2.00.

CIRCULATION: 1,200

CONTENTS: Essays on teaching of literature, composition; articles of general interest to high school teachers: methods, innovations, linguistics, interpretation; solutions to common problems, such as censorship. Spring issue devoted to writing of students in Kentucky high schools; an occasional poem. Example: "Allusion as Ingress to J. D. Salinger's 'A Perfect Day for Bananafish.'"

UNSOLICITED MSS. WELCOME? Yes; submissions acknowledged.
SPECIFICALLY WELCOMED: Materials which can get into high school classrooms at once.
MS. LENGTH: 5-10 pages; submit ONE copy.
STYLE REQUIREMENTS: Decent and reasonable.
COPYRIGHT: Kentucky Council of Teachers of English.
EDITOR'S DECISION: 1 week or permission to hold.
FROM ACCEPTANCE TO PUBLICATION: Usually 3 months.
PAYMENT/OFFPRINTS: Two complimentary issues.
REJECTED MSS.: Returned.
GENERAL: First issue, September, 1950. Usual publication length, 36 pages.
BACK ISSUES: Available from editorial address at $.75 each.

THE LEAFLET

EDITORIAL ADDRESS:
Lee E. Allen, Editor
Needham High School
609 Webster Street
Needham, Massachusetts 02194

SUBSCRIPTION ADDRESS:
Miss Frances Russell, Treasurer
P. O. Box 234
Lexington, Massachusetts 02173

PUBLISHED: 4 times during school year CIRCULATION: 1,200
COST: 1 yr.—$6.00 (included with NEATE dues); single copy—$1.00.

CONTENTS: Articles pertaining to teaching English; poems; stories; reviews; drawings; cartoons. Example: "The Multiple Ironies of Shelley's 'Ozymandias.'"

UNSOLICITED MSS. WELCOME? Yes; submissions acknowledged.
MS. LENGTH: 3,000 words maximum; submit ONE copy.

STYLE REQUIREMENTS: Typed and well-written.
COPYRIGHT: NEATE.
EDITOR'S DECISION: 3-4 months.
FROM ACCEPTANCE TO PUBLICATION: 1-4 months.
PAYMENT/OFFPRINTS: None.
REJECTED MSS.: Returned.
GENERAL: First issue, 1901. Usual publication length, 40 pages.
BACK ISSUES: Available from treasurer at $1.00 each.

LITERATURE/FILM QUARTERLY

See the section on FILM for details.

LOUISIANA ENGLISH JOURNAL

EDITORIAL ADDRESS:
James T. Nardin, Editor
Department of English
Louisiana State University
Baton Rouge, Louisiana 70803

SUBSCRIPTION ADDRESS:
Mrs. Lucille McDowell
State Department of Education
Baton Rouge, Louisiana 70804

PUBLISHED: Annually
COST: 1 yr.—$2.00.

CIRCULATION: 1,000

CONTENTS: Short articles, primarily concerned with teaching of composition and literature, with particular emphasis on literature taught in secondary schools.

UNSOLICITED MSS. WELCOME? Yes; submissions acknowledged.
SPECIFICALLY WELCOMED: Primarily articles concerned with teaching literature.
MS. LENGTH: 10-12 pages; submit ONE copy.
STYLE REQUIREMENTS: MLA STYLE SHEET.
COPYRIGHT: Member of NCTE agreement.
EDITOR'S DECISION: 2 months at most.
FROM ACCEPTANCE TO PUBLICATION: 1 year at most.
PAYMENT/OFFPRINTS: Three copies of journal; no offprints.
REJECTED MSS.: Returned.
GENERAL: First issue, 1960. Usual publication length, 60-70 pages.
BACK ISSUES: Not available.

MARYLAND ENGLISH JOURNAL

EDITORIAL ADDRESS:
Mrs. Edythe Samson, Editor
3208 Taney Road
Baltimore, Maryland 21215

SUBSCRIPTION ADDRESS:
Morris Trent
Baltimore County Board
of Education
Dumbarton House
Towson, Maryland 21204

PUBLISHED: Biannually   CIRCULATION: 1,500
COST: 1 yr.—$3.00, including membership in Maryland Council.

CONTENTS: Articles on literature, oral discussion, semantics, teacher preparation and other topics of interest to teachers of elementary, secondary schools, college levels. Examples: "In Praise of Marianne Moore"; "Children's Literature: An Insight into Life."

UNSOLICITED MSS. WELCOME? Yes, but Maryland material preferred.
SPECIFICALLY WELCOMED: Articles on how teachers used new ideas in their high school or college classes; articles on literary interpretation of frequently taught works, and curriculum suggestions.
MS. LENGTH: 8-10 pages; submit ONE OR TWO copies.
STYLE REQUIREMENTS: Informal; use first person. Minimal footnotes.
COPYRIGHT: Journal asks that its name be listed as having first printed the article.
EDITOR'S DECISION: Decisions made twice a year, August and February.
FROM ACCEPTANCE TO PUBLICATION: 6 months to 1 year.
PAYMENT/OFFPRINTS: 10 copies of magazine. Extra magazines sold at $.20 each.
REJECTED MSS.: Returned.
GENERAL: First issue, Spring, 1963. Usual publication length, 48 pages.
BACK ISSUES: Available from subscription address at cost of postage only. No complete file.

MEDIA AND METHODS

See the section on FILM for details.

MEDIA MIX: IDEAS AND RESOURCES FOR VALUE EDUCATION

EDITORIAL ADDRESS:
Jeff Schrank, Editor
145 Brentwood Drive
Palatine, Illinois 60067

SUBSCRIPTION ADDRESS:
221 West Madison Street
Chicago, Illinois 60606

PUBLISHED: 8 times during school year CIRCULATION: 1,000-2,000

COST: 1 yr.—$5.00; 2 yrs.—$9.00.

CONTENTS: Reviews of creative short and documentary films and mediagraphic data; access information on tapes, filmstrips, videosphere, books, publications of interest to high school and college educators and resource centers. Biased toward humanistic education, media, values, educational reform; illustrations.

UNSOLICITED MSS. WELCOME? No.
COPYRIGHT: Editor.
GENERAL: First issue, 1968. Usual publication length, 8 pages. Vol. 4, #8, May 15, 1973, contains the index for Vols. II-IV.
BACK ISSUES: Available from subscription address at $.75 each.

MIDWEST MODERN LANGUAGE ASSOCIATION BULLETIN

See section on SPECIALIZED TOPICS AND INTERDISCIPLINARY STUDIES: INTERDISCIPLINARY for details.

MINNESOTA ENGLISH JOURNAL

EDITORIAL ADDRESS:
Harriet Sheridan, Editor
Department of English
Carleton College
Northfield, Minnesota 55057

SUBSCRIPTION ADDRESS:

same

PUBLISHED: 2 or 3 times yearly
COST: 1 yr.—$3.00; single copy $1.50.

CIRCULATION: 800

CONTENTS: Any subject of interest and use to teachers of English and reading; occasional photographs. Example: "The Art of O. E. Rølvaag."

UNSOLICITED MSS. WELCOME? Yes; submissions acknowledged.
SPECIFICALLY WELCOMED: Essays; occasional poetry and fiction.
MS. LENGTH: Up to 12 pages; submit ONE copy.
STYLE REQUIREMENTS: Being worthy of English teachers.
COPYRIGHT: Author.
EDITOR'S DECISION: A long time.
FROM ACCEPTANCE TO PUBLICATION: Varies.
PAYMENT/OFFPRINTS: Three copies.
REJECTED MSS.: Returned.
GENERAL: First issue, October, 1965. Usual publication length, 60 pages.
BACK ISSUES: Available from editorial address at $1.50 each.

MISSOURI ENGLISH BULLETIN

EDITORIAL ADDRESS:
Hubert T. Moore, Jr., Editor
Division of Language and Literature
Northeast Missouri State University
Kirksville, Missouri 63501

SUBSCRIPTION ADDRESS:
Dorothy Matlock, Treasurer
same

PUBLISHED: Three newsletters and 1 yearbook (Jan.)

CIRCULATION: 505

COST: 1 yr.—$4.00 (includes membership in Missouri Association of Teachers of English); single copy—$.50.

CONTENTS: Poetry; articles on teaching of English in its diverse forms and content; research related to learning and teaching of English; some short book reviews; annotated bibliographies, such as "Browning's 'My Last Duchess' and the Critics." Example: "Teaching Poetry through Popular Music."

UNSOLICITED MSS. WELCOME? Yes; submissions acknowledged.
SPECIFICALLY WELCOMED: Articles with focus on secondary schools; occasional articles dealing with the teaching of English in the elementary school are accepted.
MS. LENGTH: Up to 8 pages typed pica; sometimes 9 or 10; submit ONE copy.
STYLE REQUIREMENTS: Readable; high informal to informal; colloquial at times.
COPYRIGHT: Authors.
EDITOR'S DECISION: About 6 months.
FROM ACCEPTANCE TO PUBLICATION: 6-12 months.
PAYMENT/OFFPRINTS: Contributors' copies (four or five). No offprints.
REJECTED MSS.: Returned.
GENERAL: First issue, 1943. Usual publication length, newletters, 4 pages; yearbook, about 70 pages. MATE also publishes MISSOURI'S WRITERS, about 70 pages long, containing short biographies of 50 missouri writers, some famous, some not famous.
BACK ISSUES: When available, from editorial address at $.50 each.

THE NEBRASKA ENGLISH COUNSELOR

EDITORIAL ADDRESS:
Margaret McMartin, Editor
4519 South 24th Street
South High School
Omaha, Nebraska 68107

SUBSCRIPTION ADDRESS:
Larry Andrews, Executive Secretary
Nebraska Council of Teachers
of English
University of Nebraska
Lincoln, Nebraska 68508

PUBLISHED: Quarterly (Sept., Nov., Feb., May)
COST: 1 yr.—$5.00.

CIRCULATION: 300

CONTENTS: Articles dealing with all aspects of secondary school English curriculum as it is, may be, or ought to be taught; essays about English and language arts, either subject matter or pedagogy, theoretical or practical; descriptions of activities, projects, or experiments of individual or groups of teachers. Example: "Individualized Literature Study: A Selected Bibliography."

UNSOLICITED MSS. WELCOME? Yes; submissions acknowledged.
SPECIFICALLY WELCOMED: Articles concerning effective teaching methods—either experimental or conventional.
MS. LENGTH: No preference; submit ONE copy.
STYLE REQUIREMENTS: Standard English.
COPYRIGHT: Nebraska Council of Teachers of English.
EDITOR'S DECISION: 3-6 months.
FROM ACCEPTANCE TO PUBLICATION: 3-6 months.
PAYMENT/OFFPRINTS: None.
REJECTED MSS.: Returned.
GENERAL: First issue, 1955. Usual publication length, 60 pages.
BACK ISSUES: Available from subscription address at $3.00 each (as available).

NORTH CAROLINA ENGLISH TEACHER

EDITORIAL ADDRESS:
Joseph O. Milner, Editor
English Department
Wake Forest University
Winston-Salem, North Carolina 27109

SUBSCRIPTION ADDRESS:
Dr. Elisabeth Bowles
School of Education
UNC-G
Greensboro, North Carolina 27412

PUBLISHED: Quarterly
COST: 1 yr.—$4.00.

CIRCULATION: 600

CONTENTS: Essays about teaching methods, the teaching of literature, general educational innovations. Examples: "Paperbacks on American Indian Culture"; "The Literature of North Carolina."

UNSOLICITED MSS. WELCOME? Yes; submissions acknowledged.
SPECIFICALLY WELCOMED: Articles directly related to the teaching of literature.
MS. LENGTH: Up to 2,000 words; submit ONE copy.
STYLE REQUIREMENTS: MLA STYLE SHEET.
COPYRIGHT: Author.
EDITOR'S DECISION: 2 months.
FROM ACCEPTANCE TO PUBLICATION: 2-6 months.
PAYMENT/OFFPRINTS: No payment. Two offprints per article.
REJECTED MSS.: Returned.
GENERAL: First issue, October, 1942. Usual publication length, 32 pages.
BACK ISSUES: Available from subscription address at $1.00 each.

OKLAHOMA ENGLISH BULLETIN

EDITORIAL ADDRESS:
Glenn E. Doyle, Editor
Department of English
Phillips University
Enid, Oklahoma 73701

SUBSCRIPTION ADDRESS:
John Murphy, Executive Secretary-Treasurer
Oklahoma Council of Teachers of English
501 N. W. 18th Street
Oklahoma City, Oklahoma 73103

PUBLISHED: Biannually CIRCULATION: 500-600
COST: 1 yr.—$4.00 for membership fee in Oklahoma Council of Teachers of English. All members receive the bulletin.

CONTENTS: Articles that stir minds and offer practical help to the classroom teacher of English at every level, from kindergarten to graduate instructors. Articles are sometimes detailed and specific as to special classroom procedures and sometimes are more general and theoretical and relate to education as a whole and not to English teaching. Example: "The Changing Methods Course."

UNSOLICITED MSS. WELCOME? Yes; submissions acknowledged.
SPECIFICALLY WELCOMED: Poetry is rarely printed.
MS. LENGTH: Up to 10 pages; submit ONE copy.
STYLE REQUIREMENTS: MLA STYLE SHEET.
COPYRIGHT: Author.
EDITOR'S DECISION: 2-3 weeks.
FROM ACCEPTANCE TO PUBLICATION: Within 6 months.
PAYMENT/OFFPRINTS: Three copies of issue. Generally no offprints.
REJECTED MSS.: Returned.
GENERAL: First issue, 1963-64. Maximum publication length, 40 pages.
BACK ISSUES: Available from subscription address at $1.00 each.

OUTTAKES

EDITORIAL ADDRESS:
N. Higgins and R. Sutton, Editors
2000 P Street, N. W.
Suite 308
Washington, D.C. 20036

SUBSCRIPTION ADDRESS:

same

PUBLISHED: Monthly (10 times yearly) CIRCULATION: 750
COST: 1 yr.—$5.00.

CONTENTS: Articles on media education; film and book reviews; news about conferences, workshops, and festivals of interest to media educators.

UNSOLICITED MSS. WELCOME? Yes; submissions acknowledged.
SPECIFICALLY WELCOMED: Anything on media education.

MS. LENGTH: 1-2 pages; submit ONE copy.
STYLE REQUIREMENTS: None.
COPYRIGHT: Author.
EDITOR'S DECISION: Depends.
FROM ACCEPTANCE TO PUBLICATION: Depends and varies.
REJECTED MSS.: Returned.
GENERAL: First issue, October, 1971. Usual publication length, 15-20 pages.
BACK ISSUES: Not available.

POPULAR CULTURE METHODS

EDITORIAL ADDRESS:
Sam L. Grogg, Jr., Editor
Center for the Study of Popular Culture
100 University Hall
Bowling Green State University
Bowling Green, Ohio 43403

SUBSCRIPTION ADDRESS:
Bowling Green Popular Press
same

PUBLISHED: Quarterly   CIRCULATION: 3,000
COST: Free upon request at present. A nominal subscription fee is planned.

CONTENTS: Brief articles and reports on teaching methods involving the use of popular culture materials; book reviews; bibliographies; course outlines. Generally stresses practical information for teachers. Example: "A Checklist of Materials about Detective Fiction."

UNSOLICITED MSS. WELCOME? Yes; submissions acknowledged.
MS. LENGTH: 500-1,000 words; submit ONE copy.
STYLE REQUIREMENTS: MLA STYLE SHEET, revised edition.
COPYRIGHT: Sam L. Grogg, Jr., Editor.
EDITOR'S DECISION: 1 month.
FROM ACCEPTANCE TO PUBLICATION: 6 months.
PAYMENT/OFFPRINTS: Payment is made in copies of the issue. Up to 25 offprints available.
REJECTED MSS.: Returned.
GENERAL: First issue, August, 1972. Usual publication length, 16 pages.
BACK ISSUES: First two issues are out of print; I:3 available from the Bowling Green Popular Press at no cost.

RESEARCH IN THE TEACHING OF ENGLISH

EDITORIAL ADDRESS:
Alan C. Purves, Editor
310 West Delaware
Urbana, Illinois 61801

SUBSCRIPTION ADDRESS:
National Council of Teachers of English
1111 Kenyon Road
Urbana, Illinois 61801

PUBLISHED: Tri-annually CIRCULATION: 3,150
COST: 1 yr.—$5.00; 2 yrs.—$8.00; 3 yrs.—$12.00.

CONTENTS: Empirical studies of research in the learning and teaching of language, composition, reading, and literature; reviews of research; articles dealing with educational research in English. Example: "Children and Metaphor."

UNSOLICITED MSS. WELCOME? Yes; submissions acknowledged.
SPECIFICALLY WELCOMED: Reports on research; articles summarizing research.
MS. LENGTH: 3,000-7,000 words; submit TWO copies.
STYLE REQUIREMENTS: APA; may request copy of style sheet.
COPYRIGHT: National Council of Teachers of English.
EDITOR'S DECISION: 2 months.
FROM ACCEPTANCE TO PUBLICATION: 6 months.
PAYMENT/OFFPRINTS: No payment. Two copies of journal offprints available at printing cost.
REJECTED MSS.: Returned.
GENERAL: First issue, Spring, 1967. Usual publication length, 120 pages.
BACK ISSUES: Available from subscription address at $1.50 each.

ROCKY MOUNTAIN MODERN LANGUAGE ASSOCIATION BULLETIN

See the section on AGE AND/OR NATIONALITY: AMERICAN AND ENGLISH for details.

STATEMENT

EDITORIAL ADDRESS: SUBSCRIPTION ADDRESS:
William G. McBride, Editor
English Department, same
Liberal Arts Building
Colorado State University
Fort Collins, Colorado 80521

PUBLISHED: Tri-annually CIRCULATION: 450
COST: 1 yr.—$5.00 (includes CLAS dues); $3.00 for libraries; single copy—$1.50.

CONTENTS: Articles of general interest to teachers of all levels, kindergarten through college; some "creative" work included; bibliographies. An example article on teaching about literature is "Students and Existential Literature: Involvement."

UNSOLICITED MSS. WELCOME? Yes; submissions acknowledged.

SPECIFICALLY WELCOMED: All kinds of articles, particularly those aimed at teaching.
MS. LENGTH: 10-12 pages; submit ONE copy.
STYLE REQUIREMENTS: No specific requirements.
COPYRIGHT: Not copyrighted.
EDITOR'S DECISION: 2-3 months.
FROM ACCEPTANCE TO PUBLICATION: 3-6 months.
PAYMENT/OFFPRINTS: One free copy of journal upon publication; others available at regular cost.
REJECTED MSS.: Returned.
GENERAL: First issue, December, 1965. Usual publication length, 40-50 pages. Journal is member of NCTE exchange agreement.
BACK ISSUES: Limited copies of some numbers available from editorial address at $1.50 each.

TEACHING LANGUAGE THROUGH LITERATURE

EDITORIAL ADDRESS:
Maxine G. Cutler and Jeanette Beer,
General Editors
Fordham University
Bronx, New York 10458

SUBSCRIPTION ADDRESS:

same

PUBLISHED: Biannually (Dec., April)   CIRCULATION: 500
COST: 1 yr.—$4.00.

CONTENTS: Explication de texte; methodology—teaching language through literature; laboratory program; reviews of books stressing principle of journal. Example: "EXPLICATION DE TEXTE of a Surrealist Poem by Eluard."

UNSOLICITED MSS. WELCOME? Yes; submissions not acknowledged.
MS. LENGTH: 10-15 pages; submit ONE copy.
STYLE REQUIREMENTS: MLA STYLE SHEET.
COPYRIGHT: TEACHING LANGUAGE THROUGH LITERATURE.
EDITOR'S DECISION: 1 month.
FROM ACCEPTANCE TO PUBLICATION: 1-2 issues.
PAYMENT/OFFPRINTS: Two complimentary issues. No offprints.
REJECTED MSS.: Returned.
GENERAL: First issue, 1961. Usual publication length, 50 pages. Volume I, 1961, had only one issue. All other volumes contain two issues.
BACK ISSUES: Available from General Editor at $2.00 for most issues; $3.00 for xerox copies of out-of-print issues (II, 1; III, 2; IV, 2; XI, 1).

UNIVERSITY VISION

See the section on FILM for details.

UPDATE: JOURNAL OF THE B.C.E.T.A.

EDITORIAL ADDRESS:
Rick Cooper, Editor
388 Francis Road
Richmond, British Columbia
Canada

SUBSCRIPTION ADDRESS:

same

PUBLISHED: 3 journals and newsletters; up to 6 yearly
COST: 1 yr.—$5.00.

CIRCULATION: 600

CONTENTS: Articles relating to the broad area of teaching children in English classes, particularly on the subjects of reading; brief interpretive articles on literature; articles on teaching of literature.

UNSOLICITED MSS. WELCOME? Yes; submissions acknowledged.
SPECIFICALLY WELCOMED: Curriculum material; supplemental ideas; need articles on teaching literature with high school students.
MS. LENGTH: Up to 1,500 words; submit ONE copy.
STYLE REQUIREMENTS: None.
COPYRIGHT: Author, editor, and B.C. English Teacher's Association.
FROM ACCEPTANCE TO PUBLICATION: 1-3 months.
PAYMENT/OFFPRINTS: No payment. Offprints upon request.
REJECTED MSS.: Returned.
GENERAL: First issue, 1961. Usual publication length, 40-100 pages for journal; 10 to 30 pages for newsletter. This journal is young but getting better.
BACK ISSUES: None available.

THE USE OF ENGLISH

EDITORIAL ADDRESS:
Frank Whitehead, Editor
26 Victoria Road
Broomhall
Sheffield S10 2DL
England

SUBSCRIPTION ADDRESS:
The Circulation Manager (U/E)
Scottish Academic Press
25 Perth Street
Edinburgh EH3 5DW
Scotland

PUBLISHED: Quarterly (Feb., May, Sept., Nov.)

CIRCULATION: 3,750

COST: 1 yr.—£1.50 ($4.20) net including postage. A half-price subscription of £0.75 is offered to full-time students and first year teachers for an initial year only.

CONTENTS: Articles that examine the problems of English teaching at a time when barriers between disciplines are dissolving and English is called upon to be the unifying factor; an exchange of ideas in modern educational theory; correspondence; comments and book reviews. Audience range: students and teachers of English at every level from primary school to university. Example: "Jane Austen and the Social Revolution."

UNSOLICITED MSS. WELCOME? Yes; submissions acknowledged.
SPECIFICALLY WELCOMED: Articles on the teaching/use/comprehension of English in modern society.
MS. LENGTH: Up to 5,000 words; submit TWO copies.
COPYRIGHT: Chatto & Windus Educational Ltd. (the publisher).
EDITOR'S DECISION: Variable.
FROM ACCEPTANCE TO PUBLICATION: Variable.
PAYMENT/OFFPRINTS: A small sum dependent on length of published article; offprints can be made available on request.
REJECTED MSS.: Returned.
GENERAL: First issue, September, 1949; previously entitled ENGLISH IN SCHOOLS.
BACK ISSUES: Available from The Circulation Manager at 40p each. There are several gaps in the list of back issues.

VIRGINIA ENGLISH BULLETIN

EDITORIAL ADDRESS:
Frances N. Wimer, Editor
Richmond Public Schools
301 North Ninth Street
Richmond, Virginia 23219

SUBSCRIPTION ADDRESS:
Foster B. Gresham, Business Editor
Department of English
Longwood College
Farmville, Virginia 23901

PUBLISHED: Biannually (Dec., Apr.)   CIRCULATION: 3,200
COST: 1 yr.—$2.00 (included in membership); single copy—$1.00.

CONTENTS: Articles dealing with the teaching of English, primarily in high schools and colleges. Examples: "The Virginia Author: An Essay in Definition"; "The Teaching of World Literature as a Multiple Elective."

UNSOLICITED MSS. WELCOME? Yes; submissions usually acknowledged.
SPECIFICALLY WELCOMED: Articles in areas of English, reading, humanities, communication arts.
MS. LENGTH: No preference.
STYLE REQUIREMENTS: Minimum of footnotes.
COPYRIGHT: VIRGINIA ENGLISH BULLETIN.
EDITOR'S DECISION: 1 year.
FROM ACCEPTANCE TO PUBLICATION: 1 month to 1 year.
PAYMENT/OFFPRINTS: None.
REJECTED MSS.: Returned after 1 year.
GENERAL: First issue, 1950. Usual publication length, 60 pages.
BACK ISSUES: Available from business editor at $1.00 each.

WISCONSIN ENGLISH JOURNAL

EDITORIAL ADDRESS:
Nicholas J. Karolides, Editor
Department of English
University of Wisconsin
at River Falls
River Falls, Wisconsin 54022

SUBSCRIPTION ADDRESS:

same

PUBLISHED: Tri-annually
COST: 1 yr.—$3.00; single copy—$1.25.

CIRCULATION: 1,200-1,400

CONTENTS: Articles dealing with the teaching of English at all educational levels (but primarily grades 7-12) including the teaching of literature, composition, language, and related media; articles of interpretation or analysis of these areas; bibliographies; book reviews. Example: "Students and Existential Literature: Involvement."

UNSOLICITED MSS. WELCOME? Yes; submissions acknowledged.
SPECIFICALLY WELCOMED: Articles which interpret or apply materials that are used in classroom situations that will assist teachers.
MS. LENGTH: 6-10 pages; submit ONE copy.
STYLE REQUIREMENTS: Generally standard.
COPYRIGHT: Wisconsin Council of Teachers of English.
EDITOR'S DECISION: 3-9 months.
FROM ACCEPTANCE TO PUBLICATION: 1 year.
PAYMENT/OFFPRINTS: Two copies of issue.
REJECTED MSS.: Returned.
GENERAL: First issue, March, 1959. Usual publication length, 32 pages.
BACK ISSUES: Available from editorial address at $1.00 each.

IX
LITERARY REVIEWS

(Generous representation of graphics, poetry, fiction, and/or plays; essays on literature; and essays on non-literary subjects in some)

ADAM INTERNATIONAL REVIEW

EDITORIAL ADDRESS:
Miron Grindea, Editor
28 Emperor Gate
London SW7 4HS
United Kindgom

SUBSCRIPTION ADDRESS:

same

PUBLISHED: Quarterly
COST: 1 yr.—$9.00; single copy—$2.25 (75 p).

CONTENTS: Contemporary writing, studies of comparative literature, introductions to foreign literatures; literary criticisms; poems; stories.

UNSOLICITED MSS. WELCOME? Yes; submissions acknowledged.
SPECIFICALLY WELCOMED: Stories; literary criticism; poems.
MS. LENGTH: No preference stated; submit ONE copy.
COPYRIGHT: Author.
EDITOR'S DECISION: Depends on work.
FROM ACCEPTANCE TO PUBLICATION: Irregular.
PAYMENT/OFFPRINTS: By agreement.
REJECTED MSS.: Returned.
GENERAL: Usual publication length, 104-184 pages. Articles may be submitted in English and French.
BACK ISSUES: Available from editorial address at various prices; some rare copies cost from $10 to $25.

AEGIS: A PERIODICAL IN LITERATURE & LANGUAGE

EDITORIAL ADDRESS:
Fred M. Fetrow, Robert W. Brown, and
Muriel J. Anderson Brown, Editors
Box 267
Moorhead State College
Moorhead, Minnesota 56560

SUBSCRIPTION ADDRESS:

same

PUBLISHED: Biannually
COST: 1 yr.—$3.00.

CIRCULATION: 500

CONTENTS: All kinds of articles on literature and language; criticism, scholarship, linguistics, bibliography, and comparative literature; also poetry and short fiction, and satirical shorter works. Examples: "Notes on the Reading of Black Literature"; "The Humanistic Approach to Art."

UNSOLICITED MSS. WELCOME? Yes; submissions acknowledged.
MS. LENGTH: No preference; submit ONE copy.
STYLE REQUIREMENTS: Prefer MLA STYLE SHEET formal recommendations.
COPYRIGHT: AEGIS editors; released to individual authors upon request.
EDITOR'S DECISION: 1 month.

FROM ACCEPTANCE TO PUBLICATION: 6 months to 1 year.
PAYMENT/OFFPRINTS: Either extra copies of the magazine or offprints or both.
REJECTED MSS.: Returned.
GENERAL: First issue, Spring, 1973. Usual publication length, 64 pages.
BACK ISSUES: Available from editorial address at $1.00 each.

ANN ARBOR REVIEW

EDITORIAL ADDRESS:
Fred Wolven, Editor
2118 Arlene Street
Ann Arbor, Michigan 48103

SUBSCRIPTION ADDRESS:
Fred Wolven, Editor
ANN ARBOR REVIEW
Washtenaw Community College
Ann Arbor, Michigan 48106

PUBLISHED: Tri-annually   CIRCULATION: 750-1,000
COST: $3.00 for 3 issues; single copy—$1.00; discounts on 10 copies or more (each copy—$.75).

CONTENTS: Writing and graphics stressing new directions in writing, especially poetry; emphasis is on writers who are new or emerging or those continuing to move in fresh directions; book reviews. Interest in student work; one issue per year (most is solicited).

UNSOLICITED MSS. WELCOME? Yes; submissions not acknowledged.
SPECIFICALLY WELCOMED: Poetry; short fiction; interviews; critical articles (query first); reviews of new poetry and fiction; one-act drama; art work—photos, b&w, drawings and sketches, b&w; special interest in black writers, "underground," small press, little magazine work.
MS. LENGTH: Less than 2,000 words; submit ONE copy.
STYLE REQUIREMENTS: Freedom from four-letter word spell.
COPYRIGHT: Editor, but no problem on release or reassignment.
EDITOR'S DECISION: 1 week to 1 month.
FROM ACCEPTANCE TO PUBLICATION: Varies.
PAYMENT/OFFPRINTS: Contributor's copies.
REJECTED MSS.: Returned.
GENERAL: First issue, Fall, 1967. Usual publication length, 48 pages in previous issues, 96 pages in forthcoming issues.
BACK ISSUES: Available from editor at $1.00 each, #3 through #16; microedition from Xerox University Microfilms.

ANTAEUS

EDITORIAL ADDRESS:
Daniel Halpern, Editor
1 West 30th Street
New York, New York 10001

SUBSCRIPTION ADDRESS:

same

PUBLISHED: Quarterly
CIRCULATION: 2,000
COST: 1 yr.—$8.00; 2 yrs.—$15.00; 3 yrs.—$22.00; single copy—$2.50.

CONTENTS: International assemblage of poetry, fiction, short plays, interviews with authors, such as W. H. Auden, Jorge Luis Borges, and Gabriel García Márquez; some documents; occasional photographs.

UNSOLICITED MSS. WELCOME? Yes; unsolicited submissions not acknowledged.
SPECIFICALLY WELCOMED: Poetry and fiction.
MS. LENGTH: Short story, 10-30 pages; submit ONE copy.
COPYRIGHT: Author.
EDITOR'S DECISION: 2-4 weeks.
FROM ACCEPTANCE TO PUBLICATION: 2-3 months.
PAYMENT/OFFPRINTS: Free issue of magazine; no additional offprints.
REJECTED MSS.: Returned.
GENERAL: First issue, Winter, 1970. Usual publication length, 100-140 pages.
BACK ISSUES: Available from editorial address at $3.50 each for #2 and #3; $3.00 each for #4, #5, and #6; $2.50 each for #7, and #8. Issue #1 out of print and unavailable at this time.

THE ANTIGONISH REVIEW

EDITORIAL ADDRESS:
R. J. MacSween, Editor
St. Francis Xavier University
Antigonish, Nova Scotia
Canada

SUBSCRIPTION ADDRESS:

same

PUBLISHED: Quarterly
CIRCULATION: 500
COST: 1 yr.—$5.00; $4.00 for students and agencies; single copy—$1.50.

CONTENTS: Stories; essays on literature; poems; drawings; book reviews.

UNSOLICITED MSS. WELCOME? Yes; submissions acknowledged.
MS. LENGTH: 10 pages.
STYLE REQUIREMENTS: Anything that is clear.
COPYRIGHT: Author.
EDITOR'S DECISION: 6 weeks.
FROM ACCEPTANCE TO PUBLICATION: 3-6 months.
PAYMENT/OFFPRINTS: Copies. Offprints supplied on demand.
REJECTED MSS.: Returned.

GENERAL: First issue, Spring, 1970. Usual publication length, 115 pages.
BACK ISSUES: Available from editorial address at $1.50 each.

ARIZONA QUARTERLY

EDITORIAL ADDRESS:
Albert F. Gegenheimer, Editor
University of Arizona
Tucson, Arizona 85721

SUBSCRIPTION ADDRESS:

same

PUBLISHED: Quarterly
COST: 1 yr.—$2.00; 3 yrs.—$5.00; single copy—$.50.

CONTENTS: Articles, stories, poems, book reviews appealing to a literate, general audience; biannual Arizona bibliography.

UNSOLICITED MSS. WELCOME? Yes; submissions not acknowledged.
MS. LENGTH: 2,500-3,500 words; submit ONE copy.
COPYRIGHT: The University of Arizona.
EDITOR'S DECISION: 2 weeks.
FROM ACCEPTANCE TO PUBLICATION: Varies.
PAYMENT/OFFPRINTS: Copies of issue in which work appears: 10 (poems); 20 (articles and stories); 3 (book reviews).
REJECTED MSS.: Returned.
GENERAL: First issue, Spring, 1945. Usual publication length, 96 pages.
BACK ISSUES: Volumes 1-26 available from Kraus Reprint Corp. at current prices. Xerox and microfilm copies available from Xerox University Microfilms.

THE ARLINGTON QUARTERLY: A JOURNAL OF LITERATURE, COMMENT AND OPINION

EDITORIAL ADDRESS:
Maurice I. Carlson, Editor
University of Texas at Arlington
Box 366
University Station
Arlington, Texas 76010

SUBSCRIPTION ADDRESS:

same

PUBLISHED: Quarterly

GENERAL: First issue, 1967. This periodical had not arrived by the time the entry went to press. Potential subscribers, contributors, or collectors will have to write the editor to see whether the journal still exists, and if so, to inquire about details of manuscript submission, style, back issues, and the like.

BALL STATE UNIVERSITY FORUM

EDITORIAL ADDRESS:
Merrill Rippy and Frances M. Rippy, Editors
Ball State University
Muncie, Indiana 47306

SUBSCRIPTION ADDRESS:

same

PUBLISHED: Quarterly
COST: 1 yr.—$5.00; single copy—$1.50.

CIRCULATION: 550

CONTENTS: Creative literature and criticism; occasional photographs and illustrations.

UNSOLICITED MSS. WELCOME? Yes; submissions acknowledged.
SPECIFICALLY WELCOMED: Critical essays, drama, poetry, fiction.
MS. LENGTH: No preference; submit following: 6 copies—poetry; 8 copies—short stories, essays, one-act plays; 2 copies—specific articles.
STYLE REQUIREMENTS: MLA STYLE SHEET; footnotes follow text.
COPYRIGHT: BALL STATE UNIVERSITY FORUM.
EDITOR'S DECISION: 3 months.
FROM ACCEPTANCE TO PUBLICATION: 2 years.
PAYMENT/OFFPRINTS: Ten copies of issue. Offprints available from editor.
REJECTED MSS.: Returned.
GENERAL: First issue, 1959. Usual publication length, 80 pages.
BACK ISSUES: Available from editorial address; recent issues at current price, others vary.

BERKSHIRE REVIEW

EDITORIAL ADDRESS:
S. L. Faison, E. González,
D. Park, T. Perlin, Editors
Thompson Physical Laboratory
Williams College
Williamstown, Massachusetts 01267

SUBSCRIPTION ADDRESS:

same

PUBLISHED: Biannually
COST: 1 yr.—$1.00.

CIRCULATION: 1,500

CONTENTS: Essays on general subjects; criticism; verse; fiction; photographs.

UNSOLICITED MSS. WELCOME? Yes; submissions acknowledged.
SPECIFICALLY WELCOMED: Articles of general appeal.
MS. LENGTH: 5-10 pages; submit ONE copy.
STYLE REQUIREMENTS: Few or no footnotes; materials are edited to house style.
COPYRIGHT: BERKSHIRE REVIEW; but freely assigned to author on request.
EDITOR'S DECISION: 1 month.

FROM ACCEPTANCE TO PUBLICATION: Varies.
PAYMENT/OFFPRINTS: $50 to $75 for essays; $25 for verse, plus a few copies of the magazine.
REJECTED MSS.: Returned.
GENERAL: First issue, Spring, 1965. Usual publication length, 28-32 pages.
BACK ISSUES: Available from editorial address at $.50 each.

CALIFORNIA QUARTERLY

See the section on AGE AND/OR NATIONALITY: AMERICAN for details.

CHICAGO REVIEW

EDITORIAL ADDRESS:
Alexander Besher, Editor
5757 South Drexel Avenue
The University of Chicago
Chicago, Illinois 60637

SUBSCRIPTION ADDRESS:
Steven Bookman, Managing Editor
The University of Chicago
Chicago, Illinois 60637

PUBLISHED: Quarterly
CIRCULATION: 5,000
COST: USA: 1 yr.—$5.00; 2 yrs.—$9.50; 3 yrs.—$14.00 (foreign, $6.00 first year; $5.00 each additional year). Patron subscription $25.00 includes five years. Subscribers in all 50 states plus Guam and 39 foreign countries.

CONTENTS: Fiction; drama; poetry; essays; reviews; it also is enlarging its art; photography; plans to include music articles. Original material first introduced by CR has included Burrough's NAKED LUNCH, Concrete Poetry, Philip Roth's first short story in print.

UNSOLICITED MSS. WELCOME? Yes, "we are enthusiastic about new writers"; submissions acknowledged if postcard sent.
SPECIFICALLY WELCOMED: Original, well written poetry and fiction continue to be main editorial content. Dry academic articles are not encouraged, but imaginative treatments are welcome. Originality of idea is much more important than well-tuned nicety.
MS. LENGTH: No limitations; submit ONE good copy.
STYLE REQUIREMENTS: Very flexible.
COPYRIGHT: Ordinarily the magazine, but can be negotiated.
EDITOR'S DECISION: 1-2 months.
FROM ACCEPTANCE TO PUBLICATION: 2-4 months.
PAYMENT/OFFPRINTS: Prizes in major categories; plans for payment in small amount soon. Provision of complimentary copies of magazine.
REJECTED MSS.: Returned.

GENERAL: First issue, Spring, 1946. Usual publication length, 150-220 pages. University of Chicago students, both undergrads and grads, play a major role in editing and operating the magazine. This year won $4,000 grant from Coordinating Council of Literary Magazines.
BACK ISSUES: Available from managing editor; many in stock; direct shipment same day as request of items stocked in quantity. Price varies; recent years add $.50 to base price of $1.50 for each back year; occasional discount for large orders. Some rare issues are individually negotiated. Microfilms from University Microfilms or AMS Reprint.

CIMARRON REVIEW

EDITORIAL ADDRESS:
Clinton C. Keeler, Editor
Oklahoma State University
Stillwater, Oklahoma 74074

SUBSCRIPTION ADDRESS:
Jeanne Adams Wray, Managing Editor
208 Life Sciences East
Oklahoma State University
Stillwater, Oklahoma 74074

PUBLISHED: Quarterly (Jan., Apr., July, Oct.)
COST: 1 yr.—$6.00; single copy—$2.00.

CONTENTS: Contemporary literature; letters; opinion, with emphasis upon good writing and offbeat approaches. Examples: "The Case for Robert Penn Warren's Second Best Novel"; "Religious Implications in THE CONFESSIONS OF NAT TURNER."

UNSOLICITED MSS. WELCOME? Yes; submissions acknowledged.
SPECIFICALLY WELCOMED: Fiction; articles dealing with contemporary subjects; poetry.
MS. LENGTH: 1,500-2,500 words; submit ONE copy.
STYLE REQUIREMENTS: Graceful writing; no pedantic jargon.
COPYRIGHT: OSU Board of Regents.
EDITOR'S DECISION: 4 months.
FROM ACCEPTANCE TO PUBLICATION: 12-15 months usually; in some cases, 6 months.
PAYMENT/OFFPRINTS: Payment in copies only. No offprints.
REJECTED MSS.: Returned.
GENERAL: First issue, September, 1967. Usual publication length, 76-84 pages.
BACK ISSUES: Available from editorial office at $.50 each for issues through #12 (1970); $1.00 each after #12 (some issues out-of-print).

THE COLORADO QUARTERLY

EDITORIAL ADDRESS:
Paul Carter, Editor
Hellems 134
University of Colorado
Boulder, Colorado 80302

SUBSCRIPTION ADDRESS:
Claudine Seever, Managing Editor
Same

PUBLISHED: Quarterly (Summer, Autumn, Winter, Spring)
COST: 1 yr.—$4.00.

CIRCULATION: 800

CONTENTS: Non-technical general interest articles that promote more effective communication between specialists in all academic fields and the public; fiction; poetry; translations. Example: "Campus Rebellions: Their Literary Heritage."

UNSOLICITED MSS. WELCOME? Yes; submissions not acknowledged.
SPECIFICALLY WELCOMED: Stories with plots and understandable characters.
MS. LENGTH: 4,000-6,000 words; submit ONE copy.
STYLE REQUIREMENTS: University of Chicago's A MANUAL OF STYLE.
COPYRIGHT: The University of Colorado.
EDITOR'S DECISION: 2-4 weeks.
FROM ACCEPTANCE TO PUBLICATION: 6 months to 1 year.
PAYMENT/OFFPRINTS: No payment. Offprints may be purchased through editorial office at cost.
REJECTED MSS.: Returned.
GENERAL: First issue, Summer, 1952. Usual publication length, 144 pages.
BACK ISSUES: Almost all still available from editorial office at $1.25 each plus cost of handling and mailing for large orders. Microfilm form from University Microfilms.

CONNECTICUT CRITIC (formerly NEW ENGLAND REVIEW)

EDITORIAL ADDRESS:
John DeStefano, Editor
P. O. Box 127
Cheshire, Connecticut 06410

SUBSCRIPTION ADDRESS:

same

PUBLISHED: Monthly
COST: 1 yr.—$6.50; 2 yrs—$12.00.

CONTENTS: Commentary; articles; reviews; fiction; poetry. Example: "An Art of Equilibrium: Piet Mondrian and John Updike."

UNSOLICITED MSS. WELCOME? Yes; submissions not acknowledged.
MS. LENGTH: 4,000-5,000 words; submit ONE copy.
EDITOR'S DECISION: 3-4 weeks.

FROM ACCEPTANCE TO PUBLICATION: 3 months.
PAYMENT/OFFPRINTS: Copy of issue.
REJECTED MSS.: Returned.
GENERAL: First issue, 1971. Usual publication length, 48-56 pages.
BACK ISSUES: Available from editorial address at $1.00 each.

CONTEMPORARY LITERATURE IN TRANSLATION

EDITORIAL ADDRESS:
Andreas P. Schroeder and
J. M. Yates, Editors
P.O. Box 2058
Mission City, British Columbia
Canada

SUBSCRIPTION ADDRESS:

same

PUBLISHED: Tri-annually
COST: 1 yr.—$5.00; 2 yrs.—$10.00.

CIRCULATION: 350

CONTENTS: Poetry; prose; plays; parts of novels from any language in the world translated into English. Recent examples are translations of poems by Pablo Neruda, Rene Char, and Kiskatinaw Indians (of British Columbia). Issue after issue poses problems of meaning—but not in explicit criticism, making this a unique scholarly publication.

UNSOLICITED MSS. WELCOME? Yes; submissions not acknowledged.
MS. LENGTH: No preference; submit ONE copy.
STYLE REQUIREMENTS: No specific requirements.
COPYRIGHT: Author/translator.
EDITOR'S DECISION: 2 months.
FROM ACCEPTANCE TO PUBLICATION: 4 months.
PAYMENT/OFFPRINTS: Two contributor's copies. $1 per extra copy of magazine.
REJECTED MSS.: Returned.
GENERAL: First issue, 1967-68. Usual publication length, 44 pages. Submit short biographical notes on all authors and translators along with manuscript.
BACK ISSUES: Available from editorial address at following prices: 1968—#1 ($18.00), #2 ($16.00), #3 ($13.00); 1969—#4 ($10.00), #5 ($8.00), #6 ($6.00); 1970—#7 ($4.00); #8 & #9 ($3.00 each); remaining issues—$2.00 each.

CONTEMPORARY REVIEW (incorporating THE FORTNIGHTLY)

EDITORIAL ADDRESS:
Rosalind Wade, Editor
Contemporary Review Co. Ltd.
37 Union Street
London S.E.1.
England

SUBSCRIPTION ADDRESS:
Business Manager
same

PUBLISHED: Monthly

CIRCULATION: Subscribers in over 60 countries.

COST: 1 yr.—$13.50 in U.S. and Canada (£4.02); single copy—30p. plus postage.

CONTENTS: Articles on history, international and home politics, literature and the arts; occasional poetry and short stories; social subjects; theology; book reviews. Essay example: "Jules Romains: A Last View."

UNSOLICITED MSS. WELCOME? Yes; submissions not acknowledged. A preliminary letter is helpful.
MS. LENGTH: Maximum 3,000 words; submit ONE copy.
COPYRIGHT: CONTEMPORARY REVIEW, but share fees with the authors if work is reprinted on a commercial basis.
EDITOR'S DECISION: Not more than 1 month.
FROM ACCEPTANCE TO PUBLICATION: Depends on subject.
PAYMENT/OFFPRINTS: £2.50 per 1,000 words. Offprints may be ordered in advance from the Business Manager.
REJECTED MSS.: Returned.
GENERAL: First issue, 1866. Usual publication length, 56 pages.
BACK ISSUES: Available from the Business Manager; price by arrangement.

THE DALHOUSIE REVIEW: A CANADIAN QUARTERLY OF LITERATURE AND OPINION

EDITORIAL ADDRESS:
Allan Bevan, Editor
Dalhousie University
Halifax, Nova Scotia
Canada

SUBSCRIPTION ADDRESS:
Mrs. H. Gorman, Business Manager
same

PUBLISHED: Quarterly
COST: 1 yr.—$6.00; 3 yrs.—$15.00; single copy—$2.00.

CIRCULATION: 1,000

CONTENTS: Critical essays concerning literary (in English), historical, philosophical, general subjects; some verse; occasional fiction.

UNSOLICITED MSS. WELCOME? Yes; submissions not acknowledged until decision reached.
SPECIFICALLY WELCOMED: Critical essays on works of general interest.
MS. LENGTH: 3,000-5,000 words; submit ONE copy.

COPYRIGHT: THE DALHOUSIE REVIEW.
EDITOR'S DECISION: 3 months.
FROM ACCEPTANCE TO PUBLICATION: 6-12 months.
PAYMENT/OFFPRINTS: $1.00 per page. 25 offprints and one copy of the issue.
REJECTED MSS.: Returned.
GENERAL: First issue, 1921. Usual publication length, 160 pages.
BACK ISSUES: Available from Business Manager at $2.00 to $5.00 each, depending on supply.

DELTA

EDITORIAL ADDRESS:
I. D. MacKillop, Editor
9 Sharrow View
Sheffield S7 1ND
England

SUBSCRIPTION ADDRESS:
same

PUBLISHED: Tri-annually
COST: 1 yr.—$4.00.

CONTENTS: Literary criticism; poetry; fiction. Examples: essay on Ted Hughes' CROW, one on John Gay, work by poets, extract from a novel in progress, review of a new volume of verse.

MS. LENGTH: Up to 8,000 words.
STYLE REQUIREMENTS: MLA STYLE SHEET.
PAYMENT/OFFPRINTS: 5 offprints.
GENERAL: First issue, 1953.
BACK ISSUES: Most issues past #30 available from editor at $1.25 each; remainder from Johnson Reprint Corp.

DESCANT: THE TEXAS CHRISTIAN UNIVERSITY LITERARY JOURNAL

EDITORIAL ADDRESS:
Betsy Colquitt, Editor
Department of English
Texas Christian University
Fort Worth, Texas 76129

SUBSCRIPTION ADDRESS:
same

PUBLISHED: Quarterly
COST: 1 yr.—$2.00; single copy—$.75.

CIRCULATION: 600

CONTENTS: Short stories; poems; and critical essays on recent literature, such as "The Scurrilous Parody in T. S. Eliot's Early Religious Poetry," and "Virginia Woolf and Anna Karenina."

UNSOLICITED MSS. WELCOME? Yes; submissions not acknowledged.
SPECIFICALLY WELCOMED: Stories, poems, criticism on recent literature.
MS. LENGTH: Stories, about 4,000 words; poems, usually not longer than 40 lines; submit ONE copy.
STYLE REQUIREMENTS: MLA STYLE SHEET; footnotes follow essay.
COPYRIGHT: Texas Christian University; author may request reprint permission.
EDITOR'S DECISION: Maximum 6 weeks.
FROM ACCEPTANCE TO PUBLICATION: 3 to 6 months.
PAYMENT/OFFPRINTS: Free copies.
REJECTED MSS.: Returned.
GENERAL: First issue, Fall, 1965. Usual publication length, 56-60 pages.
BACK ISSUES: Available from editorial office at $.75 each, except for a few in short supply.

THE DILIMAN REVIEW

EDITORIAL ADDRESS:
Armando F. Bonifacio, Editor
College of Arts and Sciences
University of the Philippines
Diliman, Quezon City D-505
Philippines

SUBSCRIPTION ADDRESS:
A. M. Henson, Business Manager
Publications Section
same

PUBLISHED: Quarterly
COST: 1 yr.—$12.00; single copy—$3.00.

CIRCULATION: 1,000

CONTENTS: Articles concerning the arts; letters; discussions.

UNSOLICITED MSS. WELCOME? Yes; submissions acknowledged.
SPECIFICALLY WELCOMED: Anything that is not subversive in character.
MS. LENGTH: Limit of 100 pages; submit TWO copies.
COPYRIGHT: Authors.
EDITOR'S DECISION: 2 weeks.
FROM ACCEPTANCE TO PUBLICATION: 2 weeks.
PAYMENT/OFFPRINTS: 100 copies of offprints sent by surface mail free of charge.
REJECTED MSS.: Returned.
GENERAL: First issue, January, 1953. Usual publication length, 100 pages.
BACK ISSUES: Available from the Business Manager at $3.00 each plus cost of postage/handling.

EAST-WEST REVIEW

EDITORIAL ADDRESS:
Naozo Ueno and Ken Akiyama, Editors
Doshisha University
Department of English
Kyoto
Japan

SUBSCRIPTION ADDRESS:

same

GENERAL: This periodical had not arrived by the time the entry went to press. Potential subscribers, contributors, or collectors will have to write the editor to see whether the journal still exists, and if so, to inquire about details of manuscript submission, style, back issues, and the like.

ERA: A PENNSYLVANIA MAGAZINE OF COMMENTARY AND LITERATURE

EDITORIAL ADDRESS:
Gordon Goodman, Editor
Philomathean Society
Box 17, College Hall
University of Pennsylvania
Philadelphia, Pennsylvania 19104

SUBSCRIPTION ADDRESS:

same

PUBLISHED: Annually
CIRCULATION: 1,500
COST: Single copy—$5.00; distributed free on University of Pennsylvania campus.

CONTENTS: Scholarly articles; poetry; fiction; interviews; illustrations. Example: "The Hardy Blossom: Attitudes Towards Women in Nineteenth Century America."

UNSOLICITED MSS. WELCOME? Yes; submissions acknowledged.
SPECIFICALLY WELCOMED: All kinds, especially those from U. of Pennsylvania people.
MS. LENGTH: No limit; submit ONE copy.
STYLE REQUIREMENTS: MLA STYLE SHEET.
COPYRIGHT: University of Pennsylvania.
EDITOR'S DECISION: 3-5 months.
FROM ACCEPTANCE TO PUBLICATION: Up to 6 months.
PAYMENT/OFFPRINTS: No payment. Authors may buy copies at cost.
REJECTED MSS.: Returned.
GENERAL: First issue, Fall, 1964. Usual publication length, 80 pages.
BACK ISSUES: Available from editorial address at $5.00 each.

EVERGREEN REVIEW

EDITORIAL ADDRESS:
Editor
53 East 11th Street
New York, New York 10003

SUBSCRIPTION ADDRESS:
Evergreen Review, Inc.
same

PUBLISHED: Quarterly
COST: 4 issues—$5.00; 8 issues—$9.00; foreign postage, including Canada, $1.40 additional; single copy—$1.50.

CONTENTS: Fiction; art photography; poetry; social criticism; film criticism; literary commentary. Often particularly strong on film reporting and criticism. Recent examples of film and literary appraisals: "Yevgeny Yevtushenko: The Cold Warrior as Poet" by Dotson Rader; "Is Man a Clown? Is Fellini? And What's a Clown?" by Parker Tyler; and "A Tango Strategem" by Stuart Byron.

UNSOLICITED MSS. WELCOME? Yes.
MS. LENGTH: Essays, 1,000-2,000 words; submit ONE copy.
STYLE REQUIREMENTS: Consult a recent issue.
COPYRIGHT: Evergreen Review, Inc.
GENERAL: First issue, 1957. Published in various formats recently; the latest issue was 32 pages, folio size, newspaper.
BACK ISSUES: Available from subscription address. Cost varies.

FLORIDA QUARTERLY

EDITORIAL ADDRESS:
Editor
University of Florida
Room 336 Reitz Union
Gainesville, Florida 32601

SUBSCRIPTION ADDRESS:
Business Manager
same

PUBLISHED: Tri-annually
COST: 1 yr.—$3.00; 3 yrs.—$8.00; single copy—$1.25.

CIRCULATION: 1,500

CONTENTS: Modern prose; poetry; graphics; interviews; reviews. Examples: "An Interview with John Frederick Nims"; "An Interview with John Ciardi."

UNSOLICITED MSS. WELCOME? Yes; submissions acknowledged if possible.
SPECIFICALLY WELCOMED: Modern poetry and prose.
MS. LENGTH: Up to 40 pages; submit ONE copy.
STYLE REQUIREMENTS: None.
COPYRIGHT: FLORIDA QUARTERLY; released upon request of author.
EDITOR'S DECISION: 2 weeks to 2 months.
FROM ACCEPTANCE TO PUBLICATION: Varies—2 months.
PAYMENT/OFFPRINTS: None.
REJECTED MSS.: Returned.
GENERAL: First issue, 1966. Usual publication length, 100 pages.

BACK ISSUES: Available from the Business Manager at $1.50 each.

FOUR QUARTERS

EDITORIAL ADDRESS: SUBSCRIPTION ADDRESS:
John J. Keenan, Editor
La Salle College   same
Olney Avenue at 20th Street
Philadelphia, Pennsylvania 19141

PUBLISHED: Quarterly   CIRCULATION: 700
COST: 1 yr.—$3.00; 2 yrs.—$5.00; single copy—$.75.

CONTENTS: Short stories, articles, and poetry.

UNSOLICITED MSS. WELCOME? Yes; submissions acknowledged.
SPECIFICALLY WELCOMED: Stories of high literary and artistic quality (editors avoid formula or slick stories, lean toward those centering on character); articles that are primarily literary or critical in nature, though not exclusively (have used articles on history, the arts, that are well-written); poems that demonstrate technical skill and control and that shed some light on the human situation.
MS. LENGTH: Articles and stories, under 20 pages; poems, under 35 lines; submit ONE copy.
STYLE REQUIREMENTS: Articles and stories must be literate and lively. MLA STYLE SHEET for footnotes, but heavy footnoting discouraged.
COPYRIGHT: La Salle College; available to author on request.
EDITOR'S DECISION: 6-8 weeks.
FROM ACCEPTANCE TO PUBLICATION: 6 weeks to 1 year.
PAYMENT/OFFPRINTS: Articles and stories—up to $25.00; poems—$5.00.
REJECTED MSS.: Returned.
GENERAL: First issue, November, 1951. Usual publication length, about 48 pages. Special issues published on Katherine Anne Porter (Nov.,1962), Thorton Wilder (May,1967), and Robert Penn Warren (May,1972).
BACK ISSUES: Most available from publisher at $1.00 each. Complete set or individual issues also obtainable through Xerox University Microfilms.

THE FREE LANCE: A MAGAZINE OF POETRY AND PROSE

EDITORIAL ADDRESS: SUBSCRIPTION ADDRESS:
Russell Atkins and Casper L. Jordan,
Co-editors   same
6005 Grand Avenue
Cleveland, Ohio 44104

PUBLISHED: Biannually   CIRCULATION: 500-1,000

COST: 1 yr.—$2.00; single copy—$1.00.

CONTENTS: Avant-garde, contemporary, and some traditional poetry; aesthetic theories based on science; short stories; book reviews.

UNSOLICITED MSS. WELCOME? Yes; submissions not acknowledged.
SPECIFICALLY WELCOMED: Experimental work.
MS. LENGTH: Not much over 5,000 words; submit MORE THAN ONE copy.
COPYRIGHT: Author. Copyright covers magazine only.
EDITOR'S DECISION: Varies.
FROM ACCEPTANCE TO PUBLICATION: Varies.
PAYMENT/OFFPRINTS: Payment in copy. No offprints.
REJECTED MSS.: Returned.
GENERAL: First issue, Fall-Winter, 1950. Usual publication length, 75-80 pages. Volumes 1 through 13 indexed by author and title.
BACK ISSUES: Available from Johnson Reprint Corp., 3M Microfiche, and Kraus Reprint Co. Consult them about prices.

THE GEORGIA REVIEW

EDITORIAL ADDRESS:
Edward Krickel, Acting Editor
Lustrat House
University of Georgia
Athens, Georgia 30602

SUBSCRIPTION ADDRESS:

same

PUBLISHED: Quarterly (Mar., June, Sept., Dec.)

CIRCULATION: 1,800

COST: 1 yr.—$3.00 in U.S., Canada, and Mexico; $3.50 elsewhere; 2 yrs.—$5.00 in U.S., Canada and Mexico; $6.00 elsewhere; 3 yrs.—$7.50 in U.S., Canada, and Mexico.

CONTENTS: Quality articles dealing with 19th and 20th century literature, literary criticism, art, and the history of ideas; short stories; poetry; book reviews. Examples: "Faulkner and Scott and the Legacy of the Lost Cause"; "The Man on the Quaker Oats Box: Characteristics of Recent Experimental Fiction."

UNSOLICITED MSS. WELCOME? Yes; submissions not acknowledged.
SPECIFICALLY WELCOMED: Scholarly (rather than polemical or journalistic in manner) articles, written with a general intellectual, historical, or cultural perspective.
MS. LENGTH: 1,500-8,000 words; submit ONE copy.
STYLE REQUIREMENTS: MLA STYLE SHEET; few or no footnotes
COPYRIGHT: University of Georgia.
EDITOR'S DECISION: 3-4 weeks.
FROM ACCEPTANCE TO PUBLICATION: 3 months to 1 year.
PAYMENT/OFFPRINTS: Prose, 1¢ per word; poetry, 50¢ per line. Contributor pays for offprints.

REJECTED MSS.: Returned.
GENERAL: First issue, March, 1947. Usual publication length, 128 pages.
BACK ISSUES: Almost all available from editorial office at $1.00 each. Remainder from Johnson Reprint Corp.

HARVARD ADVOCATE

EDITORIAL ADDRESS:
Rodman Paul, Editor
21 South Street
Cambridge, Massachusetts 02138

SUBSCRIPTION ADDRESS:

same

PUBLISHED: Quarterly
COST: 1 yr.—$8.00.

CIRCULATION: 3,000

CONTENTS: Articles concerning literary and cultural arts; poems; prose; photography; drawings; book reviews.

UNSOLICITED MSS. WELCOME? Yes; submissions not acknowledged.
MS. LENGTH: No book-length articles; submit ONE copy.
STYLE REQUIREMENTS: Quality in any genre.
COPYRIGHT: Editors and Trustees of the HARVARD ADVOCATE.
EDITOR'S DECISION: 1 month.
FROM ACCEPTANCE TO PUBLICATION: 3 months.
PAYMENT/OFFPRINTS: Issues of magazine upon request.
REJECTED MSS.: Returned.
GENERAL: First issue, 1866. Usual publication length, 50 pages.
BACK ISSUES: Available from Xerox University Microfilm.

HORIZON: MAGAZINE OF THE ARTS

EDITORIAL ADDRESS:
Charles L. Mee, Jr., Editor
1221 Avenue of the Americas
New York, New York 10020

SUBSCRIPTION ADDRESS:
379 West Center Street
Marion, Ohio 43302

PUBLISHED: Quarterly

CONTENTS: Articles on the arts; reviews of films, plays, authors, historically significant literary phenomena around the world. Recent literary examples: "A Historical Light on the ILIAD and the ODYSSEY"; "The Alexandrians of Lawrence Durrell"; "C. S. Lewis."

UNSOLICITED MSS. WELCOME? Consult editor before submitting ms.
MS. LENGTH: Up to 4,500 words.
COPYRIGHT: HORIZON.

PAYMENT/OFFPRINTS: Payment and 2 copies of issue.
GENERAL: First issue, 1958. Usual publication length, 120 pages.
BACK ISSUES: Available from subscription address.

THE HUDSON REVIEW

EDITORIAL ADDRESS:
Frederick Morgan, Editor
Hudson Review, Inc.
65 East 55th Street
New York, New York 10022

SUBSCRIPTION ADDRESS:
Managing Editor
Same

PUBLISHED: Quarterly

CIRCULATION: 4,000

CONTENTS: Articles on the humanities; regular features are reviews of and commentary on many books, theatre, art, films, dance, music; occasional translations, such as of the poetry of Hindu poet Nirala; creative writing, such as R. G. Vliet's short novel ROCKSPRING.

UNSOLICITED MSS. WELCOME? Yes.
SPECIFICALLY WELCOMED: Consult a recent copy of HR.
COPYRIGHT: Hudson Review, Inc.
GENERAL: First issue, Spring, 1948. Usual publication length, 150 pages.

THE HUMANITIES ASSOCIATION REVIEW/LA REVUE DE L'ASSOCIATION DES HUMANITES

EDITORIAL ADDRESS:
Phillip W. Rogers, Editor
John Watson Hall
Queen's University
Kingston, Ontario
Canada

SUBSCRIPTION ADDRESS:
Mrs. S. J. Wynne-Edwards,
Business Manager
same

PUBLISHED: Quarterly
COST: 1 yr.—$7.50.

CIRCULATION: 1,000

CONTENTS: Articles and reviews in all branches of the humanities; occasionally excerpts from poems, novels in progress and translations, with comments on procedure, method, by authors; notes and documents. Example article: "The Northern Innocent in the Fiction of Gabrielle Roy."

UNSOLICITED MSS. WELCOME? Yes; submissions acknowledged.
SPECIFICALLY WELCOMED: Articles on literature, philosophy, linguistics, fine arts, and history, as well as on all other subjects related to the concerns of the humanities. Particularly welcome are articles which survey current philosophies of, or approaches to, the various subjects, and cross-disciplinary studies.

MS. LENGTH: 10-40 pages; submit TWO copies.
STYLE REQUIREMENTS: MLA STYLE SHEET.
COPYRIGHT: Author.
EDITOR'S DECISION: 6 months.
FROM ACCEPTANCE TO PUBLICATION: Varies.
PAYMENT/OFFPRINTS: 25 offprints.
REJECTED MSS.: Returned.
GENERAL: First issue, 1951, as THE HUMANITIES ASSOCIATION BULLETIN; 1973, as HAR/RAH. Usual publication length, 75-80 pages.
BACK ISSUES: Available from Business Manager at $1.50-$2.00 each, depending on date; full runs not available.

THE IOWA REVIEW

EDITORIAL ADDRESS:
Merle E. Brown, Editor
Department of Publications
University of Iowa
17 West College Street
Iowa City, Iowa 52242

SUBSCRIPTION ADDRESS:

same

PUBLISHED: Quarterly (Winter, Spring, Summer, Autumn)
COST: 1 yr.—$6.00; 2 yrs.—$11.00; 3 yrs.—$16.00.

CIRCULATION: 800

CONTENTS: Poetry; fiction; journalit; and literary criticism (criticism generally confined to contemporary figures with special interest in young poets); occasional interview. Example essay: "Robert Bly Alive in Darkness."

UNSOLICITED MSS. WELCOME? Yes; submissions not acknowledged.
SPECIFICALLY WELCOMED: Literary criticism of young artists who are not generally covered by critical literature.
MS. LENGTH: 8,000 words or less; submit ONE copy.
STYLE REQUIREMENTS: None.
COPYRIGHT: THE IOWA REVIEW.
EDITOR'S DECISION: 1-2 months.
FROM ACCEPTANCE TO PUBLICATION: 3 months to 1 year.
PAYMENT/OFFPRINTS: Poetry, $1 per line; fiction and criticism, $10 per printed page. No offprints.
REJECTED MSS.: Returned.
GENERAL: First issue, January, 1970. Usual publication length, 130 pages.
BACK ISSUES: Available from editorial address at $1.50 each.

JAPAN QUARTERLY

EDITORIAL ADDRESS:
Kiyoshi Ebata, Editor
Asahi Shimbun Publishing Company
Yūrakuchō, Chiyoda-ku
Tokyo, Japan.

SUBSCRIPTION ADDRESS:
Business Manager
same

PUBLISHED: Quarterly
COST: 1 yr.—$7.00; single copy—$2.00.

CIRCULATION: 5,000

CONTENTS: A wide range of articles by leading authorities on social problems, international affairs, economics, politics, art, and literature. In addition, every issue contains expertly translated stories and poems by topflight Japanese writers, and essays by eminent foreign visitors; book reviews; photographs.

UNSOLICITED MSS. WELCOME? Depends upon contents; submissions acknowledged.
SPECIFICALLY WELCOMED: Novels.
MS. LENGTH: About 4,000 words; submit TWO copies.
COPYRIGHT: Contributor.
EDITOR'S DECISION: About 2 months.
FROM ACCEPTANCE TO PUBLICATION: Varies.
PAYMENT/OFFPRINTS: 10 yen per word.
REJECTED MSS.: Returned.
GENERAL: First issue, October, 1954. Usual publication length, 130 pages.
BACK ISSUES: Available from Business Manager at $1.50 each for Vols. 1-18; $2.00 each for Vols. 19 and 20.

KARAMU

EDITORIAL ADDRESS:
Allen Neff, Editor
English Department
Eastern Illinois University
Charleston, Illinois 61920

SUBSCRIPTION ADDRESS:
same

PUBLISHED: Biannually
COST: 4 issues—$3.00; single copy—$1.00.

CIRCULATION: 300

CONTENTS: Short stories (5); poetry (20 to 30); critical essay; art.

UNSOLICITED MSS. WELCOME? Yes; submissions not acknowledged.
SPECIFICALLY WELCOMED: Short stories; poetry; articles on contemporary literature.
MS. LENGTH: Short stories, under 8,000 words; submit ONE copy.
STYLE REQUIREMENTS: Clarity: traditional or experimental.
COPYRIGHT: Karamu Association; buys first rights only.

EDITOR'S DECISION: 2-5 months.
FROM ACCEPTANCE TO PUBLICATION: 7-8 months.
PAYMENT/OFFPRINTS: Copies of periodical. Offprints at $1.00 each.
REJECTED MSS.: Returned.
GENERAL: First issue, 1967. Usual publication length, 100 pages.
BACK ISSUES: Available from editorial address at $1.00 each or 4 for $3.00.

KENYON REVIEW (suspended publication)

EDITORIAL ADDRESS:
George Lanning and Ellington White,
Editors
Kenyon College
Gambier, Ohio

PUBLISHED: 5 times yearly   CIRCULATION: 6,000

CONTENTS: Fiction, criticism and verse, articles; interviews; book reviews. Examples: "Some Themes and Directions in African Literature"; "The London Theater: A Devaluation"; "This Heavy Folk Thing: An Interview with David Hostetler"; "With a Poet's Discernment"; "Through the Novelist's Looking Glass."

COPYRIGHT: Kenyon College.
GENERAL: Issued, 1939-1970. Usual publication length, 144 pages.
BACK ISSUES: Available from AMS Reprint, Inc. at $20.00 per volume; 25 year cumulative index, Vols. 1-25 (1939-1963), at $13.50.

LANDFALL

EDITORIAL ADDRESS: SUBSCRIPTION ADDRESS:
Leo Bensemann, Editor   The Caxton Press
                                  Box 25-088
                                  Christchurch
                                  New Zealand

PUBLISHED: Quarterly (Mar.,   CIRCULATION: 2,000
June, Sept., Dec.)
COST: $4.00 (NZ)—four issues.

CONTENTS: Original verse, prose, reviews, critical commentary, art.

UNSOLICITED MSS. WELCOME? Yes; submissions acknowledged.
MS. LENGTH: No preference; submit ONE copy.
COPYRIGHT: Author.
EDITOR'S DECISION: Up to 3 months.

FROM ACCEPTANCE TO PUBLICATION: Next issue.
PAYMENT/OFFPRINTS: Nominal payment. Offprints can be arranged if required.
REJECTED MSS.: Returned.
GENERAL: First issue, 1947. Usual publication length, 100 pages. As LANDFALL is designed to encourage New Zealand writers, most of the work published is by New Zealanders, either living in N.Z. or living abroad. Other work can be considered.
BACK ISSUES: Available from The Caxton Press at $1.00 (NZ) each.

THE LATIN AMERICAN LITERARY REVIEW

See the section on AGE AND/OR NATIONALITY: AFRICAN, CARIBBEAN, LATIN AMERICAN, AND NEAR EASTERN for details.

THE LAUREL REVIEW (suspended publication temporarily)

EDITORIAL ADDRESS:
W. E. Mallory, Editor
West Virginia Wesleyan College
Buckhannon, West Virginia 26201

SUBSCRIPTION ADDRESS:

same

PUBLISHED: Biannually
(Fall and Spring)
COST: 1 yr.—$3.00.

CIRCULATION: 500

CONTENTS: Critical essays; poetry; fiction. Examples: " 'Prufrock' and Huxley's CROME YELLOW"; "Proust's Elstir and the Meaning of Social Success."

UNSOLICITED MSS. WELCOME? Yes; submissions acknowledged.
MS. LENGTH: 2,000-3,000 words.
STYLE REQUIREMENTS: MLA STYLE SHEET.
COPYRIGHT: LAUREL REVIEW.
EDITOR'S DECISION: 1-3 months.
FROM ACCEPTANCE TO PUBLICATION: 6 months to 1 year.
PAYMENT/OFFPRINTS: Three copies of issue in which work appears.
REJECTED MSS.: Returned.
GENERAL: First issue, Fall, 1960. Usual publication length, 80-90 pages.
BACK ISSUES: Available from editorial address at $1.50 each or on microfilm from Xerox University Microfilms.

THE LITERARY HALF-YEARLY

EDITORIAL ADDRESS:
H. H. Anniah Gowda, Editor
52 Professors' Quarters
Mysore 9
India

SUBSCRIPTION ADDRESS:
Department of Post-graduate
Studies in English
University of Mysore
Mysore 570009
India

PUBLISHED: Biannually
COST: 1 yr.—$4.00.

CONTENTS: Critical essays about works of authors in any country and in any genre; some creative material, such as poetry, stories, plays; book reviews; poems translated into English; occasional interviews. Example: "Herman Hesse's SIDDHARTA: The Landscape of the Inner Self."

UNSOLICITED MSS. WELCOME? Yes, if they come from subscribers; submissions acknowledged.
SPECIFICALLY WELCOMED: Essays concerning writers of any genre and country.
MS. LENGTH: 2,000-3,000 words for essays; up to 30 lines for poetry; submit ONE copy.
STYLE REQUIREMENTS: MLA STYLE SHEET.
COPYRIGHT: THE LITERARY HALF-YEARLY.
EDITOR'S DECISION: 2-3 months.
FROM ACCEPTANCE TO PUBLICATION: 6 months.
PAYMENT/OFFPRINTS: Ten offprints.
REJECTED MSS.: Not returned.
GENERAL: First issue, 1960. Usual publication length, 180-190 pages.
BACK ISSUES: Those since 1968 available from subscription address at $4.00 each.

THE LITERARY REVIEW: AN INTERNATIONAL JOURNAL OF CONTEMPORARY WRITING

EDITORIAL ADDRESS:
Dr. Charles Angoff, Editor
Fairleigh Dickinson University
Rutherford, New Jersey 07070

SUBSCRIPTION ADDRESS:

same

PUBLISHED: Quarterly
COST: 1 yr.—$7.00 in U.S.; $8.00 foreign; single copy—$2.00 in U.S.; $2.50 foreign.

CONTENTS: Chiefly contemporary writing in the field of belles lettres both in the United States and abroad. TLR seeks to encourage literary excellence and its appreciation by a wider audience and to further cultural exchange among the peoples of the world. Examples: "Hemingway as Hunger Artist"; "Chekhov's Early Tales."

UNSOLICITED MSS. WELCOME? Yes; submissions not acknowledged.
SPECIFICALLY WELCOMED: Poetry; stories; articles; plays.
MS. LENGTH: Not stated; submit ONE copy.
COPYRIGHT: THE LITERARY REVIEW.
EDITOR'S DECISION: 2 months.
FROM ACCEPTANCE TO PUBLICATION: 1 to 1½ years.
PAYMENT/OFFPRINTS: Two copies of issue in which work appears. Offprints ordered through journal, but author pays printer.
REJECTED MSS.: Returned.
GENERAL: First issue, Fall, 1957. Usual publication length, 130 pages.
BACK ISSUES: Available from Johnson Reprint Corp. Kraus Reprint Co., and Xerox University Microfilms. Price depends on age and scarcity of issue.

LONDON MAGAZINE

EDITORIAL ADDRESS:
Alan Ross, Editor
30 Thurloe Place
London S. W. 7
England

SUBSCRIPTION ADDRESS:

same

PUBLISHED: 6 times yearly
COST: 1 yr.—$14.00 (£5); single copy—90p.

CONTENTS: Stories, poetry, criticism, biography, memoir, music, art, reviews, film and theatre criticism. Example: "Middle-class Heroics: The Novels of Alastair MacLean."

UNSOLICITED MSS. WELCOME? Yes; submissions not acknowledged.
MS. LENGTH: Up to 5,000 words; submit ONE copy.
STYLE REQUIREMENTS: None.
COPYRIGHT: LONDON MAGAZINE.
PAYMENT/OFFPRINTS: £5 to £40.
REJECTED MSS.: Returned.
GENERAL: First issue of new series, April, 1961. Usual publication length, 160 pages.
BACK ISSUES: About 2/3 available from Falcon Computer Bureau, 6 Burrell Row, Beckenham, Kent, Great Britain at 50p each in April/May, 1971, then 90p each for subsequent issues.

THE MALAHAT REVIEW: AN INTERNATIONAL QUARTERLY OF LIFE AND LETTERS

EDITORIAL ADDRESS:
Robin Skelton, Editor
University of Victoria
P.O. Box 1700
Victoria, British Columbia
Canada

SUBSCRIPTION ADDRESS:

same

PUBLISHED: Quarterly CIRCULATION: Less than 1,000.
COST: 1 yr.—$5.00 (£2); 3 yrs.—$12.00 (£5); single copy—$1.25 (50 n.p.).

CONTENTS: Poetry; drama; fiction; criticism; primary research material in English studies, such as letters, memoirs and the like. The journal's publications in this field have included previously unknown material by D. H. Lawrence, Edward Dahlberg, Herbert Read, and AE. Essay examples: "Between God and Notgod: Anthony Burgess' 'Tremor of Intent' "; "Shinkichi Takahashi: Contemporary Zen Poet."

UNSOLICITED MSS. WELCOME? Yes; submissions not acknowledged.
SPECIFICALLY WELCOMED: Articles, short stories and poetry, and translations of some which have not previously appeared in English.
MS. LENGTH: Prose, under 6,000 words; submit ONE copy.
STYLE REQUIREMENTS: None.
COPYRIGHT: Copyright reverts to contributor after publication in TMR.
EDITOR'S DECISION: 2 months.
FROM ACCEPTANCE TO PUBLICATION: Up to 2 years.
PAYMENT/OFFPRINTS: $10 per poem or page thereof whichever is the greater figure; $25 per thousand words of prose. Two complimentary contributor's copies of relevant issue.
REJECTED MSS.: Returned.
GENERAL: First issue, January, 1967. Usual publication length, 136 pages. Indexed for 1967-1971.
BACK ISSUES: 1967-1968 available from Kraus Reprint Co.; 1969 onwards from editorial office at $1.25 each for issues from 1969-1972; $1.50 each for issues from 1973 on.

THE MASSACHUSETTS REVIEW

EDITORIAL ADDRESS:
Jules Chametzky, John Hicks, Robert Tucker, Co-Editors
Massachusetts Review, Inc.
Amherst, Massachusetts 01002

SUBSCRIPTION ADDRESS:
Memorial Hall
University of Massachusetts
Amherst, Massachusetts 01002

PUBLISHED: Quarterly CIRCULATION: 1,500
COST: 1 yr.—$7.00 in U.S.; $8.50 elsewhere; on stands—$2.00.

CONTENTS: Literature (poetry, fiction, criticism, an occasional play); the arts; public affairs. Examples: "The Hostile Sun: the Poetry of D. H. Lawrence"; "Towards the Canonization of William Carlos Williams."

UNSOLICITED MSS. WELCOME? Usually; submissions acknowledged.
SPECIFICALLY WELCOMED: All sorts of contributions.
MS. LENGTH: 15-20 pages, prose; submit ONE OR MORE copies.
STYLE REQUIREMENTS: See recent issue.
COPYRIGHT: THE MASSACHUSETTS REVIEW, but will negotiate after publication.
EDITOR'S DECISION: 3 months.
FROM ACCEPTANCE TO PUBLICATION: ½ to 1 year.
PAYMENT/OFFPRINTS: Articles, fiction: $50.00; poetry: 35¢ per line; $8 minimum to $35 maximum.
REJECTED MSS.: Returned.
GENERAL: First issue, Autumn, 1959. Usual publication length, 200 pages.
BACK ISSUES: Available from editorial address if originals remain. Out-of-print issues from Johnson Reprint Corp; on microfilm from Xerox Co. Price varies; the more rare, the more they cost.

MEANJIN QUARTERLY: A REVIEW OF ARTS AND LETTERS

EDITORIAL ADDRESS:
Clement B. Christesen,
O.B.E., Editor
University of Melbourne
Parkville, Victoria 3052
Australia

SUBSCRIPTION ADDRESS:

same

PUBLISHED: Quarterly
COST: 1 yr.—US$10.00.

CIRCULATION: 3,500

CONTENTS: Poetry; short fiction; articles and essays on contemporary art and literature, film, drama, and on socio-political subjects; occasional illustrations. Examples: "R. K. Narayan and the Temple of Indian Fiction"; "A Bohemian's Progress: Louis Esson in Melbourne, 1904-1914."

UNSOLICITED MSS. WELCOME? Yes; submissions not acknowledged.
SPECIFICALLY WELCOMED: Top quality imaginative writing.
MS. LENGTH: 3,000-4,000 words; submit TWO copies.
STYLE REQUIREMENTS: MLA STYLE SHEET.
COPYRIGHT: Author.
EDITOR'S DECISION: 2-3 months.
FROM ACCEPTANCE TO PUBLICATION: 6 months.
PAYMENT/OFFPRINTS: Approximately $20.00 per 1000 words. Offprints subject to negotiation.
REJECTED MSS.: Returned if international reply coupons enclosed.
GENERAL: First issue, December, 1940. Usual publication length, 144 pages. Indexed.

BACK ISSUES: Available from editorial address; cost subject to negotiation. Index (1940-1965)—$30.00.

THE MICHIGAN QUARTERLY REVIEW

EDITORIAL ADDRESS:
Radcliffe Squires, Editor
3032 Rackham Building
The University of Michigan
Ann Arbor, Michigan 48104

SUBSCRIPTION ADDRESS:

same

PUBLISHED: Quarterly (Jan., Apr., July, Oct.)
COST: 1 yr.—$6.00; 2 yrs.—$11.00; 3 yrs.—$15.00; single copy—$1.50.

CIRCULATION: 2,000

CONTENTS: International literary criticism; fiction; poetry; book reviews. Example essay: "Vonnegut's Cradle: The Erosion of Comedy."

UNSOLICITED MSS. WELCOME? Yes; submissions not acknowledged.
MS. LENGTH: 2,000-4,000 words; submit ONE copy.
STYLE REQUIREMENTS: MLA STYLE SHEET.
COPYRIGHT: THE MICHIGAN QUARTERLY REVIEW.
EDITOR'S DECISION: 6 weeks.
FROM ACCEPTANCE TO PUBLICATION: 1 year.
PAYMENT/OFFPRINTS: 2¢ per word for prose; 50¢ per line for poetry. Offprints at cost.
REJECTED MSS.: Returned.
GENERAL: First issue, 1960. Usual publication length, 100-112 pages.
BACK ISSUES: Available from editorial address at $2.00 each. Also from AMS Press, Inc. and Johnson Reprint. Microfilm copies from Xerox University Microfilms.

THE MINNESOTA REVIEW

EDITORIAL ADDRESS:
Roger Mitchell, Editor
Box 5416
Milwaukee, Wisconsin 53211

SUBSCRIPTION ADDRESS:

same

PUBLISHED: Biannually
COST: 1 yr.—$3.50; 2 yrs.—$6.50; single copy—$2.00.

CIRCULATION: 600-700

CONTENTS: Mainly poems, stories, plays; limited amount of scholarly and critical essays in all fields of the arts. Prose example: "Whatever happened to Weldon Kees?"

UNSOLICITED MSS. WELCOME? Yes; submissions not acknowledged.
SPECIFICALLY WELCOMED: Poems; plays; stories; interested mostly in Marxist criticism and scholarship, in all fields of the arts; interested in reviewing small press publications or other publications not easily noticed.
MS. LENGTH: No preference; submit ONE copy.
COPYRIGHT: Author.
EDITOR'S DECISION: 1-2 months.
FROM ACCEPTANCE TO PUBLICATION: 4-8 months.
PAYMENT/OFFPRINTS: Free copies. No offprints.
REJECTED MSS.: Returned.
GENERAL: First issue, 1960. Usual publication length, 80-120 pages.
BACK ISSUES: Available from editorial address at $5.00 each.

MOJO NAVIGATOR(E)

EDITORIAL ADDRESS:
John Jacob, Editor
602 South Austin, Apt. 2-C
Oak Park, Illinois 60304

SUBSCRIPTION ADDRESS:

same

PUBLISHED: Irregularly
COST: Single copy—$1.00; 4 issues—$3.50.

CIRCULATION: 350

CONTENTS: Contemporary poetry, both from "established" and "unknown" or "small press" authors: Ginsberg and McClure to Wagner, Hiatt, and Swallow Press writers Matthias, Planz, Anania. Range expanded to include essays, book reviews, and graphics. Plans for some single author issues and an all-prose issue.

UNSOLICITED MSS. WELCOME? Very welcome; submissions not acknowledged.
SPECIFICALLY WELCOMED: Poetry; short essays related to literature; the best new work being written today.
MS. LENGTH: Depends on type; submit ONE copy.
COPYRIGHT: Reverts to author 30 days after publication.
EDITOR'S DECISION: 2 to 3 weeks.
FROM ACCEPTANCE TO PUBLICATION: 6 months.
PAYMENT/OFFPRINTS: Copies.
REJECTED MSS.: Returned.
GENERAL: First issue, November, 1969. Usual publication length, 40 pages.
BACK ISSUES: Available from editorial address at $1.00 each. Microfilms from University Microfilms.

MUNDUS ARTIUM: A JOURNAL OF INTERNATIONAL
LITERATURE AND THE ARTS

EDITORIAL ADDRESS: SUBSCRIPTION ADDRESS:
Rainer Schulte, Editor-in-Chief
English Department same
Ohio University
Athens, Ohio 45701

PUBLISHED: Biannually CIRCULATION: 1,000
COST: 1 yr.—$6.00 in U.S., Canada, and Mexico; $6.50 elsewhere; single copy—
$3.50 in U.S., Canada, and Mexico; $3.75 elsewhere.

CONTENTS: Essays on literature and the arts; fiction; poetry (some represented in bilingual form); reproductions of modern painting and sculpture; material all of a conceptual rather than descriptive nature; emphasis on interrelationship of the arts; checklists of translations-in-progress. Example: "Introduction to Contemporary African-American Poetry."

UNSOLICITED MSS. WELCOME? Yes; submissions not acknowledged.
SPECIFICALLY WELCOMED: Creative material; criticism.
MS. LENGTH: Flexible; submit ONE copy.
STYLE REQUIREMENTS: Flexible.
COPYRIGHT: Rainer Schulte, Editor.
EDITOR'S DECISION: 1 month.
FROM ACCEPTANCE TO PUBLICATION: Varies greatly.
PAYMENT/OFFPRINTS: Copies of the issue only.
REJECTED MSS.: Returned.
GENERAL: First issue, Fall, 1967. Usual publication length, 150 pages. MA is sponsored by the International Poetry Forum in Pittsburgh, Pennsylvania.
BACK ISSUES: Available from editorial address at $2.50 each for issues before Vol. VI; $3.50 each thereafter.

NEW DEPARTURES

EDITORIAL ADDRESS: SUBSCRIPTION ADDRESS:
Michael Horovitz, Editor and Publisher
Mullions, Piedmont same
Bisley, Glos GL6 7BU
United Kingdom

PUBLISHED: Highly irregularly CIRCULATION: 5,000 usually
COST: $4.00 for 4 issues. published

CONTENTS: Verse (by McClure, Ivor Cutler, Robert Bly, as examples); graphics (by Colin Self, Richard Hamilton, Adrian Henri); prose about poetry; photos, collages, reproductions; book reviews; record reviews. Occasionally the magazine appears in the form of a booklet of poems, such as THE HIGH TOWER by Frances Horovitz (No. 6), or LOVE POEMS by Michael Horovitz (No. 9).

UNSOLICITED MSS. WELCOME? Not really; submissions not acknowledged.
MS. LENGTH: Short.
COPYRIGHT: Authors and magazine on their behalf.
EDITOR'S DECISION: Up to 6 months.
FROM ACCEPTANCE TO PUBLICATION: Unpredictable.
PAYMENT/OFFPRINTS: Payment usually in complimentary copies. No offprints.
REJECTED MSS.: Returned if accompanied by IRC.
GENERAL: First issue, Summer, 1959. Usual publication length, 100-150 pages.
BACK ISSUES: Available, upon receipt of payment, from editorial address at $1.25 each for #6 and #9; $2.50 each for double issue, #7 & 8; a few of #5 available to life subscribers at $15.00 each. Nos. 1-4 out of print.

NEW EDINBURGH REVIEW

EDITORIAL ADDRESS:
M. Relich, Editor
1 Buccleuch Place
Edinburgh EH8 9LW
Scotland

SUBSCRIPTION ADDRESS:

same

PUBLISHED: Quarterly
COST: 1 yr.—60p.

CIRCULATION: 1,000

CONTENTS: General articles on culture, politics, and the arts; usually a theme in each issue; yearly "Edinburgh Festival" issue; poetry; reviews; short stories. Review articles: "New African Fiction"; "Henry James and Ibsen."

UNSOLICITED MSS. WELCOME? Yes, if they fit theme; submissions not usually acknowledged.
SPECIFICALLY WELCOMED: Poetry, reviews, short stories.
STYLE REQUIREMENTS: None.
COPYRIGHT: Board of publications or author.
EDITOR'S DECISION: 6 months.
FROM ACCEPTANCE TO PUBLICATION: 6 months.
PAYMENT/OFFPRINTS: 6 copies of issue.
REJECTED MSS.: Not returned.
GENERAL: First issue, February, 1969. Usual publication length, 40 pages.
BACK ISSUES: Available from editorial address at 10p. each.

NEW LETTERS (formerly THE UNIVERSITY REVIEW)

EDITORIAL ADDRESS:
Editor
University of Missouri—Kansas City
Kansas City, Missouri 64110

SUBSCRIPTION ADDRESS:

same

COST: 1 yr.—$6.00; 5 yrs.—$20.00; Lifetime—$100.00.

CONTENTS: Creative writing; literary criticism; photographs.

UNSOLICITED MSS. WELCOME? Yes.
SPECIFICALLY WELCOMED: In criticism as well as in creative writing, editors look for originality and for depth of insight; particularly encourage contributions from abroad.
MS. LENGTH: Average.
COPYRIGHT: NEW LETTERS.
GENERAL: First issue, 1933. Usual publication length, 40 pages.
BACK ISSUES: Available from subscription address.

NEW MORALITY: CONCERNED WITH NEW LITERATURE, ART AND CRITICISM

EDITORIAL ADDRESS:
Francine Virduzzo, Editor
Via della Penna 15
Rome
Italy

SUBSCRIPTION ADDRESS:

same

GENERAL: This periodical had not arrived by the time the entry went to press. Potential subscribers, contributors, or collectors will have to write the editor to see whether the journal still exists, and if so, to inquire about details of manuscript submission, style, back issues, and the like.

NEW ORLEANS REVIEW: A JOURNAL OF LITERATURE AND CULTURE

EDITORIAL ADDRESS:
Forrest Ingram, Editor
Loyola University
New Orleans, Louisiana 70118

SUBSCRIPTION ADDRESS:

same

PUBLISHED: Quarterly
CIRCULATION: 1,500
COST: 1 yr.—$6.00 ($5.00 with agency discount); 2 yrs.—$10.00; 3 yrs.—$14.00; single copy—$1.50.

CONTENTS: Poetry; fiction; broad range of articles; book and music reviews; interviews with national figures; art work; photography. Example: "Literature is the 'Stuffy' Art."

UNSOLICITED MSS. WELCOME? Yes; submissions acknowledged.
SPECIFICALLY WELCOMED: All types.
MS. LENGTH: Poetry, ¼ page to 6 pages; prose, 18-24 pages; submit ONE copy.
STYLE REQUIREMENTS: Standard.
COPYRIGHT: NEW ORLEANS REVIEW.
EDITOR'S DECISION: 2-4 weeks.
FROM ACCEPTANCE TO PUBLICATION: 2 months to 1 year.
PAYMENT/OFFPRINTS: Poetry, $10.00; fiction, interviews, articles, $50.00; two complimentary copies of issue. 25 offprints for $5.00.
REJECTED MSS.: Returned.
GENERAL: First issue, Fall, 1968. Usual publication length, 96 pages.
BACK ISSUES: Available from NOR office at $1.25 each up through Vol. 3, No. 1; $1.50 each for subsequent issues.

THE NEW RENAISSANCE: A MAGAZINE OF IDEAS AND OPINIONS, EMPHASIZING LITERATURE AND THE ARTS

EDITORIAL ADDRESS: SUBSCRIPTION ADDRESS:
Louise T. Reynolds, Editor
9 Heath Road
Arlington, Massachusetts 02174

PUBLISHED: 1 or 2 times yearly   CIRCULATION: 1,000
COST: 4 issues—$5.50 in U.S. and Canada; $6.50 elsewhere; single copy—$1.60 in U.S. and Canada; $1.90 elsewhere.

CONTENTS: Fiction; poetry; lead articles; essays; reviews; art work.

UNSOLICITED MSS. WELCOME? Yes, generally, but overstocked, at present, with poetry and fiction.
SPECIFICALLY WELCOMED: Literary or theatre or political essays.
MS. LENGTH: Under 35 pages; submit ONE copy.
STYLE REQUIREMENTS: None.
COPYRIGHT: THE NEW RENAISSANCE.
EDITOR'S DECISION: 10-16 weeks.
FROM ACCEPTANCE TO PUBLICATION: 12-16 months.
PAYMENT/OFFPRINTS: Payment depends upon length after publication. Offprints at cost to magazine, plus postage.
REJECTED MSS.: Returned.
GENERAL: First issue, Fall, 1968. Usual publication, 68, sometimes 72, pages.
BACK ISSUES: Available from editorial address at regular rates ($1.60 each in U.S. and Canada; $1.90 elsewhere) except Vol. 1, #1 at $3.20 in all countries.

NORTH AMERICAN REVIEW

EDITORIAL ADDRESS:
Robley Wilson, Jr., Editor
University of Northern Iowa
Cedar Falls, Iowa 50613

SUBSCRIPTION ADDRESS:

same

PUBLISHED: Quarterly (Mar., June, Sept., Dec.)
CIRCULATION: 2,700
COST: 1 yr.—$6.00 in U.S. and possessions; $6.15 in Canada and Latin America; $7.00 elsewhere.

CONTENTS: Fiction; poetry; articles especially focusing on environmental concerns; some reviews and literary pieces; occasional political editorials. Examples: "Hamlet and the Animals"; "THE DEVIL TREE: An Interview with Jerzy Kosinski."

UNSOLICITED MSS. WELCOME? Yes, fiction and poems but query on articles; submissions not acknowledged.
SPECIFICALLY WELCOMED: Writings having a "general interest."
MS. LENGTH: No restrictions; submit ONE copy.
STYLE REQUIREMENTS: None specifically.
COPYRIGHT: Assigned on request.
EDITOR'S DECISION: 6-10 weeks.
FROM ACCEPTANCE TO PUBLICATION: 3-9 months.
PAYMENT/OFFPRINTS: $10 per published page. Contributors may buy extra magazines at discount.
REJECTED MSS.: Returned.
GENERAL: First issue, 1815-1940; revived—Spring, 1964. Usual publication length, 80 pages.
BACK ISSUES: 1969-1973 available from publisher at $1.50 each for those in print. 1815-1902, 1964-1969, from AMS Reprint Company. Microfilm 1815 to present, from Xerox University Microfilms.

NORTHEAST

EDITORIAL ADDRESS:
John Judson, Editor
Juniper Press
1310 Shorewood Drive
La Crosse, Wisconsin 54601

SUBSCRIPTION ADDRESS:

same

PUBLISHED: 2 NE and 2 Juniper Books yearly; also some special issues.
CIRCULATION: 500
COST: 1 yr.—$6.00; single copy of NE—$1.00; single copy of Jupiper Book—$2.50.

CONTENTS: Poetry; book reviews; experimental fiction.

UNSOLICITED MSS. WELCOME? Yes; submissions not acknowledged.
SPECIFICALLY WELCOMED: Has typically published poetry and reviews, but interested in essays on poetics and on experimental fiction.
MS. LENGTH: No restrictions; submit ONE copy.
STYLE REQUIREMENTS: None.
COPYRIGHT: NORTHEAST buys only first N.A. rights; authors retain others.
EDITOR'S DECISION: 6-8 weeks.
FROM ACCEPTANCE TO PUBLICATION: 6-12 months.
PAYMENT/OFFPRINTS: Copies of the issue in which material is printed.
REJECTED MSS.: Returned.
GENERAL: First issue, 1962. Usual publication length, 40-100 pages.
BACK ISSUES: Available from editorial or specified dealers. Write for price sheet.

NORTHWEST REVIEW

EDITORIAL ADDRESS:
Patricia Brooks, Managing Editor
University of Oregon
Eugene, Oregon 97403

SUBSCRIPTION ADDRESS:

same

PUBLISHED: Quarterly:
3 issues per year.

CIRCULATION: 500

COST: 1 yr.—$4.00, $3.00 for students; 2 yrs.—$7.00, $5.00 for students; 3 yrs.—$10.00; single copy—$1.50.

CONTENTS: Poetry, fiction, art, and reviews; occasional articles, critical or reportive (the latter regional); occasional special issues on the work of a particular writer.

UNSOLICITED MSS. WELCOME? Yes, but most articles are solicited; submissions not acknowledged.
SPECIFICALLY WELCOMED: Poetry, fiction, art of highest quality.
MS. LENGTH: Any length considered; submit one original.
STYLE REQUIREMENTS: None.
COPYRIGHT: NORTHWEST REVIEW; assigned to author only on request.
EDITOR'S DECISION: 1-3 months.
FROM ACCEPTANCE TO PUBLICATION: Published in next issue.
PAYMENT/OFFPRINTS: Three complimentary copies of issue in which work appears. Offprints available at nominal cost.
REJECTED MSS.: Returned.
GENERAL: First issue, Spring, 1957. Usual publication length, 128 pages.
BACK ISSUES: Available from editorial office at $1.50 each.

THE OHIO REVIEW: A JOURNAL OF THE HUMANITIES

EDITORIAL ADDRESS:
Stanley W. Lindberg,
Managing Editor
346 Ellis Hall
Ohio University
Athens, Ohio 45701

SUBSCRIPTION ADDRESS:

same

PUBLISHED: Tri-annually CIRCULATION: 800-1,000
COST: 1 yr.—$5.00; 3 yrs.—$12.00; single copy—$2.00

CONTENTS: Essays; poetry; fiction; book reviews; a series of interviews with major contemporary poets, such as Adrienne Rich, Mark Strand, William Matthews, Galway Kinnell, Charles Simic, and Louis Simpson, Joyce Carol Oates, James Tate, Marvin Bell, and Louise Glück; occasional photographs. Examples: "Black Humor: Beyond Satire"; "All About Talk: Arthur Miller's THE PRICE."

UNSOLICITED MSS. WELCOME? Yes, although TOR normally does own interviewing; submissions not acknowledged.
SPECIFICALLY WELCOMED: Essays, selected to appeal across disciplinary lines, must be of general humanistic interest and view their subjects against a broad intellectual background; poetry; fiction.
MS. LENGTH: Under 6,000 words; submit TWO copies.
STYLE REQUIREMENTS: MLA STYLE SHEET (for essays).
COPYRIGHT: Negotiable; normally fiction and poetry copyright is reassigned.
EDITOR'S DECISION: 8-10 weeks.
FROM ACCEPTANCE TO PUBLICATION: Less than 1 year.
PAYMENT/OFFPRINTS: $5 per page and up, plus a one-year complimentary subscription. 20 offprints, plus 2 copies of the complete issue.
REJECTED MSS.: Returned.
GENERAL: First issued, 1959-1971, as THE OHIO UNIVERSITY REVIEW; 1971—, THE OHIO REVIEW. Usual publication length, 112-120 pages.
BACK ISSUES: Those since Fall, 1971, available from the editorial address. Others from Kraus Reprint Co. Rates upon request.

PARTISAN REVIEW

EDITORIAL ADDRESS:
William Phillips, Editor
Partisan Review Inc.
1 Richardson Street
New Brunswick, New Jersey 08903

SUBSCRIPTION ADDRESS:

same

PUBLISHED: Quarterly
COST: 1 yr.—$5.50; 2 yrs.—$10.50.

CONTENTS: Articles of literary, cultural, and political interest; reviews of books; stories; poems. Examples: "Writing about Movies"; "Is There a Science of Literature?"; "The Melodramatic Imagination."

UNSOLICITED MSS. WELCOME? Yes; submissions not acknowledged.
SPECIFICALLY WELCOMED: Short stories, poems, essays.
MS. LENGTH: Not established; submit ONE copy.
STYLE REQUIREMENTS: None.
COPYRIGHT: PARTISAN REVIEW.
EDITOR'S DECISION: 3 months.
FROM ACCEPTANCE TO PUBLICATION: 1 year.
PAYMENT/OFFPRINTS: Payment varies. No offprints.
REJECTED MSS.: Returned.
GENERAL: First issue, 1934. Usual publication length, 196 pages.
BACK ISSUES: Available from editorial address at $1.50 each, plus $.20 postage.

PERSPECTIVE: A QUARTERLY OF MODERN LITERATURE

EDITORIAL ADDRESS:
Jarvis Thurston and
Mona Van Duyn, Editors
Washington Univeristy P.O.
St. Louis, Missouri 63130

SUBSCRIPTION ADDRESS:

same

PUBLISHED: Irregularly
COST: $1.00 per issue.

CIRCULATION: 500-600

CONTENTS: Contemporary short stories, poetry, and criticism, such as "Art as Communion: Auden's 'The Sea and the Mirror.' "

UNSOLICITED MSS. WELCOME? Yes; submissions not acknowledged.
SPECIFICALLY WELCOMED: Fiction; poetry; outstanding critical articles.
MS. LENGTH: 2,000-4,000 words; submit ONE copy.
COPYRIGHT: Author.
EDITOR'S DECISION: Two months.
FROM ACCEPTANCE TO PUBLICATION: Varies.
PAYMENT/OFFPRINTS: No provision.
REJECTED MSS.: Returned.
GENERAL: First issue, 1947. Usual publication length, 80 pages.
BACK ISSUES: Many available from editorial office; some from Johnson Reprint Corp.

PRAIRIE SCHOONER

EDITORIAL ADDRESS:
Bernice Slote, Editor
Andrews Hall
University of Nebraska
Lincoln, Nebraska 68508

SUBSCRIPTION ADDRESS:
Business Office
Nebraska Hall
University of Nebraska
901 North 17th Street
Lincoln, Nebraska 68508

PUBLISHED: Quarterly
COST: 1 yr.—$3.00.

CONTENTS: Short fiction; poetry; reviews; occasional articles, such as "Primitivism in Melville."

UNSOLICITED MSS. WELCOME? Yes.
MS. LENGTH: Articles up to 2,500 words.
COPYRIGHT: University of Nebraska Press.
PAYMENT/OFFPRINTS: Copy of issue.
GENERAL: First issue, 1927. Usual publication length, 106 pages. Indexed by volume.

QUARTERLY REVIEW OF LITERATURE

EDITORIAL ADDRESS:
T. Weiss and Renée Weiss, Editors
26 Haslett Avenue
Princeton, New Jersey 08540

SUBSCRIPTION ADDRESS:

same

COST: 2 double issues—$5.00.

CONTENTS: Translations of works of well known authors, such as Sartre's "Mallarmé"; poetry; short stories; occasional interview, such as "Conversation with Marianne Moore"; occasional issue centers on one author, such as Hölderlin; plays; novellas; unpublished or little known material of relevant older American writers.

UNSOLICITED MSS. WELCOME? Yes.
COPYRIGHT: QUARTERLY REVIEW OF LITERATURE.
GENERAL: Usual publication length, 250 pages. Mss. are not read between May and Sept.

THE SEWANEE REVIEW

EDITORIAL ADDRESS:
Andrew Lytle, Editor

SUBSCRIPTION ADDRESS:
The University of the South
Sewanee, Tennessee 37375

PUBLISHED: Quarterly
COST: 1 yr.—$5.00 (foreign, add $1.00).

CONTENTS: Essays, such as "T. S. Eliot and the Ghost of S.T.C."; fiction; verse; and articles in "Arts and Letters" section, such as "The Art and the Conscience of Jean Genet."

UNSOLICITED MSS. WELCOME? Yes.
MS. LENGTH: 2,000-8,000 words.
STYLE REQUIREMENTS: MLA STYLE SHEET.
COPYRIGHT: Journal.
PAYMENT/OFFPRINTS: Payment.
GENERAL: First issue, 1892.
BACK ISSUES: Available from Kraus Reprints; for recent back issues, contact subscription address.

SHENANDOAH: THE WASHINGTON AND LEE UNIVERSITY REVIEW

EDITORIAL ADDRESS:
James Boatwright, Editor
Box 722
Lexington, Virginia 24450

SUBSCRIPTION ADDRESS:

same

PUBLISHED: Quarterly
COST: 1 yr.—$4.00; 2 yrs.—$7.00; single copy—$1.25.

CONTENTS: Criticism, fiction, poetry, reviews, interviews.

UNSOLICITED MSS. WELCOME? Yes; submissions not acknowledged.
MS. LENGTH: Prose, 3-20 pages; submit ONE copy.
STYLE REQUIREMENTS: Lucid.
COPYRIGHT: Variable.
EDITOR'S DECISION: 1 month.
FROM ACCEPTANCE TO PUBLICATION: Variable, 3 months at most.
PAYMENT/OFFPRINTS: Payment by arrangement. Copies of magazine at contributor's discount.
REJECTED MSS.: Returned.
GENERAL: First issue, 1950. Usual publication length, 100 pages.
BACK ISSUES: Available from editorial address at $1.75 each.

SOUTH CAROLINA REVIEW

EDITORIAL ADDRESS:
Richard Calhoun, Robert Hill,
William Koon, Editors
Department of English
Clemson University
Clemson, South Carolina 29631

SUBSCRIPTION ADDRESS:

same

PUBLISHED: Biannually
COST: 1 yr.—$2.00; 2 yrs.—$3.50.

CIRCULATION: 300

CONTENTS: Poetry; short fiction; book reviews; literary criticism and interpretations; critical essays that concern any topic of general interest. The journal does not limit itself to Caroliniana. Essay example: "The Literature of Laputa."

UNSOLICITED MSS. WELCOME? Yes; submissions not acknowledged.
SPECIFICALLY WELCOMED: Poetry, short fiction, critical essays, book reviews.
MS. LENGTH: 1,500-2,500 words, except poetry; submit ONE copy.
STYLE REQUIREMENTS: MLA STYLE SHEET.
COPYRIGHT: SOUTH CAROLINA REVIEW.
EDITOR'S DECISION: 1 month.
FROM ACCEPTANCE TO PUBLICATION: Within 1 year.
PAYMENT/OFFPRINTS: Six copies of journal; additional copies at $.50 each.
REJECTED MSS.: Returned.
GENERAL: First issue, November, 1968. Usual publication length, 75 pages.
BACK ISSUES: Available from editorial address at $1.00 each.

SOUTH DAKOTA REVIEW

EDITORIAL ADDRESS:
John R. Milton, Editor
Box 111
University Exchange
Vermillion, South Dakota 57069

SUBSCRIPTION ADDRESS:

same

PUBLISHED: Quarterly
COST: 1 yr.—$4.00 in U.S. and Canada, $5.00 elsewhere; 2 yrs.—$7.00 in U.S. and Canada, $9.00 elsewhere; single copy—usually $1.25.

CIRCULATION: 600-1,000

CONTENTS: Fiction, poetry, literary criticism, interviews, regional history, photographs on occasional. Emphasis on Western America, but not limited to that. Examples: "Anne Gilchrist, Critic of Walt Whitman"; "The Kachina Characters of Frank Waters' Novels."

UNSOLICITED MSS. WELCOME? Yes, generally; submissions not acknowledged.

SPECIFICALLY WELCOMED: Top-notch fiction (with some preference going to western writers), literary criticism of a non-stuffy nature (but well written).
MS. LENGTH: 5,000 words; submit ONE copy.
STYLE REQUIREMENTS: Informal, but very correct; avoid extremes (academic or unlettered).
COPYRIGHT: University of South Dakota, but only for writers' protection.
EDITOR'S DECISION: Varies.
FROM ACCEPTANCE TO PUBLICATION: 2 months to 1 year.
PAYMENT/OFFPRINTS: One to four free copies of journal, depending on item.
REJECTED MSS.: Returned.
GENERAL: First issue, December, 1963. Usual publication length, 100 pages.
BACK ISSUES: Available from editorial address usually at cover price although varies according to scarcity of issue. All available on microfilm from Xerox University Microfilms.

SOUTHERN HUMANITIES REVIEW

EDITORIAL ADDRESS:
Norman A. Brittin and Eugene
Current-Garcia, Editors
Auburn University
9088 Haley Center
Auburn, Alabama 36830

SUBSCRIPTION ADDRESS:

same

PUBLISHED: Quarterly
COST: 1 yr.—$4.00; single copy—$1.25.

CIRCULATION: 400

CONTENTS: Critical and/or scholarly essays in fields of literature, history, philosophy, languages, and fine arts; plus short fiction; poetry; and book reviews of works in humanities areas. Example: "Symbolism in T. S. Eliot's 'Landscapes.'"

UNSOLICITED MSS. WELCOME? Yes; submissions acknowledged.
SPECIFICALLY WELCOMED: Critical and/or scholarly interpretations of individual writers and writings, particularly those bearing serious treatment of humanities themes, ideas.
MS. LENGTH: Under 4,000 words; submit ONE copy.
STYLE REQUIREMENTS: MLA STYLE SHEET.
COPYRIGHT: Auburn University through SHR.
EDITOR'S DECISION: 3-4 months.
FROM ACCEPTANCE TO PUBLICATION: 6-8 months.
PAYMENT/OFFPRINTS: Two free copies of entire issue, plus 15 offprints of piece published.
REJECTED MSS.: Returned.
GENERAL: First issue, Spring, 1967. Usual publication length, 100 pages; occasionally up to 20 more.
BACK ISSUES: Original issues of first three years are now exhausted; these are available from AMS Reprint Co. A few back issues of more recent years are still on hand at the editorial office at $1.25 each, but some of these are also quite scarce.

SOUTHERN REVIEW

EDITORIAL ADDRESS:
Ian Reid, Editor
Department of English
University of Adelaide
Adelaide
South Australia

SUBSCRIPTION ADDRESS:
Business Manager
same

PUBLISHED: Tri-annually
COST: 1 yr.—$4.00 (Aust.) in Australia; $4.50 (Aust.) elsewhere.

CONTENTS: Critical articles on literature, mainly (but not exclusively) literature in English; inter-disciplinary and inter-regional essays; poems; short stories; book reviews; occasional interview. Example: "T. S. Eliot: The Psychobiographical Approach."

UNSOLICITED MSS. WELCOME? Yes; submissions, except poems, acknowledged.
SPECIFICALLY WELCOMED: Interdisciplinary and inter-regional essays, i.e. discussions or demonstrations of how literary study relates to the study of society, philosophy, religion, science and of how one national literature relates to another.
MS. LENGTH: Any length; submit ONE copy.
STYLE REQUIREMENTS: MLA STYLE SHEET.
COPYRIGHT: Author.
EDITOR'S DECISION: 2-3 months.
FROM ACCEPTANCE TO PUBLICATION: 2-3 months.
PAYMENT/OFFPRINTS: Poem, at least $5; short story, at least $10. 20 free offprints of article; 10 of review or poems; limited number of extra offprints are available, but must be ordered and paid for in advance.
REJECTED MSS.: Returned.
GENERAL: First issue, 1963. Usual publication length, 90-96 pages.
BACK ISSUES: Available from Business Manager at $1.35 (Aust.) each in Australia; $1.50 (Aust.) elsewhere. Vol. I, No. 1 not available.

SOUTHWEST REVIEW

EDITORIAL ADDRESS:
Margaret L. Hartley, Editor
Southern Methodist University Press
Dallas, Texas 75275

SUBSCRIPTION ADDRESS:
same

PUBLISHED: Quarterly
COST: 1 yr.—$4.00; 2 yrs.—$7.00; 3 yrs.—$10.00; single copy—$1.00.

CONTENTS: Contemporary literature and discussion combining quality fiction and verse with studies in current affairs, historical research, literary criticism; accounts of achievements in the lively arts; essays of personal opinion; book reviews. Essay example: "All the New Vibrations: Romanticism in 20th-Century America."

UNSOLICITED MSS. WELCOME? Yes; submissions acknowledged.
SPECIFICALLY WELCOMED: Poetry, fiction, and scholarly articles dealing with contemporary affairs, history, literary criticism (contemporary American literature), art, music, and the theater.
MS. LENGTH: 3,000-5,000 words; submit ONE copy.
STYLE REQUIREMENTS: University of Chicago's A MANUAL OF STYLE.
COPYRIGHT: Southern Methodist University Press.
EDITOR'S DECISION: 3 months.
FROM ACCEPTANCE TO PUBLICATION: Length, subject matter, season considered when scheduling poems; stories and articles—first or second issue after date accepted.
PAYMENT/OFFPRINTS: $5.00 per poem; ½¢ per word of prose. Offprints provided at cost.
REJECTED MSS.: Returned.
GENERAL: First issue, June, 1915 (entitled TEXAS REVIEW from 1915-1924). Usual publication length, 96-112 pages. Indexed by volume.
BACK ISSUES: Available from Southern Methodist University Press at $1.00 each, except rare or scarce issues (inquire about cost).

TRIQUARTERLY

EDITORIAL ADDRESS: SUBSCRIPTION ADDRESS:
Charles Newman, Editor
University Hall 101 same
Northwestern University
Evanston, Illinois 60201

PUBLISHED: Tri-annually CIRCULATION: 6,000
COST: 1 yr.—$7.00; 2 yrs.—$12.00; 3 yrs.—$17.00; foreign subscriptions add $.75 per year for postage; single copies—usually $2.95.

CONTENTS: International arts, letters, and opinion; fiction; theater; foreign perspectives; critical essays on such topics as The Art of Sylvia Plath, Eastern European Literature, Writers Under Thirty, Latin American Literature, Vladimir Nabokov, Edward Dahlberg, Jorge Luis Borges, and Literature in Revolution. Example: "The Myth of the Postmodernist Breakthrough."

UNSOLICITED MSS. WELCOME? Yes; submissions not acknowledged.
SPECIFICALLY WELCOMED: Contemporary American fiction, and critical essays related thereto.
MS. LENGTH: No preference; submit ONE copy.
STYLE REQUIREMENTS: Good English grammar/usage.

COPYRIGHT: Blanket copyright on magazine by Northwestern University Press.
EDITOR'S DECISION: 6 weeks.
FROM ACCEPTANCE TO PUBLICATION: Varies greatly.
PAYMENT/OFFPRINTS: Varies from nothing to a great deal, about $10 per page. No offprints, but reasonable number of copies sent.
REJECTED MSS.: Returned.
GENERAL: First issue, Fall, 1964. Usual publication length, 250 pages. Index of issues 1 through 22 available.
BACK ISSUES: Available from editorial office, Kraus Reprint Co., and Xerox University Microfilms. Price varies widely (many are collectors' items priced at $25).

UNICORN: A MISCELLANEOUS JOURNAL

EDITORIAL ADDRESS:
Karen Rockow, Editor
1153 East 26 Street
Brooklyn, New York 11210

SUBSCRIPTION ADDRESS:
same

PUBLISHED: Tri-annually   CIRCULATION: 500
COST: 1 yr.—$2.50 (library—$3.50); single copy—$1.00 (library—$1.50).

CONTENTS: Essays, from personal essays to scholarly papers directed at a general audience; poetry; satire; graphics; light verse; a few short stories; many reviews. Examples: "Robert Creeley and the Surprise of Zen"; "Three Notes on Edward Lear."

UNSOLICITED MSS. WELCOME? Yes; submissions not acknowledged.
SPECIFICALLY WELCOMED: Folklore, popular culture (esp. fantasy literature, detective fiction, children's books), medieval studies, essays, and "gracefully scholarly" papers.
MS. LENGTH: Up to 3,000 words, but will consider series of articles; submit ONE OR TWO copies.
STYLE REQUIREMENTS: Footnotes (if any) should follow MLA form.
COPYRIGHT: UNICORN, but authors may have a release on request.
EDITOR'S DECISION: 2-4 weeks.
FROM ACCEPTANCE TO PUBLICATION: Varies; for essays usually no longer than 6 months, usually much less.
PAYMENT/OFFPRINTS: $5 honorarium for each article or essay accepted plus copies and 3 to 5 offprints, depending on length; more on special request.
REJECTED MSS.: Returned.
GENERAL: First issue, 1967. Usual publication length, 32 pages.
BACK ISSUES: All are in print and available from editorial address at $1.00 each for individuals; $1.50 each for libraries.

THE UNIVERSITY OF DENVER QUARTERLY: A JOURNAL OF MODERN CULTURE

EDITORIAL ADDRESS:
Burton Feldman, Editor
Department of English
University of Denver
Denver, Colorado 80210

SUBSCRIPTION ADDRESS:

same

PUBLISHED: Quarterly
COST: 1 yr.—$6.00; 2 yrs.—$10.00.

CIRCULATION: 700

CONTENTS: Poetry; fiction; articles; reviews.

UNSOLICITED MSS. WELCOME? Yes; submissions not acknowledged.
MS. LENGTH: No preferred length; submit ONE copy.
COPYRIGHT: Author.
EDITOR'S DECISION: 1-3 months.
FROM ACCEPTANCE TO PUBLICATION: Varies.
PAYMENT/OFFPRINTS: Minimum rates of $5 per page, prose; $10 per page, poetry. Offprints are available.
REJECTED MSS.: Returned.
GENERAL: First issue, Spring, 1966. Usual publication length, 140 pages.
BACK ISSUES: Available from editorial office at $3.00 each or $6.00 per volume.

UNIVERSITY OF WINDSOR REVIEW

EDITORIAL ADDRESS:
Eugene McNamara, Editor
Department of English
University of Windsor
Windsor, Ontario N9B 3P4

SUBSCRIPTION ADDRESS:

same

PUBLISHED: Biannually (Fall, Spring)   CIRCULATION: 400
COST: 1 yr.—$2.50 plus postage—$.30 to U.S. (agency rates—$2.00 plus postage).

CONTENTS: Poems; short stories; book reviews; fiction; criticism.

UNSOLICITED MSS. WELCOME? Yes; submissions not acknowledged.
SPECIFICALLY WELCOMED: Poetry; short fiction (limited space for these); articles on untouched areas of literary criticism.
MS. LENGTH: 2,000-3,000 words; submit ONE copy.
STYLE REQUIREMENTS: MLA STYLE SHEET.
COPYRIGHT: Author.
EDITOR'S DECISION: 1-2 months.
FROM ACCEPTANCE TO PUBLICATION: Varies.
PAYMENT/OFFPRINTS: Two copies of issue; 20 offprints.

REJECTED MSS.: Returned.
GENERAL: First issue, Spring, 1965.
BACK ISSUES: Available from editorial address at current prices.

WASCANA REVIEW

EDITORIAL ADDRESS:
H. C. Dillow, Editor
English Department
University of Saskatshewan-
Regina Campus
Regina, Saskatchewan, S4S OA2
Canada

SUBSCRIPTION ADDRESS:
M. Bergbusch,
Managing Editor
same

PUBLISHED: Biannually (May, Nov.)   CIRCULATION: 300
COST: 1 yr.—$2.50; 3 yrs.—$6.00; single copy—$1.50.

CONTENTS: Critical articles, mainly but not exclusively on literary subjects; poems of 4 to 100 lines in length; short stories up to 6,000 words; book reviews.

UNSOLICITED MSS. WELCOME? Yes, but not book reviews; submissions acknowledged.
SPECIFICALLY WELCOMED: A wide variety of articles, poems, and short stories. Editors do not prefer any particular literary style, but judge each work on its merits.
MS. LENGTH: Articles and stories, up to 6,000 words; poems, 4-100 lines; submit ONE copy.
STYLE REQUIREMENTS: Prefer articles to follow MLA STYLE SHEET but do not insist on this.
COPYRIGHT: WASCANA REVIEW.
EDITOR'S DECISION: 4-6 weeks.
FROM ACCEPTANCE TO PUBLICATION: Not more than 6 months.
PAYMENT/OFFPRINTS: $10 per page for poetry; $3 per page for prose; $4 per page for commissioned prose. Two copies of issue in which work appears. Offprints available from printers; information supplied upon publication.
REJECTED MSS.: Returned.
GENERAL: First issue, Spring, 1966. Usual publication length, 80 pages.
BACK ISSUES: Available from Managing Editor at subscription rates cited above.

WEBSTER REVIEW

EDITORIAL ADDRESS:
Harry J. Cargas and
Nancy Schapiro, Editors
Webster College
Webster Groves, Missouri 63119

SUBSCRIPTION ADDRESS:

same

PUBLISHED: Quarterly
COST: 1 yr.—$5.00.

CONTENTS: Contemporary poetry, fiction, and literary criticism from Africa, Asia, South America, Europe, Australia, the Middle East, as well as from North America. Example: U.S. Indian writings will make up the Summer, 1974, issue.

UNSOLICITED MSS. WELCOME? Yes.
GENERAL: First issue, February, 1974.

WESTERN HUMANITIES REVIEW

EDITORIAL ADDRESS:
Jack Garlington, Editor
University of Utah
Salt Lake City, Utah 84112

SUBSCRIPTION ADDRESS:
OSH 331
University of Utah
Salt Lake City, Utah 84112

PUBLISHED: Quarterly (Winter, Spring, Summer, Autumn)

CIRCULATION: 1,000

COST: 1 yr.—$5.00; straight yearly subscription only, up to 3 years in advance.

CONTENTS: Short stories; poetry; book and film reviews; articles on the humanities and related fields; a poetry column; an events in the humanities column. Examples: "Brecht: An Historical Perspective"; "Malamud's Trial: THE FIXER and the Critics."

UNSOLICITED MSS. WELCOME? Yes; submissions not acknowledged.
SPECIFICALLY WELCOMED: All kinds of contributions.
MS. LENGTH: No limits; submit ONE copy.
STYLE REQUIREMENTS: MLA STYLE SHEET.
COPYRIGHT: WESTERN HUMANITIES REVIEW.
EDITOR'S DECISION: 4-6 weeks.
FROM ACCEPTANCE TO PUBLICATION: 4-6 months.
PAYMENT/OFFPRINTS: Payment varies from $35 to $100 according to item. Twenty-five offprints for stories and articles provided; more can be ordered.
REJECTED MSS.: Returned.
GENERAL: First issue, 1947. Usual publication length, 100-120 pages.
BACK ISSUES: WHR has limited back issues at $1.50 each for 1970-1973 issues; $2.00 each for 1960-1969 issues; $3.00 each prior to 1960. Volumes 1-20 available from Johnson Reprint Corp. Also available on microfilm from Xerox University Microfilms.

THE WIDENING CIRCLE

EDITORIAL ADDRESS:
Richard R. Centing, Editor
111 West Hudson, Apt. 2-C
Columbus, Ohio 43202

SUBSCRIPTION ADDRESS:

same

PUBLISHED: Quarterly
COST: 1 yr.—$3.00.

CIRCULATION: 600

CONTENTS: Short stories, poetry, articles on modern literature. Prose example: "About Nijinsky's Diary." Recent issue was devoted to Gertrude Stein.

UNSOLICITED MSS. WELCOME? Yes; submissions acknowledged.
MS. LENGTH: 1,000 words; submit ONE copy.
COPYRIGHT: Author.
EDITOR'S DECISION: 2 months.
FROM ACCEPTANCE TO PUBLICATION: 4 months.
PAYMENT/OFFPRINTS: $5 to $15. Contributors receive 2 copies.
REJECTED MSS.: Returned.
GENERAL: First issue, Winter, 1973. Usual publication length, 24 pages.
BACK ISSUES: Available from editorial address at $.75 each.

WORKS: A QUARTERLY OF WRITING

EDITORIAL ADDRESS:
Lee Hatfield, Editor
AMS Press, Inc.
56 East 13th Street
New York, New York 10003

SUBSCRIPTION ADDRESS:

same

PUBLISHED: Quarterly
COST: $1.50 per issue; 4 issues—$5.00; 8 issues—$9.00; 12 issues—$12.50.

CIRCULATION: 2,500

CONTENTS: Poetry; fiction; drama; commentary; book reviews that are occasionally long critical essays, such as that on C.P. Cavafy; graphics; translations. Examples: "Literature of Dada"; essay on Maine poets.

UNSOLICITED MSS. WELCOME? Yes; submissions not acknowledged.
SPECIFICALLY WELCOMED: Poetry, fiction, translations of the highest quality.
MS. LENGTH: No set requirements; submit ONE copy.
STYLE REQUIREMENTS: No specific style requirements.
COPYRIGHT: WORKS retains first North American serial rights only.
EDITOR'S DECISION: 4-6 weeks.
FROM ACCEPTANCE TO PUBLICATION: 3-4 months.
PAYMENT/OFFPRINTS: Poetry, 25¢ a line ($10 minimum). Payment variable for prose.
REJECTED MSS.: Returned.

GENERAL: First issue, Fall, 1967. Usual publication length, 96-120 pages.
BACK ISSUES: Available from editorial office. Cost varies, depending on issue; prices on request.

X

GENERAL REVIEWS

(Essays from Various Fields included with some literary appraisals; poems or short stories on occasion)

THE ABERDEEN UNIVERSITY REVIEW

See the section on AGE AND/OR NATIONALITY: ENGLISH, AND BRITISH COMMONWEALTH for details.

ABRAXAS: A JOURNAL FOR THE THEORETICAL STUDY OF PHILOSOPHY, THE HUMANITIES, AND THE SOCIAL SCIENCES
(suspended publication)

EDITORIAL ADDRESS: SUBSCRIPTION ADDRESS:
Jorge García-Gómez, Editor
Humanities Division same
Southampton College
Southampton, New York 11968

PUBLISHED: Quarterly CIRCULATION: 600
COST: 1 yr.—$6.00 (students); $8.00 (individuals); $10.00 (libraries).

CONTENTS: Essays, studies, reviews, bibliographies on philosophy, the humanities, and social sciences.

GENERAL: First issue, 1970; ceased publication, Spring, 1971. Usual publication length, 100 pages.
BACK ISSUES: Available from editor at $3.00 each.

AGORA: A JOURNAL IN THE HUMANITIES AND SOCIAL SCIENCES

EDITORIAL ADDRESS: SUBSCRIPTION ADDRESS:
Martin A. Bertman and
Onnik K. Keshishian, Editors same
State University of New York
College at Potsdam
Potsdam, New York 13676

PUBLISHED: Biannually (Fall, Spring) CIRCULATION: 1,200
COST: 1 yr.—$4.00.

CONTENTS: Philosophical and critical examination of problems in wide ranging fields; book reviews. Example: "Bananas, Anti-Imperialism and Miguel Angel Asturias."

UNSOLICITED MSS. WELCOME? Yes; submissions acknowledged.
SPECIFICALLY WELCOMED: Researched articles; no "creative" writing.
MS. LENGTH: 15-20 pages; submit ONE copy.
STYLE REQUIREMENTS: MLA STYLE SHEET; footnotes follow essay.
COPYRIGHT: AGORA.

EDITOR'S DECISION: 2 months.
FROM ACCEPTANCE TO PUBLICATION: 1 year.
PAYMENT/OFFPRINTS: Twelve issues of journal.
REJECTED MSS.: Returned.
GENERAL: First issue, Spring, 1970. Usual publication length, 90 pages.
BACK ISSUES: Available from editorial office at $3.00 each.

THE AMERICAN SCHOLAR: A QUARTERLY FOR THE INDEPENDENT THINKER

EDITORIAL ADDRESS:
Hiram Haydn, Editor
1811 Q Street, N.W.
Washington, D.C. 20009

SUBSCRIPTION ADDRESS:

same

PUBLISHED: Quarterly CIRCULATION: 45,000
COST: 1 yr.—$6.50; 2 yrs.—$11.00; 3 yrs.—$15.00.

CONTENTS: Articles on art, politics, literature, social sciences, history.

UNSOLICITED MSS. WELCOME? Yes; submissions acknowledged.
SPECIFICALLY WELCOMED: No fiction.
MS. LENGTH: 3,500-4,000 words; submit ONE OR TWO copies.
COPYRIGHT: AMERICAN SCHOLAR, unless author wants it.
EDITOR'S DECISION: 2-3 weeks.
FROM ACCEPTANCE TO PUBLICATION: Up to 1 year.
PAYMENT/OFFPRINTS: $150 for articles; $35 for poems. Offprints charged per 100 copies according to number of pages.
REJECTED MSS.: Returned.
GENERAL: First issue, 1932. Usual publication length, 150-170 pages.
BACK ISSUES: Available from editorial office. Price varies, depending on date.

ANTHELION

EDITORIAL ADDRESS:
R. W. Whitney, Editor
P. O. Box 21441
Dallas, Texas 75211

SUBSCRIPTION ADDRESS:

same

PUBLISHED: Quarterly CIRCULATION: 2,800-3,200
COST: 1 yr.—$5.00 for individuals; $10.00 for institutions. Two-year discount of 10%.

CONTENTS: Articles about the fields of literature, social commentary, and philosophy; striving for the best in new literary talents, reviews, articles, and commentary concerning the current scene. Example: "Sartre and Marcel: On Love."

UNSOLICITED MSS. WELCOME? Yes; submissions not acknowledged.
SPECIFICALLY WELCOMED: Articles and fiction; looking for the original in style and content.
MS. LENGTH: 2,500 words maximum; submit ONE copy.
STYLE REQUIREMENTS: None.
COPYRIGHT: Anthelion Press.
EDITOR'S DECISION: 4-6 weeks.
FROM ACCEPTANCE TO PUBLICATION: 2-4 months.
PAYMENT/OFFPRINTS: Payment schedule ranges from contributors copies to 5-7½¢ per word. Offprints for $.10 a page.
REJECTED MSS.: Returned.
GENERAL: First issue, Fall, 1971. Usual publication length, 32-48 pages.
BACK ISSUES: Available from Anthelion Press, above address, at $2.00 each. Very limited on back issue copies.

THE ANTIOCH REVIEW

EDITORIAL ADDRESS:
Lawrence Grauman, Jr., Editor
Antioch Press
Yellow Springs, Ohio 45387

SUBSCRIPTION ADDRESS:
P.O. Box 148
Yellow Springs, Ohio 45387

PUBLISHED: Quarterly
CIRCULATION: 6,000
COST: 1 yr.—$6.00; 2 yrs.—$11.00; 3 yrs.—$16.00; single copy—$1.75.

CONTENTS: Critical and creative prose; features lively cultural analysis, fiction, poetry, parody, polemics, reviews and regular editorial columns; only occasional articles on literature. Once or twice a year a special issue gathers a group of articles on a topic of contemporary interest and importance. Contributors include unknown as well as established American and foreign writers.

UNSOLICITED MSS. WELCOME? Yes; submissions not acknowledged unless requested.
MS. LENGTH: 2,000-8,000 words; submit TWO copies.
STYLE REQUIREMENTS: Must be exceptionally well-written; use University of Chicago's A MANUAL OF STYLE.
COPYRIGHT: THE ANTIOCH REVIEW.
EDITOR'S DECISION: 3-8 weeks.
FROM ACCEPTANCE TO PUBLICATION: 3-6 months.
PAYMENT/OFFPRINTS: $8 per printed page, payable upon publication. Offprints provided at cost upon request.
REJECTED MSS.: Returned.
GENERAL: First issue, Spring, 1941. Usual publication length, 160 pages.
BACK ISSUES: Recent ones available from editorial address; older ones from A.M.S. Reprint Co. Prices vary with the issue; prices available upon request.

ARTES LIBERALES (formerly ARTS AND LETTERS)

EDITORIAL ADDRESS:
Edwin W. Gaston, Jr., Editor
School of Liberal Arts
Stephen F. Austin State University
Nacogdoches, Texas 75961

SUBSCRIPTION ADDRESS:

same

PUBLISHED: Biannually (Fall, Spring)   CIRCULATION: 1,000
COST: 1 yr.—$3.00.

CONTENTS: Articles from all intellectual disciplines ordinarily associated with liberal arts; original poems and stories. Editor plans to devote one issue a year to humanistic studies and one issue a year to behavioral scientific studies, interlacing each issue with poems and stories. Example: "The Curse of Kafka."

UNSOLICITED MSS. WELCOME? Yes; submissions acknowledged upon receipt.
MS. LENGTH: Up to 10,000 words.
STYLE REQUIREMENTS: MLA STYLE SHEET.
COPYRIGHT: Author.
EDITOR'S DECISION: 1 month.
FROM ACCEPTANCE TO PUBLICATION: 1-6 months.
PAYMENT/OFFPRINTS: Three copies of the journal, but no offprints of an article, will be furnished the author.
REJECTED MSS.: Returned, with explanation.
GENERAL: First issue, Spring, 1968, as ARTS AND LETTERS; Fall, 1973, as ARTES LIBERALES. Usual publication length, 60 pages.
BACK ISSUES: Available from the editor at $1.50 each.

ARTS IN SOCIETY

EDITORIAL ADDRESS:
Edward L. Kamarack, Editor
Room 728 Lowell Hall
610 Langdon Street
University of Wisconsin—Extension
Madison, Wisconsin 53706

SUBSCRIPTION ADDRESS:

same

PUBLISHED: Tri-annually   CIRCULATION: 4,500
COST: 1 yr.—$7.50; 2 yrs.—$14.00; 3 yrs.—$20.00; foreign, add $1.00 per year for postage.

CONTENTS: Articles that discuss, interpret, and illustrate the various functions of the arts in contemporary civilization, and that present the insights of experience, research and theory in support of educational and organizational efforts to enhance the position of the arts in America; photographs and reproductions of art. Essay example: "Humanism for Our Time."

UNSOLICITED MSS. WELCOME? Yes, but it is usually good to query first; submissions not acknowledged.
SPECIFICALLY WELCOMED: Articles dealing with four areas—the teaching and learning of the arts; aesthetics and philosophy; social analysis; and other examples of creative expression.
MS. LENGTH: 3,000-4,000 words; submit ONE copy.
STYLE REQUIREMENTS: No special requirements.
COPYRIGHT: ARTS IN SOCIETY.
EDITOR'S DECISION: 1-2 months.
FROM ACCEPTANCE TO PUBLICATION: 3-6 months.
PAYMENT/OFFPRINTS: Honorarium. Offprints available at cost.
REJECTED MSS.: Returned.
GENERAL: First issue, 1958. Usual publication length, 160 pages. Indexed by volume.
BACK ISSUES: Vols. 1-5 available from Johnson Reprints Corp.; Vols. 6-present from editorial offices. Price varies; query.

THE ARYAN PATH

EDITORIAL ADDRESS:
Sophia Wadia, Editor
40 New Marine Lines
Bombay 400 020
India

SUBSCRIPTION ADDRESS:
Business Department
Theosophy Hall
same

PUBLISHED: Monthly (but no issue in June or July)
COST: 1 yr.—$5.50; single copy—$.65.

CIRCULATION: 800-900

CONTENTS: Study and comparison of ancient and modern, Eastern and Western ideas and of mystical, philosophical, literary, and social reformist perspectives.

UNSOLICITED MSS. WELCOME? Yes; preferable to discuss scope with editor beforehand; submissions acknowledged unless decision is made soon.
SPECIFICALLY WELCOMED: Comparative religion and philosophy; East-West relations; literary criticism, not too technical; social and educational problems.
MS. LENGTH: 1,800-2,400 words; submit ONE copy (no carbon).
STYLE REQUIREMENTS: Must be intelligible to eastern and western readers, educated and not necessarily scholarly.
COPYRIGHT: THE ARYAN PATH has first-publication and reprint rights; author may reprint elsewhere acknowledging previous publication in TAP.
EDITOR'S DECISION: 1 week to 1 month.
FROM ACCEPTANCE TO PUBLICATION: 1-5 months.
PAYMENT/OFFPRINTS: Payment by arrangement and on acceptance in India and U.K. only. Up to 6 offprints free on request; further copies at cost.
REJECTED MSS.: Returned.
GENERAL: First issue, January, 1930. Usual publication length, 48 pages.

BACK ISSUES: Available from Business Department at following prices: from 1930-1963 (Vols. 1-34), $6.00 per volume or $.70 per issue; from 1964-1971 (vols. 35-42), $10.00 per volume or $1.20 per issue; from 1971 onwards, $11.00 per volume or $1.30 per issue.

THE ATLANTIC MONTHLY

EDITORIAL ADDRESS:
Robert Manning, Editor-in-Chief
8 Arlington Street
Boston, Massachusetts 02116

SUBSCRIPTION ADDRESS:

same

PUBLISHED: Monthly
COST: 1 yr.—$11.50; single copy—$1.00.

CIRCULATION: 325,000

CONTENTS: Articles on literature and public affairs, the arts, and other antic pursuits, which assume on the part of its readers a modest sophistication in literary and political matters, and a willingness to be challenged by tendentious and sometimes conflicting points of view.

UNSOLICITED MSS. WELCOME? Yes; submissions from agents and some others acknowledged.
SPECIFICALLY WELCOMED: Art, biography, economics, education, history, humanities, journalism, literary and political reviews, literature, music, political science, psychology, science, sociology.
MS. LENGTH: 2,000-5,000 words; submit ONE copy.
STYLE REQUIREMENTS: Consult past issues.
COPYRIGHT: AM buys first-serial rights. Copyright reverts to author.
EDITOR'S DECISION: 4-8 weeks.
FROM ACCEPTANCE TO PUBLICATION: Immediate to several months.
PAYMENT/OFFPRINTS: Approximately $100 per page, but depends on quality and length.
REJECTED MSS.: Returned.
GENERAL: First issue, November, 1857. Usual publication length, 116-138 pages.
BACK ISSUES: Available from editorial address at original cost of issue.

BOSTON UNIVERSITY JOURNAL: SCHOLARLY PERIODICAL WITH ARTICLES OF GENERAL INTEREST

EDITORIAL ADDRESS:
Paul Kurt Ackermann, Editor
Boston University Graduate School
Box 357, Boston University Station
Boston, Massachusetts 02215

SUBSCRIPTION ADDRESS:

same

PUBLISHED: Tri-annually   CIRCULATION: 3,000
COST: 1 yr.—$5.50; single copy—$1.95.

CONTENTS: Articles from scholars and experts in various fields, as well as literary criticism, poetry, and graphic art. Examples: "Artaud as Playwright"; "Octavio Paz: Roots and Branches."

UNSOLICITED MSS. WELCOME? Yes; submissions acknowledged.
SPECIFICALLY WELCOMED: Material of relatively lasting importance written so that it is appealing and understandable to a general intelligent audience.
MS. LENGTH: 15-25 pages; submit ONE copy.
STYLE REQUIREMENTS: Clarity.
COPYRIGHT: By arrangement.
EDITOR'S DECISION: 6 weeks.
FROM ACCEPTANCE TO PUBLICATION: 3 months.
PAYMENT/OFFPRINTS: 20 copies of issue. Journal will arrange for offprints.
REJECTED MSS.: Returned.
GENERAL: First issue, Winter, 1966. Usual publication length, 72 pages.
BACK ISSUES: Available from editorial office at $1.00 each.

BUCKNELL REVIEW: A SCHOLARLY JOURNAL OF LETTERS, ARTS AND SCIENCES

EDITORIAL ADDRESS: SUBSCRIPTION ADDRESS:
Harry R. Garvin, Editor
Chairman of the English Department   same
Bucknell University
Lewisburg, Pennsylvania 17837

PUBLISHED: Tri-annually

CONTENTS: Scholarly and interdisciplinary articles for both the specialist and the generalist.

UNSOLICITED MSS. WELCOME? Yes; submissions acknowledged.
SPECIFICALLY WELCOMED: Humanistic, critical, and philosophical approaches to the arts and sciences are preferred.
MS. LENGTH: 12-25 pages; submit ONE copy.
STYLE REQUIREMENTS: MLA STYLE SHEET.
COPYRIGHT: BUCKNELL REVIEW.
EDITOR'S DECISION: 2-4 weeks.
FROM ACCEPTANCE TO PUBLICATION: Within 1 year.
PAYMENT/OFFPRINTS: Two copies of REVIEW; 5 offprints; nominal charges for additional ones.
REJECTED MSS.: Returned.
GENERAL: First issue, 1940. Usual publication length, 150 pages.
BACK ISSUES: Available from Ellen Clarke Bertrand Library, Bucknell University, at $2.50 each.

CAMBRIDGE REVIEW

EDITORIAL ADDRESS:
The Editor
7 Green Street
Cambridge CB2 3JU
England

SUBSCRIPTION ADDRESS:

same

PUBLISHED: Biannually   CIRCULATION: 2,500

CONTENTS: Articles and reviews on literary, historical, political, and philosophical figures and themes.

UNSOLICITED MSS. WELCOME? Yes, but material usually commissioned; submissions acknowledged.
MS. LENGTH: 2,500 words; submit ONE copy.
STYLE REQUIREMENTS: Standard.
COPYRIGHT: CAMBRIDGE REVIEW.
EDITOR'S DECISION: 1 month.
FROM ACCEPTANCE TO PUBLICATION: Not more than 6 months.
PAYMENT/OFFPRINTS: Copies of journal provided.
REJECTED MSS.: Returned.
GENERAL: First issue, 1879. Usual publication length, 32 pages.
BACK ISSUES: Available from editorial address.

THE CHRISTIAN CENTURY

EDITORIAL ADDRESS:
James M. Wall, Editor
407 South Dearborn Street
Chicago, Illinois 60605

SUBSCRIPTION ADDRESS:

same

PUBLISHED: Weekly   CIRCULATION: 30,000
COST: 1 yr.—$12.00; 2 yrs.—$20.00; 3 yrs.—$27.00.

CONTENTS: Information, intelligent articles, reviews aimed at the liberal Protestant background. Examples: "Film Repression in Eastern Europe"; "The New Arts in Europe"; "Teachings of Don Juan from a Buddhist Perspective."

UNSOLICITED MSS. WELCOME? Yes; submissions acknowledged.
SPECIFICALLY WELCOMED: Interpretative articles where theology and culture intersect.
MS. LENGTH: 500-2,500 words; submit ONE copy.
COPYRIGHT: THE CHRISTIAN CENTURY.
EDITOR'S DECISION: 3-4 weeks.
FROM ACCEPTANCE TO PUBLICATION: 6-8 weeks.
PAYMENT/OFFPRINTS: Payment varies. Offprints at cost.
REJECTED MSS.: Returned.
GENERAL: First issue, 1900. Usual publication length, 24 and 32 pages.

BACK ISSUES: Available from editorial address at $.50 each; complete year at $14.00.

COMMENTARY

EDITORIAL ADDRESS:
Norman Podhoretz, Editor
165 East 56th Street
New York, New York 10022

SUBSCRIPTION ADDRESS:

same

PUBLISHED: Monthly   CIRCULATION: 65,000
COST: 1 yr.—$12.00; single copy—$1.25.

CONTENTS: Articles on general, political and cultural subjects; some fiction; articles on matters of Jewish concern; book reviews; and shorter "observations."

UNSOLICITED MSS. WELCOME? Yes; submissions not acknowledged.
SPECIFICALLY WELCOMED: Fiction; serious literary criticism.
MS. LENGTH: Articles—5,000-7,000 words; book reviews—2,000 words; submit ONE copy.
STYLE REQUIREMENTS: No specific style requirement.
COPYRIGHT: American Jewish Committee.
EDITOR'S DECISION: 4-6 weeks.
FROM ACCEPTANCE TO PUBLICATION: Usually within 6 months.
PAYMENT/OFFPRINTS: $150 for book review; $350 to $500 for article. Up to six copies free.
REJECTED MSS.: Returned.
GENERAL: First issue, November, 1946. Usual publication length, 96 pages.
BACK ISSUES: Not generally available except for recent (6 months to a year) issues—$1.50 each.

COMMONWEAL

EDITORIAL ADDRESS:
James O'Gara, Editor
232 Madison Avenue
New York, New York 10016

SUBSCRIPTION ADDRESS:
Andrea Coar, Circulation Manager
same

PUBLISHED: Weekly, bi-weekly June   CIRCULATION: 27,000
through mid-Sept.
COST: 1 yr.—$14.00; special 17 week trial subscription—$3.00.

CONTENTS: Articles on public affairs, literature, and the arts, edited by Catholic laymen; strong film review section; book reviews.

UNSOLICITED MSS. WELCOME? Yes, if of pertinent interest to reading public; submissions acknowledged.
SPECIFICALLY WELCOMED: Poetry; non-fictional pieces concerning today's topics of interest (no fictional work).
MS. LENGTH: 1,500 words at most; submit ONE copy.
COPYRIGHT: Commonweal Publishing Co., Inc.
EDITOR'S DECISION: Varies.
FROM ACCEPTANCE TO PUBLICATION: Varies.
PAYMENT/OFFPRINTS: Set amount of payment for set length. Two copies free of charge, usually, maybe more.
REJECTED MSS.: Returned.
GENERAL: First issue, November, 1924. Usual publication length, 24 pages.
BACK ISSUES: Available from circulation manager at $.40 each, plus postage and handling, if they are in stock; if not, from Xerox University Microfilms.

THE CRESSET: A REVIEW OF LITERATURE, THE ARTS, AND PUBLIC AFFAIRS.

EDITORIAL ADDRESS:
Kenneth F. Korby, Editor
Valparaiso University Press
Valparaiso University
Valparaiso, Indiana 46383

SUBSCRIPTION ADDRESS:

same

PUBLISHED: Monthly, except July, August
COST: 1 yr.—$3.00; 2 yrs.—$5.50; students—$1.00.

CIRCULATION: 5,500

CONTENTS: Essays exploring issues and questions relating to the general areas of study in the University; topics that lend themselves to theological discussion; a representative sermon from the University chapel; reviews of books, films, recordings, and theater; articles on law and ethics, politics and urban life, education and teaching; items of value to churches. Example: "Gorky and Beckett: Bitterness and Despair."

UNSOLICITED MSS. WELCOME? Yes; submissions acknowledged.
SPECIFICALLY WELCOMED: Where solid exploration on topics can be expressed in such a way that people who do not use conceptual, abstract language in their daily work can find materials for thought and reflection.
MS. LENGTH: 5-10 pages; submit ONE copy.
STYLE REQUIREMENTS: University of Chicago's A MANUAL OF STYLE.
COPYRIGHT: Valparaiso University Press.
EDITOR'S DECISION: 1-2 months.
FROM ACCEPTANCE TO PUBLICATION: 6 months.
PAYMENT/OFFPRINTS: $5.00 per printed page. Ten copies of issue; up to 30 will be given if desired.
REJECTED MSS.: Returned.
GENERAL: First issue, November, 1937. Usual publication length, 28 pages.
BACK ISSUES: Available from editorial address at $.35 each.

CULTURAL HERMENEUTICS: AN INTERNATIONAL JOURNAL FOR THE PHILOSOPHICAL INTERPRETATIONS OF THE SPECIAL LANGUAGES OF THE HUMAN SCIENCES

EDITORIAL ADDRESS:
David M. Rasmussen, Editor
Department of Philosophy
Boston College
Chestnut Hill, Massachusetts 02167

SUBSCRIPTION ADDRESS:
D. Reidel Publishing Co.
P.O. Box 17
Dordrecht
Holland

PUBLISHED: Quarterly
COST: 1 yr.—$26.78 in U.S. (D fl. 75,—).

CIRCULATION: 400

CONTENTS: Articles of critical social and cultural theory; book reviews; index.

UNSOLICITED MSS. WELCOME? Yes; submissions acknowledged.
SPECIFICALLY WELCOMED: Any contributions will be considered which relate to the meaning, interpretation, or transformation of the social and cultural contexts of life.
MS. LENGTH: 20-30 pages; submit ONE copy.
STYLE REQUIREMENTS: No specific requirements.
COPYRIGHT: Reidel, the publisher.
EDITOR'S DECISION: About 1 month.
FROM ACCEPTANCE TO PUBLICATION: About 3 or 4 months.
PAYMENT/OFFPRINTS: 25 free offprints.
REJECTED MSS.: Returned.
GENERAL: First issue, 1970. Usual publication length, 100 pages.
BACK ISSUES: From D. Reidel Publishing Co.; inquire about cost.

DURHAM UNIVERSITY JOURNAL

EDITORIAL ADDRESS:
M. E. James, Editor
43 North Bailey
University of Durham
Durham, England

SUBSCRIPTION ADDRESS:
University of Durham
Old Shire Hall
Durham, England

CIRCULATION: 750-800
COST: 1 yr.—£1.15; single copy—35 n.p.

CONTENTS: Scholarly essays on literature, history, philosophy and theology. Articles on science, sociology, and political thought are also included. Ample space is given to specialist reviews of books which cover a wide range of topics. Examples: "The Method of Auden's "The Orators' "; "Tennyson and Evolution."

UNSOLICITED MSS. WELCOME? Yes; submissions acknowledged.
MS. LENGTH: 8,000-10,000 words; submit ONE copy.

STYLE REQUIREMENTS: Scholarly, with footnotes and detailed bibliographical references.
EDITOR'S DECISION: 2-3 months.
FROM ACCEPTANCE TO PUBLICATION: 12 months.
PAYMENT/OFFPRINTS: Contributors receive 25 free offprints.
REJECTED MSS.: Returned.
GENERAL: First issue, 1876. Usual publication length, 100 pages.
BACK ISSUES: Available from subscription address at 35 n.p. each. Microfilms of past issues, 1876-1967, available from University Microfilms.

ENGLISH MISCELLANY: A SYMPOSIUM OF HISTORY, LITERATURE AND THE ARTS

See the section on AGE AND/OR NATIONALITY: ENGLISH, AND BRITISH COMMONWEALTH for details.

FORUM

EDITORIAL ADDRESS:
William Lee Pryor, Editor
English Department
University of Houston
Cullen Boulevard
Houston, Texas

SUBSCRIPTION ADDRESS:

same

PUBLISHED: Tri-annually
COST: 1 yr.—$3.00; single copy—$1.00.

CONTENTS: Articles in the humanities, the fine arts, and the sciences; also some bearing on business and technology (but not specialized interests involving highly technical or special vocabularies). Generally an art section is devoted to photographs, variously, of paintings, drawing, architecture.

UNSOLICITED MSS. WELCOME? Yes; submissions acknowledged.
SPECIFICALLY WELCOMED: Both the scholarly approach and originality.
MS. LENGTH: 12-15 pages; submit ONE copy.
STYLE REQUIREMENTS: University of Chicago's A MANUAL OF STYLE and Kate Turabian's manual.
COPYRIGHT: Writer.
EDITOR'S DECISION: 1 or 2 months.
FROM ACCEPTANCE TO PUBLICATION: 7 months.
PAYMENT/OFFPRINTS: Ten copies of magazine; up to 50 offprints.
REJECTED MSS.: Returned.
GENERAL: First issue, 1956. Usual publication length, 48 pages.
BACK ISSUES: Limited supply available from editorial address at $1.00 each.

FURMAN STUDIES

EDITORIAL ADDRESS:
Alfred S. Reid, Editor
Department of English
Furman University
Greenville, South Carolina 29613

SUBSCRIPTION ADDRESS:

same

PUBLISHED: Biannually
COST: Free on request.

CIRCULATION: 300

CONTENTS: Interdisciplinary scholarship—articles in any discipline, such as art, chemistry, economics, education, engineering, English, geology, history, library science, modern languages, music, philosophy, political science, psychology, religion, sociology, theater. Example: "Melville's Reading of Dante."

UNSOLICITED MSS. WELCOME? Yes, but space is limited; submissions not acknowledged.
SPECIFICALLY WELCOMED: Worthwhile scholarship.
MS. LENGTH: 15 pages maximum; submit ONE copy.
STYLE REQUIREMENTS: Those applicable to the best practice in a discipline.
COPYRIGHT: FURMAN STUDIES, but will transfer on request.
EDITOR'S DECISION: 2 weeks.
FROM ACCEPTANCE TO PUBLICATION: 6 months to 1 year.
PAYMENT/OFFPRINTS: Extra copies of issue.
REJECTED MSS.: Returned.
GENERAL: First issue, May, 1928. Usual publication length, 30 to 50 pages.
BACK ISSUES: Available from Editor or from Furman librarian at no cost.

HARPER'S MAGAZINE

EDITORIAL ADDRESS:
Robert Shnayerson, Editor-in-Chief
2 Park Avenue
New York, New York 10016

SUBSCRIPTION ADDRESS:
381 West Center Street
Marion, Ohio 43302

PUBLISHED: Monthly
COST: 1 yr.—$8.50; 3 yrs.—$21.00.

CIRCULATION: 325,000

CONTENTS: Articles on a variety of subjects: politics, science, education, personalities, literary matters, the arts, entertainment, business, travel, foreign affairs. Usually publish one piece of notable fiction per month; some poetry. Special departments: Wraparound, Commentary, Letters, Contest, Countersigns (written by the Editors).

UNSOLICITED MSS. WELCOME? Not without query first (except poetry). Send a 300 word specific summary to Queries Editor. Submissions not acknowledged.

SPECIFICALLY WELCOMED: Articles; essays; short stories; poetry.
MS. LENGTH: Articles—2,000-5,000 words; fiction—2,000-4,000 words; commentary—750 words; submit ORIGINAL.
STYLE REQUIREMENTS: Editors seek the highest quality writing.
COPYRIGHT: HARPER'S MAGAZINE, but copyright will be reassigned upon request.
EDITOR'S DECISION: 3 weeks.
FROM ACCEPTANCE TO PUBLICATION: At least 2 months; can be much longer.
PAYMENT/OFFPRINTS: Payment varies according to piece. Two copies of magazine. Offprints if author purchases them.
REJECTED MSS.: Returned.
GENERAL: Usual publication length, 115 pages (including advertising).
BACK ISSUES: Available from Back Issues Department at editorial address at $1.25 each paid in advance.

THE HUMANIST

EDITORIAL ADDRESS:
Paul Kurtz, Editor
923 Kensington Avenue
Buffalo, New York 14215

SUBSCRIPTION ADDRESS:
Patricia Pliss
same

PUBLISHED: Bi-monthly
CIRCULATION: 23,000
COST: 1 yr.—$7.00; 2 yrs.—$12.00; 3 yrs.—$16.50; single copy—$1.25.

CONTENTS: Articles dealing with moral and social matters from a humanistic and secular viewpoint; editorials; poetry; ethical forums; film reviews; book reviews; drama critiques, such as "A Black Cherry Orchard" and "Intimations of Revolution."

UNSOLICITED MSS. WELCOME? Yes; submissions acknowledged.
SPECIFICALLY WELCOMED: Articles on contemporary moral problems. Topics include ecclesiastical affairs, cultural affairs, education, literature, philosophy.
MS. LENGTH: 2,000-3,000 words.
STYLE REQUIREMENTS: New York TIMES style book.
COPYRIGHT: THE HUMANIST.
EDITOR'S DECISION: 4-8 weeks.
FROM ACCEPTANCE TO PUBLICATION: 2 months to 1 year.
PAYMENT/OFFPRINTS: Minimum $50.00. Five copies of issue furnished; offprints on request.
REJECTED MSS.: Returned.
GENERAL: First issue, 1940. Usual publication length, 48 pages.
BACK ISSUES: Available from subscription address at $2.00 each or from Johnson Reprint Corp.

ILLINOIS QUARTERLY (formerly ILLINOIS STATE UNIVERSITY JOURNAL)

EDITORIAL ADDRESS:
Editor
Illinois State University
Normal, Illinois 61761

SUBSCRIPTION ADDRESS:

same

PUBLISHED: Quarterly (Sept., Dec., Feb., Apr.)
COST: Free, at present.

CONTENTS: Articles on areas of literature, social sciences, education, the humanities, and other disciplines. Example: "Hardy's Poetic Technique."

UNSOLICITED MSS. WELCOME? Yes.
SPECIFICALLY WELCOMED: Manuscripts of merit on all topics, not purely Illinois topics. Writers do not need to have an Illinois connection.
MS. LENGTH: No preference; submit TWO copies.
STYLE REQUIREMENTS: MLA STYLE SHEET.
GENERAL: First issue, 1938, as TEACHER EDUCATION: 1964, as THE ILLINOIS STATE UNIVERSITY JOURNAL; 1970, as ILLINOIS QUARTERLY. Usual publication length, 64 pages.

JOURNAL OF JEWISH STUDIES

See the section on AGE AND/OR NATIONALITY: AFRICAN, CARIBBEAN, LATIN AMERICAN, AND NEAR EASTERN for details.

KANSAS QUARTERLY

See the section on AGE AND/OR NATIONALITY: AMERICAN for details.

KOVAVE: JOURNAL OF NEW GUINEA LITERATURE

See the section on AGE AND/OR NATIONALITY: ENGLISH, AND BRITISH COMMONWEALTH for details.

LUSO-BRAZILIAN REVIEW: DEVOTED TO THE CULTURE OF THE
PORTUGUESE SPEAKING WORLD

See the section on AGE AND/OR NATIONALITY: AFRICAN, CARIBBEAN, LATIN AMERICAN, AND NEAR EASTERN for details.

THE MAGAZINE OF FURTHER STUDIES

EDITORIAL ADDRESS:
George Butterick, John Clarke,
Albert Glover, Editor
The Institute of Further Studies
Buffalo, New York

SUBSCRIPTION ADDRESS:

same

CONTENTS: Poetry; research; studies (for example, "a poem can become a bibliographical note on Pleistocene Man.") Issues often center around theme, such as one devoted to Olson and his work.

UNSOLICITED MSS. WELCOME? Consult editors.
GENERAL: First issue, Spring, 1965.
BACK ISSUES: Numbers 1-6 available on microfilm (one reel—$7.50) from Walter J. Johnson, Inc.

MICHIGAN ACADEMICIAN: PAPERS OF THE MICHIGAN ACADEMY
OF SCIENCE, ARTS, AND LETTERS

EDITORIAL ADDRESS:
Ronald L. Trowbridge, Editor
2117 Washtenaw Avenue
Ann Arbor, Michigan 48104

SUBSCRIPTION ADDRESS:

same

PUBLISHED: Quarterly (Summer, Fall, Winter, Spring)
CIRCULATION: 2,500
COST: 1 yr.—$12.00, individuals; $15.00, libraries; $10.00, institutional members.

CONTENTS: Articles that cover academic fields of science, arts, and letters; books reviews. Example: "The End of the World in Medieval Art and Drama."

UNSOLICITED MSS. WELCOME? No. Paper must be read at annual convention of MASAL. Membership required for publication.
SPECIFICALLY WELCOMED: Articles from all academic fields.
MS. LENGTH: 5-20 pages; submit TWO copies.
STYLE REQUIREMENTS: Consistent with respective discipline.
COPYRIGHT: MICHIGAN ACADEMICIAN.
EDITOR'S DECISION: 2-4 months.

FROM ACCEPTANCE TO PUBLICATION: 3-12 months.
PAYMENT/OFFPRINTS: No payment. Offprints available at cost.
REJECTED MSS.: Returned.
GENERAL: First issue, Winter, 1969. Usual publication length, 128 pages.
BACK ISSUES: Available from editorial address at $4.00 each.

THE MIDWEST QUARTERLY: A JOURNAL OF CONTEMPORARY THOUGHT

EDITORIAL ADDRESS:
Rebecca Patterson, Editor-in-Chief
Kansas State College of Pittsburg
Pittsburg, Kansas 66762

SUBSCRIPTION ADDRESS:

same

PUBLISHED: Quarterly (Jan., Apr., July, Oct.)
COST: 1 yr.—$2.50 (10% discount to recognized agents); single copy—$1.00.

CONTENTS: Scholarly, analytical articles with a broad range of subjects of current interest, predominantly history, political science, literature, humanities in general; poetry. Examples: "A Chaser of Phantoms: Mark Twain and Romanticism"; "Spark and Waugh: Similarities by Coincidence."

UNSOLICITED MSS. WELCOME? Yes.
SPECIFICALLY WELCOMED: Articles on subjects of contemporary significance. Articles should be interesting and readable—analytic, speculative, not heavily documented or overspecialized.
MS. LENGTH: 5,000 words maximum; submit the ORIGINAL.
COPYRIGHT: THE MIDWEST QUARTERLY, Kansas State College of Pittsburg.
PAYMENT/OFFPRINTS: Payment in copies of issue only; no offprints.
GENERAL: First issue, 1959. Usual publication length, 15-20 pages.
BACK ISSUES: Available from editorial address at $1.00 each (a few early issues are out of print); also from University Microfilms, Inc.

THE NATION

EDITORIAL ADDRESS:
Carey McWilliams, Editor
333 Sixth Avenue
New York, New York 10014

SUBSCRIPTION ADDRESS:

same

PUBLISHED: Weekly (except biweekly in July, Aug.) CIRCULATION: 30,000
COST: 1 yr.—$15.00; 2 yrs.—$27.50; add $1 per year postage for Canada and Mexico; $2 elsewhere; single copy—$.50.

CONTENTS: Articles on social issues, education, the law, labor, consumer subjects, foreign policy, racial issues, environmental topics, science; reviews of books, theatre, films, art, music, dance.

UNSOLICITED MSS. WELCOME? Yes; submissions acknowledged.
SPECIFICALLY WELCOMED: Book reviews; poetry.
MS. LENGTH: 1,000-2,500 words; submit ONE copy.
COPYRIGHT: Reassigned to author upon request.
EDITOR'S DECISION: 1-3 weeks.
FROM ACCEPTANCE TO PUBLICATION: Varies.
PAYMENT/OFFPRINTS: $30 to $50 for book reviews. Offprints sent automatically.
REJECTED MSS.: Returned.
GENERAL: First issue, July, 1865. Usual publication length, 32 pages.
BACK ISSUES: If available, from publication office at $.50 each.

NATIONAL REVIEW

EDITORIAL ADDRESS:
William F. Buckley, Jr., Editor
150 East 35th Street
New York, New York 10016

SUBSCRIPTION ADDRESS:
Circulation Manager
same

PUBLISHED: Fortnightly
COST: 1 yr.—$14.00; single copy—$.50.

CIRCULATION: 120,000-130,000

CONTENTS: Political and social analysis; comments on current affairs; reviews of books, music, theatre, art—from a conservative viewpoint.

UNSOLICITED MSS. WELCOME? Yes; submissions acknowledged.
SPECIFICALLY WELCOMED: Articles dealing with some current topic of political or sociological interest; short humorous fillers.
MS. LENGTH: Articles, 1,000-5,000 words; humorous fillers, under 700 words; submit ONE copy.
STYLE REQUIREMENTS: Good English prose; non-technical enough to be understood by a layman.
COPYRIGHT: National Review.
EDITOR'S DECISION: 1 month.
FROM ACCEPTANCE TO PUBLICATION: Up to 1 year.
PAYMENT/OFFPRINTS: $75 per 1,000 words. Extra copies of magazine at cost.
REJECTED MSS.: Returned.
GENERAL: First issue, November, 1955. Usual publication length, 44-60 pages.
BACK ISSUES: Available from NATIONAL REVIEW's Research Library at above address at $.50 each.

NEW STATESMAN

EDITORIAL ADDRESS:
Anthony Howard, Editor
10 Great Turnstile
London WC1V 7HJ
England

SUBSCRIPTION ADDRESS:

same

PUBLISHED: Weekly CIRCULATION: 64,300
COST: 1 yr.—$21.00 or £8.50 by surface mail; $28.00 to North America, £10.25 to Europe by air mail; single copy—$.60 or 15p.

CONTENTS: Articles for a radical journal of opinion dealing with literature, the arts, and politics; book reviews.

UNSOLICITED MSS. WELCOME? No. All articles and book reviews are commissioned.
GENERAL: First issue, April, 1913.
BACK ISSUES: Available from editorial address at 20p to 30p each, and on microfilm from Xerox University Microfilms.

RESEARCH STUDIES

EDITORIAL ADDRESS:
Henry Grosshans, Editor
Washington State University
Pullman, Washington 99163

SUBSCRIPTION ADDRESS:

same

PUBLISHED: Quarterly CIRCULATION: 900
COST: 1 yr.—$4.00.

CONTENTS: Articles and shorter commentaries upon literary, historical, social, and cultural aspects of contemporary period—18th century and later. Examples: "Thoreau as Mythologist"; "Updike's COUPLES: A Barthian Parable."

UNSOLICITED MSS. WELCOME? Yes; submissions acknowledged.
SPECIFICALLY WELCOMED: Speculative.
MS. LENGTH: 10-15 pages; submit ONE copy.
STYLE REQUIREMENTS: None.
COPYRIGHT: Not copyrighted.
EDITOR'S DECISION: 4 weeks.
FROM ACCEPTANCE TO PUBLICATION: 4-6 months.
PAYMENT/OFFPRINTS: No payment. Offprints provided at cost.
REJECTED MSS.: Returned.
GENERAL: First issue, 1929. Usual publication length, 72 pages.
BACK ISSUES: Available from Washington State University Press, Pullman, Washington 99163 at $1.00 each.

SCOTTISH INTERNATIONAL REVIEW

See the section on AGE AND/OR NATIONALITY: ENGLISH, AND BRITISH COMMONWEALTH for details.

THE SOUTH ATLANTIC QUARTERLY

EDITORIAL ADDRESS:
Oliver W. Ferguson, Editor
Duke University Press
Box 6697
Durham, North Carolina 22708

SUBSCRIPTION ADDRESS:

same

PUBLISHED: Quarterly (Jan., Apr., July, Oct.)
COST: 1 yr.—$7.00.

CIRCULATION: 1,300

CONTENTS: Essays and articles of general interest on literature, the arts, historical and recent events. Examples: "George Eliot as Mary Ann Cross"; "The Romantics as Therapists: Shelley and Keniston."

UNSOLICITED MSS. WELCOME? Yes; submissions not acknowledged.
SPECIFICALLY WELCOMED: No particular guidelines, but detailed analyses of a single literary work generally not accepted.
MS. LENGTH: Maximum 4,500 words; submit ONE copy.
COPYRIGHT: Duke University Press and author.
EDITOR'S DECISION: 1-2 months.
FROM ACCEPTANCE TO PUBLICATION: 12-18 months.
PAYMENT/OFFPRINTS: No payment. Offprints ordered from printer at author's expense.
REJECTED MSS.: Returned.
GENERAL: First issue, January, 1902. Usual publication length, 150 pages.
BACK ISSUES: Available from Duke University Press at $2.50 each.

THE SOUTHERN QUARTERLY

EDITORIAL ADDRESS:
William H. Hatcher, Editor
University of Southern Mississippi
Box 78
Southern Station
Hattiesburg, Mississippi 39401

SUBSCRIPTION ADDRESS:

same

PUBLISHED: Quarterly
COST: 1 yr.—$3.00 ($2.55 by Subscription Agency).

CIRCULATION: 600

CONTENTS: Scholarly articles or essays relating to any of the humanities or social sciences.

UNSOLICITED MSS. WELCOME? Yes, if submitted by faculty or graduate students of USM; submissions acknowledged.
SPECIFICALLY WELCOMED: Scholarly articles and essays.
MS. LENGTH: No preference; submit ONE copy.
STYLE REQUIREMENTS: MLA STYLE SHEET.
COPYRIGHT: Publisher.
EDITOR'S DECISION: 3 months.
FROM ACCEPTANCE TO PUBLICATION: 6 months.
PAYMENT/OFFPRINTS: 20 free offprints.
REJECTED MSS.: Returned.
GENERAL: First issue, October, 1962. Usual publication length, 100 pages.
BACK ISSUES: Available from editorial address at $1.00 each.

TEXAS QUARTERLY

EDITORIAL ADDRESS:
Tom Cranfill and Miguel Gonzalez-Gerth, Editors
Box 7517 University Station
Austin, Texas 78712

SUBSCRIPTION ADDRESS:
same

PULISHED: Irregularly
CIRCULATION: 2,500
COST: 1 yr.—$4.00 in U.S.; $5.00 foreign.

CONTENTS: General articles, poetry, artwork. Some specific or less general articles are used for special issues.

UNSOLICITED MSS. WELCOME? Yes; submissions not generally acknowledged.
SPECIFICALLY WELCOMED: Short stories; articles; varied materials for the general reader.
MS. LENGTH: 6,000 words maximum; submit ONE copy.
STYLE REQUIREMENTS: University of Chicago's A MANUAL OF STYLE.
COPYRIGHT: TQ has first serial rights.
EDITOR'S DECISION: 4-6 weeks.
FROM ACCEPTANCE TO PUBLICATION: Varies.
PAYMENT/OFFPRINTS: 50 offprints for any article or several poems; others available at nominal fee.
REJECTED MSS.: Returned.
GENERAL: First issue, 1958. Usual publication length, 200 pages.
BACK ISSUES: Available from Jenkins Publishing Company, Austin, Texas, or from editorial address. Some available at regular price.

TEXAS STUDIES IN LITERATURE AND LANGUAGE: A JOURNAL OF
THE HUMANITIES

See the section on AGE AND/OR NATIONALITY: COMPREHENSIVE IN SCOPE for details.

THOUGHT

EDITORIAL ADDRESS:
Joseph E. O'Neill, Editor
Fordham University
441 East Fordham Road
Bronx, New York 10458

SUBSCRIPTION ADDRESS:
Fordham University Press
Box L, Fordham University
Bronx, New York 10458

PUBLISHED: Quarterly (Mar., June, Sept., Dec.)
CIRCULATION: 1,770
COST: 1 yr.—to subscribers, $10.00; to wholesale agents, $8.00; single copy (current issue)—to subscriber, $3.50; to wholesale agent, $2.80.

CONTENTS: Scholarly but not excessively technical or specialized articles in every field of learning and culture on questions of permanent value and contemporaneous interest; reviews of books. Examples: "Burke and Swift"; "Dostoevsky: Seer of Totalitarianism."

UNSOLICITED MSS. WELCOME? Yes; submissions acknowledged.
SPECIFICALLY WELCOMED: Articles dealing with the whole work of a man or of one aspect of his work or a thorough study of one or more of his works.
MS. LENGTH: 3,000-10,000 words; submit ONE copy.
STYLE REQUIREMENTS: No special ones, but University of Chicago's A MANUAL OF STYLE preferred.
COPYRIGHT: THOUGHT, Fordham University Press.
EDITOR'S DECISION: 1 month.
FROM ACCEPTANCE TO PUBLICATION: 1 year.
PAYMENT/OFFPRINTS: 25 bound offprints of author's article.
REJECTED MSS.: Returned.
GENERAL: First issue, June, 1926. Usual publication length, 160 pages.
BACK ISSUES: Available in microfilm only from Xerox University Microfilms. Request price list.

UNIVERSITY OF PORTLAND REVIEW

EDITORIAL ADDRESS:
Thompson M. Faller, Editor
University of Portland
5000 North Willamette Boulevard
Portland, Oregon 92703

SUBSCRIPTION ADDRESS:
Circulation Editor
same

PUBLISHED: Biannually (Spring, Fall)
CIRCULATION: 1,000
COST: 1 yr.—$1.00; 2 yrs.—$2.00; single copy—$.50.

CONTENTS: Articles which bring the content of particular disciplines to bear on the problems of contemporary society and culture; poetry; book reviews.

UNSOLICITED MSS. WELCOME? Yes; submissions not acknowledged.
SPECIFICALLY WELCOMED: Articles should be in terms which presuppose a liberal arts background, but not necessarily a technical one.
MS. LENGTH: 1,500-2,000 words; submit ONE copy.
STYLE REQUIREMENTS: None.
COPYRIGHT: University of Portland.
EDITOR'S DECISION: Up to 3 months.
FROM ACCEPTANCE TO PUBLICATION: 1 to 2 years at most.
PAYMENT/OFFPRINTS: Four complimentary copies.
REJECTED MSS.: Returned.
GENERAL: First issue, Fall, 1948. Usual publication length, 45 pages.
BACK ISSUES: Available from circulation editor at $.50 each.

THE VISVA-BHARATI QUARTERLY: JOURNAL OF GENERAL CULTURAL INTEREST

EDITORIAL ADDRESS:
Sisirkumar Ghose, Editor
P. O. Santiniketan
Dist. Birbhum
West Bengal
India

SUBSCRIPTION ADDRESS:

same

PUBLISHED: Quarterly
CIRCULATION: 1,000
COST: 1 volume—$4.00 or £1.00 or Rs. 10/ (post-paid); single copy—$1.00 or 5sh or Rs.2=50 (postage extra).

CONTENTS: Articles and reviews concerned with philosophy, religion and mysticism, literary criticism, biography, cultural studies, fine arts; translations from other languages; poetry of general cultural interest and not too technical in presentation.

UNSOLICITED MSS. WELCOME? Yes; submissions acknowledged.
MS. LENGTH: 2,500-7,000 words; submit ONE copy.
STYLE REQUIREMENTS: Typed on foolscap sheet (30 × 20 cm.); broad margin for editing; alternative spellings for diacritical marks.
COPYRIGHT: THE VISVA-BHARATI QUARTERLY.
EDITOR'S DECISION: 4-6 weeks.
FROM ACCEPTANCE TO PUBLICATION: 12-24 weeks.
PAYMENT/OFFPRINTS: Minimum Rs. 25/ to maximum Rs.50/ in Indian currency or up to 100 free offprints to foreign contributors in lieu of payment. 20 free offprints when payment is made for articles.

REJECTED MSS.: Returned, within India.
GENERAL: First issue, April, 1923; New Series, May, 1935. Usual publication length, 90 pages of 350 words each. Each volume beings in May and is completed in April of the following year. Hence, subscriptions are accepted volume-wise and not annually according to calendar year.
BACK ISSUES: Available from subscription address at 25% extra on the current price. Complete sets from Vol. 19 to date.

THE YALE REVIEW

EDITORIAL ADDRESS:
J. E. Palmer, Editor
1902A Yale Station
New Haven, Connecticut 06520

SUBSCRIPTION ADDRESS: same

PUBLISHED: Quarterly CIRCULATION: 6,500
COST: 1 yr.—$6.00; 2 yrs.—$11.00; 3 yrs.—$15.00; single copy—$1.75 plus postage of $.25 (postage of $.50 for Canada and Mexico; postage of $1.00 elsewhere).

CONTENTS: Articles; reviews of new books and records; verse.

UNSOLICITED MSS. WELCOME? Yes, within reason; submissions not acknowledged.
SPECIFICALLY WELCOMED: Consult the magazine.
MS. LENGTH: Consult recent issue; submit ONE copy.
STYLE REQUIREMENTS: Any prospective contributor should consult the magazine itself to learn its publishing policies.
COPYRIGHT: Yale University, for first year.
EDITOR'S DECISION: 2 months.
FROM ACCEPTANCE TO PUBLICATION: 2 years.
PAYMENT/OFFPRINTS: Articles—from $75 to $100; poetry—$.50 per line. Contributors order offprints at their own expense.
REJECTED MSS.: Returned.
GENERAL: First issue, Autumn, 1911. Usual publication length, 160 pages.
BACK ISSUES: Available from editorial office at $2.25 each.

XI
BIBLIOGRAPHICAL AND LIBRARY RESOURCES

AFRO-AMERICAN HISTORY AND CULTURE: NEW BOOKS QUARTERLY CHECKLIST SERIES

EDITORIAL ADDRESS:
Editor
Bibliography Press
7139 Hopkins Road
P. O. Box 138
Mentor, Ohio 44060

SUBSCRIPTION ADDRESS:

same

PUBLISHED: Quarterly
(Feb., May, Aug., Nov.)
COST: 1 yr.—$12.00 (institutions—$15.00); outside U.S. and Canada, add $1.50.

CONTENTS: Each issue includes the titles of books and monographs in Afro-American Studies cataloged by the Library of Congress for the past three months. Topics included are history, political science, law, education, music, literature, bibliography, and such related topics as race relations, minority studies, integration, and civil rights. November issue contains annual index.

THE AMERICAN BOOK COLLECTOR

EDITORIAL ADDRESS:
Jason A. Nogee, Editor
1434 South Yale Avenue
Arlington Heights, Illinois 60005

SUBSCRIPTION ADDRESS:

same

PUBLISHED: Bimonthly
COST: 1 yr.—$7.50; 2 yrs.—$15.00; 3 yrs.—$19.50.

CIRCULATION: 2,455

CONTENTS: Illustrated articles on American first editions, private presses, rare books, and auction reports with prices realized. Articles and book reviews are directed at bibliophiles and book collectors, both private and otherwise. Examples: "Hemingway Items: What are the Limits?"; "Propaganda in the Novel: or Art for Heart's Sake."

UNSOLICITED MSS. WELCOME? Yes; submissions acknowledged.
SPECIFICALLY WELCOMED: Articles or book reviews that deal with "books about books" or any material that deals with book collecting.
MS. LENGTH: Approximately 2,000 words; submit ONE copy.
COPYRIGHT: Author.
EDITOR'S DECISION: 1½ months.
FROM ACCEPTANCE TO PUBLICATION: 2-4 months.
PAYMENT/OFFPRINTS: From 7 to 12 copies of particular issue. Offprints can be made available at an additional cost.
REJECTED MSS.: Returned.
GENERAL: First issue, September, 1950. Usual publication length, 32-40 pages; the index is usually larger.
BACK ISSUES: Available from the editorial address at $1.25 each plus postage.

AMERICAN LITERATURE ABSTRACTS: A REVIEW OF CURRENT SCHOLARSHIP IN THE FIELD OF AMERICAN LITERATURE

EDITORIAL ADDRESS:
James K. Bowen and Richard
Van Der Beets, Editors
Department of English
California State University, San Jose
San Jose, California 95114

SUBSCRIPTION ADDRESS:

same

PUBLISHED: Biannually
COST: 1 yr.—$4.00; 2 yrs.—$7.50; 3 yrs.—$11.00.

CIRCULATION: 550

CONTENTS: Author-prepared abstracts of articles published relating to American literature, 1607-present, for bibliographic and reference guide.

UNSOLICITED MSS. WELCOME? Abstracts requested from authors of original articles.
MS. LENGTH: 250 words maximum; submit ONE copy.
STYLE REQUIREMENTS: MLA Abstract System Recommendations.
COPYRIGHT: Journal.
GENERAL: First issue, December, 1967 to June, 1972 (temporarily suspended). Plans to reissue. Usual publication length, 50 pages.
BACK ISSUES: Available from University Microfilms.

THE BIBLIOTHECK

EDITORIAL ADDRESS:
Douglas S. Mack, Editor
The University Library
University of Stirling
Stirling
Scotland

SUBSCRIPTION ADDRESS:
Secretary
same

PUBLISHED: Tri-annually
(beginning 1974) plus supplement.
COST: 1 yr.—$8.00 or £2.70.

CIRCULATION: 310

CONTENTS: Articles; reviews; notes and queries on bibliography; textual criticism and related subjects. Journal specializes in material of Scottish interest or association. The annual supplement (ANNUAL BIBLIOGRAPHY OF SCOTTISH LITERATURE) is a bibliography of books, reviews, essays, and articles in the field of Scottish literature published during the preceding year. Authors covered include Dunbar, Boswell, David Hume, Adam Smith, Smollett, Carlyle, Hogg, Scott, MacDiarmid.

UNSOLICITED MSS. WELCOMED? Yes; submissions acknowledged.

SPECIFICALLY WELCOMED: Articles and notes on bibliography and related subjects embodying original material based on manuscripts or printed books of Scottish interest or association.
MS. LENGTH: 500-10,000 words; submit ONE copy.
STYLE REQUIREMENTS: THE LIBRARY Style Sheet.
COPYRIGHT: Author.
EDITOR'S DECISION: 3 months.
FROM ACCEPTANCE TO PUBLICATION: 1 year to 18 months.
PAYMENT/OFFPRINTS: Six free offprints; additional copies supplied at cost.
REJECTED MSS.: Returned.
GENERAL: First issue, 1956. Usual publication length, 32 pages; supplement, 50 pages. Separate subscriptions may be placed for the supplement, the ANNUAL BIBLIOGRAPHY OF SCOTTISH LITERATURE, at 35p. or $1.00 p.a. The ABSL is free to subscribers of The BIBLIOTHECK.
BACK ISSUES: Complete sets are available from the secretary; individual issues at 75p. each or £1.50 p.a.

BIBLIOTHÈQUE D'HUMANISME & RENAISSANCE

EDITORIAL ADDRESS:
A. Dufour, Editor
Librairie Droz S. A.
11, rue Massot
Geneva
Switzerland

SUBSCRIPTION ADDRESS:

same

PUBLISHED: Tri-annually
COST: 1 yr.—65 Swiss francs.

CIRCULATION: 1,000

CONTENTS: Studies in literature and history of the 15th and 16th centuries. Examples: "Pernette Du Guillet's Poetry of Love and Desire"; "The Theatre, Diplomacy and Censorship in the Reign of Henri IV."

UNSOLICITED MSS. WELCOME? Only the best; submissions not acknowledged.
SPECIFICALLY WELCOMED: Researched works supplying something new.
MS. LENGTH: Up to 20 pages; submit ONE copy.
STYLE REQUIREMENTS: In French, English, Italian, or German.
COPYRIGHT: The editorial staff.
EDITOR'S DECISION: 3 months.
PAYMENT/OFFPRINTS: None.
REJECTED MSS.: Returned.
GENERAL: First issue, 1933. Usual publication length, 700 pages.
BACK ISSUES: Reprinting of out of print volumes in preparation; last two years available. 75 Swiss francs for one year (3 numbers) for 1969, 1971, 1972, 1973. The series 1-24 available by sending 2100 Swiss francs to the Librairie Droz S. A. HUMANISME ET RENAISSANCE is in reprint and available by sending 700 Swiss francs to Librairie Droz S.A.

THE BODLEIAN LIBRARY RECORD

EDITORIAL ADDRESS:
Bodleian Library
Oxford OX1 3BG
England

SUBSCRIPTION ADDRESS:

same

PUBLISHED: Irregularly, 1 or 2 yearly   CIRCULATION: 2,000
COST: 50p per issue, plus postage.

CONTENTS: Bibliography; palaeography; library history. For the most part, material is based on or relating to objects in the Library's own collections or those of the colleges' libraries. Examples: "On the Text of Some Letters by Shelley"; "Joyce Cary's Published Writings."

UNSOLICITED MSS. WELCOME? Yes; submissions acknowledged.
MS. LENGTH: Up to 4,000 words; submit ONE copy.
COPYRIGHT: Library and author jointly.
EDITOR'S DECISION: A few weeks.
FROM ACCEPTANCE TO PUBLICATION: Very variable.
PAYMENT/OFFPRINTS: 25 free offprints; others at cost if ordered in advance.
REJECTED MSS.: Returned.
GENERAL: First issue, 1938 (BLR replaced BODLEIN QUARTERLY RECORD). Usual publication length, 56 pages.
BACK ISSUES: Vols. I-VI available from Kraus Reprint. Vol. VII onwards available from Bodleian Library at 50p each.

THE BOOK COLLECTOR

EDITORIAL ADDRESS:
Nicolas Barker, Editor
58 Frith Street
London W1V 6BY
England

SUBSCRIPTION ADDRESS:
The Collector Ltd.
same

PUBLISHED: Quarterly (Mar.,   CIRCULATION: 16,000
June, Sept., Dec.)
COST: 1 yr.—$17.50 (USA & Canada); single copy—$4.38.

CONTENTS: Articles of interest to book collectors, bibliographers, antiquarian booksellers, and custodians of rare books; bibliophily, all aspects from medieval to modern first editions. Regular features: contemporary collectors, unfamiliar libraries, English bookbindings, English autographs, bibliographical notes and queries, uncollected authors, collector's piece, news and comments, notes on sales, book reviews, illustrations. Example: "Douglas Sladen (1856-1947): An Anatomy."

UNSOLICITED MSS. WELCOME? Yes; submissions acknowledged.
SPECIFICALLY WELCOMED: Anything regarding Antiquarian Books.

MS. LENGTH: 2,000-5,000 words, submit THREE copies.
EDITOR'S DECISION: 3 months.
FROM ACCEPTANCE TO PUBLICATION: Varies.
PAYMENT/OFFPRINTS: Offprints of articles supplied.
REJECTED MS.: Returned.
GENERAL: First issue, Spring, 1952. Usual publication length, 120-160 pages.
BACK ISSUES: Available from subscription address at $2.50 each.

BOOKS AT BROWN

EDITORIAL ADDRESS:
David A. Jonah, George
Monteiro et al, Editors
Brown University Library
Box A
Providence, Rhode Island 02912

SUBSCRIPTION ADDRESS:

same

PUBLISHED: Occasionally   CIRCULATION: 500
COST: Subscription is only open to educational institutions (cost is determined on a per volume basis). BOOKS AT BROWN is sent to all members of the Friends of the Library of Brown University.

CONTENTS: Articles on special collections, gifts to the Library and of a literary nature. Articles are usually written by, but not limited to, faculty members, graduate students, and members of the local community with an affiliation with Brown. Examples: "Whitman and the Providence Literate"; "The Poe-Chivers Controversy: A New Letter."

UNSOLICITED MSS. WELCOME? Yes, if the author does not mind waiting an indeterminate length of time for publication; submissions acknowledged.
SPECIFICALLY WELCOMED: Articles on some aspect of literature or history, mainly American literature.
MS. LENGTH: No preference; submit ONE copy.
COPYRIGHT: Brown University.
FROM ACCEPTANCE TO PUBLICATION: Varies but may be quite a while.
PAYMENT/OFFPRINTS: 12 free copies of periodical. Authors may order offprints at time of journal's order; payment upon delivery.
REJECTED MSS.: Returned.
GENERAL: First issue, 1938. Usual publication length, 150 pages.
BACK ISSUES: Available from editorial address at $5.00 each for Vols. 1-22; $10.00 each for Vols. 23 & 24.

BRITISH BOOK NEWS

EDITORIAL ADDRESS:
Gillian Dickinson, Editor
Albion House
59 New Oxford Street
London WC1A 1BP
England

SUBSCRIPTION ADDRESS:

same

PUBLISHED: Monthly
COST: 1 yr.—$9.00 or £3.60 (includes surface postage and annual index).

CONTENTS: Reviews of approximately 250 books in each issue in the fields of general works, philosophy and psychology, religion, social sciences, language, pure sciences, technology, the arts, literature, geography and history, and fiction. Literature sections include English Poetry, English Drama, English Fiction, Spanish Literature, Latin and Greek Literature, Russian Literature, German Literature, French Literature, Norwegian Literature, and others; publishing news; one or two articles on such subjects as "Recent Fiction."

UNSOLICITED MSS. WELCOME? No.
COPYRIGHT: The British Council.
GENERAL: First issue, 1940. Indexed annually.

BULLETIN OF BIBLIOGRAPHY AND MAGAZINE NOTES

EDITORIAL ADDRESS:
Carol Felsenthal, Editor
15 Southwest Park
Westwood, Massachusetts 02090

SUBSCRIPTION ADDRESS:
F. W. Faxon Company, Inc.
15 Southwest Park
Westwood, Massachusetts 02090

PUBLISHED: Quarterly
COST: 1 yr.—$14.00; single copy—$4.00 (calendar year only).

CIRCULATION: 1,500

CONTENTS: Topical and studious bibliographies; reference studies; articles on operational methods applicable to libraries; reviews of reference works; and a record of new, ceased, and changed titles in the periodical world.

UNSOLICITED MSS. WELCOME? Yes; submissions acknowledged.
SPECIFICALLY WELCOMED: Bibliographies; articles of interest to librarians.
MS. LENGTH: No preference; submit TWO copies.
STYLE REQUIREMENTS: MLA STYLE SHEET.
COPYRIGHT: Not copyrighted.
EDITOR'S DECISION: 1 month.
FROM ACCEPTANCE TO PUBLICATION: 1 year.
PAYMENT/OFFPRINTS: Ten copies of Bulletin; no offprints.
REJECTED MSS.: Returned.
GENERAL: First issue, 1897. Usual publication length, 48 pages.

BACK ISSUES: Up to 1971, back issues available from J. S. Canner; 1972-73 from Faxon Company. Refer all inquiries to J. S. Canner.

BULLETIN OF THE CENTER OF CHILDREN'S BOOKS

EDITORIAL ADDRESS:
Mrs. Zena Sutherland, Editor
Graduate Library School
University of Chicago
Chicago, Illinois

SUBSCRIPTION ADDRESS:
The University of Chicago Press
5801 Ellis Avenue
Chicago, Illinois 60637

PUBLISHED: 11 issues yearly   CIRCULATION: 10,000 plus
COST: 1 yr.—$8.00; $7.00 for each additional subscription to same address; $6.00 for students.

CONTENTS: Critical analyses of the general content, reading level, importance, usefulness, weaknesses in style, subject treatment, and strengths of books for children and young people; bibliographies and reference reading lists for parents, librarians, and teachers; no articles and advertisements.

UNSOLICITED MSS. WELCOME? No.
GENERAL: First issue, 1945. Usual publication length, 16 pages. Indexed by volume.
BACK ISSUES: Available from University of Chicago Press or Kraus Reprints; microfilm editions from Xerox University Microfilms. Cost—Vol. 17-22, $4.00; Vol. 23-26, $5.00; earliest volumes out of print.

BULLETIN OF THE NEW YORK PUBLIC LIBRARY

EDITORIAL ADDRESS:
David V. Erdman, Editor
New York Public Library
Room 58
Fifth Avenue and 42nd Street
New York, New York 10018

SUBSCRIPTION ADDRESS:
Readex Books
101 Fifth Avenue
New York, New York 10003

PUBLISHED: Quarterly   CIRCULATION: 2,000
COST: 1 yr.—$7.50.

CONTENTS: Illustrated articles on new or neglected holdings of the New York Public Library.

UNSOLICITED MSS. WELCOME? Yes; submissions acknowledged.

SPECIFICALLY WELCOMED: "Original critical study of anything on, about, or in books and manuscripts, and any useful bibliographical tools for such study"; essays useful to librarians, scholars, bookmen. Do not send "book reviews, essays in criticism or explications of familiar texts, or surveys of well-trodden grounds."
MS. LENGTH: No preference; submit ONE copy.
STYLE REQUIREMENTS: MLA STYLE SHEET with some modifications. Consult recent issue or query editor before typing ms.
COPYRIGHT: The New York Public Library.
EDITOR'S DECISION: 3 months.
FROM ACCEPTANCE TO PUBLICATION: 1-2 years.
PAYMENT/OFFPRINTS: Four complimentary copies of issue. Authors may purchase offprints at cost if ordered before publication.
REJECTED MSS.: Returned.
GENERAL: First issue, 1897. Usual publication length, 128 pages, beginning in Fall, 1973.
BACK ISSUES: Some are available; query editor RE specific issue.

COLBY LIBRARY QUARTERLY

See the section on AGE AND/OR NATIONALITY: AMERICAN for details.

COLLEGE AND RESEARCH LIBRARIES

EDITORIAL ADDRESS:
Richard M. Dougherty, Editor
University of California Libraries
Berkeley, California 94720

SUBSCRIPTION ADDRESS:
American Library Association
50 East Huron Street
Chicago, Illinois 60611

PUBLISHED: 17 issues yearly
COST: Membership only.

CIRCULATION: 15,000

CONTENTS: Articles reporting scholarly research in all aspects of academic librarianship.

UNSOLICITED MSS. WELCOME? Yes.
MS. LENGTH: 10 pages; submit ONE copy.
STYLE REQUIREMENTS: University of Chicago's A MANUAL OF STYLE; MLA STYLE SHEET.
COPYRIGHT: American Library Association.
EDITOR'S DECISION: 6-8 weeks.
FROM ACCEPTANCE TO PUBLICATION: 9 months.
PAYMENT/OFFPRINTS: 25 free offprints; author may order additional ones.
REJECTED MSS.: Not returned.
GENERAL: First issue, 1939. Usual publication length, 72 pages.
BACK ISSUES: Available from University Microfilms; see its catalog for prices.

THE CRITICAL QUARTERLY

See the section on AGE AND/OR NATIONALITY: AMERICAN AND ENGLISH for details.

ELIZABETHAN BIBLIOGRAPHIES SUPPLEMENTS

EDITORIAL ADDRESS:
Charles A. Pennel, Editor
Nether Press
25 Whitehall Park
London N. 19
England

SUBSCRIPTION ADDRESS:

same

GENERAL: This periodical had not arrived by the time the entry went to press. Potential subscribers, contributors, or collectors will have to write the editor to see whether the journal still exists, and if so, to inquire about details of manuscript submission, style, back issues, and the like.

HANDBOOK OF LATIN AMERICAN STUDIES

EDITORIAL ADDRESS:
Henry E. Adams, Editor
HLAS, Hispanic Foundation
Library of Congress
Washington, D.C. 20540

SUBSCRIPTION ADDRESS:

same

PUBLISHED: Annually

CIRCULATION: 3,000

CONTENTS: Inter-disciplinary annotated bibliography of works published about Latin America during any age.

GENERAL: First issue, 1936.

HARVARD LIBRARY BULLETIN

EDITORIAL ADDRESS:
Edwin E. Williams, Editor
505 Lamont Library
Cambridge, Massachusetts 02138

SUBSCRIPTION ADDRESS:
Harvard University Press
79 Garden Street
Cambridge, Massachusetts 02138

PUBLISHED: Quarterly
COST: 1 yr.—$15.00; single copy—$4.00.

CIRCULATION: 1,600

CONTENTS: Articles on collections of the Harvard libraries and their significance for scholarship; articles embodying research based on materials in Harvard libraries and museums; articles on research libraires and in particular on the policies, plans, and problems of the Harvard Library; articles of general intellectual appeal on developments in the world of books and scholarship; occasional illustrations. Examples: "Irony in the Tragedies of Racine"; "Keats on Kean: An Early Version."

UNSOLICITED MSS. WELCOME? Yes; submissions acknowledged.
MS. LENGTH: 5-40 pages; submit ONE copy.
STYLE REQUIREMENTS: MLA STYLE SHEET in general.
COPYRIGHT: HLB holds copyright, but for benefit of author.
EDITOR'S DECISION: 2-3 weeks.
FROM ACCEPTANCE TO PUBLICATION: 6 months to 1 year.
PAYMENT/OFFPRINTS: 50 free offprints; additional offprints at cost.
REJECTED MSS.: Returned.
GENERAL: First issue, Winter, 1947. Usual publication length, 110 pages.
BACK ISSUES: 1947-1967 available from Johnson Reprint Corp.; 1948 to date from Harvard University Press at $15.00 per year.

THE HOPKINS RESEARCH BULLETIN

EDITORIAL ADDRESS:
The Editor
Hopkins Secretariat
114 Mount Street
London W1Y 6AH
England

SUBSCRIPTION ADDRESS:
For North American members:
The Director of Libraries
Crosby Library
Gonzaga University
East 502 Boone Avenue
Spokane, Washington 99202

PUBLISHED: Annually
COST: 1 yr.—$6.00, regular subscription; $12.00, library; $30.00, patron; $300, benefactor. Dues payable March 1 of each year.

CONTENTS: Unpublished material of the poet; an annual bibliography; other items of interest; a selective index.

UNSOLICITED MSS. WELCOME? Yes, of type specified; submissions acknowledged.
SPECIFICALLY WELCOMED: Poet's biographical background; bibliographical material; research in progress.
MS. LENGTH: No preference; submit ONE copy.
STYLE REQUIREMENTS: MLA STYLE SHEET.
COPYRIGHT: Editor of HRB.
EDITOR'S DECISION: 3 months.
FROM ACCEPTANCE TO PUBLICATION: 1-2 years.
PAYMENT/OFFPRINTS: Two copies.
REJECTED MSS.: Returned.

GENERAL: First issue, 1970. Usual publication length varies (e.g., 28, 24, 40 pages). Subscribers receive postage free copies of the annual lectures and the annual sermons, all sponsored by The Hopkins Society. Also, the Society is represented in North America by The Hopkins Collection, Crosby Library, at subscription address. The Library's Hopkins holdings are enumerated and described by Ruth Seelhammer in her book HOPKINS COLLECTED AT GONZAGA (Chicago: Loyola University Press, 1970).
BACK ISSUES: Volumes 1, 2, 3, and 4 (1970-1973) available from Hopkins Secretariat, "Roselands," 162 Turkey Street, Enfield, Middlesex EN1 4NW, England at 40p or US$1.00 each plus postage and packing.

THE HUNTINGTON LIBRARY QUARTERLY: A JOURNAL FOR THE HISTORY AND INTERPRETATION OF ENGLISH AND AMERICAN CIVILIZATION

EDITORIAL ADDRESS:
John M. Steadman, Editor
Henry E. Huntington Library
and Art Gallery
San Marino, California 91108

SUBSCRIPTION ADDRESS:

same

PUBLISHED: Quarterly
(Nov., Feb., May, Aug.)
COST: 1 yr.—$7.50; single copy—$2.50.

CIRCULATION: 1,250

CONTENTS: Articles on English history and literature, medieval to twentieth century; American history and literature, emphasis on colonial period, Civil War, and western Americana; British art history, emphasis on eighteenth and early nineteenth centuries; notes and documents; illustrations. Examples: "Three Sets of Religious Poems"; "A Source for Shakespeare's Malvolio: The Elizabethan Controversy with the Puritans."

UNSOLICITED MSS. WELCOME? Yes, within limits; submissions acknowledged.
SPECIFICALLY WELCOMED: Research articles on material from Huntington Library collections; a smaller number of critical-interpretative articles; a few notes.
MS. LENGTH: Articles—20-30 pages; notes—5-10 pages; submit ONE copy.
STYLE REQUIREMENTS: MLA STYLE SHEET.
COPYRIGHT: HUNTINGTON LIBRARY QUARTERLY.
EDITOR'S DECISION: 1-3 months.
FROM ACCEPTANCE TO PUBLICATION: 15-18 months.
PAYMENT/OFFPRINTS: 25 free offprints; others may be ordered from printer.
REJECTED MSS.: Returned.
GENERAL: First issue, October, 1937, replacing HUNTINGTON LIBRARY BULLETIN. Usual publication length, 104 pages.

BACK ISSUES: Vols. I-XXVII available from Kraus Reprints; a partial file of subsequent volumes is available from Huntington Library; Kraus can supply those lacking. Microfilms of separate volumes of HLQ may be purchased by subscribers only from University Microfilms.

INDEX TO AUSTRALIAN BOOK REVIEWS

EDITORIAL ADDRESS:
Libraries Board of
South Australia
Box 419, G.P.O.
Adelaide
South Australia 5001

SUBSCRIPTION ADDRESS:
State Library of
South Australia
same

PUBLISHED: Mar., June, Sept.,
Annual cumulation in Dec.
COST: A$4.70 (postage included).

CIRCULATION: 200

CONTENTS: An index of reviews of books of Australian interest which are published in a selected group of Australian journals and newspapers. Reviews of the following material are included: (1) books by Australian authors, whether published in Australia or overseas; (2) books published in Australia; (3) books of Australian interest published overseas.

GENERAL: First issue, March, 1965. Usual publication length, 250-300 pages for annual cumulation; 40 to 75 for others.
BACK ISSUES: Available from State Library of South Australia at A$4.70 (only cumulated volumes available).

INTERNATIONAL P.E.N. BULLETIN OF SELECTED BOOKS

EDITORIAL ADDRESS:
Kathleen Nott, Editor
62/3 Glebe Place
London SW3 5JB
England

SUBSCRIPTION ADDRESS:
Stechert-Hafner, Inc.
31 East 10th Street
New York, New York 10003

PUBLISHED: Quarterly
COST: 1 yr.—$2.60.

CIRCULATION: 2,000

CONTENTS: Articles and reviews referring only to "literature of lesser currency" (i.e., anything except English, American, and French). A number of special issues devoted to one literature only (contemporary). Examples: "Literary Criticism in the West."

UNSOLICITED MSS. WELCOME? Yes, within range indicated above; submissions not acknowledged.
MS. LENGTH: Articles—1,500 words; reviews—600 words.
COPYRIGHT: The Bulletin.
EDITOR'S DECISION: 1 month.
FROM ACCEPTANCE TO PUBLICATION: 1-3 months.
PAYMENT/OFFPRINTS: About £2.00 for a review and about £5.00 for an article.
REJECTED MSS.: Returned.
GENERAL: First issue, 1950. Usual publication length, 24-28 pages. Published jointly by PEN and Unesco in English and French.
BACK ISSUES: Available from editorial address at 17p each.

JOURNAL OF THE RUTGERS UNIVERSITY LIBRARY

EDITORIAL ADDRESS:
Editor
Rutgers University
New Brunswick, New Jersey 08901

SUBSCRIPTION ADDRESS:

same

PUBLISHED: Biannually

GENERAL: First issue, 1937. This periodical had not arrived by the time the entry went to press. Potential subscribers, contributors, or collectors will have to write the editor to see whether the journal still exists, and if so, to inquire about details of manuscript submission, style, back issues, and the like.

THE LIBRARY: A QUARTERLY JOURNAL OF BIBLIOGRAPHY

EDITORIAL ADDRESS:
Peter Davison, Editor
Department of English
St. David's University College
Lampeter
Cardiganshire, Wales
United Kingdom

SUBSCRIPTION ADDRESS:
Hon. Secy.,
Bibliographical Society
Reference Section
British Library
Gt Russell Street
London, WC1B 3DG
United Kingdom

PUBLISHED: Quarterly   CIRCULATION: 1,800
COST: £5.25—membership of society; includes Society's other publications.

CONTENTS: Historical, analytical, descriptive bibliography; manuscripts; history of printing, publishing, bookselling, book collecting, and bookbinding; illustrations. Example: "Early Manuscripts of Virgiliana."

UNSOLICITED MSS. WELCOME? Yes; submissions acknowledged.

MS. LENGTH: No preference; submit ONE copy.
STYLE REQUIREMENTS: MHRA preferred.
COPYRIGHT: Author and journal.
EDITOR'S DECISION: 4-6 weeks.
FROM ACCEPTANCE TO PUBLICATION: Depends on nature of article/review but likely date given at acceptance.
PAYMENT/OFFPRINTS: 25 free offprints for articles; 12 for bibliographic notes; 6 for reviews.
REJECTED MSS.: Returned.
GENERAL: First issue, 1893. Usual publication length, 90 pages.
BACK ISSUES: Available from Oxford University Press for last five years; from Kraus (Liechtenstein) for earlier years.

THE LIBRARY CHRONICLE

EDITORIAL ADDRESS: SUBSCRIPTION ADDRESS:
William E. Miller, Editor
University of Pennsylvania Library same
Philadelphia, Pennsylvania 19174

PUBLISHED: Biannually CIRCULATION: 400-500
COST: 1 yr.—$6.00; Friends of the Library receive free (Membership—$25.00)

CONTENTS: Articles and notes of bibliophile or bibliographic interest, especially about books and manuscripts owned by the University of Pennsylvania Libraries; occasional literary studies not in the above categories. Examples: "Dreiser's Novels: The Editorial Problem"; "Some Swinburne Letters."

UNSOLICITED MSS. WELCOME? Yes; submissions acknowledged.
MS. LENGTH: Not a criterion; submit ONE copy.
STYLE REQUIREMENTS: MLA STYLE SHEET is the general, but not absolute, guide.
COPYRIGHT: Authors (if they care to take one out); LC does not copyright.
EDITOR'S DECISION: 1-4 months.
FROM ACCEPTANCE TO PUBLICATION: 1-2 years.
PAYMENT/OFFPRINTS: 25 free offprints. Extra offprints may be purchased at cost.
REJECTED MSS.: Returned.
GENERAL: First issue, 1933. Usual publication length, 60-70 pages.
BACK ISSUES: Available from University of Pennsylvania Library at $3.00 each.

THE LIBRARY CHRONICLE OF THE UNIVERSITY OF TEXAS AT AUSTIN

EDITORIAL ADDRESS:
F. W. Roberts, Editor
Box 7219
University of Texas
Austin, Texas 78712

SUBSCRIPTION ADDRESS:

same

PUBLISHED: Tri-annually
COST: 1 yr.—$10.00.

CIRCULATION: 400

CONTENTS: Articles on literary, photographic, theatrical, scientific, historical, and iconographic collections in the Humanities Research Center as well as articles on the Texas History and Latin American collections. Examples: "Fifty Unpublished Letters from Joseph Conrad"; "Herman Charles Bosman."

UNSOLICITED MSS. WELCOME? Yes; submissions acknowledged.
MS. LENGTH: 10-20 pages; submit ONE copy.
STYLE REQUIREMENTS: MLA STYLE SHEET.
COPYRIGHT: Humanities Research Center.
EDITOR'S DECISION: 3-4 weeks.
FROM ACCEPTANCE TO PUBLICATION: 4 months to 1½ years, depending on backlog.
PAYMENT/OFFPRINTS: None.
REJECTED MSS.: Returned.
GENERAL: Usual publication length, 60-100 pages.

THE LIBRARY QUARTERLY

EDITORIAL ADDRESS:
Lester Asheim, Managing Editor
Graduate Library School
University of Chicago
Chicago, Illinois 60637

SUBSCRIPTION ADDRESS:
Journals Department
The University of Chicago Press
5801 Ellis Avenue
Chicago, Illinois 60637

PUBLISHED: Quarterly
CIRCULATION: 3,700
COST: 1 yr.—$10.00; 2 yrs.—$19.00; 3 yrs.—$28.00; outside of U.S. add $1.00 for each year's subscription for postage; single copy—$3.00.

CONTENTS: Articles and book reviews dealing with problems of library and information science in general; problems of service for specific types of library: public, academic, special, school; bibliographic studies (but not bibliographies); history of libraries, books, printing, and scholarship; studies of reading and readers; international comparative librarianship. Examples: "The Culturally Deprived Reader: Research Diagnosis and Prescriptions"; "Book Selection and Book Collection Usage in Academic Libraries."

UNSOLICITED MSS. WELCOME? Yes; submissions acknowledged.

SPECIFICALLY WELCOMED: Reports of research and investigation and scholarly articles of some depth.
MS. LENGTH: Normally 40-60 pages maximum; submit ONE copy.
STYLE REQUIREMENTS: Will send information on request.
COPYRIGHT: University of Chicago Press.
EDITOR'S DECISION: 3-6 weeks.
FROM ACCEPTANCE TO PUBLICATION: 6-9 months.
PAYMENT/OFFPRINTS: 50 free offprints; additional offprints at charge to author.
REJECTED MSS.: Returned.
GENERAL: First issue, January, 1931. Usual publication length, 88-104 pages. Index in October issue.
BACK ISSUES: Available from 1962 (Vol. 32) from publisher at $3.75 each; $13.00 per volume (four issues). Single issues and reprinted volumes through 1961 (Vols. 1-31) available from Walter J. Johnson, Inc.; microfilm copies from University Microfilms; microfiche from J. S. Canner & Co.

LIBRARY REVIEW: A QUARTERLY MAGAZINE ON LIBRARIES AND LITERATURE

EDITORIAL ADDRESS:
W. H. Aitken, Editor
W. & R. Holmes (Books)
98-100 Holm Street
Glasgow G2 6SN
Scotland

SUBSCRIPTION ADDRESS:

same

PUBLISHED: Quarterly
COST: 1 yr.—£2.00 ($6.60).

CONTENTS: Critical articles on literature and libraries, 'bookish' librarianship; sections on "Library Publications," "Books for Young Readers," "Books of General Interest," "Notes and News." Examples: "Stephen Crane—A Distant Echo"; "The Walter de la Mare Centenary."

UNSOLICITED MSS. WELCOME? Yes; submissions acknowledged.
SPECIFICALLY WELCOMED: Critical articles of all kinds.
MS. LENGTH: 2,000-5,000 words; submit ONE copy.
STYLE REQUIREMENTS: Clarity, precision, and understanding.
COPYRIGHT: Author.
EDITOR'S DECISION: 6 weeks.
FROM ACCEPTANCE TO PUBLICATION: 1 year.
PAYMENT/OFFPRINTS: £3 to £4 per 1,000 words. Offprints, by arrangement, at cost.
REJECTED MSS.: Returned.
GENERAL: First issue, 1927. Usual publication length, 48 pages.
BACK ISSUES: Vols. 1-20 (1927-66 inclusive) reprinted by Kraus Reprint in Nendeln, Liechtenstein; write for prices. Later issues available from editorial address at 50p. ($1.65) each.

MLA ABSTRACTS

EDITORIAL ADDRESS:
Walter S. Achtert, Compiler
Modern Language Association
of America
62 Fifth Avenue
New York, New York 10011

SUBSCRIPTION ADDRESS:

same

PUBLISHED: Annually
COST: Available to MLA members.

CONTENTS: Abstracts of journal articles on the modern languages and literatures in "a three volume annual following the arrangement of the MLA INTERNATIONAL BIBLIOGRAPHY." Vol. I: General, English, American, Medieval and Neo-Latin, Celtic Literatures, and Folklore. Vol. II: European, Asian, African, and Latin American Literatures. Vol. III: Linguistics. Usually, the authors of the original articles write the abstract.

MS. LENGTH: 200 words.
GENERAL: Usual publication length, 240 pages.

MLA INTERNATIONAL BIBLIOGRAPHY OF BOOKS AND ARTICLES ON THE MODERN LANGUAGES AND LITERATURES

EDITORIAL ADDRESS:
Harrison T. Meserole, Editor
Department of English
117 Burrowes Building
Pennsylvania State University
University Park, Pennsylvania 16802

SUBSCRIPTION ADDRESS:

same

PUBLISHED: Annually (Four separate paperbound vols.; one clothbound "Library Edition," all 4 vols. in one)
COST: $8.00 per volume.

CIRCULATION: 35,000

CONTENTS: Vol. I: General, English, American, Medieval and Neo-Latin, and Celtic Literatures; and Folklore. Vol. II: European, Asian, African, and Latin American Literatures. Vol. III: Linguistics. Vol. IV: Pedagogy.

GENERAL: First issue, 1922. Usual publication length of Vol. I, 230-250 pages; Vol. II, 330-350 pages; Vol. III, 175-200 pages; Vol. IV, 75-100 pages. Until 1968, the BIBLIOGRAPHY appeared in its parent journal PMLA.
BACK ISSUES: Available from Kraus Reprint Co.

MODERN FICTION STUDIES

See the section on GENRES: PROSE for details.

THE NEW YORK REVIEW OF BOOKS

See the section on AGE AND/OR NATIONALITY: COMPREHENSIVE IN SCOPE for details.

THE NEW YORK TIMES BOOK REVIEW

See the section on AGE AND/OR NATIONALITY: COMPREHENSIVE IN SCOPE for details.

NEWBERRY LIBRARY BULLETIN

EDITORIAL ADDRESS:
James M. Wells, Editor
Office of the Associate Director
60 West Walton Street
Chicago, Illinois 60610

SUBSCRIPTION ADDRESS:

same

PUBLISHED: Irregularly
COST: Free to subscribers.

CIRCULATION: 2,000

CONTENTS: Articles relating to Newberry Library and its collections; reflecting research done at the Library in its strengths: American and European history and literature to W.W.I, midwestern authors, Renaissance, Spanish and Portuguese colonial history through wars of independence, history of printing, history of music, American Indian history, history of cartography, Philippines; Library notes of major events and acquisitions. Example: "The Nostalgia of WINESBURG, OHIO."

UNSOLICITED MSS. WELCOME? Yes, but editor should be queried beforehand; submissions acknowledged.
MS. LENGTH: 3,000-5,000 words; submit ONE copy.
STYLE REQUIREMENTS: MLA STYLE SHEET or University of Chicago's A MANUAL OF STYLE.
COPYRIGHT: Newberry.
EDITOR'S DECISION: 3 months.
FROM ACCEPTANCE TO PUBLICATION: 1 year.
PAYMENT/OFFPRINTS: Copies of entire bulletin.
REJECTED MSS.: Returned.

GENERAL: First issue, November, 1944. Usual publication length, 40 pages.
BACK ISSUES: Available from The Newberry Library, editorial address, at $.75 each; $5.00 per volume.

OLD ENGLISH NEWSLETTER

See section on AGE AND/OR NATIONALITY: ENGLISH, AND BRITISH COMMONWEALTH for details.

THE PAPERS OF THE BIBLIOGRAPHICAL SOCIETY OF AMERICA (PBSA)

EDITORIAL ADDRESS:
William B. Todd, Editor
Department of English
University of Texas
Austin, Texas 78712

SUBSCRIPTION ADDRESS:
P. O. Box 397
Grand Central Station
New York, New York 10017

PUBLISHED: Quarterly
COST: 1 yr.—$15.00

CIRCULATION: 1,700

CONTENTS: Researched articles; bibliographical notes; news, notes, and queries section; long reviews; briefer mention of other publications; occasional illustrations. Example: "The Italian Imprimaturs in Milton's AREOPAGITICA."

UNSOLICITED MSS. WELCOME? Yes; submissions acknowledged.
SPECIFICALLY WELCOMED: Articles on editorial problems; descriptive and enumerative bibliography; history of the book trade.
MS. LENGTH: Articles, 2,000-5,000 words; notes 100-1,000 words; submit ONE copy.
STYLE REQUIREMENTS: MLA STYLE SHEET.
COPYRIGHT: Bibliographical Society; reprints only on permission of author.
EDITOR'S DECISION: 4 months.
FROM ACCEPTANCE TO PUBLICATION: 8 months.
PAYMENT/OFFPRINTS: 20 gratis offprints for articles, 10 for other contributions; additional offprints at cost.
REJECTED MSS.: Returned.
GENERAL: First issue, 1907. Usual publication length, 120 pages. Indexed by volume.
BACK ISSUES: Available from Kraus Reprint Corporation. Cost varies.

THE PRINCETON UNIVERSITY LIBRARY CHRONICLE

EDITORIAL ADDRESS:
Alfred L. Bush, Chairman
Editorial Board
Princeton University Library
Princeton, New Jersey 08540

SUBSCRIPTION ADDRESS:

same

PUBLISHED: Tri-annually   CIRCULATION: 2,000
COST: 1 yr.—$7.50; or free with membership in the Friends of the Princeton University Library ($10.00 per yr.).

CONTENTS: Articles about or based on printed, manuscript or other material in the Princeton University Library collections. Examples: "F. Scott Fitzgerald's Work in the Film Studios"; "Restoration Plays at Princeton."

UNSOLICITED MSS. WELCOME? Yes; submissions acknowledged.
SPECIFICALLY WELCOMED: Articles concerning or based on the Princeton collections.
MS. LENGTH: About 20 pages; submit ONE copy.
STYLE REQUIREMENTS: University of Chicago's A MANUAL OF STYLE.
EDITOR'S DECISION: 1 month.
FROM ACCEPTANCE TO PUBLICATION: Varies.
PAYMENT/OFFPRINTS: Two copies of the issue and 50 offprints.
REJECTED MSS.: Returned.
GENERAL: First issue, June, 1930. Usual publication length, 80 pages.
BACK ISSUES: Available from Princeton University Library from $1.50 to $2.50 per issue.

PROOF: THE YEARBOOK OF AMERICAN BIBLIOGRAPHICAL AND TEXTUAL STUDIES

EDITORIAL ADDRESS:
Joseph Katz, Editor
Department of English
University of South Carolina
Columbia, South Carolina 29208

STANDING ORDER ADDRESS:
Order Department
University of South Carolina Press
Columbia, South Carolina 29208

PUBLISHED: Annually   CIRCULATION: 800
COST: $20.00 per issue (20% discount to institutions and individuals who enclose payment with order).

CONTENTS: A collection of scholarly essays, articles, and reviews dealing with the study of books and manuscripts and their contribution to the American cultural experience. Proof is concerned with works of Americans printed here and abroad and foreign works published in America; it approaches the study of literature and the arts in America through explorations in the transmission and recovery of their records. Examples: "Mark Twain in Knee Pants: The Expurgation of Tom Sawyer Abroad"; "Hawthorne and the Pirates."

UNSOLICITED MSS. WELCOME? Yes; submissions acknowledged.
SPECIFICALLY WELCOMED: Essays on the theory and practice of bibliography and textual criticism and on printing, publishing, and bookselling history.
MS. LENGTH: No limit; submit two copies.
STYLE REQUIREMENTS: Consult most recent issue.
COPYRIGHT: Joseph Katz.
EDITOR'S DECISION: 1-2 months.
FROM ACCEPTANCE TO PUBLICATION: 18-24 months.
PAYMENT/OFFPRINTS: $25 to $50 token payment. 50 free offprints of article.
REJECTED MSS.: Returned.
GENERAL: First issue, 1971. Usual publication length, 450-550 pages. Each volume is fully indexed and heavily illustrated.
BACK ISSUES: Available from University of South Carolina Press at $20.00 each.

QUARTERLY CHECK-LIST OF CLASSICAL STUDIES

EDITORIAL ADDRESS:
Publisher
American Bibliographic Service
Darien, Connecticut 06820

SUBSCRIPTION ADDRESS:

same

PUBLISHED: Quarterly
COST: 1 yr.—$8.00.

CONTENTS: Catalogues new and recent non-periodical materials in Western languages of cultural and political studies of Greek and Roman civilizations, critical editions and translations of Latin and Greek texts; all available bibliographic data, together with list-prices and publishers' addresses; annual index of authors, editors and translators.

BACK ISSUES: Available from publisher. Cost varies with each volume.

QUARTERLY CHECK-LIST OF LITERARY HISTORY: AN INTERNATIONAL INDEX OF CURRENT BOOKS, MONOGRAPHS, BROCHURES & SEPARATES

EDITORIAL ADDRESS:
Publisher
American Bibliographic Service
Darien, Connecticut 06820

SUBSCRIPTION ADDRESS:

same

PUBLISHED: Quarterly
COST: 1 yr.—$11.00.

CONTENTS: A current, running catalogue of non-periodical materials on English, American, French, and German literary history in Western languages as published throughout the world; all available bibliographic data for each entry, together with list-prices and publishers' addresses. Includes translations, new and revised editions, and paperbacks, and an annual index of authors, editors, and translators.

GENERAL: First issue, 1958. Usual publication length, 60 pages.
BACK ISSUES: Available from publisher. Cost varies with each volume.

QUARTERLY CHECK-LIST OF MEDIEVALIA

EDITORIAL ADDRESS:
Publisher
American Bibliographic Service
Darien, Connecticut 06820

SUBSCRIPTION ADDRESS:
same

PUBLISHED: Quarterly
COST: 1 yr.—$9.00.

CONTENTS: Catalogues new and recent non-periodical materials in the Western languages on ecclesiastical and political history, language and literature, arts and crafts, social, political and economic institutions of Byzantium and Western Europe in the Middle Ages; all available bibliographic data for each entry, together with list-prices and publishers' addresses. Includes translations, new and revised editions, and paperbacks, and an annual index of authors, editors, and translators.

BACK ISSUES: Available from publisher. Cost varies with each volume.

QUARTERLY CHECK-LIST OF ORIENTAL STUDIES

EDITORIAL ADDRESS:
Publisher
American Bibliographic Service
Darien, Connecticut 06820

SUBSCRIPTION ADDRESS:
same

PUBLISHED: Quarterly
COST: 1 yr.—$9.50.

CONTENTS: Catalogues non-periodical political, economic, social and cultural studies of the ancient Near East, Central and South Asia, Far East and Southeast Asia in Western languages as published throughout the world; all available bibliographic data for each entry, together with list-prices and publishers' addresses. Includes translations, new and revised editions, and paperbacks, and an annual index of authors, editors, and translators.

BACK ISSUES: Available from publisher. Cost varies with each volume.

QUARTERLY CHECK-LIST OF RENAISSANCE STUDIES

EDITORIAL ADDRESS:
Publisher
American Bibliographic Service
Darien, Connecticut 06820

SUBSCRIPTION ADDRESS:

same

PUBLISHED: Quarterly
COST: 1 yr.—$5.00.

CONTENTS: Catalogues non-periodical materials in the Western languages as published throughout the world on the European scene during the Renaissance and Reformation: history, religion, philosophy, arts, and sciences; all available bibliographic data for each entry, together with list-prices and publishers' addresses. Includes translations, new and revised editions, and paperbacks, and an annual index of authors, editors, and translators.

BACK ISSUES: Available from publisher. Cost varies with each volume.

RESOURCES FOR AMERICAN LITERARY STUDY

See the section on AGE AND/OR NATIONALITY: AMERICAN for details.

REVISTA INTERAMERICANA DE BIBLIOGRAFIA: INTER-AMERICAN REVIEW OF BIBLIOGRAPHY

EDITORIAL ADDRESS:
Armando Correia Pacheco, Editor
Division of Philosophy and Letters
General Secretariat
Organization of American States
Washington, D.C. 20006

SUBSCRIPTION ADDRESS:
Sales and Promotion Division
same

PUBLISHED: Quarterly   CIRCULATION: 3,000
COST: 1 yr.—$3.00 in Americas; $3.50 in other countries; single copy—$1.00.

CONTENTS: Articles devoted to the study of the various aspects of the culture of the Western Hemisphere, particularly in the field of humanities and the social sciences; book reviews; bibliography of books and pamphlets; notes and news; recent books; publications of the OAS and its specialized organizations. The last issue of each volume includes also a list of new journals; annual index and table of contents.

UNSOLICITED MSS. WELCOME? Occasionally; submissions acknowledged.
SPECIFICALLY WELCOMED: Articles or reviews dealing with humanistic subjects, and relating to the culture of the Americas only.
MS. LENGTH: 20 pages; submit ONE copy.
STYLE REQUIREMENTS: University of Chicago's A MANUAL OF STYLE.
COPYRIGHT: The Organization of American States.
EDITOR'S DECISION: 1 month or less.
FROM ACCEPTANCE TO PUBLICATION: 6 months to 1 year.
PAYMENT/OFFPRINTS: Only solicited articles are paid.
REJECTED MSS.: Returned.
GENERAL: First issue, January-March, 1951. Usual publication length, 128 pages. Articles may be written in English, Spanish, Portuguese, or French.
BACK ISSUES: Recent issues available from OAS at $1.00 each; 1951-1962 from Johnson Reprint Corporation; all available from University Microfilms.

SCHOLARLY PUBLISHING: A JOURNAL FOR AUTHORS & PUBLISHERS

EDITORIAL ADDRESS:
Eleanor Harman, Editor
University of Toronto Press
Toronto, Ontario M5S 1A6
Canada

SUBSCRIPTION ADDRESS:
Journals Department
same

PUBLISHED: Quarterly
COST: 1 yr.—$10.00; single copy—$3.50.

CIRCULATION: 1,200-1,300

CONTENTS: Articles on all phases of scholarly publishing—editorial, promotion, finance, management, organization. International publishing featured. Examples: "The Critic as Mediator"; "Scholarly Publishing in the Philippines."

UNSOLICITED MSS. WELCOME? Yes, however, a previous inquiry is welcome; submissions acknowledged.
MS. LENGTH: 5,000 words maximum; submit ONE copy.
COPYRIGHT: University of Toronto Press.
EDITOR'S DECISION: 1-2 months.
FROM ACCEPTANCE TO PUBLICATION: 3-6 months.
PAYMENT/OFFPRINTS: Fees modest; 100 free offprints.
REJECTED MSS.: Returned.
GENERAL: First issue, October, 1969. Usual publication length, 96 pages.
BACK ISSUES: Available from Journals Department at $3.50 each; $15.00 per volume, cloth bound.

THE SERIF: QUARTERLY OF THE KENT STATE UNIVERSITY LIBRARIES

EDITORIAL ADDRESS:
Dean Keller and Alex Gildren, Editors
Kent State University Libraries
Kent, Ohio 44242

SUBSCRIPTION ADDRESS:
Sandy Clark
Kent State University Press
Kent, Ohio 44242

PUBLISHED: Quarterly (Winter, Spring, Summer, Fall)
COST: 1 yr.—$6.00; single copy—$2.00.

CONTENTS: Articles on bibliography and book arts; annual issue on a single author. Example: "Jean-Claude van Itallie: Playwright-of-the-Ensemble: Open Theater."

UNSOLICITED MSS. WELCOME? Yes; submissions acknowledged.
SPECIFICALLY WELCOMED: Bibliographies; checklists; book-as-art articles.
MS. LENGTH: No preference; submit ONE copy.
COPYRIGHT: Author.
EDITOR'S DECISION: 2 weeks.
FROM ACCEPTANCE TO PUBLICATION: Varies.
PAYMENT/OFFPRINTS: Copies.
REJECTED MSS.: Returned.
GENERAL: First issue, April, 1964. Usual publication length, 40-60 pages. Indexed by volume.
BACK ISSUES: Available from Kent State University Press at $2.00 each.

SMALL PRESS REVIEW

EDITORIAL ADDRESS:
Len Fulton, Editor
5218 Scottwood Road
Paradise, California 95969

SUBSCRIPTION ADDRESS:

same

PUBLISHED: Quarterly
COST: 1 yr.—$3.50; 2 yrs.—$6.50; outside U.S., Canada, and Mexico—$5.00 p.a.

CONTENTS: News, lists, and reviews of small press little magazines and books worldwide; books received; interim updating to annual DIRECTORY OF LITTLE MAGAZINES AND SMALL PRESSES; answers to: What are the small presses publishing? Example: "The Poetry of Courage"; "The Good, the Bad, and the Abominable" (on little mags).

UNSOLICITED MSS. WELCOME? Yes.
MS. LENGTH: Articles under 3,000 words.
PAYMENT/OFFPRINTS: Copies of issue.
GENERAL: First issue, 1966. Usual publication length, 28-38 pages.

STUDIES IN BIBLIOGRAPHY: PAPERS OF THE BIBLIOGRAPHICAL SOCIETY OF THE UNIVERSITY OF VIRGINIA

EDITORIAL ADDRESS:
Fredson Bowers, Editor
c/o University Press of Virginia
Charlottesville, Virginia 22903

SUBSCRIPTION ADDRESS:
Secretary-Treasurer
Bibliographical Society of
University of Virginia
University of Virginia Library
Charlottesville, Virginia 22901

PUBLISHED: Annually
COST: 1 yr.—$15.00; $10 to members.

CIRCULATION: 1,200

CONTENTS: Articles on analytical and textual bibliography and textual criticism; articles on descriptive and historical bibliography.

UNSOLICITED MSS. WELCOME? Yes; submissions acknowledged.
MS. LENGTH: No preference; submit ONE copy.
STYLE REQUIREMENTS: MLA STYLE SHEET.
COPYRIGHT: Author substantially although STUDIES IN BIBLIOGRAPHY copyrights.
EDITOR'S DECISION: 2 months.
FROM ACCEPTANCE TO PUBLICATION: 1 year.
PAYMENT/OFFPRINTS: 15 to 25 free reprints.
REJECTED MSS.: Returned.
GENERAL: First issue, 1948. Usual publication length, 20-30 pages.
BACK ISSUES: Available from Secretary-Treasurer of the Society at $15 each to non-members; $12 each to members.

STUDIES ON VOLTAIRE AND THE EIGHTEENTH CENTURY

EDITORIAL ADDRESS:
Editor
Voltaire Foundation
Thorpe Manderville House
Banbury, Oxfordshire
England

SUBSCRIPTION ADDRESS:

same

PUBLISHED: Irregularly
COST: Varies with size of volume.

CIRCULATION: Varies

CONTENTS: Bibliography of studies on Voltaire and the eighteenth century published by the Voltaire Foundation.

UNSOLICITED MSS. WELCOME? Yes, submissions acknowledged.
SPECIFICALLY WELCOMED: Scholarly contributions.
MS. LENGTH: No limit; submit ONE copy.
STYLE REQUIREMENTS: Volumes published by Voltaire Foundation must use STUDIES style.

COPYRIGHT: Voltaire Foundation.
EDITOR'S DECISION: A few weeks.
FROM ACCEPTANCE TO PUBLICATION: 6 months.
PAYMENT/OFFPRINTS: 50 special offprints free.
REJECTED MSS.: Not returned.
GENERAL: First issue, 1955. Volumes range up to 2,000 pages. Already published 120 volumes.
BACK ISSUES: Available from Voltaire Foundation. Price varies.

TRACE (suspended publication)

EDITORIAL ADDRESS:
James Boyer May, Editor
P. O. Box 1068
Hollywood, California 90028

SUBSCRIPTION ADDRESS:

same

PUBLISHED: Quarterly

CIRCULATION: 2,000

CONTENTS: New writings and art of all types, and featuring bibliographies of little magazines and small presses.

GENERAL: Issued June, 1952-1970; final issue, No. 72/73. Usual publication length, from small beginning to over 300 pages at the end.
BACK ISSUES: Partial backfile remains available from the editor. Listings supplied upon request. Cost varies on basis of scarcity from $1.00 to $5.00 each.

TRANSACTIONS OF THE CAMBRIDGE BIBLIOGRAPHICAL SOCIETY

EDITORIAL ADDRESS:
Editor
University Library
Cambridge
England

SUBSCRIPTION ADDRESS:

same

PUBLISHED: Annually

GENERAL: First issue, 1949. This periodical had not arrived by the time the entry went to press. Potential subscribers, contributors, or collectors will have to write the editor to see whether the journal still exists, and if so, to inquire about details of manuscript submission, style, back issues, and the like.

VICTORIAN PERIODICALS NEWSLETTER

See the section on AGE AND/OR NATIONALITY: ENGLISH, AND BRITISH COMMONWEALTH for details.

YEARBOOK OF COMPARATIVE AND GENERAL LITERATURE

See the section on AGE AND/OR NATIONALITY: COMPREHENSIVE IN SCOPE for details.

Tracing Literary Periodicals:
An Afterword

This "Afterword" is concerned with some of the problems faced by researchers, be they academic bibliographers or amateur literary sleuths, who require some guidance in locating bibliographic information about the hundreds of literary periodicals which have come into existence in the last few decades, particularly those publishing scholarship. Historians of literary periodicals have at their disposal numerous reference tools to lead them to retrospective studies, and it is not my intention to survey them here. The BIBLIOGRAPHY OF BRITISH LITERARY BIBLIOGRAPHIES (Oxford, 1969) has a section on periodicals, as does the BIBLIOGRAPHY OF BIBLIOGRAPHIES IN AMERICAN LITERATURE (Bowker, 1970). They can lead one to the pertinent studies.

Checklists of contemporary literary periodicals can be found in many sources, too, but none of them are comprehensive, and researchers must consult dozens of sources while tracing an elusive periodical. The researcher is happiest when the periodical he is hunting can be found in an annotated checklist, such as "Literary Magazines and Commonwealth Literature," a chapter in Goodwin's NATIONAL IDENTITY (London: Heinemann, 1970), which lists thirty-two literary magazines from Africa, Australia, India, Malta, and other Commonwealth countries. "Australian Literary Magazines," an annotated list of eleven Australian literary magazines, was published in WORLD LITERATURE WRITTEN IN ENGLISH, XI (November, 1972). Articles in the SMALL PRESS REVIEW are highly recommended. Most recently it has provided articles on "Drama Mags: A Survey of Little Magazines Devoted Exclusively to the Theatre" (issue 13:vol.4, no. 1) and "A Survey of Film Magazines" (issue 17: vol. 5, no. 1). Roger D. Sween has compiled a TITLE INDEX TO "MAGAZINES," which is an index to the column called "Magazines" edited by Bill Katz and which appears regularly in LIBRARY JOURNAL. Many of the titles are literary, and anyone desiring a copy of the first edition of 1,000 copies can obtain a copy from the Index Company, 465 Division Street, Platteville, Wisconsin 53818.

All too often, directories of periodicals do not provide the researcher enough information about the periodical, and many have inadequate indexes. The ninth edition of the INTERNATIONAL DIRECTORY OF LITTLE MAGAZINES & SMALL PRESSES (1973-74) has a listing for UNDER THE SIGN OF PISCES: ANAÏS NIN AND HER CIRCLE, but it is necessary to read from A-U until one finds the title, because there is no index in the DIRECTORY listing Nin, Anaïs. The same problem faults the STANDARD PERIODICAL DIRECTORY (1973). The highly respected MLA INTERNATIONAL BIBLIOGRAPHY (1972) was compiled from a master list of approximately 2,300 periodicals; the master list precedes each volume of the BIBLIOGRAPHY, a mammoth, alphabetical list, totally without classification, with no addresses and no annotations. The pamphlet DIRECTORY OF JOURNALS & SERIES IN THE HUMANITIES is a data list of the periodical sources on the master list of the MLA INTERNATIONAL BIBLIOGRAPHY. The compilers describe it as a "Directory in Progress." It assigns an acronym for each title and states frequency of publication and year of first issue. It indicates whether or not the journal on the list reviews books, but it has no descriptions of contents or topics sought.

THE DIRECTORY OF PUBLISHING OPPORTUNITIES (Academic Media, 1973) is a promising venture, although far from comprehensive, but its price of $39.50 is not justified. Gerstenberger and Hendrick's THIRD DIRECTORY OF PERIODICALS PUBLISHING ARTICLES ON ENGLISH AND AMERICAN LITERATURE AND LANGUAGE was last issued by Swallow in 1970; their focus, by definition however, omits the many journals of foreign literatures except a few comparative literature journals. A new, seven-volume area study series called ACADEMIC WRITER'S GUIDE TO PERIODICALS (Kent State University Press) covers periodicals devoted to the disciplines within the humanities and social sciences. The first two volumes are out, and a thorough check on those periodicals described as publishing literary criticism and history revealed that, when the Harmons asked the same editors to describe the contents of their periodicals, nearly half did not indicate, on their own, an interest in literary criticism or history. Thus, what appeared to be a thorough effort, though the listing is alphabetically arranged, may be seriously flawed through the use of a checklist method of soliciting information from the periodicals.

Science fiction is an important genre in modern literature, and it has produced a large body of criticism. Thomas D. Clareson's SCIENCE FICTION CRITICISM; AN ANNOTATED CHECKLIST (Kent State University Press, 1973) is the best guide to the field. Clareson excludes fanzines from his survey, those specialized, irregular, inexpensively produced periodicals issued by the thousands in science fiction fandom. Howard De Vore, a science fiction dealer (Dearborn Heights, Michigan), estimates that thirty thousand unique fanzine titles have been published. Many of these fanzines have been concerned with single authors, like Ron Miller's DAKKAR which was devoted to Jules Verne (Columbus, Ohio: 1968-69), and some were edited by writers who later became famous s-f writers, like Harlan Ellison, whose SCIENCE FANTASY BULLETIN, was issued in the early fifties (Cleveland, Ohio).

An early checklist of fanzines was done by Robert Pavlat and Bill Evans in the late fifties, but it has been long out-of-print. I have been conducting research on Ohio fanzines and have published a short checklist of them in COZINE THREE (March 30, 1972), the newsletter of the Central Ohio Science Fiction Society, and someday I hope to muster the bibliographic enthusiam to index an uncataloged collection of fanzines housed in the Division of Special Collections of The Ohio State University Libraries. At the present, Dr. Fredric Wertham's THE WORLD OF FANZINES: A SPECIAL FORM OF COMMUNICATION (Southern Illinois University Press, 1973), which studies fanzines in the fields of science fiction, fantasy, and comics, and which includes a checklist of fanzines in Wertham's collection, is the only book on the subject. A current article is Albert Drake's "Fanzines: The Mag of the Future," in SMALL PRESS REVIEW (issue 17: June, 1973).

Richard D. Altick's SELECTIVE BIBLIOGRAPHY FOR THE STUDY OF ENGLISH AND AMERICAN LITERATURE (1971) contains a list of "Scholarly Periodicals" and adds in a note that "there are many informal organs of specialized groups" dealing with single authors; he lists no source where a researcher can find a list of such periodicals. William White's articles in THE AMERICAN BOOK COLLECTOR (November, 1957; March, 1967; and September, 1972) were the first to draw attention to the burgeoning list of societies and periodicals devoted to a single author. An essay on "Academic Newsletters" by Earl Wilcox appeared in CHOICE (December, 1970), which listed and discussed the history of single author newsletters. Most recently, excellent lists of author newsletters were published in LITERARY SKETCHES (October, 1971) and Katz' MAGAZINES FOR LIBRARIES (1972). Margaret C. Patterson's checklist, "V.I.P. Publications: An International Bibliography of 300 Newsletters,

Journals, and Miscellanea," which appeared in the BULLETIN OF BIBLIOGRAPHY (October-December, 1973), is basically concerned with author newsletters, and includes no less than thirty-four items for Conan Doyle (active and defunct). Now we have Gary L. Harmon and Susanna M. Harmon's SCHOLAR'S MARKET which includes, among other categories, the first comprehensive list of periodicals dealing with particular authors and periods of literary history. It is important for librarians to be aware of these specialized literary periodicals, not only for reasons of acquisition and reference, but also for purposes of interlibrary loan, because institutions which issue single author newsletters are often developing special collections of that author's work.

SCHOLAR'S MARKET is not a directory of creative arts, little magazines, though their book contains a large section of those that occasionally publish literary criticism. There are many existing sources for finding information on periodicals that publish poetry, short stories, and other literature. THE INTERNATIONAL WHO'S WHO IN POETRY (1972-73) has an appendix on over 900 little magazines which publish poetry in Europe, North and South America, and Canada. A more selective list of approximately 150 little magazines can be found in THE NEW YORK QUARTERLY (Autumn, 1972), which published their third annual annotated list of literary magazines and other markets for poetry manuscripts. Katz' MAGAZINES FOR LIBRARIES (1972) has sections on poetry magazines and literary reviews. WRITER'S MARKET is a classic source, with sections on little magazines and those that specialize in poetry. The Negro Bibliographic and Research Center (Washington, D.C.) has written me that they have plans for updating the DIRECTORY OF BLACK LITERARY MAGAZINES (1970).

Two other aspects important in tracing periodicals are special issues of periodicals and periodical sales catalogues. Special issues of creative writing periodicals are often devoted to a single author. RENDEZVOUS (Idaho State University) devoted their Winter, 1970, issue to Ernest Hemingway, and THE WIDENING CIRCLE (Columbus, Ohio) celebrated the centennial of the birth of Gertrude Stein by turning over its Fall, 1973, issue to a study of her work. Reference librarians should be aware of these special issues, as they often draw together all the current thinking about an author and are valuable to scholars and to students beginning their library research. Abrahams Magazine Service published a LITERATURE CATALOGUE: SERIALS IN ORIGINAL AND REPRINTED EDITIONS, which lists 507 major creative writing periodicals. They are only one example of a publisher making available sales catalogues which can also serve as periodical directories. NCR's ANNOUNCED REPRINTS, GUIDE TO REPRINTS, and GUIDE TO MICROFORMS IN PRINT can keep one posted on the many journals now being reprinted. Some catalogues of book dealers, like the one issued by L. W. Currey Rare Books Incorporated, MODERN LITERATURE AND LITERARY PERIODICALS (Catalogue Eighteen: Winter 1971-72), are very informative, and usually contain notes about contributors and editors of the periodicals. A CATALOGUE OF LITERARY PERIODICALS with an index of principal contributors was issued by The Crane Bookshop Ltd. (Haslemere, England: Autumn, 1973).

The reference tools necessary for the verification of literary periodicals now exist, especially after the publication of this outstanding directory. It only remains for libraries to purchase the periodicals listed herein, so they are available to the scholarly community.

                        Richard R. Centing
                        Reference Librarian
December, 1973   The Ohio State University
                        Editor:
                            UNDER THE SIGN OF PISCES: ANAÏS NIN
                            AND HER CIRCLE
                            and
                            THE WIDENING CIRCLE

APPENDIX A

PUBLISHING CONVENTIONS FOR MANUSCRIPT SUBMISSIONS

1. Inspect a recent issue or two of the periodical you plan to send an article.

2. If an editor has indicated in our book that you should inquire first about possible interest in your article, spell out as many aspects of your intended contribution as possible in your inquiry letter. Inquiry first may save time.

3. Type and double-space all manuscript submissions.

4. If you wish to have your submitted manuscript returned—in case it is rejected—send a self-addressed, STAMPED envelope (or, enclose an international reply coupon to cover postage for foreign periodicals). If you do not, you should not expect a return.

5. When (and if) your contribution is rejected, consider William White's advice in his Introduction to this book.

6. On matters of style, when the MLA STYLE SHEET is listed herein as the style source, this refers to the SECOND EDITION, unless otherwise noted. References to the Turabian MANUAL (University of Chicago Press) are for the third edition (1967), and references to the University of Chicago's A MANUAL OF STYLE are for the 12th edition (1969). Should editions supersede these, it is assumed that the latest edition is the proper one.

APPENDIX B
REPRINT COMPANIES MOST OFTEN CITED

a. Kraus Reprint Company   (a new address as of summer, 1973)
   Route 100
   Millwood
   New York 10546

   And for overseas journals:
   FL94401 Nendeln
   LIECHTENSTEIN

b. Walter J. Johnson, Inc.
         or
   Johnson Reprint Corporation
   111 Fifth Avenue
   New York, New York 10003

c. AMS Press, Inc.
         or
   AMS Reprint Co.
   56 East 13th Street
   New York, New York 10003

d. Dawson Reprint
   For Journals:
   Wm. Dawson and Sons, Ltd.
   16 West Street
   Farnham, Surrey
   ENGLAND

   For books:
   Dawsons of Pall Mall
   16 Pall Mall
   London, S.W. 1
   ENGLAND

e. Swets and Zeitlinger
   Keizersgracht 487
   Amsterdam
   HOLLAND

MICROFILM AND MICROFICHE COMPANIES

a. Xerox University Microfilms
   300 North Zeeb Road
   Ann Arbor, Michigan 48106

b. J. S. Canner and Co.
   49-65 Landsdowne Street
   Boston, Massachusetts 02215

c. 3M International Microfilm Press
   3M Center, 220-9E
   St. Paul, Minnesota 55101

AUTHOR INDEX

[Addison, Joseph] — The Scriblerian and the Kit-Cats, 85

[Alger, Horatio] — Newsboy, 5

[Arbuthnot, John] — The Scriblerian and the Kit-Cats, 85

[Arthur, King] — Bibliographical Bulletin of the International Arthurian Society, 45

[Bacon, Francis] — Baconiana (formerly Bacon Society Journal), 45

[Barnes, William] — The Thomas Hardy Yearbook, 68

[Baum, L. Frank] — The Baum Bugle, 5, 467

[Blake, William] — Blake Newsletter, 46
Blake Studies, 47

[Bramah, Ernest] — Presenting Moonshine, 57

[Brecht, Bertolt] — Brecht Heute/Brecht Today, 48
Communications: The Brecht Newsletter, 48

[Brontë, Charlotte, Emily, and Anne] — Brontë Society Transactions, 49

[Browning, Robert and Elizabeth Barrett] — Browning Institute Studies, 50
Browning Society Notes, 51
The New York Browning Society Bulletin, 52
Studies in Browning and His Circle, (formerly The Browning Newsletter), 53

[Bryant, William Cullen] — American Transcendental Quarterly, 31, 134

[Burke, Edmund] — Studies in Burke and His Time (formerly The Burke Newsletter), 53

[Burns, Robert] — Burns Chronicle, 54

[Burroughs, Edgar Rice] — The Burroughs Bulletin, 6, 468
ERB-dom and The Fantasy Collector, 6, 470
The Gridley Wave, 6, 472

[Byron, George Gordon] — Keats-Shelley Journal, 72
The Keats-Shelley Memorial Bulletin, 72

[Cabell, James Branch] — The Cabellian: A Journal of the Second American Renaissance (suspended publication), 6
Kalki: Studies in James Branch Cabell, 7

[Carleton, William]	Carleton Newsletter, 55
[Cather, Willa]	Willa Cather Pioneer Memorial and Educational Foundation Newsletter, 8
[Chamberlain, J. S.]	Amra, 464
[Chaney, William H.]	The Chaney Chronical, 8
[Chaucer, Goeffrey]	The Chaucer Review: A Journal of Medieval Studies and Literary Criticism, 55
[Christy, Dame Agatha]	The Pontine Dossier, 85, 484
[Claudel, Paul]	Claudel Studies (formerly Claudel Newsletter), 56
[Clemens, Samuel Langhorne]	American Transcendental Quarterly, 31, 134 The Mark Twain Journal, 9 Mark Twain Memorial Newsletter, 10 The Twainian, 10
[Coleridge, Samuel Taylor]	The Charles Lamb Bulletin: The Journal of the Charles Lamb Society, 74 The Wordsworth Circle, 101
[Collier, John]	Presenting Moonshine, 57
[Congreve, William]	The Scriblerian and the Kit-Cats, 85
[Conrad, Joseph]	Conradiana: A Journal of Joseph Conrad, 57 Conradiana Newsletter, 58
[Cooper, James Fenimore]	American Transcendental Quarterly, 31, 134 Natty Bumpo Review, 11, 148
[Crane, Stephen]	Stephen Crane Newsletter, 11
[Curwood, James Oliver]	The Curwood Collector, 12
[Dante Alighieri]	Dante Studies (with The Annual Report of the Dante Society), 59
[Defoe, Daniel]	Johnsonian News Letter, 68
[Derleth, August]	The Pontine Dossier, 85, 484 IS: A Quarterly of Popular Literature and Popular Culture, 475

[DeQuincey, Thomas]	The Charles Lamb Bulletin: The Journal of the Charles Lamb Society, 74 The Wordsworth Circle, 101
[Dickens, Charles]	Broadstairs Dickens Festival Programme, 60 The Dickensian, 60 Dickens Studies Annual, 61 Dickens Studies Newsletter, 62
[Dickinson, Emily]	American Transcendental Quarterly, 31, 134 Emily Dickinson Bulletin, 13 Higginson Journal of Poetry, 13
[Dos Passos, John]	Lost Generation Journal, 145
[Dostoevsky, Fedor]	International Dostoevsky Society Bulletin, 62
[Doyle, Sir Arthur Conan]	The Baker Street Journal, 63, 466 The Commonplace Book, 63, 468 The Holmesian Observer, 64, 472 The Hurlstone Papers, 64, 474 The Pontine Dossier, 85, 484 The Sherlock Holmes Journal (suspended publication), 64, 489
[Dreiser, Theodore]	The Dreiser Newsletter, 14
[Dryden, John]	The Scriblerian and the Kit-Cats, 85
[Emerson, Ralph Waldo]	American Transcendental Quarterly: Journal of New England Writers, 31, 134 ESQ: A Journal of the American Renaissance (formerly Emerson Society Quarterly), 15, 140
[Erasmus, Desiderius]	Erasmus in English, 64
[Faulkner, William]	Faulkner Concordance Newsletter, 16 Faulkner Studies (suspended publication), 16
[Faust, Frederick]	The Faust Collector, 17, 471
[Fitzgerald, F. Scott]	Fitzgerald-Hemingway Annual, 17 The Fitzgerald Newsletter (suspended publication), 18
[Frederic, Harold]	The Frederick Herald, 18
[Galdós, Benito Perez]	Anales Galdosianos, 65

[Gay, John]	The Scriblerian and the Kit-Cats, 85
[Gissing, George]	The Gissing Newsletter, 66
[Godwin, William]	Keats-Shelley Journal, 72
[Goethe, Johann W. von]	The English Goethe Society: Publications, 66
[Graves, Robert]	Focus on Robert Graves, 67
[Grey, Zane]	The Zane Grey Collector, 19
[Hardy, Thomas]	The Thomas Hardy Yearbook, 68
[Harris, George Washington]	The Lovingood Papers (suspended publication), 20
[Hartmann, Sadakichi]	Sadakichi Hartmann Newsletter, 20
[Hawthorne, Nathaniel]	American Transcendental Quarterly: Journal of New England Writers, 31, 134 ESQ: A Journal of American Renaissance, 15, 140 Nathaniel Hawthorne Journal. 21
[Hazlitt, William]	The Keats-Shelley Memorial Bulletin, 72 Keats-Shelley Journal, 72 The Wordsworth Circle, 101
[Hemingway, Ernest]	Fitzgerald-Hemingway Annual, 17 Hemingway Notes, 22 Lost Generation Journal, 145
[Higginson, T. W.]	Higginson Journal of Poetry, 13
[Holmes, Oliver Wendell]	American Transcendental Quarterly, 31, 134
[Howard, Robert E.]	Amra, 464 The Howard Collector, 22, 473
[Hunt, Leigh]	Keats-Shelley Journal, 72 The Keats-Shelley Memorial Bulletin, 72
[Irving, Washington]	American Transcendental Quarterly, 31, 134
[Jeffers, Robinson]	Robinson Jeffers Newsletter, 23
[Johnson, Samuel]	Johnsonian News Letter, 68 New Rambler: Journal of the Johnsonian Society of London, 69

[Joyce, James]	James Joyce Quarterly, 70
	The James Joyce Review
	  (suspended publication), 71
	A Wake Newslitter: Studies of James
	  Joyce's Finnegans Wake, 71

[Keats, John]	Keats-Shelley Journal, 72 The Keats-Shelley Memorial Bulletin, 72
[Kipling, Rudyard]	The Kipling Journal, 73
[Lamb, Charles]	The Charles Lamb Bulletin: The Journal of the Charles Lamb Society, 74 The Wordsworth Circle, 101
[Lawrence, D. H.]	The D. H. Lawrence Review, 74
[Lessing, Gotthold Ephraim]	The Lessing Yearbook, 75
[Lewis, C. S.]	The Bulletin of the New York C. S. Lewis Society, 76 Mythlore, 97, 480 Mythprint, 97, 481
[Lewis, Sinclair]	Sinclair Lewis Newsletter, 23
[London, Jack]	Jack London Newsletter, 24 The London Collector, 25 What's New About London, Jack?, 25
[Longfellow, Henry Wadsworth]	American Transcendental Quarterly, 31, 134
[Lorca, Garcia]	Garcia Lorca Review, 77
[Lovecraft, H. P.]	The Arkham Collector (suspended publication), 465 Nyctalops, 77, 483
[MacDonald, John D.]	The John D. MacDonald Bibliophile, 26, 475
[Machen, Arthur]	Arthur Machen Society Occasional, 77
[Malraux, Andre]	Malraux Miscellany, 78
[Markham, Edwin]	The Markham Review, 26, 146
[Marlowe, Christopher]	Shakespeare Studies, 92

[Melville, Herman]	American Transcendental Quarterly: Journal of New England Writers, 31, 134 Extracts/An Occasional Newsletter (formerly The Melville Society Newsletter), 27
[Mencken, H. L.]	Menckeniana, 28
[Mill, John Stuart]	Mill News Letter, 79
[Miller, Henry]	The Henry Miller Literary Society Newsletter (suspended publication), 28 The International Henry Miller Letter (suspended publication), 29 Lost Generation Journal, 145 Under the Sign of Pisces: Anaïs Nin and her Circle, 30
[Milton, John]	Milton Quarterly (formerly The Milton Newsletter), 79 Milton Society of America Newsletter, 80 Milton Studies, 81
[Moore, Thomas]	Keats-Shelley Journal, 72
[More, Thomas]	Moreana: A Bilingual Quarterly, 82
[Morris, William]	The Journal of the William Morris Society, 82 News From Anywhere, 83
[Munro, H. H.]	Presenting Moonshine, 57
[Neihardt, John G.]	The Neihardt Foundation Newsletter, 29
[Nin, Anaïs]	Under the Sign of Pisces: Anaïs Nin and her Circle, 30
[O'Connor, Flannery]	The Flannery O'Connor Bulletin, 31
[Peacock, Thomas Love]	Keats-Shelley Journal, 72
[Petronius, Gaius]	The Petronian Society Newsletter, 84
[Pirandello, Luigi]	Pirandello Studies, 84
[Poe, Edgar Allan]	American Transcendental Quarterly: Journal of New England Writers, 31, 134 ESQ: A Journal of the American Renaissance, 14, 140 The Poe Messenger, 32 Poe Studies (formerly Poe Newsletter), 33

[Pons, Sol ar]	The Pontine Dossier, 85, 484
[Pope, Alexander]	The Scriblerian and the Kit-Cats, 85
[Pound, Ezra]	Paideuma: A Journal Devoted to Ezra Pound Scholarship, 33 The Pound Newsletter (suspended publication), 34
[Powys family]	The Thomas Hardy Yearbook, 68
[Proust, Marcel]	Proust Research Association Newsletter, 86
[Queen, Ellery]	The Ellery Queen Review (formerly The Queen Canon Bibliophile), 470
[Rank, Otto]	The Journal, 35
[Richardson, Samuel]	Johnsonian News Letter, 68
[Rohmer, Sax]	The Rohmer Review, 86, 487
[Schnitzler, Arthur]	Modern Austrian Literature, 259
[Shakespeare, William]	Folger Library Newsletter, 87 Shakespeare-Jahrbuch, 88 The Shakespeare Newsletter, 88 Shakespeare Oxford Society News-Letter, 89 Shakespeare's Proclamation, 91 Shakespeare Quarterly, 90 Shakespearean Research and Opportunities, 87 Shakespeare Studies (Japan), 91 Shakespeare Studies: An Annual Gathering of Research, Criticism, and Reviews, 92 Shakespeare Survey, 93
[Shaw, George Bernard]	The Independent Shavian, 94 The Shavian, 94 The Shaw Review, 95
[Shelley, Percy Bysshe]	Keats-Shelley Journal, 72 The Keats-Shelley Memorial Bulletin, 72
[Smith, Clark Ashton]	Nyctalops, 77, 483
[Smollett, Tobias]	Johnsonian News Letter, 68
[Southey, Robert]	The Wordsworth Circle, 101
[Spenser, Edmund]	Spenser Newsletter, 96

[Steele, Richard]	The Scriblerian and the Kit-Cats, 85
[Stein, Gertrude]	The Widening Circle (Fall, 1973), 593
[Steinbeck, John]	Steinbeck Quarterly (formerly Steinbeck Newsletter), 35
[Stevens, Wallace]	The Wallace Stevens Newsletter, 36
[Stuart, Jesse]	Jack London Newsletter, 24
[Swift, Jonathan]	The Scriblerian and the Kit-Cats, 85
[Synge, John Millington]	Yeats Studies [#2], 102
[Tennyson, Alfred]	Tennyson Research Bulletin, 96
[Thoreau, Henry David]	American Transendental Quarterly: Journal of New England Writers, 31, 134 The Concord Saunterer, 36 ESQ: A Journal of the American Renaissance, 15, 140 Thoreau Journal Quarterly, 37 The Thoreau Society Bulletin, 38
[Tolkien, J. R. R.]	Mythlore, 97, 480 Mythprint, 97, 481 Niekas, 97, 482
[Vanbrugh, John]	The Scriblerian and the Kit-Cats, 85
[Vergil]	Vergilian Society Newsletter, 98 Vergilius, 98
[Voltaire, Francois M. A.]	Studies on Voltaire and the Eighteenth Century, 99, 272, 648
[Wallace, Edgar]	Edgar Wallace Society Newsletter (formerly Edgar Wallace Club Newsletter), 99, 469
[Ward, Arthur Sarsfield]	See Rohmer, Sax
[Waugh, Evelyn]	Evelyn Waugh Newsletter, 99

[Whitman, Walt]	American Transcendental Quarterly: Journal of New England Writers, 31, 134 Calamus: An International Whitman Quarterly, 38 Walt Whitman Birthplace Bulletin (suspended publication), 39 Walt Whitman Review (formerly Walt Whitman Newsletter), 39
[Whittier, John Greenleaf]	American Transcendental Quarterly, 31, 134 Whittier Newsletter, 40
[Williams, Charles]	Mythlore, 97, 480 Mythprint, 97, 481
[Wollstonecraft, Mary]	Keats-Shelley Journal, 72 Mary Wollstonecraft Newsletter, 100
[Woolf, Virginia]	Virginia Woolf Quarterly, 101
[Wordsworth, William]	The Wordsworth Circle, 101 The Wordsworth Society: Transactions (suspended publication), 102
[Yeats, William Butler]	Yeats Studies: An International Journal, 102

TITLE INDEX

AAASS Newsletter, 277

The Aberdeen University Review, 187, 597

Abraxas: A Journal for the Theoretical Study of Philosophy, the Humanities and the Social Sciences, 597

Action, 409

Adam International Review, 547

Aegis: A Periodical in Literature & Language, 547

African Arts, 313, 371

African Literature Today: An Annual Review (formerly African Literature Today: A Journal of Explanatory Criticism), 313, 371

Afro-American History and Culture: New Books Quarterly Checklist Series, 371, 632

Agenda, 331

Agora: A Journal in the Humanities and Society Sciences, 597

ALAC-ALAS Papers [Latin America], 314

Alberta English, 187, 511

Algol: A Magazine about Science Fiction, 463

The Alien Critic, 463

The American Book Collector, 623

American Hungarian Review, 129, 245

American Imago, 445

American Jewish Historical Quarterly, 372

American Journal of Philology, 159

American Literary Realism, 1870-1910, 129

American Literary Scholarship: An Annual, 130

American Literature: A Journal of Literary History, Criticism, and Bibliography, 130

American Literature Abstracts: A Review of Current Scholarship in the Field of American Literature, 131, 624

American Notes & Queries, 131

The American Poetry Review, 331

American Quarterly, 132

The American-Scandinavian Review, 245

The American Scholar: A Quarterly for the Independent Thinker, 598

American Studies, 132

American Studies: An International Newsletter, 133

American Transcendental Quarterly: Journal of New England Writers [Poe, Emerson, Thoreau, Hawthorne, Melville, Whitman], 31, 134

American West, 134

Americas, 314

Amerikastudien (formerly Jahrbuch für Amerikastudien), 134

Amistad: Writings on Black History and Culture (suspended publication), 372

Amra, 464

Anales Galdosianos [Galdós, Benito Perez], 65

Andy Warhol's Interview, 409

The Anglo-Welsh Review, 187

Ann Arbor Review, 548

Annuale Mediaevale, 227

Antaeus, 549

Anthelion, 598

The Antigonish Review, 549

The Antioch Review, 599

Archiv fur das Studium der Neueren Sprachen und Literaturen, 159, 227, 246

Arctic Anthropology, 391

Arethusa, 271

Argentine Science Fiction Review, 409, 465

Ariel: A Review of International English Literature (formerly A Review of English Literature), 109

Arion, 217

Arizona and the West, 135

Arizona English Bulletin, 511

Arizona Quarterly, 550

The Arkham Collector (suspended publication), 465

The Arlington Quarterly: A Journal of Literature, Comment and Opinion, 550

The Armchair Detective, 466

Årsbok, Slaviska Institutionen vid Lunds Universitet, 277

Artes Liberales (formerly Arts and Letters), 600

Arthur Machen Society Occasional, 77

Arts in Society, 600

The Aryan Path, 109, 601

Asian Affairs: Journal of the Royal Central Asian Society, 299

Asian Folklore Studies, 299, 391

Asian Theatre Bulletin, 299, 347

ASTR: American Society for Theatre Research Newsletter, 347

Athanor, 361

The Atlantic Monthly, 602

AUMLA: A Journal of Literary Criticism, Philosophy and Linguistics, 188

Australian Literary Studies, 189

AV Guide: The Learning Media Magazine, 410

Aztlán: Chicano Journal of the Social Sciences and the Arts, 373

Baconiana (formerly Bacon Society Journal) [Bacon, Francis], 45

The Baker Street Journal [Doyle, Arthur Conan], 63, 466

Balkan Studies, 278

Ball State University Forum (formerly Ball State Teachers College Forum), 551

The Baum Bugle [Baum, L. Frank], 5, 467

Beau-Cocoa, 373

Berkshire Review, 551

Bibliographical Bulletin of the International Arthurian Society, 45

The Bibliotheck, 624

Bibliotheque d'Humanisme & Renaissance, 625

The Bilingual Review/La Revista Bilingue, 136

Black Academy Review: Quarterly of the Black World, 315, 374

The Black Arts Magazine, 375

Black Books Bulletin, 375

Black Review, 376

The Black Scholar: Journal of Black Studies and Research, 376

Black Theatre, 348, 377

Black World (formerly Negro Digest), 377

Blake Newsletter: An illustrated quarterly [Blake, William] 46

Blake Studies [Blake, William], 47

The Bodleian Library Record, 626

The Book Collector, 626

Books Abroad: An International Literary Quarterly, 109

Books and Bookmen, 159

Books at Brown, 627

Books in Canada, 190

Boston University Journal: Scholarly Periodical with Articles of General Interest (formerly Boston University Graduate Journal), 602

Brecht Heute/Brecht Today [Brecht, Bertolt], 48

British Book News, 628

Broadstairs Dickens Festival Programme [Dickens, Charles], 60

Bronte Society Transactions [Bronte, Charlotte, Emily, & Anne], 49

Browning Institute Studies [Browning, Robert & Elizabeth Barrett], 50

Browning Society Notes [Browning, Robert and Circle], 51

Bucknell Review: A Scholarly Journal of Letters, Arts and Sciences, 603

Bulgarian Review, 278

Bulletin of Bibliography and Magazine Notes, 628

Bulletin of the Center of Children's Books, 505, 629

Bulletin of the Comediantes, 228

Bulletin of Hispanic Studies, 246, 315

The Bulletin of the New York C. S. Lewis Society, 76

Bulletin of the New York Public Library, 629

Burns Chronicle [Burns, Robert], 54

The Burroughs Bulletin [Burroughs, Edgar Rice], 6, 468

The Cabellian: A Journal of the Second American Renaissance (suspended publication) [Cabell, James Branch], 6

Calamus: An International Whitman Quarterly, 38

California Quarterly, 136, 552

Cambridge Review, 604

Canadian Literature/Litterature Canadienne: A Quarterly of Criticism and Review, 190

The Canadian Modern Language Review, 191

The Canadian Review of American Studies, 137, 191

Canadian Slavonic Papers—Revue Canadienne des Slavistes, 279

Canyon Cinemanews, 410

Caribbean Review: A Quarterly Journal Dedicated to Caribbean, Latin America and Their Emigrant Groups (formerly San Juan Review), 315

Caribbean Studies, 316

Carleton Newsletter [Carleton, William], 55

CEAA Newsletter: An Occasional Publication of the Center for Editions of American Authors, 138

The CEA Critic (College English Association), 512

The CEA Forum, 513

The Centennial Review (formerly Centennial Review of Arts and Science), 445

Centrum: Working Papers of the Minnesota Center for Advanced Studies in Language, Style, and Literary Theory, 495

The Chaney Chronical [Chaney, William H.], 8

The Charles Lamb Bulletin: The Journal of the Charles Lamb Society, 74

The Chaucer Review: A Journal of Medieval Studies and Literary Criticism [Chaucer, Geoffrey, and Others], 55

Chicago Review, 552

Children's Literature, 505

Chinese Literature/Litterature Chinoise, 299

The Christian Century, 604

Christianity and Literature, 446

Chronica, 229

Cimarron Review, 553

Cineaste, 411

Cinema, 411

Cinema Canada (formerly Canadian Cinematographer), 412

Cinema Journal, 413

Cinema Studies, 413

CLA Journal: Official Quarterly Publication of the College Language Association, 110, 378

Classic Film Collector, 414

The Classical Bulletin, 218

The Classical Journal, 219, 513

Classical Philology, 219

Claudel Studies (formerly Claudel Newsletter) [Claudel, Paul], 56

CLIO: An Interdisciplinary Journal of Literature, History, and the Philosophy of History, 446

Colby Library Quarterly [Maine writers], 138, 630

College and Research Libraries, 630

College English, 495, 514

College English Association Critic, 512

College Literature, 515

The Colorado Quarterly, 554

Commentary, 605

The Commonplace Book [Doyle, Arthur Conan], 63, 468

Commonweal, 605

Comitatus, 229

Communications—The Brecht Newsletter [Brecht, Bertolt], 48

Comparative Drama, 348

Comparative Literature, 111, 496

Comparative Literature Studies, 112, 246, 316

Computer Studies in the Humanities and Verbal Behavior, 447

Concerning Poetry, 332

The Concord Saunterer [Thoreau, Henry David], 36

The Connecticut Critic (formerly New England Review), 554

Connecticut English Journal, 515

Connections II (formerly Connections: The Radical American Studies Journal), 516

Conradiana: A Journal of Joseph Conrad, 57

Conradiana Newsletter, 58

Contemporary Literary Scene, 139

Contemporary Literature (formerly WSCL), 160

Contemporary Literature in Translation, 555

Contemporary Poetry: A Journal of Poetry Criticism, 332

Contemporary Review (incorporating The Fortnightly), 556

The Count Dracula Society Quarterly, 414

Creative Moment, 333

The Cresset: A Review of Literature, the Arts, and Public Affairs, 606

Critic (formerly Film Critics' Guild Bulletin), 415

The Critical Quarterly, 160, 631

The Critical Review: Melbourne, 161

Criticism: A Quarterly for Literature and the Arts, 162, 496

Critique: Studies in Modern Fiction, 113

CTVD (Cinema-TV-Digest), 415

Cultural Hermeneutics: An International Journal for the Philosophical Interpretation of the Special Languages of the Human Sciences, 607

The Curwood Collector [Curwood, James Oliver], 12

Dada/Surrealism, 416, 447

Dalhousie Review: A Canadian Quarterly of Literature and Opinion, 556

Dante Studies (with The Annual Report of the Dante Society), 59

December: A Magazine of the Arts and Opinion, 416

Delta, 557

Descant: The Texas Christian University Literary Journal, 557

Dhara: A Quarterly Review of Indian Literature in English Language, 300

The D. H. Lawrence Review, 74

Diacritics: A Review of Contemporary Criticism, 496

Dialogue for English Teachers in West Virginia, 517

The Dickensian [Dickens, Charles], 60

Dickens Studies Annual [Dickens, Charles], 61

Dickens Studies Newsletter [Dickens, Charles], 62

The Diliman Review, 558

Dimension: Contemporary German Arts and Letters, 247

Dragonfly: A Quarterly of Haiku Highlights, 333

Drama and Theatre (formerly First Stage), 349

The Dreiser Newsletter [Dreiser, Theodore], 14

The Dublin Magazine: Ireland's Quarterly of Literature and Art, 191

Durham University Journal, 607

Early American Literature, 139

East Slavic Languages and Literatures, 280

East-West Review, 559

Edgar Wallace Society Newsletter (formerly Edgar Wallace Club Newsletter), 99, 469

Educational Theatre Journal, 349, 517

Eighteenth-Century Studies, 162

Eire-Ireland: A Journal of Irish Studies, 192

Elementary English, 517

El Grito: Journal of Contemporary Mexican American Thought, 378

ELH, 163

Elizabethan Bibliographies Supplements, 192, 631

The Ellery Queen Review (formerly The Queen Canon Bibliophile), 470

Emily Dickinson Bulletin, 13

The Emporia State Research Studies, 114

English, 193

English Education, 518

English in Texas, 519

English Journal, 519

English Language Notes, 164

English Literary Renaissance, 193

English Literature, Criticism, Teaching, 520

English Literature in Transition: 1800-1920, 194

English Miscellany: A Symposium of History, Literature and the Arts, 195, 608

The English Quarterly, 521

The English Record, 521

English Studies: A Journal of English Language and Literature, 165

English Studies in Africa: A Journal of the Humanities, 195

English Symposium Papers, 196, 334, 361

Enlightenment Essays, 165

Era: A Pennsylvania Magazine of Commentary and Literature, 559

Erasmus in English [Erasmus, Desiderius], 64

The Erasmus Review, 166

ERB-dom and The Fantasy Collector [Burroughs, Edgar Rice], 6, 470

ESQ: A Journal of the American Renaissance, 15

Essays in Criticism: A Quarterly Journal of Literary Criticism, 167

Essays in Literature [U. of Denver], 167

Essays in Literature [W. Illinois U.], 168

Etudes Anglaises, 168

European Studies Review, 247

Evelyn Waugh Newsletter, 99

Evergreen Review, 560

Exercise Exchange: A Journal for Teachers of English in high schools and colleges, 522

The Explicator, 114

Explorations: A Journal of Literary Criticism, 196, 301

Extracts/An Occasional Newsletter (formerly The Melville Society Newsletter) [Melville, Herman], 27

Extrapolation: A Journal of Science Fiction and Fantasy, 471

Fabula: Journal of Folktale Studies, 392

Far-Western Forum, 115

Faulkner Concordance Newsletter [Faulkner, William], 16

Faulkner Studies (suspended publication) [Faulkner, William], 16

The Faust Collector [Faust, Frederick], 17, 471

Fiction International, 169, 361

Film, 416

Film Comment, 417

Film Critic (formerly Film Society Review), 418

Film Culture, 418

The Film-English/Humanities Journal, 419

Film Facts, 419

Film Fan Monthly, 420

Film Heritage, 420

Film Information, 421

The Film Journal, 421

Film Library Quarterly, 422

Filmmakers Newsletter, 423

Filmograph, 424

Film Quarterly, 424

Film Review, 425

Films and Filming, 425

Films Illustrated, 426

Films in Review, 426

Film World, 427

Fitzgerald Newsletter (suspended publication), 18

Fitzgerald-Hemingway Annual (formerly The Fitzgerald Newsletter) [Fitzgerald, F. Scott; Hemingway, Ernest], 17

The Flannery O'Connor Bulletin, 31

Florida Council of Teachers of English Newsletter, 523

Florida English Journal, 523

Florida Quarterly, 560

Focus! Chicago's Film Journal, 428

Focus on Robert Graves, 67

Folger Library Newsletter [Shakespeare, William], 87

Folklore, 392

Folklore Annual of the University Folklore Association, 393

Folklore Forum: A Communication for Students of Folklore, 393

Forum, 608

Forum Italicum: A Quarterly of Italian Studies, 248

Four Quarters, 561

The Frederic Herald (formerly Seth's Brother's Banner) [Frederic, Harold], 18

Freedomways: A Quarterly Review of the Freedom Movement, 316, 379

The Free Lance: A Magazine of Poetry and Prose, 561

French Notes & Queries, 249

The French Review, 249

French Studies: A Quarterly Review, 250

From the Sourdough Crock, 394

Furman Studies, 609

Garcia Lorca Review, 77

Genre, 362

The Georgia Review, 562

Germanic Notes, 250

The Germanic Review: Devoted to Studies Dealing with the Germanic Languages and Literatures, 251

German Life and Letters: A Quarterly Review, 252

The German Quarterly, 252

The Gissing Newsletter [Gissing, George], 66

The Great Lakes Review: A Journal of Midwest Culture, 140

Greek, Roman and Byzantine Studies, 220

The Gridley Wave [Burroughs, Edgar Rice], 6, 472

Handbook of Latin American Studies, 316, 631

Harper's Magazine, 609

Hartford Studies in Literature: A Journal of Interdisciplinary Criticism, 448

Harvard Advocate, 563

Harvard Journal of Asiatic Studies, 301

Harvard Library Bulletin, 631

Ha-sifrut: Quarterly for the Study of Literature, 497

Hawaii Review, 141

Hemingway Notes [Hemingway, Ernest], 22

The Henry Miller Literary Society Newsletter (suspended publication), 28

Hesperia: Journal of the American School of Classical Studies at Athens, 220

Higginson Journal of Poetry [Dickinson, Emily; Higginson, T. W.], 13

Hiram Poetry Review, 334

Hispania, 316, 524

Hispanic Review: A Quarterly Journal Devoted to Research in the Hispanic Languages and Literatures, 253, 317

Hispanofila, 254, 317

The Hollins Critic, 142

The Holmesian Observer [Doyle, Arthur Conan], 64, 472

Hopkins Research Bulletin, 632

Horizon [South Carolina Council of Teachers of English], 525

Horizon: Magazine of the Arts, 350, 428, 563

The Horn Book Magazine, 505

The Howard Collector [Howard, Robert E.], 22, 473

The Hudson Review, 564

The Humanist, 610

The Humanities Association Review/La Revue de l'Association des Humanites, 564

The Huntington Library Quarterly: A Journal for the History and Interpretation of English and American Civilization, 169, 633

The Hurlstone Papers [Doyle, Arthur Conan], 64, 474

Illinois English Bulletin, 528

Illinois Quarterly, 611

The Independent Shavian: Journal of the New York Shavians, Inc. [Shaw, George Bernard], 94

Index to Australian Book Reviews, 197, 634

Indiana English Journal, 526

Indiana Folklore, 395

The Indian Historian, 317, 379

Indian Journal of American Studies, 142

The Indian Journal of English Studies, 169

Indian Literature, 302

The Indian Review: Devoted to the Discussion of All Topics of Interest, 303

Indian Writing Today, 303

The Intercollegiate Review: A Journal of Scholarship and Opinion, 449

International Dostoevsky Society Bulletin [Dostoevsky, Fedor], 62

The International Fiction Review, 115, 363

The International Henry Miller Letter (suspended publication), 29

International Journal of Slavic Linguistics and Poetics, 280

International Journal of Symbology, 449

International P.E.N. Bulletin of Selected Books, 634

International Poetry Review, 335

Interpretation: A Journal of Bible and Theology, 450

Iowa English Bulletin: Yearbook, 526

The Iowa Review, 565

Irish University Review: A Journal of Irish Studies, 197

IS: A Quarterly of Popular Literature and Popular Culture, 475

Islands: A New Zealand Quarterly of Arts and Letters, 197

Italian Quarterly, 254

Italica, 230, 255, 527

Jack London Newsletter, 24

James Joyce Quarterly, 70

The James Joyce Review (suspended publication), 71

Japan Quarterly, 566

The John D. MacDonald Bibliophile, 26, 475

John Edwards Memorial Foundation Quarterly, 395

Johnsonian News Letter [Johnson, Samuel], 68

Journal [The Utah Council of Teachers of English], 528

The Journal [Rank, Otto], 35

Journal of Aesthetic Education, 528

The Journal of Aesthetics and Art Criticism, 497

Journal of American Folklore, 143, 396

Journal of the American Oriental Society, 304

Journal of American Studies, 143

Journal of Baltic Studies (formerly Bulletin of Baltic Studies), 281

Journal of Biblical Literature, 450

Journal of Canadian Studies/Revue d'etudes canadiennes, 198

Journal of Commonwealth Literature, 199

Journal of English and Germanic Philology: A Quarterly Devoted to the English, German, and Scandinavian Languages and Literatures, 255

Journal of English Teaching Techniques, 529

Journal of the Folklore Institute, 397

Journal of the Folklore Society of Greater Washington, 397

Journal of the Gypsy Lore Society, 398

The Journal of Indian Writing in English, 304

The Journal of Interdisciplinary History, 451

Journal of Jewish Studies, 317, 380, 611

Journal of Literary Semantics, 452

The Journal of Medieval and Renaissance Studies, 230

Journal of Modern Literature, 144, 255

The Journal of Narrative Technique, 170, 335, 364

Journal of Near Eastern Studies, 318

Journal of the New African Literature and the Arts, 319, 380

Journal of Popular Culture, 476

Journal of Popular Film, 428

Journal of the Rutgers University Library, 635

Journal of South Asian Literature (formerly Mahfil: A Quarterly of South Asian Literature), 305

Journal of Spanish Studies: Twentieth Century, 255, 319

Journal of the University Film Association, 429

Journal of the Warburg and Courtauld Institutes, 453

The Journal of the William Morris Society, 82

Kalki: Studies in James Branch Cabell, 7

Kansas English, 530

Kansas Quarterly, 144, 611

Karamu, 566

Keats-Shelley Journal [Keats, John; Shelley, Percy Bysshe], 72

The Keats-Shelley Memorial Bulletin, 72

Kentucky English Bulletin, 531

Kentucky Folklore Record, 398

Kentucky Romance Quarterly, 256

Kenyon Review (suspended publication), 567

Keystone Folklore Quarterly, 399

The Kipling Journal [Kipling, Rudyard], 73

Kovave: Journal of New Guinea Literature, 199, 611

Kritikon Litterarum: International Book Review of American, English, Romance, and Slavic Studies, 281

La Coronica, 231

Landfall, 567

La Luz, 381

Language and Style: An International Journal, 498

The Language of Poems, 336

La Revista Chicano-Reguena, 319, 381

The Latin American Literary Review, 319, 382, 568

Latin American Theatre Review: A Journal Devoted to the Theatre and Drama of Spanish and Portuguese America, 320, 350

The Laurel Review, 568

The Leaflet, 531

L'Esprit Createur, 257

Lessing Yearbook [Lessing, Gotthold Ephraim], 75

The Library: A Quarterly Journal of Bibliography, 635

The Library Chronicle [University of Pennsylvania], 636

The Library Chronicle of the University of Texas at Austin, 637

The Library Quarterly, 637

Library Review: A Quarterly Magazine on Libraries and Literature, 638

The Literary Criterion, 145, 200, 306

The Literary Half-Yearly, 115, 569

The Literary Review: An International Journal of Contemporary Writing, 569

Literary Sketches, 170

Literary Studies: A Quarterly Review of Literature and Criticism from the Panjab (suspended publication), 306

Literature & Idealogy, 453

Literature and Psychology, 454

Literature East and West, 306, 320

Literature/Film Quarterly, 430, 532

Literature, Music, Fine Arts: A Review of German-Language Research Contributions on Literature, Music, and Fine Arts, 257

Literatur in Wissenschaft und Unterricht, 145, 258

Litterature Polonaise, 285

Lituanus: The Lithuanian Quarterly, 282

Locus, 477

The London Collector [London, Jack], 25

London Magazine, 570

Lost Generation Journal, 145

Louisiana English Journal, 532

The Lovingood Papers (suspended publication) [Harris, George Washington], 20

Luna Monthly, 477

Luna (Prime), 478

Luso-Brazilian Review: Devoted to the Culture of the Portuguese Speaking World, 320, 612

The Magazine of Further Studies, 612

The Malahat Review: An International Quarterly of Life and Letters, 571

Malraux Miscellany [Malraux, Andre], 78

Many Smokes: Native American Magazine, 382

The Markham Review, 26, 146

The Mark Twain Journal [Clemens, Samuel Langhorne], 9

Mark Twain Memorial, Newsletter [Clemens, Samuel Langhorne], 10

Maryland English Journal, 533

The Mary Wollstonecraft Newsletter [women writers], 100, 200, 506

The Massachusetts Review, 571

The Masterkey: For Indian Lore and History, 321, 383

Meanjin Quarterly: A Review of Arts and Letters, 572

Media and Methods (formerly School Paperback Journal), 431, 533

Media Mix: Ideas and Resources for Value Education, 533

Mediaeval Studies, 231

Medievalia et Humanistics: Studies in Medieval and Renaissance Culture, 232

Medium Aevum, 233

Melanges Malraux Miscellany [See Malraux Miscellany], 78

Melbourne Slavonic Studies, 283

Menckeniana [Mencken, H. L.], 28

Mexico Quarterly Review, 321

Michigan Academician: Papers of the Michigan Academy of Science, Arts, and Letters, 612

The Michigan Quarterly Review (formerly Michigan Alumnus Quarterly Review), 573

Mid-America, 146

Mid-South Folklore, 399

Midwest Modern Language Association Bulletin, 455, 498, 534

The Midwest Quarterly: A Journal of Contemporary Thought, 613

The Mill News Letter [Mill, John Stuart], 79

Milton Quarterly (formerly The Milton Newsletter) [Milton, John], 79

Milton Society of America [Milton, John], 80

Milton Studies [Milton, John], 81

Minnesota English Journal, 534

The Minnesota Review, 573

Mississippi Folklore Register, 400

The Mississippi Quarterly: the Journal of Southern Culture, 147

Missouri English Bulletin, 535

MLA Abstracts, 639

MLA International Bibliography of Books and Articles on the Modern Languages and Literatures, 639

MLN, 171

Modern Austrian Literature, 259

Modern Drama, 351

Modern Fiction Studies, 115, 365, 640

Modern Haiku, 336

Modern Language Quarterly, 171

The Modern Language Review, 259

Modern Philology: A Journal Devoted to Research in Medieval and Modern Literature, 234, 260

Modern Poetry in Translation, 337

Modern Poetry Studies, 338

Mojo Navigator(e), 147, 574

Monatshefte: A Journal Devoted to the Study of German Language and Literature, 260

Monthly Film Bulletin, 431

Moreana: A Bilingual Quarterly [More, Thomas], 82

Mosaic: A Journal for the Comparative Study of Literature and Ideas, 116

Mundus Artium: A Journal of International Literature and the Arts, 575

The Muslim World, 322, 456

The Mystery & Detection Annual, 478

The Mystery Reader's Newsletter (formerly The Mystery Lover's Newsletter), 479

The Mystery Trader, 479

Mythlore, 97, 480

Mythprint, 97, 481

Mythril, 481

Nathaniel Hawthorne Journal, 21

The Nation, 613

National Review, 614

Natty Bumpo Review [Cooper, James Fenimore and Others], 11, 148

The Nebraska English Counselor, 535

Negro American Literature Forum, 383

Negro History Bulletin, 384

The Neihardt Foundation Newsletter [Neihardt, John G.], 29

Neo-Hellenika: Annual Publication of the Center for Neo-Hellenic Studies, 221

Neophilologus, 234, 261, 498

Neuphilologische Mitteilungen: Bulletin of the Modern Language Society, 235, 261

Newberry Library Bulletin, 640

New Departures, 575

New Edinburgh Review, 576

The New England Quarterly: An Historical Review of New England Life and Letters, 148

The New Hungarian Quarterly, 262

New Letters (formerly The University Review successor to University of Kansas City Review), 577

New Literary History: A Journal of Theory and Interpretation, 499

New Morality: Concerned with New Literature, Art and Criticism, 577

New Orleans Review, 577

The New Rambler: Journal of the Johnson Society of London [Johnson, Samuel], 69

the new renaissance: a magazine of ideas and opinions, 578

Newsboy [Alger, Horatio], 5

News from Anywhere [Morris, William], 83

The News-Letter of the Society for the Study of Southern Literature, 148

New Statesman, 615

New World Review, 283

The New York Browning Society, Inc. Bulletin [Browning, Robert], 52

New York Folklore Quarterly, 401

The New York Review of Books, 116, 640

The New York Times Book Review, 117, 640

Niekas, 97, 482

Nineteenth-Century Fiction, 171

Nineteenth-Century French Studies, 263

Nineteenth Century Theatre Research, 352

North American Review, 579

North Carolina English Teacher, 536

North Carolina Folklore, 401

Northeast, 579

Northeast Folklore, 402

Northwest Review, 580

Nostalgia News, 482

Notes and Queries, 172

Notes on Contemporary Literature, 117

Notes on Mississippi Writers, 149

Notre Dame English Journal, 173

Nottingham French Studies, 263

Nottingham Mediaeval Studies, 235

Novel: A Forum on Fiction, 365

Nyctalops [Lovecraft, H. P., and Others], 77, 483

Obzor: Bulgarian Quarterly Review of Literature and the Arts, 284

Odu: A Journal of West African Studies, 322

Ohioana Quarterly (formerly Ohioana), 149

The Ohio Review: A Journal of the Humanities, 581

Oklahoma English Bulletin, 537

Old English Newsletter, 201, 641

On Film, 432

Orbis Litterarum: International Review of Literary Studies, 150, 264

Orot: Journal of Hebrew Literature, 323

Outlook: A Magazine of Literary Criticism, 118

Outtakes, 537

Paideuma: A Journal Devoted to Ezra Pound Scholarship, 33

The Pakistan Review, 307

The Papers of the Bibliographical Society of America (PBSA), 641

Papers of the MMLA, 174, 338

Papers on Language and Literature, 173

Parma Eldalamberon (Book of the Elven Tongues), 484

Parnassus: Poetry in Review, 338

Partisan Review, 581

Paunch, 456

The Pendulum of Time and the Arts, 457

Pennsylvania Folklife, 402

Perspective: A Quarterly of Modern Literature, 582

The Petronian Society Newsletter [Petronius, Gaius], 84

Philological Quarterly, 150, 221, 265

Philologica Pragensia [Germanic and Romance], 265

Phoenix: Journal of the Classical Association of Canada, 222

Photon, 432

Phylon: The Atlanta University Review of Race and Culture, 385

Pirandello Studies [Pirandello, Luigi], 84

Players: The Magazine of American Theatre, 150, 352

Plays and Players, 353

PMLA: Publications of the Modern Language Association of America, 118

The Poe Messenger [Poe, Edgar Allan], 32

Poe Studies (formerly Poe Newsletter) [Poe, Edgar Allan], 33

Poet and Critic, 339

Poetics: International Review for the Theory of Literature, 500

Poet Lore: A National Quarterly of World Poetry, 339

Poetry, 340

Poetry Review, 340

Polish Literature/Litterature Polonaise, 285

Polish Perspectives, 285

The Polish Review, 286

The Pontine Dossier, 85, 484

Popular Culture Methods, 538

The Pound Newsletter (suspended publication) [Pound, Ezra], 34

Prairie Schooner, 583

Presenting Moonshine [Collier, John; Munro, H. H., and Others], 57

The Princeton University Library Chronicle, 642

Proceedings of the British Academy, 201

Proceedings of the Comparative Literature Symposium, 175

Proof: The Yearbook of American Bibliographical and Textual Studies, 642

Prose, 366

Proust Research Association Newsletter [Proust, Marcel], 86

The Psychoanalytic Review, 458

Publications of the English Goethe Society: New Series, 66

Pucred, 506

The Pulp Era (formerly JD-Argassy), 485

Quarterly Check-List of Classical Studies, 222, 643

Quarterly Check-List of Literary History, 175, 643

Quarterly Check-List of Medievalia, 236, 644

Quarterly Check-List of Oriental Studies, 307, 644

Quarterly Check-List of Renaissance Studies, 645

Quarterly Review of Literature, 583

Queen's Quarterly: A Canadian Review, 202

Rackham Literary Studies, 119

Recovering Literature: A Journal of Contextualist Criticism, 176, 500

Remember When, 486

Renaissance and Modern Studies, 236, 266

Renaissance and Reformation, 237

Renaissance Drama, 202, 237, 353

Renaissance Papers, 238

Renaissance Quarterly (formerly Renaissance News), 238

Renascence: Essays on Values in Literature, 176

Research in African Literatures, 323, 385

Research Opportunities in Renascence Drama, 239, 353

Research Studies, 615

Research in the Teaching of English, 538

Resources for American Literary Study, 151, 645

Restoration and 18th Century Theatre Research (formerly 17th and 18th Century Theatre Research), 354

Review: A Magazine of Poetry and Criticism, 341

The Review of English Studies: A Quarterly Journal of English Literature and the English Language, 202

Review of National Literatures, 119

Revista de Estudios Hispanicos, 266, 323

Revista Interamericana de Bibliografia: Inter-American Review of Bibliography, 324, 645

Revue de Litterature Comparee, 120

Revue des Etudes Sud-Est Europeennes, 286

Revue des Langues Vivantes/Tijdschrift voor Levende Talen, 203, 266

Riverside Quarterly, 486

Rivista di letterature moderne e comparate, 267

Robinson Jeffers Newsletter, 23

Rocky Mountain Modern Language Association Bulletin, 177, 539

The Rohmer Review [Rohmer, Sax], 86, 487

Romance Notes, 268

Romance Philology, 268

Romanian Review, 287

The Romanic Review, 269

Rumanian Studies, 287

Russian Literature Triquarterly: A Journal of Translation and Criticism, 288

The Russian Review: An American Quarterly Devoted to Russia Past and Present, 289

Sadakichi Hartmann Newsletter, 20

Satire Newsletter, 507

Scandinavian Studies: The Journal of the Society for the Advancement of Scandinavian Study, 270

Scholarly Publishing: A Journal for Authors & Publishers, 646

Science-Fiction Studies, 487

Scottish International Review, 203, 616

Scottish Studies, 204, 403

Screen, 433

The Scriblerian and the Kit-Cats [Pope, Swift, and their Circle], 85

Seattle Folklore Society Journal (formerly Seattle Folklore Society Newsletter), 403

The Serif: Quarterly of the Kent State University Libraries, 647

Seventeenth-Century News (including The Neo-Latin News), 178

The Sewanee Review, 584

SF Commentary, 488

Shakespearean Research and Opportunities, 87

Shakespeare-Jahrbuch, 88

The Shakespeare Newsletter, 88

The Shakespeare Oxford Society News-letter, 89

Shakespeare Quarterly, 90

Shakespeare's Proclamation, 91

Shakespeare Studies [Japan], 91

Shakespeare Studies: An Annual Gathering of Research, Criticism, and Reviews, 92

Shakespeare Survey, 93

The Shavian [Shaw, George Bernard], 94

The Shaw Review, 95

Shenandoah: The Washington and Lee University Review, 584

The Sherlock Holmes Journal [Doyle, Arthur Conan], 64, 489

Sight and Sound: The International Film Quarterly, 433

Sightlines, 434

The Silent Picture, 435

Sinclair Lewis Newsletter, 23

Slavic and East European Journal, 289

Slavic Review: American Quarterly of Soviet and East European Studies, 290

Slovakia, 291

Small Press Review, 647

Society for the Study of Midwestern Literature Newsletter, 151

Soundings: An Interdisciplinary Journal, 458

South Asian Review: The Journal of the Royal Society for India, Pakistan and Ceylon, 308

South Atlantic Bulletin: A Quarterly Journal Devoted to Research and Teaching in the Modern Languages and Literature, 178

The South Atlantic Quarterly, 616

South Australiana: A Journal for the Publication and Study of South Australian Historical and Literary Manuscripts, 205

The South Carolina Review, 585

The South Central Bulletin, 179

South Dakota Review, 585

Southerly: A Quarterly Review of Australian Literature, 205

Southern Folklore Quarterly, 404

Southern Humanities Review, 586

Southern Literary Journal, 152

The Southern Quarterly, 616

Southern Review [Australia], 587

The Southern Review [U.S.A.], 153

South Slavic and Balkan Languages and Literatures, 292

Southwestern American Literature, 153, 405

Southwest Review, 587

Soviet Film (An Illustrated Monthly Magazine), 292, 435

Soviet Jewish Affairs: A Journal on Jewish Problems in the USSR and Eastern Europe, 292

Soviet Literature, 293

Soviet Studies in Literature, 294

The Sparrow Magazine, 341

Specialia: A Multidisciplinary Journal [Latin America], 324

Special Studies [Latin America], 325

Speculum, 240

Spenser Newsletter [Spenser, Edmund], 96

Statement, 539

Steinbeck Quarterly (formerly Steinbeck Newsletter) [Steinbeck, John], 35

Stephen Crane Newsletter, 11

Studi Americani, 154

Studia Monastica, 121

Studies in American Fiction, 155, 367

Studies in Bibliography: Papers of the Bibliographical Society of the University of Virginia, 648

Studies in Black Literature, 325, 386

Studies in Browning and His Circle (formerly The Browning Newsletter) [Browning, Robert], 53

Studies in Burke and His Time (formerly The Burke Newsletter), [Burke, Edmund], 53

Studies in Comparative Communism: An Interdisciplinary Journal, 459

Studies in Contemporary Satire: A Creative and Critical Journal, 507

Studies in English, 180

Studies in English Literature/Eibungaku Kenkyu, 180

Studies in English Literature: 1500-1900, 206

Studies in the Humanities, 181, 436, 460

Studies in Literary Imagination, 181

Studies in the Novel, 367

Studies in Philology, 270

Studies in the Renaissance, 241

Studies in Romanticism, 271

Studies in Scottish Literature, 207

Studies in Short Fiction, 368

Studies in the 20th Century, 121, 155, 272

Studies on Voltaire and the Eighteenth Century, 99, 272, 648

Style, 121, 501

Symposium: A Quarterly Journal in Modern Foreign Literatures, 122

Take One, 436

Tamkang Review: A Journal Mainly Devoted to Comparative Studies between Chinese and Foreign Literatures, 122, 308

Tamlacht, 489

TDR: The Drama Review, 354

Teaching Language through Literature, 540

Tennessee Folklore Society Bulletin, 405

Tennessee Poetry Journal, 342

Tennessee Studies in Literature, 182

Tennyson Research Bulletin [Tennyson, Alfred Lord], 96

Texas Quarterly, 617

Texas Studies in Literature and Language: A Journal of the Humanities, 123, 618

Theatre Annual, 355

Theatre Arts, 355

Theatre Studies: The Journal of the Ohio State University Theatre Research Institute (formerly The OSU Theatre Collection Bulletin), 356

Theatre Survey: The American Journal of Theatre History, 356

The Thomas Hardy Yearbook, 68

Thoreau Journal Quarterly [Thoreau, Henry David], 37

The Thoreau Society Bulletin [Thoreau, Henry David], 38

Thoth, 182

Thought, 618

The Times Literary Supplement, 123

Trace, 649

Traditio: Studies in Ancient and Medieval History, Thought and Religion, 222

Transactions of the Cambridge Bibliographical Society, 649

TriQuarterly: An International Journal of Arts, Letters, and Opinion, 588

Tulane Studies in English, 183

The Twainian [Clemens, Samuel Langhorne], 10

Twentieth Century Literature, 124

Twentieth Century Studies, 125

Under the Sign of Pisces: Anaïs Nin and her Circle, 30

Unicorn: A Miscellaneous Journal, 490, 589

The University of Denver Quarterly: A Journal of Modern Culture, 590

University of Portland Review, 618

University of Toronto Quarterly, 207

University of Windsor Review, 590

University Vision, 437, 540

Update: Journal of the B.C.E.T.A., 541

The Use of English, 541

Vector: Journal of the British Science Fiction Association, 490

The Velvet Light Trap: A Quarterly Journal of Film History and Criticism, 437

Venture: Bi-Annual Review of English Language and Literature, 155, 208, 309

Vergilian Society Newsletter, 98

Vergilius, 98

Viator: Medieval and Renaissance Studies, 241, 294

The Victorian Newsletter, 208

Victorian Periodicals Newsletter, 209, 650

Victorian Poetry: A Critical Journal of Victorian Literature, 209

Victorians Institute Journal, 210

Victorian Studies, 211

Views & Reviews: Quarterly Magazine of the Reproduced Arts, 438

Virginia English Bulletin, 542

The Virginia Quarterly Review, 125

Virginia Woolf Quarterly, 101

The Visva-Bharati Quarterly: Journal of General Cultural Interest, 619

A Wake Newslitter: Studies of James Joyce's Finnegans Wake, 71

The Wallace Stevens Newsletter, 36

Walt Whitman Birthplace Bulletin (suspended publication), 39

Walt Whitman Review (formerly Walt Whitman Newsletter), 39

Wascana Review, 591

Webster Review, 592

The Weewish Tree: A Magazine of Indian America for Young People, 387

Western American Literature, 155

Western Folklore, 406

Western Humanities Review, 592

The Westigan Review, 343

West Slavic Languages and Literature, 294

What's New About London, Jack? [London, Jack], 25

Whittier Newsletter [Whittier, John Greenleaf], 40

The Widening Circle , 593

Willa Cather Pioneer Memorial and Educational Foundation Newsletter, 8

Wisconsin English Journal, 543

WLWE: World Literature Written in English (formerly WLWE Newsletter, and CBCL Newsletter), 211

The Wordsworth Circle [Wordsworth, William], 101

Wordsworth Society: Transactions (suspended publication) [Wordsworth, William], 102

Working Papers in Cultural Studies, 439

Works: A Quarterly of Writing, 593

Yale French Studies, 272

The Yale Review, 620

yale/theatre, 357

Yandro, 491

Yeats Studies: An International Journal [Yeats, William Butler], 102

Yearbook of Comparative and General Literature, 126, 650

The Zane Grey Collector, 19

Zeitschrift für Anglistik und Amerikanistik, 183

Ref
Z
6944
S3
H3